AF473929

THE ART OF PRINTING

THE ART OF PRINTING

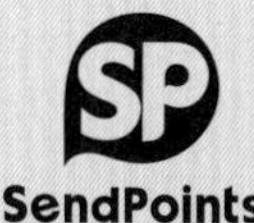

EDITED & PUBLISHED BY SendPoints Publishing Co., Ltd.
PUBLISHER: Lin Gengli
PUBLISHING DIRECTOR: Lin Shijian
ASSISTANT PUBLISHING DIRECTOR: Chen Ting
CHIEF EDITOR: Lin Shijian
LEAD EDITOR: Lin Qiumei
EXECUTIVE EDITOR: Akira Ho Claire Wei
DESIGN DIRECTOR: Lin Shijian
EXECUTIVE ART EDITOR: Ou Xiaoyu
PROOFREADING: James Powell

REGISTERED ADDRESS: Room 15A Block 9 Tsui Chuk Garden, Wong Tai Sin, Kowloon, Hong Kong
TEL: +852-35832323 / **FAX:** +852-35832448
OFFICE ADDRESS: 7F, 9th Anning Street, Jinshazhou, Baiyun District, Guangzhou, China
TEL: +86-20-89095121 / **FAX:** +86-20-89095206
BEIJING OFFICE: Room 107, Floor 1, Xiyingfang Alley, Ande Road, Dongcheng District, Beijing, China
TEL: +86-10-84139071 / **FAX:** +86-10-84139071
SHANGHAI OFFICE: Room 307, Building 1, Hong Qiang Creative Zhabei District, Shanghai, China
TEL: +86-21-63523469 / **FAX:** +86-21-63523469

SALES MANAGER: Sissi
TEL: +86-20-81007895
EMAIL: sales@sendpoints.cn
WEBSITE: www.sendpoints.cn / www.spbooks.cn

ISBN 978-988-78494-1-4

Printed and bound in China.

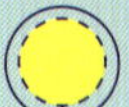

FOREWORD

Printing may be the most frequently used way of turning a creative idea into an actual product. Thus ideas have been printed on paper, fabric, plastic, and even plant, broadening the spectrum of expressive forms available to the literary and graphic arts.

A Three-Party Interview

This book begins with a chapter entitled "A Three-Party Interview." The interweaving strands of dialogue offer readers an engaging reading experience.

Significant Moments in the History of Printing

Next we highlight important advances in the history of printing, featuring, in chronological order, 18 printing methods.

Four Major Printing Methods

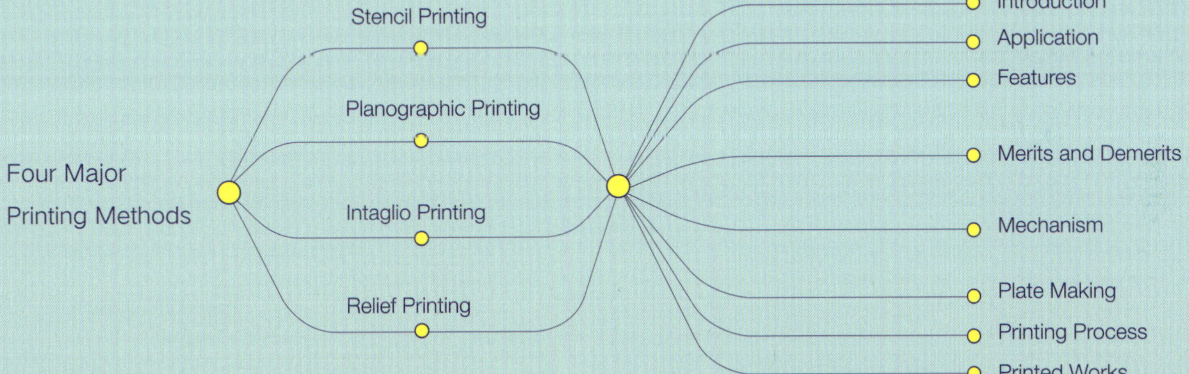

Printing techniques, depending on the character of the printing plate used, are divided into four major categories: stencil printing, planographic printing, intaglio printing, and relief printing. The last section is divided into four chapters, each of the four easy-to-understand chapters describing one printing method, illustrating its features and principles: how the printing plate is made, and how the printing process proceeds. Over 90 printed works are featured in this book. Most printing examples include a detailed description of the printing method, substrate, and inks.

CONTENTS

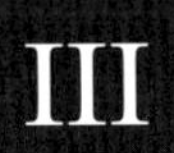

Intaglio Printing

164-193

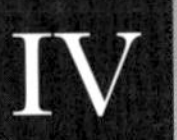

Relief Printing

194-253

Paper Mill X Printer X Designer

A THREE-PARTY INTERVIEW

From design to print, three parties are involved in the process: designers, paper mill experts, and printers. In this chapter, we invited each to talk with one another: asking any questions they may have had. Although all were at the top of their respective fields, gaining some knowledge of related fields was of great advantage in their work. Their stimulating dialogue offers readers an engaging reading experience.

Paper Mill: Zhiwang Ou

HANDSOME HALL
CEO
Engaged in the paper industry for 15 years

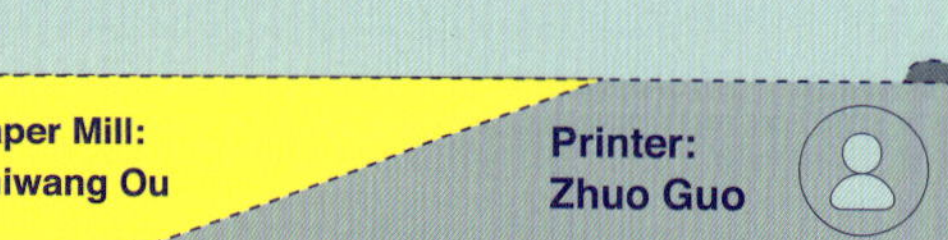

Many designers want to print high resolution photos and buy papers from us. Sometimes the quality of printing is related to halftone screening methods*. Could you please talk about that?

FM Screening (Frequency Modulated Screening) and AM Screening (Amplitude Modulated Screening) are halftone screening methods. There is no regularly-spaced pattern of dots in FM screening. Dark tones are rendered with more dots and light tones with fewer dots. FM screening creates more detailed pictures. But it is relatively less used due to the high printing requirement. AM screening is characterized by its geometric and fixed spacing dots. It is more commonly used now, because it is more suitable for printing machines.

Some papers may generate dust and lint during printing, the problem is usually with the papers, right?

I don't think so. There are mainly two reasons for that. First, because of poor quality paper, loose material on the surface may cause dust and lint. Second, if the ink is too thick and adhesive, papers can generate dust and lint easily. So it is important to have more communication between us, then we can recommend proper papers for you.

*The halftone screening method is the measure of how many halftone lines are printed in a linear inch. The original picture is divided into small dots. Changing the size and space between dots will change the tone of a picture.

In FM screening, the size of dots is fixed. Colors are changed by modulating the frequency of dots: with darker tones generated by a greater density of dots.

In AM screening, the number of dots is fixed. It changes the color by modulating the size of the dots. It is based on a graphic grid where a dot stays fixed in its position in the center of any grid cell.

Printer: Zhuo Guo | **Designer: Shijian Lin**

You've been engaged in the design industry for many years. There must have been times when things did not go smoothly. Could you please share some stories?

Once we wanted to coat a soft-touch film on the cover of one book to achieve a desired tactile feeling. It turned out, however, applying hot foil stamping technique on the soft touch film was difficult to realize. The film was incompatible with the gold foil. If I had known more about printing, things might have got better. Therefore, it is always better to know some knowledge about printing (smile).

Vibrant colors may result in the problem of "print-through." What can designers do to prevent this?

Usually, there are two causes. One is the thin paper, and the other is the heavy ink. We normally suggest that the designer change to another kind of paper instead of modifying the design file.

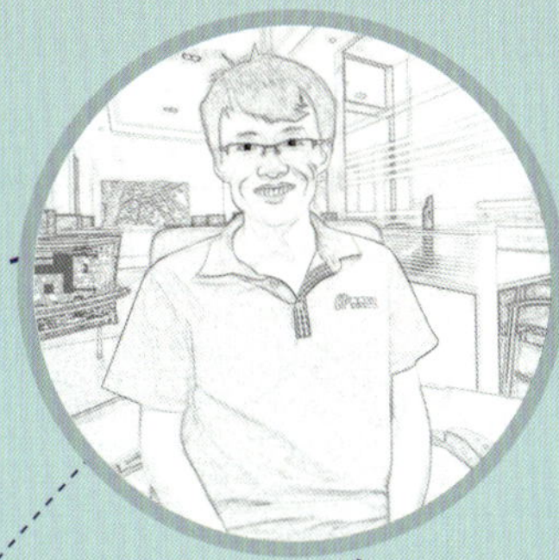

Printer: Zhuo Guo

HUAYU PRINTING
CEO Assistant
Engaged in the printing industry for 9 years

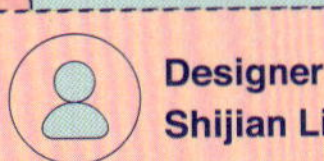

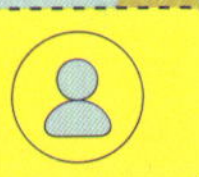

Designer: Shijian Lin | **Paper Mill: Zhiwang Ou**

Are there any economical options when choosing papers?

Well, some low-weight specialty papers produce the same performance as high-weight specialty papers do. See, the price of the 150g paper is 25% cheaper than that of 200g papers. And even some 130g specialty papers have the same stiffness and thickness of 200g specialty papers, but at a much lower price.

Now many designers contact us for good advice. They attach more and more importance to knowledge of paper and printing. In your opinion, what should designers do to guarantee the printing result?

First of all, designers should provide a reasonable design. Some designers may have lots of creative ideas, but the technology may fail to keep pace. An experienced designer will keep this in mind. A novice designer should communicate more often with paper mill experts and printers and take the initiative to master the knowledge of papers and printing. For example, if I want to achieve a hollowed-out effect, I will discuss it with the paper mill expert and choose proper papers that with the desired stiffness and thickness. And then decide whether to do laser engraving or die-cutting, according to the degree of the fineness of the design. Better communication will yield better results.

The birth of a printed work

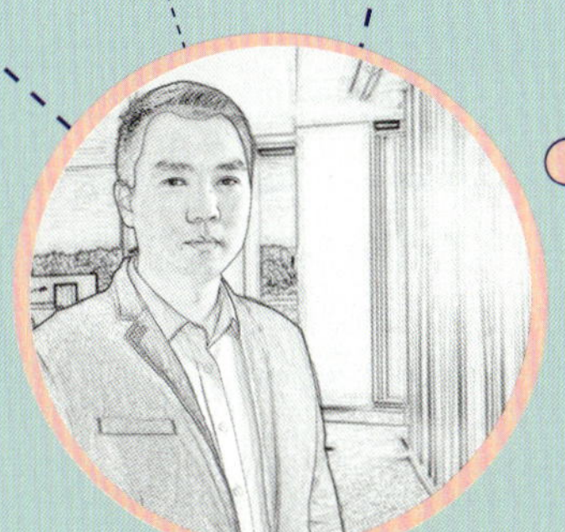

Designer: Shijian Lin

SendPoints Publishing Co., Ltd.
Publishing Director & Chief Editor
Engaged in the publishing industry for 10 years

Six Tips for Using Specialty Papers

- Interviewee: Zhiwang Ou

  HANDSOME HALL (GUANGZHOU) TRADING CO., LTD.
  CEO

- Editor: Akira/Claire

1 Do not go against the grain

A paper's grain is the direction in which most of the fibers lie, and is generated during paper formation. When the paper is cut into sheets, it will be either long-grain (if the fibers are aligned parallel to the sheet's longer dimension) or short-grain (if the fibers are aligned parallel to the sheet's shorter dimension). The paper will tear and fold more easily with the grain and with greater difficulty against the grain. When pages are bound in books, the grain should be parallel to the binding edge.

2 Pay attention to color reproduction when printed on colored papers

Cream papers are widely used for inside pages now. Printing on cream papers that are not white will adversely affect color reproduction. Therefore, yellow ink should be less when mixing colors during the printing process. The quality of color reproduction will be better after adjusting colors.

3 Choose proper specialty papers

Some specialty papers may generate dust and lint when printed with too much ink. There is no point in using specialty papers for full-page printing because it will obscure the unique features of specialty papers. Coated papers are usually more suitable for full-page printing. Uncoated papers with rough surfaces are not appropriate for full-page printing.

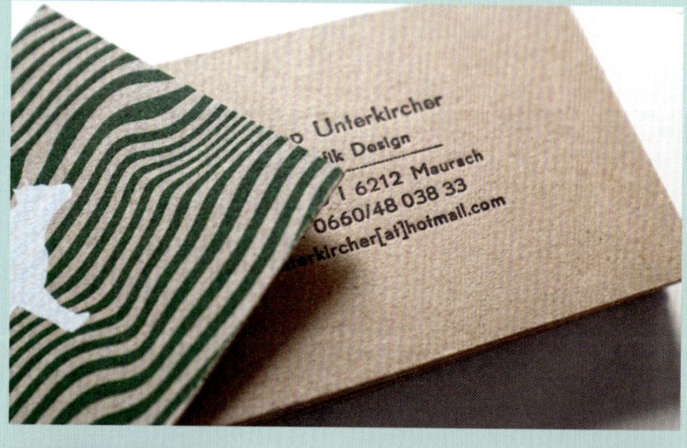

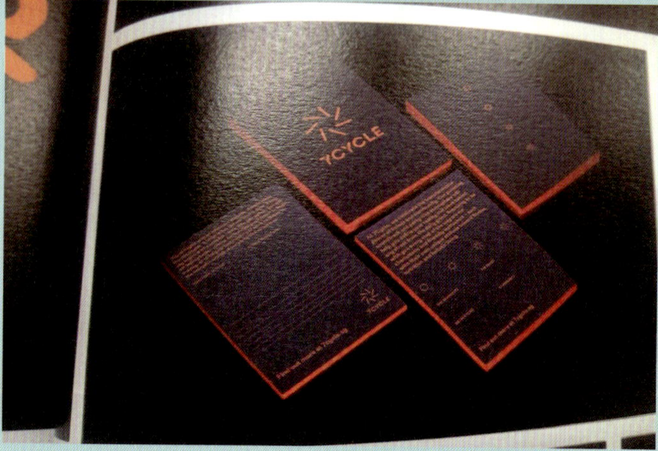

Uncoated Paper

Coated Paper

4 Do not use extra printing techniques

Specialty papers will produce good output printed with a simple method. They will lose their unique features after lamination. Printing methods should be carefully chosen according to the features of the papers used.

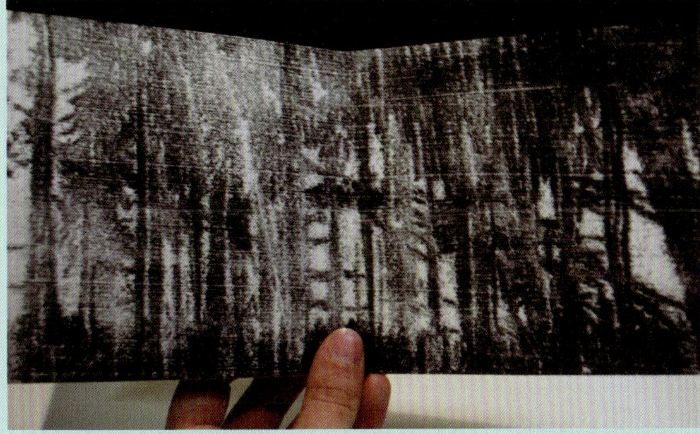

5 Carefully choose printing content based on the features of papers

Printing content should be carefully chosen based on the features of papers. Some papers with a glossy surface usually produce good quality of color reproduction and thus are suitable for high-quality printing: such as imported matte coated paper and glossy coated paper. In Hong Kong, art paper includes glossy coated paper and matte coated paper. The advantages of art coated paper lies in the quality of color reproduction and easy printing. The drawbacks of art paper are that it lacks textures and distinctive features.

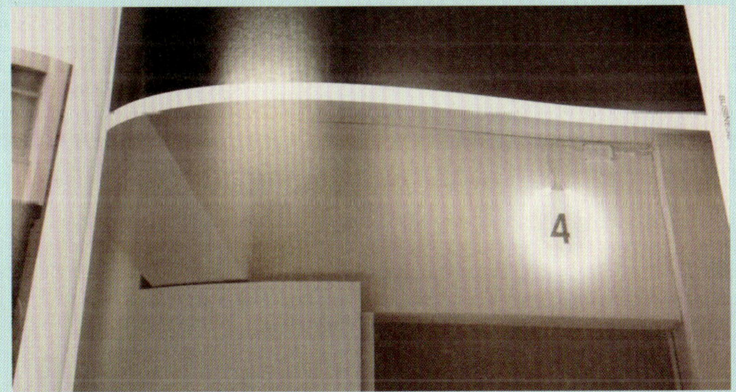

Art Paper

6 Avoid white edge in the folded areas of dyed papers

There are two kinds of specialty paper: pulp and dyed. Pulp papers refer to unbleached papers, which remain the original color. Dyed papers refer to papers with only the surface dyed. If the surface appears red, the interior may be white when exposed. Therefore, a white edge in the folded area should be avoided when a dyed paper is used for a cover. Besides, the price of dyed papers is much lower than that of pulp papers. And the stiffness and tenacity may also not be as good as those of pulp papers.

Exposed white edge of papers

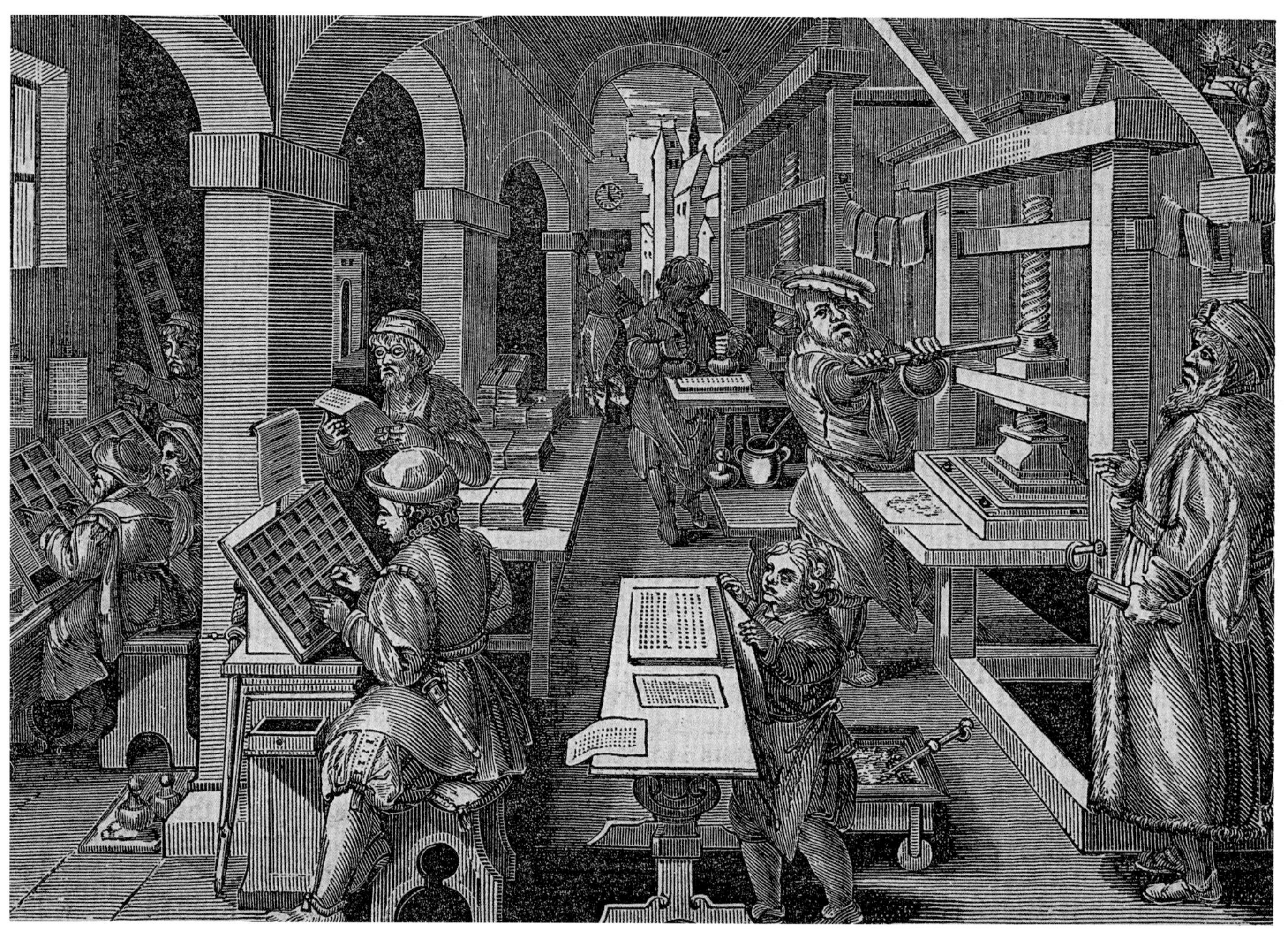

SIGNIFICANT MOMENTS IN THE HISTORY OF PRINTING

There are many different types and crafts of printing

Conventional printing technology includes woodblock printing, movable type, and stencil printing. Printing methods introduced in modern times include offset printing, collotype printing, aquatint and so on.

200 BC Woodblock Printing

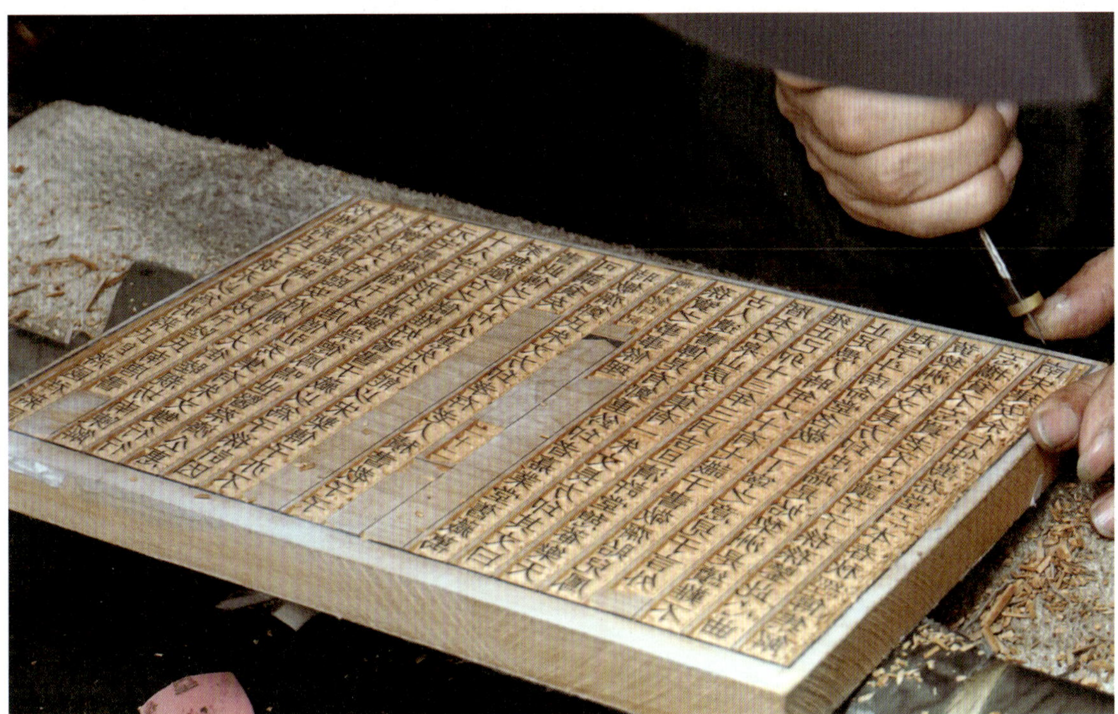

"**Woodblock printing is the greatest invention with initiation significance.**"

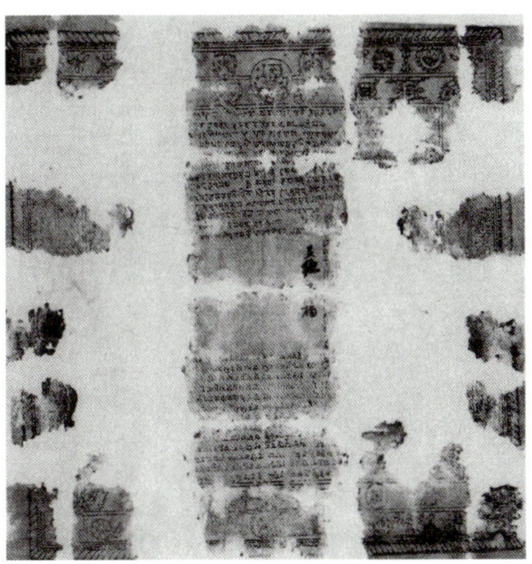

On November 20th 1996, the Shaanxi Historic Relic Identification Committee invited experts to identify some unearthed relics: five *Dharani Sutra* and other artifacts, including bronze mirrors. The earliest printing found on them was in Sanskrit: thus in 2006 the *Dharani Sutra* woodblock printing technique was added to the list of the state-level intangible cultural heritage.

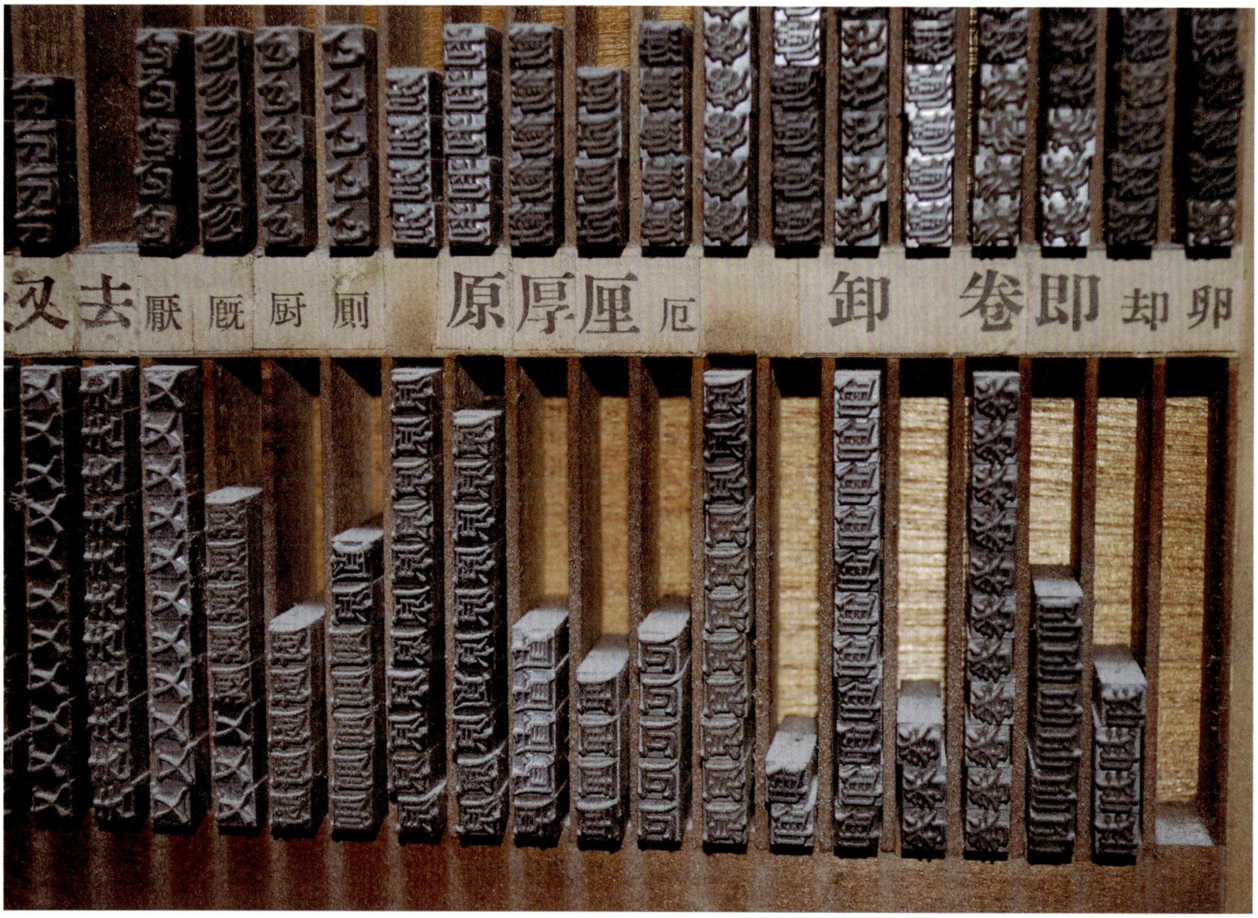

©Katorisi

In the 1040s Movable Type

Movable type was invented by the genius worker Bi Sheng in the Northern Song Dynasty (1041-1048) in China. Movable characters were first made by wood, then by clay. They were the earliest type in the world, more than 400 years earlier than the type used in the Gutenburg press.

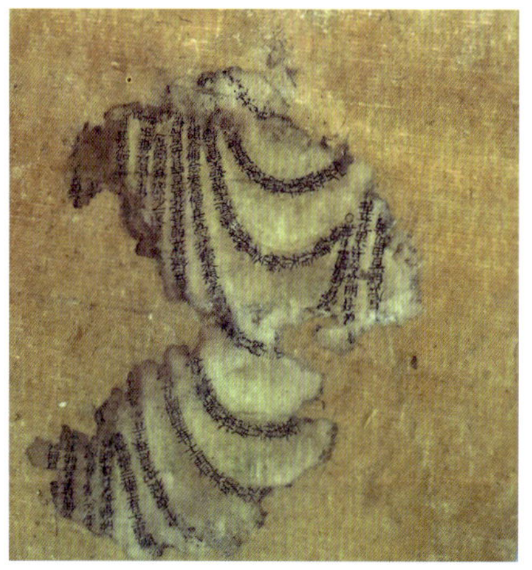

"The Earliest Buddhist Scriptures"

The printing methods Chinese people invented (including woodblock printing and movable type) preserved their traditional handicrafts, which are basic compared to modern printing. However, fundamentals such as the three basic procedures (carving or casting characters, composing, printing) already existed in the Song Dynasty.

The *Amitayurdhyana Sutra* in the Northern Song Dynasty (1103) is believed to be the earliest survivor of the first movable type printing works.

Movable Type in the East

North Korea took advantage of its favorable geographical position and to become the first culture that borrowed woodblock printing from China to print many books.

The oldest book in the world printed in metallic movable type is *Jikji*, printed in Korea in 1377. Later, Korea established a font-casting institution, and movable type printing developed rapidly.

In 1366, in North Korea appeared wooden movable type *Tong Jian Gang Mu* (《通鉴纲目》).

And then, in 1436, in North Korea appeared lead-type printing *Tong Jian Gang Mu* (《通鉴纲目》).

Woodblock printing spread to Japan in the eighth century. Wooden movable type came in Japan in the sixteenth century, under the influence of China and Korea.

In the late sixteenth century, *Classic of Filial Piety* (《古文孝经》) and *Exhortation to Study* (《劝学文》) were printed in Japan with movable type.

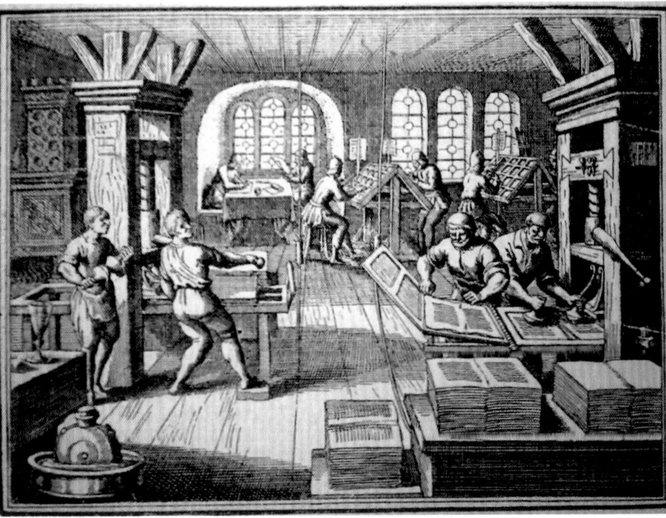

Movable Type in the West

In Germany, around 1440, Johannes Gutenburg integrated several techniques already existing in Europe. As a result, movable type spread in Europe quickly, promoting the industrialization of printing. Before Gutenberg, Western countries also mastered block printing, which can print one copy or many more. But one big problem with this method is that printing every new book needs a new woodblock or forme. Thus, it is unrealistic to print many different books. Although movable type had appeared several hundred years before in China, it had never spread. Besides, Chinese movable type is handmade. Thus, modern European movable type printing originates mainly from Gutenburg's combinations, innovations, and modifications.

The Historical Significance of Movable Type

Before movable type, the only method was woodblock printing: requiring much time, space, and management. The birth of movable type was an earth-shaking event for printing and disseminating knowledge. Movable type became an important pillar of modern civilization: deemed by Westerners as the "mother of civilization."

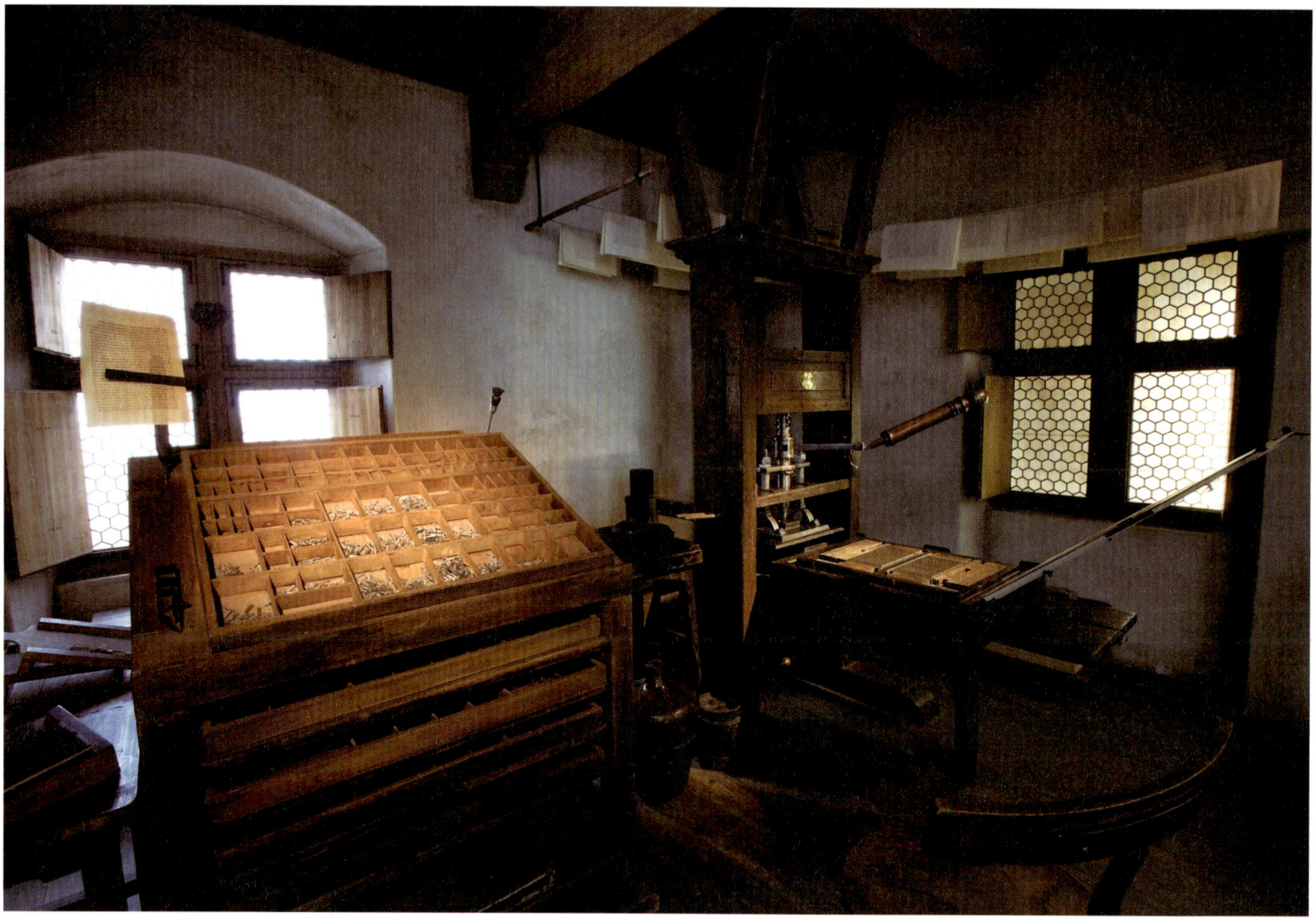

©Jorge Royan

In the 1440s Printing Press

Johannes Gutenberg's first movable printing workshop was in 1449.

> " **An important media revolution in contemporary history** "

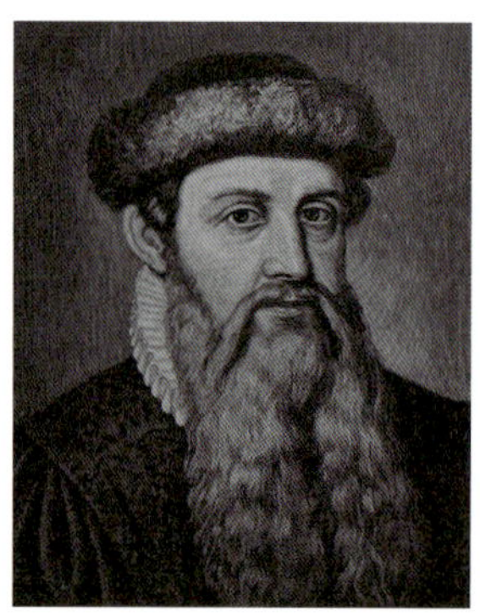

Johannes Gutenberg

Gutenberg's method for making type is traditionally considered to have included a type of metal alloy and a hand mould for casting type. The alloy was a mixture of lead, tin, and antimony that melted at a relatively low temperature for faster and more economical casting, cast well, and created a durable type. His major work, the Gutenberg Bible (also known as the 42-line Bible), has been acclaimed for its high aesthetic and technical quality.

In the 1450s Intaglio Printing

Intaglio printing, or gravure, is one of the four major printing methods. There are two kinds of intaglio printing. One is engraving art, invented in 1452 by Italian goldsmith M. Finiguela. Another is photogravure, created in the early nineteenth century by French inventor Nicéphore Niépce. He tried using light-sensitive and acid-resistant properties to make plates.

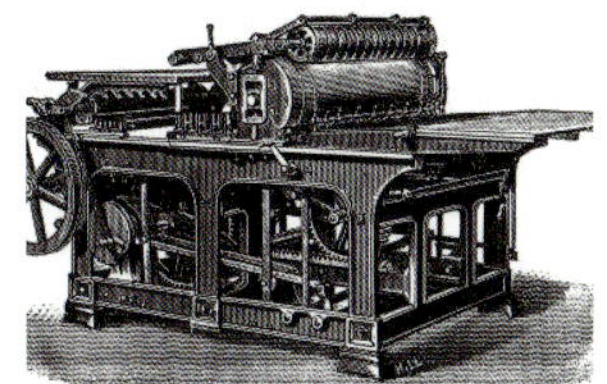

> " **A number of technologies invented and used from the eighteenth to the twentieth centuries laid a solid foundation for changes in gravure plate-making technology.** "

- In 1782, potassium was found to be sensitized.
- In 1839, photographic technology was invented.
- In 1891, carbon tissue was invented.
- In 1895, Klimch invented the rotogravure printing method.

In the early 1500s Etching Prints

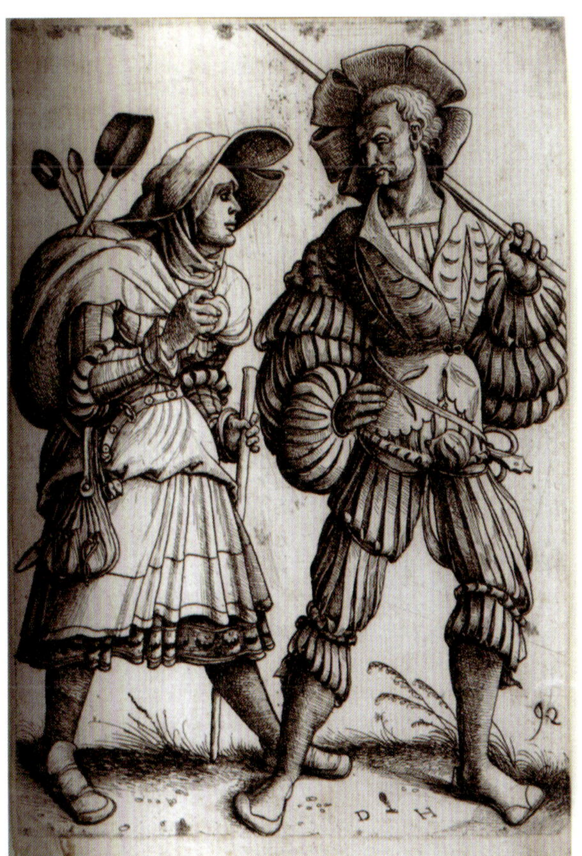

Etching was invented by a German, Daniel Hopefel, and applied in printmaking. Etching is a way of drawing prints. Strong acid or mordant is used to cut into the unprotected parts of a metal surface to create a design in intaglio in the metal. In modern manufacturing, other chemicals may be used on other types of material.

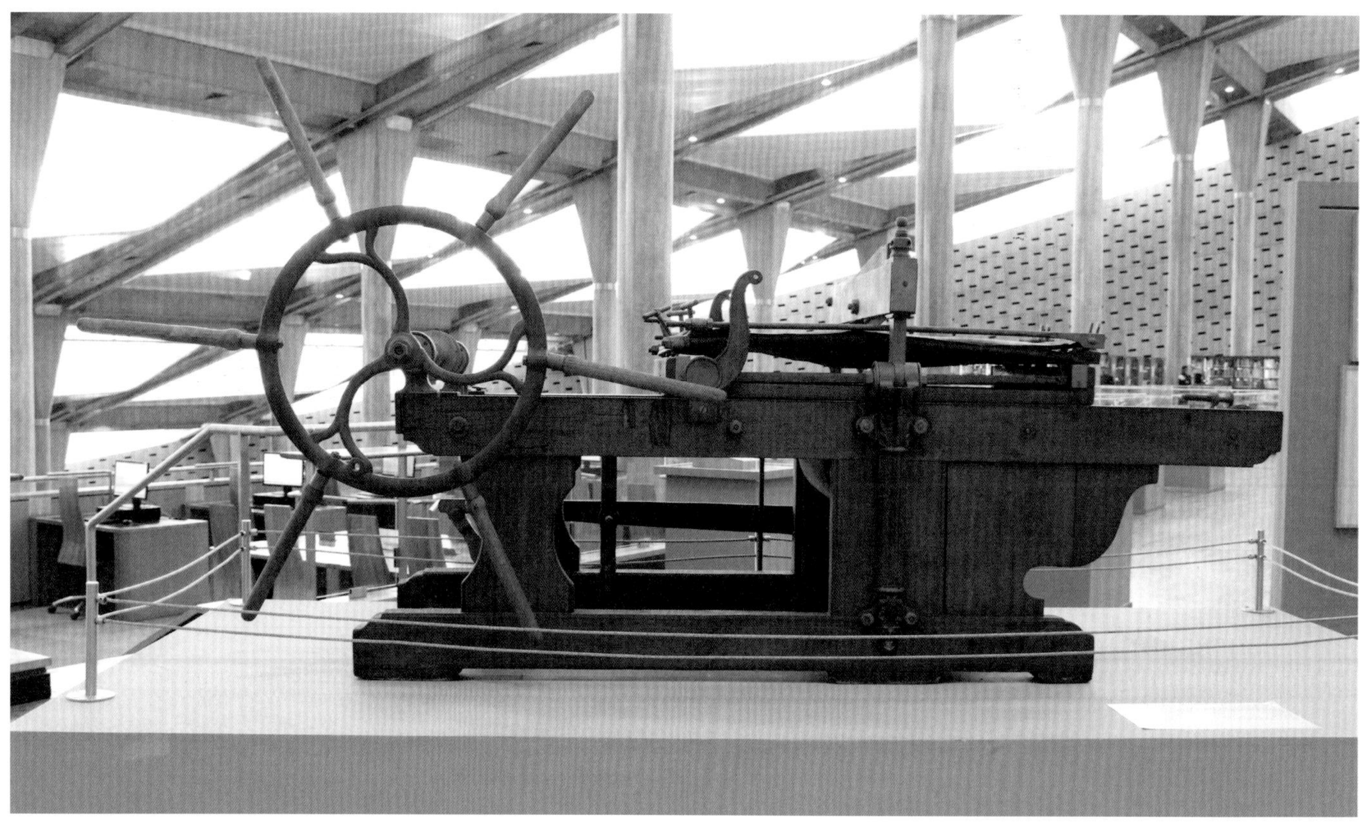

In the late 1700s   Lithography

Lithography was invented in 1798 by author and actor Alois Senefelder. It was the first new printing technique since typography was created in 15th century and has become the most widely used one. It uses a flat forme to print. In the early years of lithography, it originally used a smooth, level lithographic limestone plate. That is why its name is from "stone" in ancient Greek.

In the 1830s   Chromolithography

Chromolithography is a method for making multi-color prints. It was invented in 1837. This type of color printing stemmed from lithography and includes all types of lithography printed in color. It replaced hand coloring and became a true art form.

In the 1840s The Rotary Printing Press

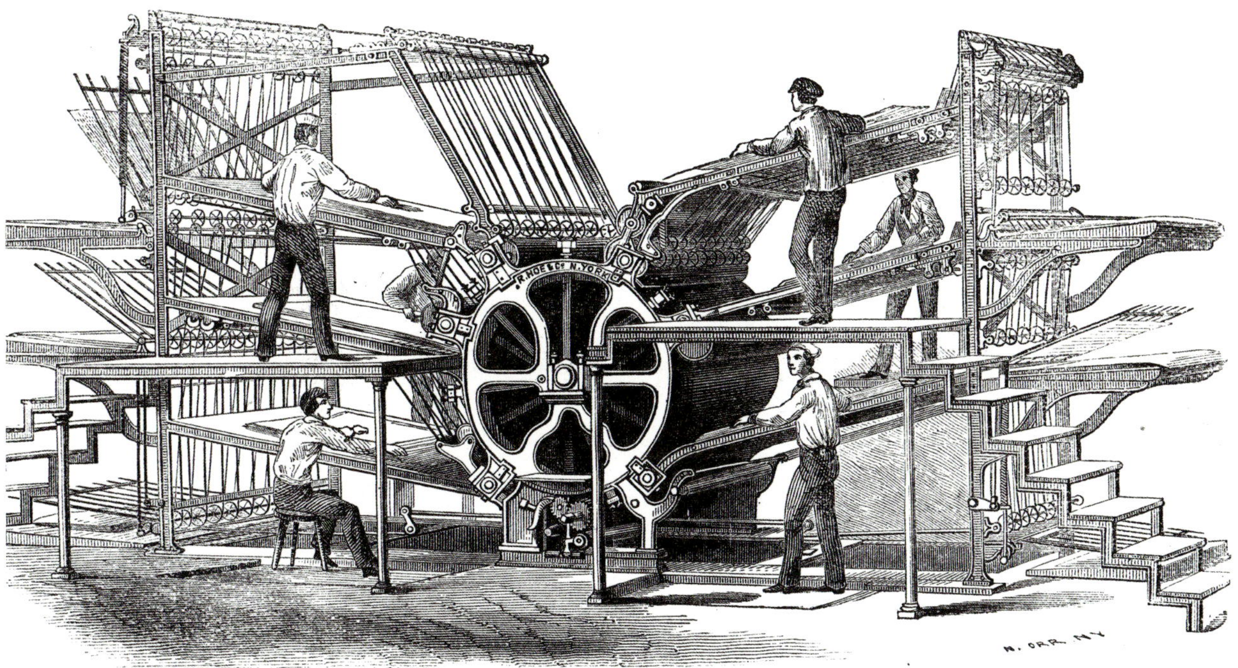

Hoe's six cylinder printing press.

In 1847, Richard March Hoe invented rotary drum printing. Today, there are three main types of rotary printing press: offset (including web offset), rotogravure, and flexography. Although the three types use cylinders to print, they vary in method.

In the 1870s Web Offset

Offset printing, also known as offset lithography, is a widely used printing technique in which the inked image is transferred from a plate to a rubber blanket, then to the printing surface. As one type of lithographic printing, it is also based on the repulsion of oil and water which avoids water and ink carried to printing materials together.

In the 1880s Mimeograph

In 1886, came mimeographing, a printing method using waxed paper before computer printing prevailed. Because the tools and materials required are simple, it was once popular in schools and companies. The main tools are transcribing steel, copying pen, waxed paper, ink and blank paper.

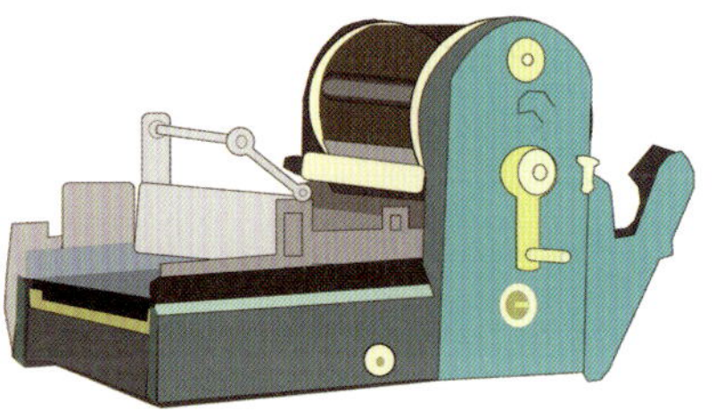

In the early 1900s Screen Printing

Screen printing first appeared in China more than 2,000 years ago. Dating back to the Qin and Han dynasties, "Jiaxie," an ancient Chinese technique of printing and dying, already existed. The printing principle is the same as to today's screen printing, but using printing blocks instead of silkscreen.

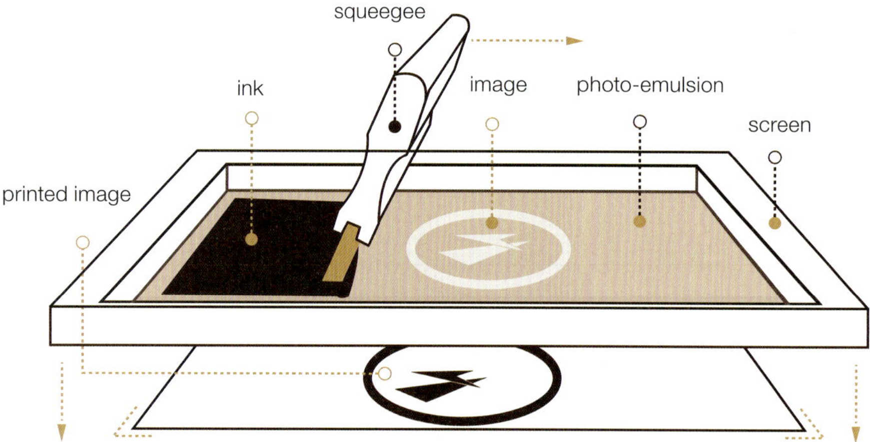

The principle of screen printing

In the Sui Dynasty, people began to use the tulle frame to print, which developed clip dye to silk-screen printing. According to historical records, the delicate clothes worn in the court during the Tang Dynasty were printed in this way. To the Song Dynasty, silk-screen printing progressed and improved the original oil painting. Printers began to add starch powder to the dye to make it into pulp. As a result, the screen printing products became more colorful.

In the 1930s Xerography

The usual copy is one kind of xerography. Its fundamental principle was invented by American physicist Chester Carlson in 1938 and was awarded a U.S. Patent on October 6,1942.

In the 1950s Inkjet Printing

Inkjet printing, is a kind of printing without contact, pressure or forme. If the information is input into the machine, it can be printed at once. Inkjet printing usually adopts a direct ink-jet model. As the name implies, this method involves imaging on the surface of the printed material.

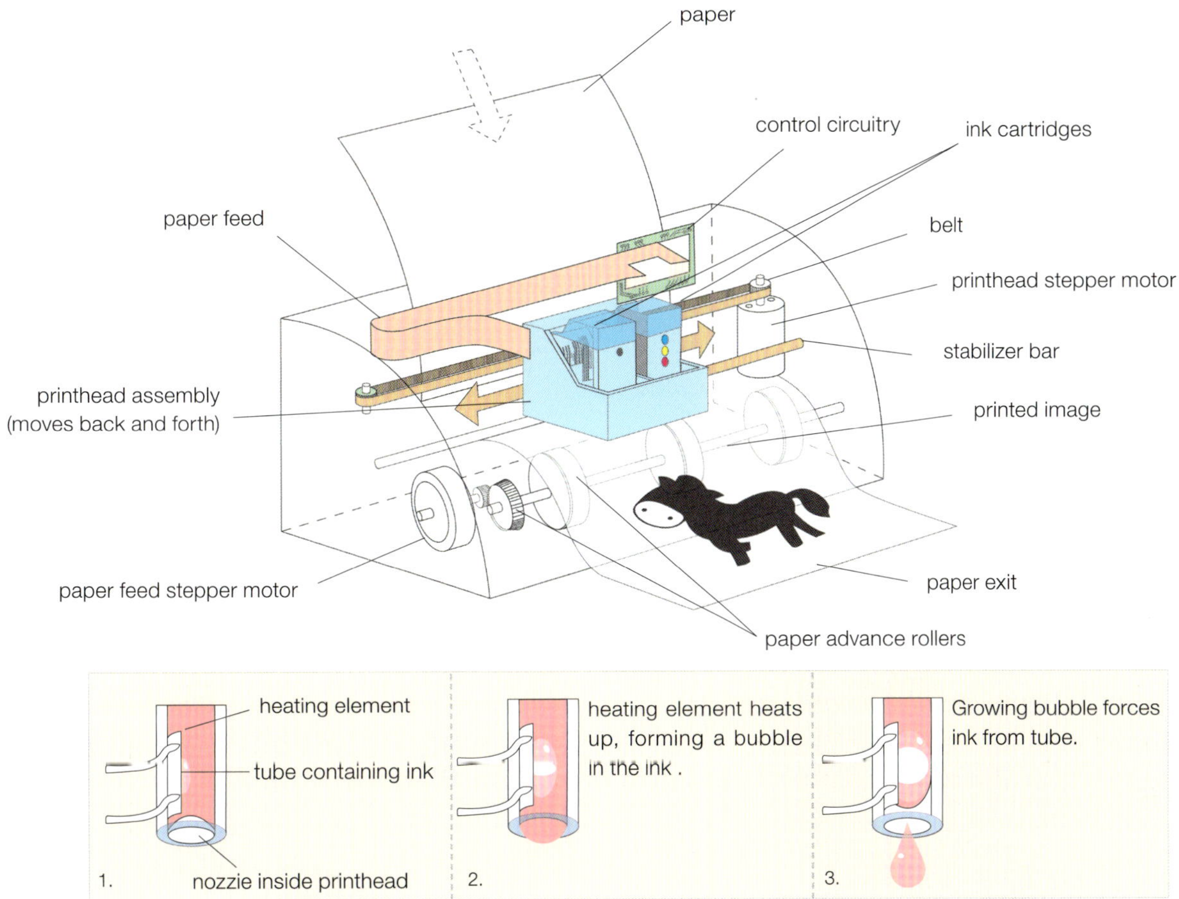

The principle of inkjet

In the 1950s Dye-Sublimation Printing

Many consumer and professional dye-sublimation printers are designed and used for producing photographic prints, ID cards, clothing, and more. Traditional dye-sublimation requires specialized printing paper and ribbon (usually yellow, green and red). It can print only one primary color at a time, so each photo must be typed three times. The printing process is complicated, and the cost is relatively high.

In the 1960s Dot Matrix Printing

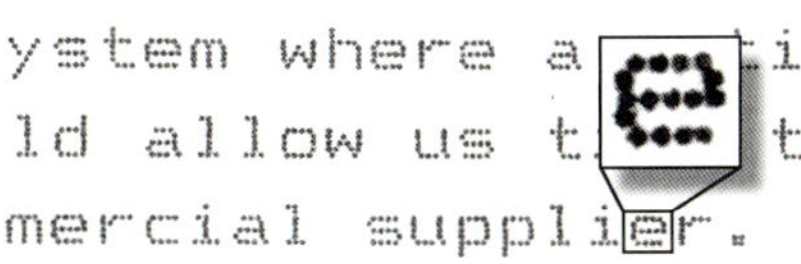

The dot matrix printer, also called a needle printer, forms a larger image with a set of pixels or dots. It applies the print mechanism on a typewriter, which uses a print head to form dots accurately. More advanced than a typewriter, it can print graphics besides texts. However, the quality of printing texts is lower than with typewriters with an independent matrix.

In the 1960s Laser Printing

In the late 1960s, Gary Starkweather of the Xerox Corporation invented the laser printer. Then, by the mid 1970s, the company was producing a commercial laser printer. Images produced by the laser (Dover) achieved speeds of 60 pages per minute (one page a second). It was sold at the price of 300,000 dollars.

1. laser-scanning unit
2. glass copier window
3. mirror
4. lens
5. mirror
6. image transfer belt
7. image developer
8. paper and paper feed mechanism
9. fuser

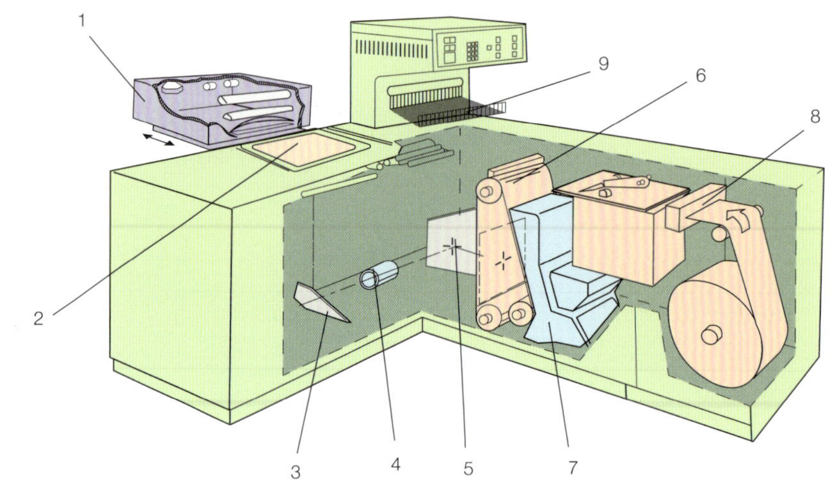

In the 1970s Thermal Printing

Thermal printing is a digital printing process. It generally uses two methods: direct thermal printing and thermal transfer printing.

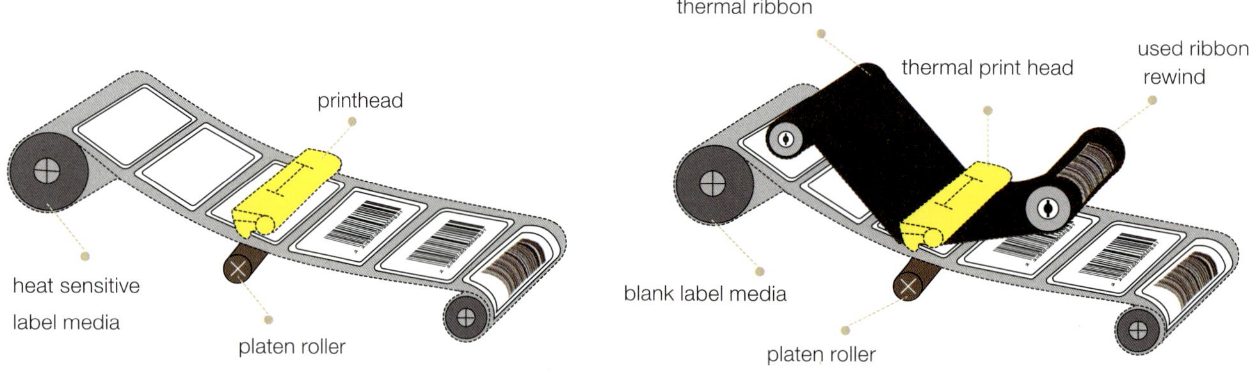

Direct thermal printing produces a printed image by selectively heating coated thermal paper. The coating turns black when the paper passes over the thermal print head.

Thermal transfer printing uses a heat-sensitive ribbon. The material is applied to paper by melting a coating of ribbon so that it stays glued to the material on which the print is applied.

In the late 1990s Digital Printing

Digital printing refers to methods of printing from a digital-based image directly onto a variety of media. Digital printing has a higher cost per page than more traditional offset printing methods, but this price is usually offset by avoiding the cost of all the technical steps required to make printing plates.

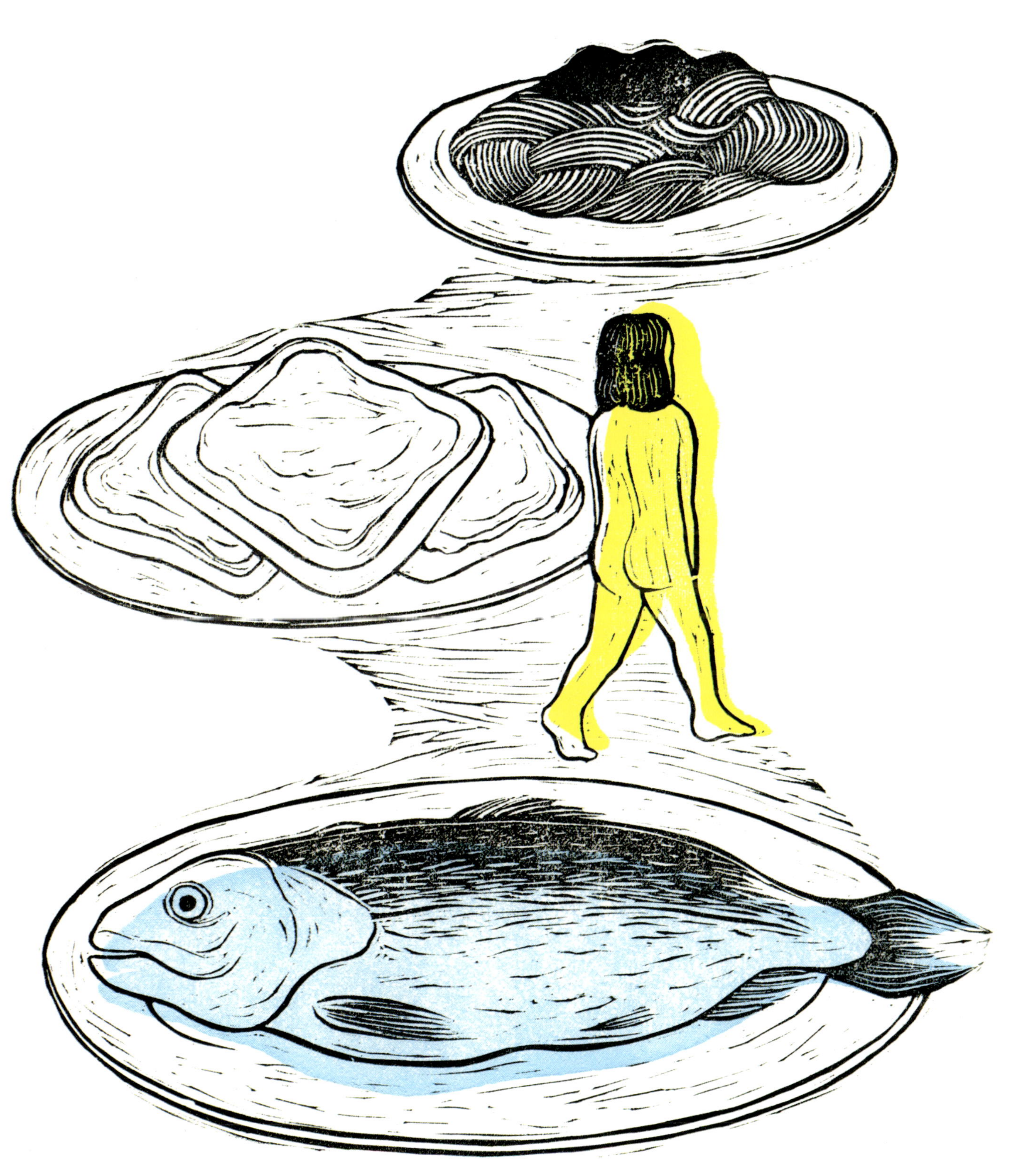

Photo by RITARDO

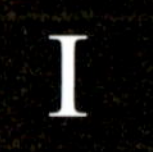

Stencil Printing

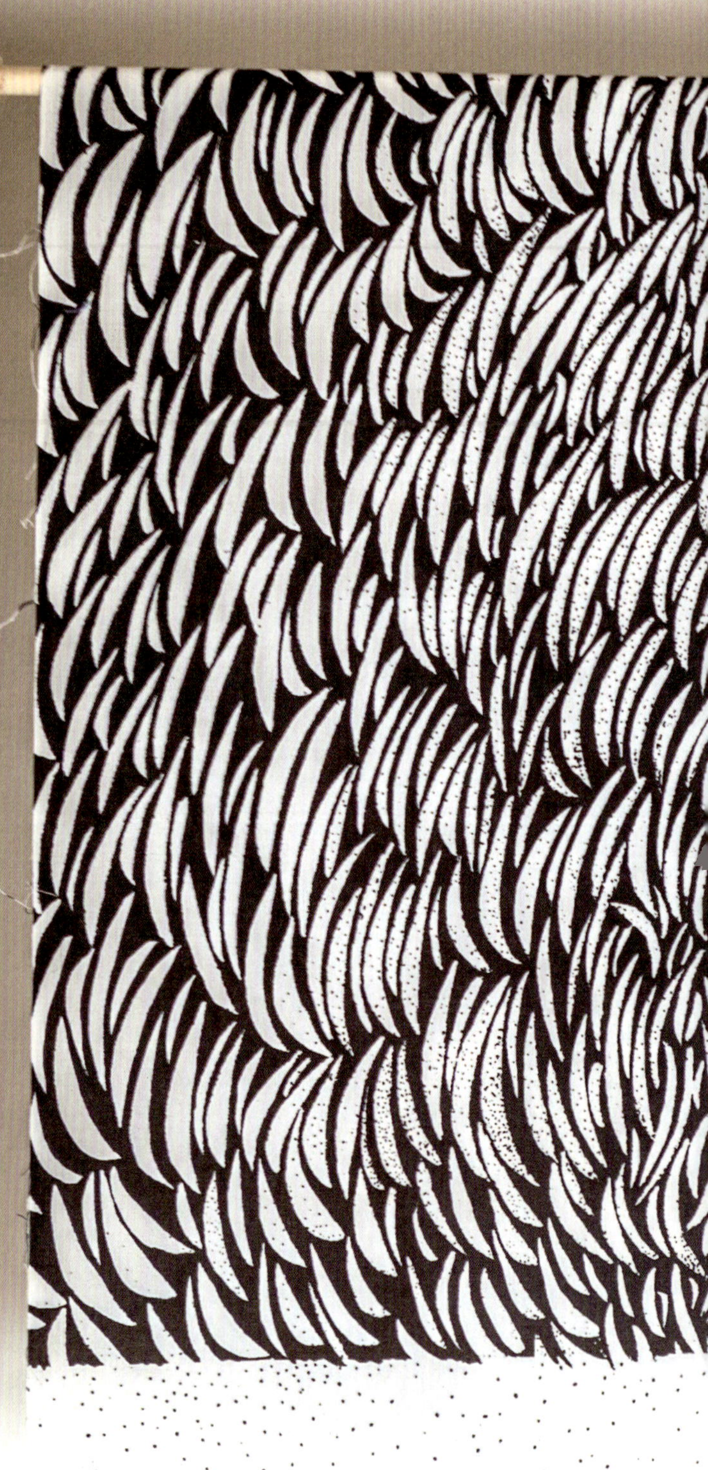

Stencil Printing

1 Introduction

The stencil printing technique is a printing technique whereby a mesh is used to transfer ink onto a substrate. There are several types of stencil printing, including mimeograph, type stencil printing, and screen printing. Each process offers several different plate-making methods. Among them, screen printing is a widely applied printing method. Traditionally the process is called silkscreen printing because silk was used in the process prior to the invention of polyester mesh. Actually, there are special-use mesh materials of cotton and stainless steel available to screen printers. Currently, synthetic threads are commonly used in the screen printing process, which is better and more durable than silk.

2 Application

① short-run printing of posters and graphics ② traffic signs ③ vehicle parts and instrument dials
④ printed circuit boards ⑤ photoelectric components ⑥ CD ⑦ textiles ⑧ decorations, labels, and wallpapers

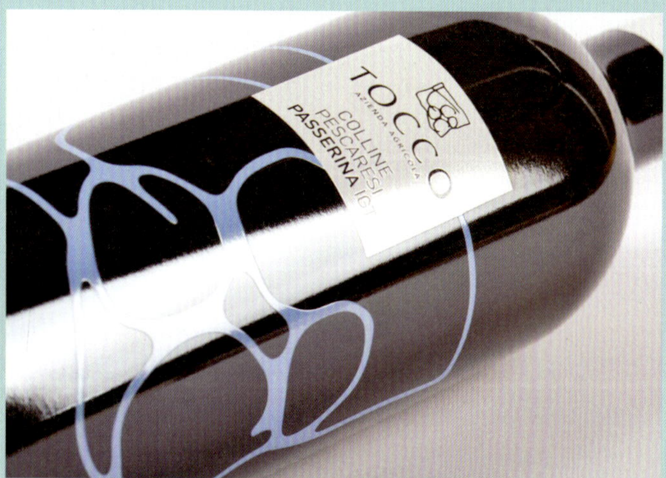

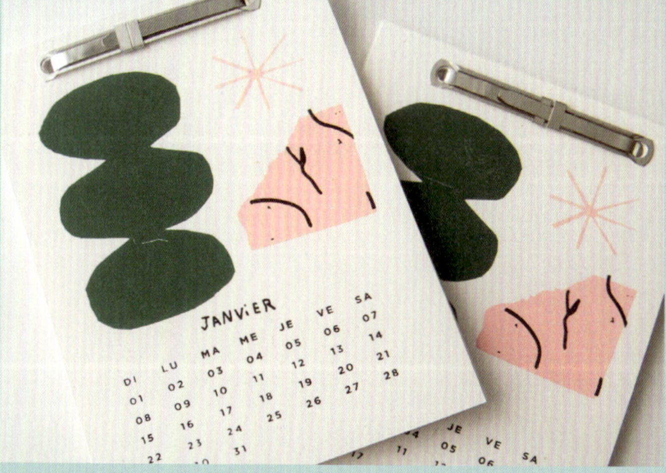

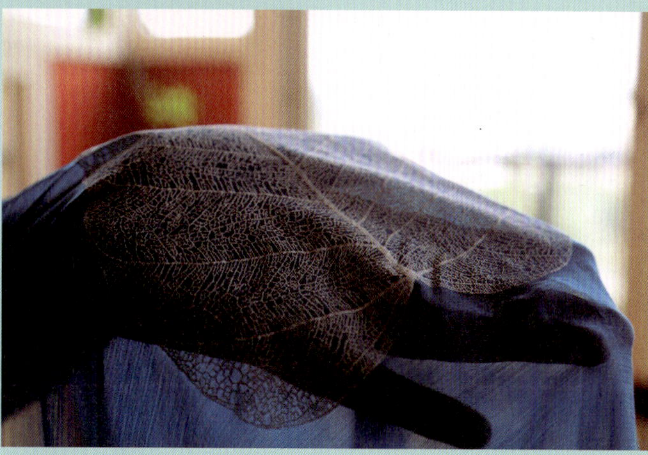

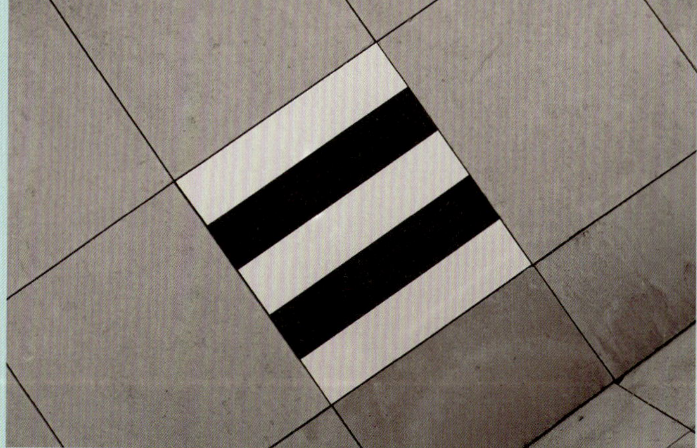

3 Features

- The thickness of ink is visible to the naked eye.
- The ink is matte.
- The process offers a direct printing method.

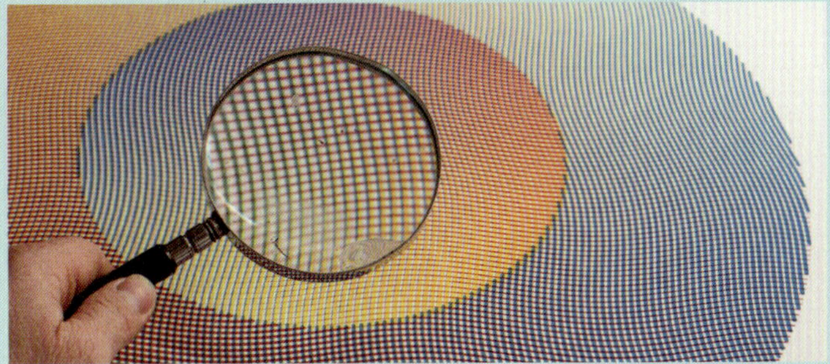

The pattern of screen printing is visible after the image is enlarged.

4 Merits and Demerits

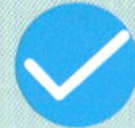

- The principle of plate making is simple and the equipment easy to operate.
- The substrate can be any object except for liquid or gas.

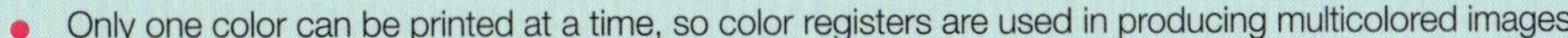

- Only one color can be printed at a time, so color registers are used in producing multicolored images.
- Poor color registration may occur.
- This makes it difficult to operate if printing gradient colors.
- Unsuitable for small scale printing due to the high cost of plate making and proofing processes.

Sreen Printing with Plants.

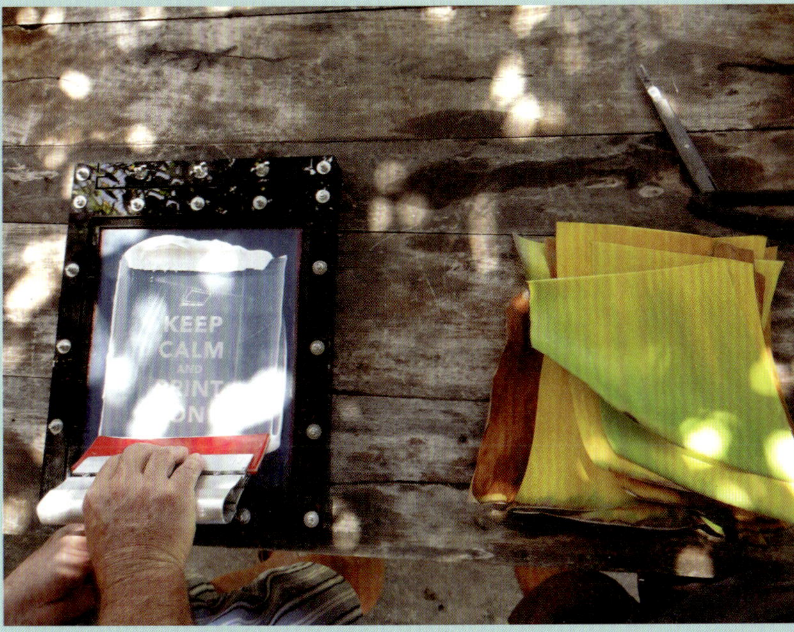

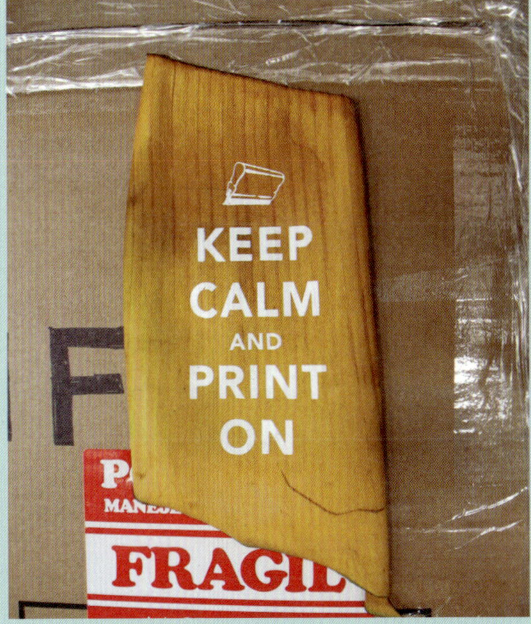

5 Mechanism

A Function View

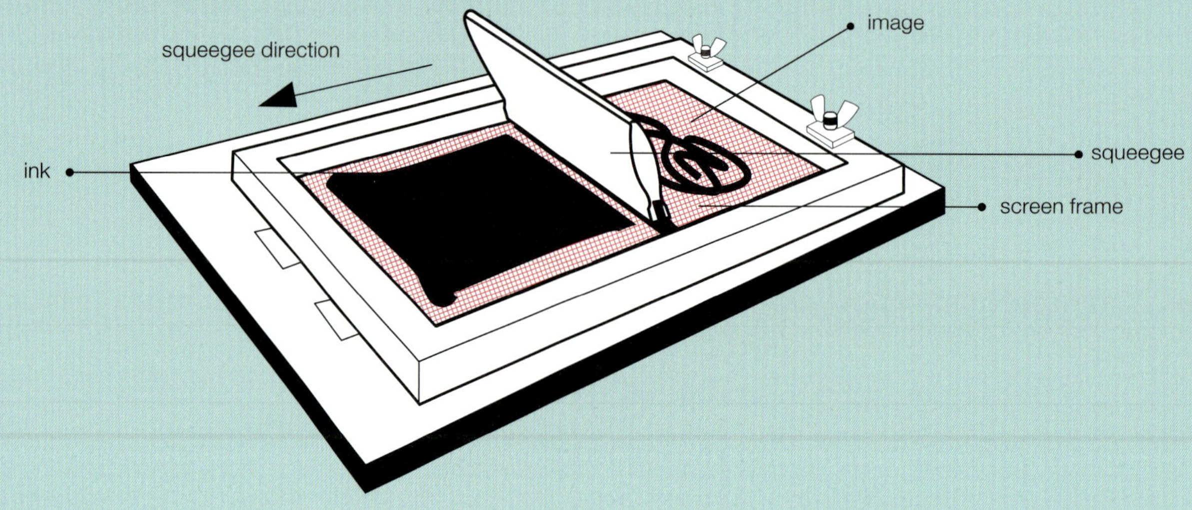

B Top View

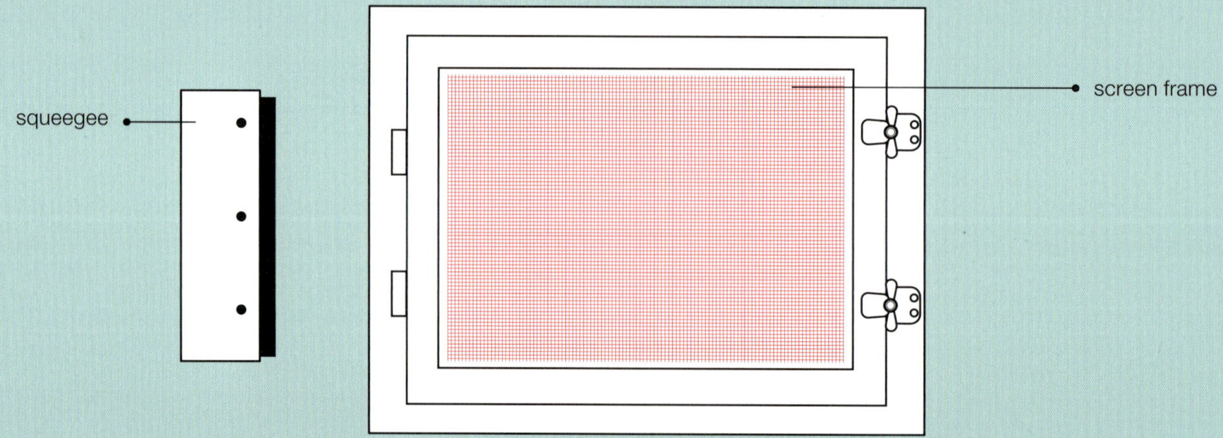

C Side View

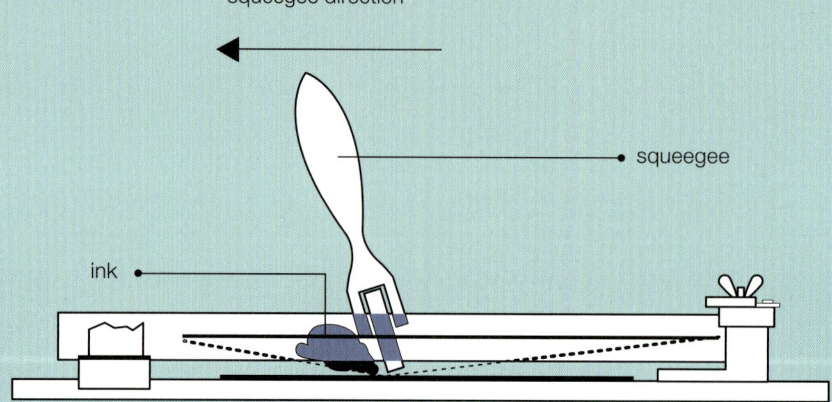

D Printing Method

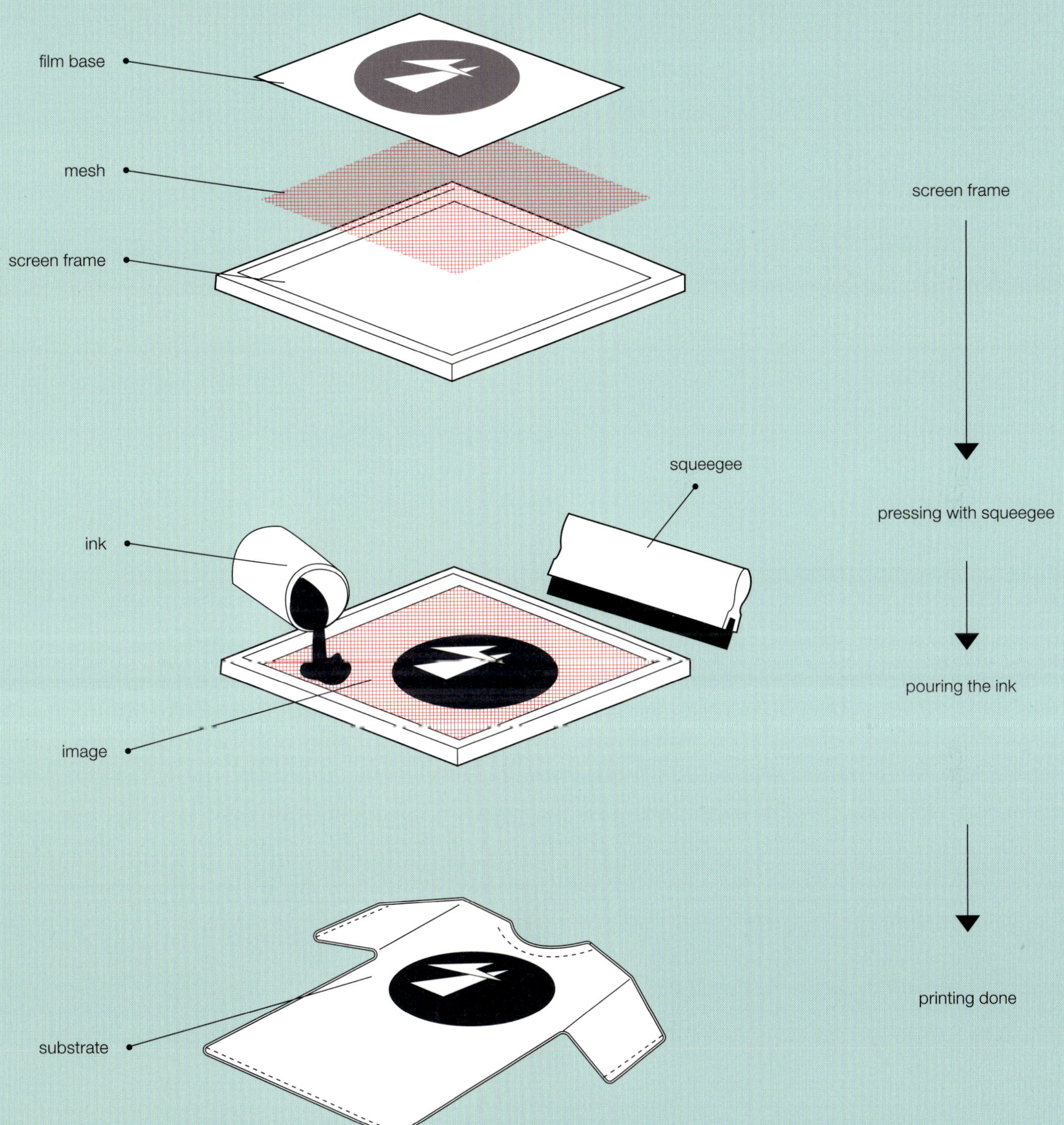

Principle

In screen printing, the image is printed by forcing ink through the stencil openings and onto the substrate to form graphics and text. Because the ink goes directly into the substrate, the ink remains thick. Therefore, the quality of color reproduction produced by screen printing ranks first among the four major printing methods.

E Structure

A screen printing press consists mainly of a feeder, a rotary turret, a drying unit, and a controlling unit. There are at least four ink-printing stations arranged around a rotary turret. One separate printer prints one color at a time. The color register can be done as long as the substrate makes a round on the rotary turret. The heating stations and cooling stations will dry the ink quickly because the ink for screen printing is thick.

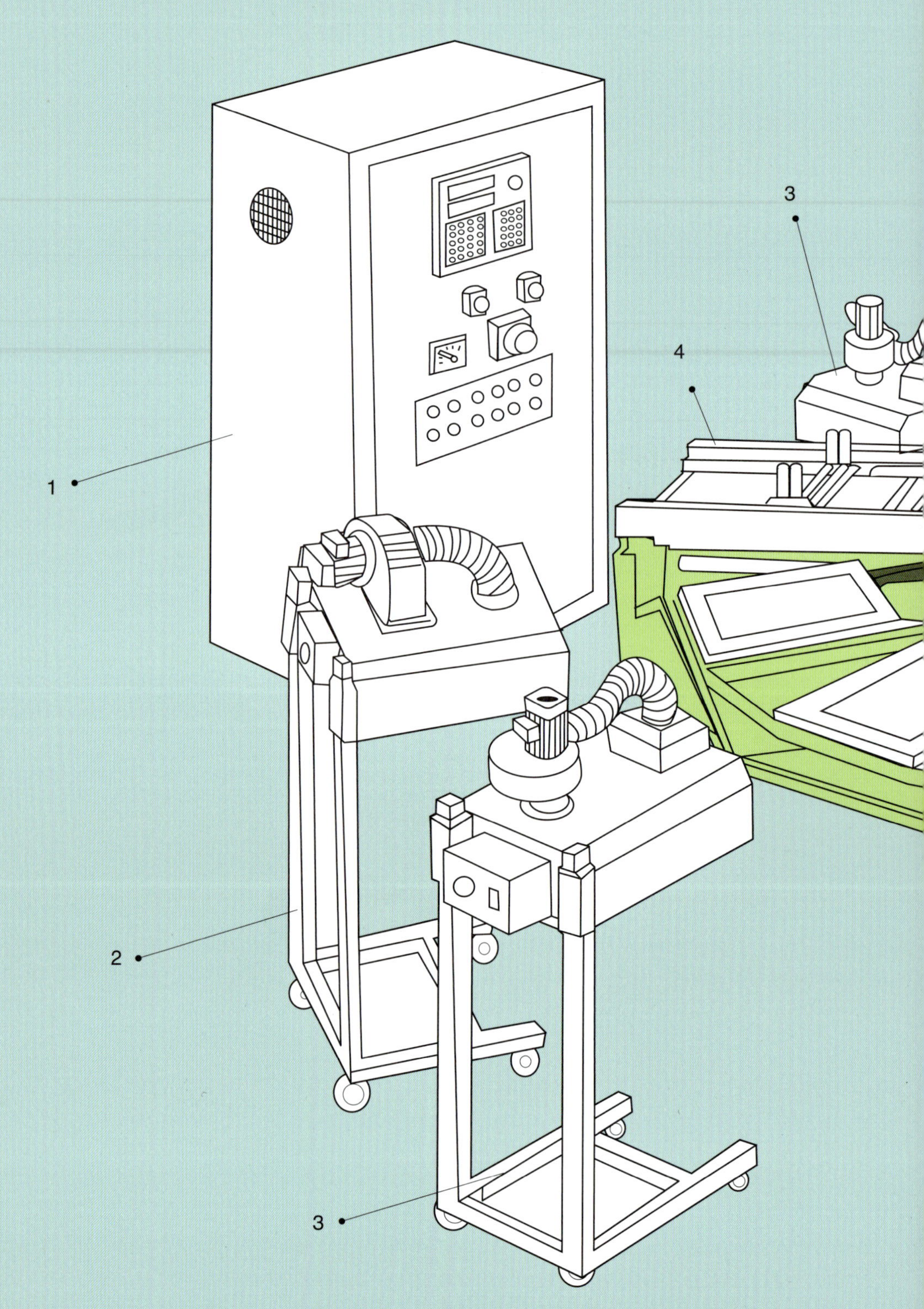

1.controlling unit

2.cooling station

3.heating station

4.rotary turret

5.feeder

6.central pin

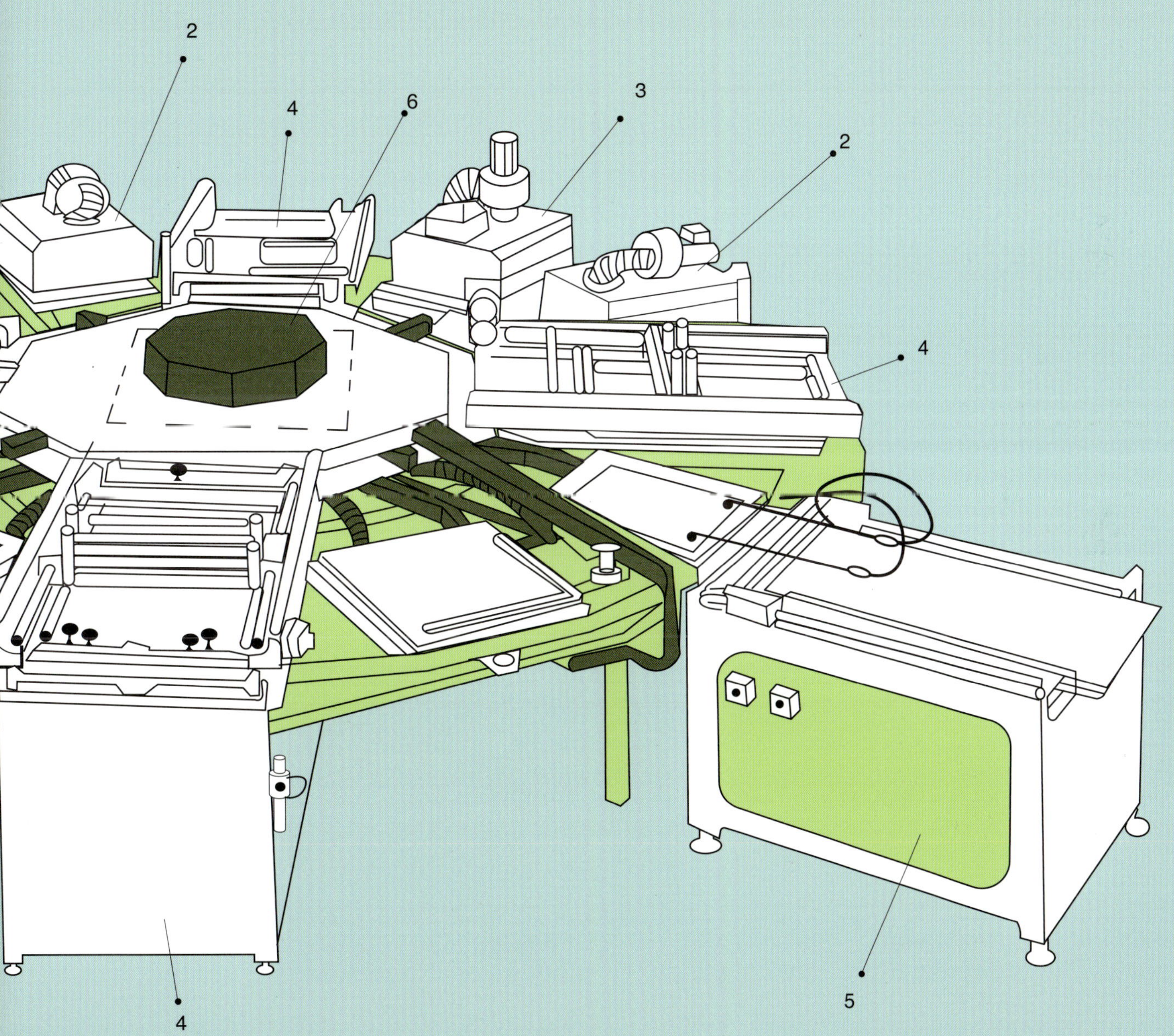
2
4
6
3
2
4
5
4

6 Plate Making

Currently, the plate-making methods of screen printing consist of manual plate making, sensitizer stencil making and wire mesh plate making. The methods could be divided into direct plate making, indirect plate-making and mix & match plate-making methods.

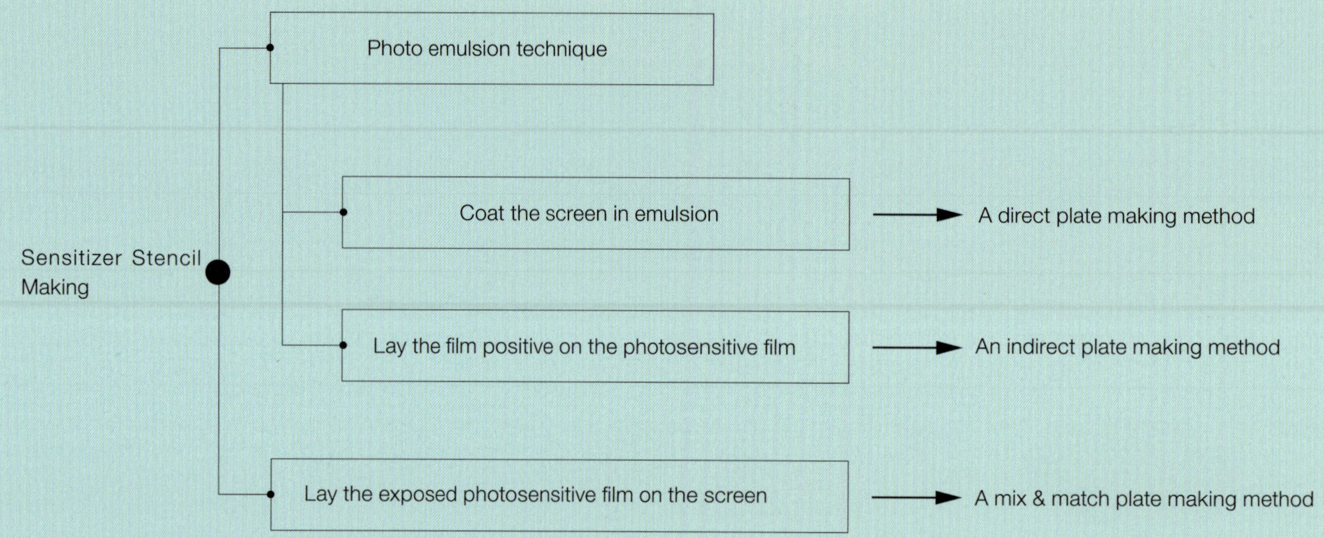

a. Direct plate-making method

Process

The direct plate-making method is the most widely used method. Coat the screen with a layer of photo-reactive emulsion and then wash it to remove all the extra emulsion, leaving only the image behind. After exposure and development, the plate is made ready for printing.

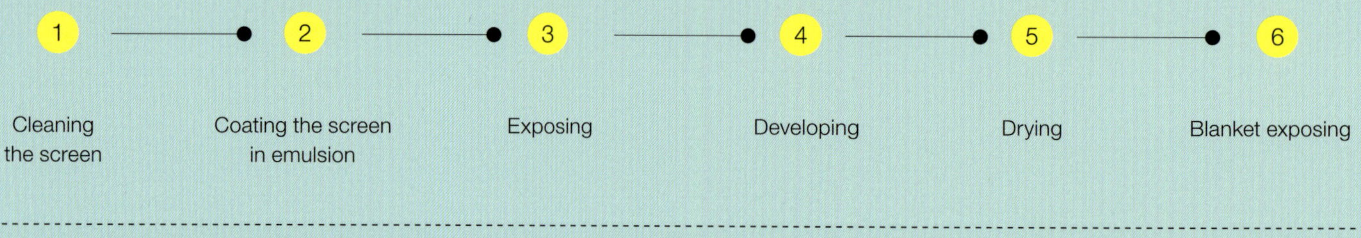

1 Cleaning the screen

Use a screen cleaning agent to clean the screen base to facilitate better adhesion between the emulsion and the screen.

2 Coating the screen in emulsion

Put the emulsion into a stainless steel container and lay down the screen at a 70° angle. Use a squeegee to spread the emulsion on the screen. Repeat the process until the layer is even and thick enough.

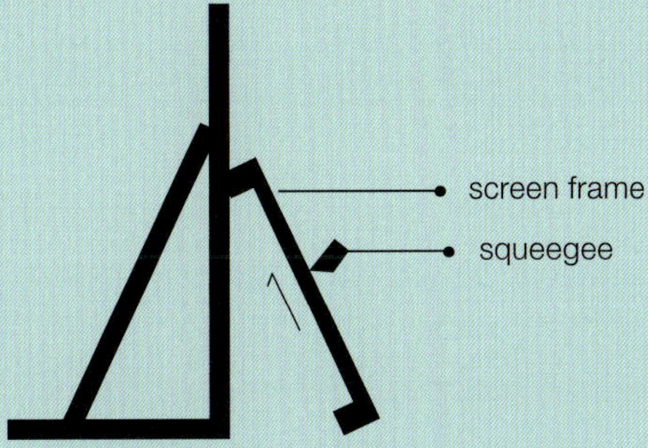

Coating the screen in emulsion

3 Exposing

Lay the film positive on the screen layer and put it into an exposure unit. Exposure time depends on various factors including the property of the emulsion, the distance from the light source, and so on. During the process, a thick sponge is placed on the screen to hold the film positive tightly. A matte black cloth between the sponge and the screen blocks the light from getting to the screen (as shown in the picture).

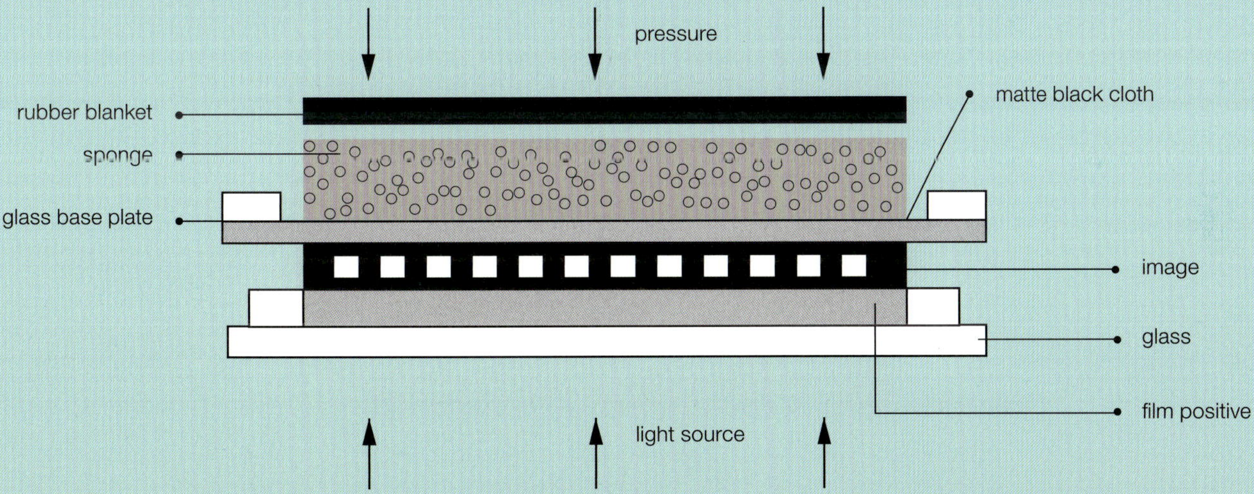

4 Developing

Place the exposed screen frame in water and spray it with cold water from a shower head until the image starts to appear more as the emulsion washes away.

5 Drying

Dry the screen immediately after the image develops. Use an absorbent paper to absorb the water on both sides of the screen. Then dry it with a warm-air dryer. If small halftones become clogged, use a needle to clear them.

6 Blanket exposing

Expose the dry screen once more to make it more durable.

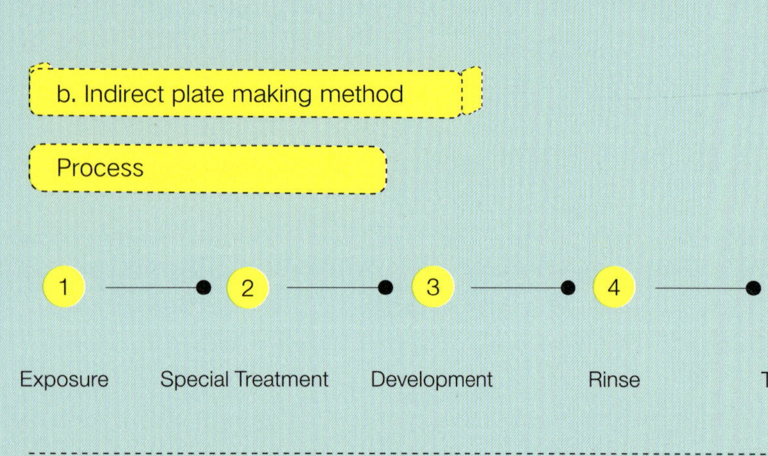

b. Indirect plate making method

Process

1 Exposure → 2 Special Treatment → 3 Development → 4 Rinse → 5 Transfer → 6 Coating → 7 Peel off the layer → 8 Finishing

1 Exposure

Lay the film positive on the photosensitive film for exposure.

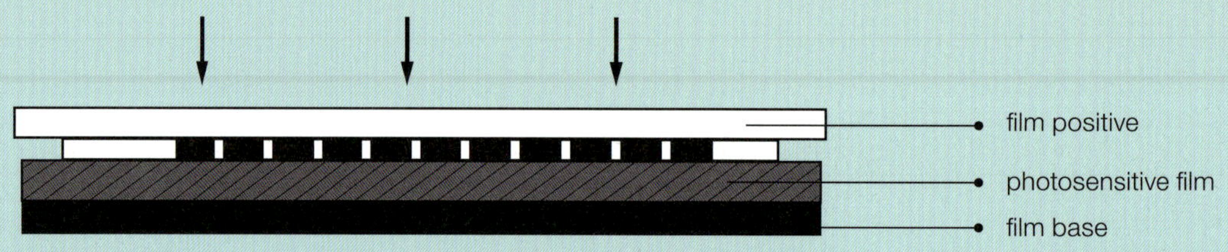

2 Special Treatment

Soak the screen in 1.5% ~ 3% hydrogen peroxide solutions for 1 to 2 minutes, to avoid the image to being broken during transfer.

3 Development

Use warm water to develop the image.

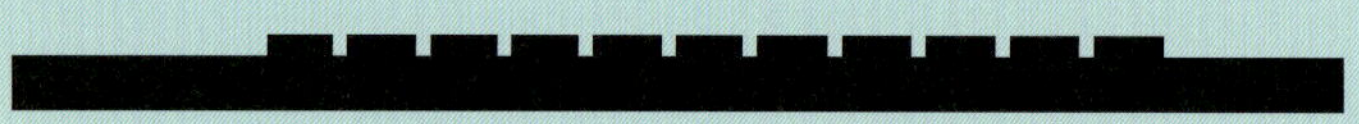

4 Flush

Flush it in cold water.

5 Transfer

Wash the treated screen base with clear water. Lay the film on the desk, place the stretched screen on it, and press with rubber roll.

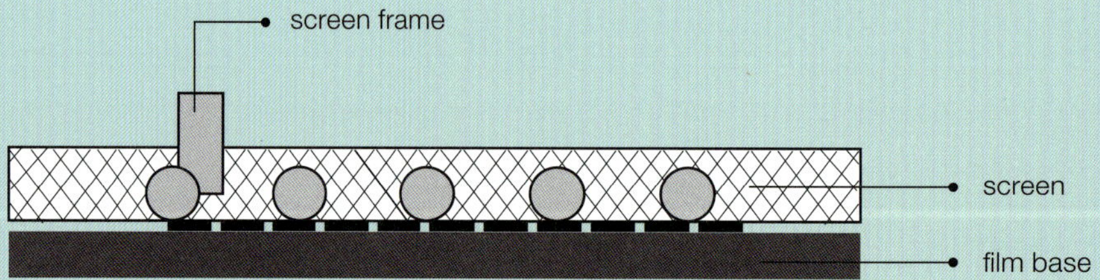

6 **Coating**

Coat the screen with specially made emulsion and dry it in hot air.

7 **Peel off the layer**

Peel off the layer to get a stencil ready for printing.

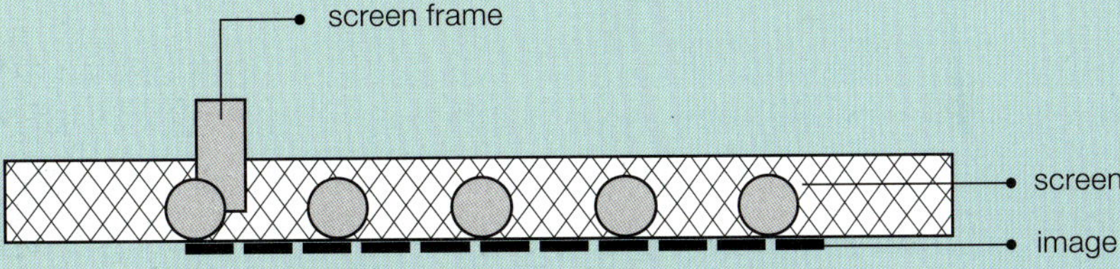

8 **Finishing**

Make some adjustments.

c.The mix & match plate-making method

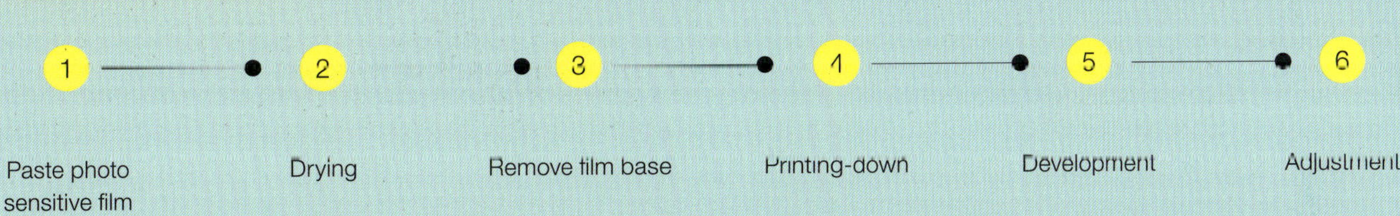

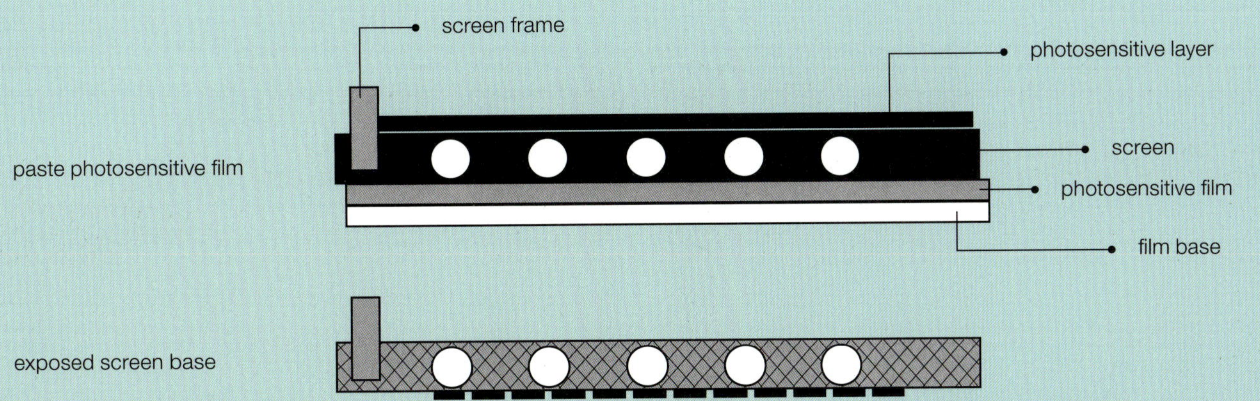

This method shares the features of direct and indirect plate-making methods. In plate making, lay the prepared photo sensitive film on the screen, and coat the emulsion on the screen, pressing the coating with a squeegee to hold the photo sensitive film tightly on the screen. Once it is dry, remove the screen base and start burning. When the image appears, a screen plate ready to print is done.

7 Printing Process

Studio: tind

Designer: Chrisanthos Angelakis & Manolis Angelakis

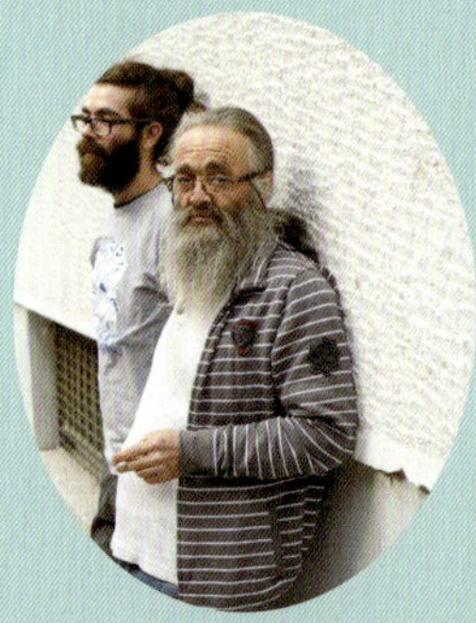

The father-and-son team of Chrisanthos Angelakis and Manolis Angelakis truly push silkscreen printing to its maximum limits. As they put it: "There are no materials they cannot print, no colours they cannot match, and no dimensions, large or small, they cannot handle." The screen print studio, based in Athens, Greece, experiments with all kinds of materials and colours to achieve what they have never expected.

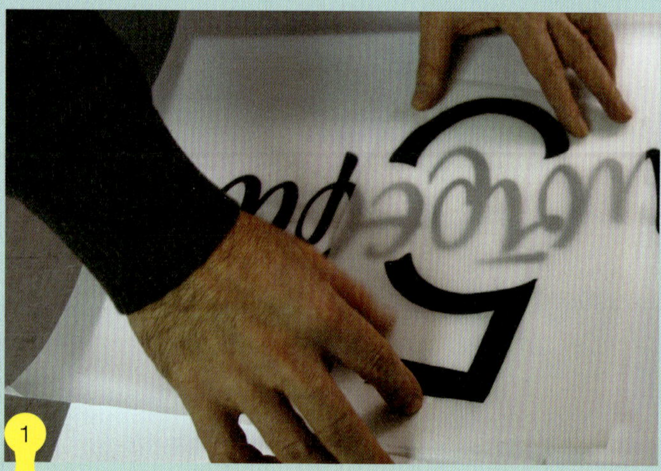

1 Create a design on the computer and then print it onto a transparency sheet, or draw on the sheet directly.

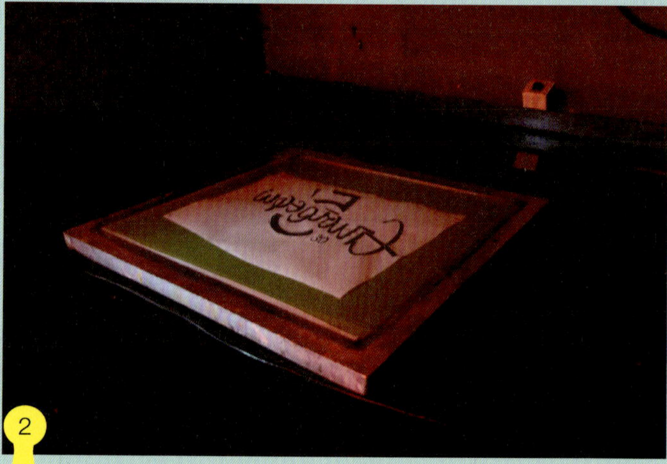

2 Cover the screen with a layer of photo-reactive emulsion and dry it thoroughly. Then put the transparency stencil on the screen and apply pressure on it to make sure the stencil stays flush with the screen.

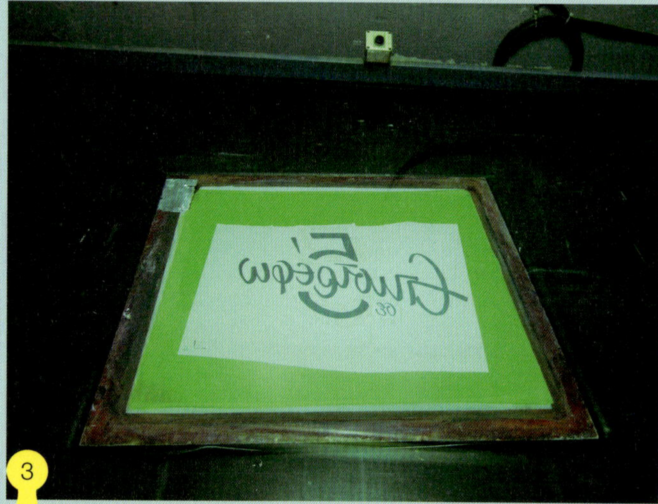

3 After that, shine UV lights on the screen to set the design.

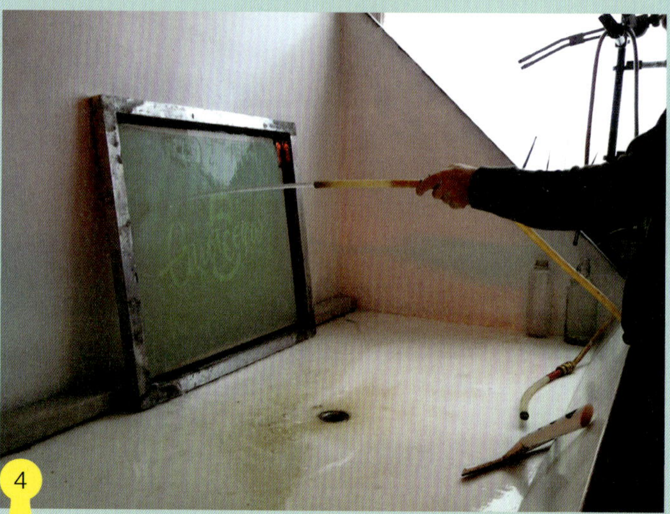

4 The blank areas coated with emulsion become impermeable after shining UV lights and will not be washed out, while the image areas will be washed out, leaving openings on the screen.

Photo by tind

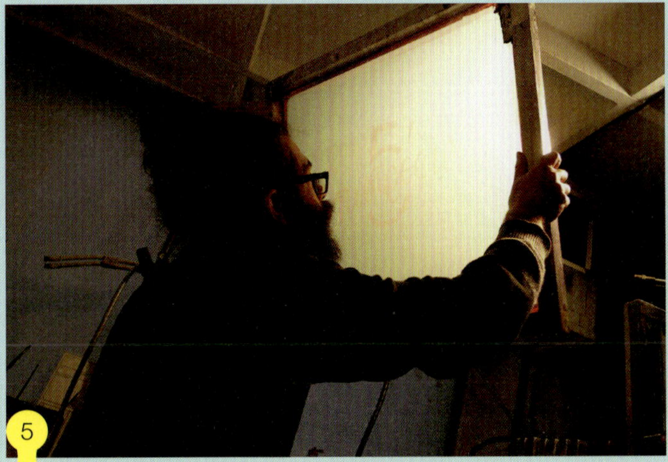

5 The silkscreen is produced, ready for printing.

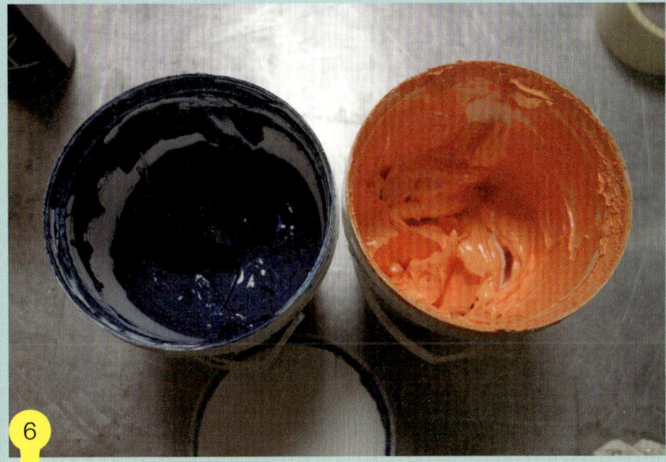

6 Prepare screen printing color.

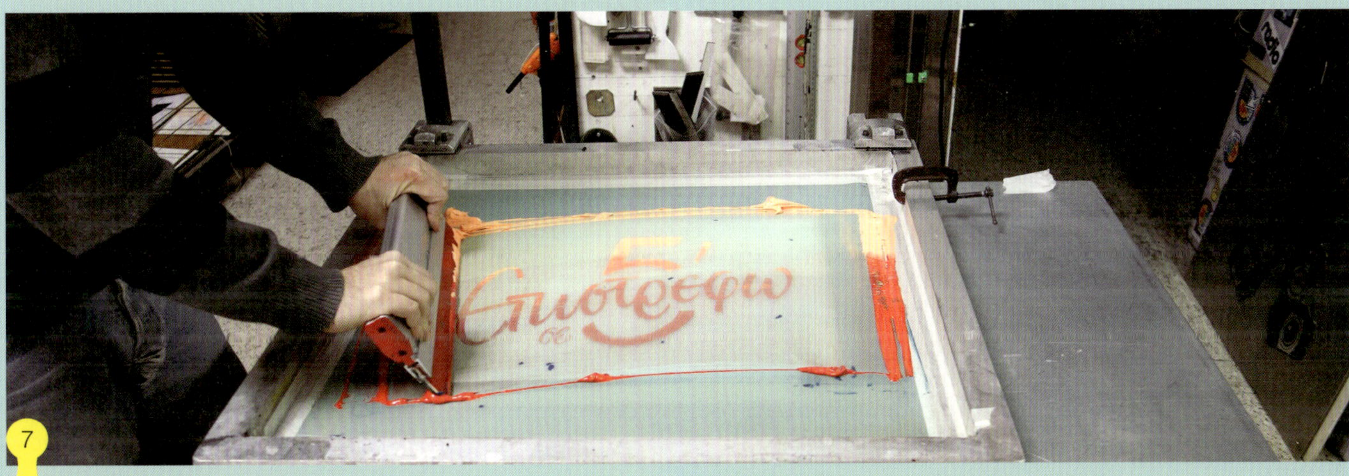

7 Put silkscreen ink onto the screen and push it through the screen with a squeegee, and the ink is transferred onto the substrate.

8 A silkscreen print work is finished.

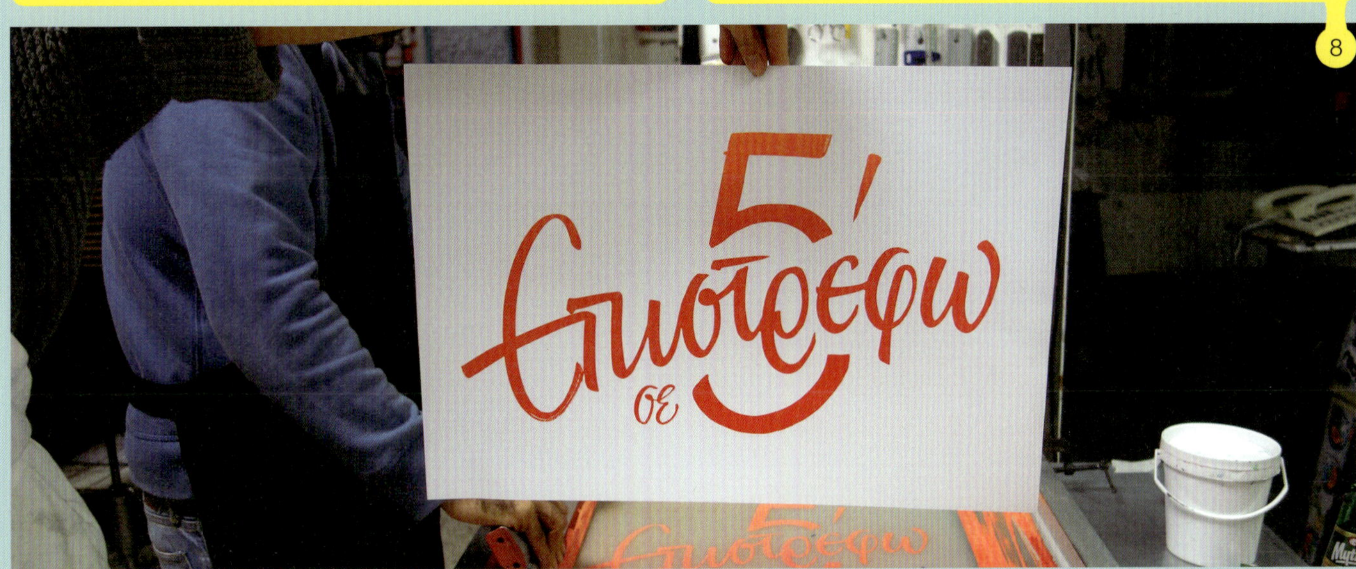

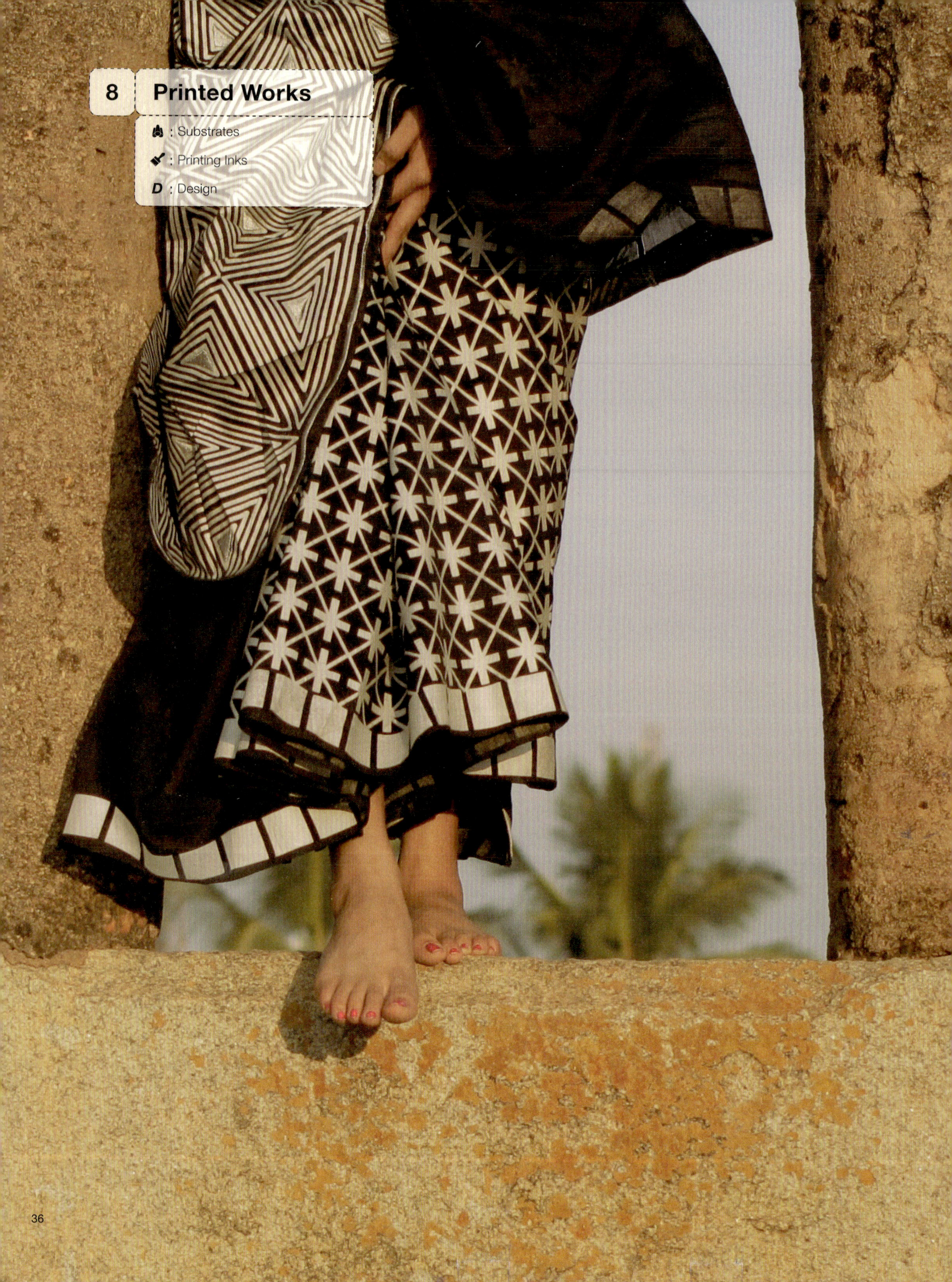

8 Printed Works

: Substrates

: Printing Inks

D : Design

Alice's Adventures in Wonderland

180g paper

screen printing ink

Illustrations and layout developed for the novel *Alice's Adventures in Wonderland* by Lewis Carroll. The illustrations were developed by hand. And afterwards they were improved using the computer. In the end they were printed using the silkscreen technique. The designer thinks that the silkscreen adds a special touch to the design and really makes the illustrations came alive. In the end, this technique offers the illustrations a unique final touch.

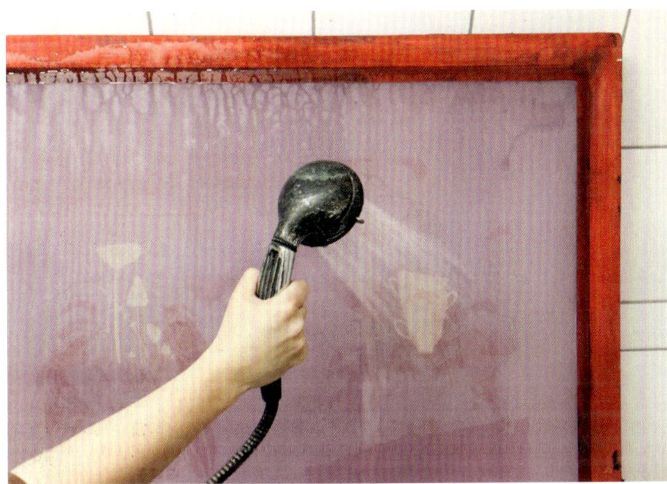

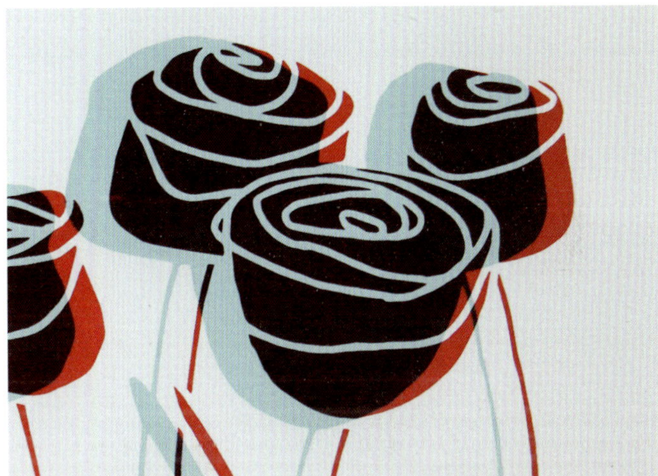

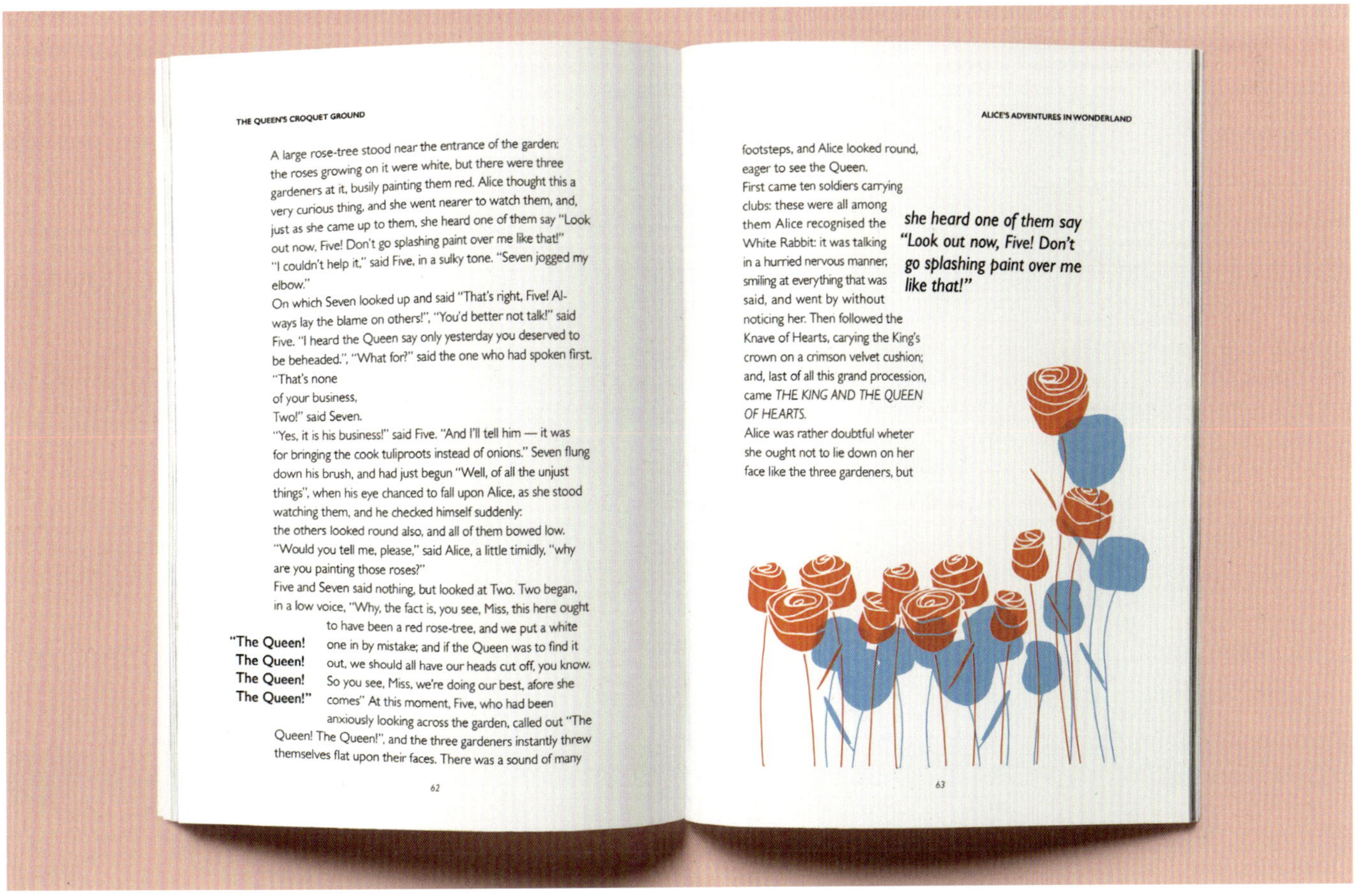

THE QUEEN'S CROQUET GROUND

A large rose-tree stood near the entrance of the garden: the roses growing on it were white, but there were three gardeners at it, busily painting them red. Alice thought this a very curious thing, and she went nearer to watch them, and, just as she came up to them, she heard one of them say "Look out now, Five! Don't go splashing paint over me like that!" "I couldn't help it," said Five, in a sulky tone. "Seven jogged my elbow."
On which Seven looked up and said "That's right, Five! Always lay the blame on others!", "You'd better not talk!" said Five. "I heard the Queen say only yesterday you deserved to be beheaded.", "What for?" said the one who had spoken first. "That's none of your business, Two!" said Seven.
"Yes, it is his business!" said Five. "And I'll tell him — it was for bringing the cook tuliproots instead of onions." Seven flung down his brush, and had just begun "Well, of all the unjust things", when his eye chanced to fall upon Alice, as she stood watching them, and he checked himself suddenly: the others looked round also, and all of them bowed low. "Would you tell me, please," said Alice, a little timidly, "why are you painting those roses?"
Five and Seven said nothing, but looked at Two. Two began, in a low voice, "Why, the fact is, you see, Miss, this here ought to have been a red rose-tree, and we put a white one in by mistake; and if the Queen was to find it out, we should all have our heads cut off, you know. So you see, Miss, we're doing our best, afore she comes" At this moment, Five, who had been anxiously looking across the garden, called out "The Queen! The Queen!", and the three gardeners instantly threw themselves flat upon their faces. There was a sound of many

"The Queen! The Queen! The Queen! The Queen!"

62

ALICE'S ADVENTURES IN WONDERLAND

footsteps, and Alice looked round, eager to see the Queen. First came ten soldiers carrying clubs: these were all among them Alice recognised the White Rabbit: it was talking in a hurried nervous manner, smiling at everything that was said, and went by without noticing her. Then followed the Knave of Hearts, carying the King's crown on a crimson velvet cushion; and, last of all this grand procession, came *THE KING AND THE QUEEN OF HEARTS.*
Alice was rather doubtful wheter she ought not to lie down on her face like the three gardeners, but

she heard one of them say "Look out now, Five! Don't go splashing paint over me like that!"

63

Tarangati

- fabric (cotton and silk)
- a mix of fabric colour dye and the printing binder

Tarangati is a collection of Saree's, inspired from Bidriward, a silver and metal craft from Bidar. The designer translated the origins of the design into different prints and distributed them across 6 mt fabric yardage worn as an Indian style sari. The medium was screen printing, and the designer used primarily silver binder and paste for her printing process. She also finished the product with highlights of details in silver hand embroidery.

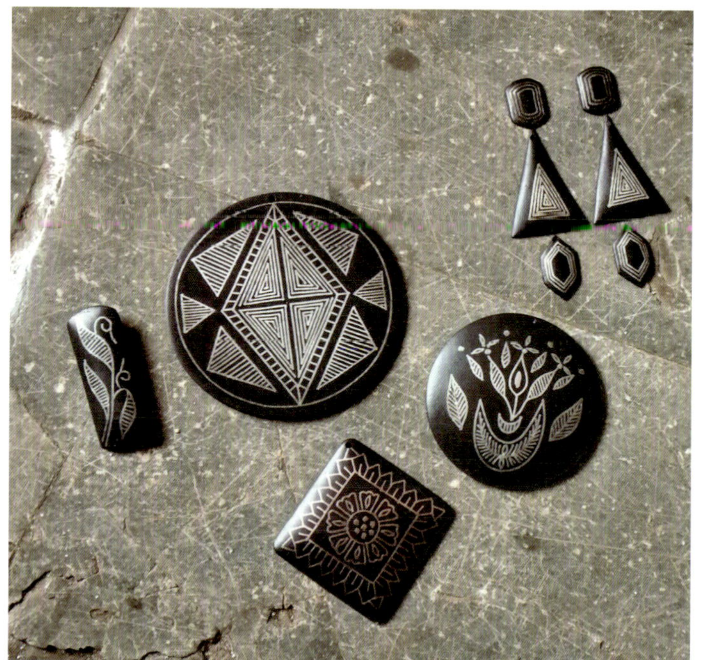

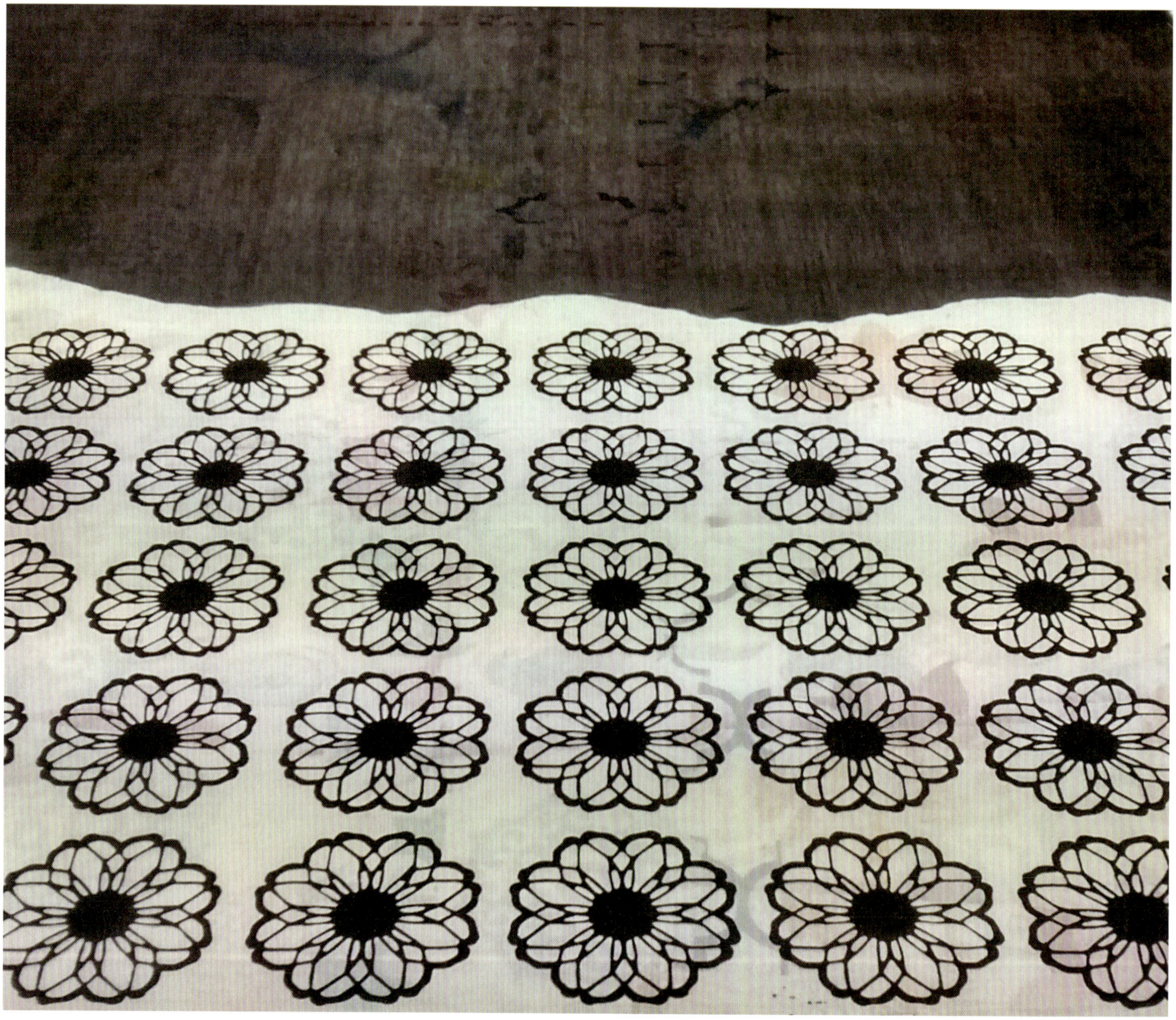

D: Achala Athreya

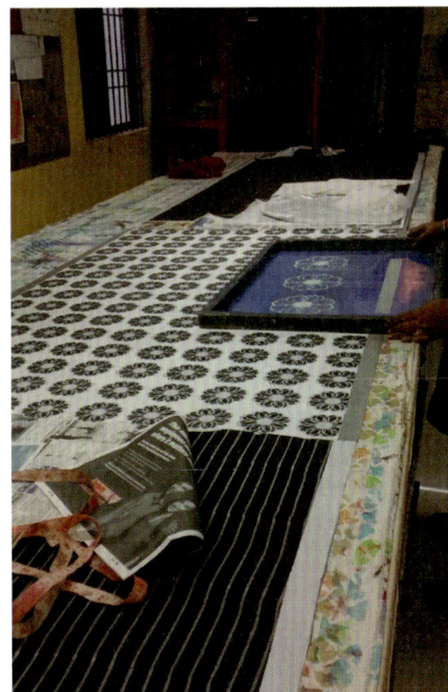

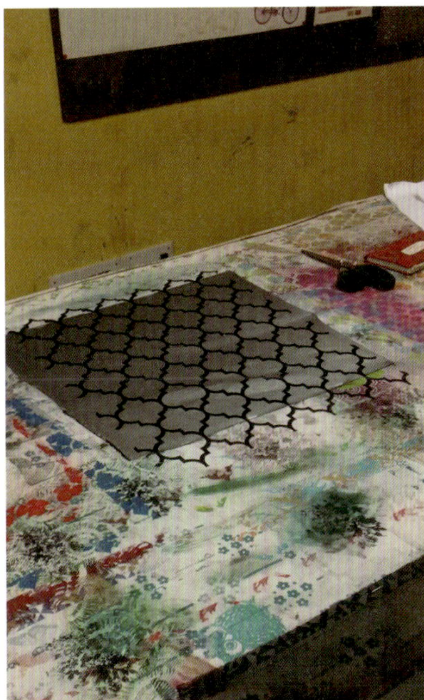

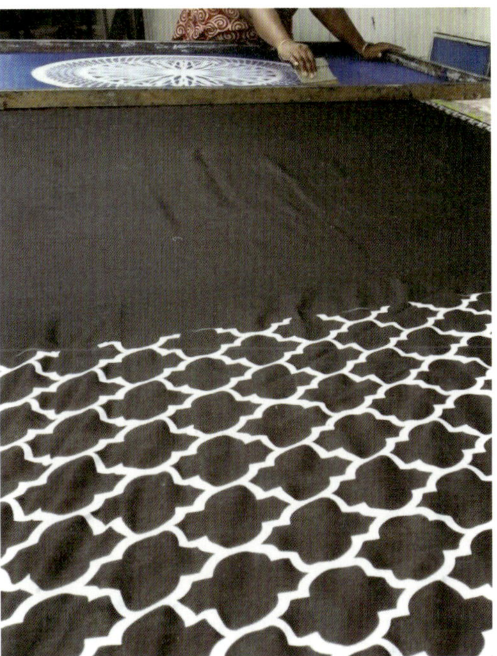

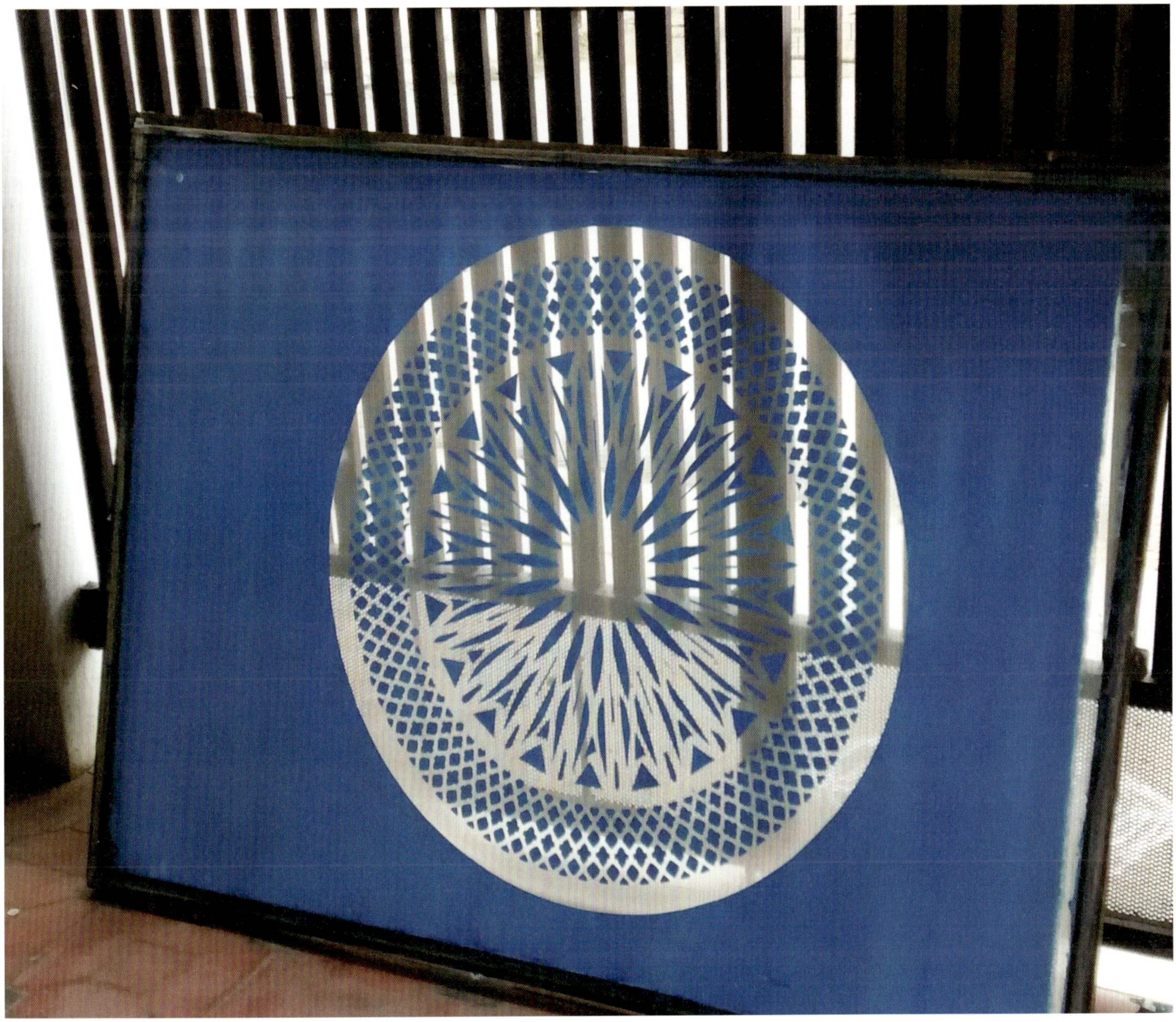

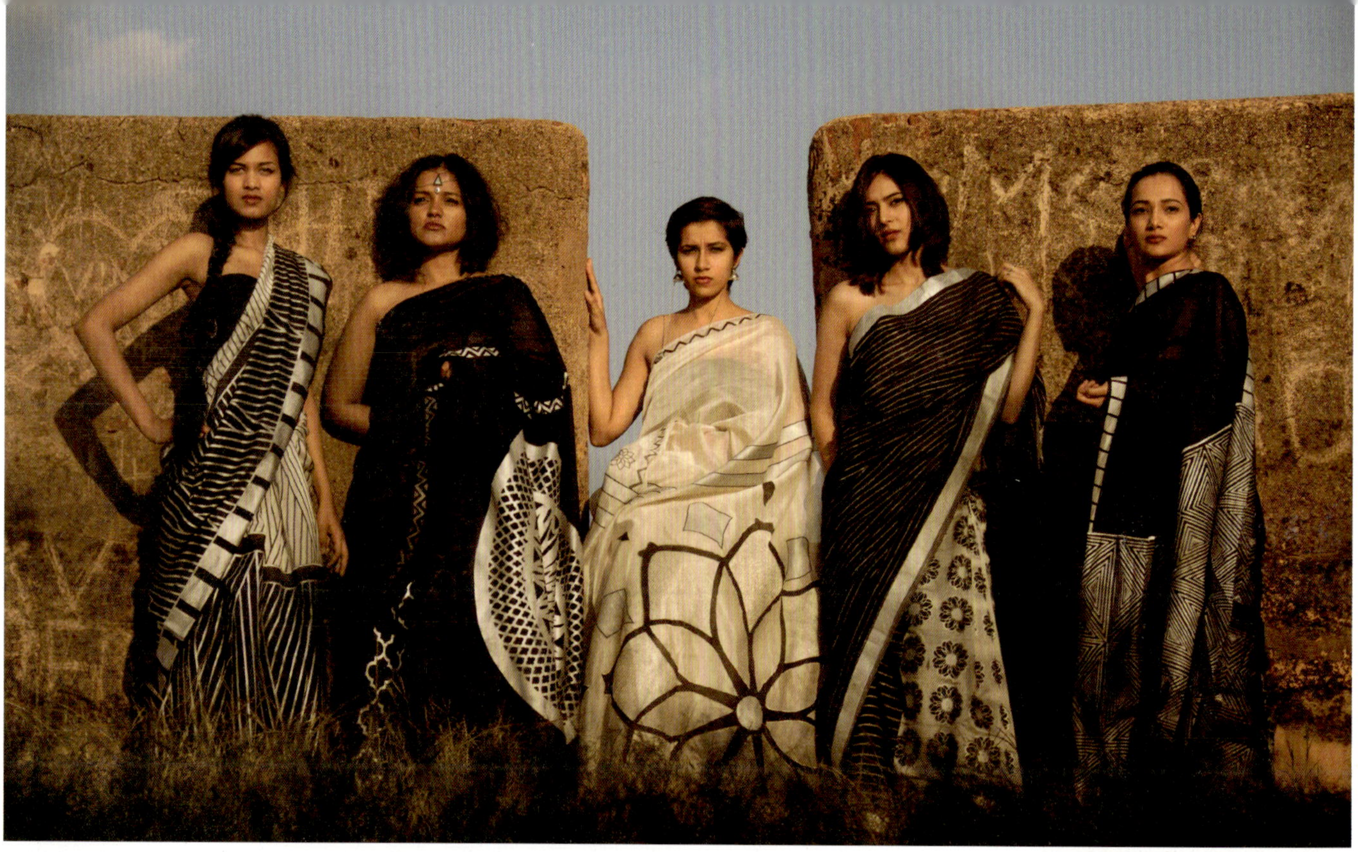

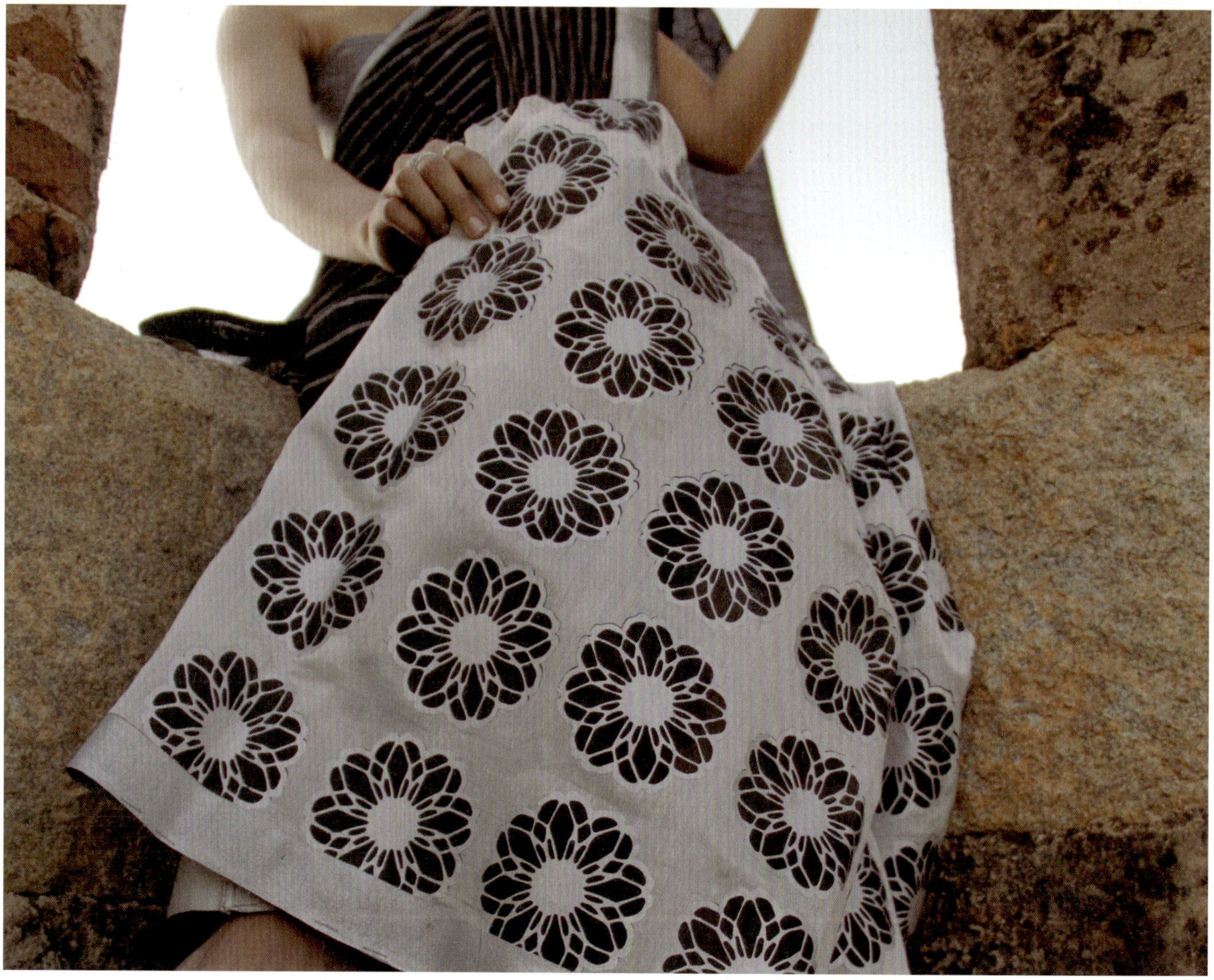

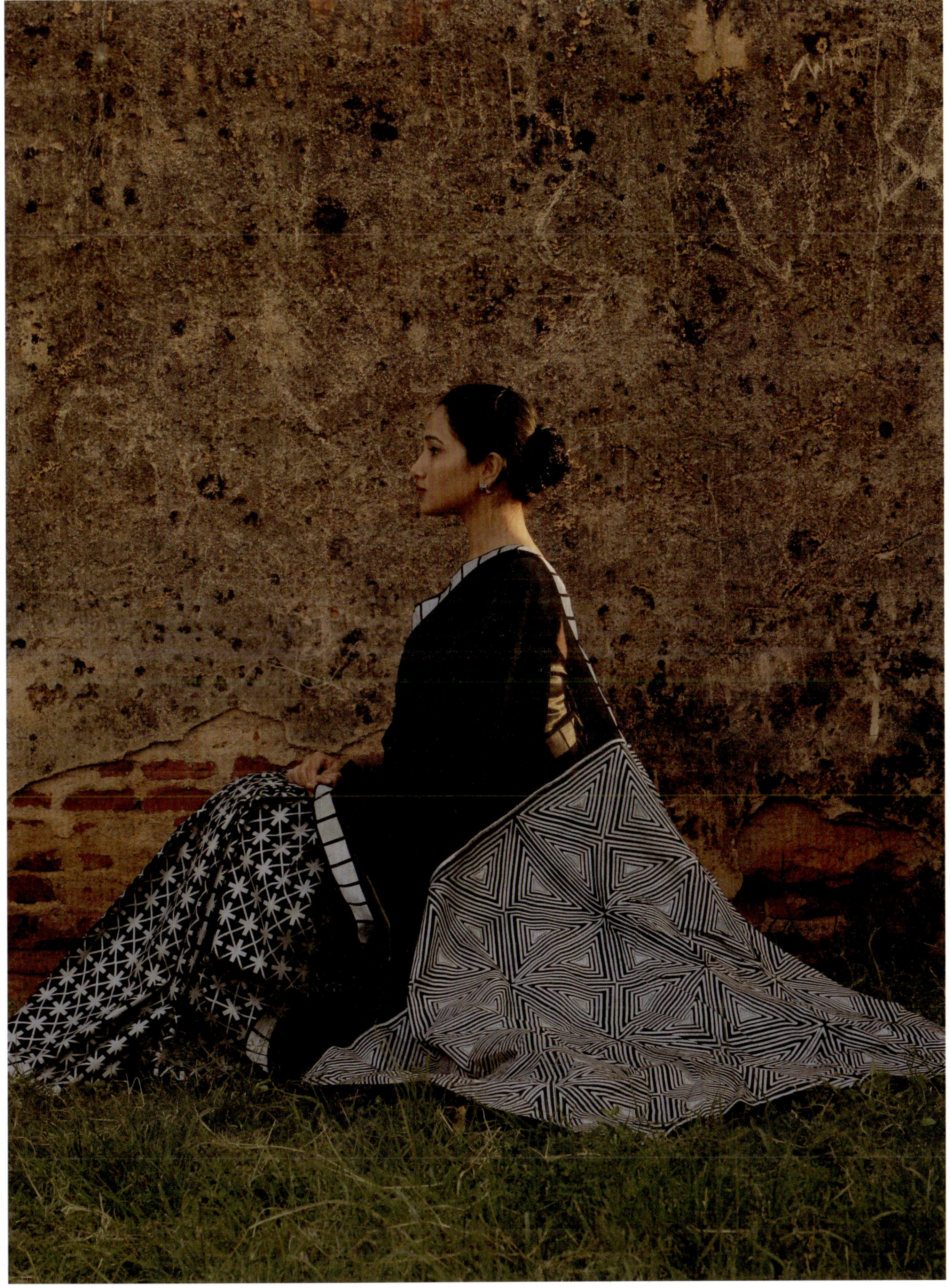

Inspired by the Botanical

- fabric (cotton and silk)
- a mix of fabric color dye and the printing binder

This project looked at botanical motifs (leaves) and their translation through different screen print media (fabric and paste). The designer looked specifically into the microscopic world of plants in terms of the design and aesthetic. She used lighter fabric bases to work with creating layers between different prints. The designer experimented with print puff paste (which raises the print after the printing process upon heating) and gold and silver binders besides regular color dye paste. All designs are hand drawn and replicated by the designer herself.

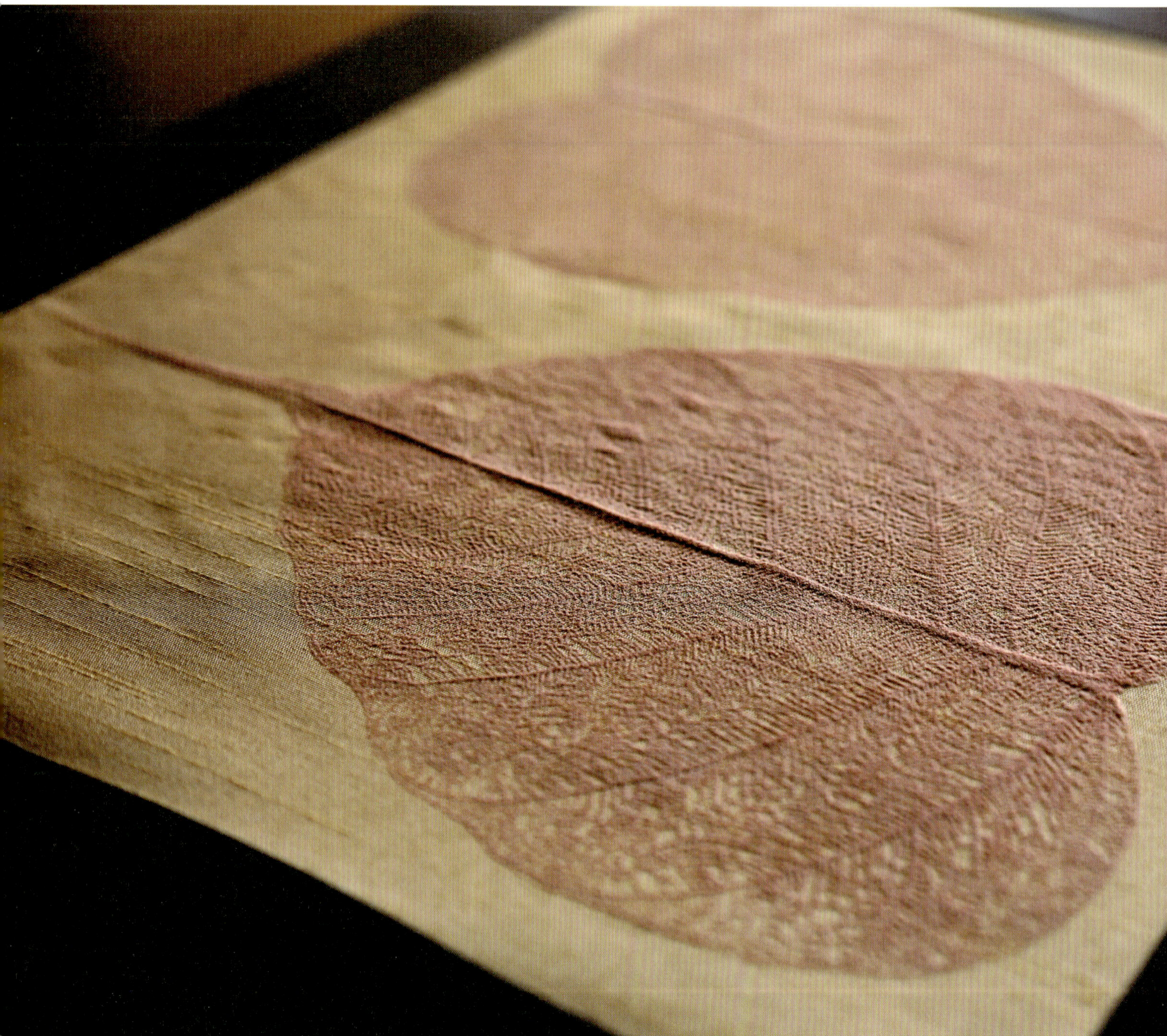

***D*:** Achala Athreya

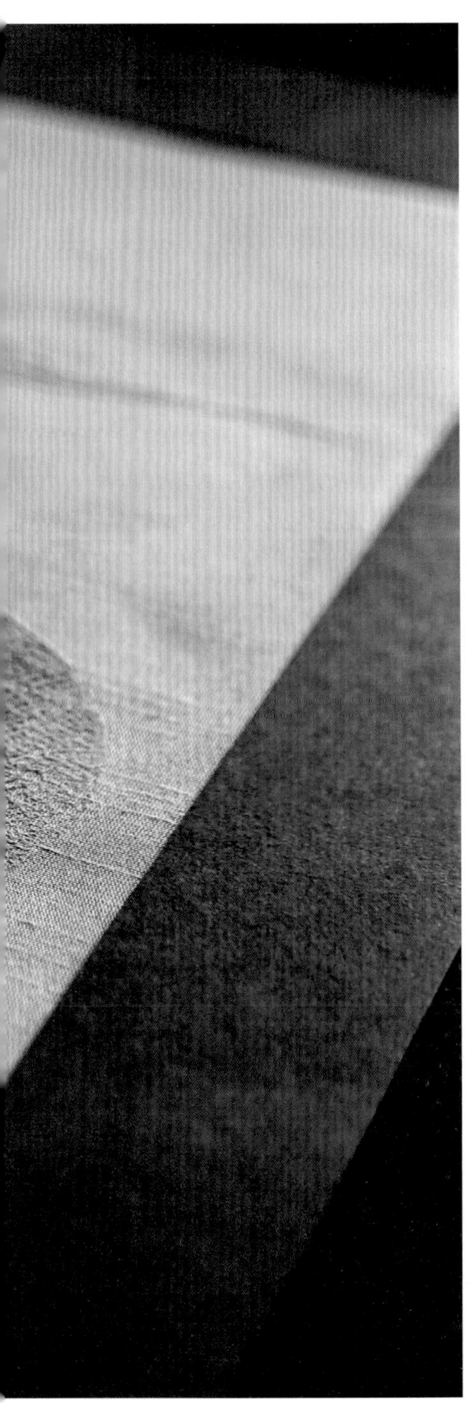

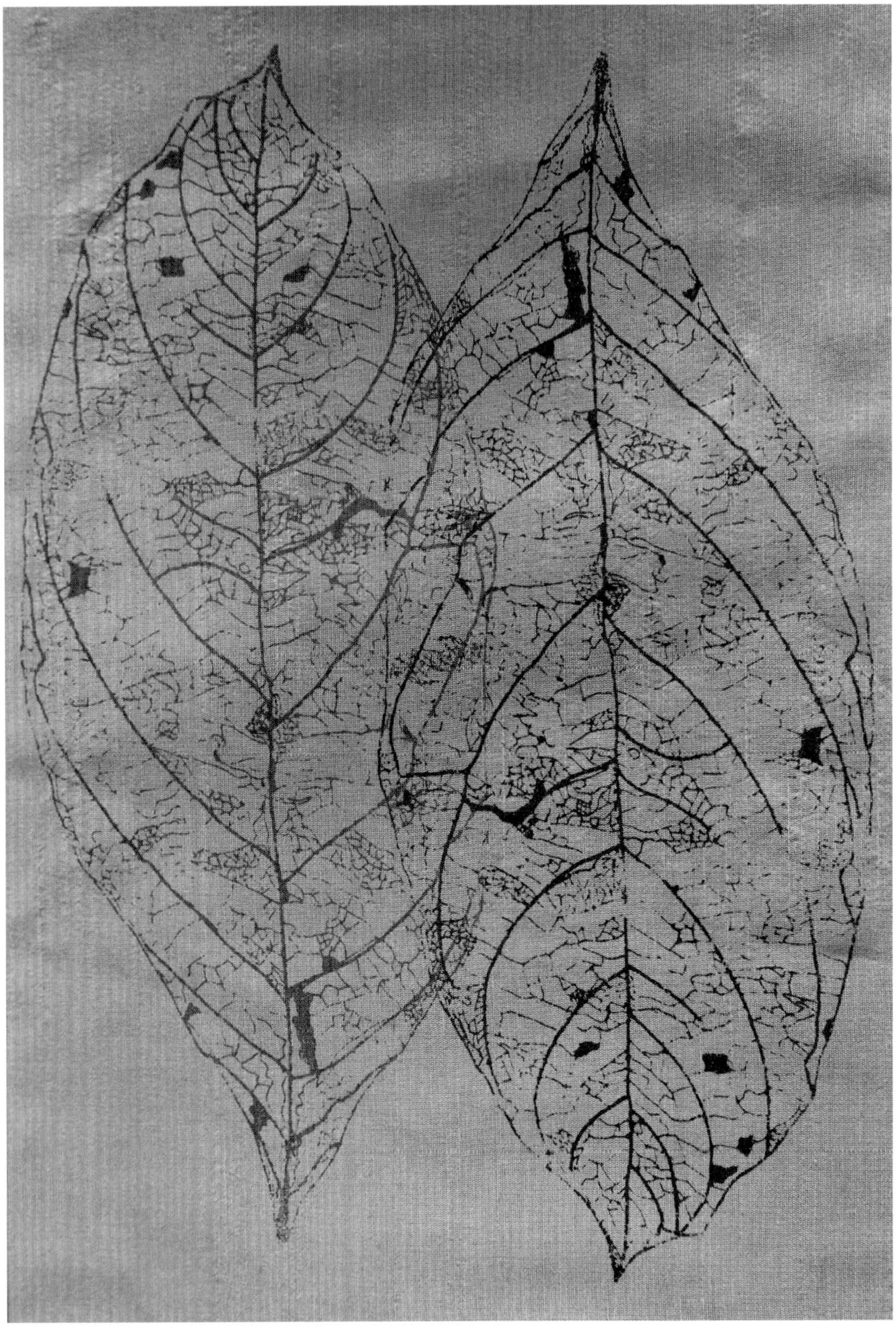

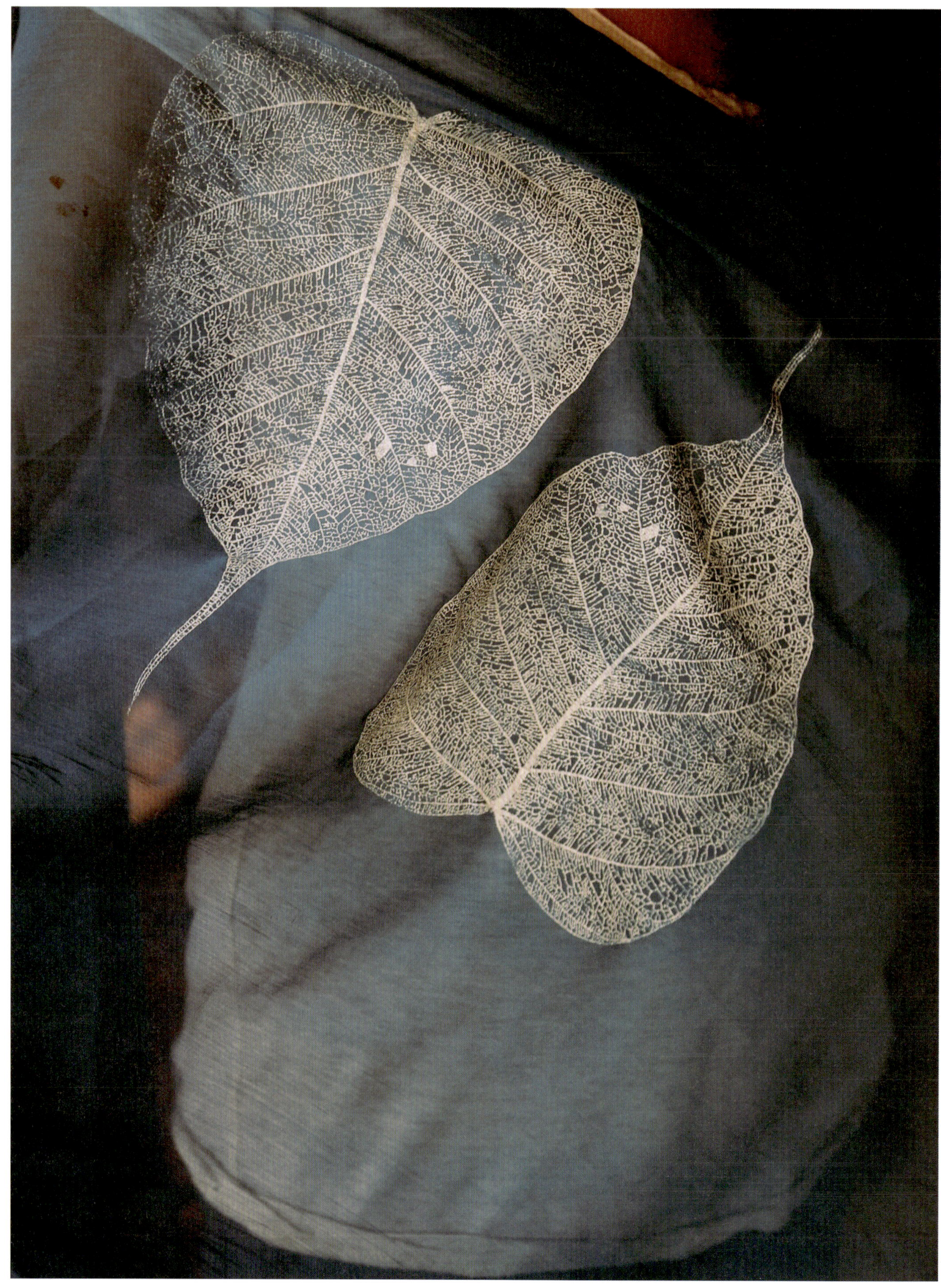

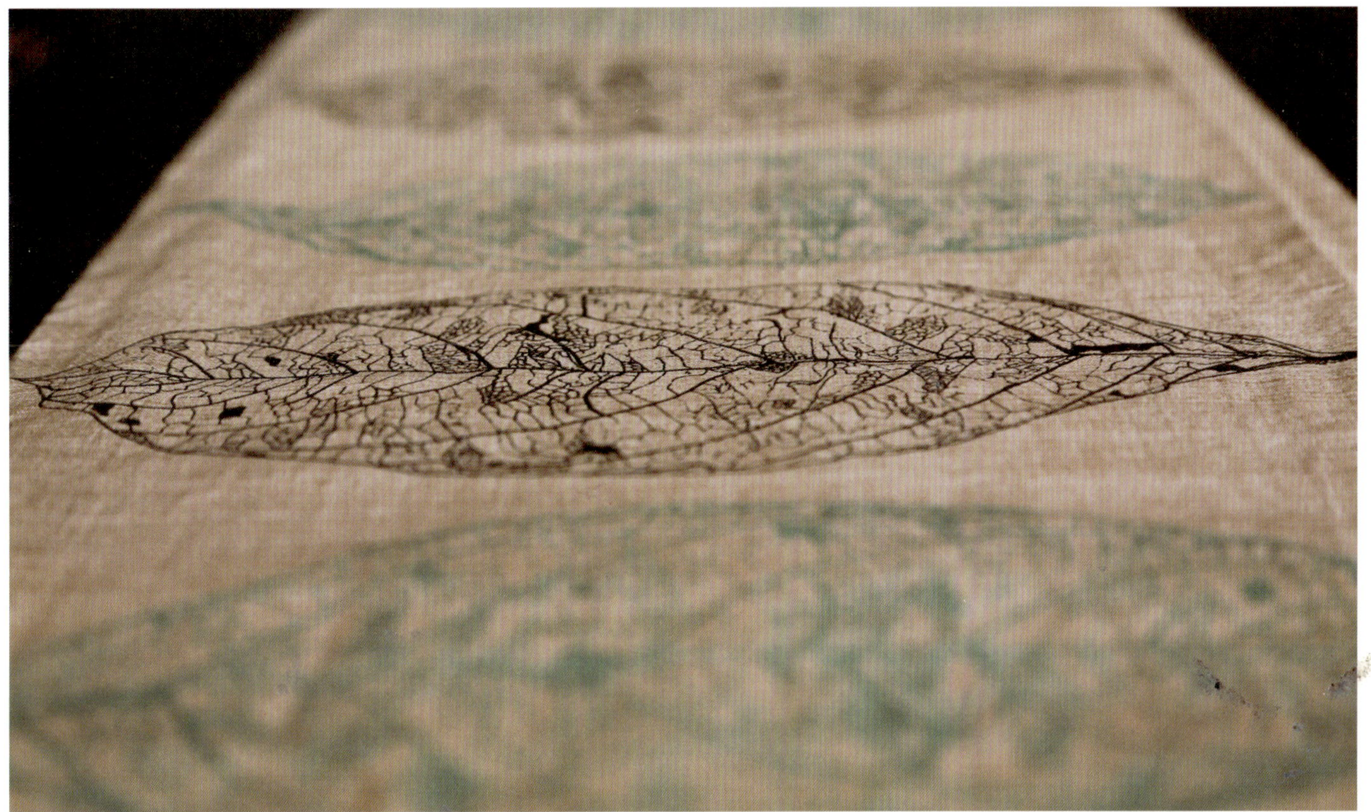

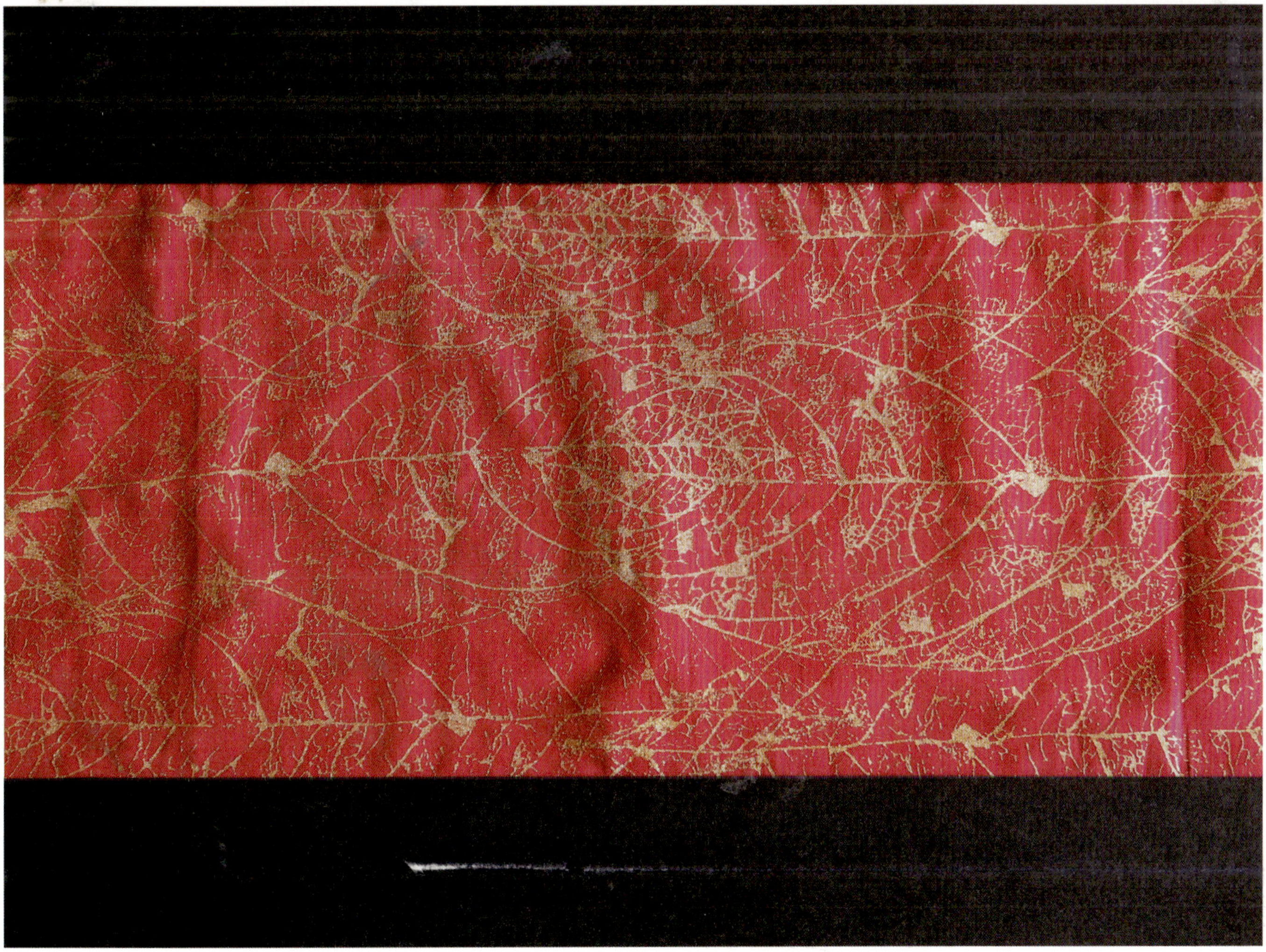

Erato

170g Munken Pure Rough paper

Non Solvent Based

During March of 2017, tind challenged collaborators and visitors of Synergastirion to doodle the second layer of a 70x100 cm silkscreen printed poster. The first layer, a vector design of a Satyrus, was designed by Manolis Angelakis, using visual basic custom macro-tools. The second layer was created on a film at Synergastirion on the light table, which was filled in by hand with black markers, by whoever passed by and wished to contribute.

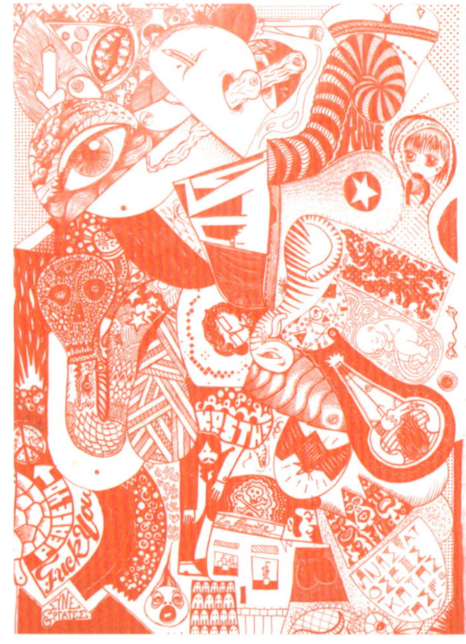

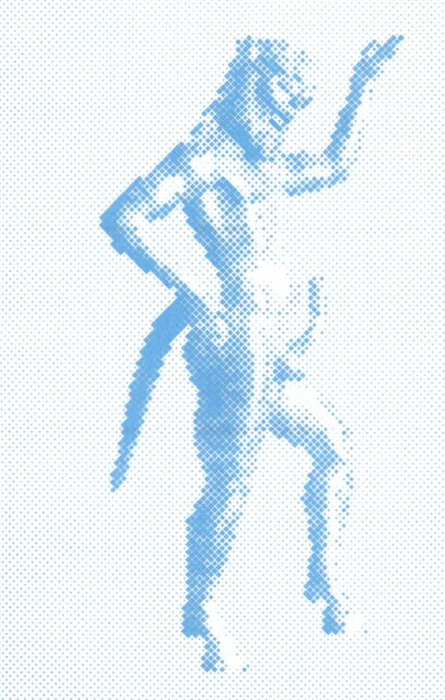

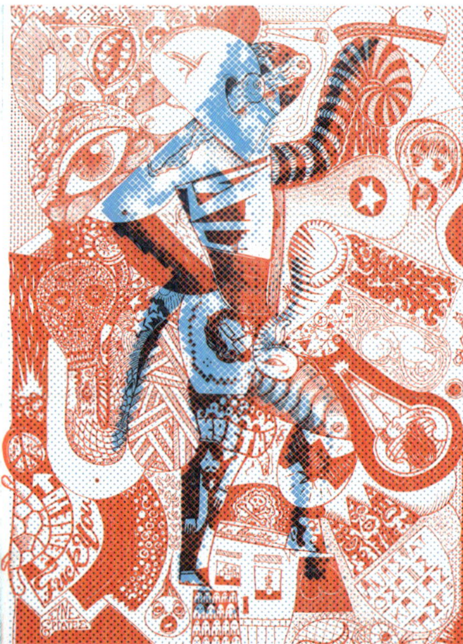

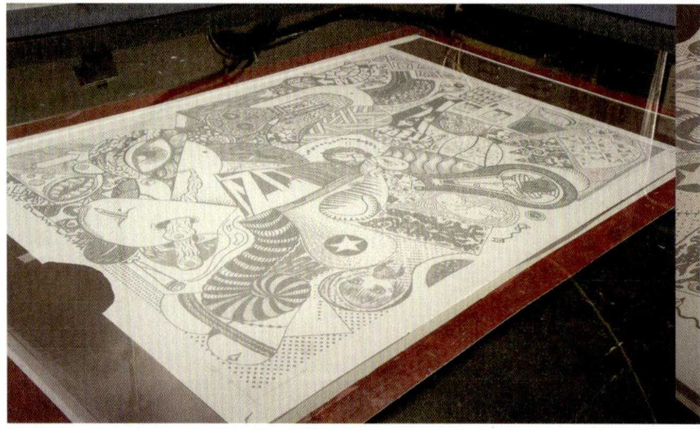

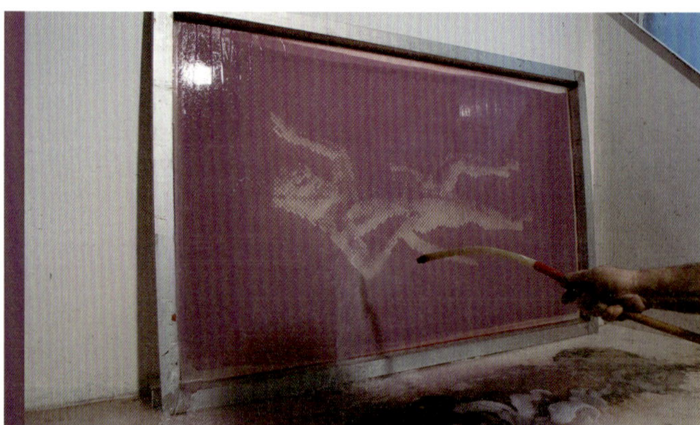

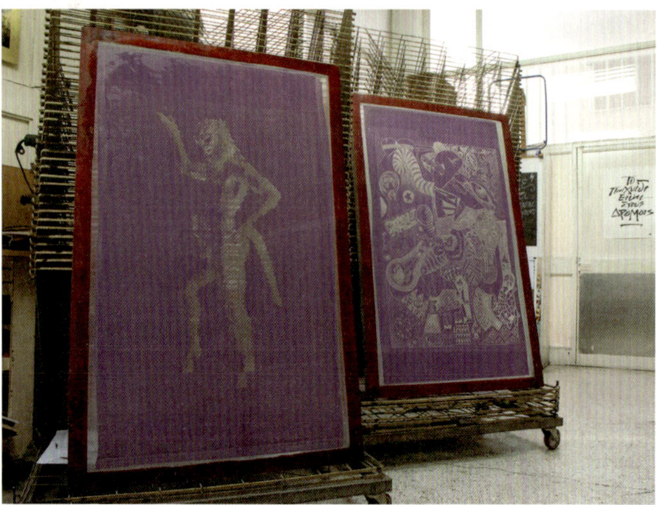

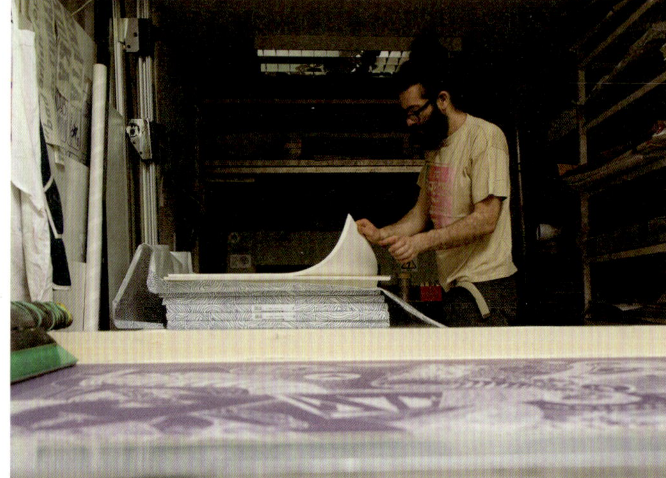

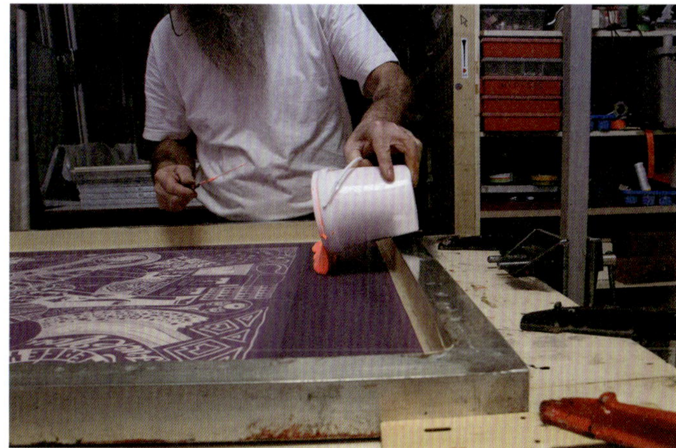

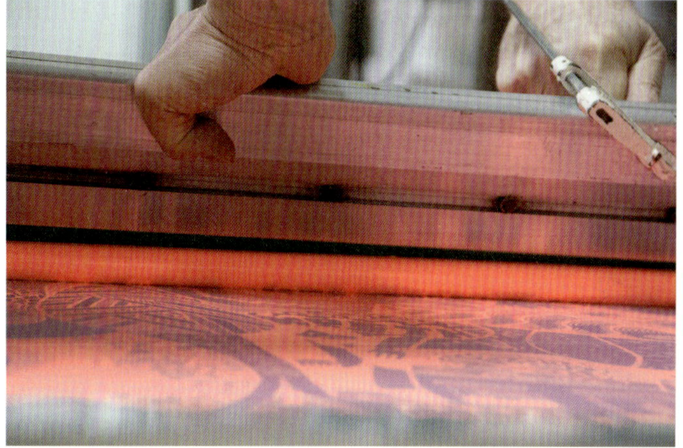

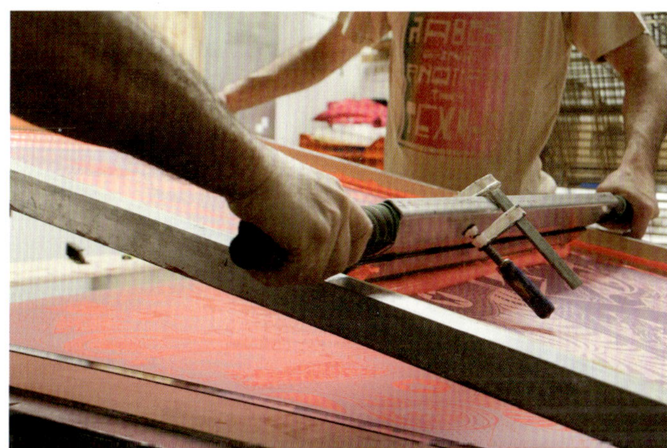

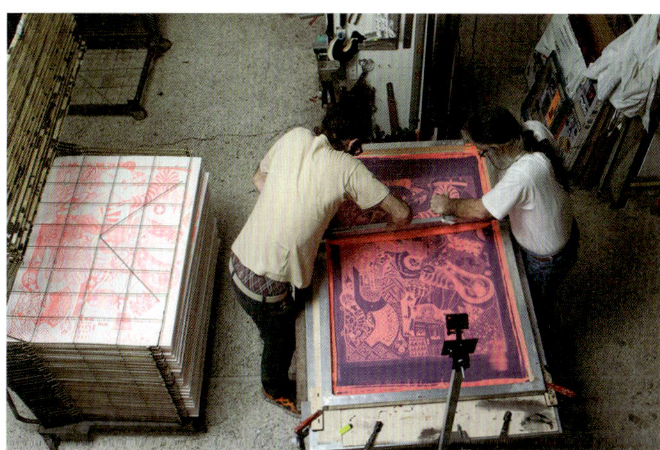

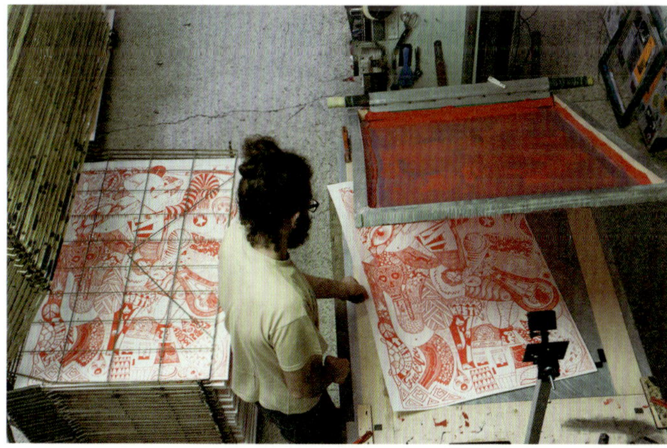

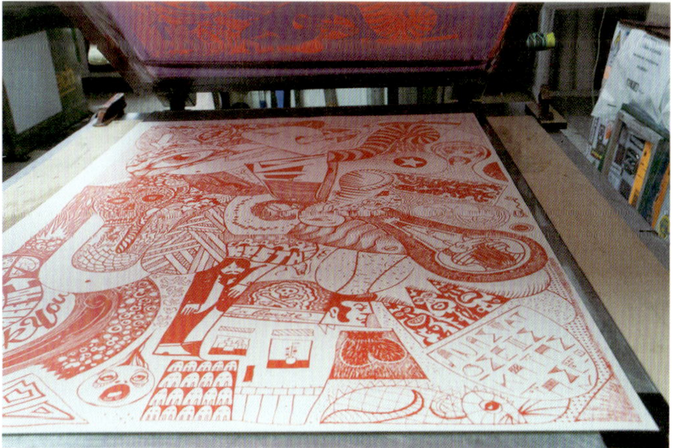

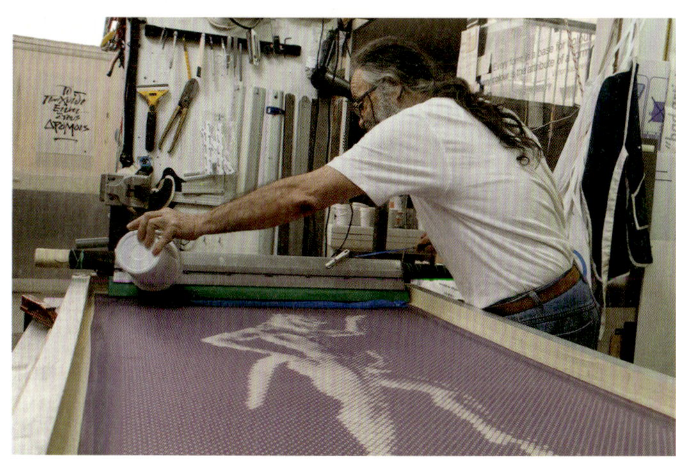

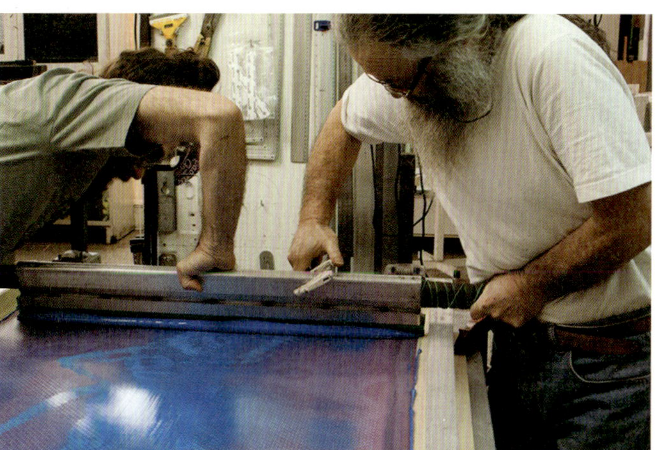

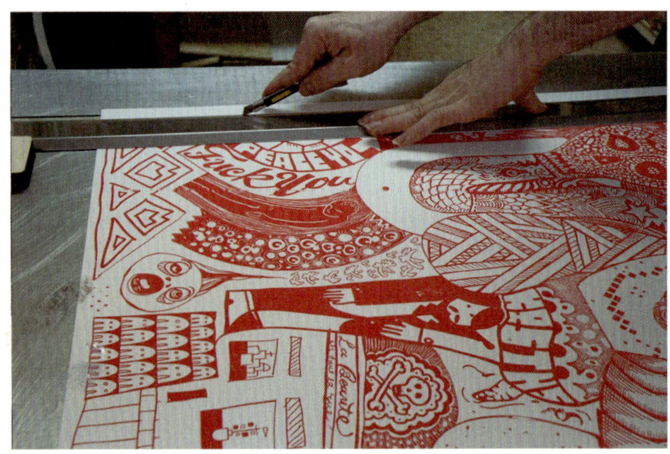
Fuck You

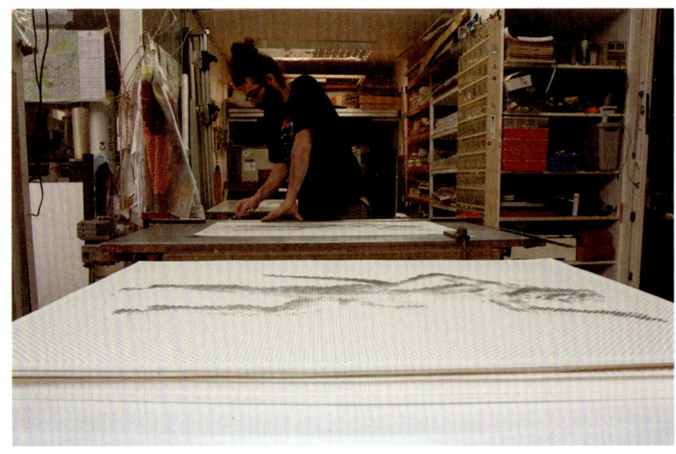

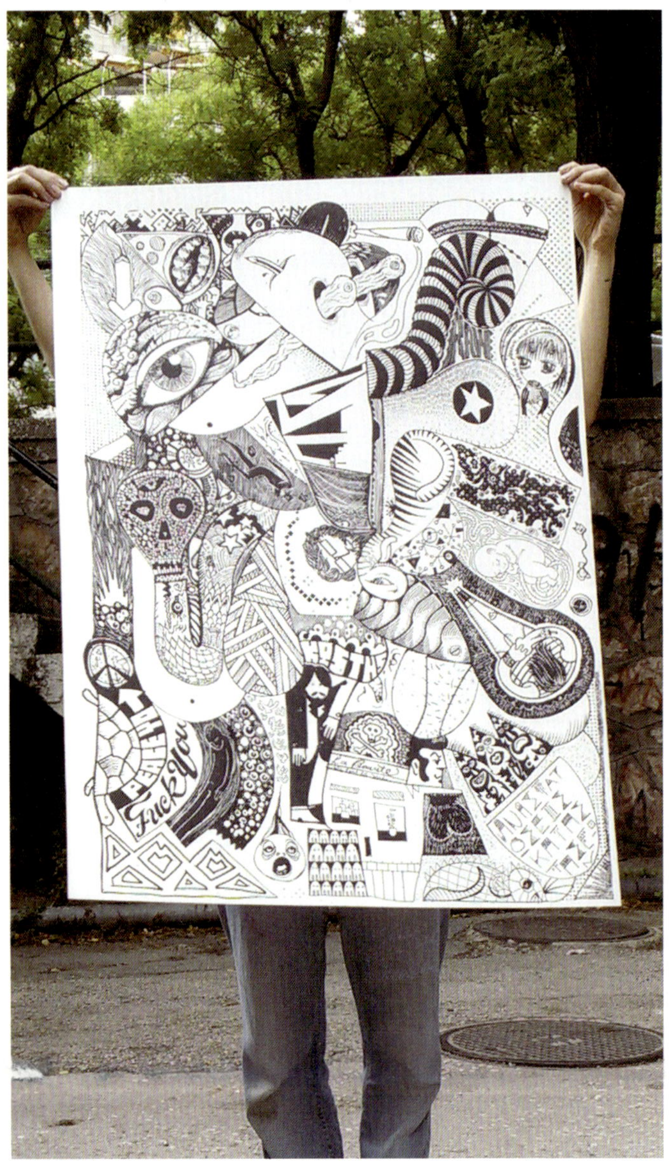
Fuck You

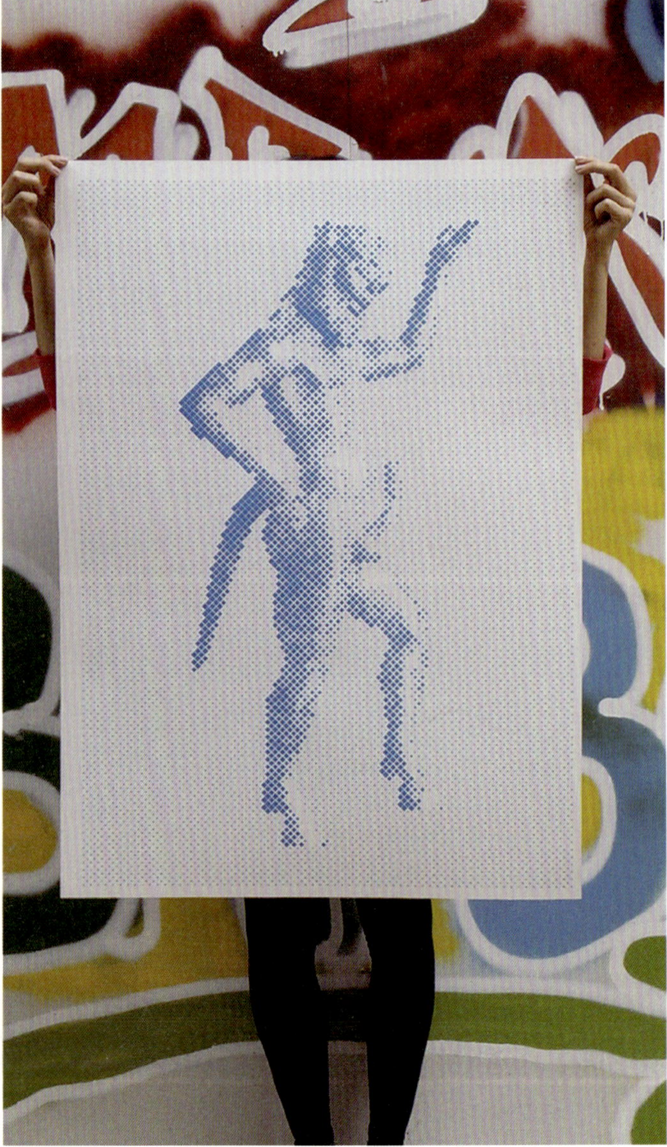

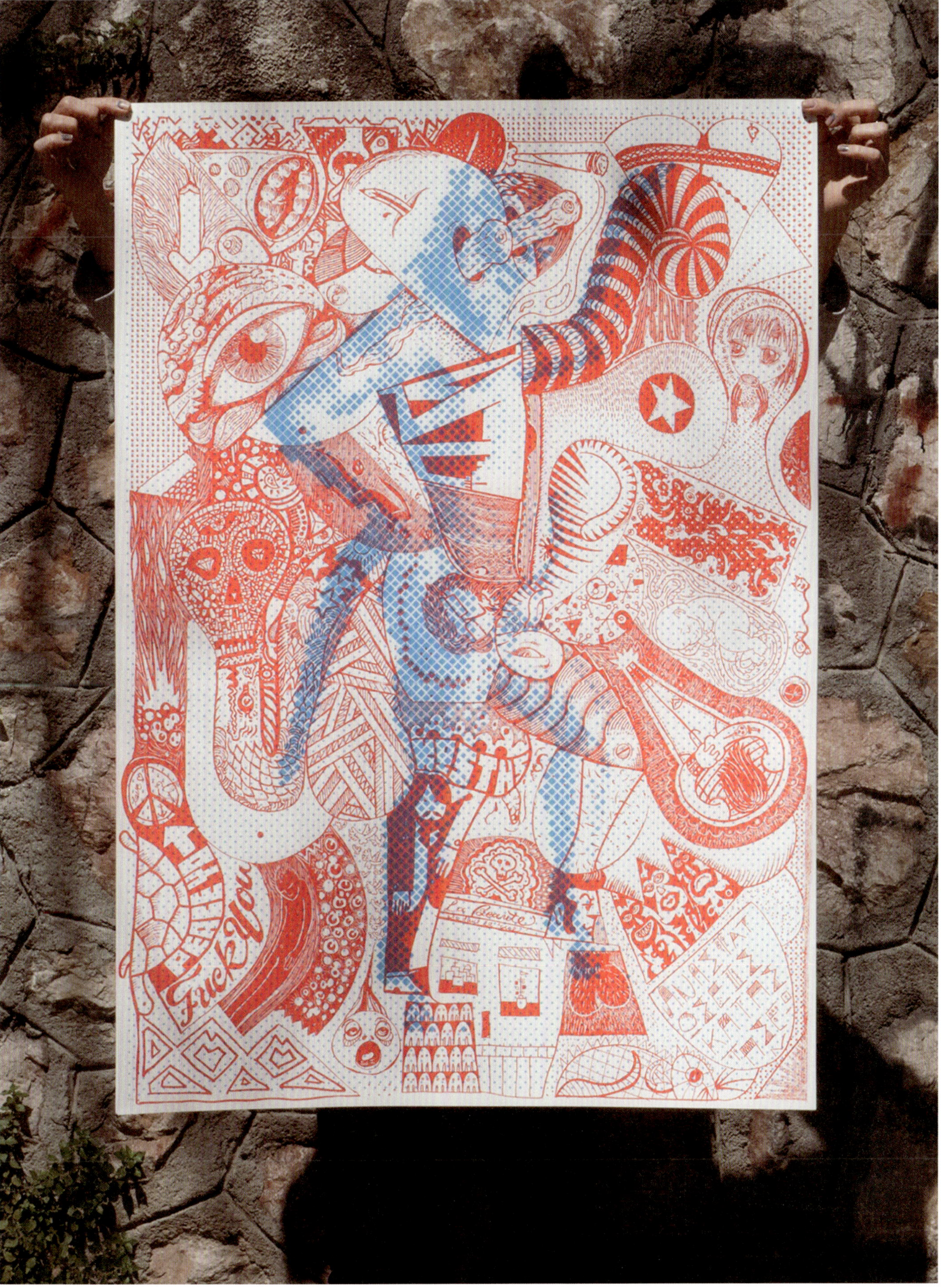
Fuck You

Zeus or Poseidon

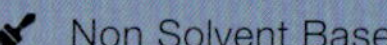

Non Solvent Based

The Artemision Bronze, often called the God from the Sea, is an ancient Greek sculpture that was recovered from the sea off Cape Artemision, in northern Euboea. It represents either Zeus or Poseidon. It was the central theme of the 1,000 drachma bill before the euro became the official currency of the Eurozone. This print is a love letter to the past, with a focus on the challenging printing level it required.

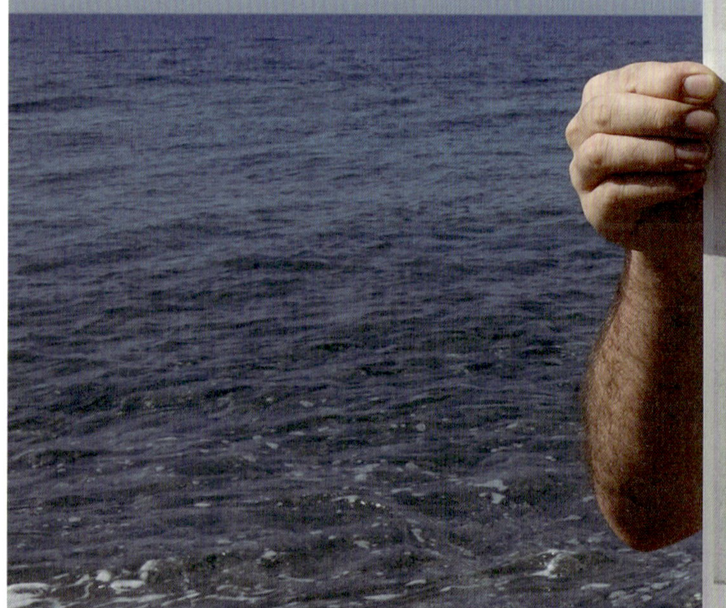

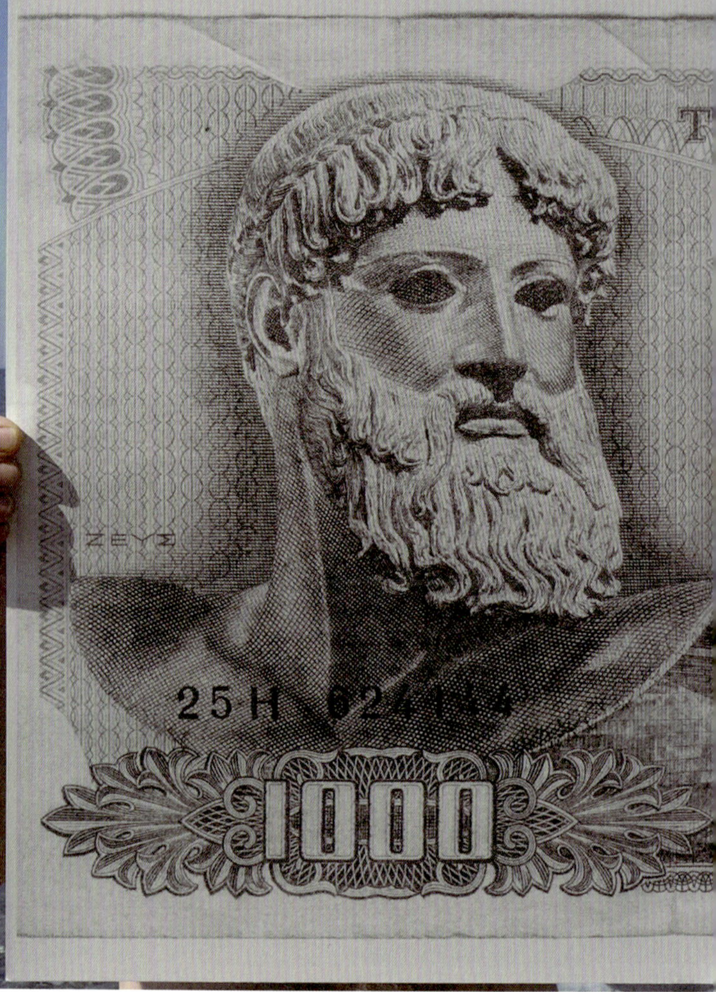

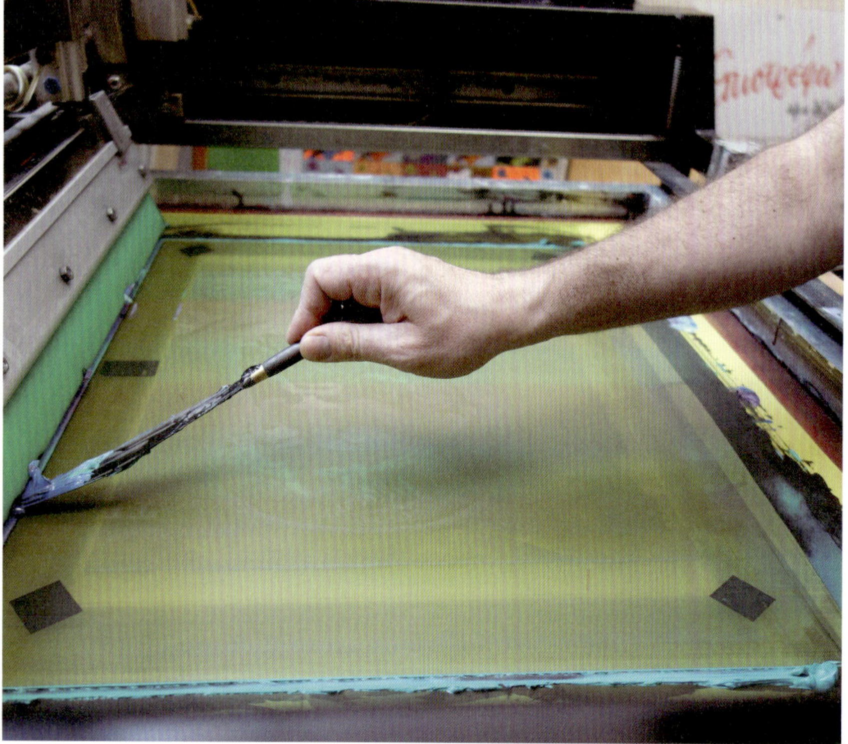

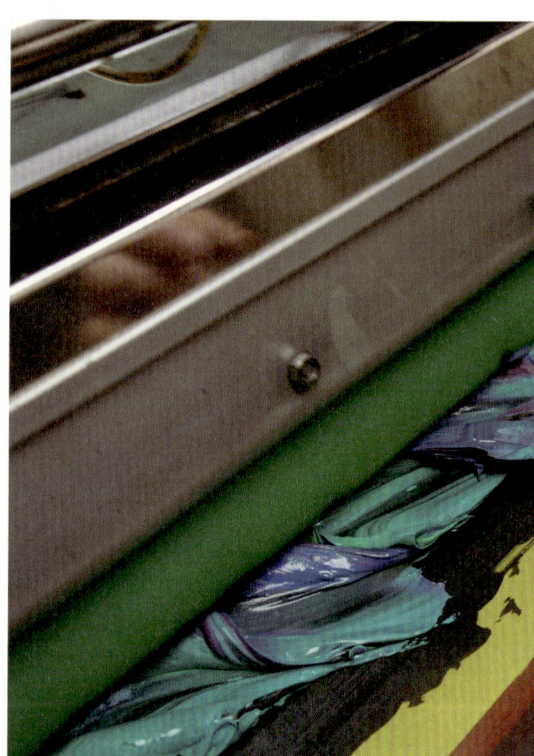

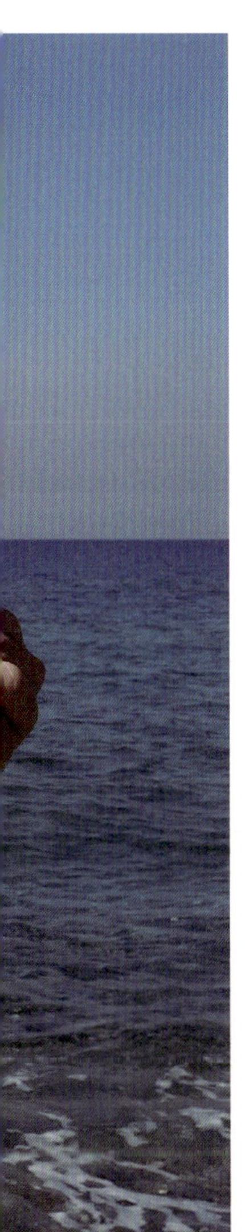

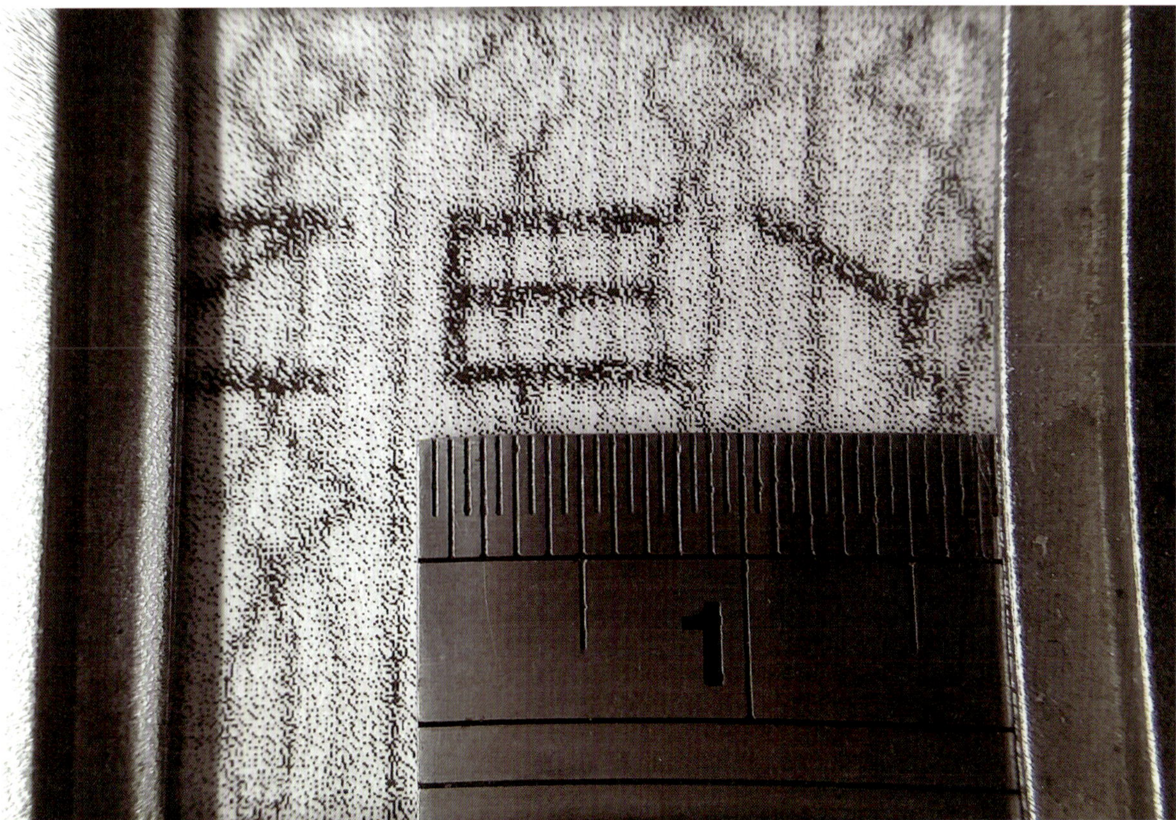
1

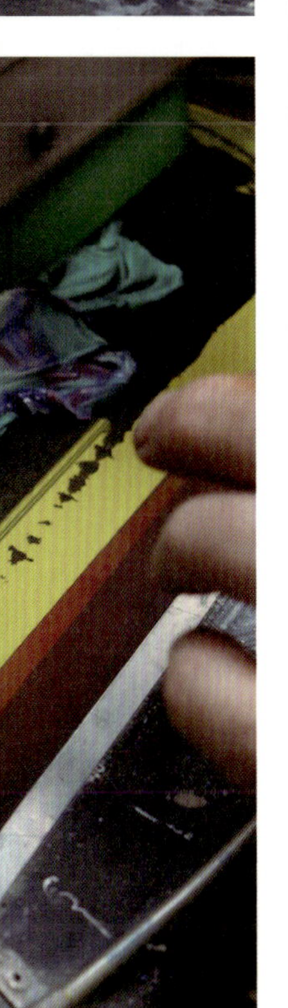

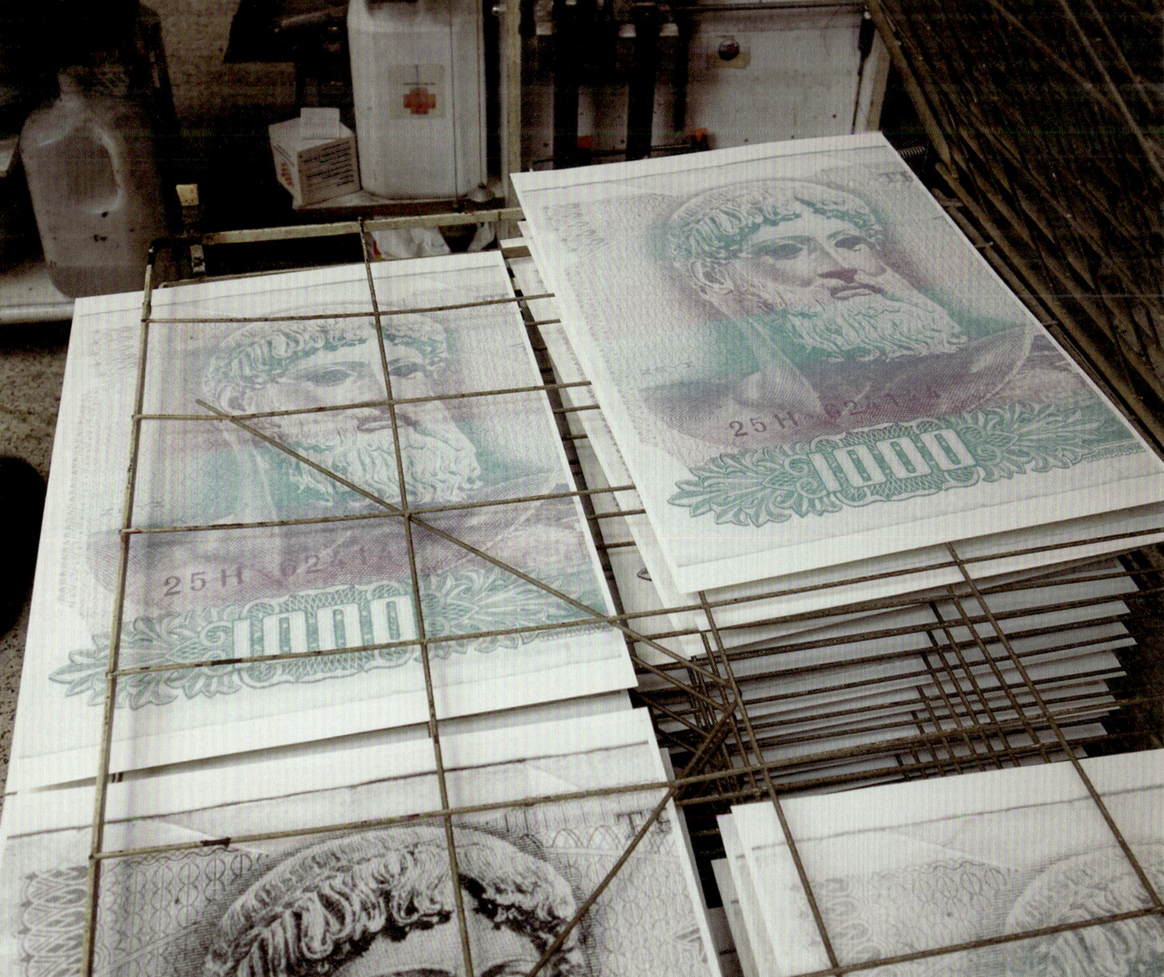
1000
1000

Die Rakete the return

300g white paper

phosphorescent ink

Design wise is a love letter to the space age that never came, at least up until today. Behind this is a need to always try new materials with screen printing and, just like an ant, to gather stuff to try. The designers also try to use their gut feelings. They find the best way to deal with the process, screen printing. Screen printing requires, above all else, curiosity, mixing, experimenting, taking a step back and repeating.

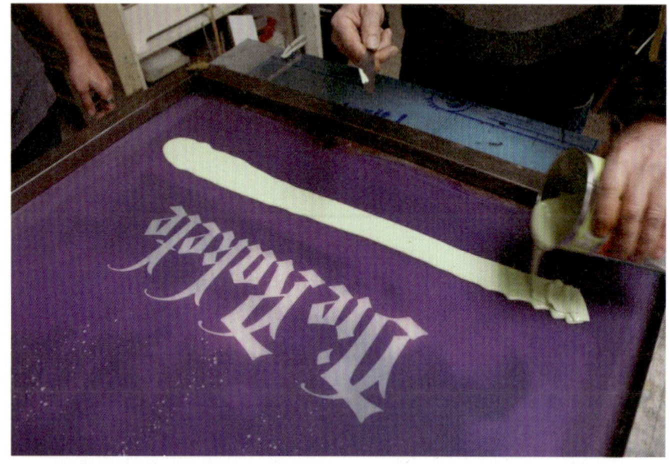

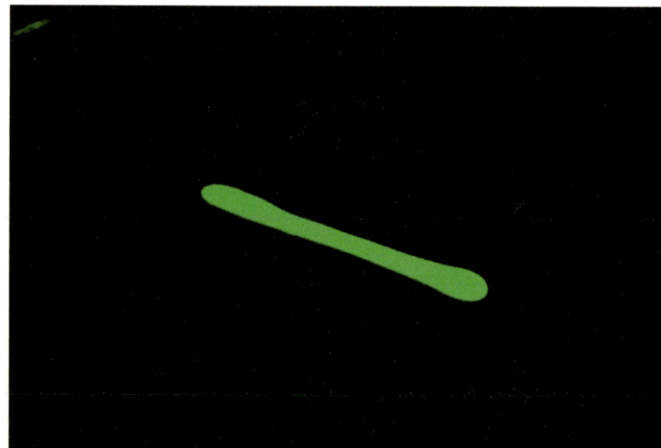

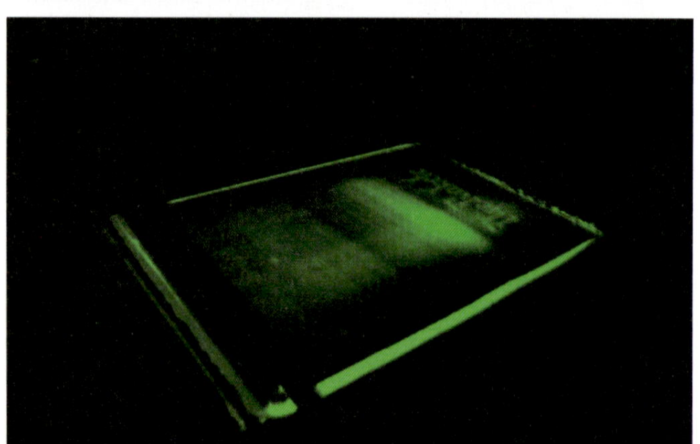

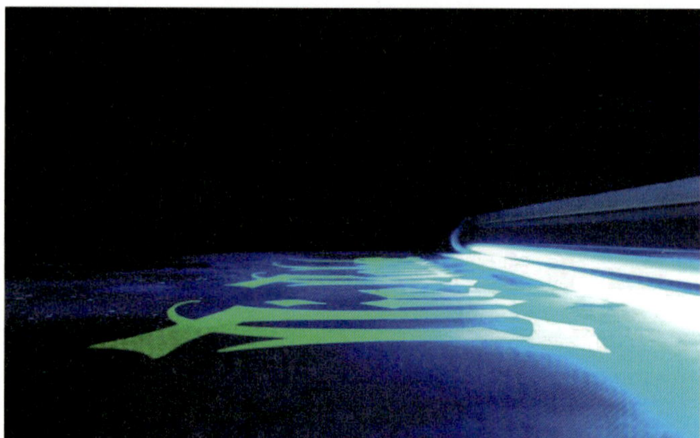

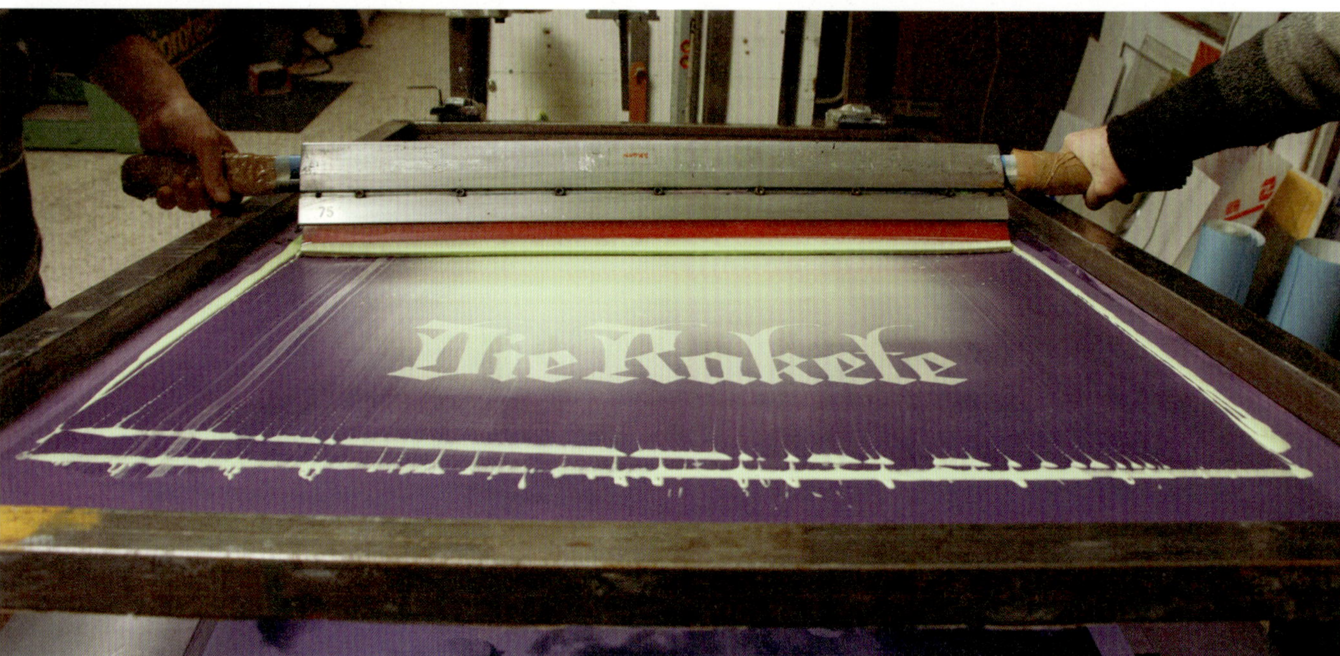

***D*:** tind

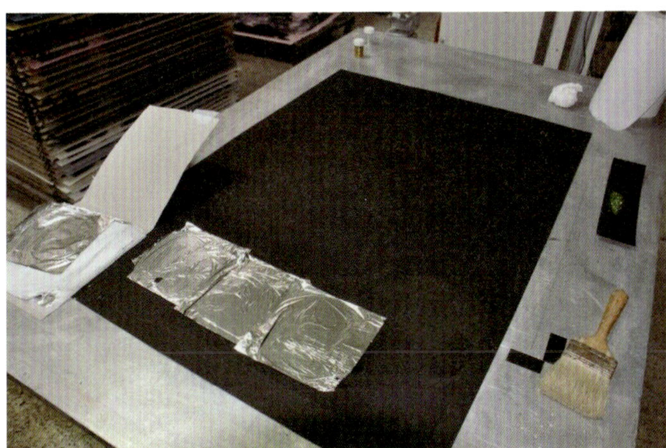

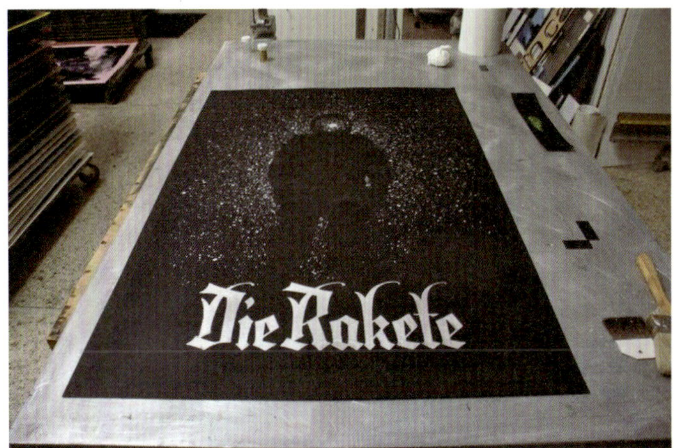
Die Rakete

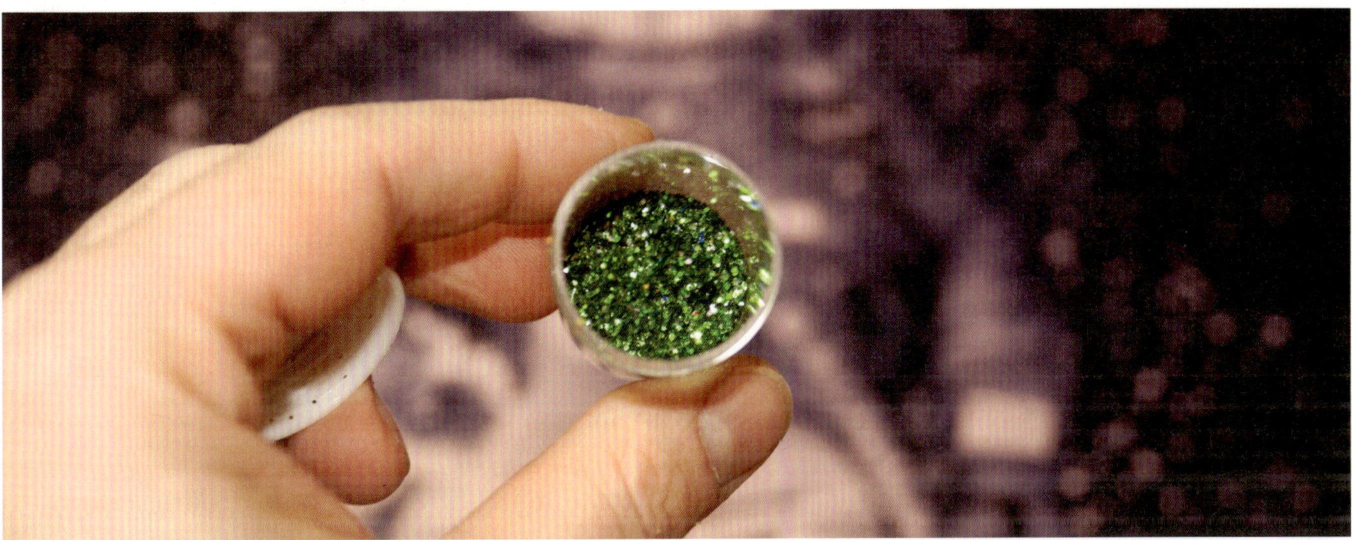

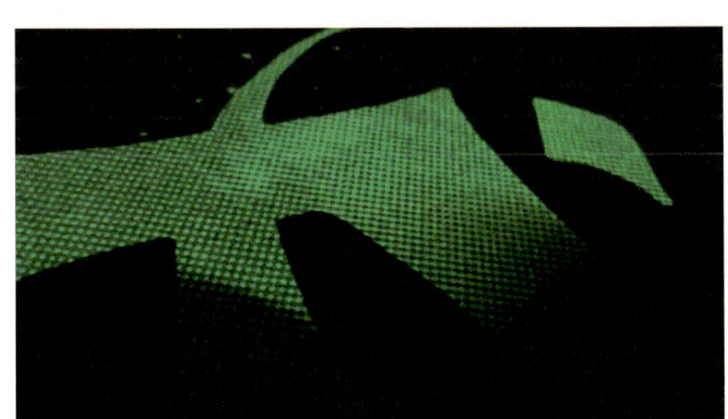

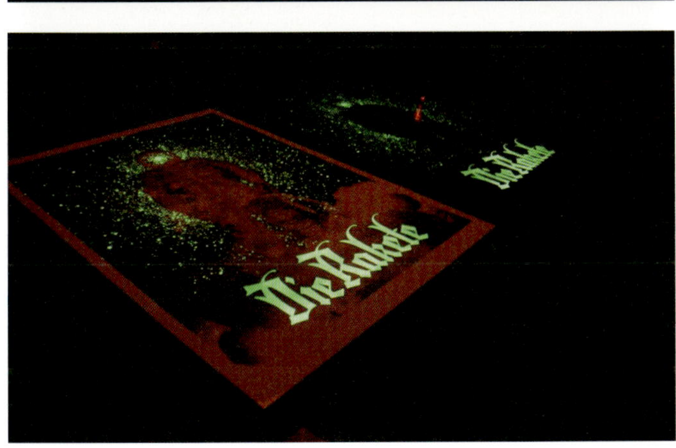
Die Rakete

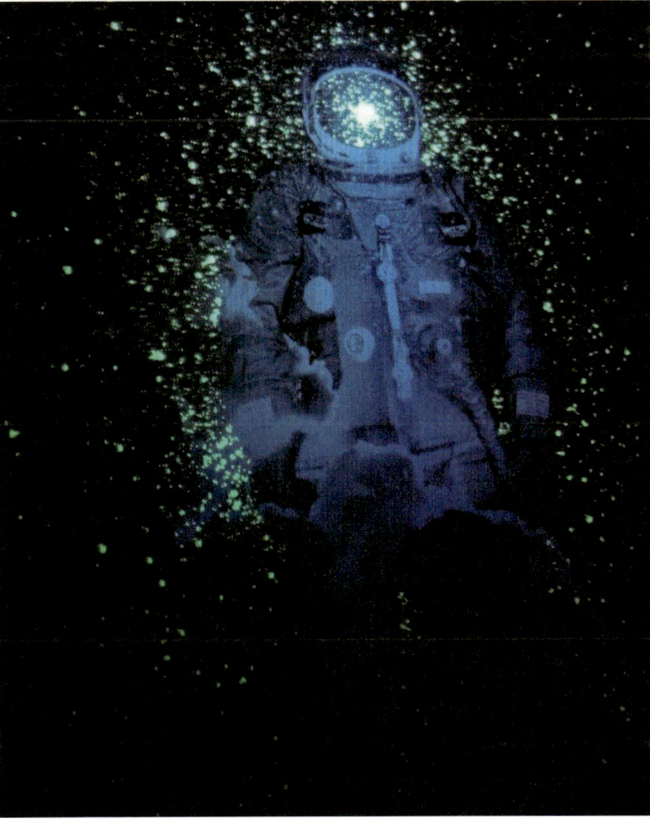

Feathers Construction

- light cotton fabrics
- pigment and reactive dyes

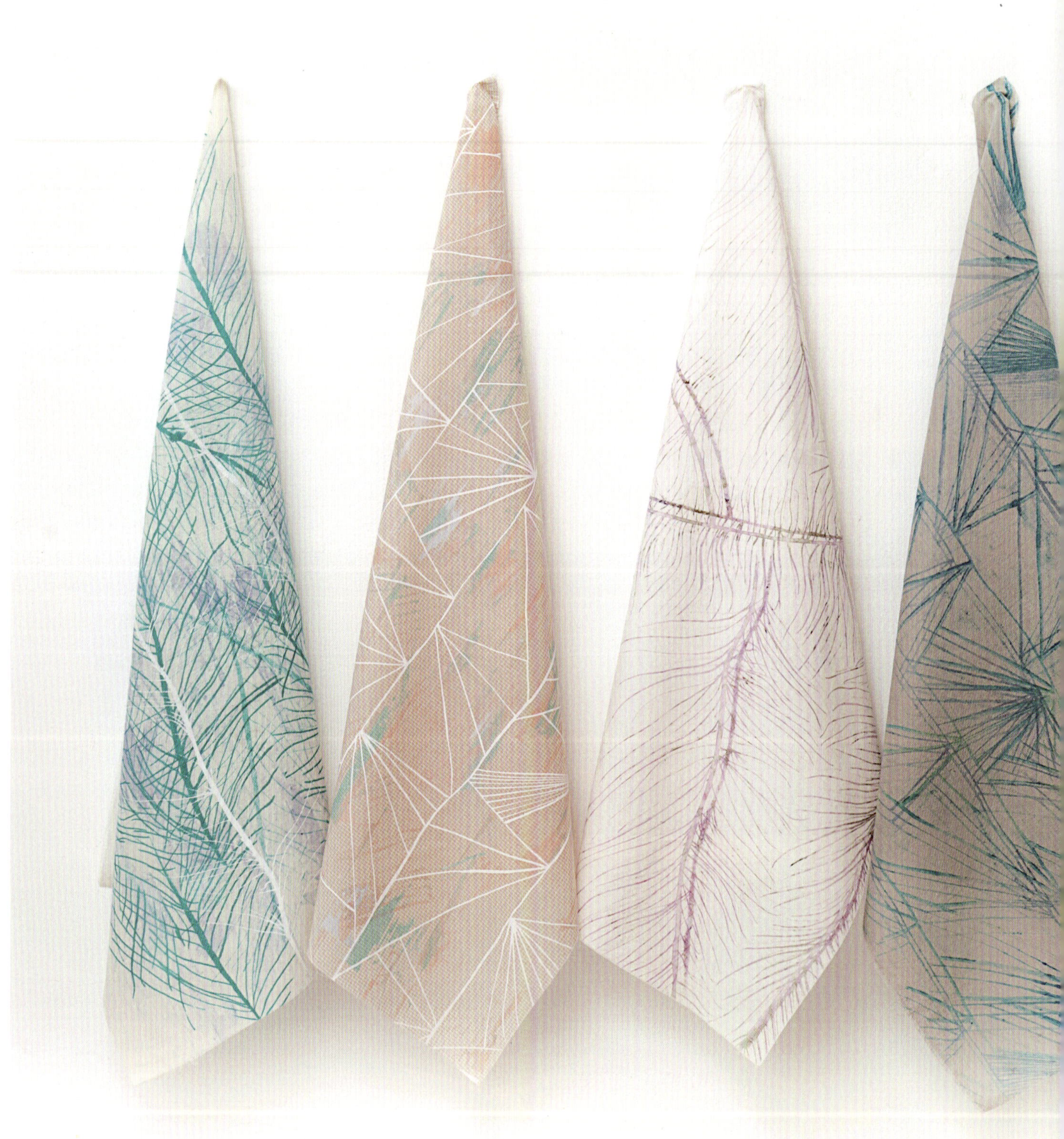

 D: Mor Svirsky

The designer chose reactive dyes and a monoprint technique so each piece is one of a kind, a few reactive dyes mixed in different colors with water and painted on the screen with a brush. In some cases, the designer repeated the same action twice or more on the same structure, which gave the print a faded feel resembling a feather, its mixture of lightness and intensity at the same time. For some prints, white pigment paste was added as a final layer.

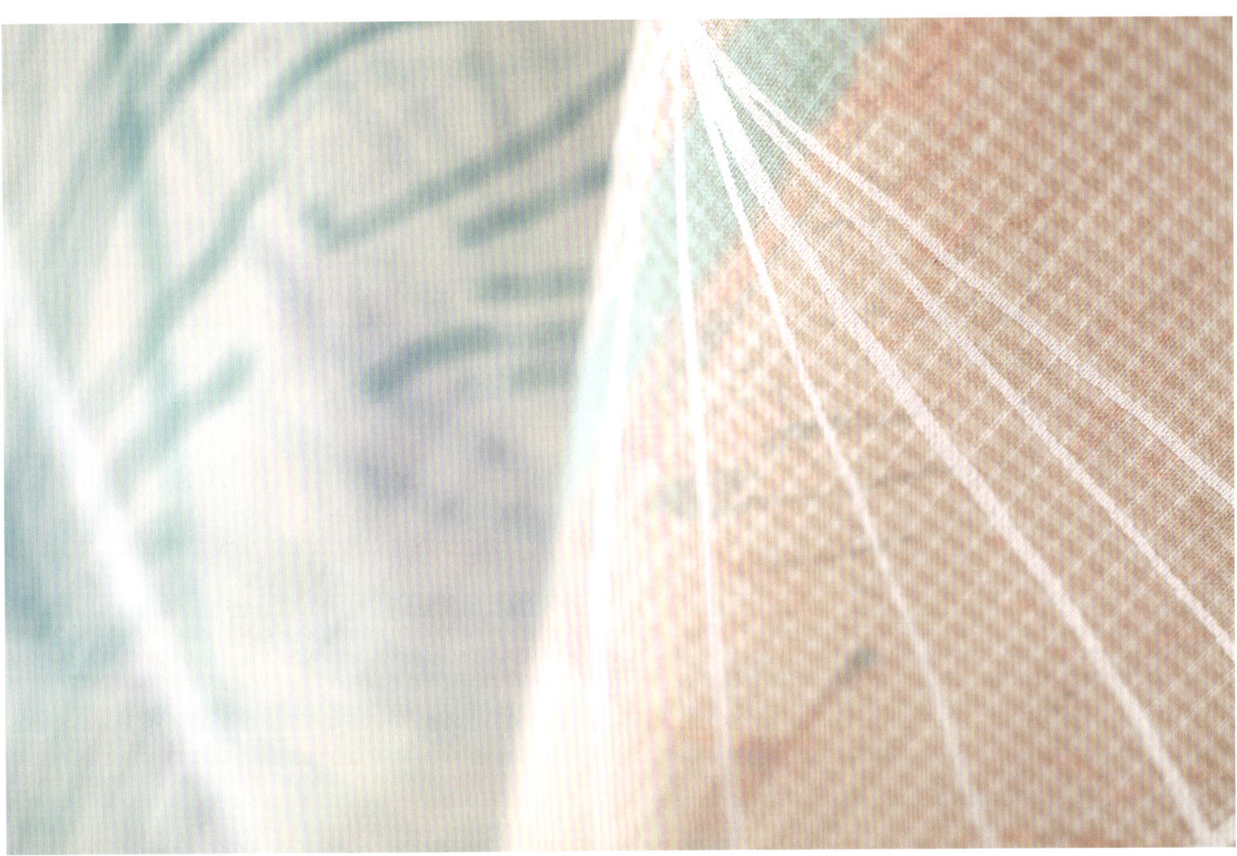

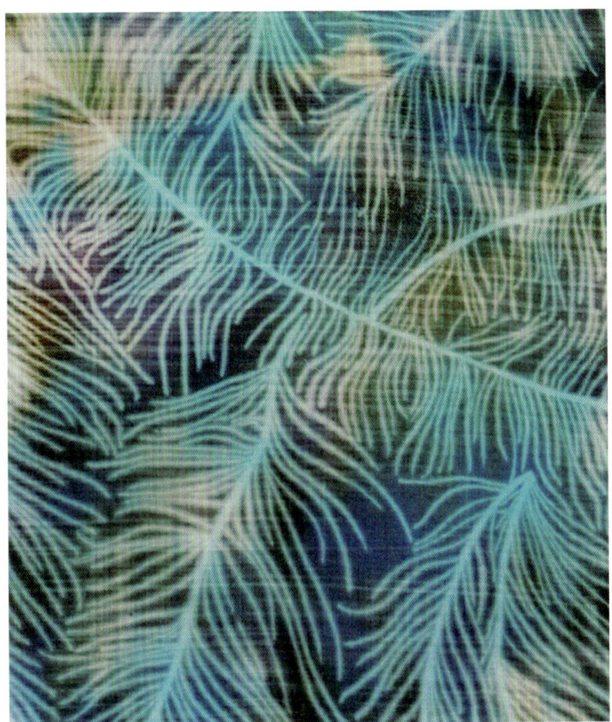

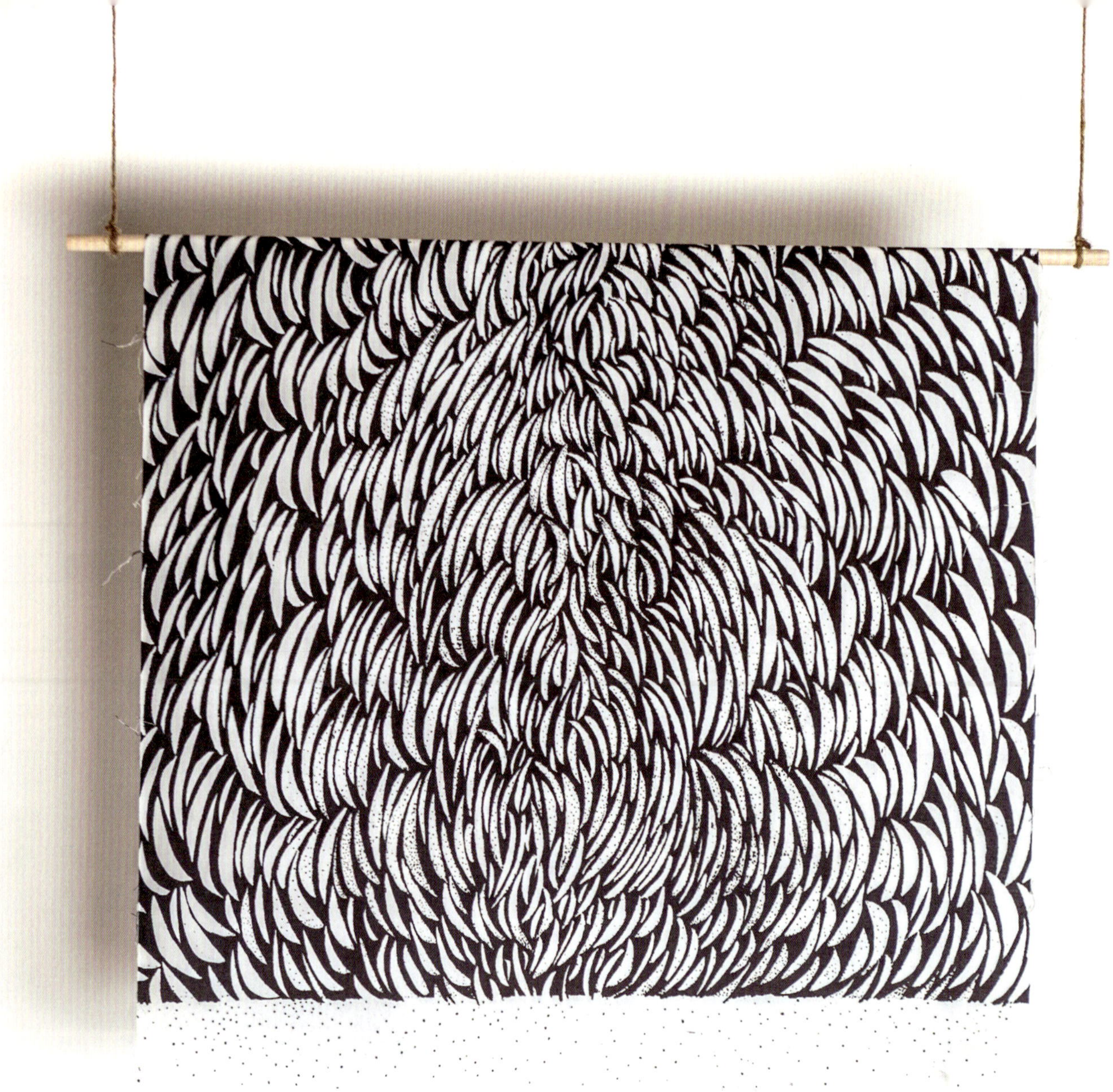

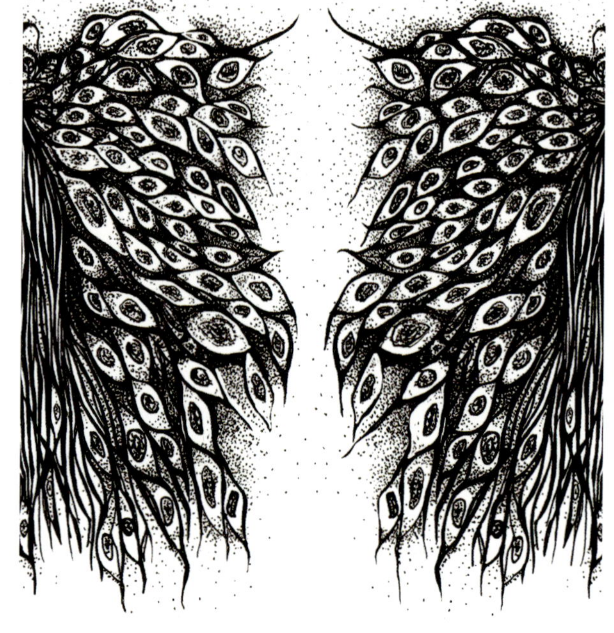

Glorious Visions

cotton fabrics

reactive dyes, discharge, foil.

A collection of screen printed fabrics for home decoration. The motifs are inspired by saintly and gothic cathedrals. The prints were created after illustrations, using black pens of 2 mm & 3 mm. Some of the illustrations are combined into repeated patterns. The designer chose reactive dyes on heavy cotton fabrics, and the prints, mostly, are one layered. In some cases, discharge and monoprinting techniques are combined.

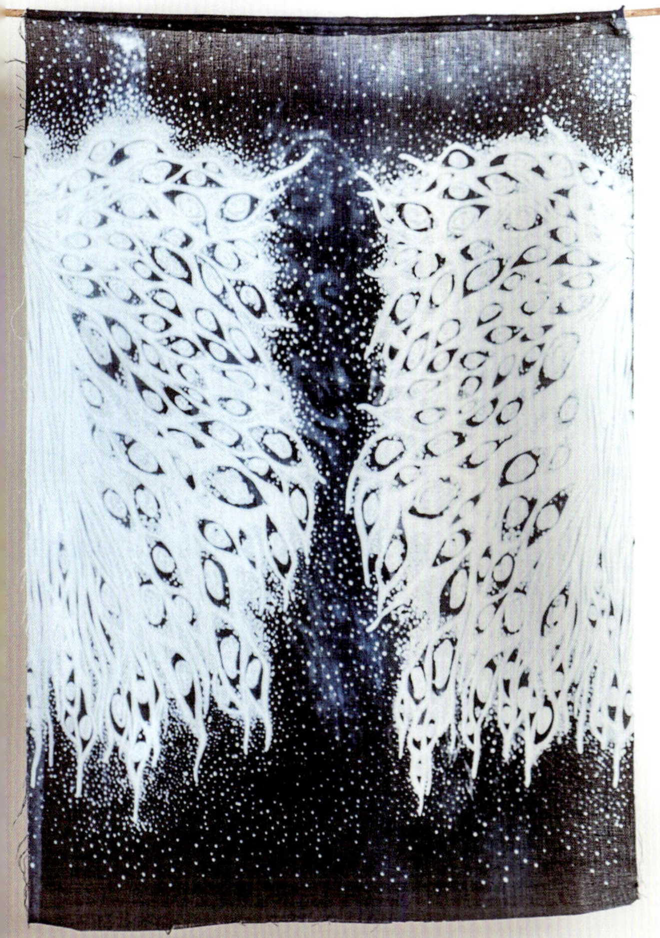

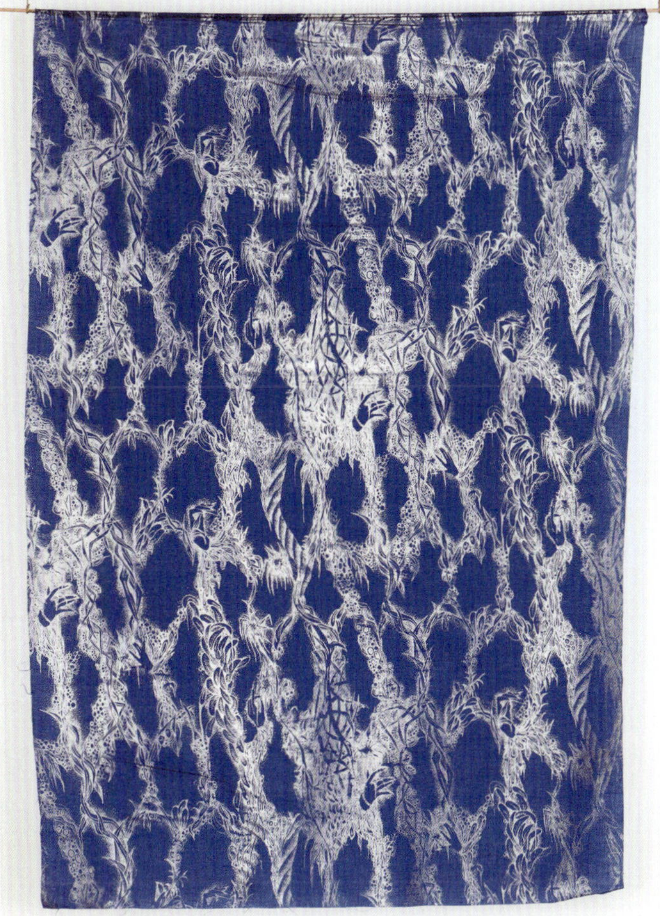

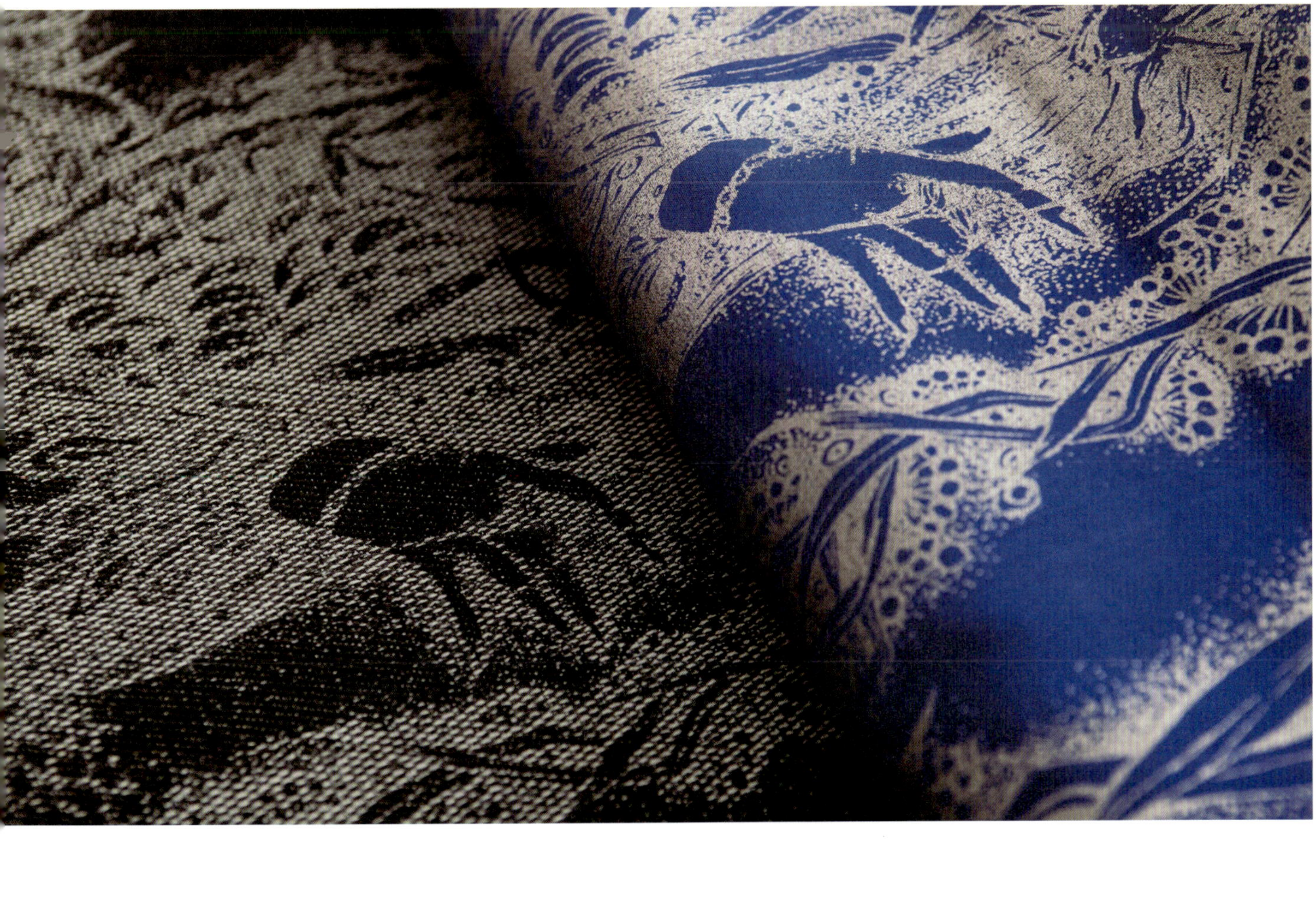

Supernova

paper

water-based screenprint inks

Photo by Julie Pradier

Designers wanted to experiment transparency and color superposing effects. A series of original patterns were created and printed on both sides of large paper sheets. They were then assembled randomly to create rhythm in shapes and colors. Light offered a way to reveal those combinations. The 3D object evokes a balloon or flower.

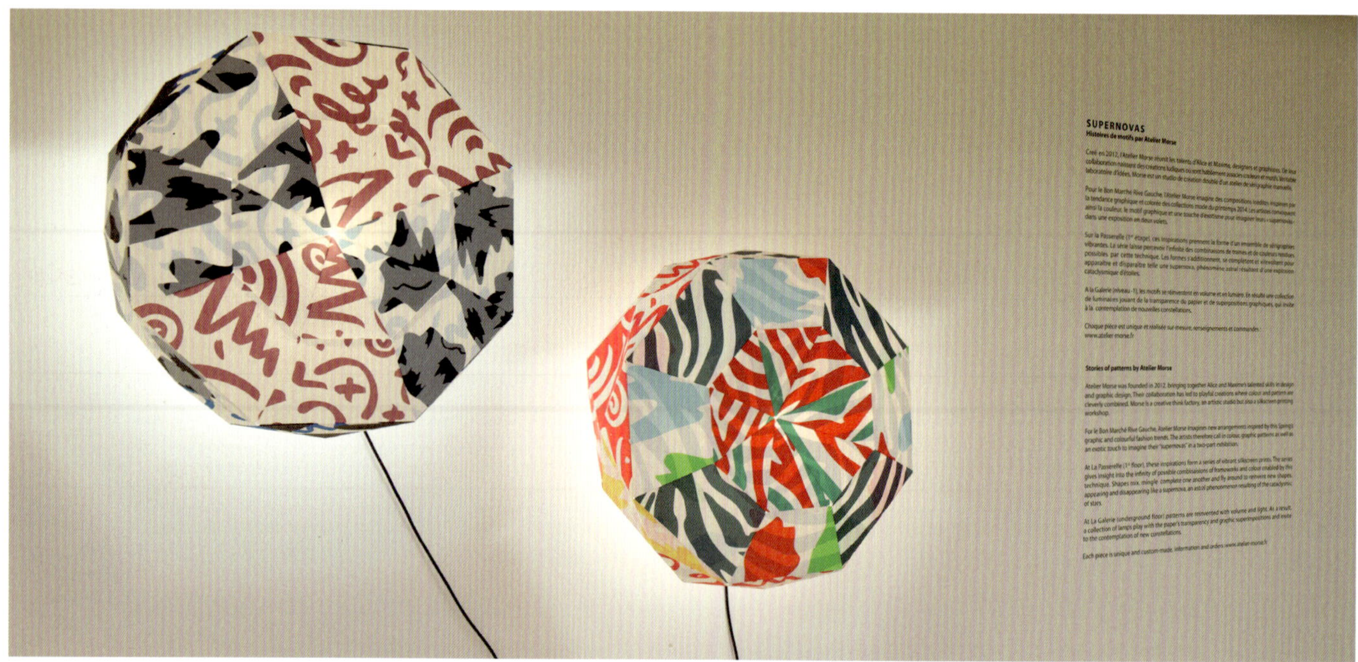

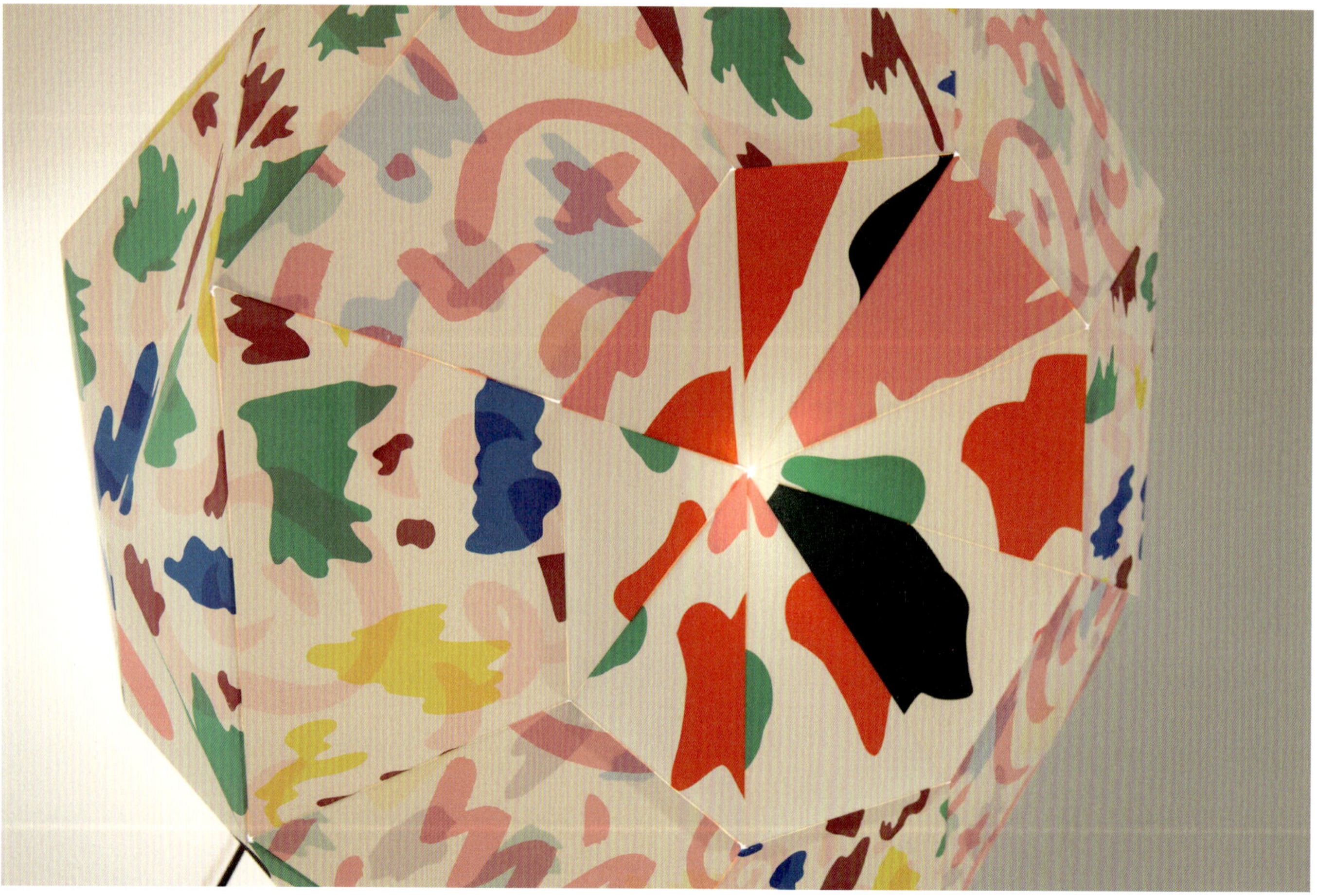

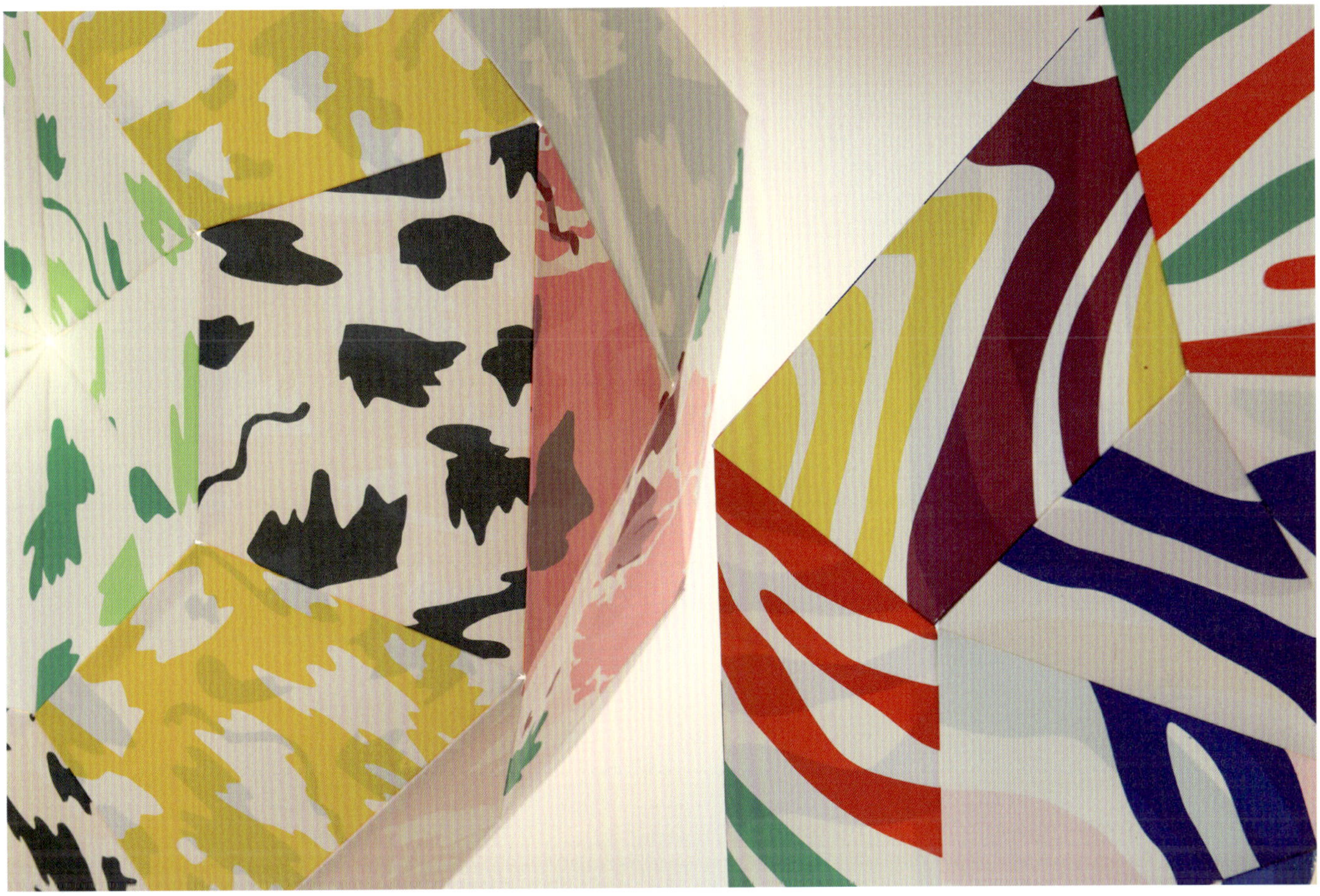

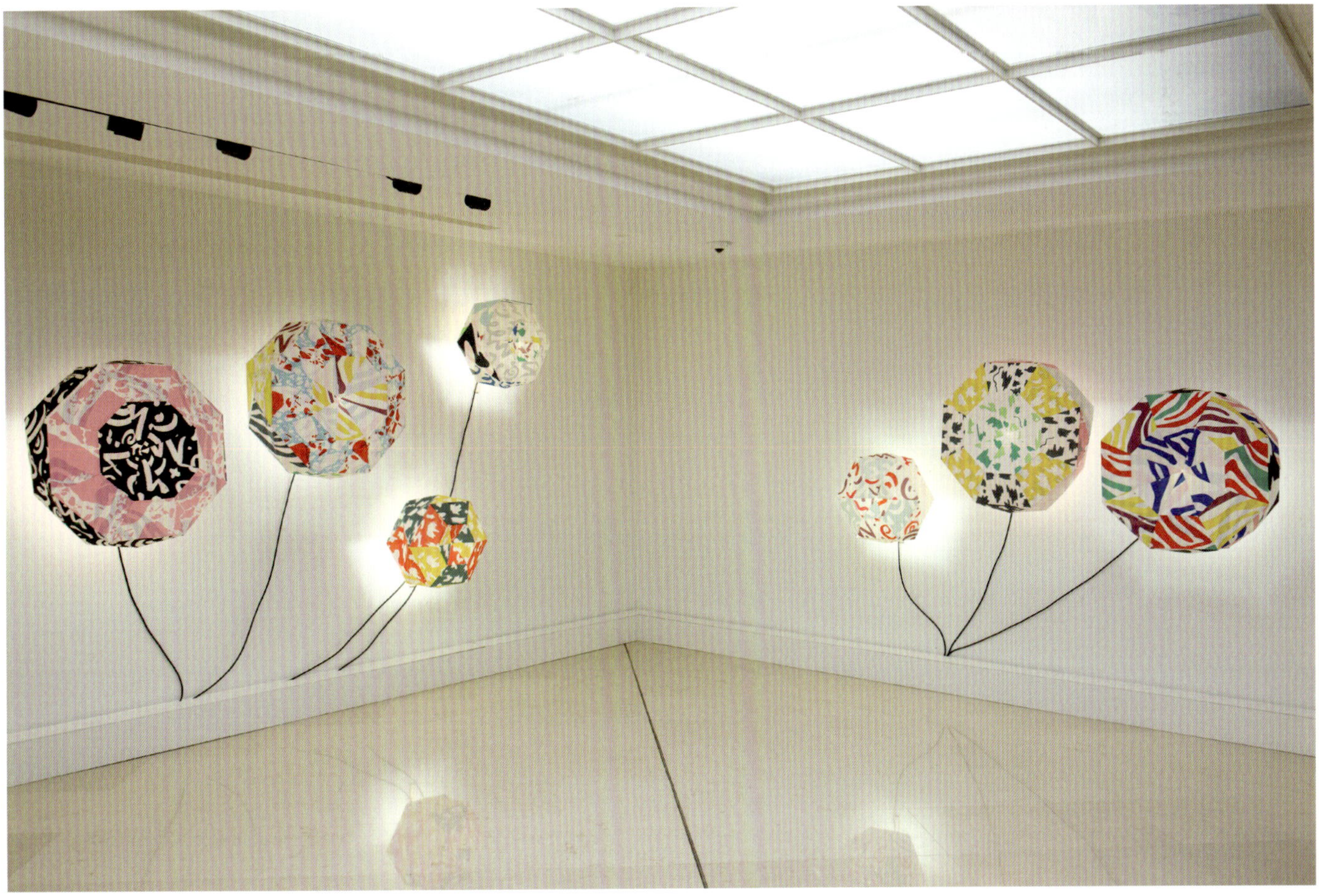

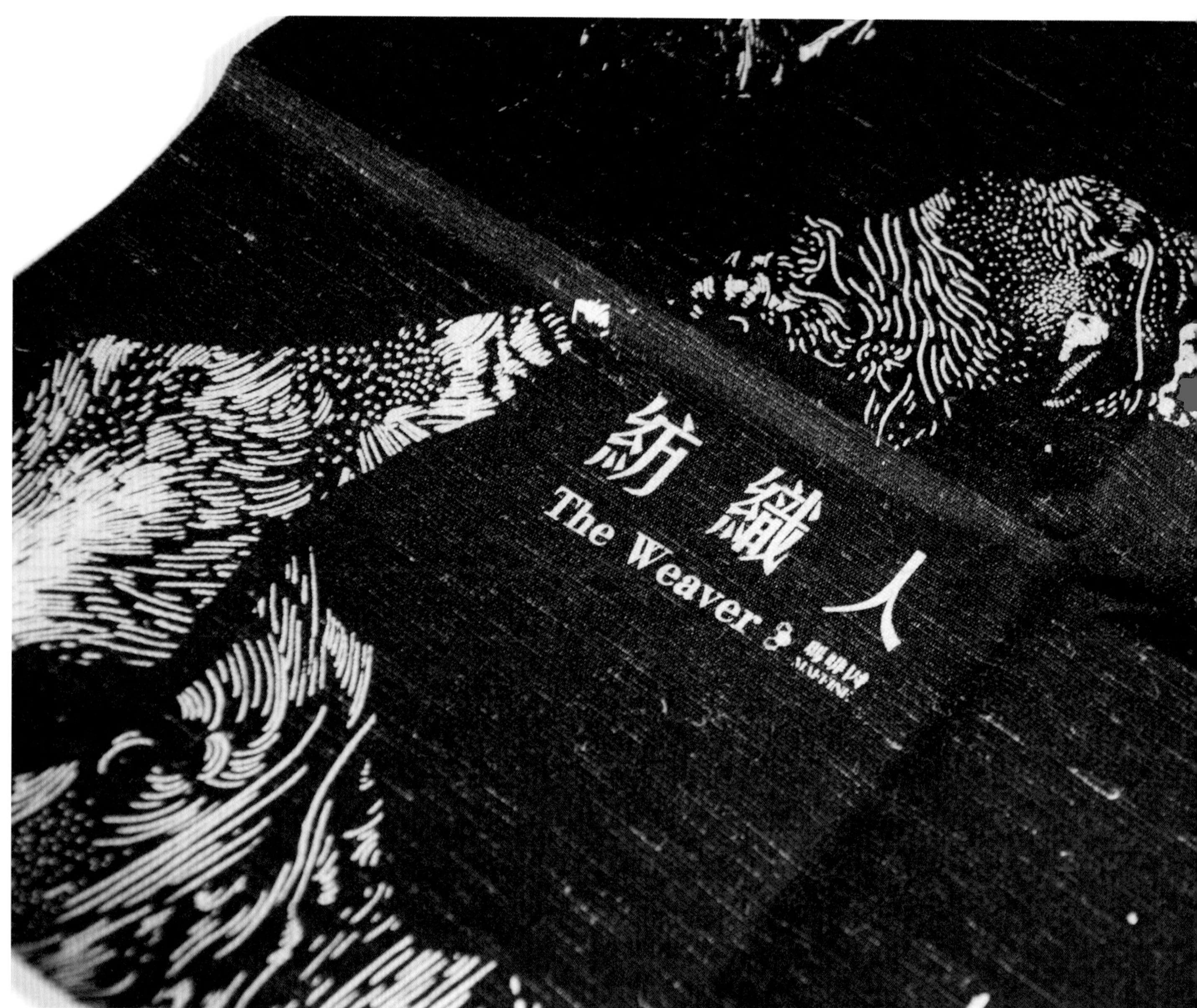

The Weaver

tracing paper, yunyan weaving fabrics

uv ink, black ink, silver ink

The loom has often been described, like fate, as a continuous time warp. The "warp of the loom" is the same as time, which will never stops. What color, what pattern, and what image will we choose to apply on the textile to become the "weft of the loom," all looking forward to see what it will emerge at the end. The packaging of Maffine's album "The Weaver," released in 2015, echoes the theme of the album. The designer used tracing paper as the outer packing, which contains the cloth lyric book and the CD in layer upon layer: design elements interweave to influence each one other in this unique creation.

D: Yun-Fang Ho

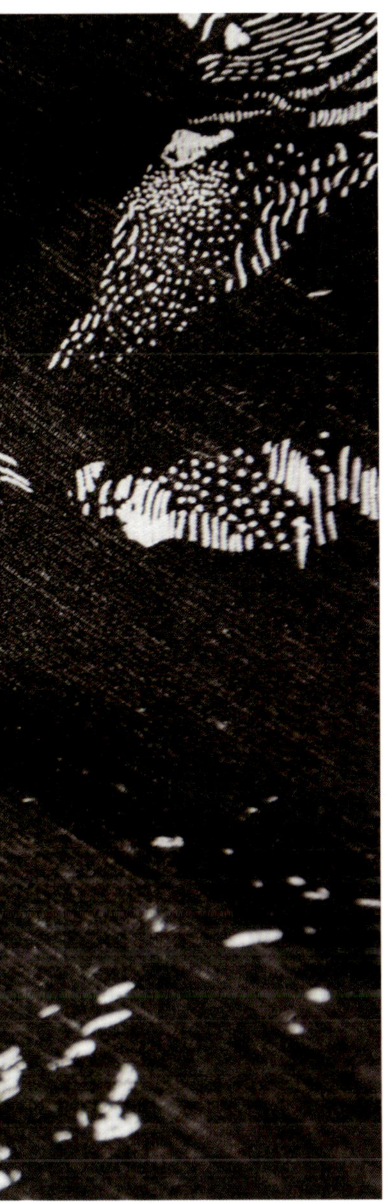

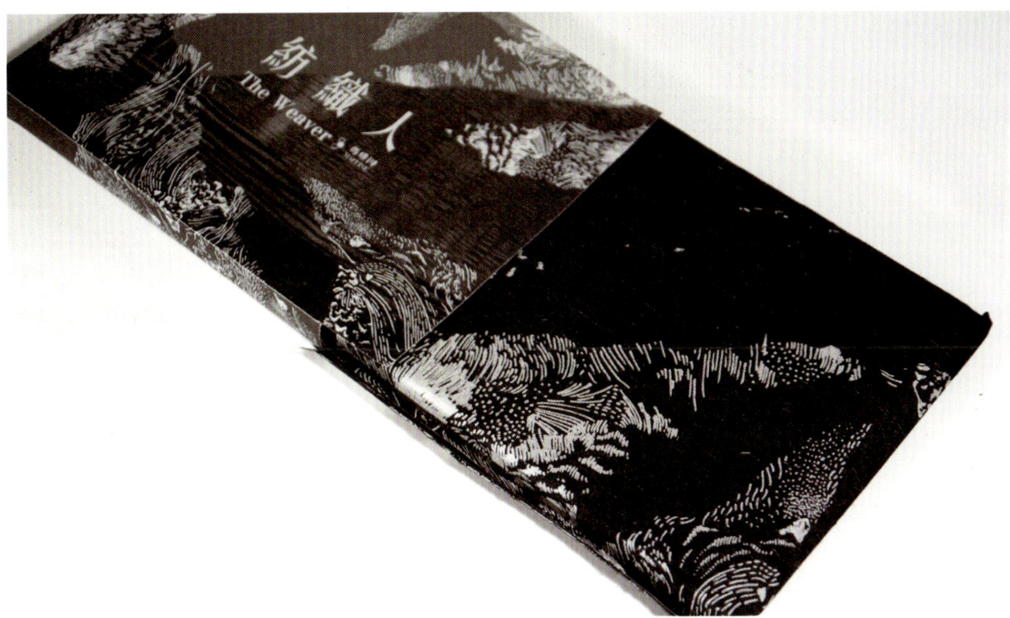
紡織人
The Weaver 3

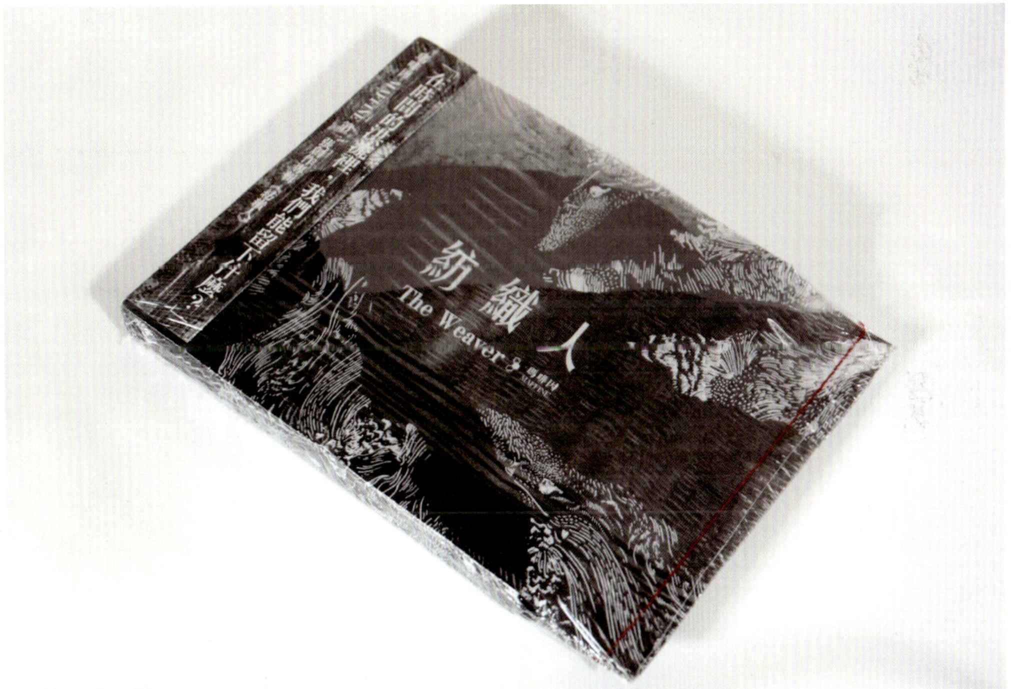
紡織人
The Weaver 3

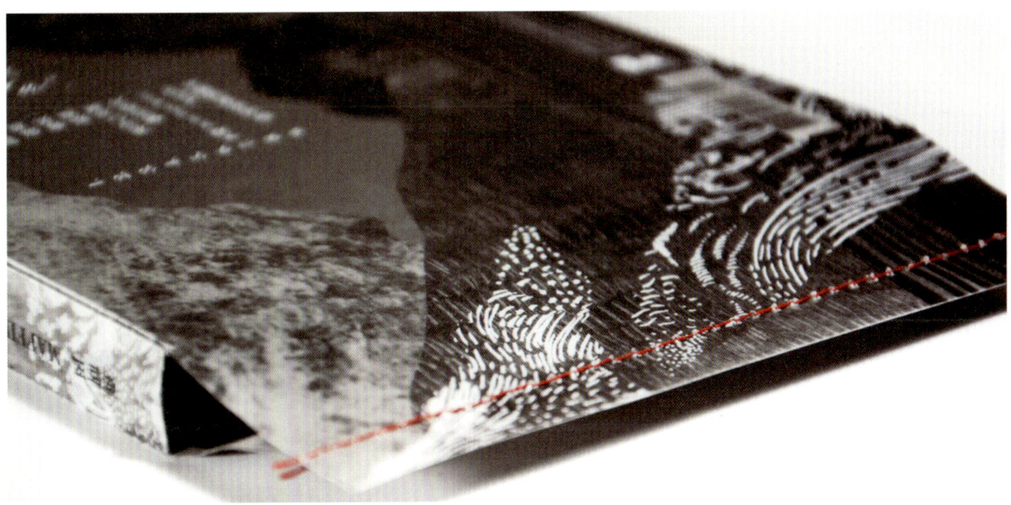

Names of Prostitutes

80g Munken paper

gouache paint

Prostitutes form a special group. During ancient dynasties there were various names for referring to them. This book introduces over 100 names of prostitutes, with typography design, and illustrations. The illustrations were printed with a screen printing method. Phloxine paint was used to hint of women and sex.

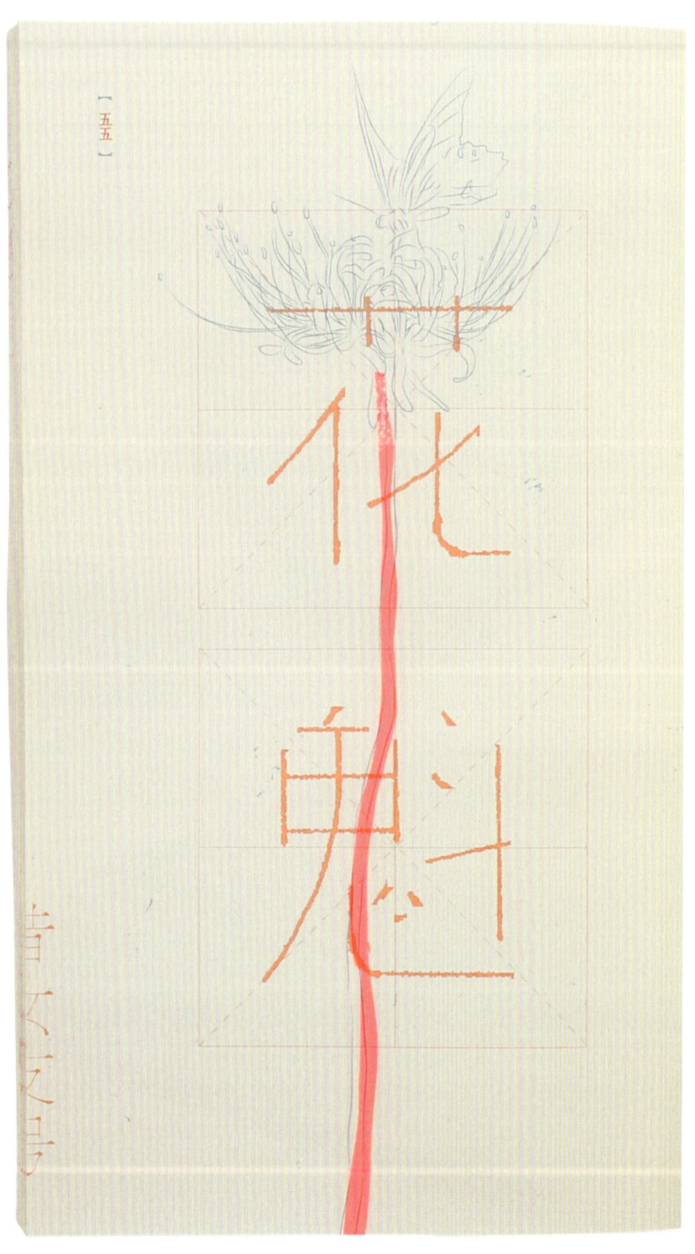

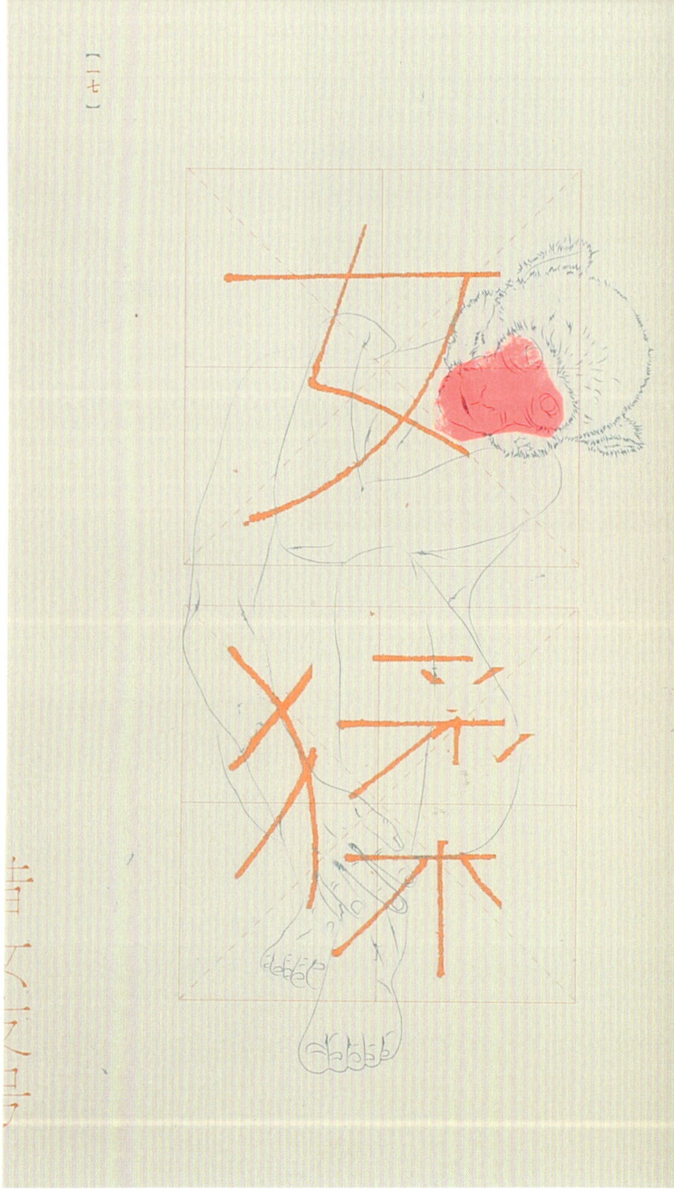

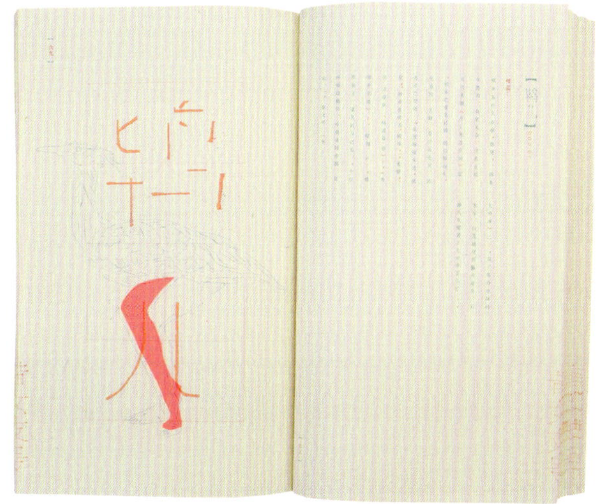

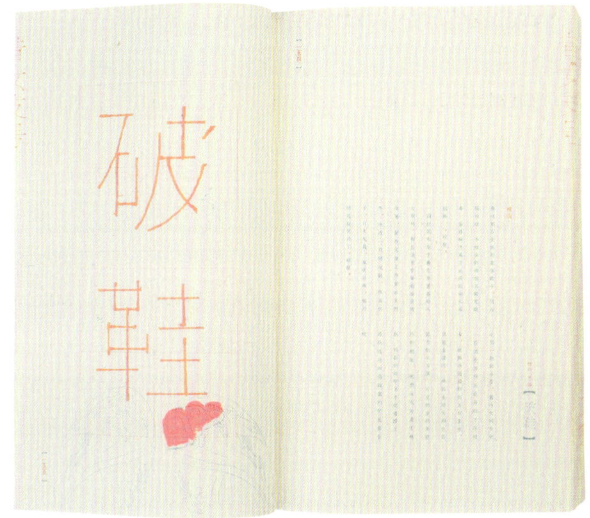

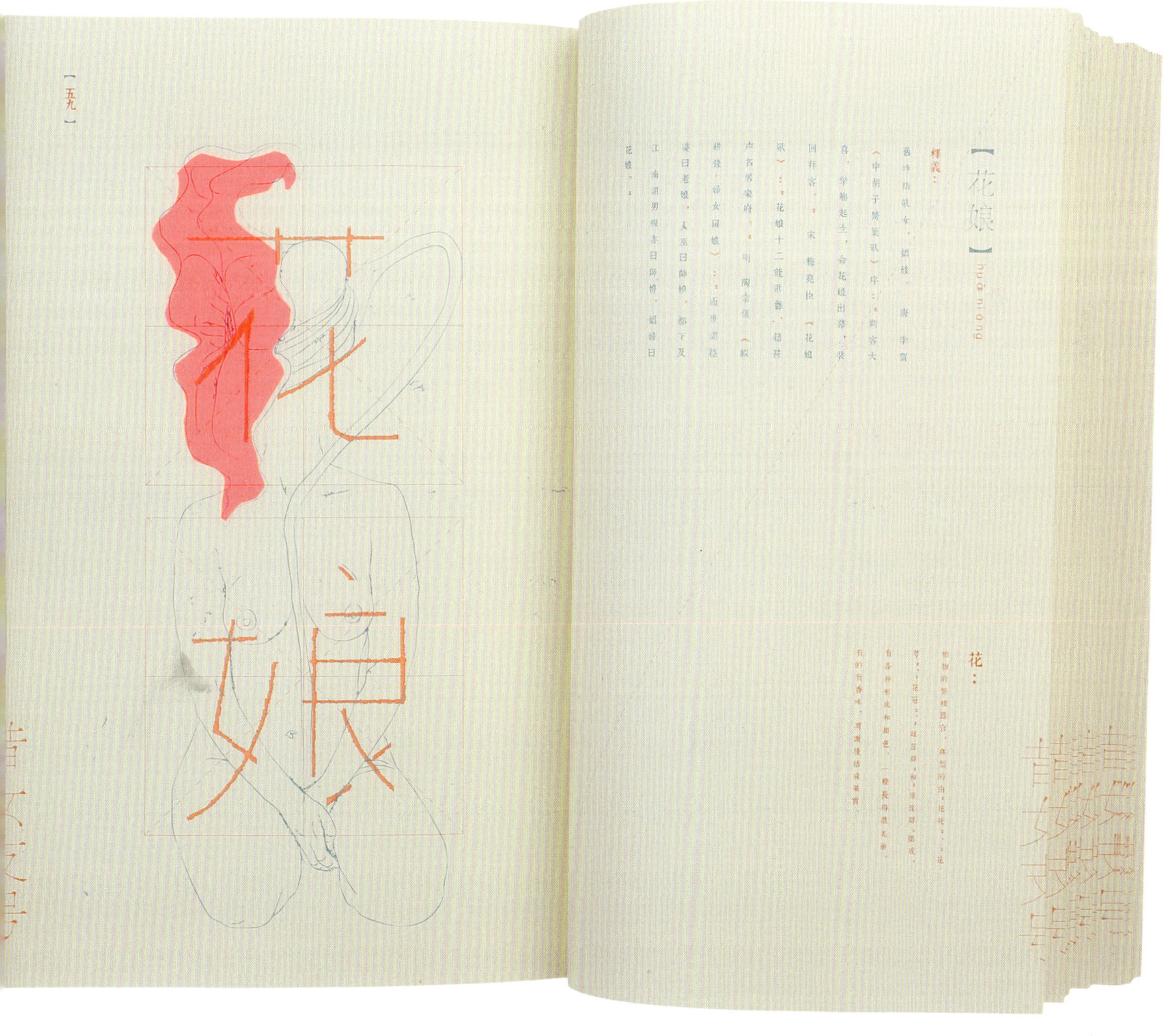

TALLINN-TARTU-TALLINN

oil paint

This set of three books is about the designer's perception of the landscape between Tallinn and Tartu, on her first trip through Estonia. She noticed especially the forest that covers almost the whole country, and the light playing between the pine trunks. A set of three leporello books, are held together – when folded – by a strip. The route between the two towns is outlined on this strip as well as at the back of each book. She chose monotype because it allows her to be flexible and quick when drawing, as well as creating beautiful textures that suits her theme.

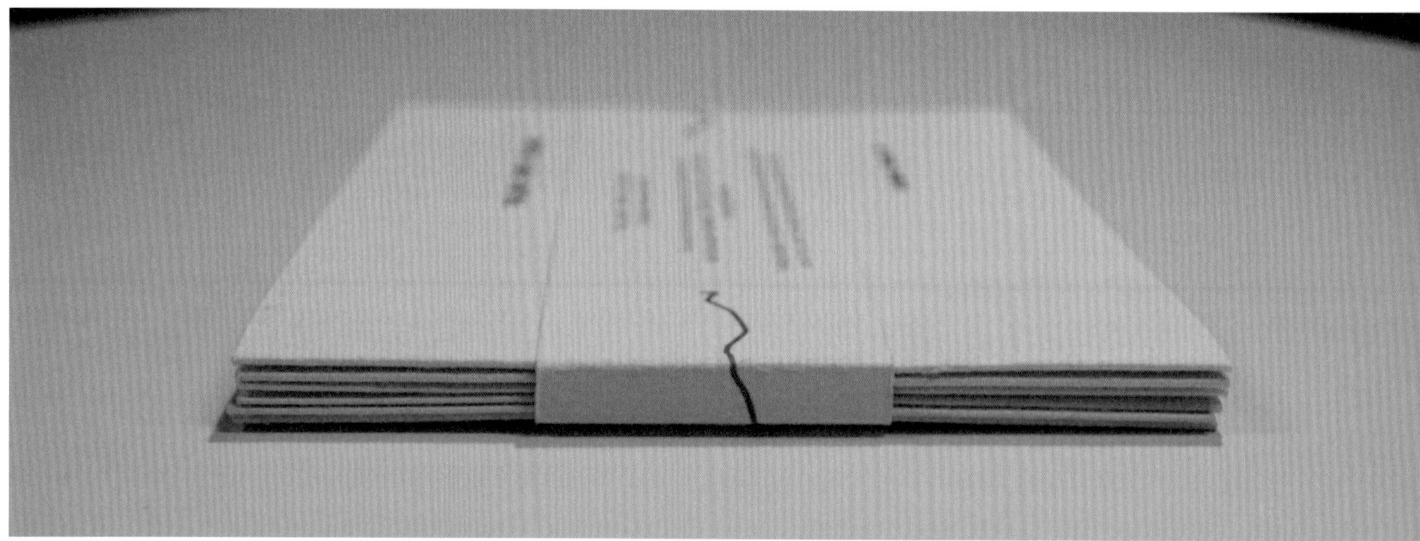

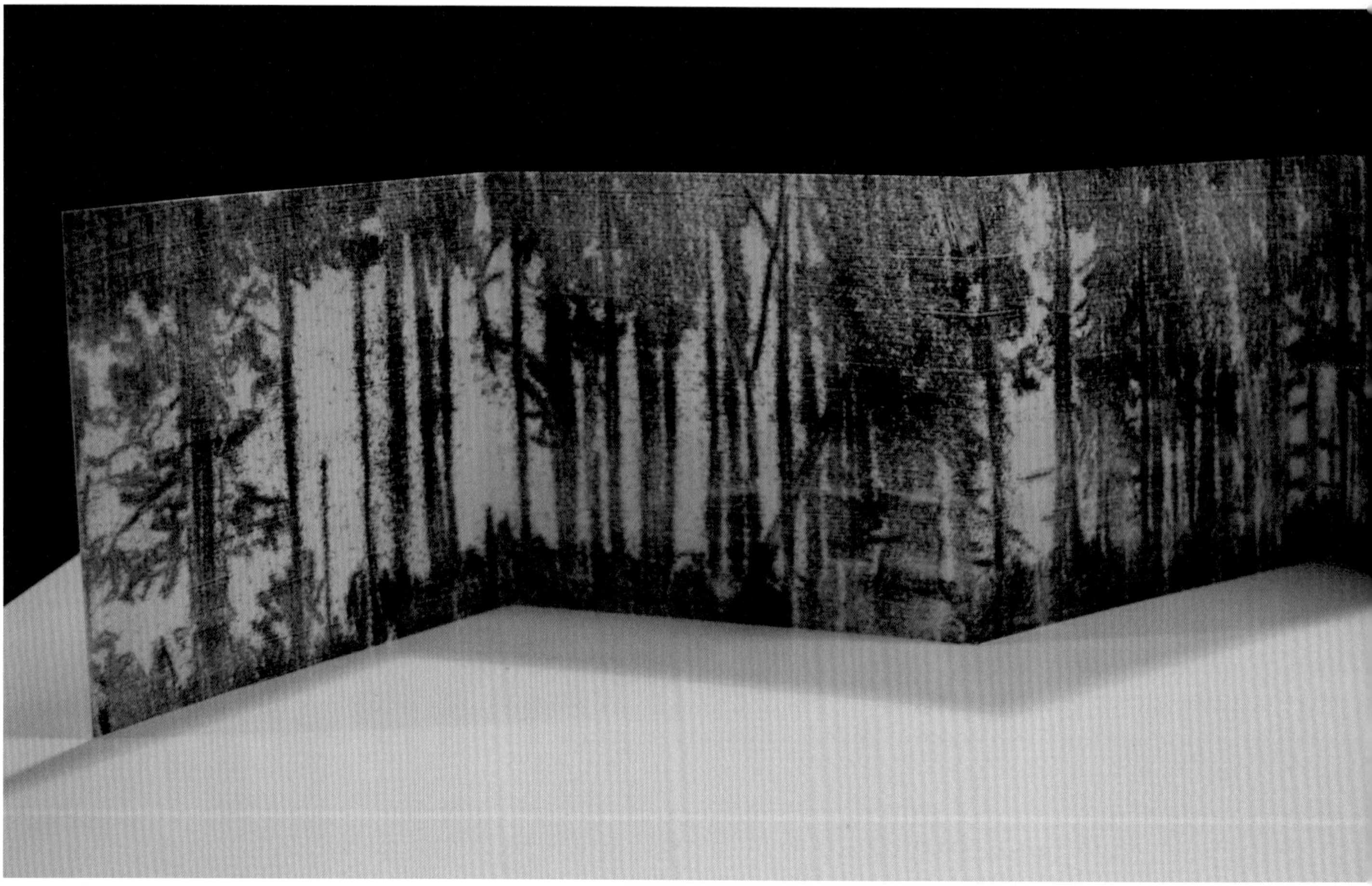

D: Jeanne Tocqueville

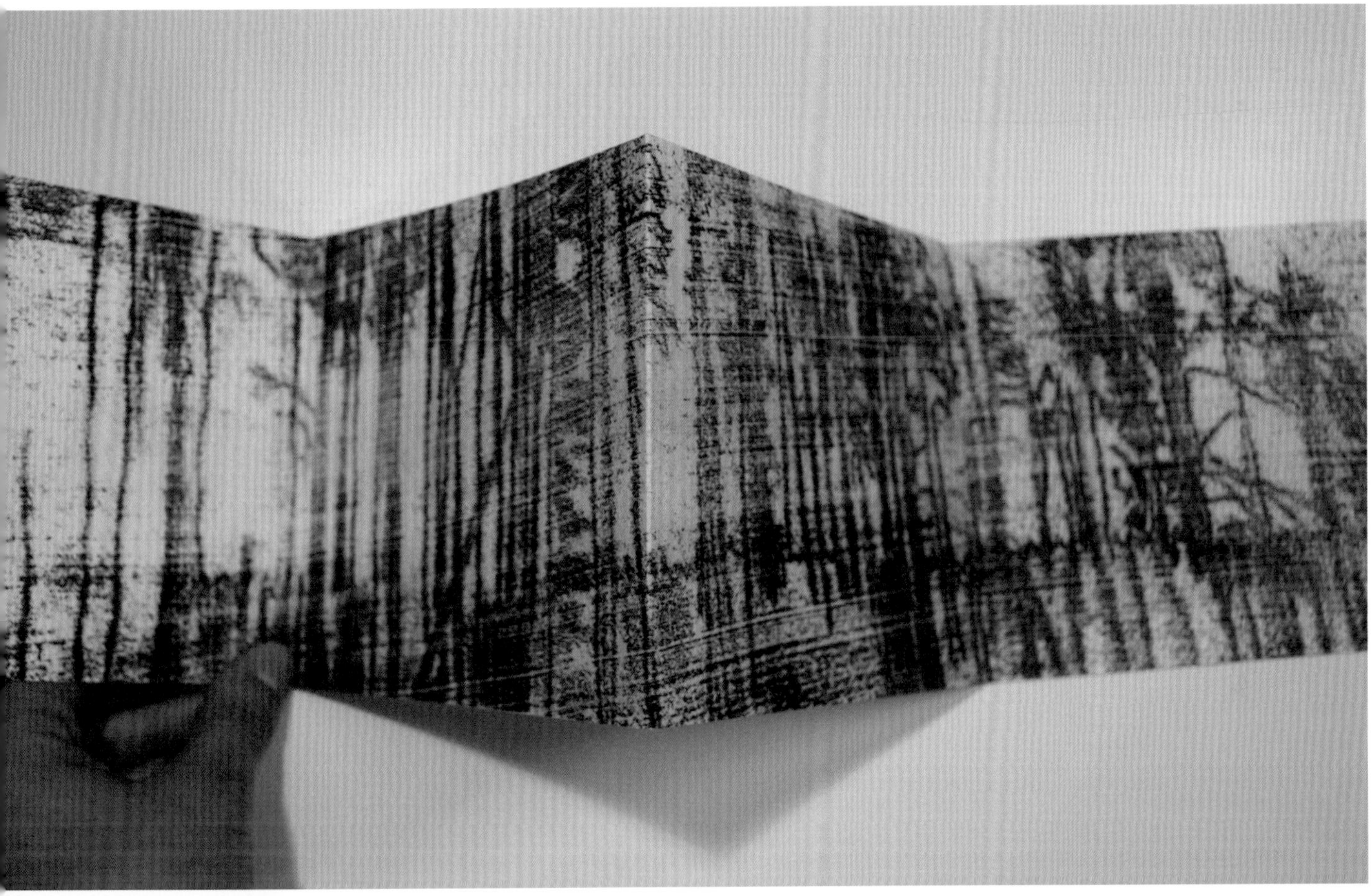

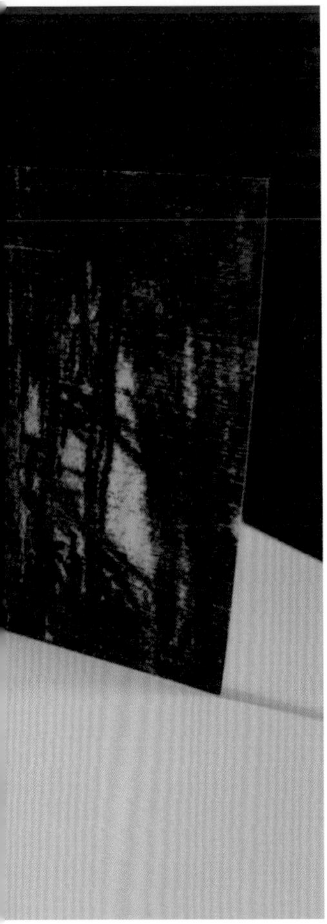

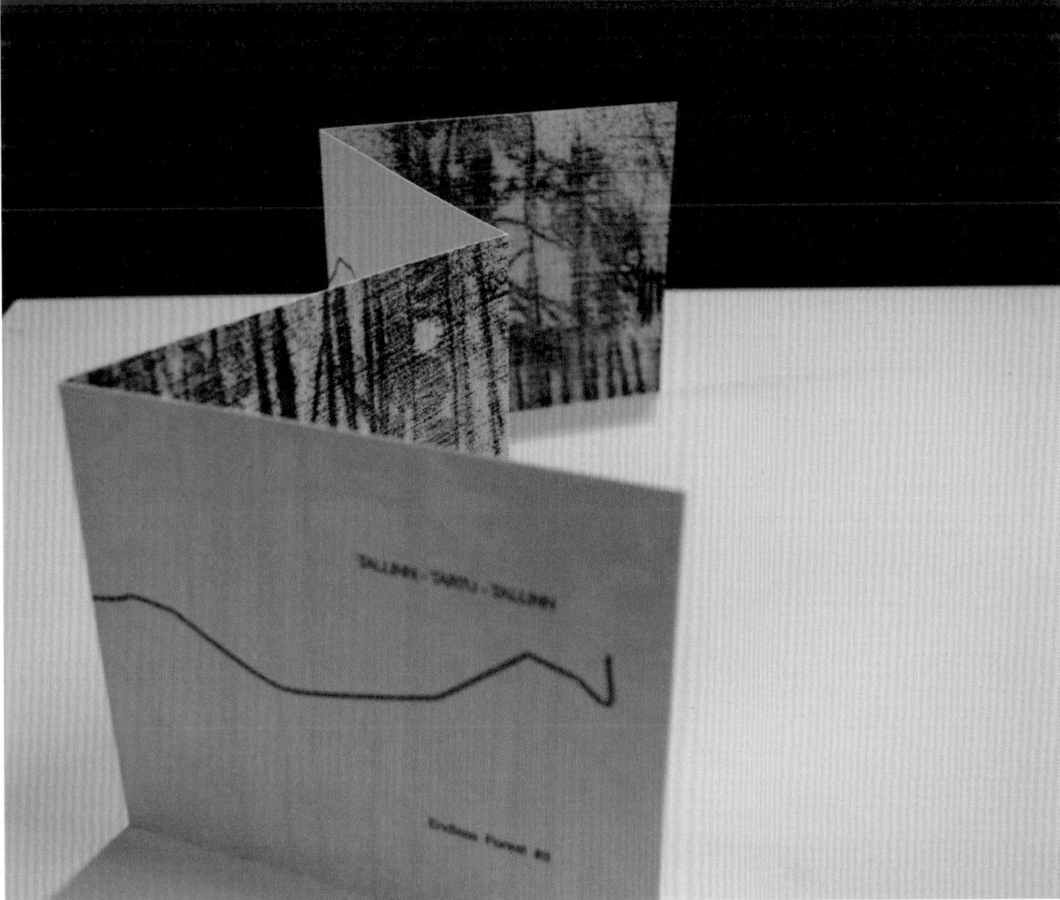
TALLINN - TARTU - TALLINN

Memórias Encantadas Da Terra Brincante (ENCHANTED MEMORIES FROM JOKER'S LAND)

Fabriano paper

"Memórias encantadas da terra brincante" is a four-color silkscreen featuring Brazil's popular folk festivals. This piece is 100 cm long and was originally designed to be a concertina postcard printing. Brazil is a country filled with the richest expressions of popular culture. Revelries, festivals, and games are present in all regions and take place throughout the year. These expressions are part of a large treasure of memories and traditions passed down from generation to generation and form popular imagery. As a tribute to the Brazilian soul and to those who keep alive their origins, these postcards illustrate some of the most charming faces of the beloved "joker's land."

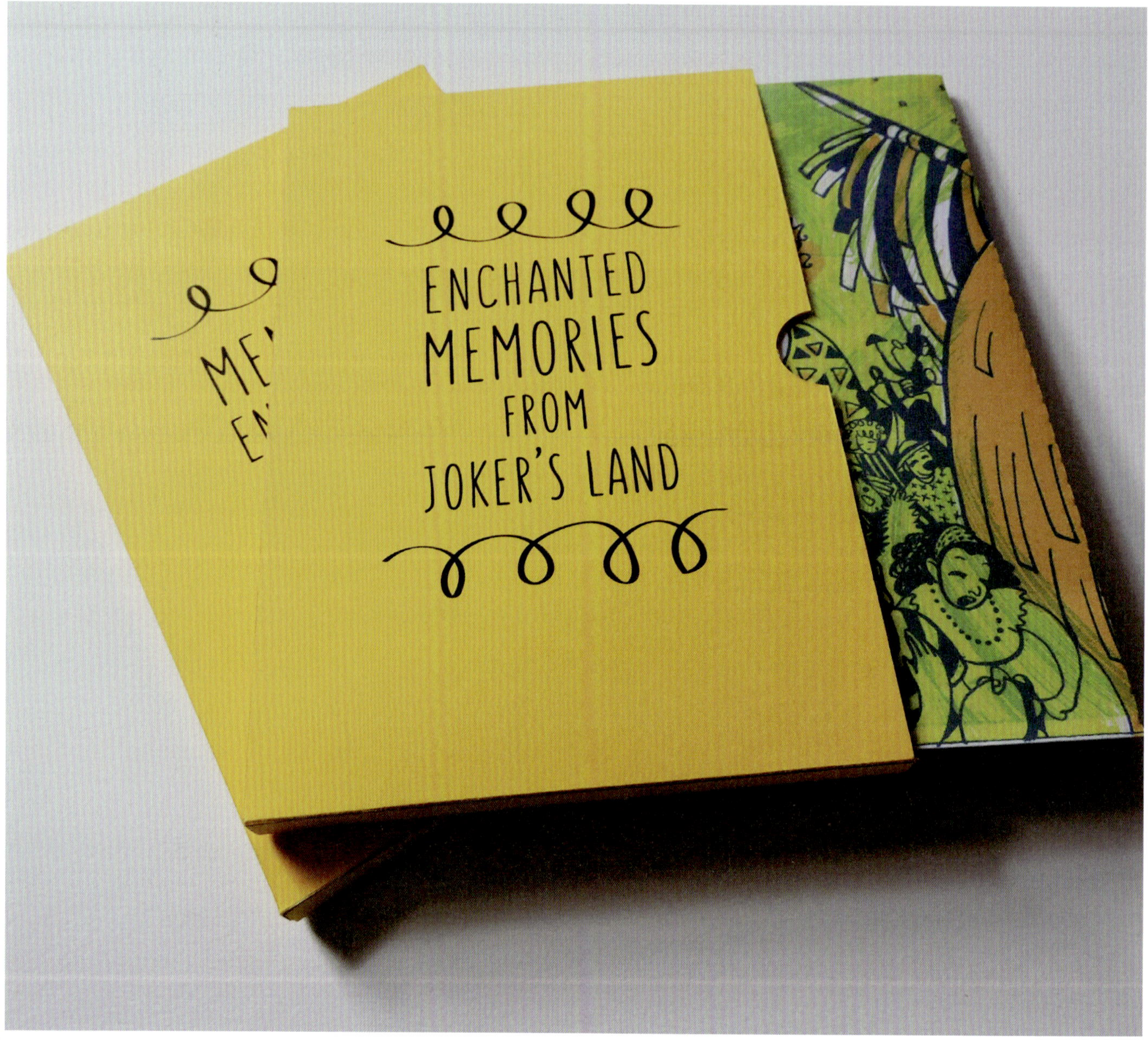

D: Mayara Lista

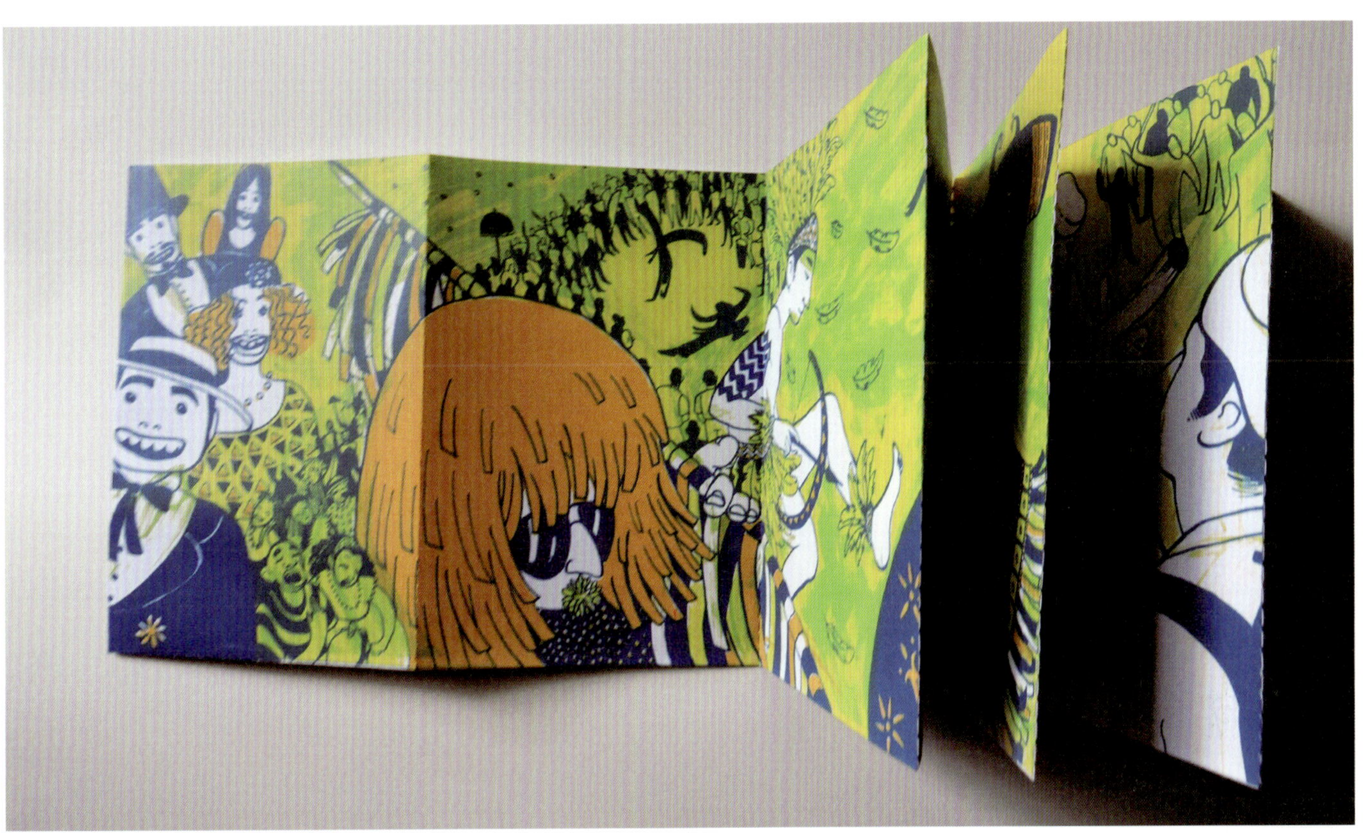

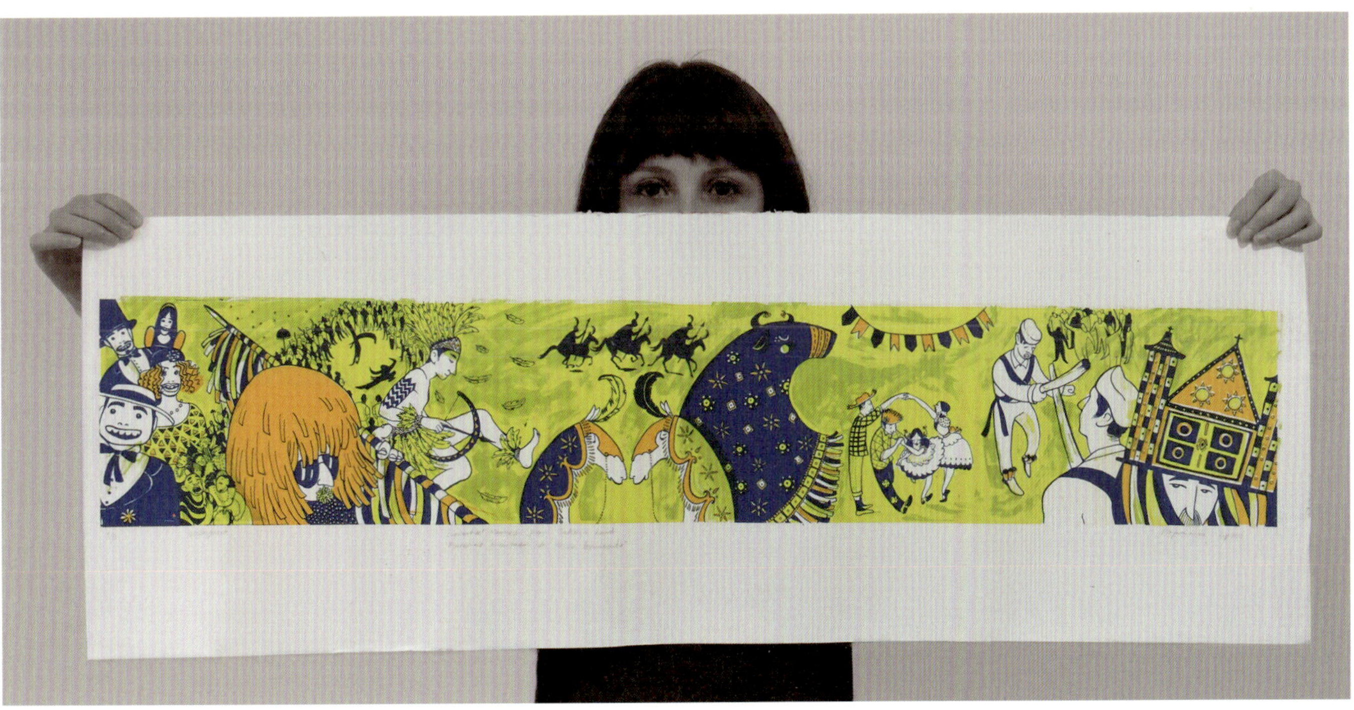

The Lost Spring

This is a four-color risography printing created by the designer. A book written in both Czech and English, its author is Anna Bobreková. The designer used black and gray pens for the original graphics, which she then printed. The original story relates to Japanese mythology and the Czech tradition of Masopust. She decided to use the Japanese harvesting myths of a pair of gods well known in Japan. In this story each god has name: Inari and Miketsu. They are portrayed as a bridge between the Japanese and Czech natures. The material chosen was from the oldest story about Japanese gods "Kojiki," and the Czech spring festival, "Masopust."

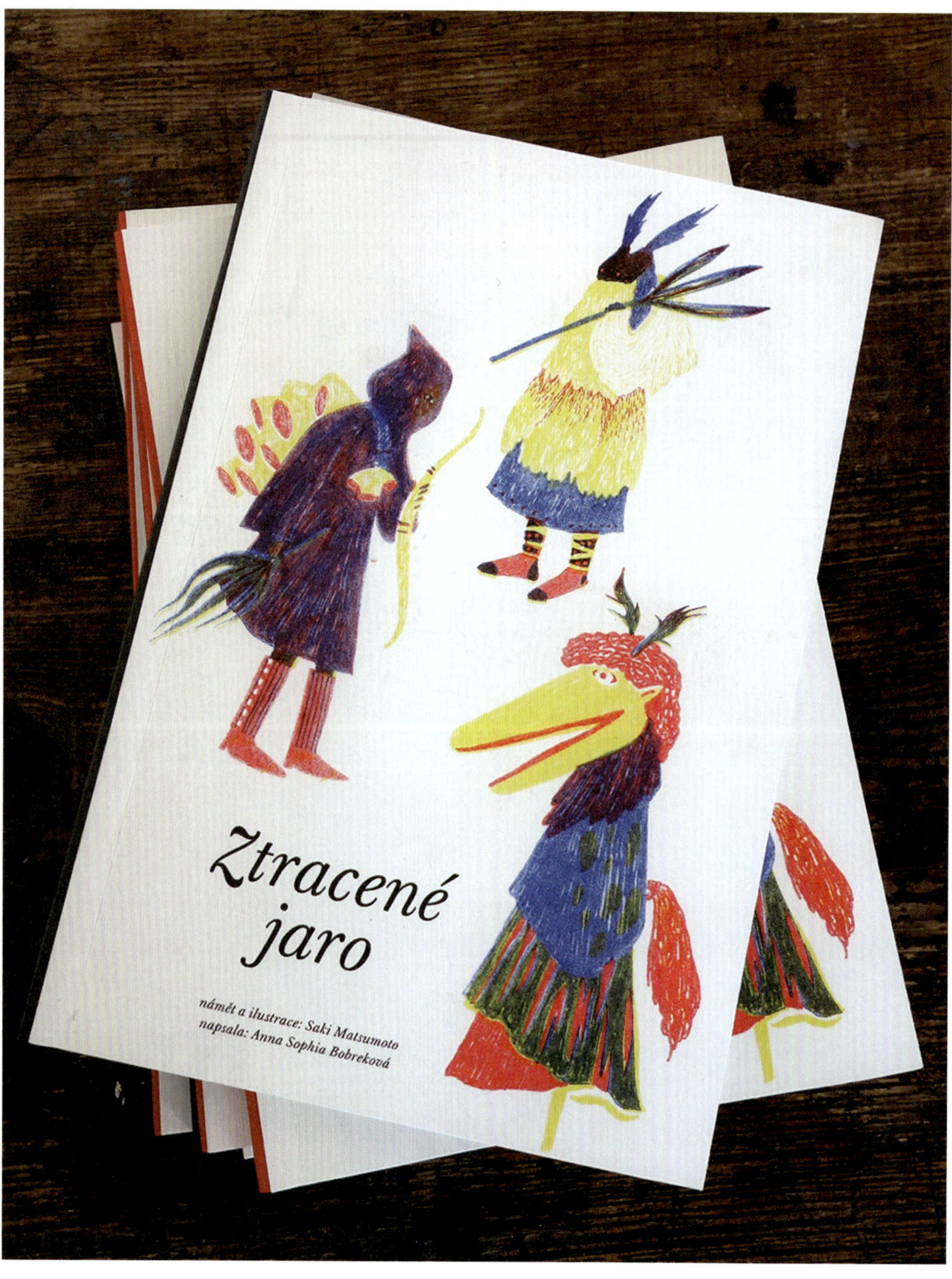

D: Saki Matsumoto

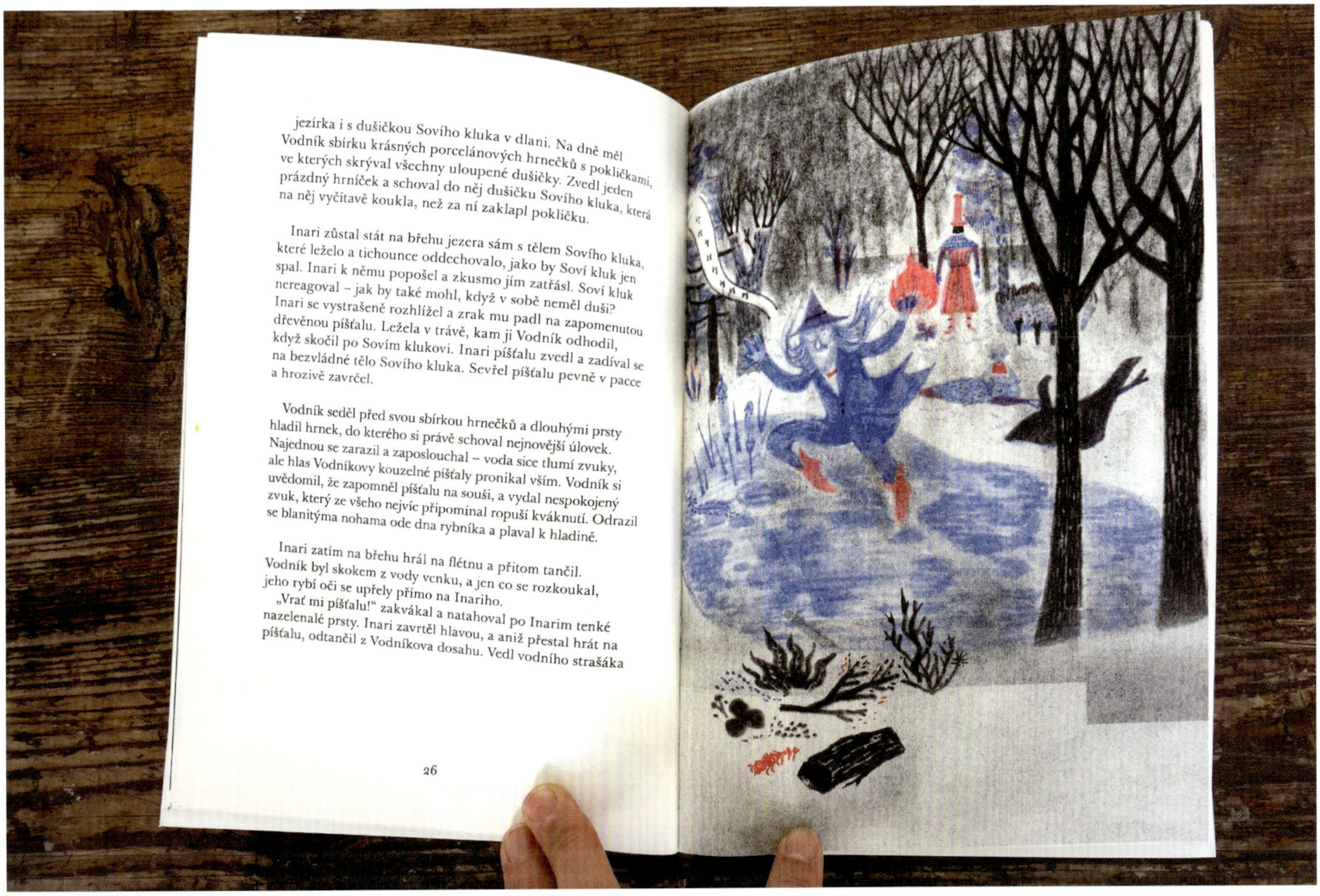

jezírka i s dušičkou Sovího kluka v dlani. Na dně měl
Vodník sbírku krásných porcelánových hrnečků s pokličkami,
ve kterých skrýval všechny uloupené dušičky. Zvedl jeden
prázdný hrníček a schoval do něj dušičku Sovího kluka, která
na něj vyčítavě koukla, než za ní zaklapl pokličku.

Inari zůstal stát na břehu jezera sám s tělem Sovího kluka,
které leželo a tichounce oddechovalo, jako by Soví kluk jen
spal. Inari k němu popošel a zkusmo jím zatřásl. Soví kluk
nereagoval – jak by také mohl, když v sobě neměl duši?
Inari se vystrašeně rozhlížel a zrak mu padl na zapomenutou
dřevěnou píšťalu. Ležela v trávě, kam ji Vodník odhodil,
když skočil po Sovím klukovi. Inari píšťalu zvedl a zadíval se
na bezvládné tělo Sovího kluka. Sevřel píšťalu pevně v pacce
a hrozivě zavrčel.

Vodník seděl před svou sbírkou hrnečků a dlouhými prsty
hladil hrnek, do kterého si právě schoval nejnovější úlovek.
Najednou se zarazil a zaposlouchal – voda sice tlumí zvuky,
ale hlas Vodníkovy kouzelné píšťaly pronikal vším. Vodník si
uvědomil, že zapomněl píšťalu na souši, a vydal nespokojený
zvuk, který ze všeho nejvíc připomínal ropuší kváknutí. Odrazil
se blanitýma nohama ode dna rybníka a plaval k hladině.

Inari zatím na břehu hrál na flétnu a přitom tančil.
Vodník byl skokem z vody venku, a jen co se rozkoukal,
jeho rybí oči se upřely přímo na Inariho.
„Vrať mi píšťalu!“ zakvákal a natahoval po Inarim tenké
nazelenalé prsty. Inari zavrtěl hlavou, a aniž přestal hrát na
píšťalu, odtančil z Vodníkova dosahu. Vedl vodního strašáka

26

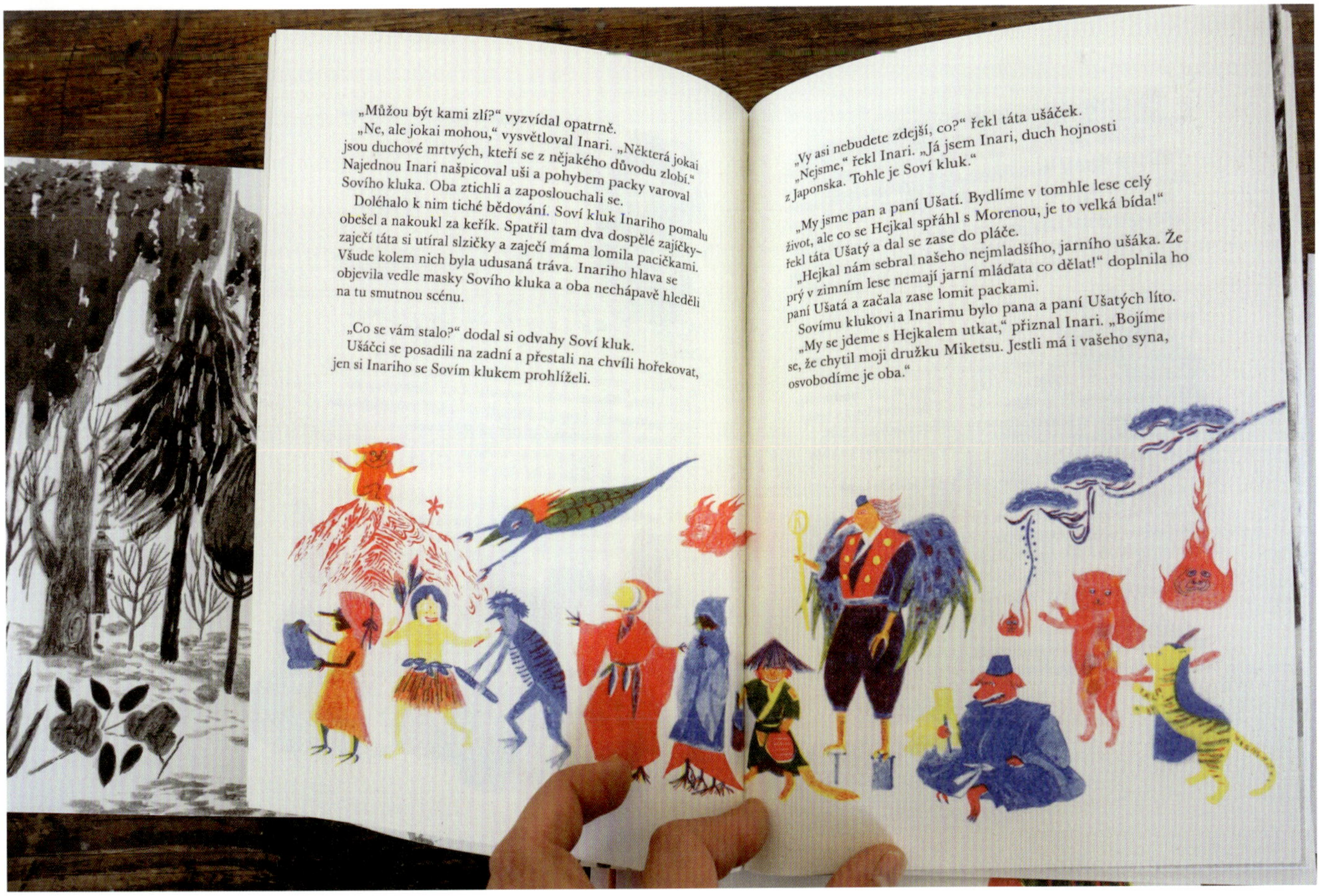

„Můžou být kami zlí?“ vyzvídal opatrně.
„Ne, ale jokai mohou,“ vysvětloval Inari. „Některá jokai
jsou duchové mrtvých, kteří se z nějakého důvodu zlobí.“
Najednou Inari našpicoval uši a pohybem packy varoval
Sovího kluka. Oba ztichli a zaposlouchali se.
Doléhalo k nim tiché bědování. Soví kluk Inariho pomalu
obešel a nakoukl za keřík. Spatřil tam dva dospělé zajíčky–
zaječí táta si utíral slzičky a zaječí máma lomila pacičkami.
Všude kolem nich byla udusaná tráva. Inariho hlava se
objevila vedle masky Sovího kluka a oba nechápavě hleděli
na tu smutnou scénu.

„Co se vám stalo?“ dodal si odvahy Soví kluk.
Ušáčci se posadili na zadní a přestali na chvíli hořekovat,
jen si Inariho se Sovím klukem prohlíželi.

„Vy asi nebudete zdejší, co?“ řekl táta ušáček.
„Nejsme,“ řekl Inari. „Já jsem Inari, duch hojnosti
z Japonska. Tohle je Soví kluk.“

„My jsme pan a paní Ušatí. Bydlíme v tomhle lese celý
život, ale co se Hejkal spřáhl s Morenou, je to velká bída!“
řekl táta Ušatý a dal se zase do pláče.
„Hejkal nám sebral našeho nejmladšího, jarního ušáka. Že
prý v zimním lese nemají jarní mláďata co dělat!“ doplnila ho
paní Ušatá a začala zase lomit packami.
Sovímu klukovi a Inarimu bylo pana a paní Ušatých líto.
„My se jdeme s Hejkalem utkat,“ přiznal Inari. „Bojíme
se, že chytil moji družku Miketsu. Jestli má i vašeho syna,
osvobodíme je oba.“

Train Journey Over the Highlands

etching ink

The book was conceived after the designer came back from a solo trip to Scotland. She took a lot of footage when she was there, fascinated by the horizon line that kept reappearing and disappearing into the fog. The pictures are taken from one of those videos, and she used monotype to recreate the foggy, dark, and wet atmosphere of that day. The picture also plays with the ink: what can be made to disappear, or obversely, what can be enlighted. The cover has an embossing, a simple line that symbolizes the horizon of the precise landscape of the book.

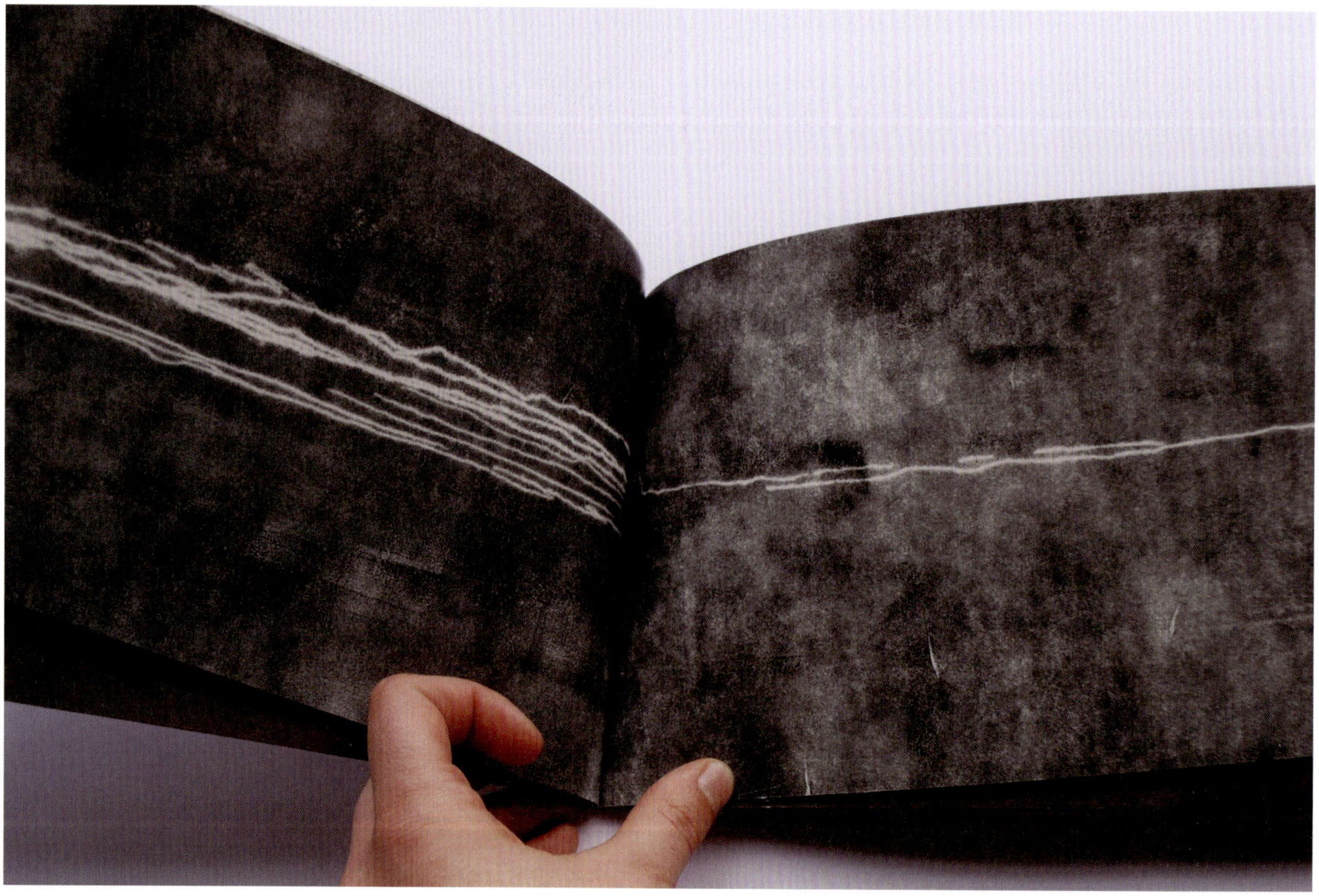

***D*:** Jeanne Tocqueville

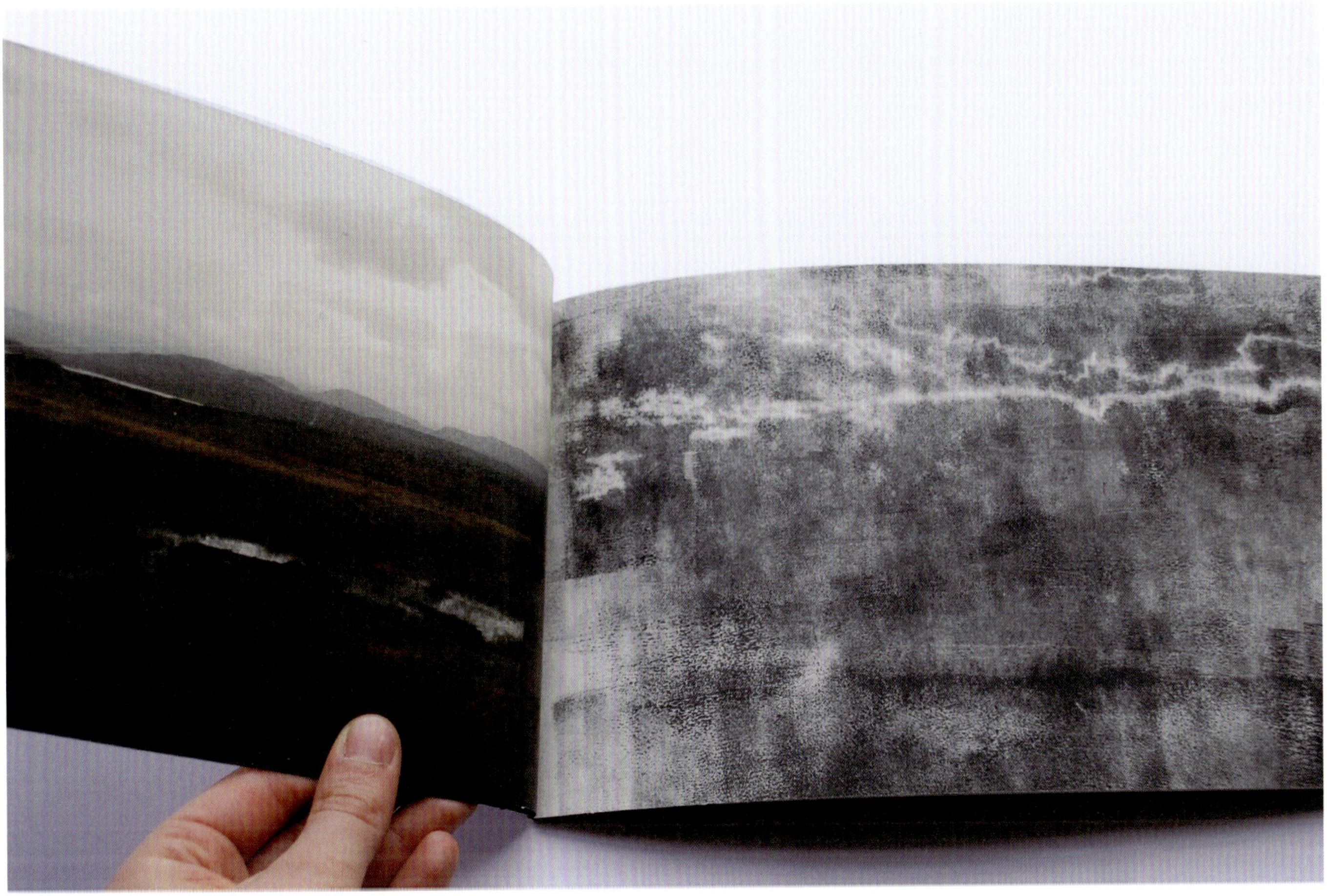

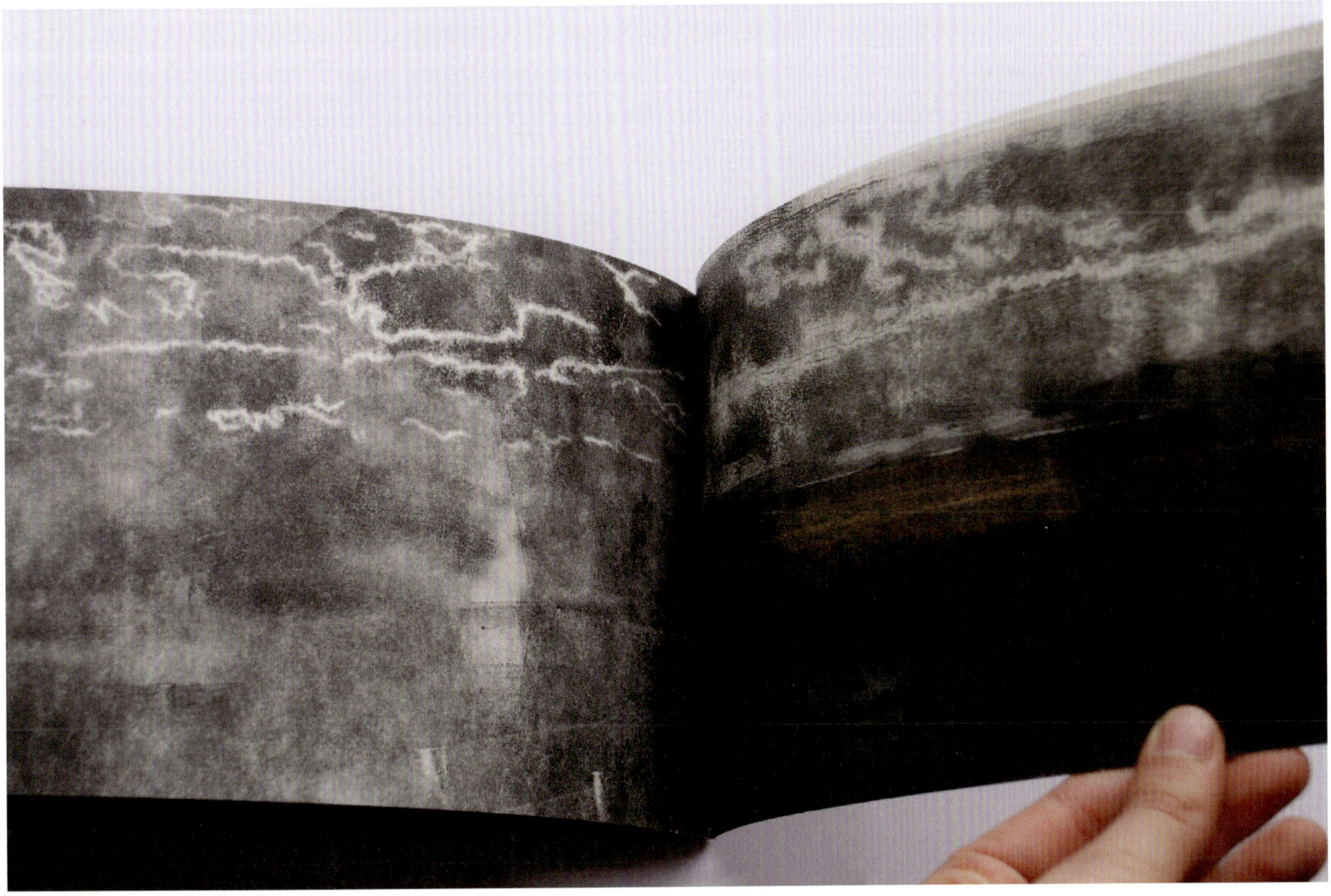

Typographic Poster

- white Manila paper
- black ink

This poster is the result of a four-day workshop on typographic poster design. The inspiration for this poster originates from the meaning of Eleusis, which comes from the Greek word: ἐλεύθω (eleftho) – arriving. An old photo of the city's landmarks like the factory chimneys and the ancient ruins were used as background.

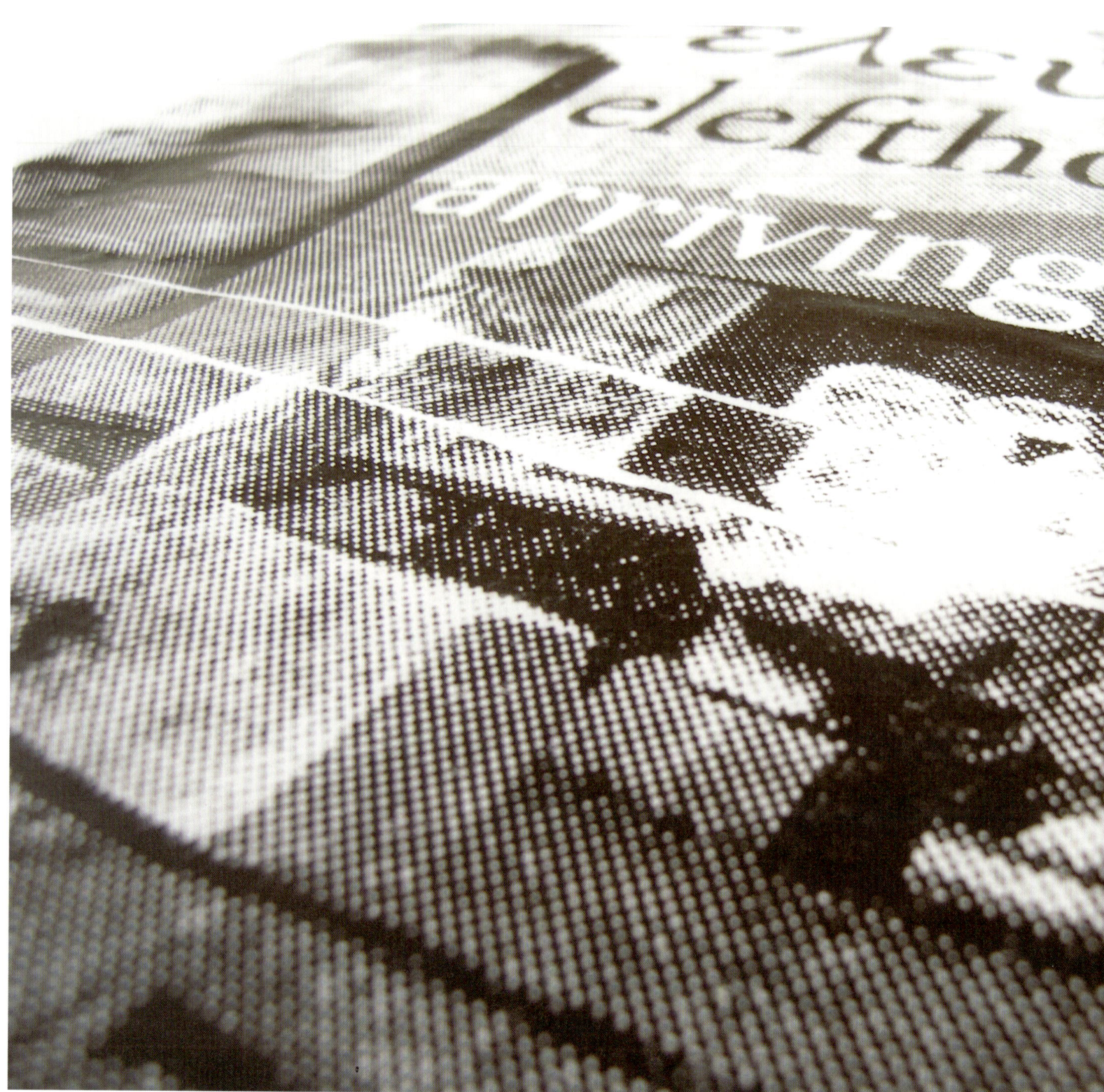

D: Dora Grigoropoulou

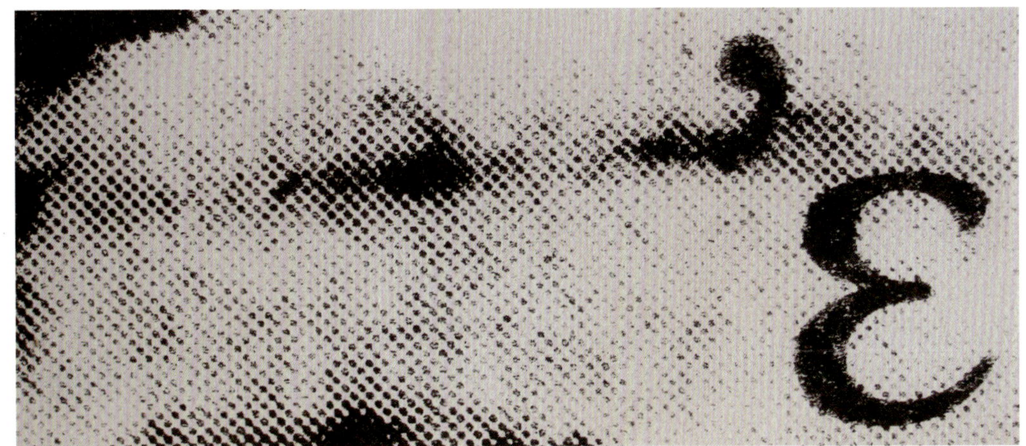

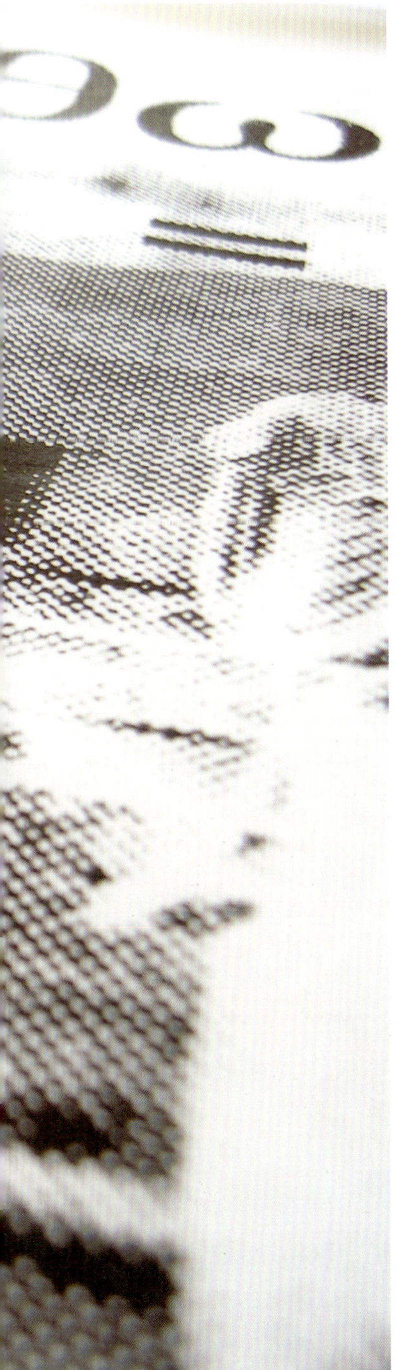

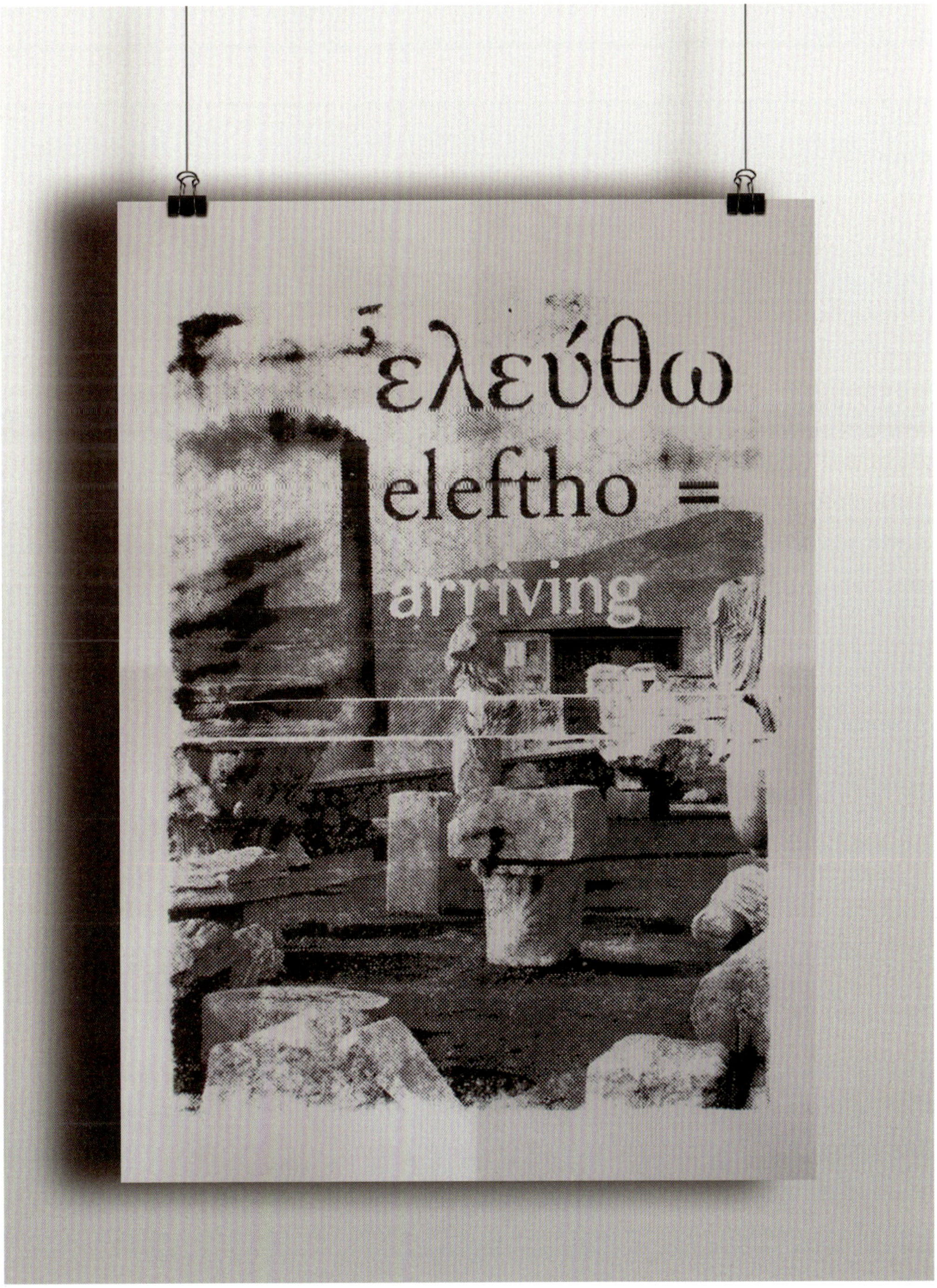

Olio D'oliva

glass, aluminium

The motivation behind this resourceful vessel came from the new laws in southern Europe that forbid the use of refillable oil bottles at public eateries. The solution is to incorporate this often-metal oil spout accessory into the sleek packaging—positioned right into the front sticker. The circular section of the label can be peeled off easily and curled into the mouth of the glass neck. This has the double function of producing a round window that exposes the beautiful color of the contents and also helps the viewer to see how much of the product is left in the bottle. When it's emptied, the entire bottle can be recycled, and a fresh new one can be opened as a practical and economical solution for restaurants.

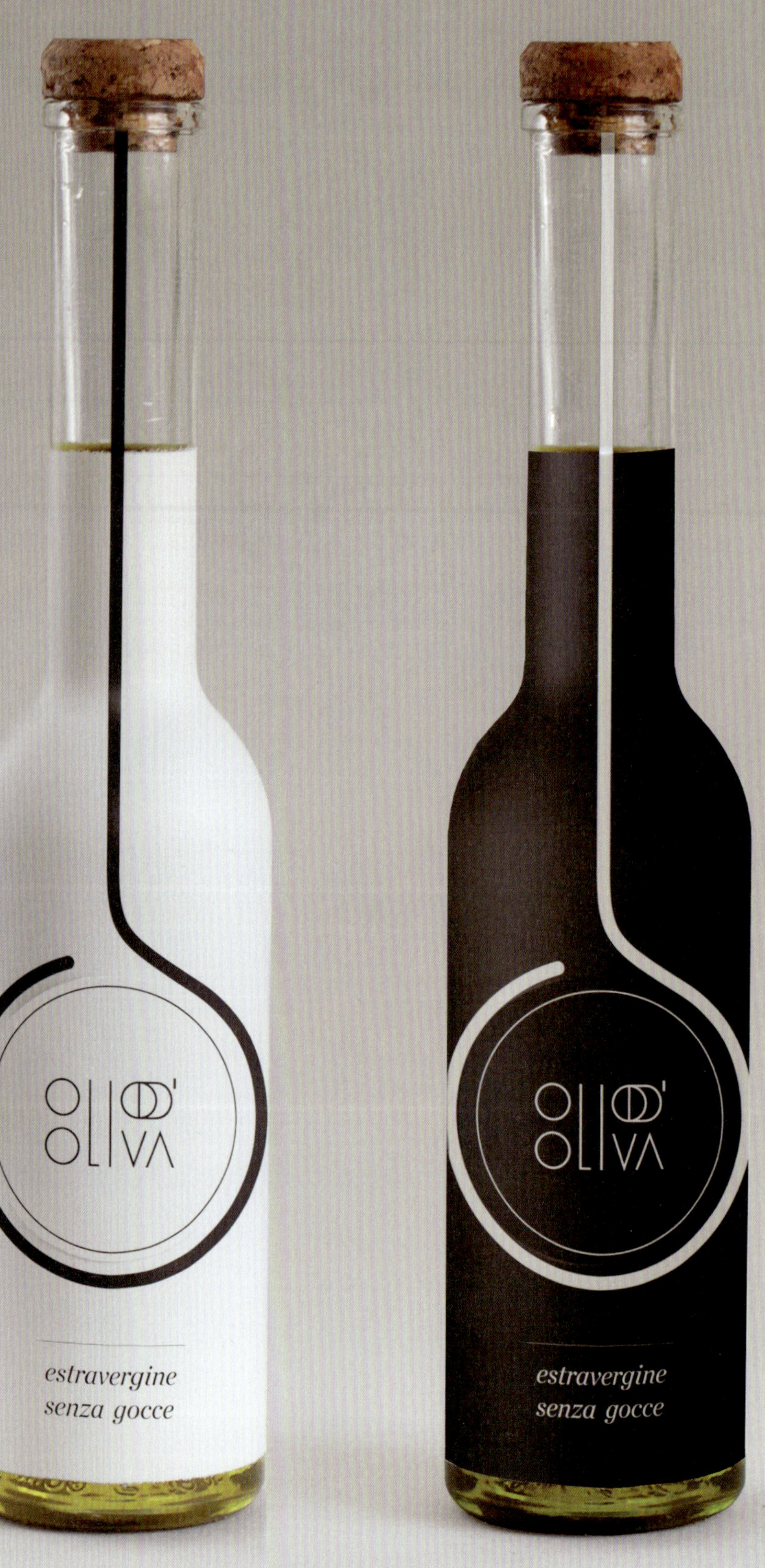

D: Alessia Sistori

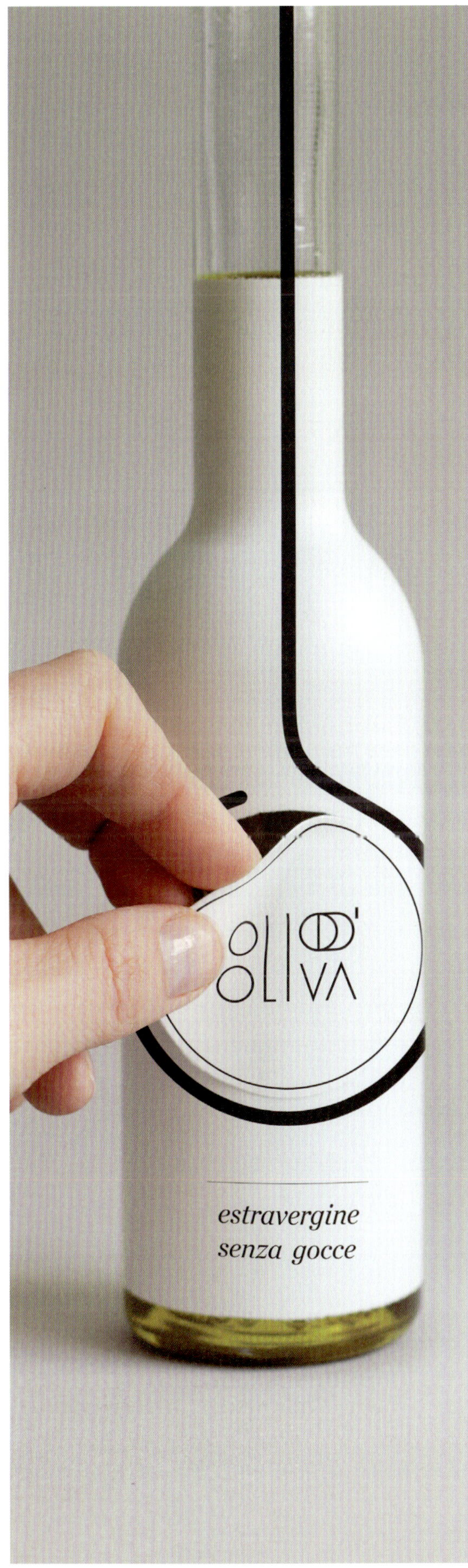
OLIO D'
OLIVA
estravergine
senza gocce

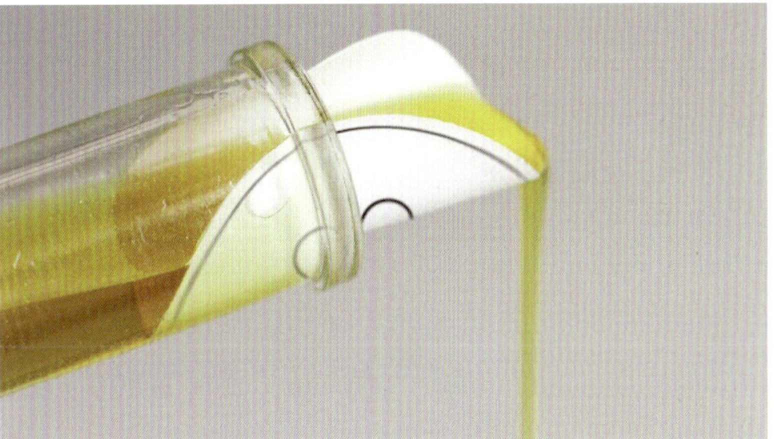

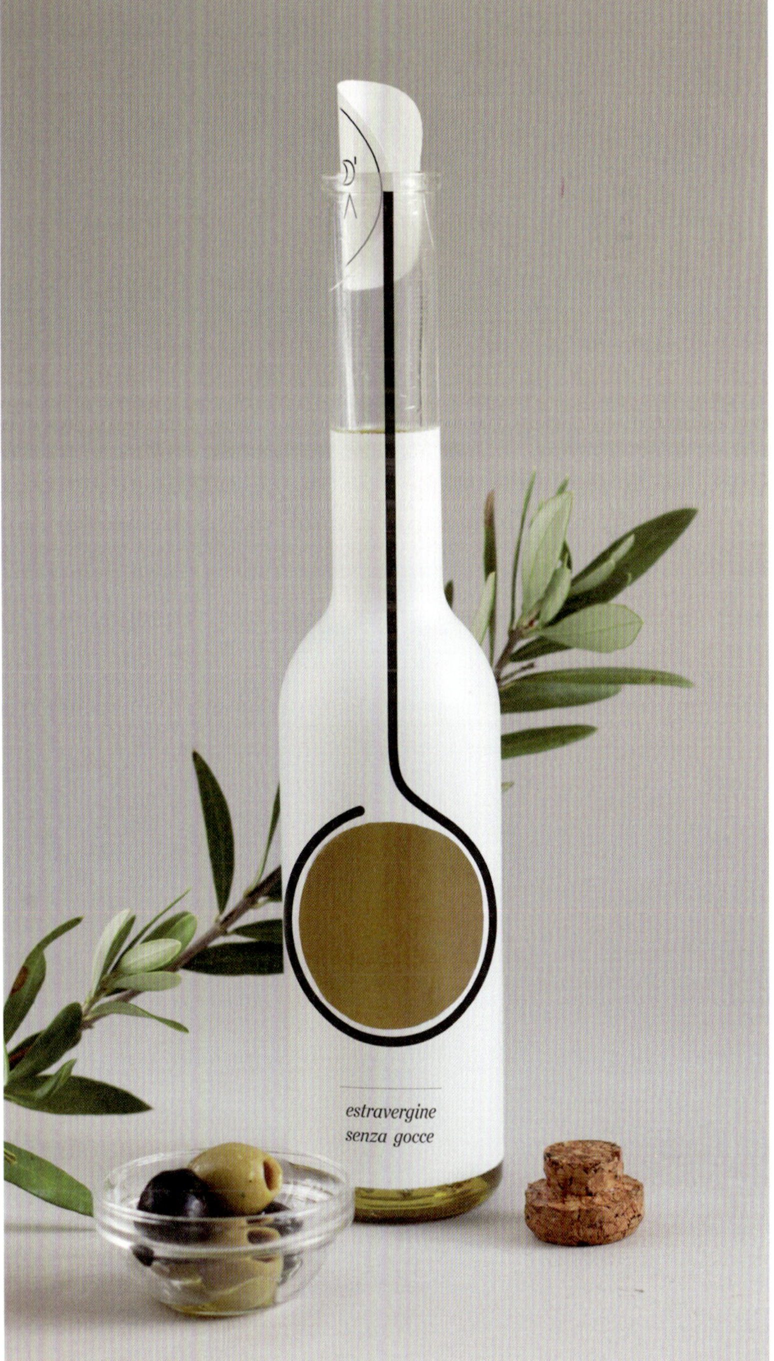
estravergine
senza gocce

We Wrocławiu

ceramics, glass

This project was born of impressions of the Polish city of Wroclaw, in which the designer was studying. It is about people and architecture, and silkscreen helped her to bring her impressions alive. This technique can create perfectly resistant images with fine details and saturated colors. Because first of all she is a graphic artist, she used ceramics and glass like paper, with silkscreen allowing her to transfer her drawings. That is why the ceramics were white and the glass was transparent. She used only two colors with glass and one color with ceramics, but for her the idea was enough. The designer is really satisfied with this project: she created beautiful and useful objects.

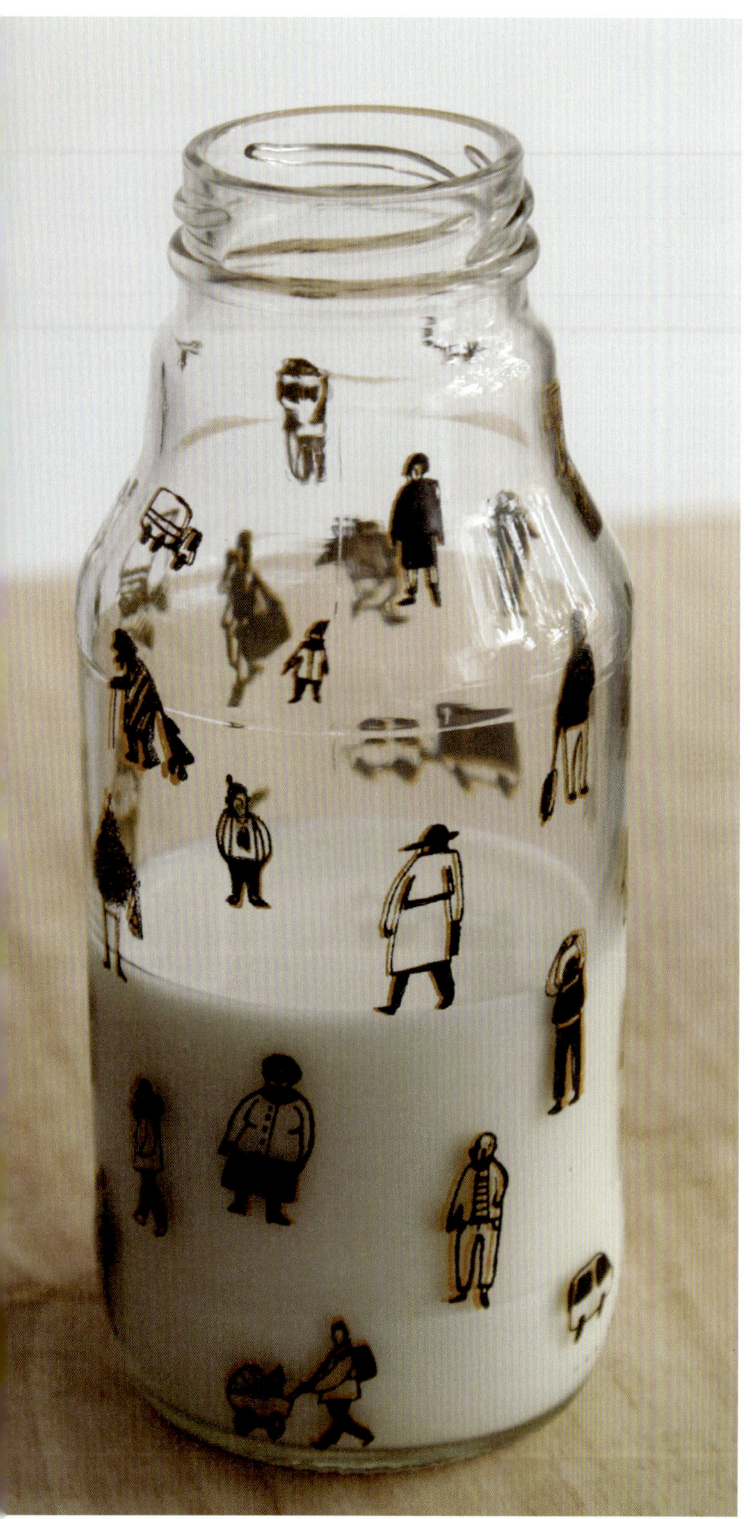

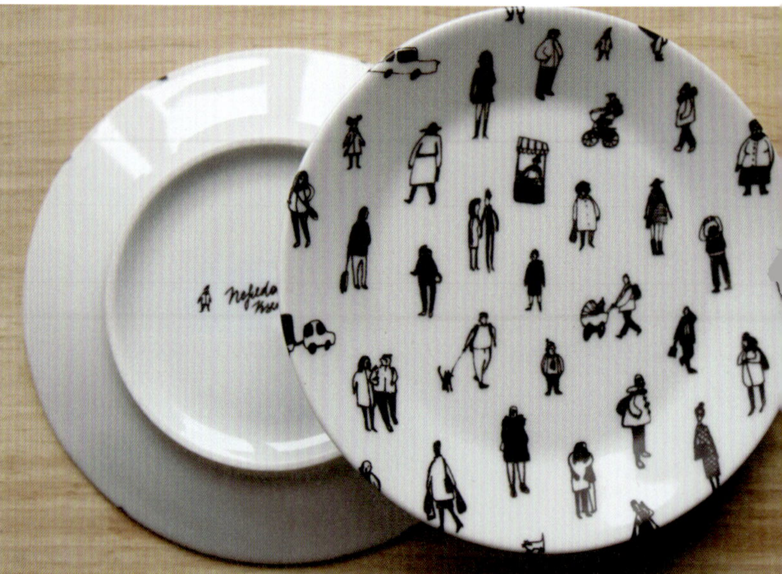

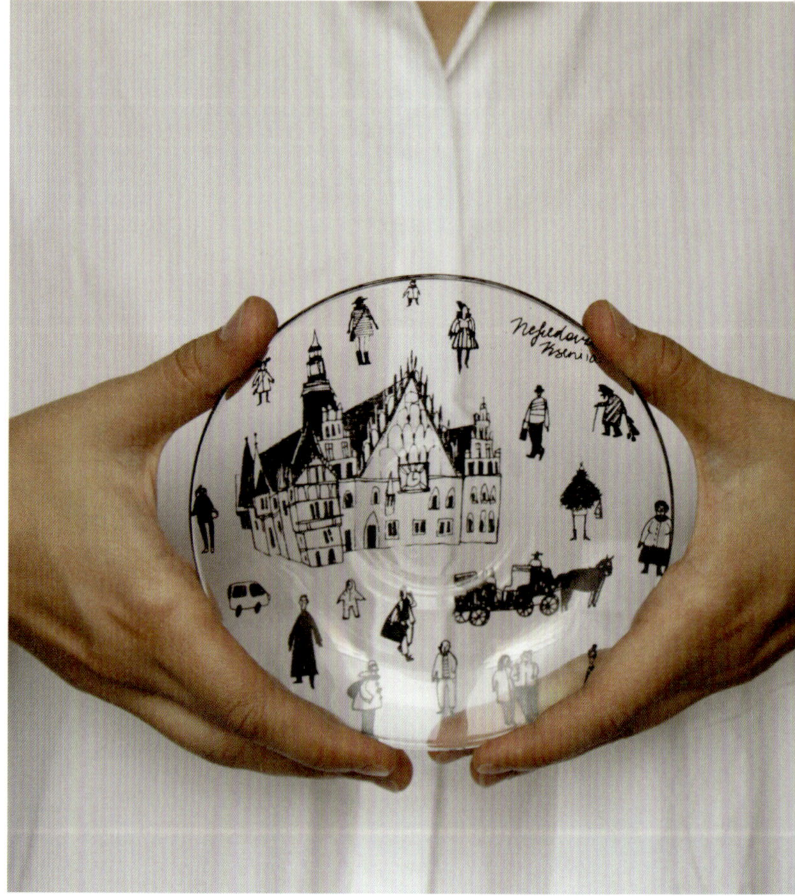

D: Nefedova Kseniia

Tocco Wine

glass

This project boasts a strong visual effect, which reflects the young and dynamic feature of this enterprise. The restyling of the corporate image improves the brand awareness and ranks the identity elements correctly. The designers chose the silkscreen printing method to make the product innovative, unique, and original.

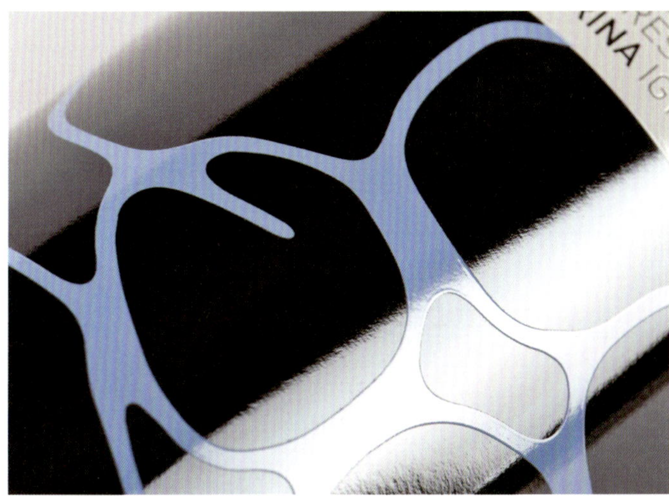

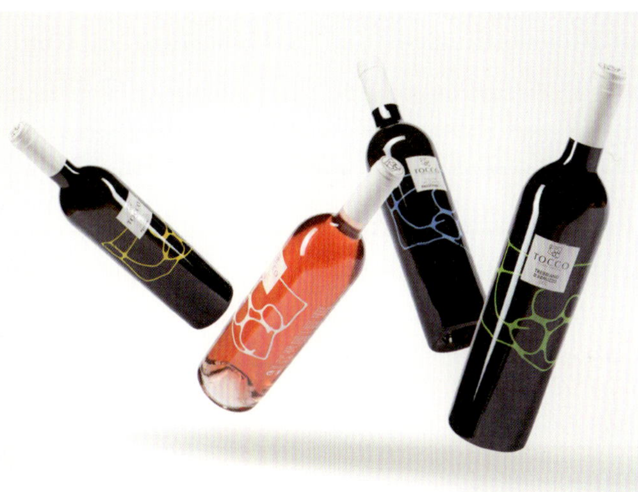

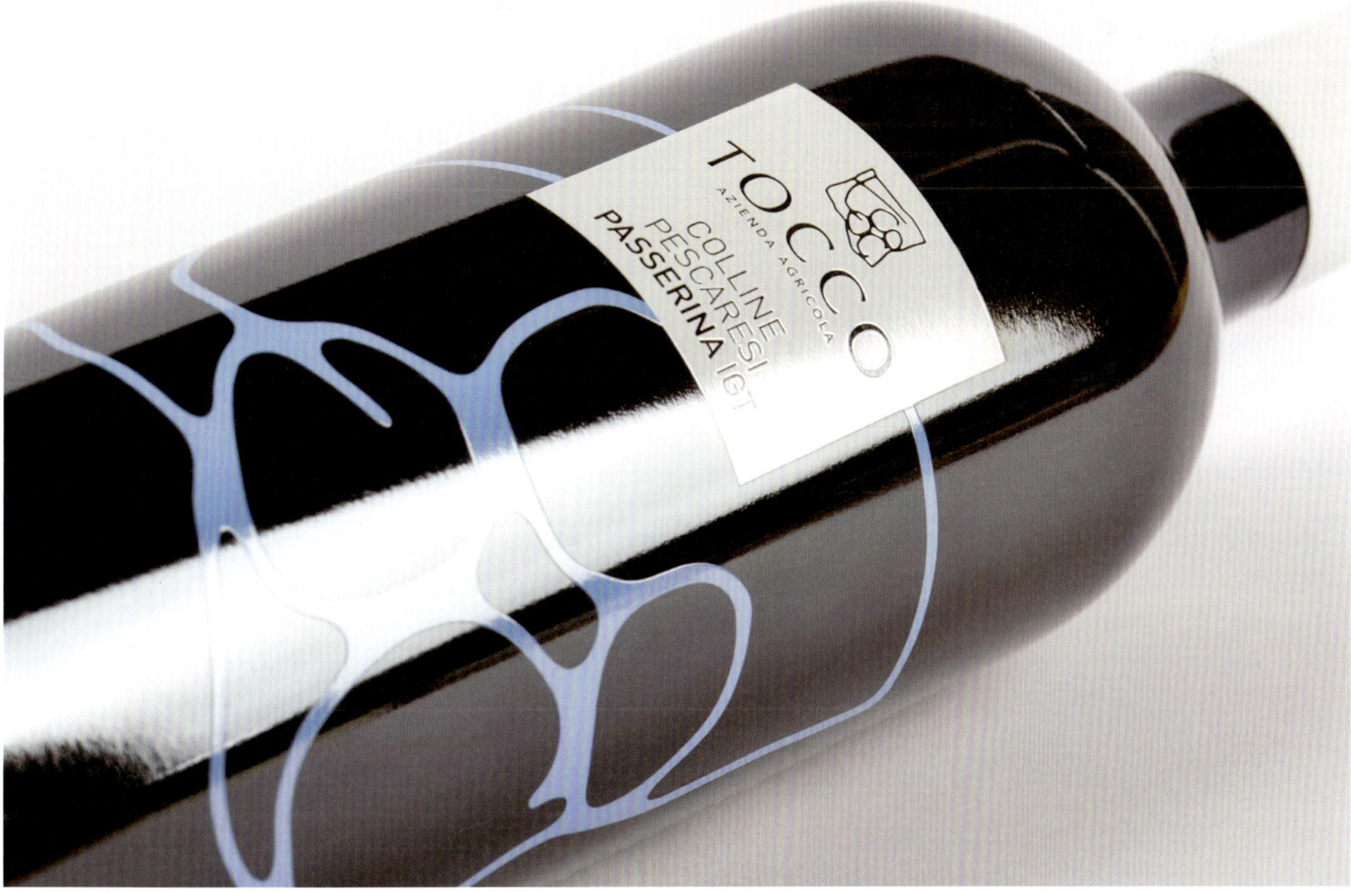

D: Marco D'Aroma

2017 Rooster Year Card

- cream white paper
- Risograph ink (red/black/yellow)

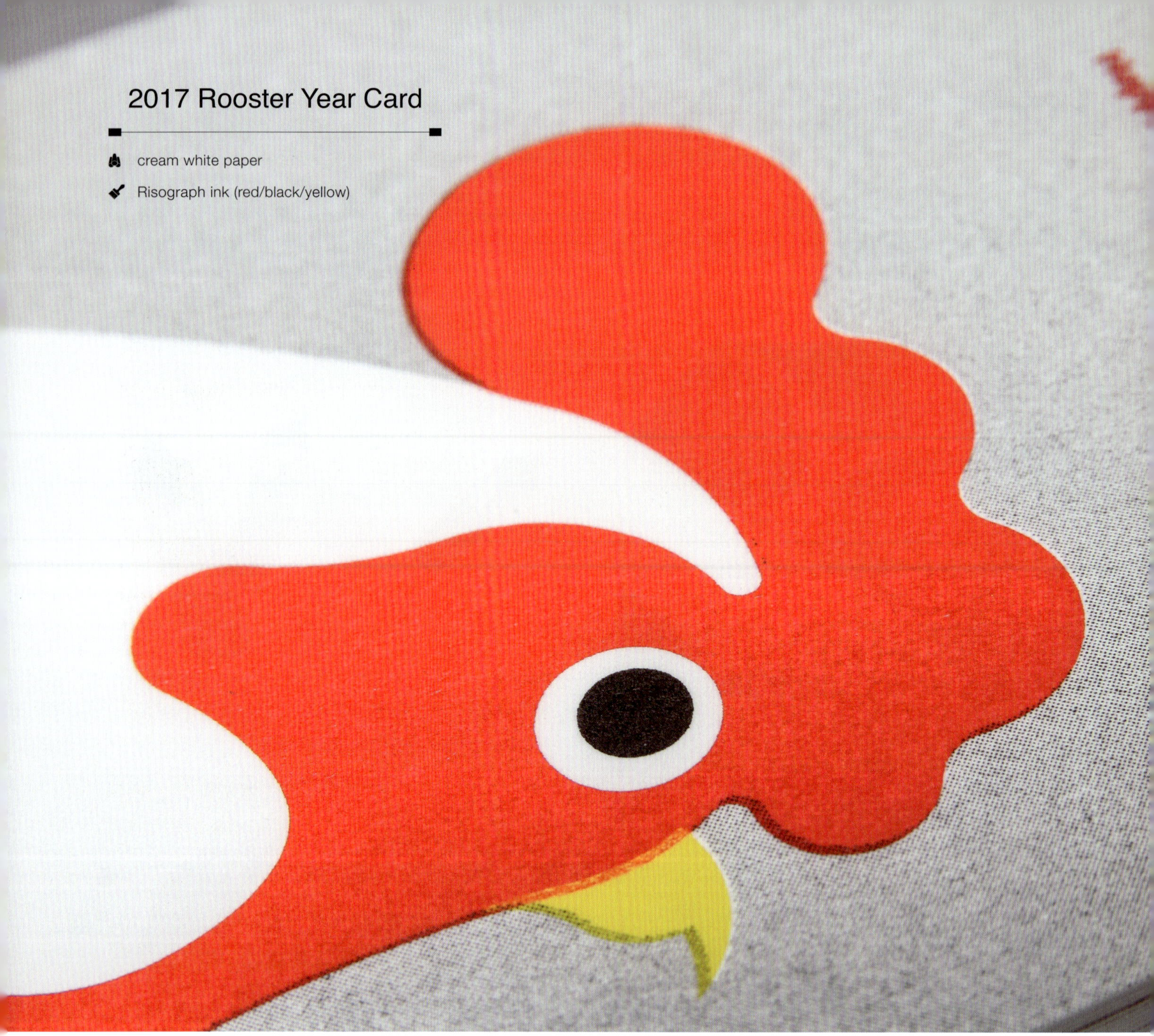

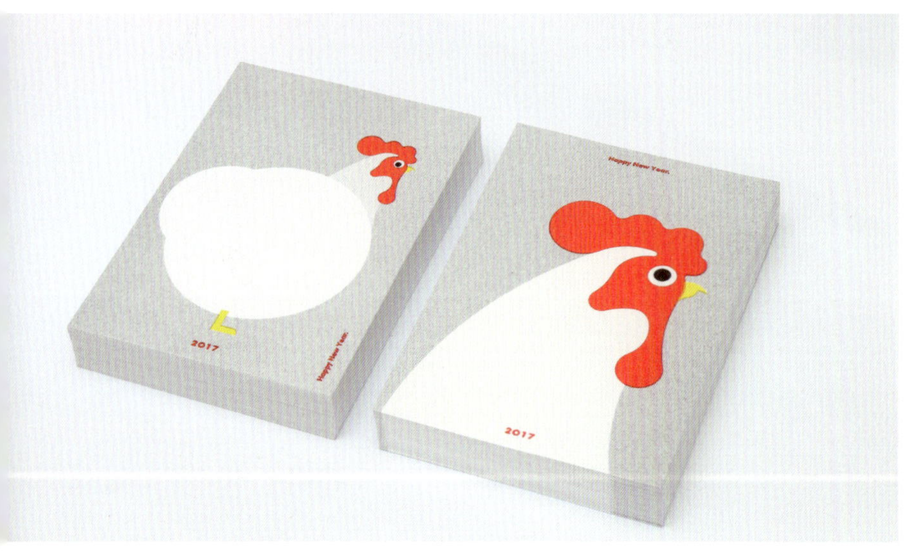

In the second half of 2016, the designer went freelance. Support from predecessors, friends, and business partners' arrived in one warm wave after another. Therefore, the designer decided to produce two types of cards before the Spring Festival of 2017. The postcards were made by round scale and printed in risography printing, in a limited print run. The designer sent them only to his relatives and close friends.

Black Bouquet Series

French White Wash paper

metallic gold ink

The Carpenter Collective is the studio of designers Jessica and Tad Carpenter. These are three prints of the Black Bouquet series. Each is an 11x14 silk screen print using metallic gold ink.

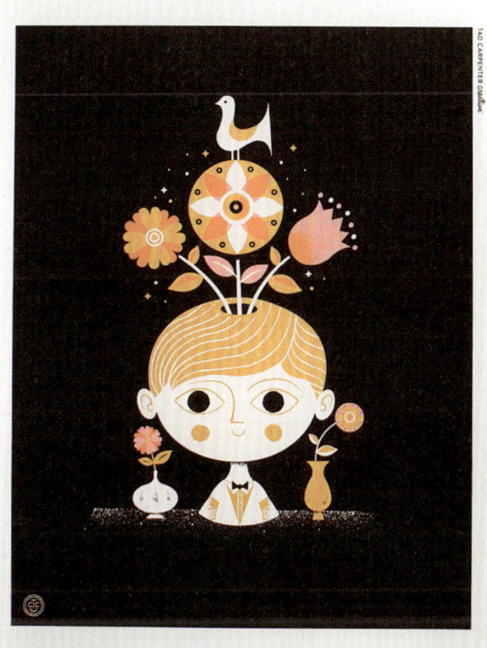

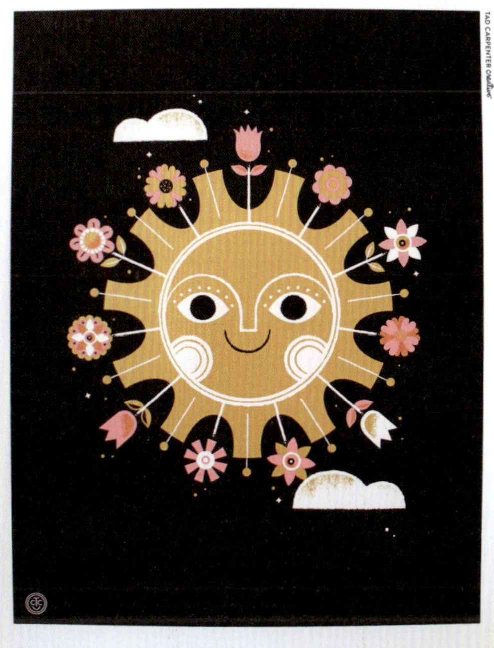

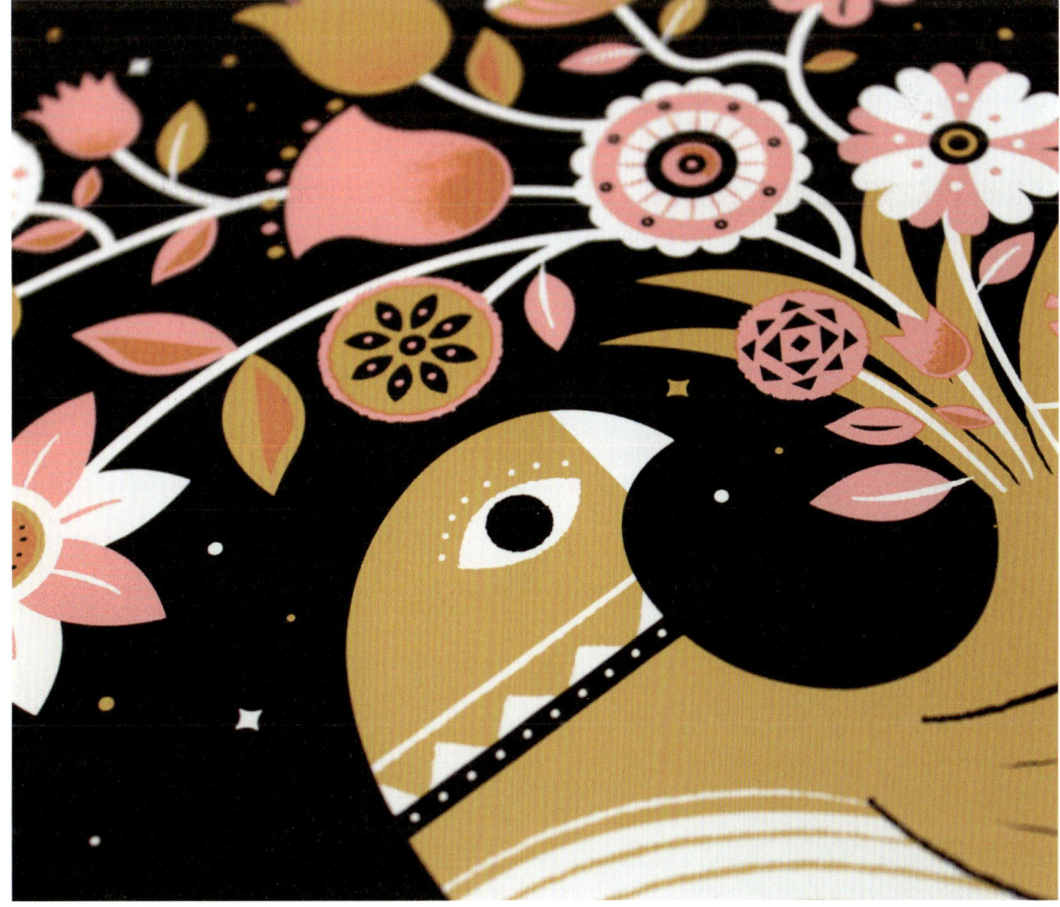

D: Tad Carpenter, Jessica Carpenter

Typeface Calendar, 2017

200g Munken Polar paper

vegetable spot color ink

The designer thought that risography printing produces a sharper color representation than any other printing method, so he chose to print in this way.

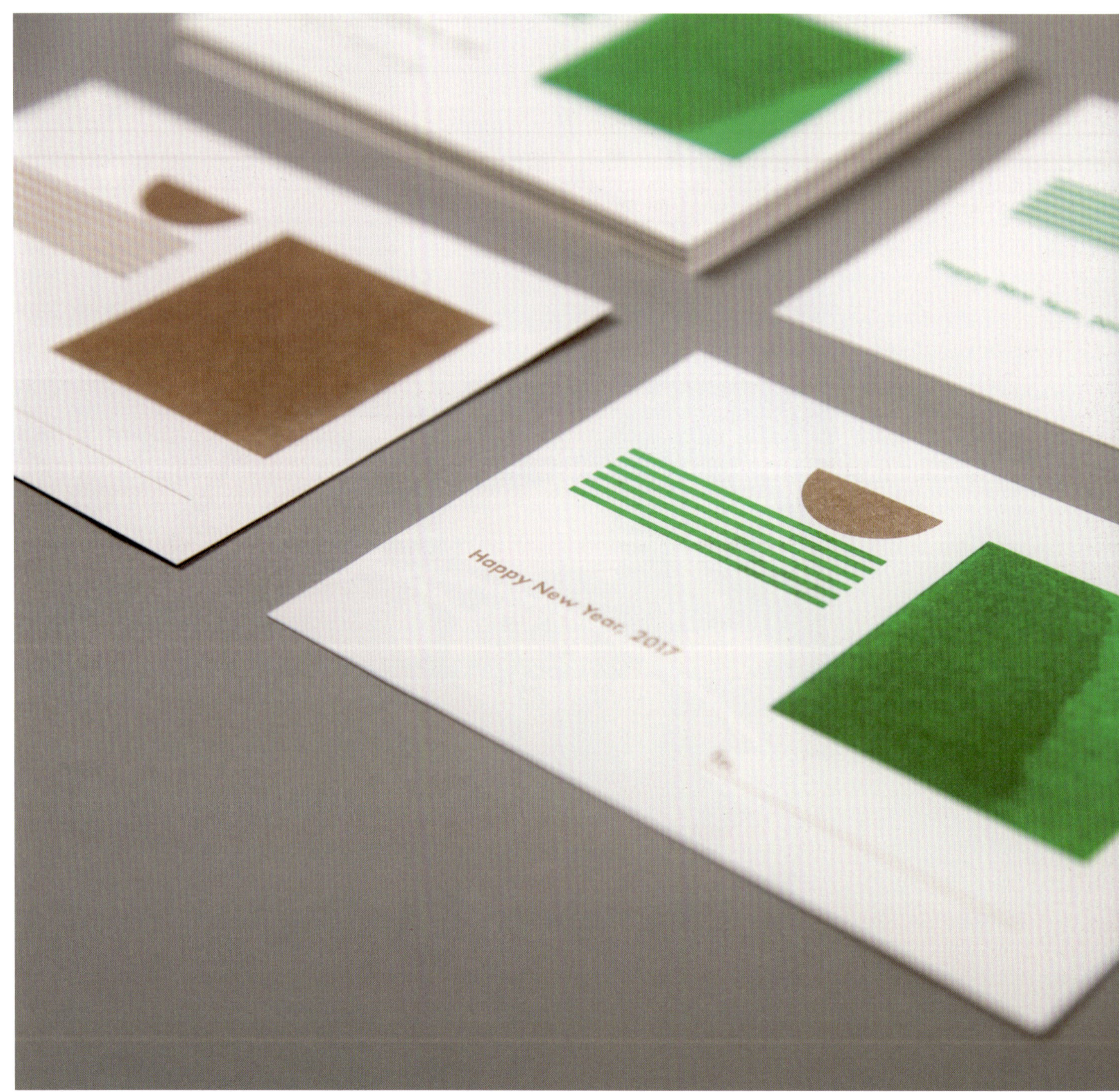

D: Lee jaegoo (Studio 1989)

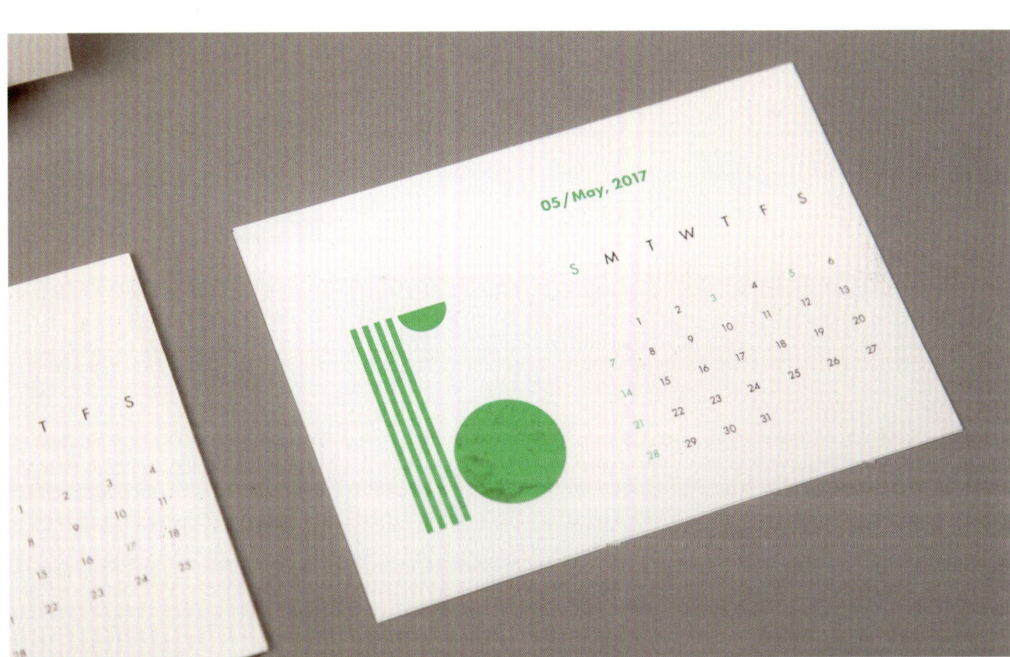
05/May, 2017
S M T W T F S

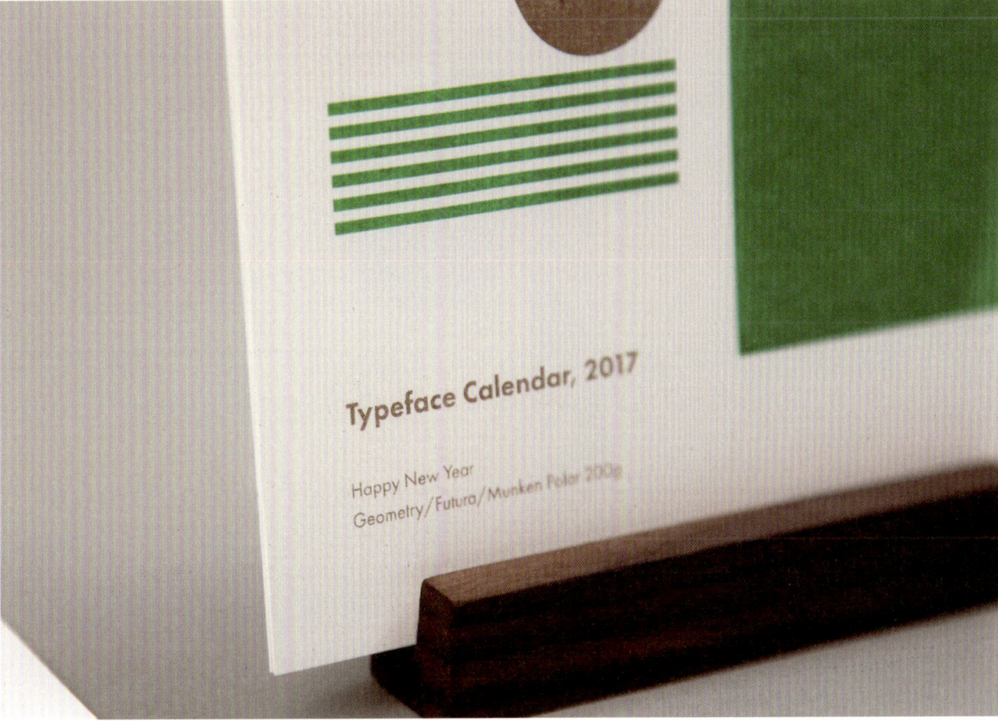
Typeface Calendar, 2017
Happy New Year
Geometry/Futura/Munken Polar 200g

Hypebox

cardboard, paper

Hypebox is an event management company based in Mexico City. The icon is an abstract "H" in the shape of a box. The minimal shape of the logo lets the quality of the brand stand out and underlines the elegant image of the events organized by Hypebox. The branding uses black cardboard, screen-printed in white which reflects the calm and stable temperament of Hypebox.

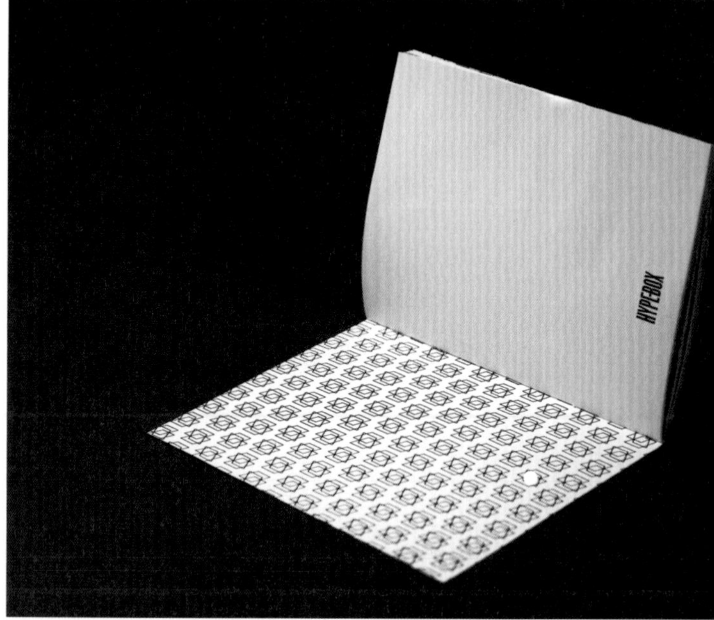

D: Alessia Sistori

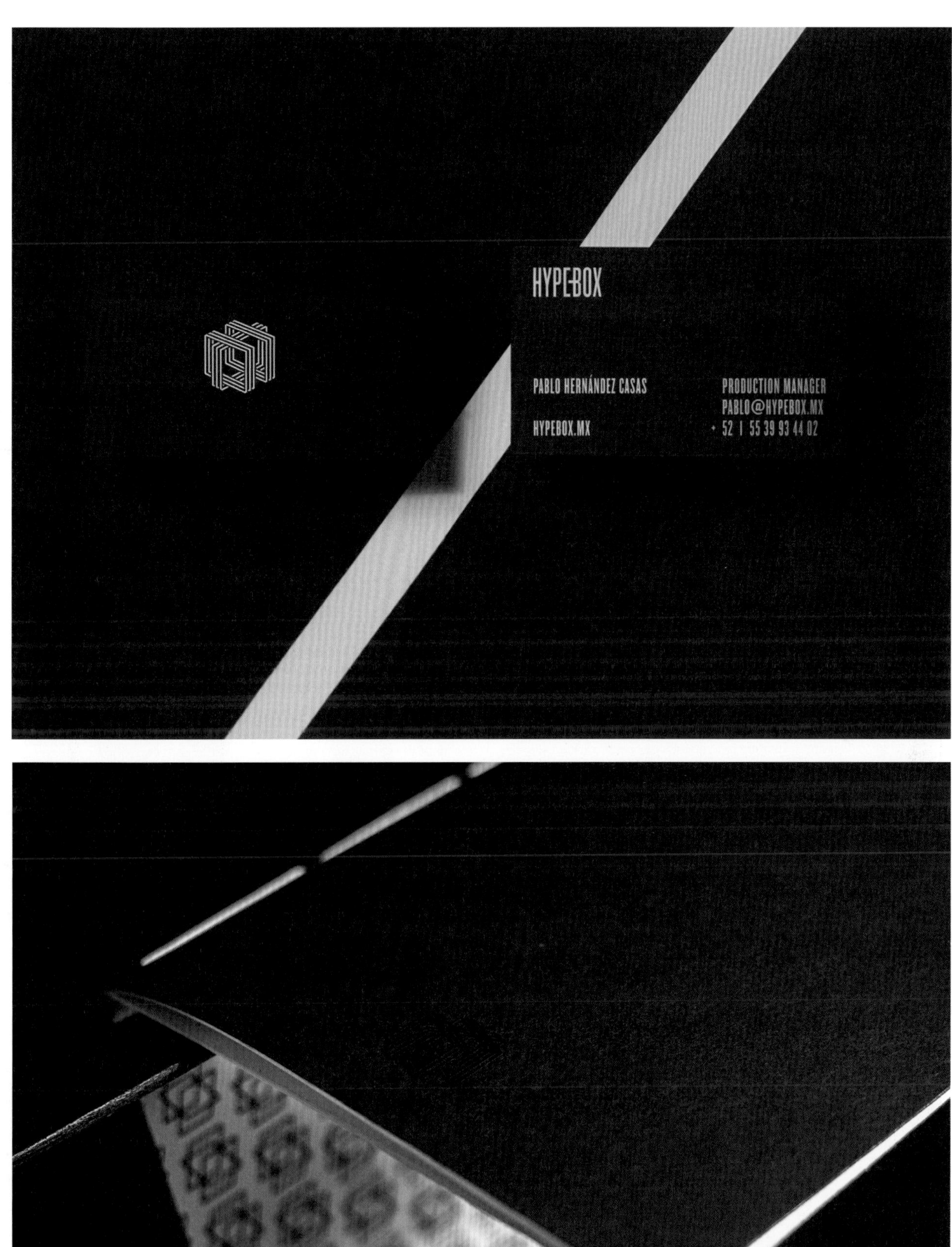
HYPEBOX
PABLO HERNÁNDEZ CASAS
HYPEBOX.MX
PRODUCTION MANAGER
PABLO@HYPEBOX.MX
+ 52 1 55 39 93 44 02

MUM

paper, aluminium foil

"Mum chocolate factory" produces the finest organic chocolates for the whole family. Using a child-friendly aesthetic, the design for their summer edition is based on two risography illustrations that communicate perfectly the positive feelings of summer and the extravagant products. The rough printing texture of the risograph transmits the handmade character of the product, and the friendly illustrations invite everyone to try out the unique taste of this delicious chocolate.

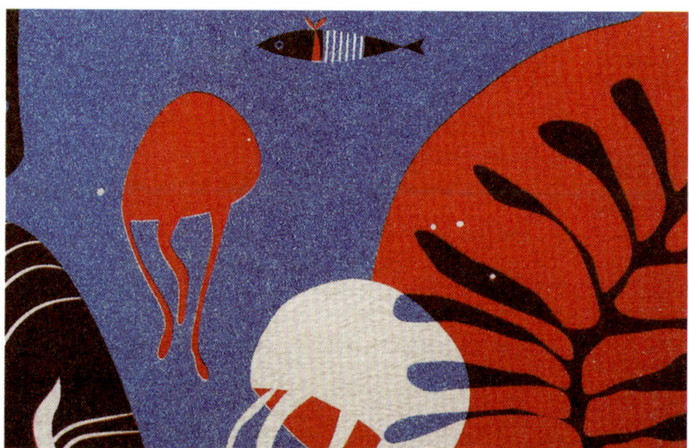

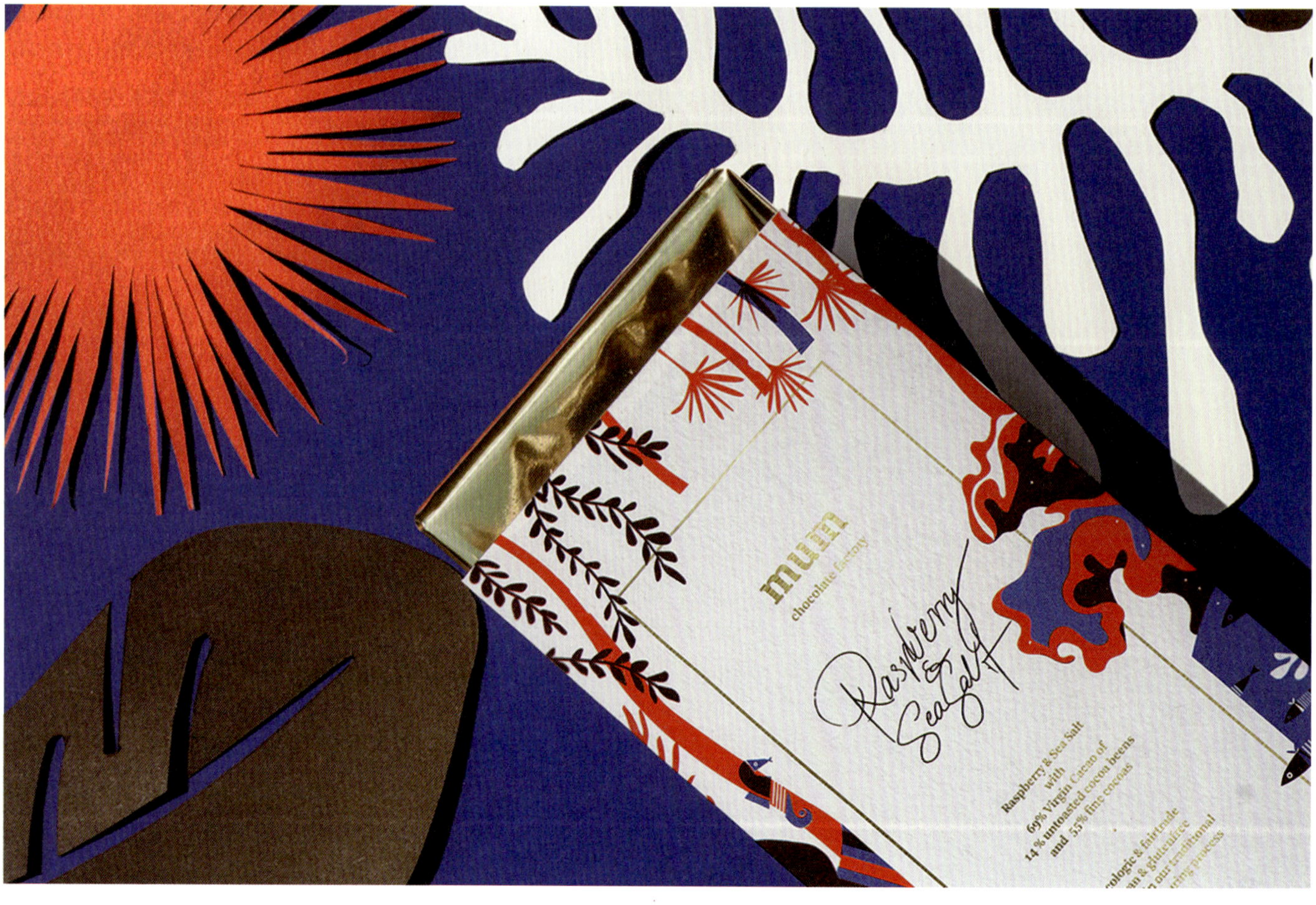

D: Alessia Sistori

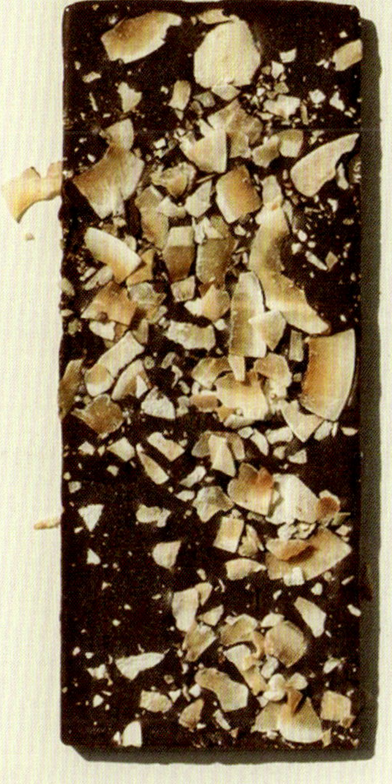

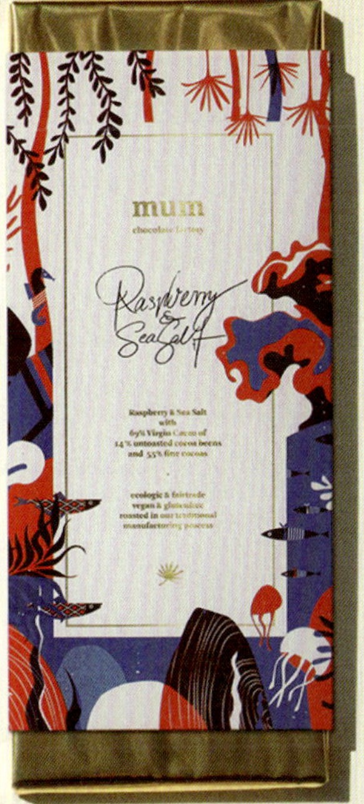
mum

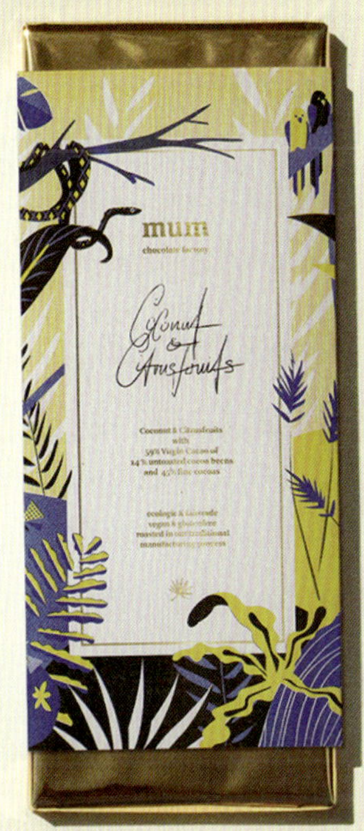
mum

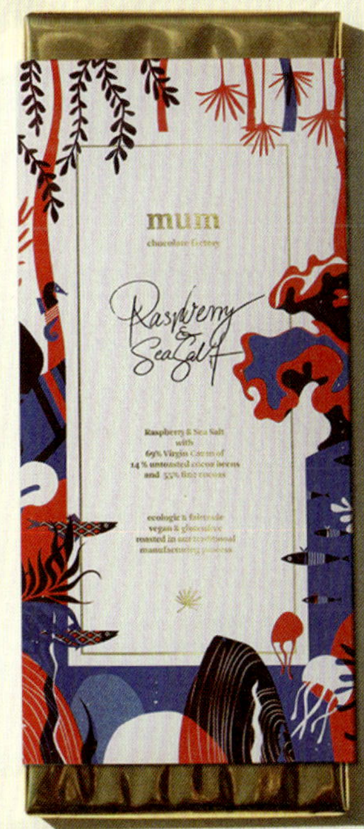
mum

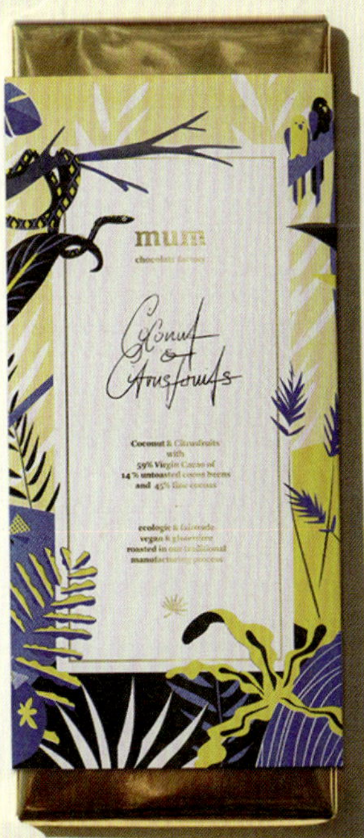
mum

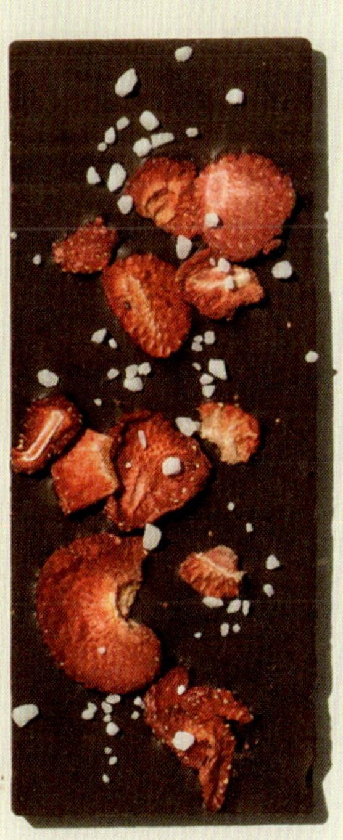

Meerbier

cardboard

The goal of this redesign was to create a six-pack carrier that offers flexibility to the user, can be reused, and at the same time uses the same amount of material as conventional ones. The wavy shape increases the stability of the cardboard and gives the product its name, Meerbier, whose sound has two meanings in German: "beer of the sea" or "more beer." The name communicates a positive summer feeling and at the same time underlines that this product is offering more to the user and also our environment.

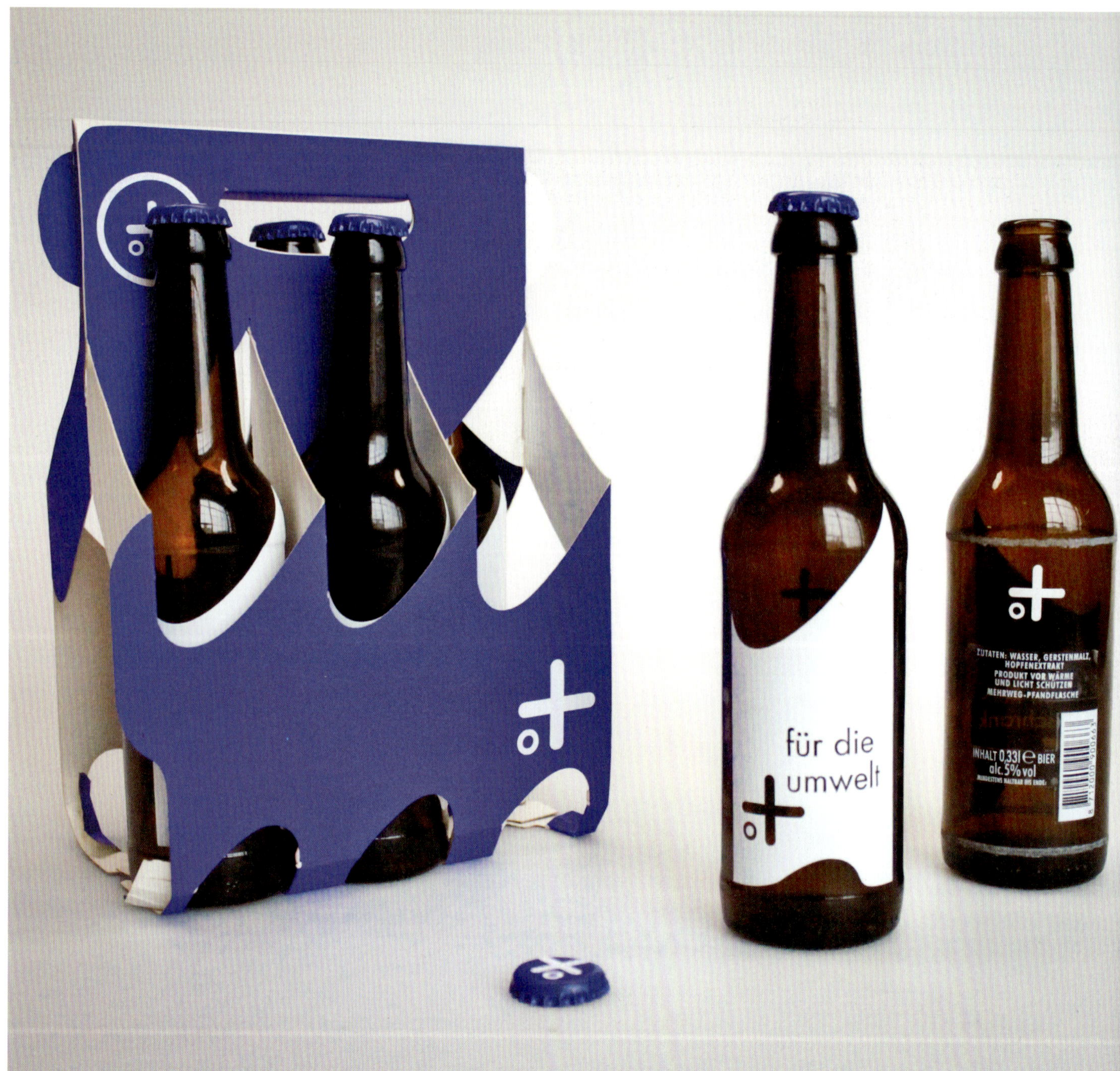

D: Alessia Sistori

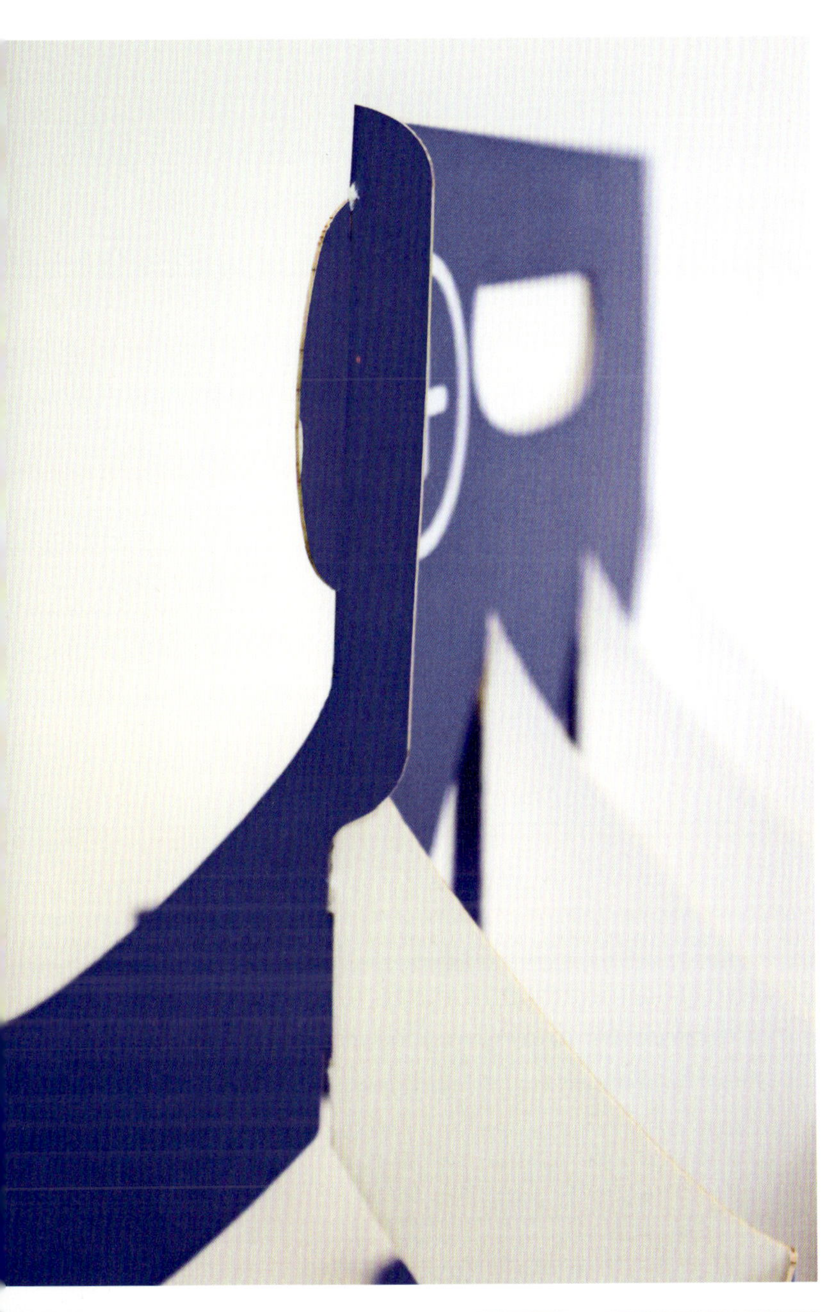

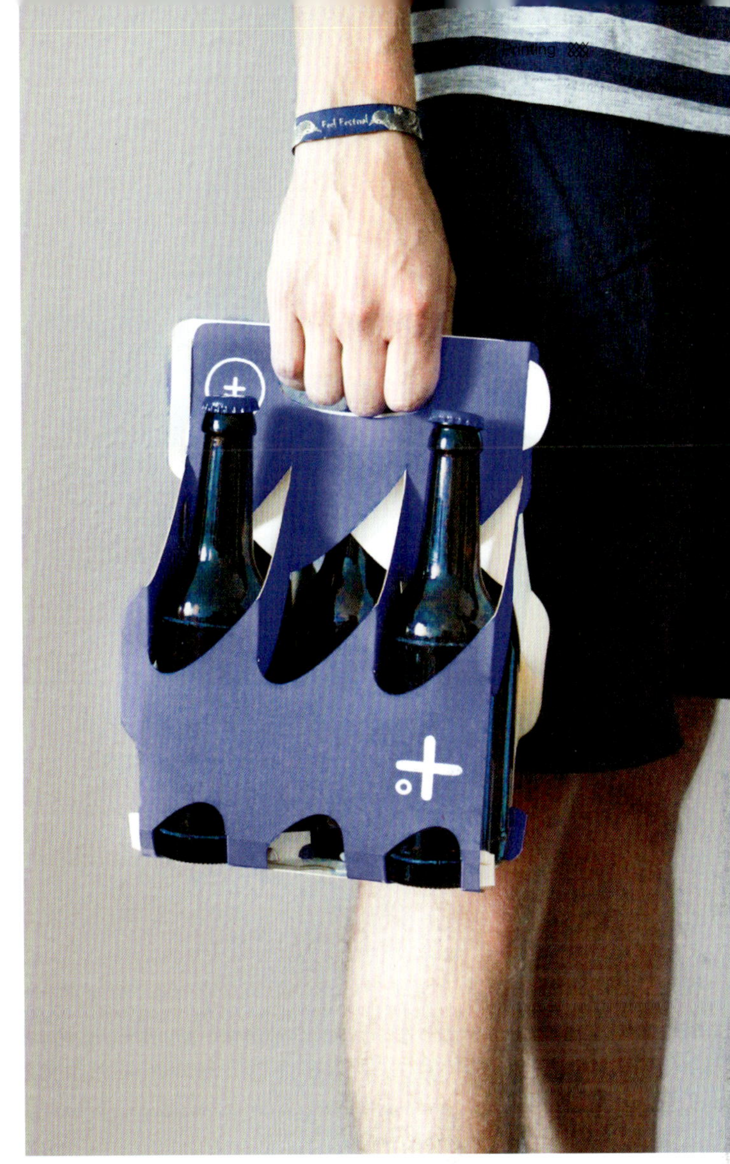

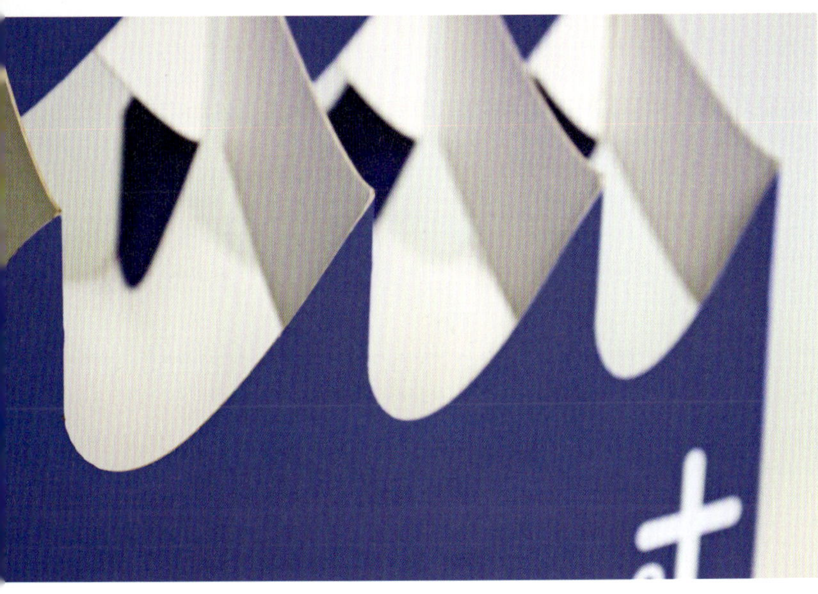

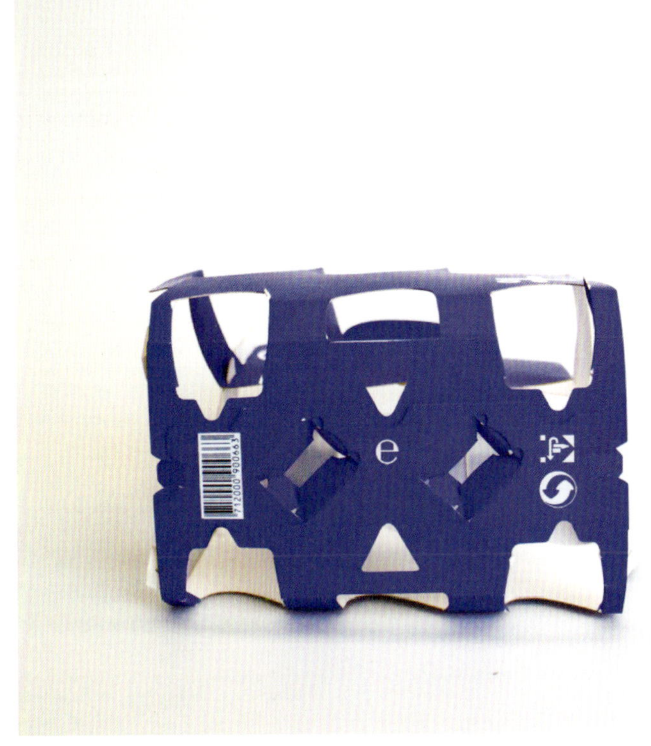

Vispera Coffee

Vispera, which is Spanish, means "evening" or the day before a holiday and evokes serenity, but also a positive, expectant atmosphere. Vispera responds to a global demand for a conceptual, premium brewing coffee that lives up to high product ideals, quality, and design—often referred to as affordable luxury. The box is printed in three-color screen printing.

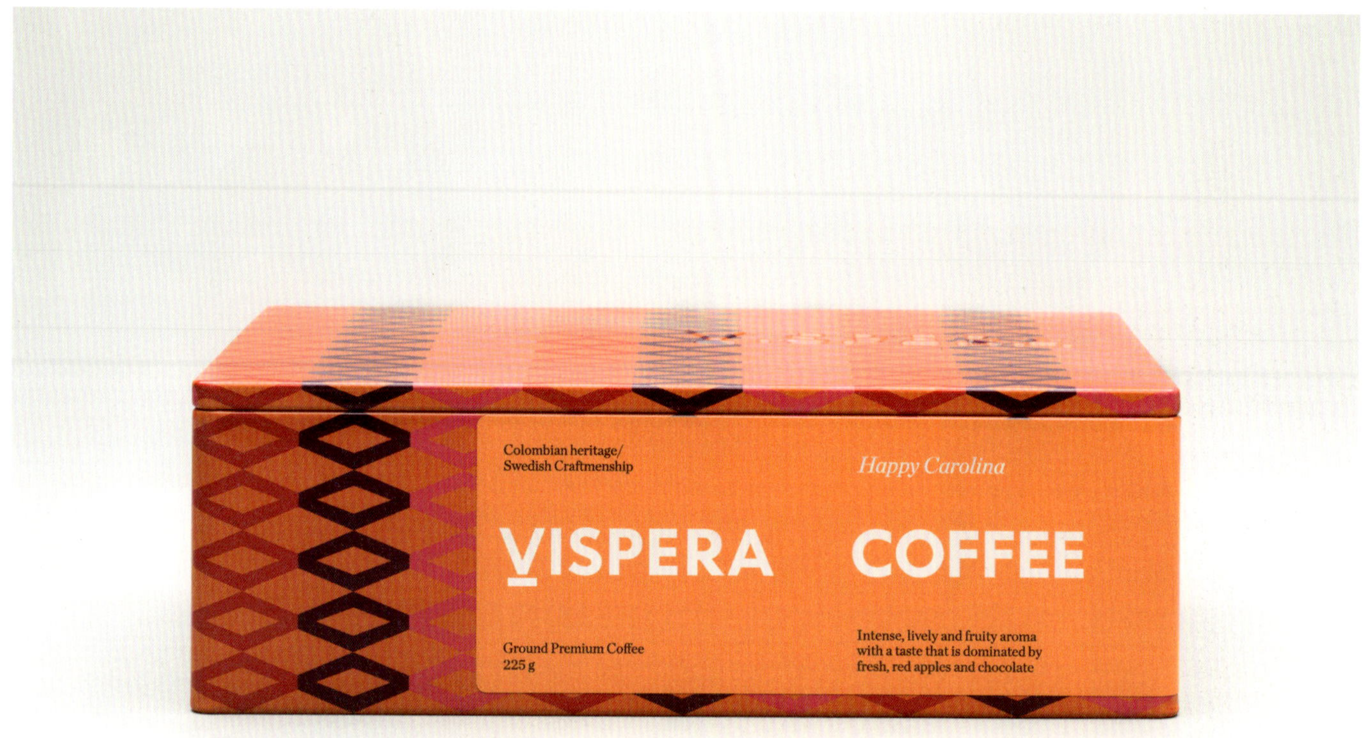

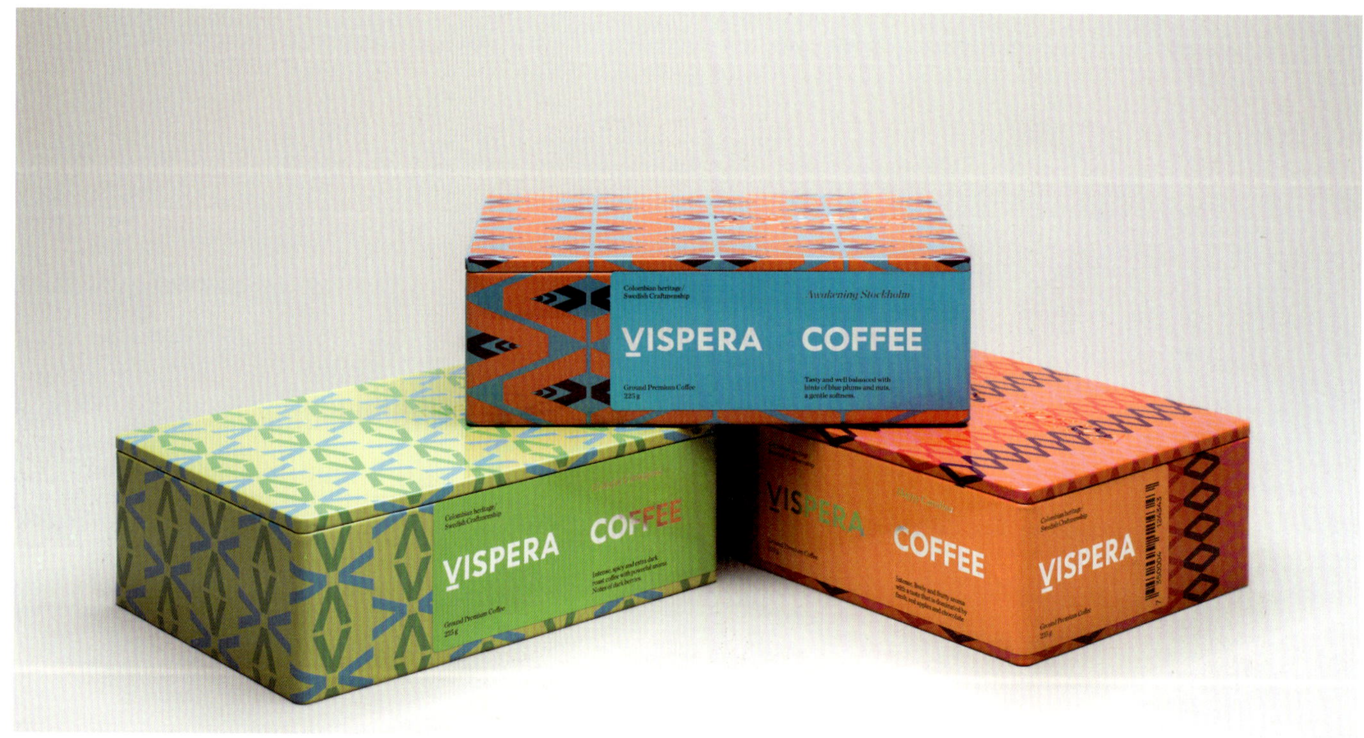

LP "Exposito"

plastic films, 300g Papago black paper

The design came as a result of hand drawing sketches based on the concept of the LP, "Exposito." There is a figure being "exposed" in an unfriendly landscape. In the background a tornado threatens, and a crow stands on a wooden pile as a memento mori, holding an eye in its mouth and being both exposed and watched. The design is build up on two layers/colors printed on 300g Pagago black paper. The choice of printing on black was made because of the strong contrast between the colors and the background. Screen-print was chosen as the print method because of the accuracy of the print and the flatness and brightness of the colors.

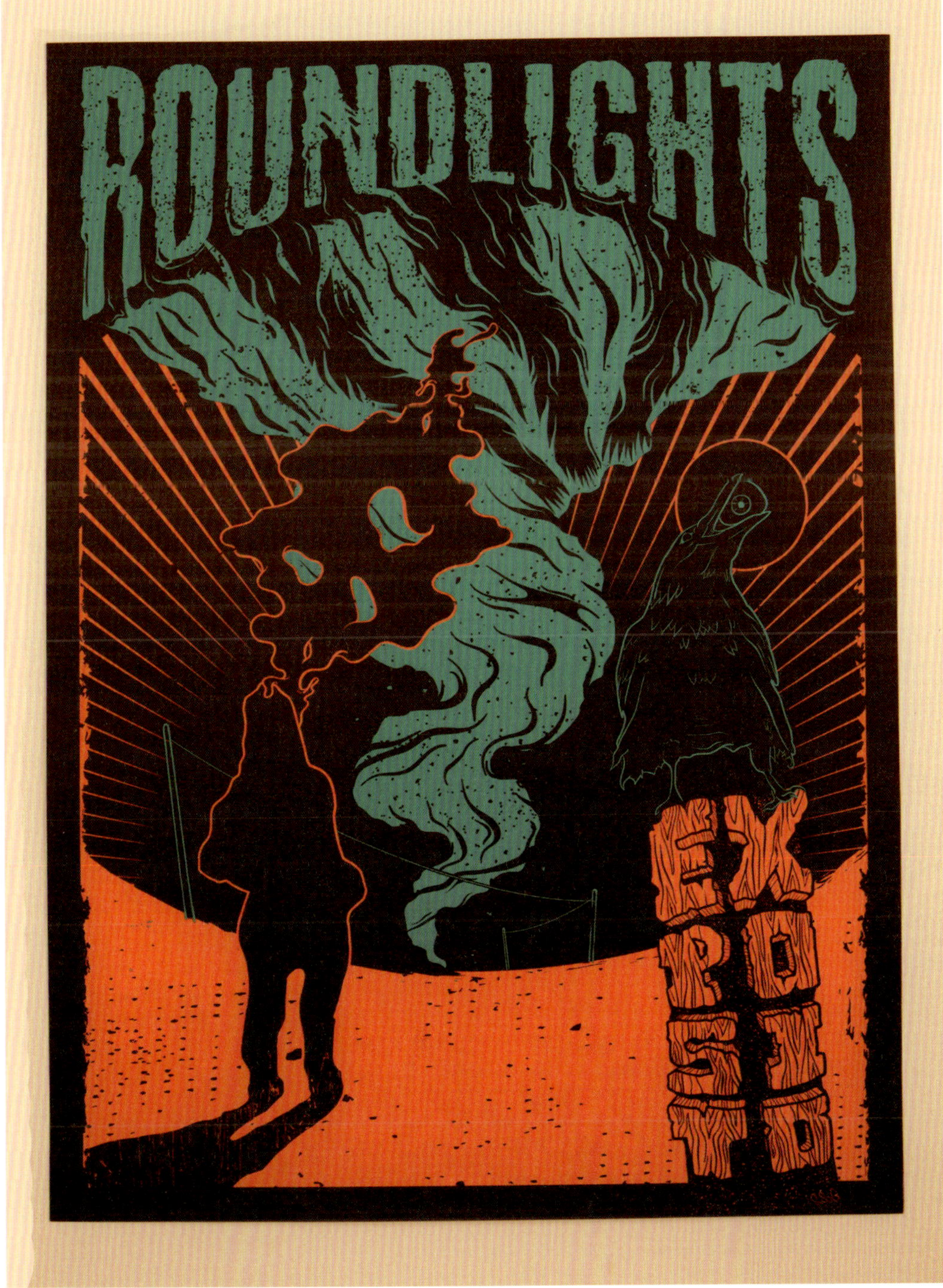

***D*:** Yiorgos Chatzivasilakis

Greek Democracy

- 300g Curious Matter Black Truffle paper
- white ink, silver ink, white ink and varnish (typography)

The inspiration comes from a quote by Ray Bradbury: "The terrible tyranny of the majority." The designer used the image of a snake and the color of black to create a dark atmosphere. This work is printed via silkscreen by Chris Angelakis and tind.

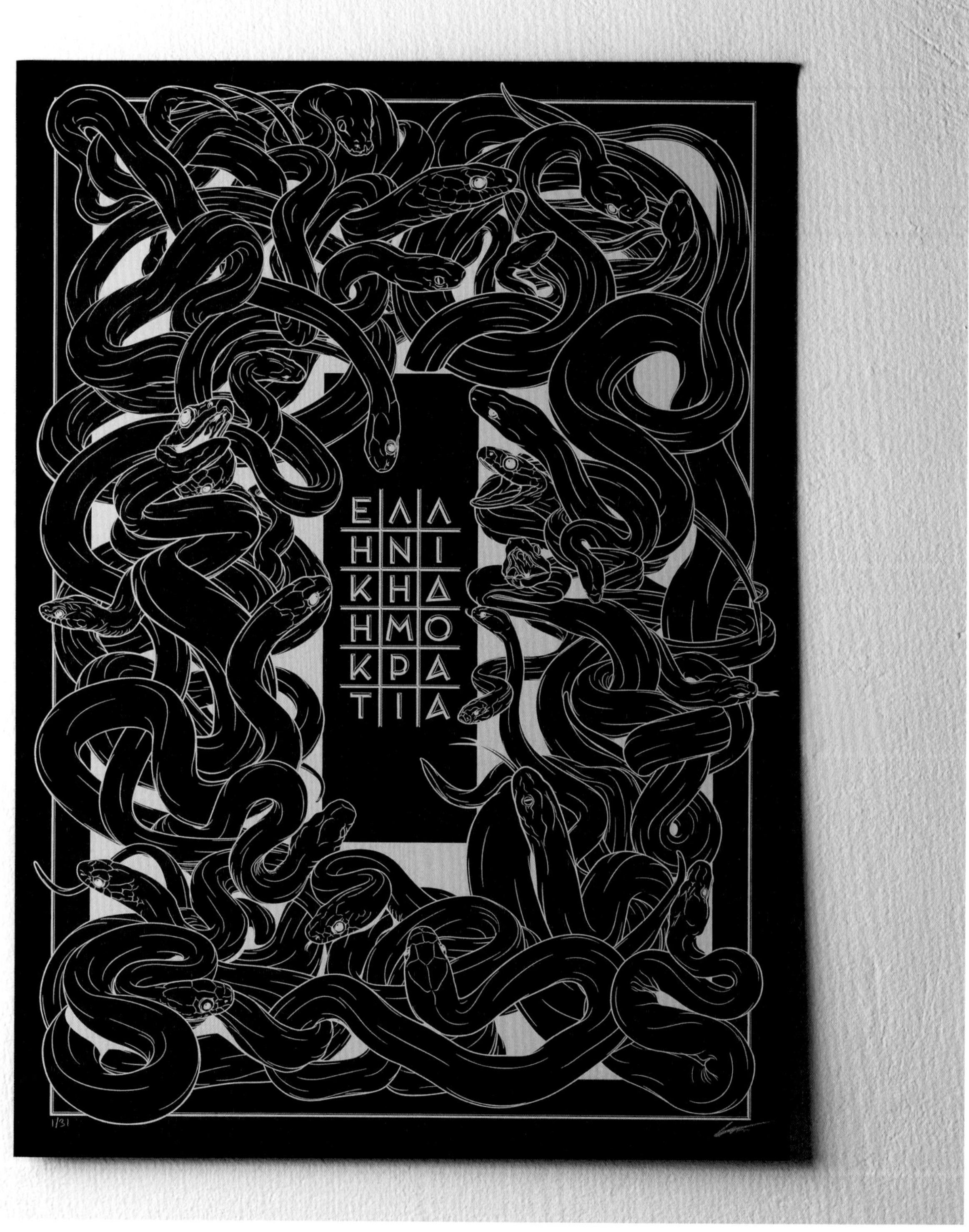

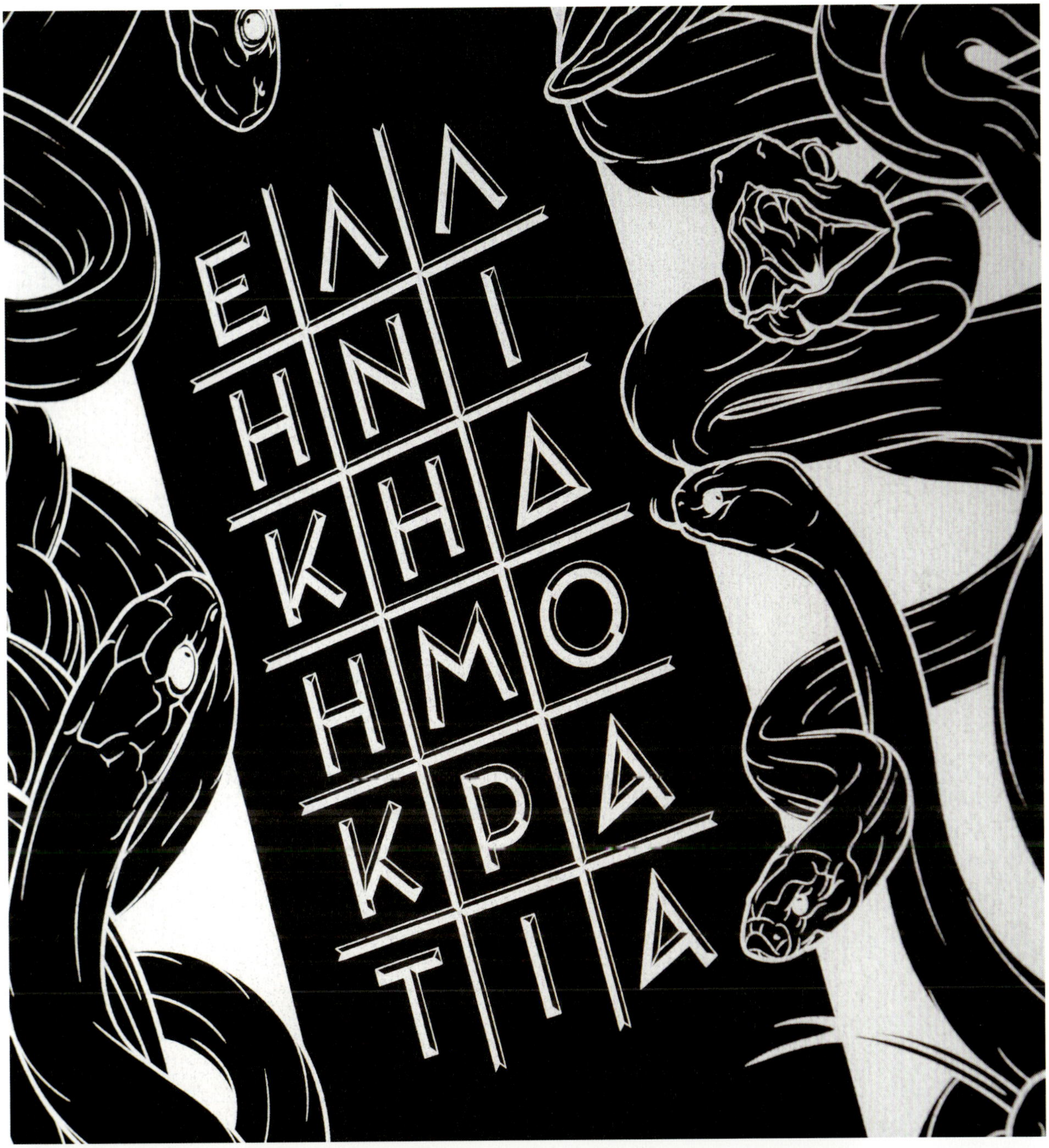

ΕΛΛ
ΗΝΙ
ΚΗΔ
ΗΜΟ
ΚΡΑ
ΤΙΑ

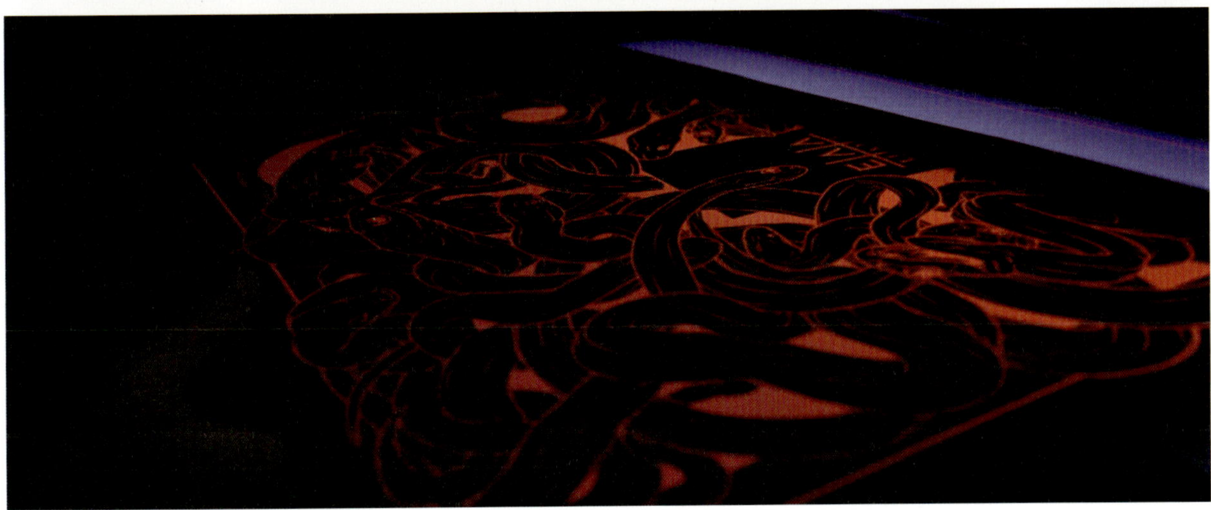

Whow - Anyone Can Win!

120g matte white paper

This game was developed from scratch as a group project based on the game strategy, the type of board, the target audience, the illustration, right up to the packaging itself. The packaging and cover of the book are printed on laminated paper to offer more resistance. All the Pop-Up elements were developed, cut, and glued to the board game by hand.

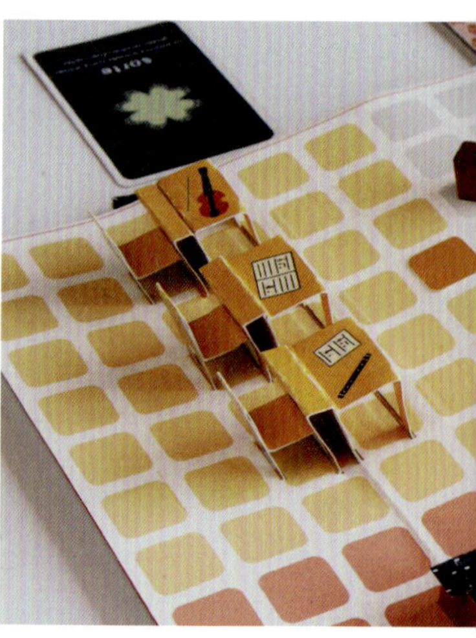

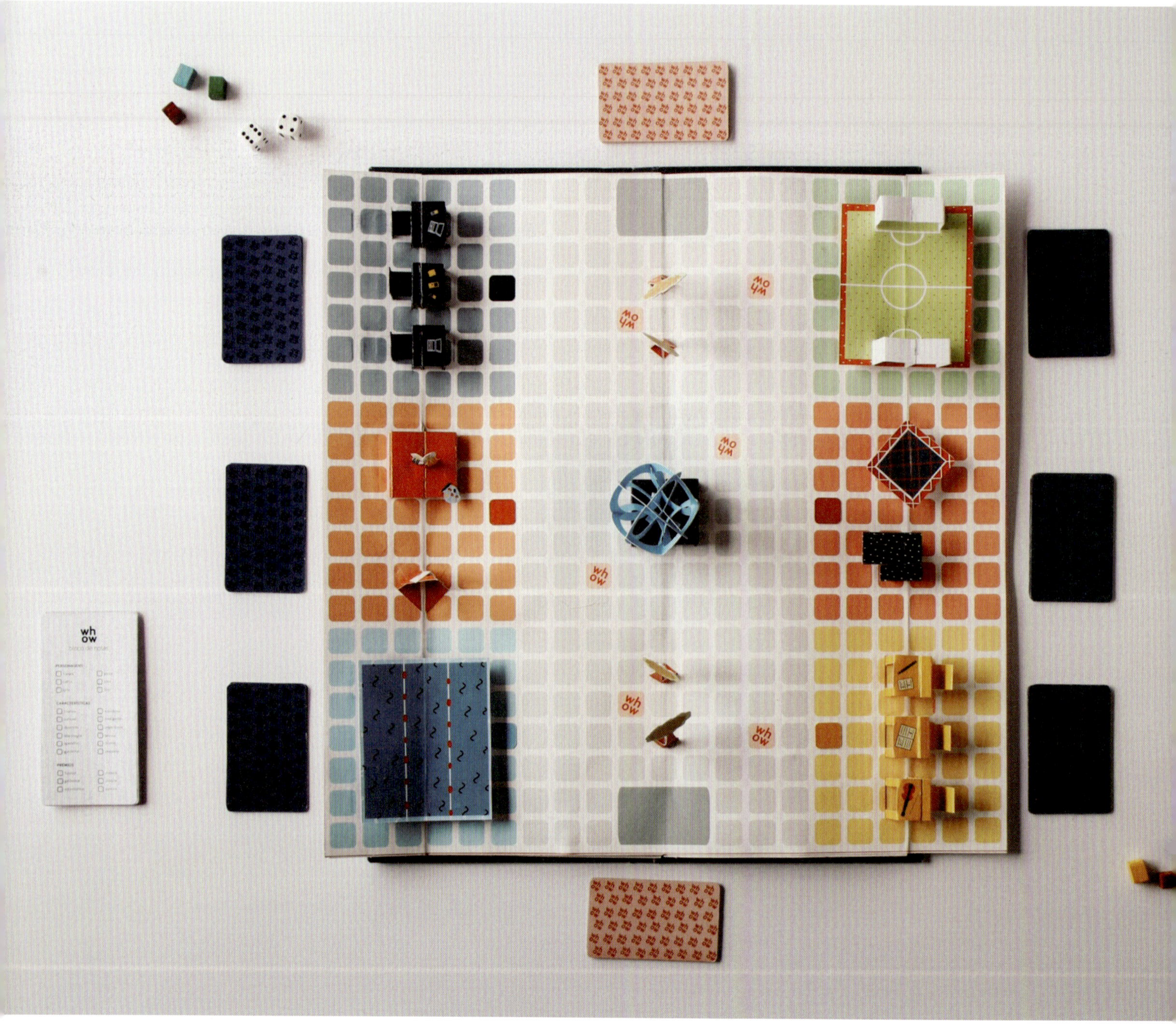

D: Carolina Rainho, Joana Carolina Capela, Sofia Oliveira

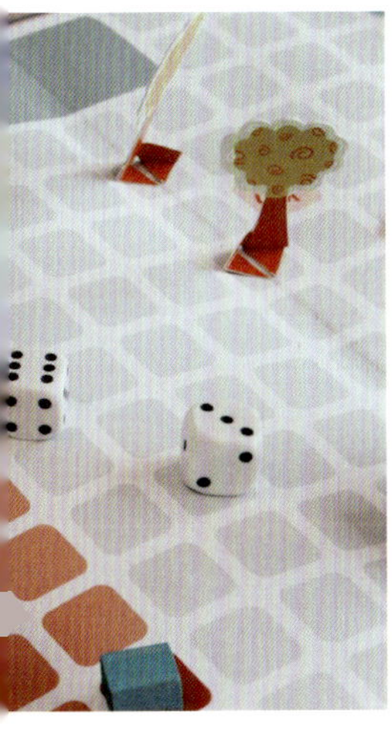

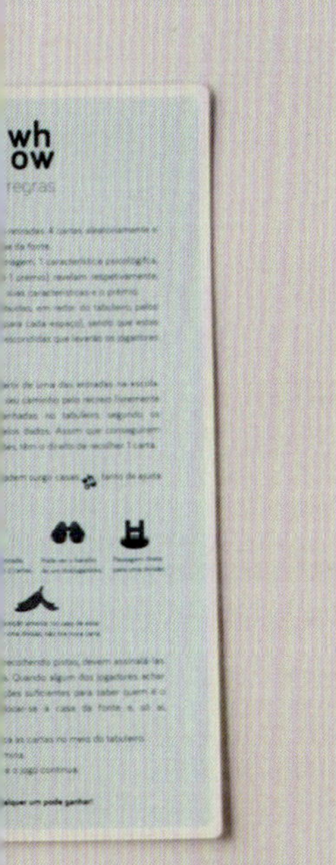

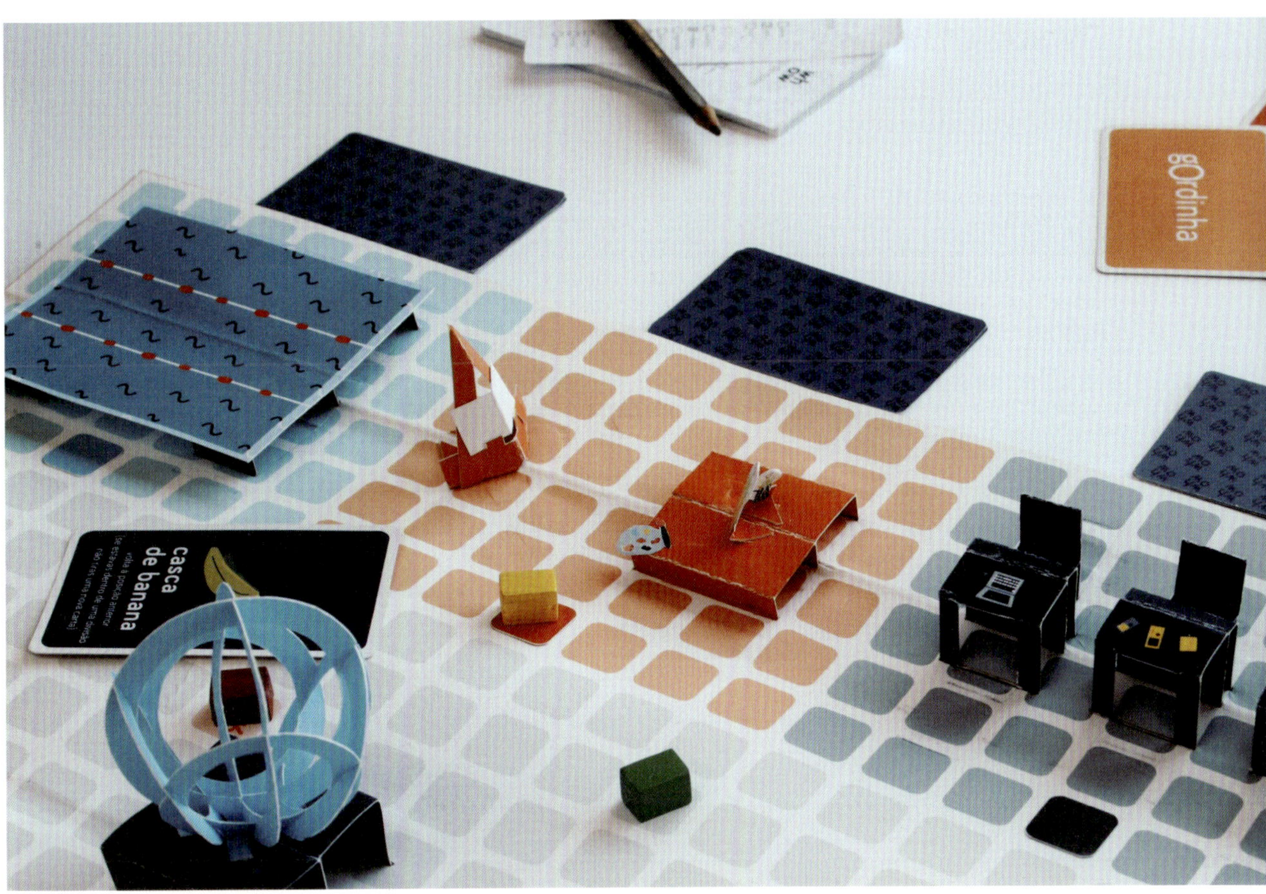
casca
de banana
gOrdinha

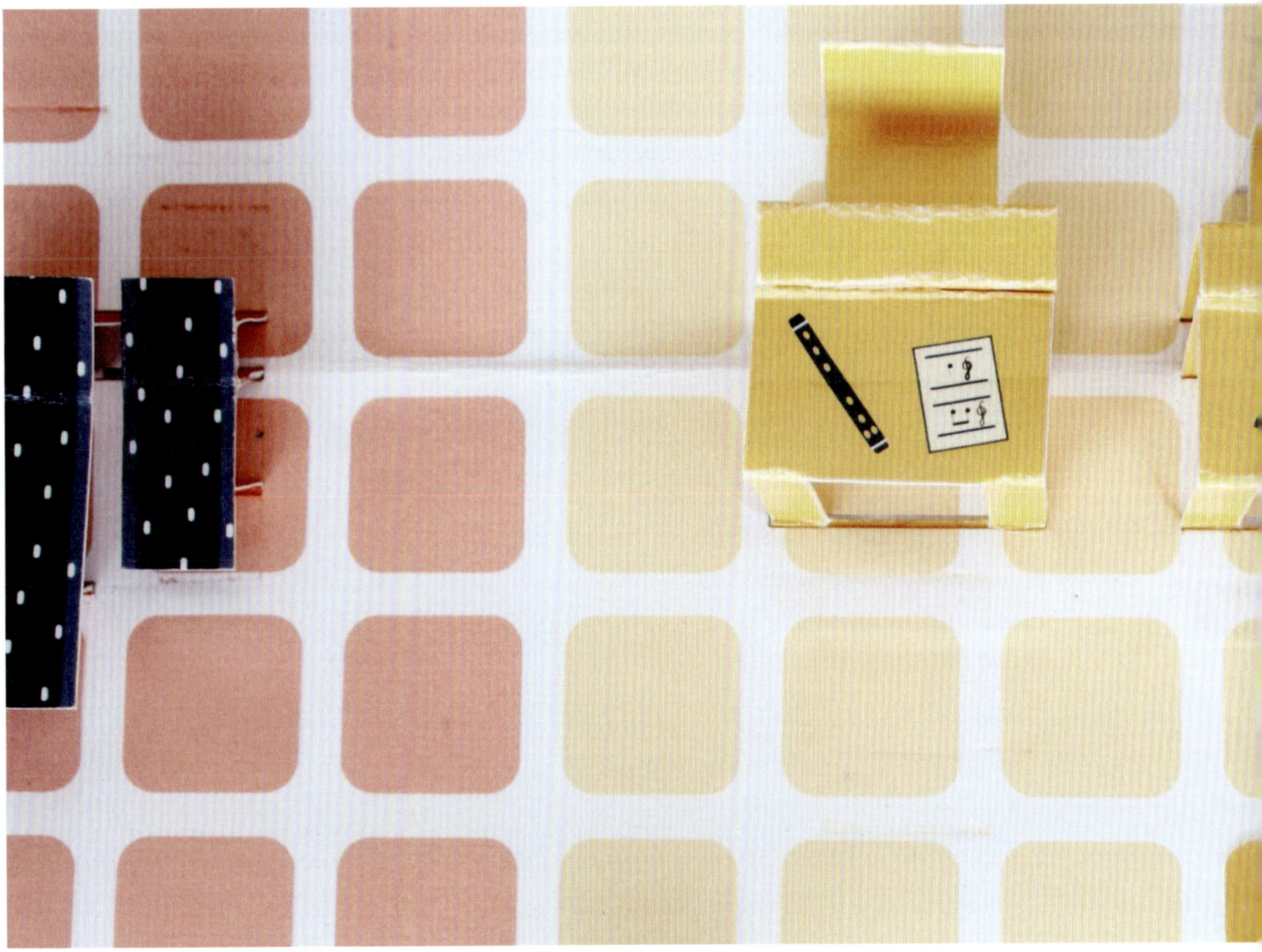

Personal Business Card

450g uncoated paperboard

When you are born right in the middle of the Alps, you are automatically surrounded by huge mountains, green pastures, and an incredibly high number of grass-chewing cows. Austrians, especially western Austrians, are a folk who live close to nature. The designer turned this obvious and almost ridiculous proudness into a visual theme on the rear side of his calling card. He then printed the cards using an old, traditional printing method: the front side with letterpress; the three different sides, with serigraphy. The canvas is 450g uncoated paperboard.

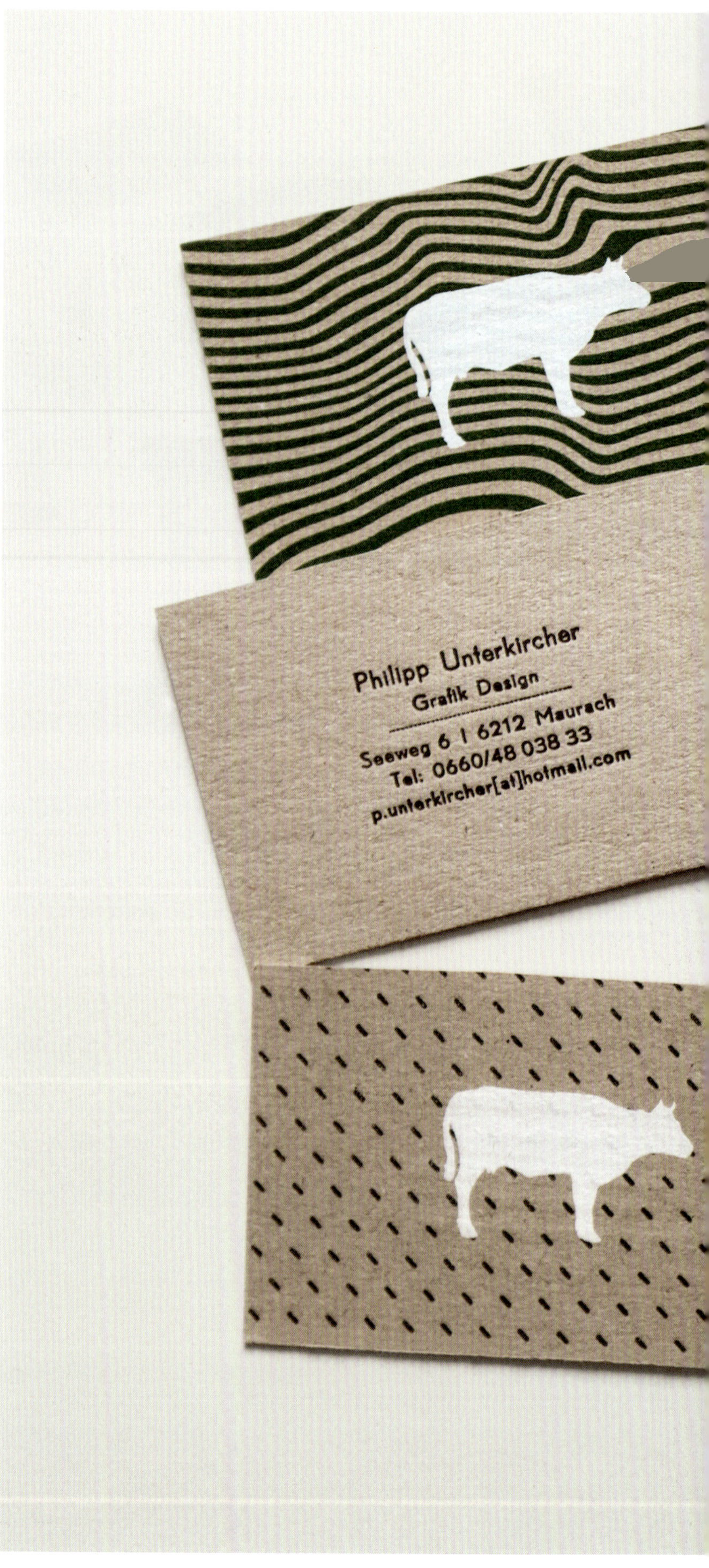

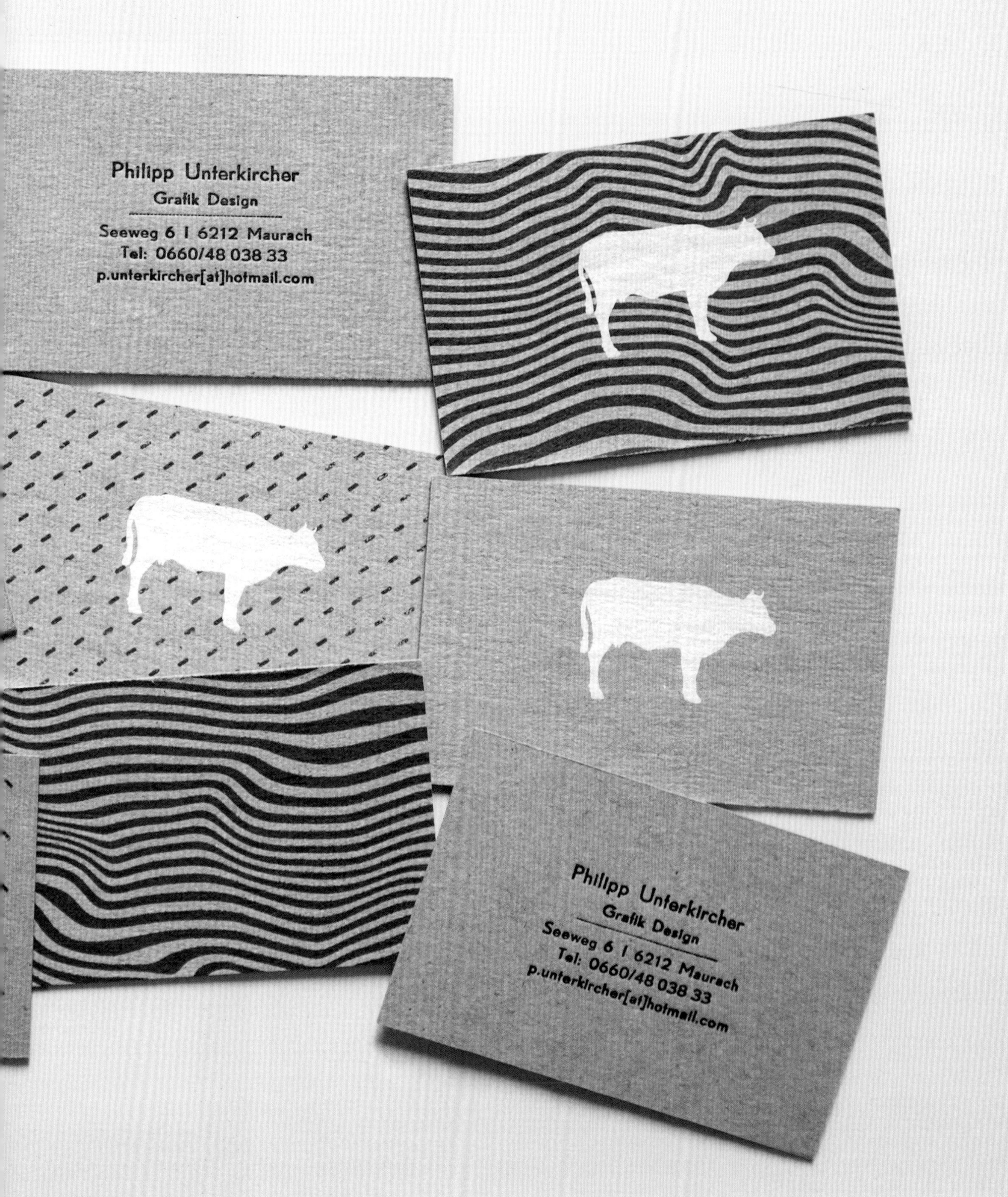
Philipp Unterkircher
Grafik Design
Seeweg 6 I 6212 Maurach
Tel: 0660/48 038 33
p.unterkircher[at]hotmail.com
Philipp Unterkircher
Grafik Design
Seeweg 6 I 6212 Maurach
Tel: 0660/48 038 33
p.unterkircher[at]hotmail.com

Calendar 2017

heavyweight paper

screen printing ink

Calendar screen printed in three colors. Each collage is a semi-abstract reinterpretation of the month it represents. The series explores the relationship between shape and line. Screen printing was an obvious choice for this project, as it is a printing method that brings great depth to any print matter. It is an interesting medium because it enables to print a myriad of vivid colors usually not printable in process and CMYK printing. Screen printing also offers a chance to experiment with happy accidents.

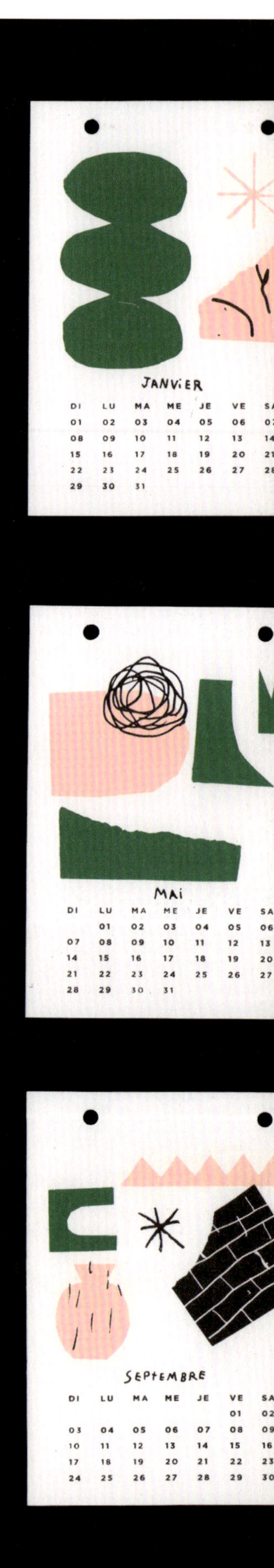

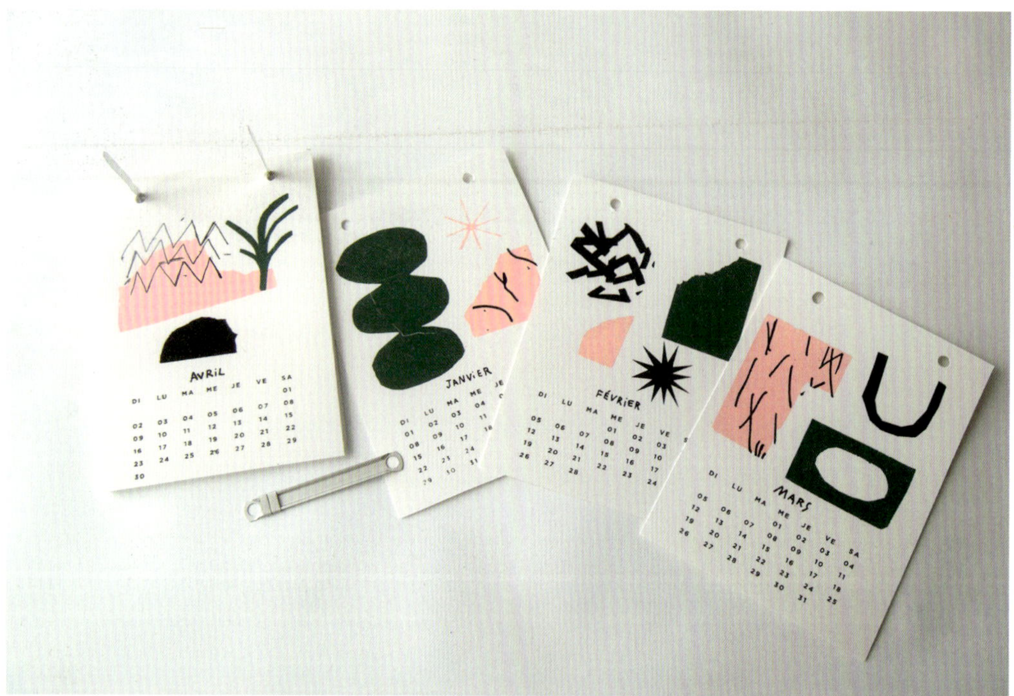

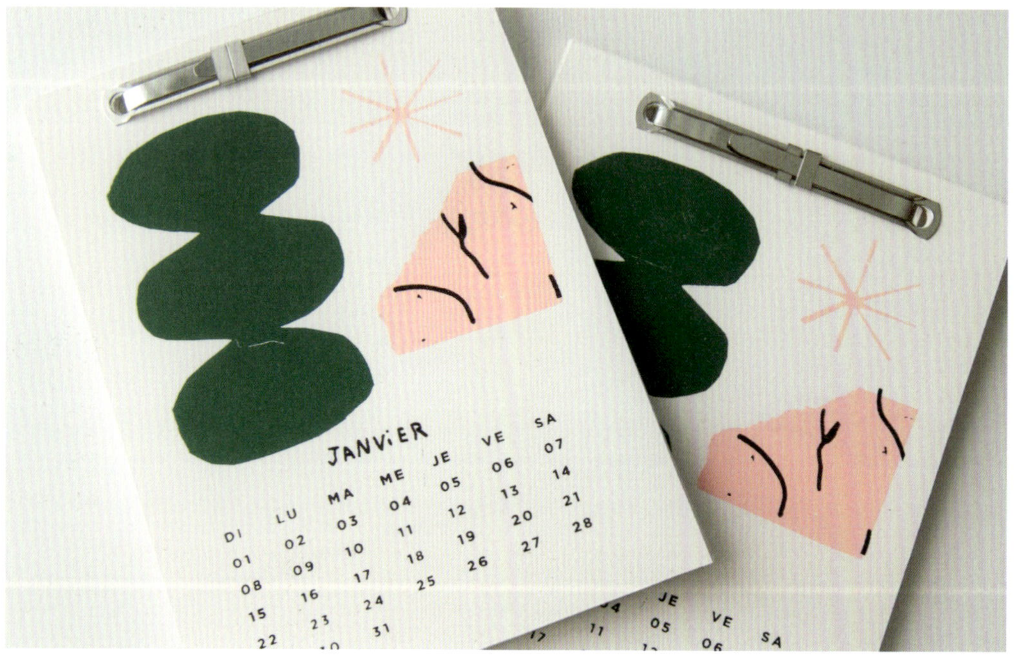

D: Amélie Lehoux

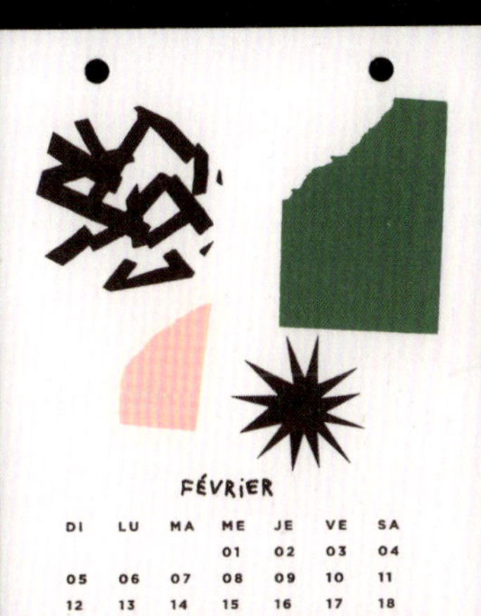
FÉVRIER
DI LU MA ME JE VE SA
01 02 03 04
05 06 07 08 09 10 11
12 13 14 15 16 17 18
19 20 21 22 23 24 25
26 27 28

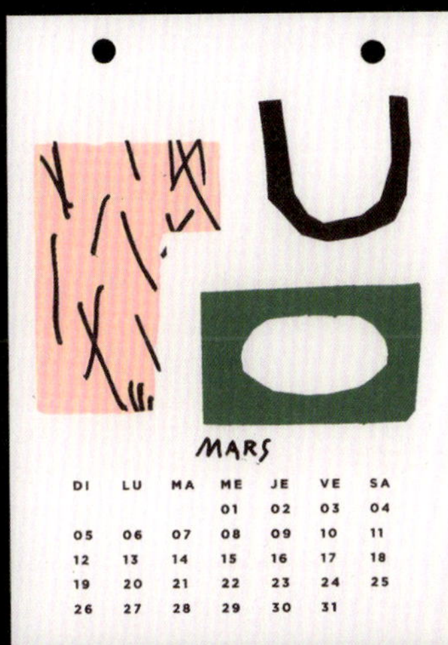
MARS
DI LU MA ME JE VE SA
01 02 03 04
05 06 07 08 09 10 11
12 13 14 15 16 17 18
19 20 21 22 23 24 25
26 27 28 29 30 31

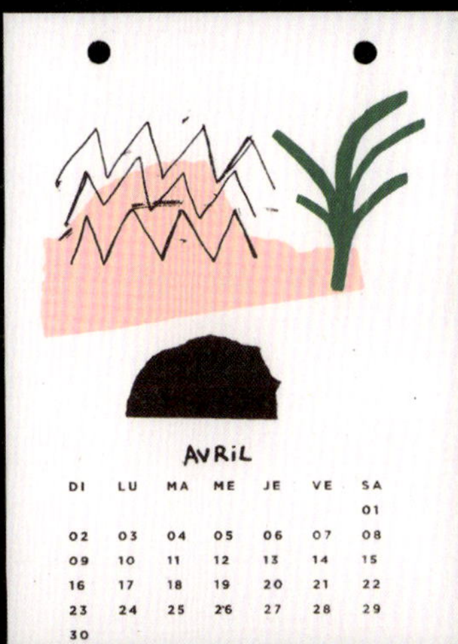
AVRIL
DI LU MA ME JE VE SA
01
02 03 04 05 06 07 08
09 10 11 12 13 14 15
16 17 18 19 20 21 22
23 24 25 26 27 28 29
30

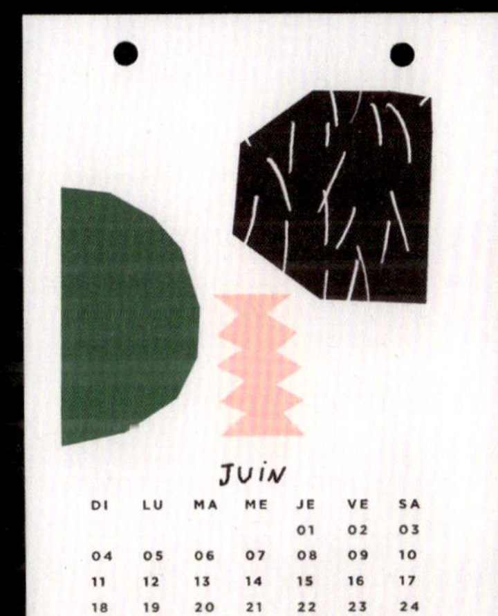
JUIN
DI LU MA ME JE VE SA
01 02 03
04 05 06 07 08 09 10
11 12 13 14 15 16 17
18 19 20 21 22 23 24
25 26 27 28 29 30

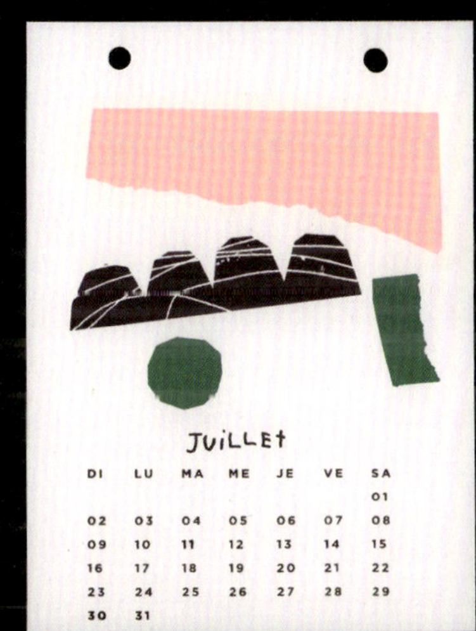
JUILLET
DI LU MA ME JE VE SA
01
02 03 04 05 06 07 08
09 10 11 12 13 14 15
16 17 18 19 20 21 22
23 24 25 26 27 28 29
30 31

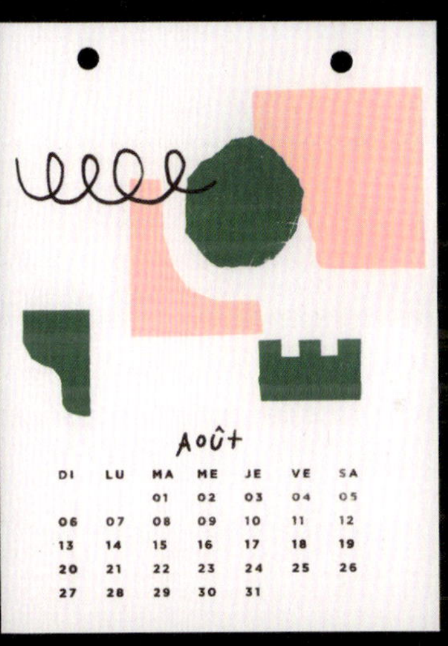
AOÛT
DI LU MA ME JE VE SA
01 02 03 04 05
06 07 08 09 10 11 12
13 14 15 16 17 18 19
20 21 22 23 24 25 26
27 28 29 30 31

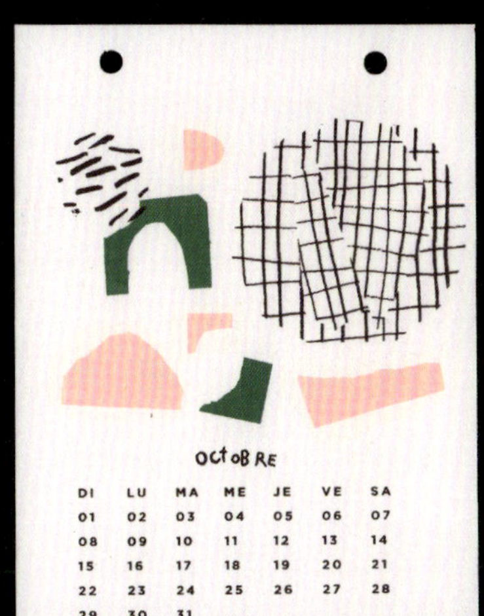
OCTOBRE
DI LU MA ME JE VE SA
01 02 03 04 05 06 07
08 09 10 11 12 13 14
15 16 17 18 19 20 21
22 23 24 25 26 27 28
29 30 31

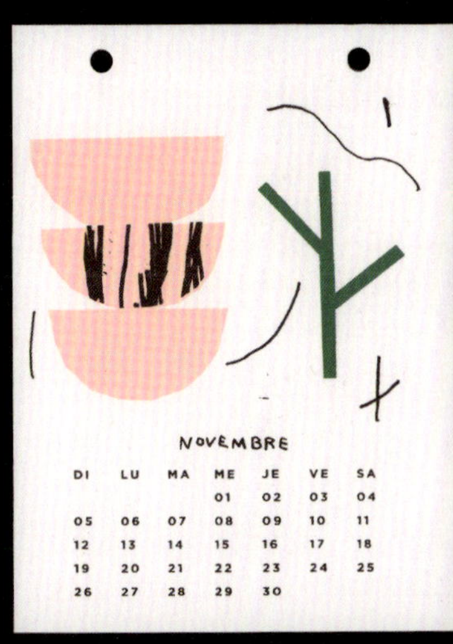
NOVEMBRE
DI LU MA ME JE VE SA
01 02 03 04
05 06 07 08 09 10 11
12 13 14 15 16 17 18
19 20 21 22 23 24 25
26 27 28 29 30

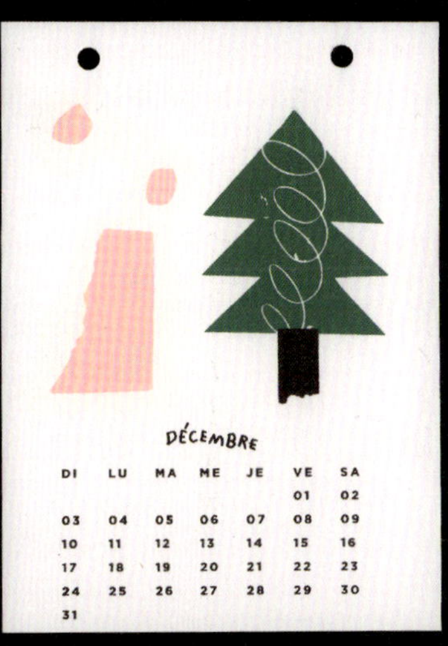
DÉCEMBRE
DI LU MA ME JE VE SA
01 02
03 04 05 06 07 08 09
10 11 12 13 14 15 16
17 18 19 20 21 22 23
24 25 26 27 28 29 30
31

Universe

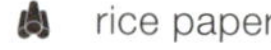

rice paper

black ink

The theme of this packaging is derived from the first line of the *Thousand Character Classic*, "The sky was black and earth yellow; space and time vast, limitless." For the external packaging, the designer choose rice paper, with ribbon-like patterns at its base and navy-dyed paper: using different coloring for the front and the back of the paper to present "thick" or "daily." The silkscreen printing method was used because the designers wanted to present the special effect of silkscreen printing. Another reason is that the designers wanted to avoid errors made by the more commonly used process of offset printing.

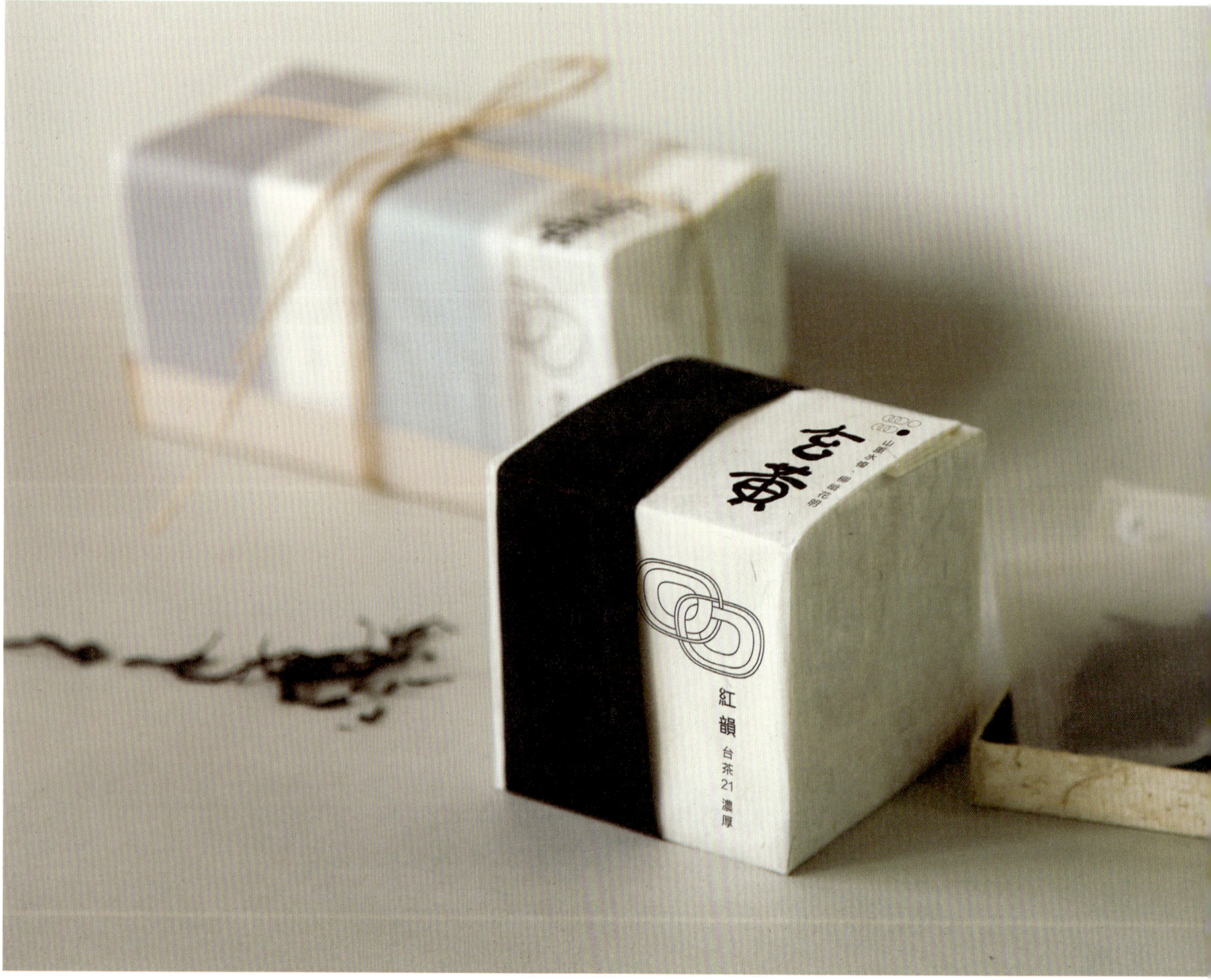

D: Yu-Fang Huang/Chun-Ta Chu

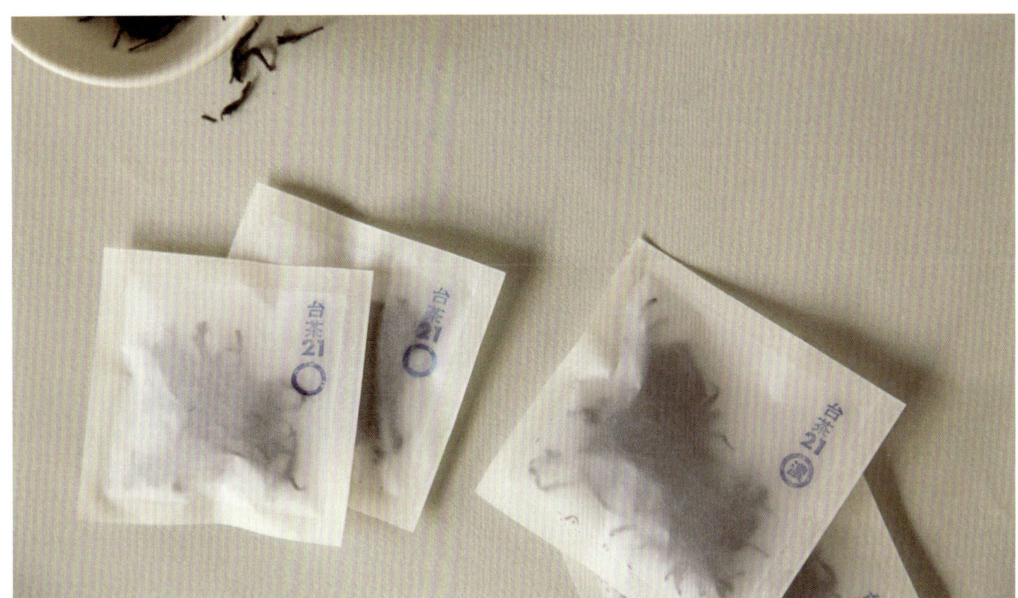
台茶21
台茶21
台茶21

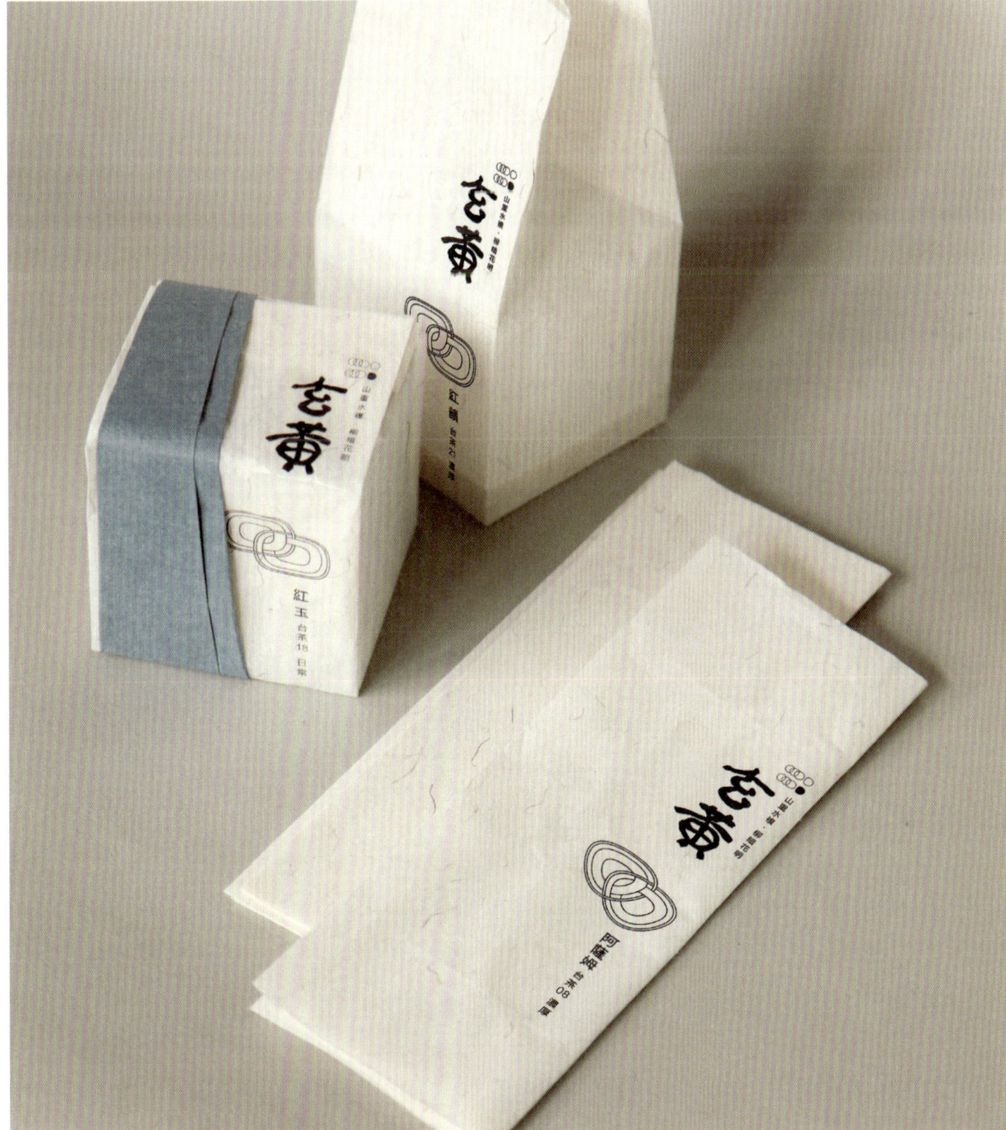
紅玉
台茶18 日常

II

Planographic Printing

1 Introduction

2 Application

3 Features

4 Merits and Demerits

5 Mechanism

6 Plate Making

7 Printing Process

8 Printed Works

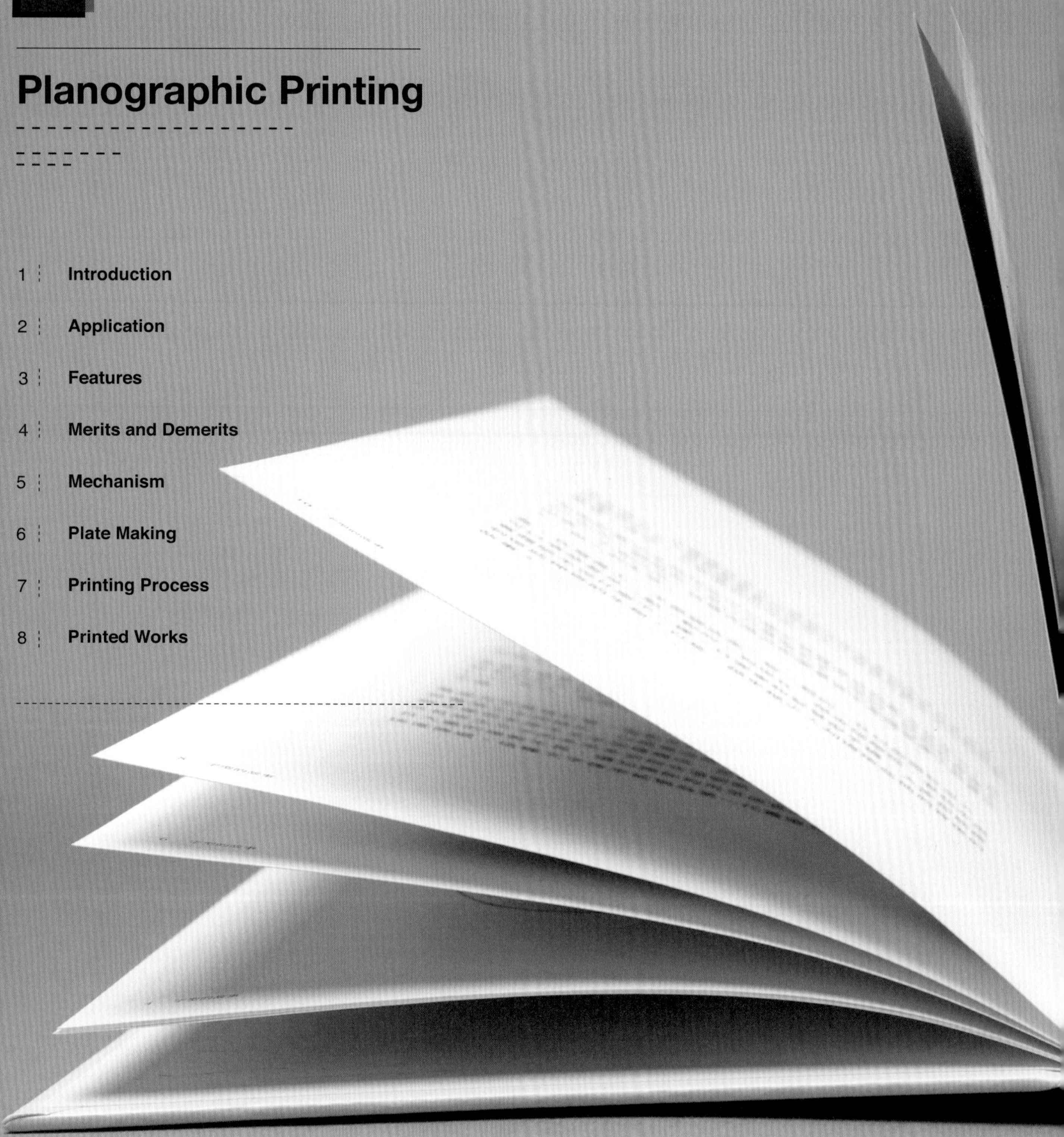

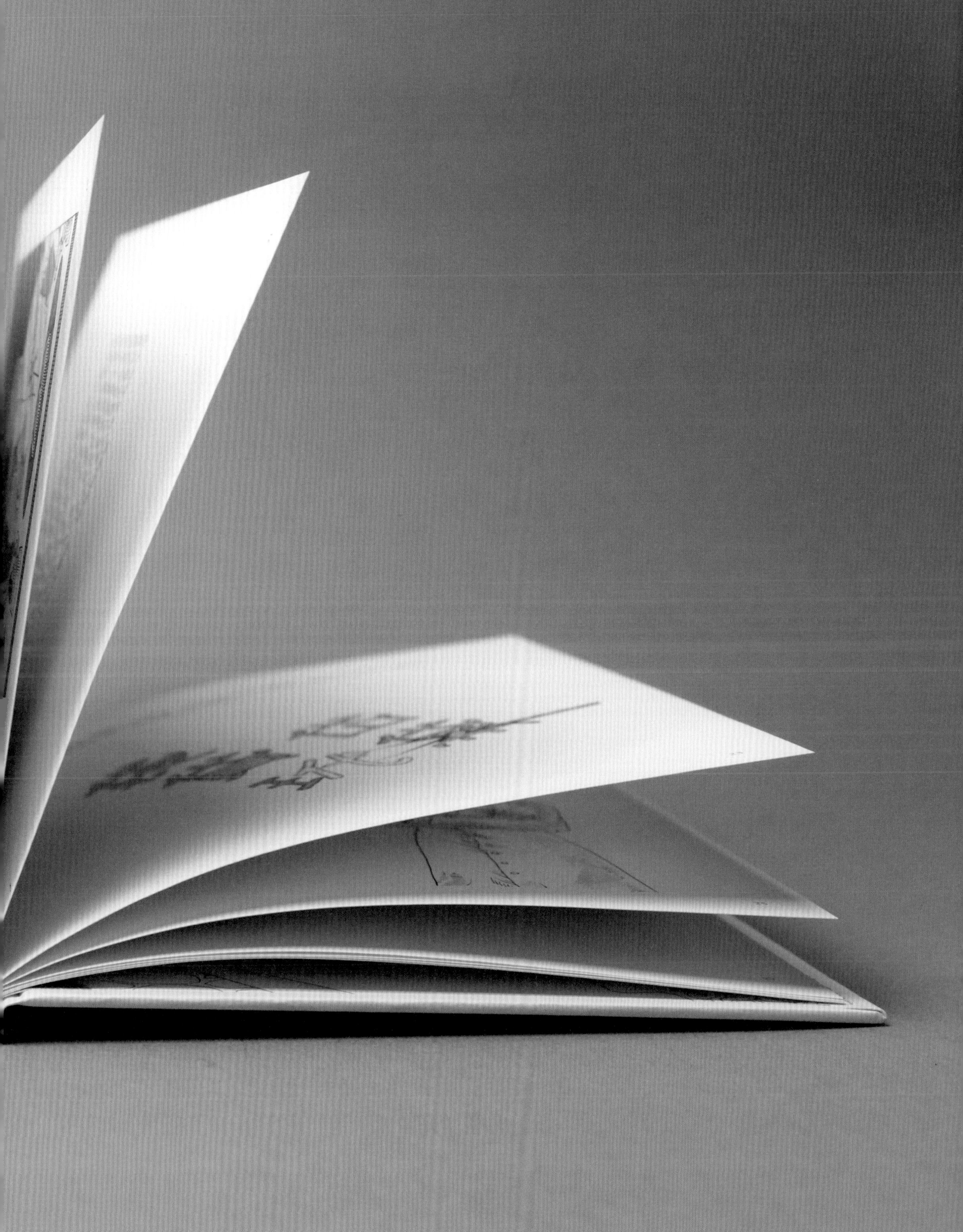

Planographic Printing

1 Introduction

Planographic printing is a commonly used commercial printing method that means printing from a flat surface. Offset printing is one kind of planographic printing. It is called "offset" because the inked image is not printed directly on the substrate. Rather, it is transferred to the printing surface through the interaction between the plate and a rubber blanket roller.

2 Application

① posters ② magazines ③ newspapers ④ picture books ⑤ packaging ⑥ calendar, etc.

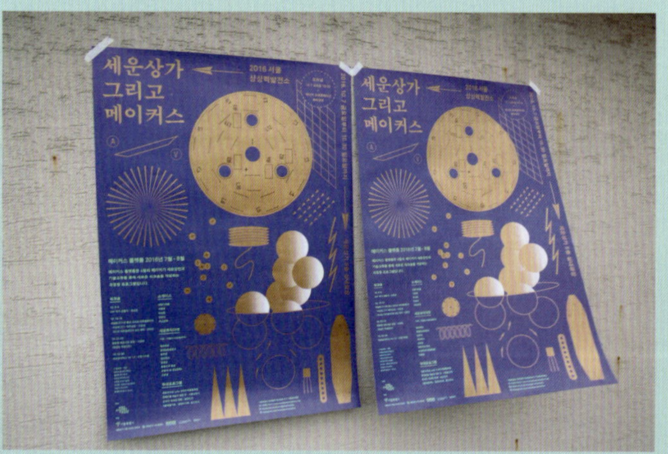

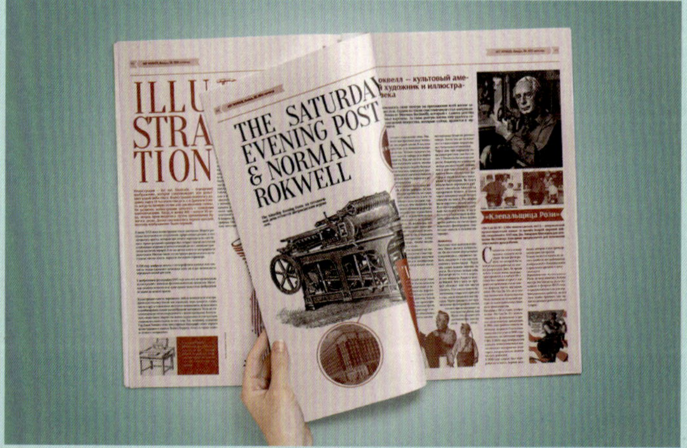

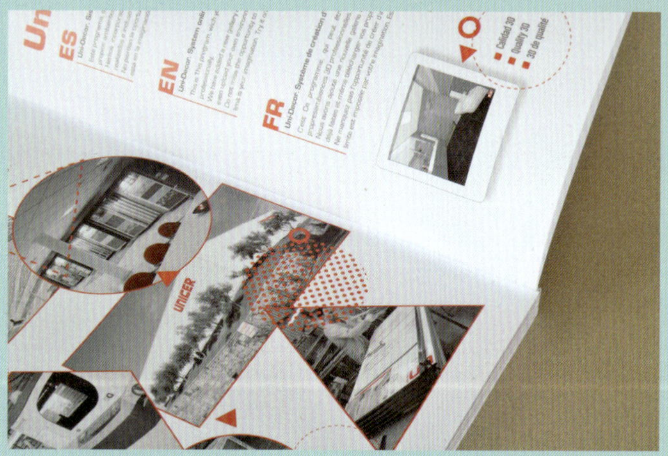

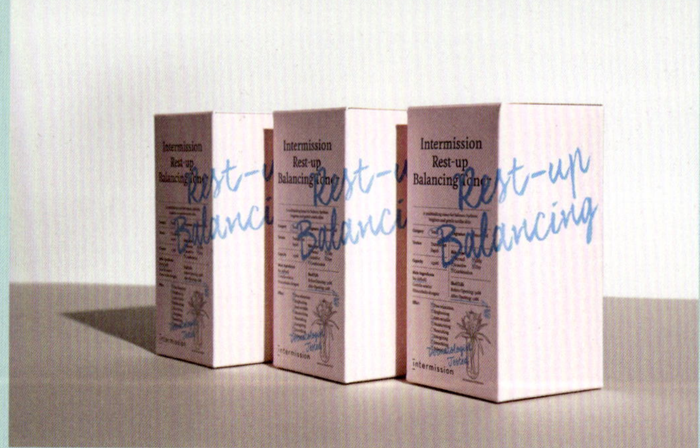

3 Features

- A flat printing surface
- Direct-read texts and images
- An indirect printing method

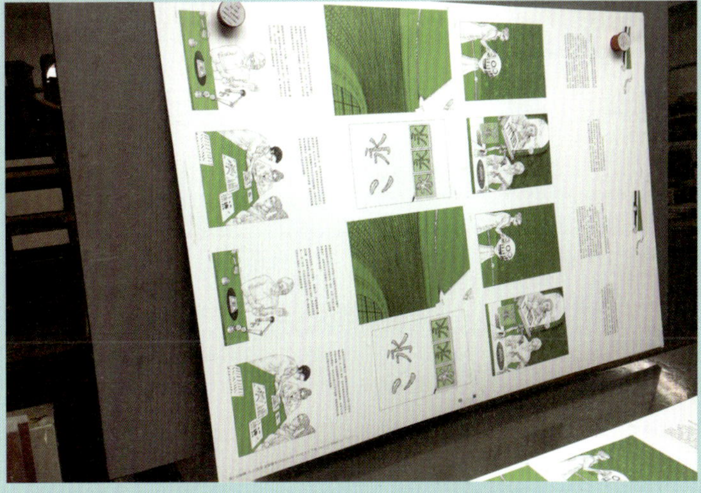

Press check for colors.

4 Merits and Demerits

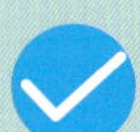

- Easy plate-making method
- High accuracy of color register
- Clear images and texts with exquisite colors

- Relatively poor quality of color reproduction

a lithography stone used for early lithography printing.

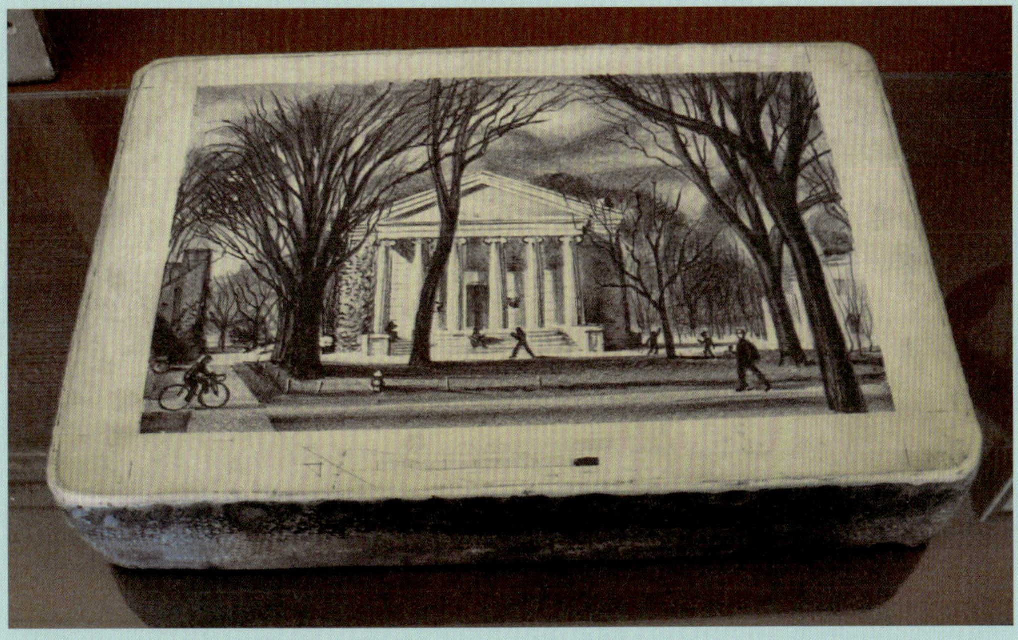

5 Mechanism

A Function View

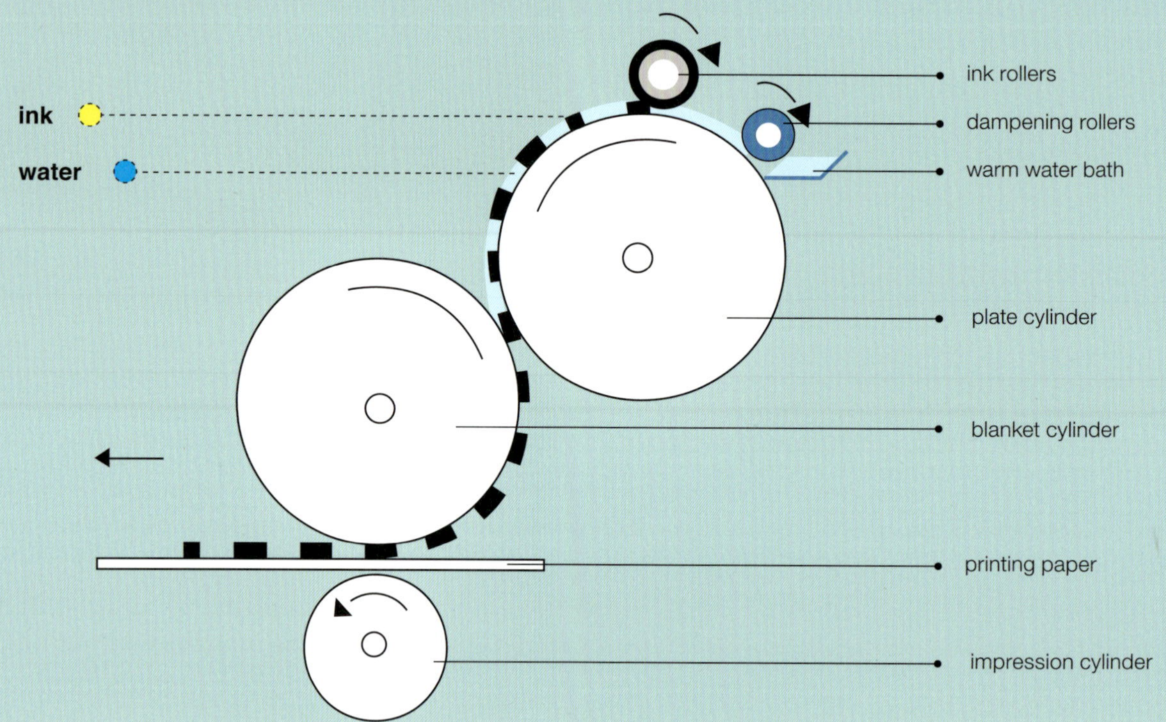

B Top View

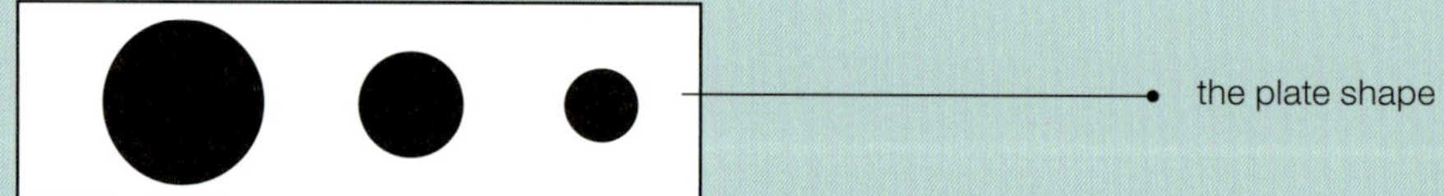

C Side View

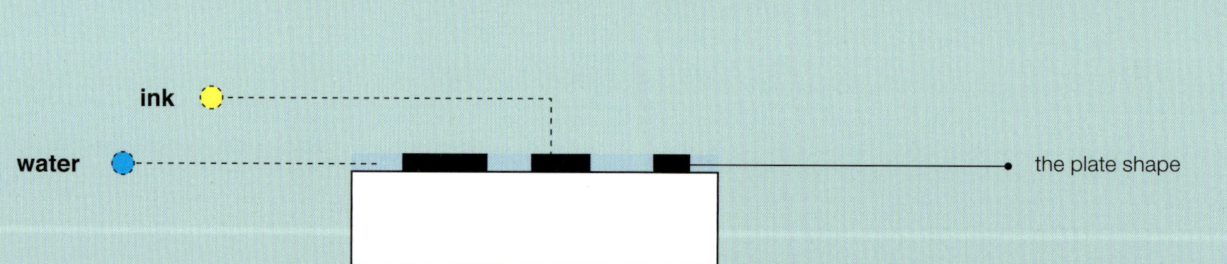

D Printing Method

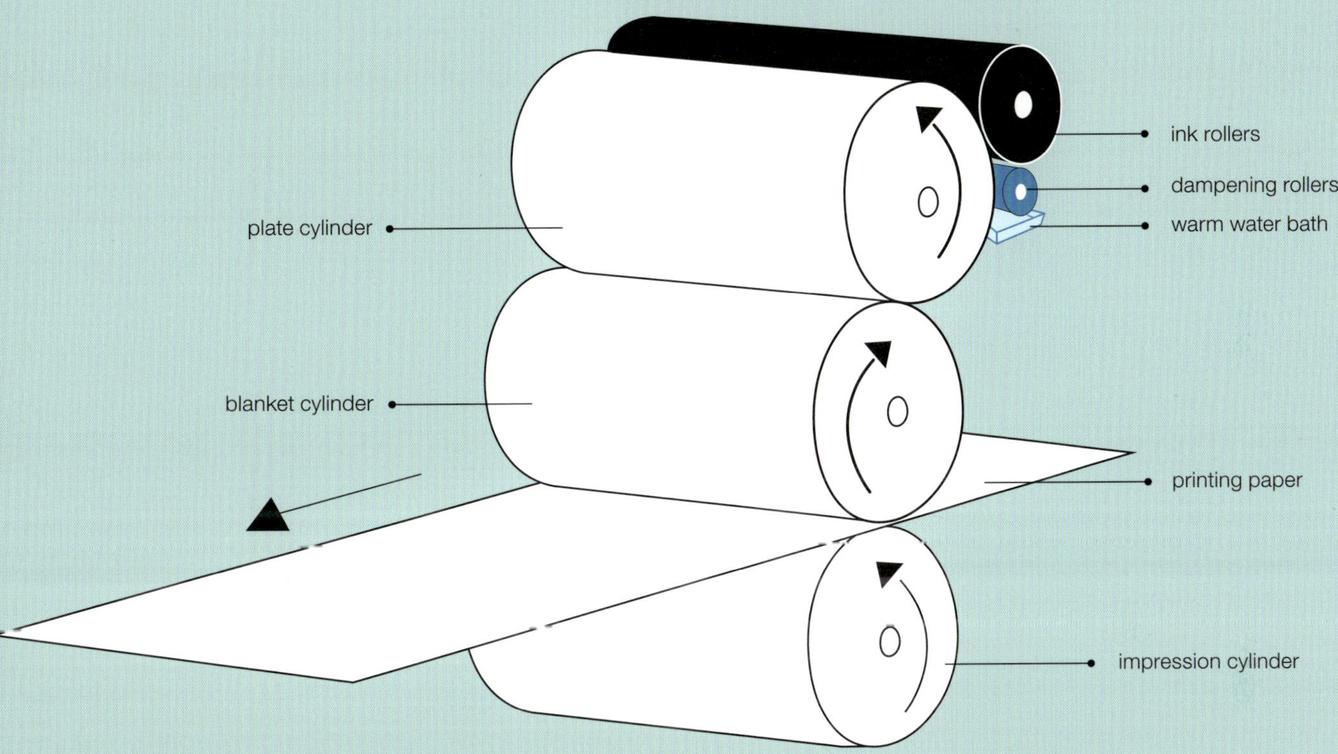

Principle

The printing process is based on the principle that water and oil do not mix. It is definite that the ink is denser the closer it is to the center of the line. This manifestation, from light edge to dark center, is a basic characteristic of planographic printing. Due to the water gel and indirect printing method, the average hue concentration is lower than with the other three printing methods, with a 60% to 70% ink expression. In other words, planographic-printed works look softer.

E ⁞ Structure

Generally, a whole planographic printing machine consists of a sheet feeder, a printing unit and a delivery unit. The paper transfers from the sheet feeder to the printing unit via the conveyor. Every machine prints one color once. The plate is dampened first by water fountains, then ink rollers. The ink adheres to the image area, the water to the non-image area.

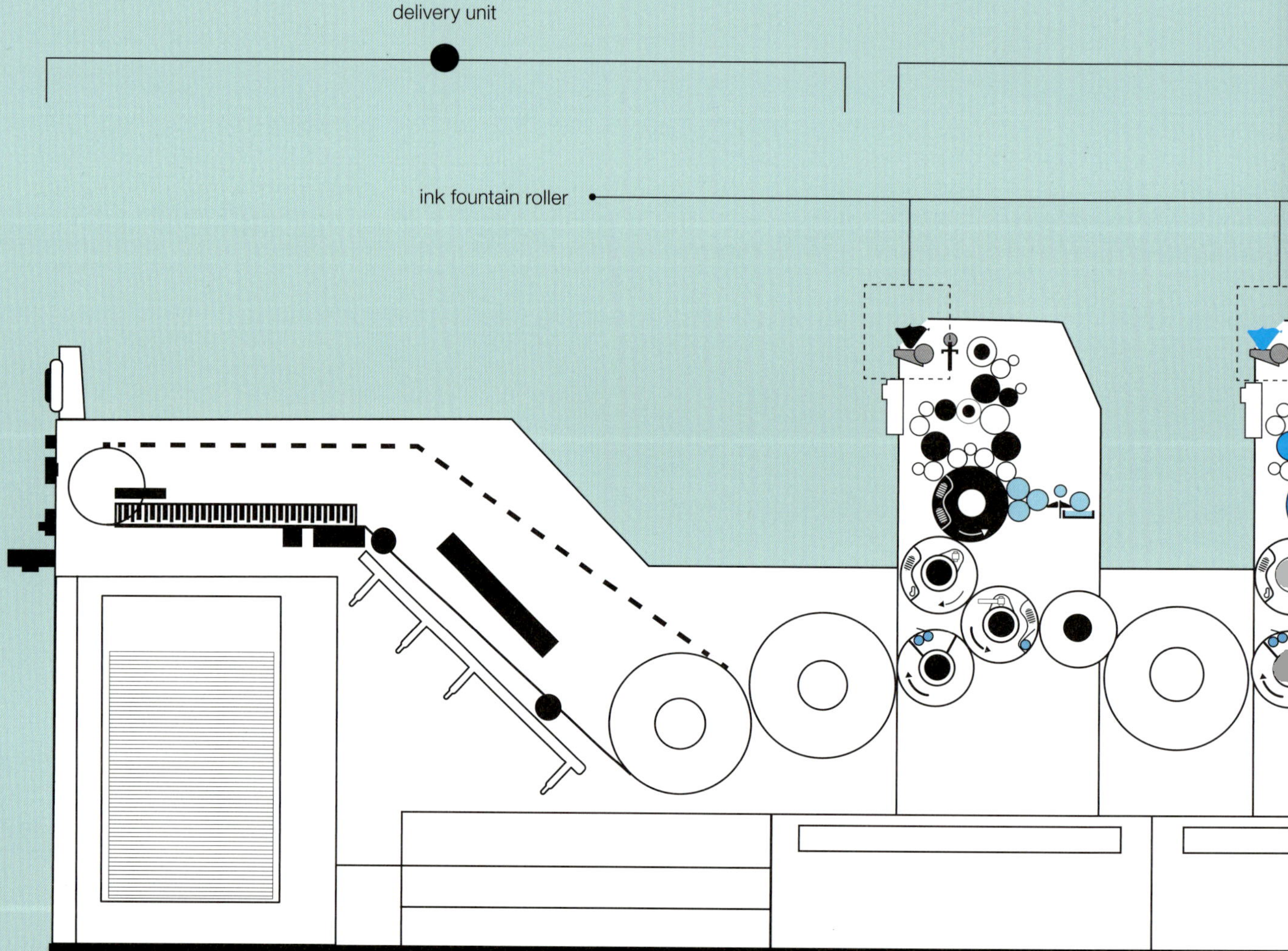

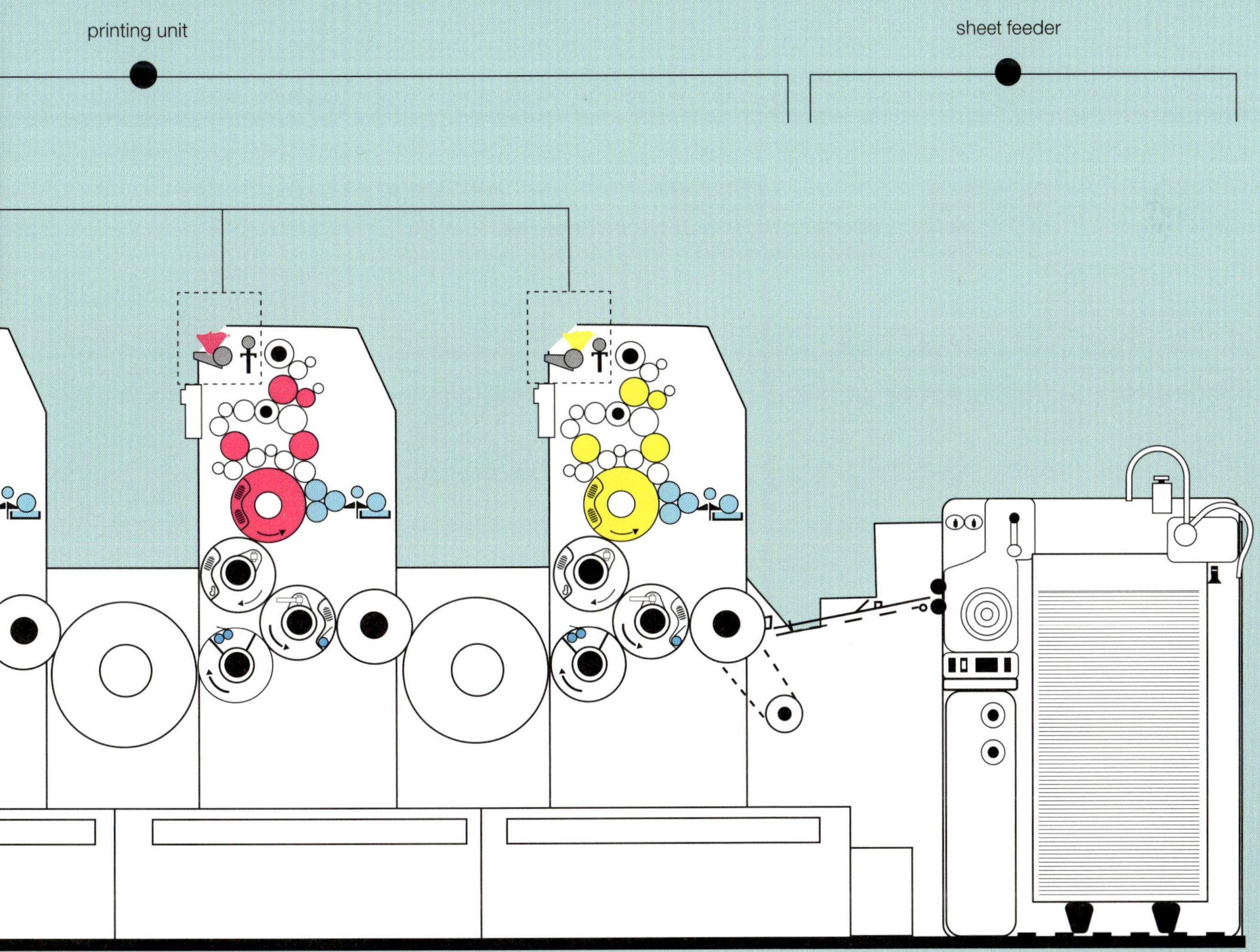
printing unit
sheet feeder

6 Plate Making

Most of the plates are made from metals such as aluminum or zinc, with aluminum being a better choice. And the most popular type is the PS plate, which is a presensitized aluminum board.

A table of hydrophilic and lipophilic of metals

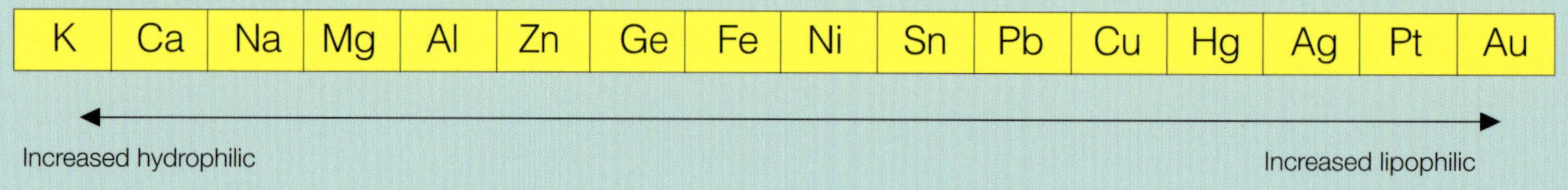

K	Ca	Na	Mg	Al	Zn	Ge	Fe	Ni	Sn	Pb	Cu	Hg	Ag	Pt	Au

Increased hydrophilic ←→ Increased lipophilic

Structure of PS plates

A PS plate is short for presensitized plate. The base is an aluminium board with a thickness of 0.5 mm, 0.3 mm or 0.15 mm. It was previously treated so that its surface was water-accepting, and was developed with a photopolymer coating.
There are two types of PS plates, namely, photopolymerization and photolysis. The former uses negative film for plate burning and the later uses positive film for plate burning.

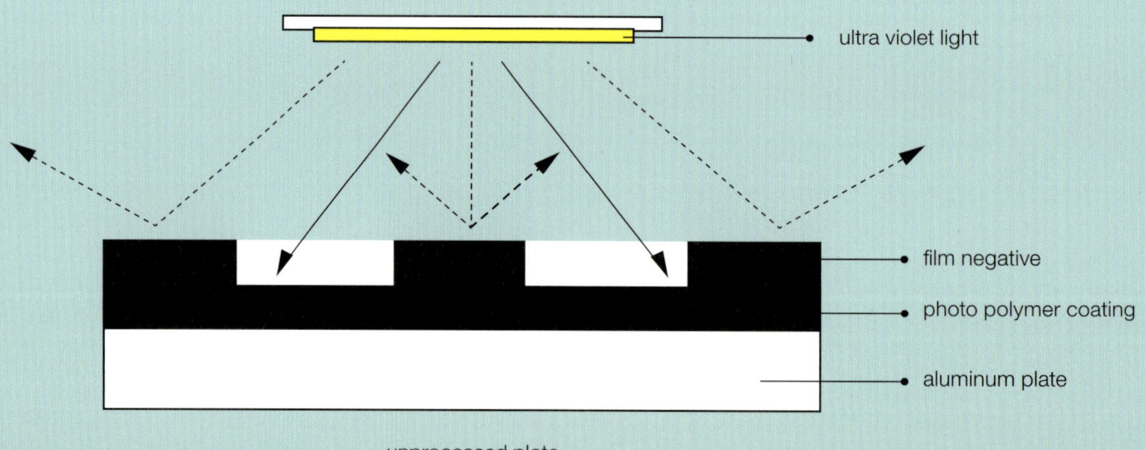

unprocessed plate

Why is the image area ink-receptive whereas the non-image area is water-receptive?

Indeed it is due to the making of the printing plate. Images from film negatives are transferred to the plates in much the same way as photographs are exposed.

① When the exposure starts, the light will pass through the clear areas and get to the polymer; which is then hardened due to the photochemical reaction, resulting in the formation of an image.
② Coat the negative with developer inks and the hardened polymer can absorb the ink to form an oil-receptive base. The light, on the contrary, is reflected away from the dark portions of the negative without causing hardening of the polymer, which can be dissolved by water during later processing. Thus the water-accepting plate shows through.

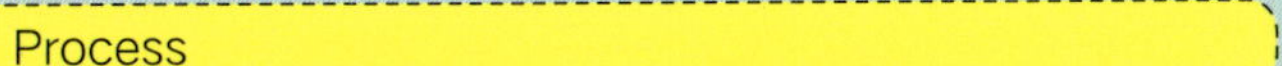

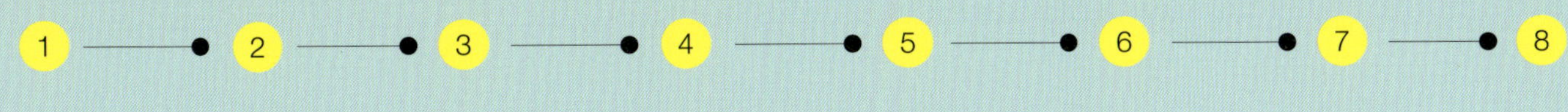

Placing the film — Printing-down — Developing — Rinsing — Drying — Finishing — Burning — Coating

1 Placing the film

Photopolymerization PS plates use positive film, and photolysis PS plates use negative film. Carefully lift the glass board of the printing-down machine and position the film on the PS plates. Set the time of printing down and put it into a vacuum unit.

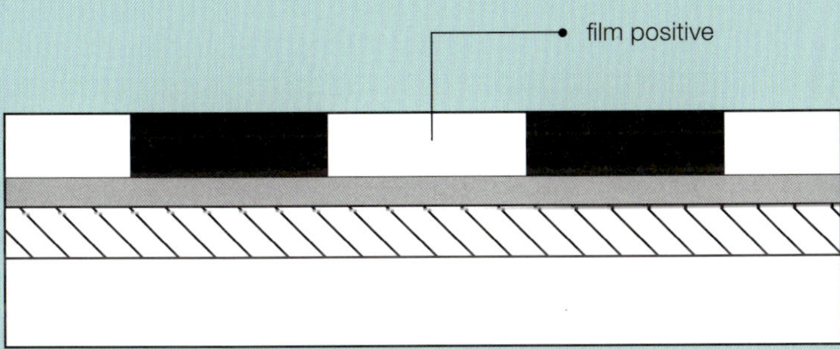

2 Printing-down

The exposed light is usually Iodine gallium ultra violet light. The exposed parts of the PS plates are dissolved (photopolymerization) or polymerized (photolysis). Remove the photosensitive resin of the non-printing area.

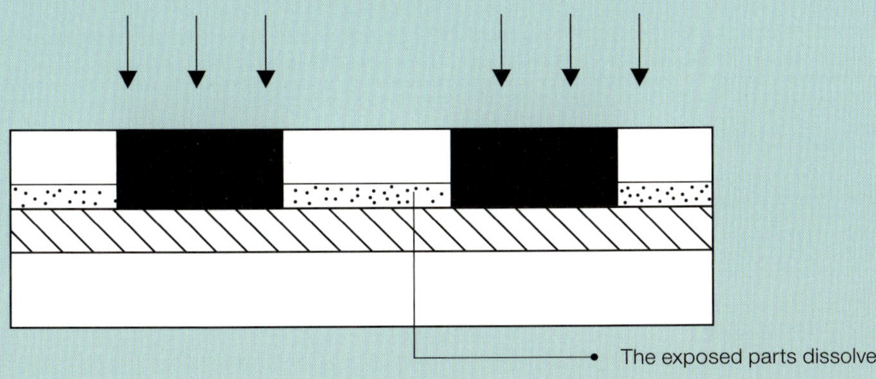

3 Developing

The developer bath is a weak alkaline solution. The exposed area of photosensitive resin (positive film PS plates) layer is removed. The unexposed area of ink-receptive photosensitive resin remains.

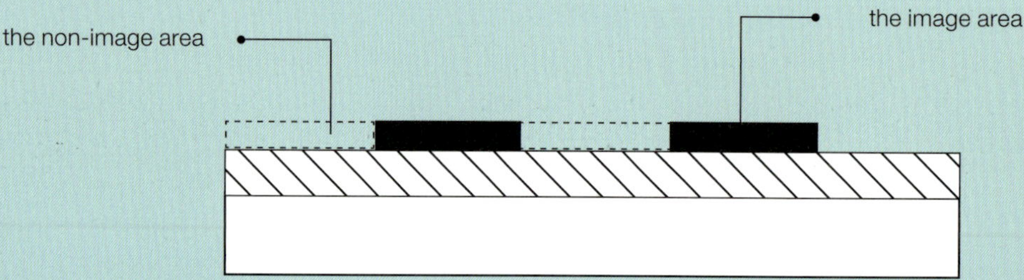

4 Rinsing

Rinse the plate in water to remove the remaining bath of developer.

5 Drying

Remove the water on the surface of the plate.

6 Finishing

Remove the extra photosensitive resin. Scrub the plate gently with clear water or cleansing paste.

7 Burning

Bake the plate in the whirler machine, with a steady temperature of 230°C~250°C for 5 to 8 minutes in order to make the plate more durable.

8 Coating

The plate is coated with a solution of Gum Arabic to ensure the water loving property of the plate is protected.

7 Printing Process

Studio: Supergraphic

Designer: Bill Fick & Brian Garner

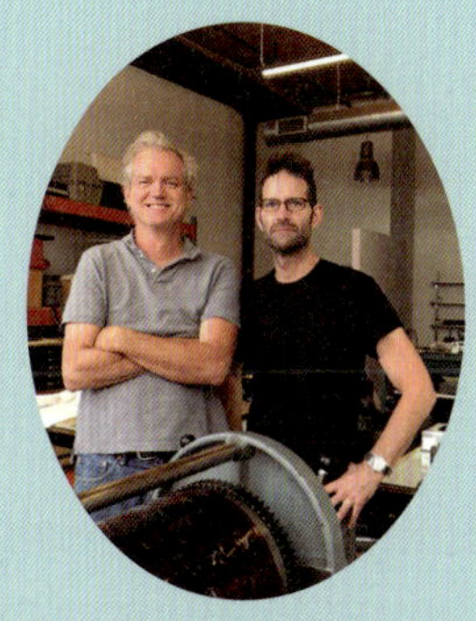

Located in Durham, North Carolina, Supergraphic is a contract print studio owned by Printmaker Bill Fick and Master Printer Brian Garner. The studio is dedicated to the production of fine art prints, with expertise in lithography, relief prints, screen prints, and etchings. For its latest project, Supergraphic cooperated with artist David Brown to produce lithographic prints, through which the technique of offset printing was used.

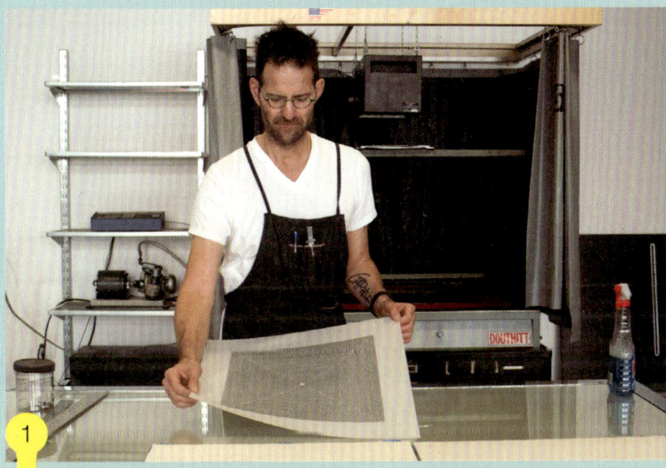

1 Master printer Brian Garner is inspecting David Brown's oil-based, ink pen drawing on a sheet of frosted Mylar (a polyester film). The image on the Mylar will be exposed on to the photo positive lithographic plate.

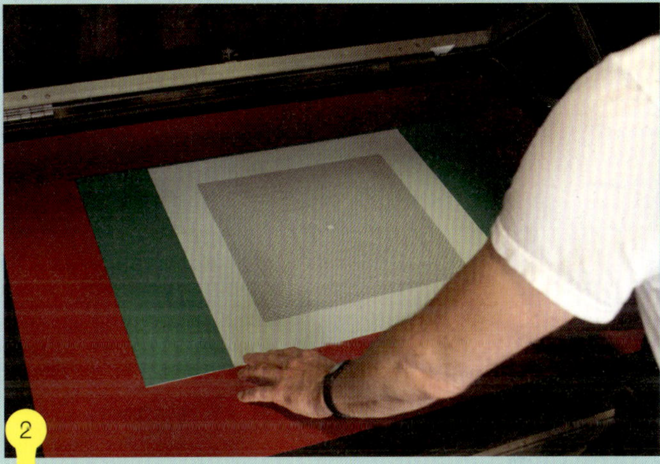

2 Placing the Mylar on to the unexposed photo-positive lithographic metal plate.

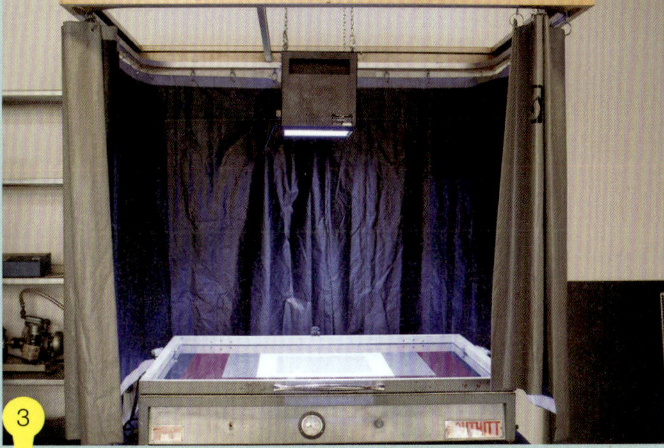

3 Exposing the plate to ultra violet light on the exposure unit. The exposure time is 60 seconds.

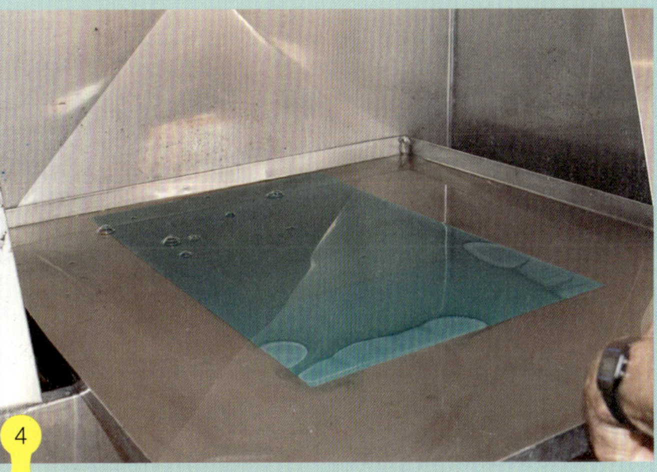

4 Processing the plate in a bath of developer. This usually takes about 60 seconds.

Photo by Supergraphic

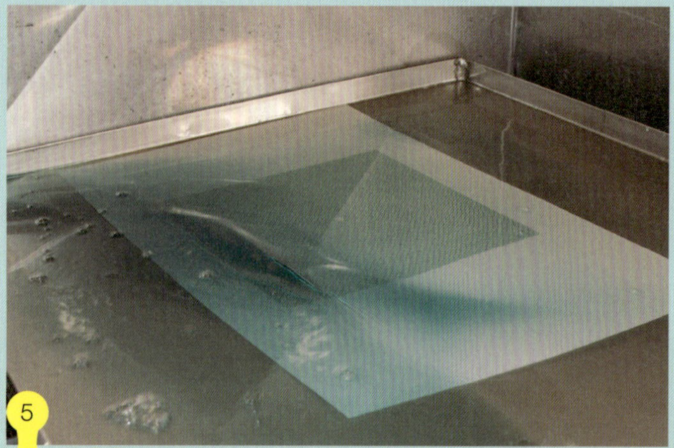

5

During image developing, the non-image area will dissolve and be removed from the plate, while the image area remains.

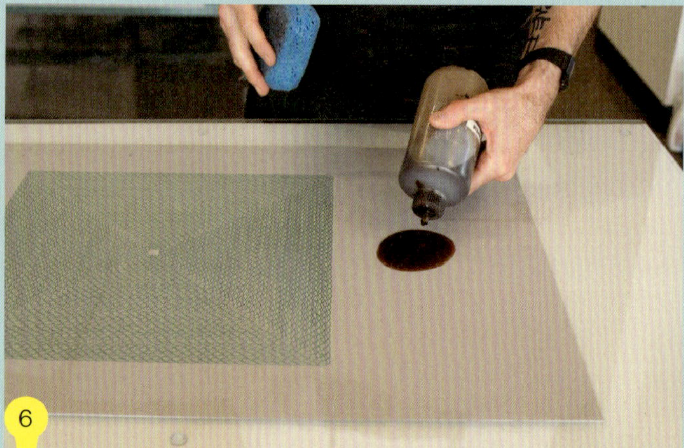

6

Dispensing the gum Arabic. This will desensitize the non-image area, enabling it to become hydrophilic, and at the same time make the photo emulsion receptive to the ink.

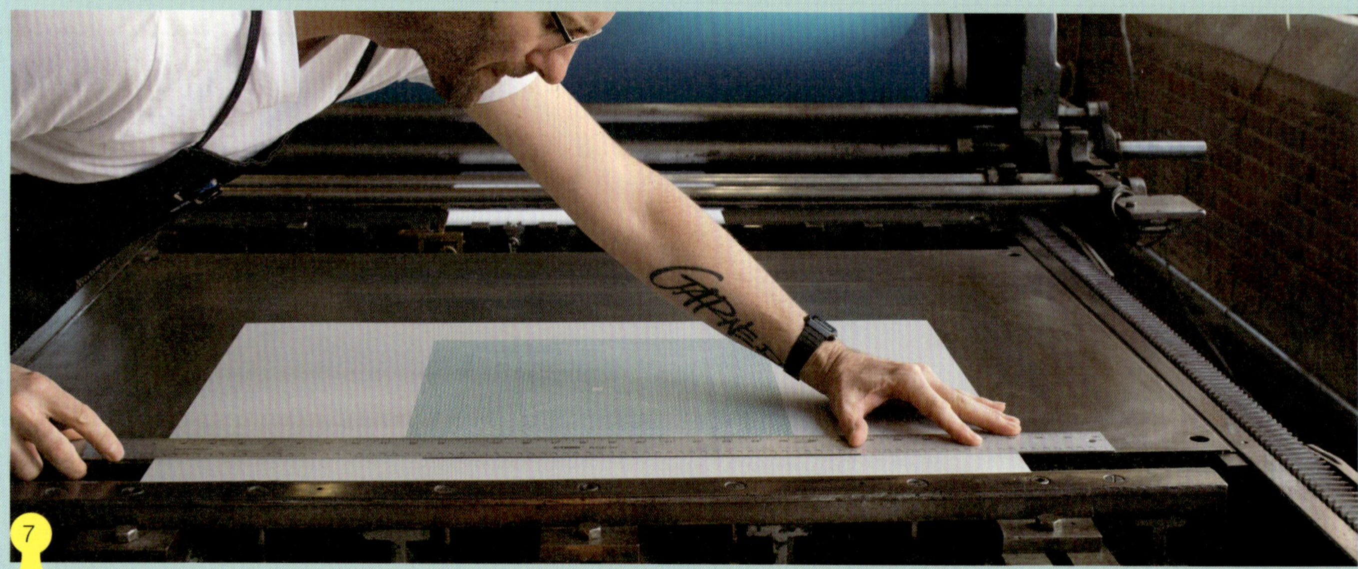

7

Registering the plate on the offset press.

Rolling the ink out on to the palette.

8

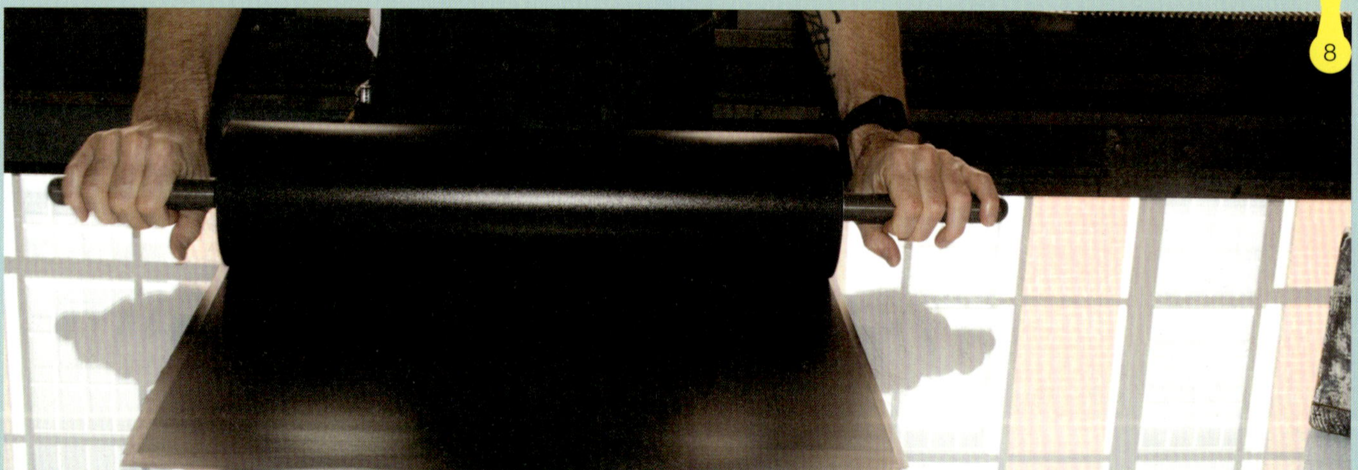

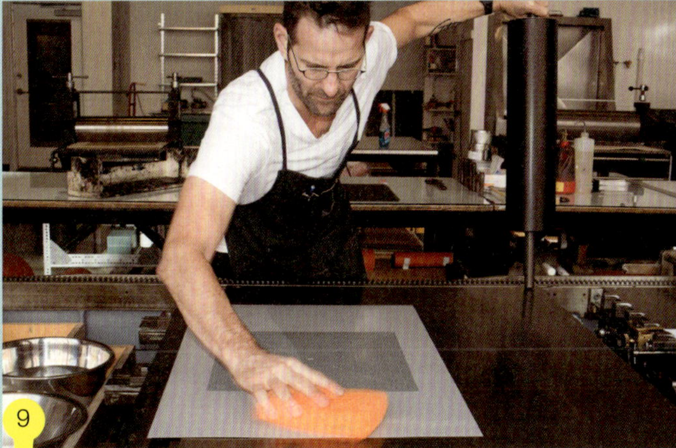

9

The plate is sponged with a thin film of water to create a hydrophobic barrier in the non image areas, which make sure no ink adheres to non-image area.

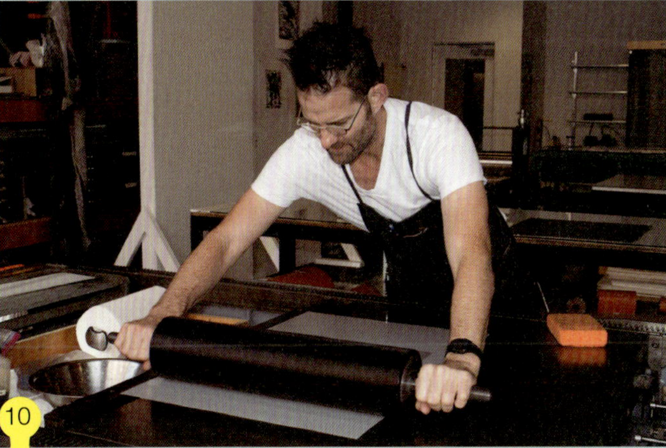

10

Rolling ink on to the plate.

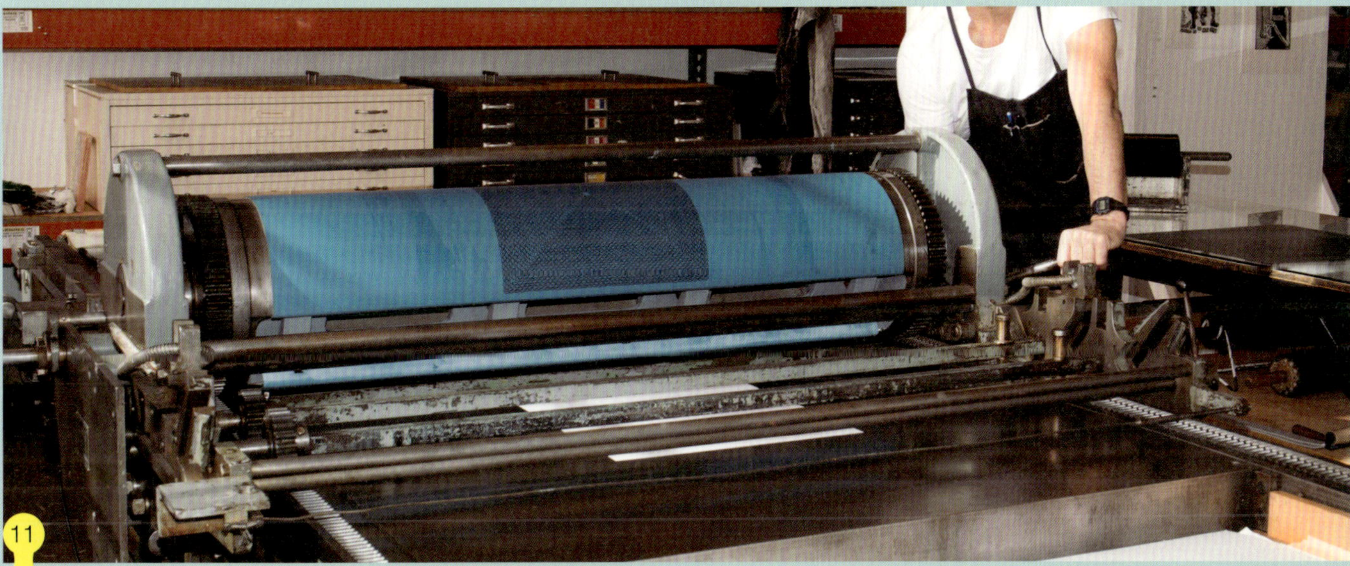

11

Printing the plate using the offset press. The image has been offset on to blue rubber blanket and will be deposited on the sheet of paper.

The printed image on paper.

12

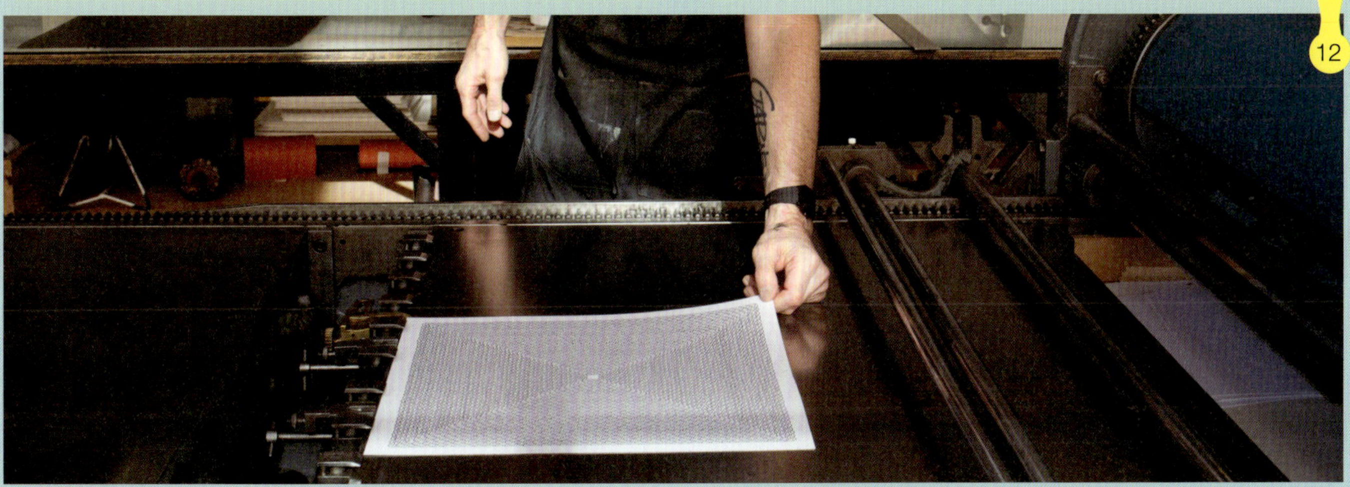

8	Printed Works
	: Substrates
	: Printing Inks
	D : Design

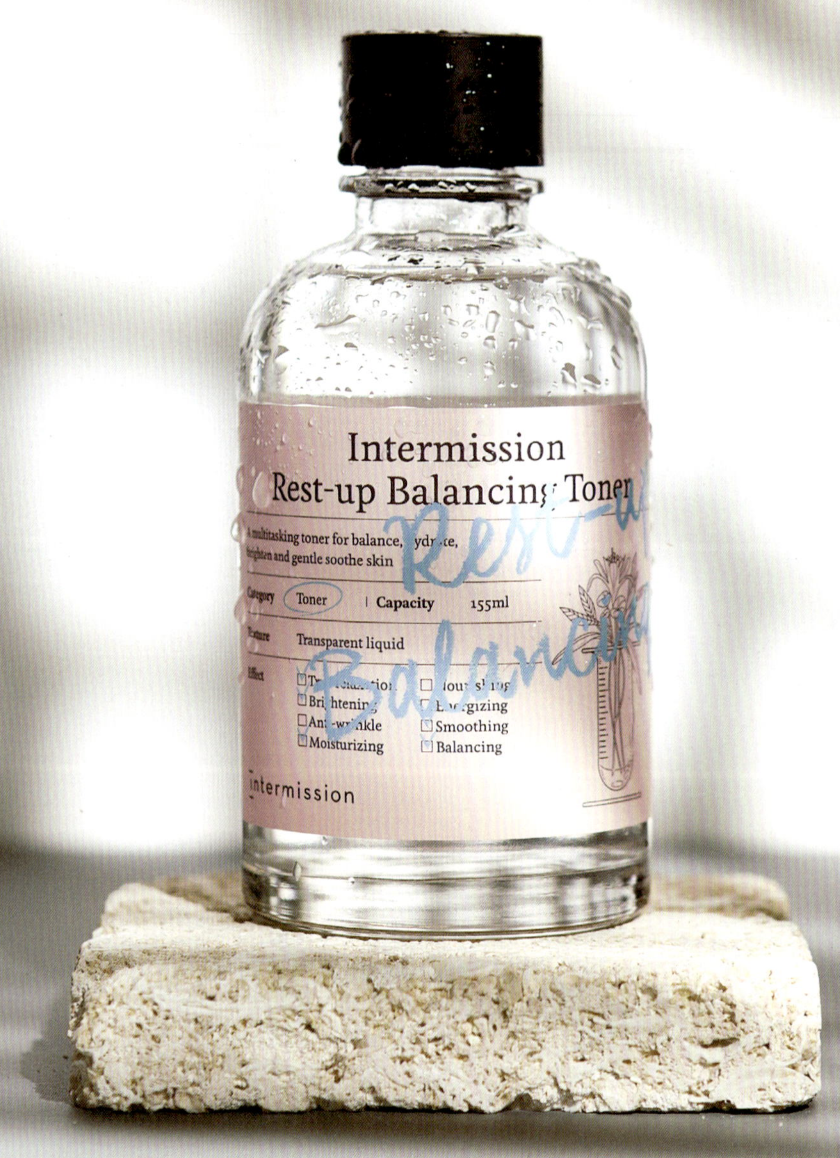

Intermission Branding & Packaging

300g TNB Paper, Moolim Paper

This brand identity is designed for a brand-new skincare brand Intermission: a brand belonging to a cosmetic company. Considering the balance of emotional and functional benefits of the product, CFC developed a symbol with a test tube and flower: each representing science and emotion. They also created a packaging system with the same concept: systematic charts for science, calligraphic letters for emotion.

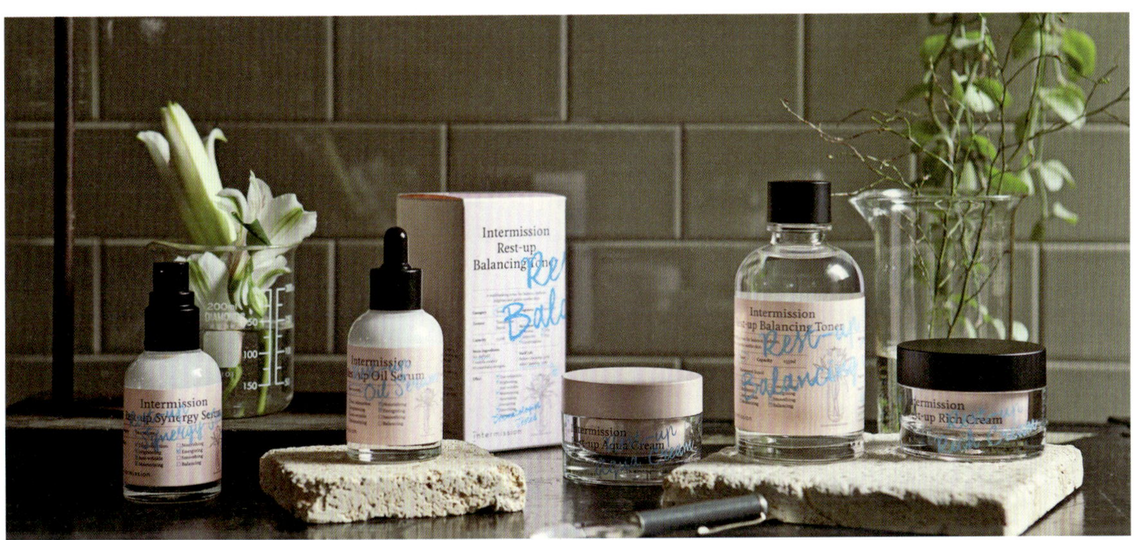

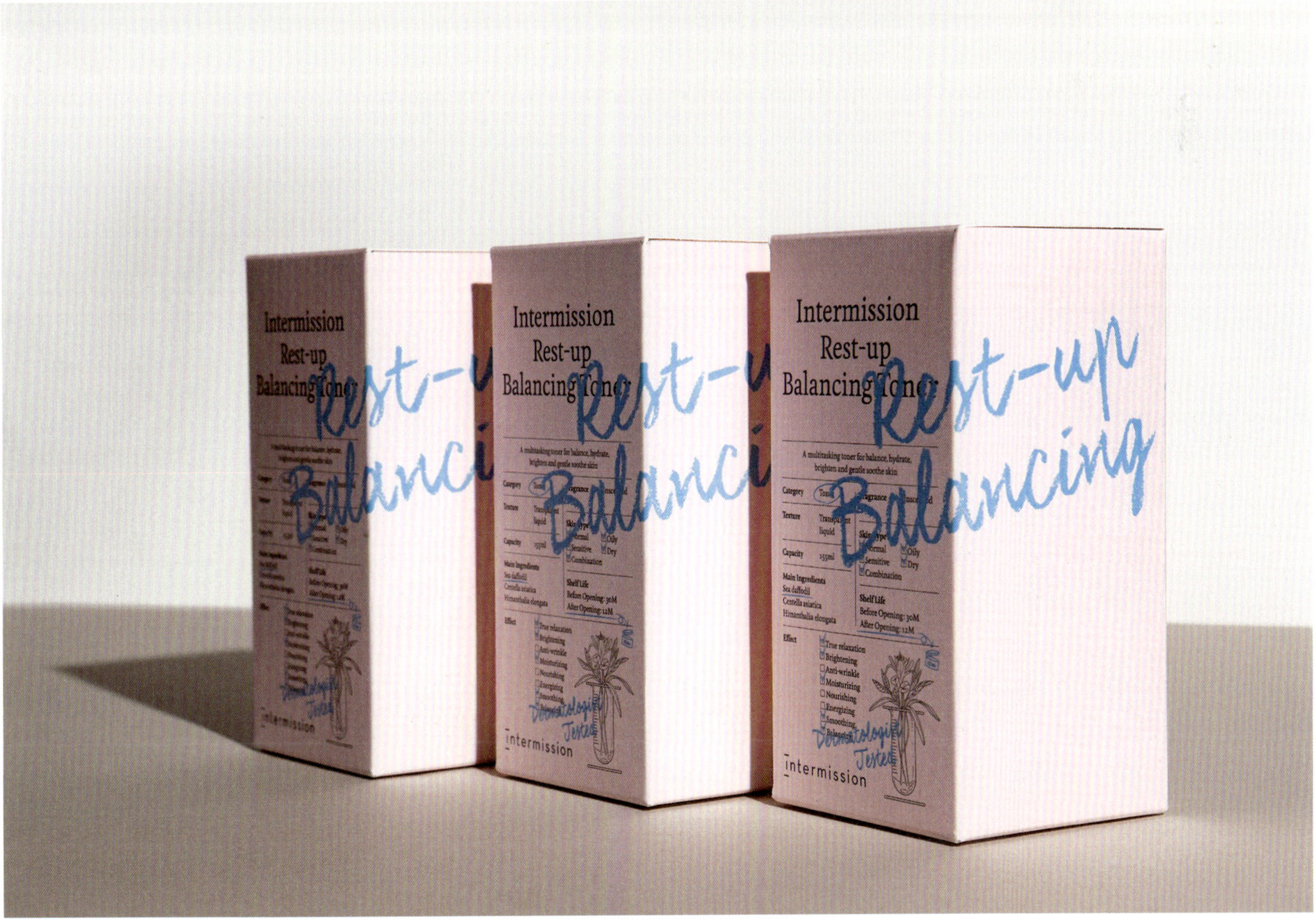

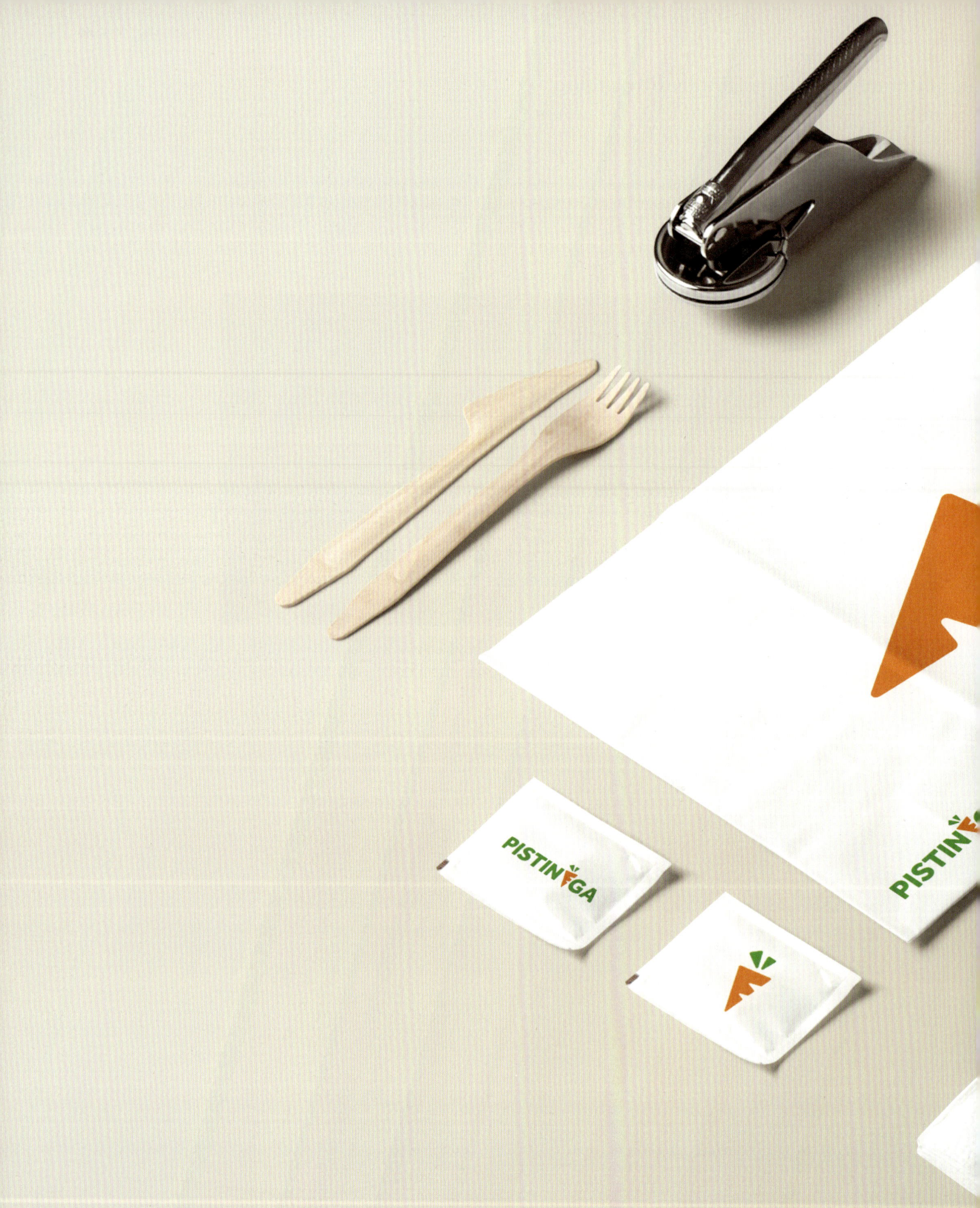
PISTINEGA

Pistinèga

The designer was invited to define the identity of Pistinèga, a specialized juices bar recently opened in the Italian city of Bologna. "Pistinèga" is a word used in the Bolognese dialect to name the carrot. The Pistinèga logo merges the "È" of Pistinèga's carrot and juice drink and refers to the most representative aspects of the bar. The resulting logo is a clean and fun design, where orange and green colors are consistently used. Different materials made for Pistinèga have been printed in several ways to exalt the final result. The designer has supervised the print team to keep the color rendering under control. The colors used are Pantone P 154-8 (green) and Pantone P 20-8 (orange).

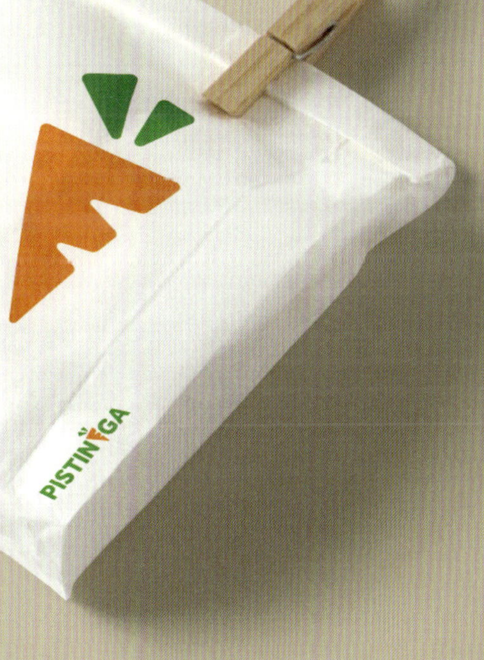

D: Maurizio Pagnozzi

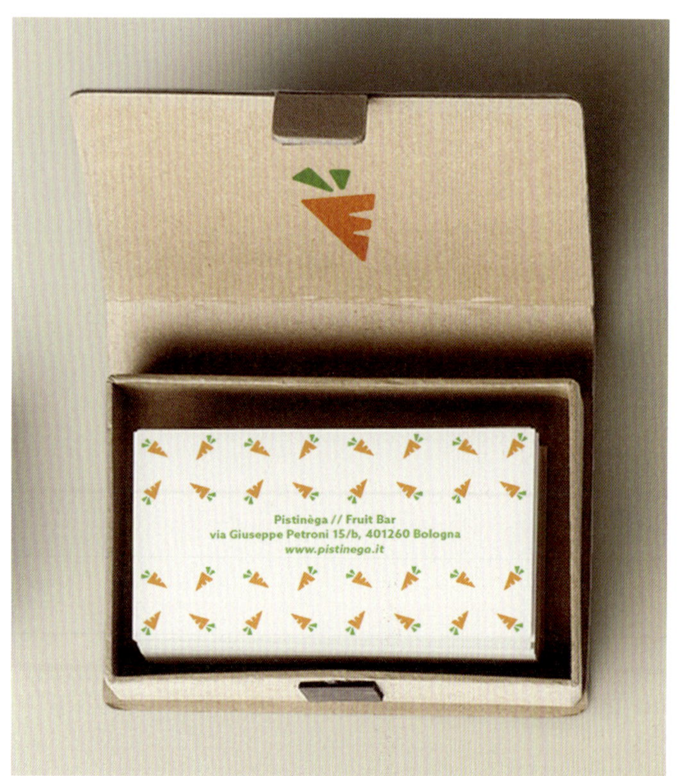
Pistinèga // Fruit Bar
via Giuseppe Petroni 15/b, 401260 Bologna
www.pistinega.it

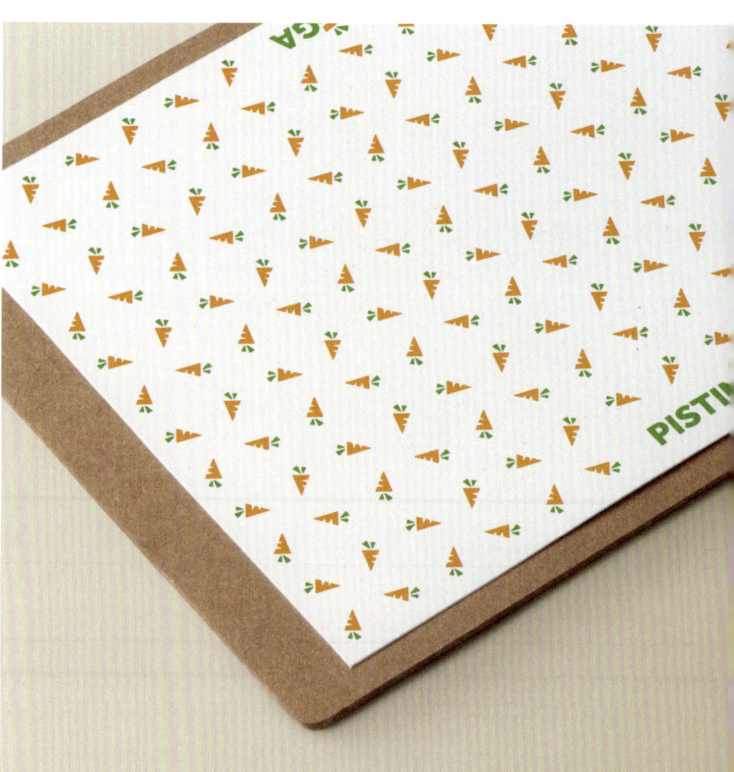

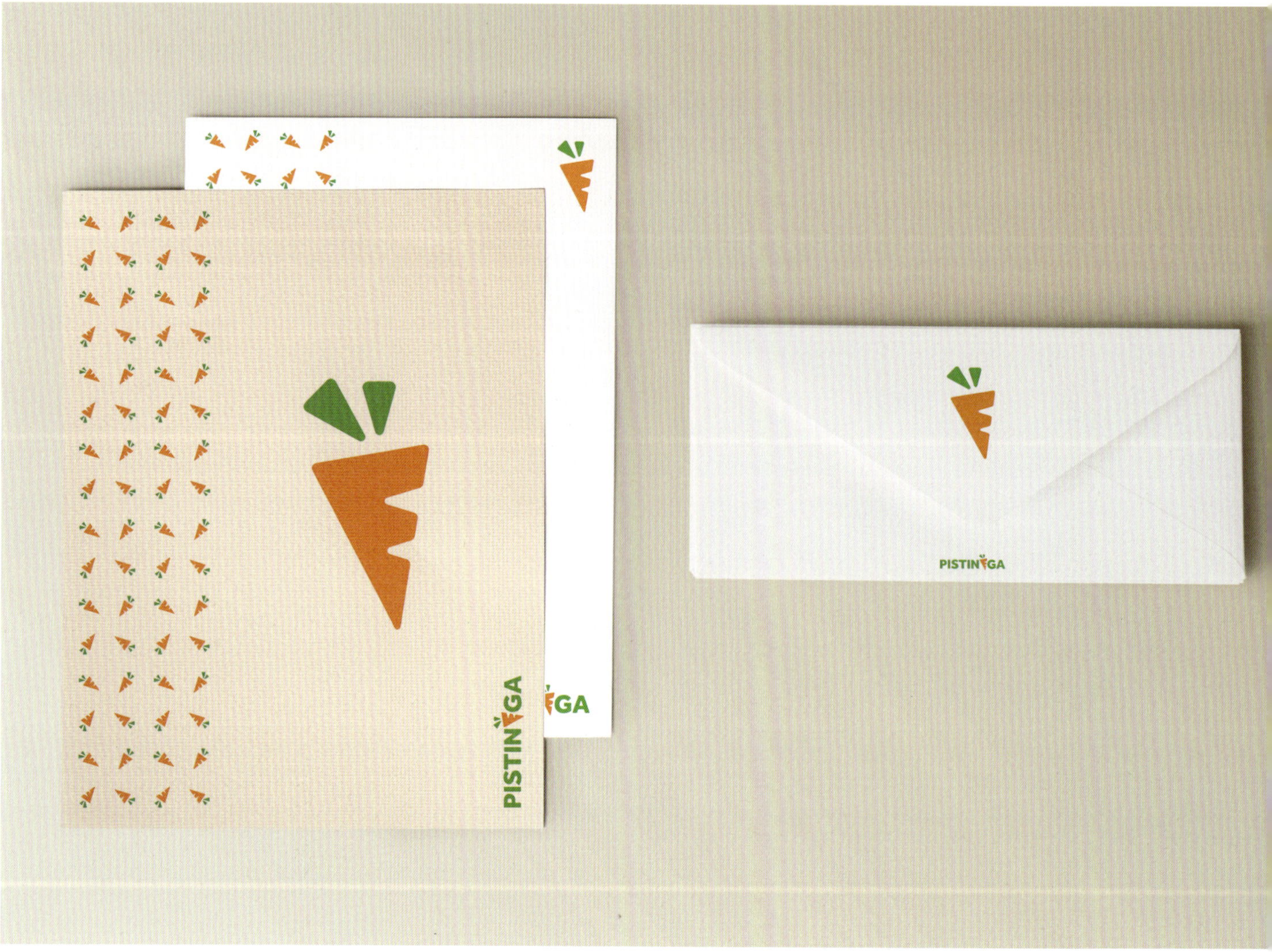

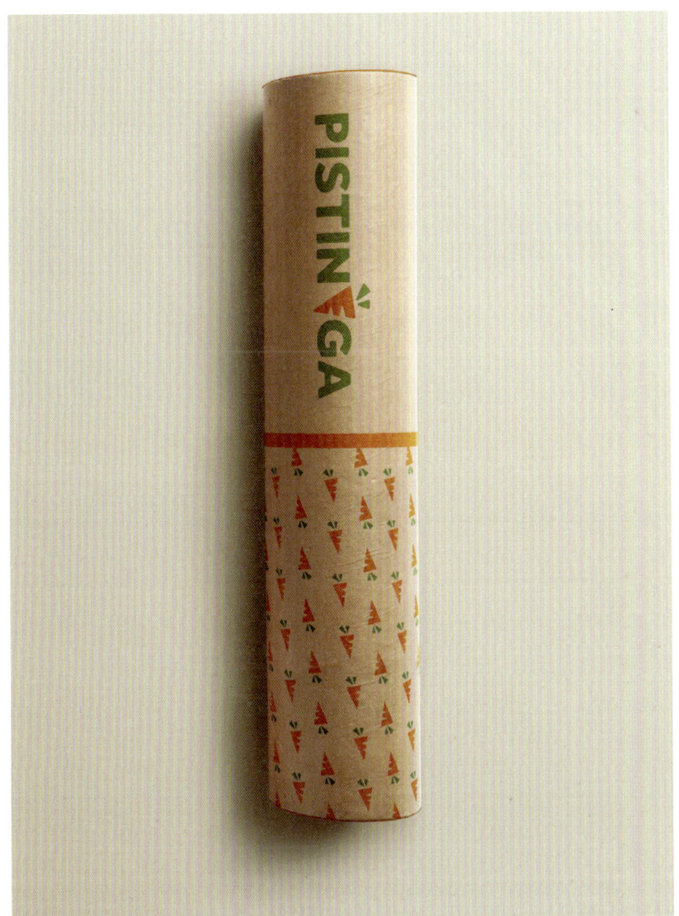
PISTIN GA

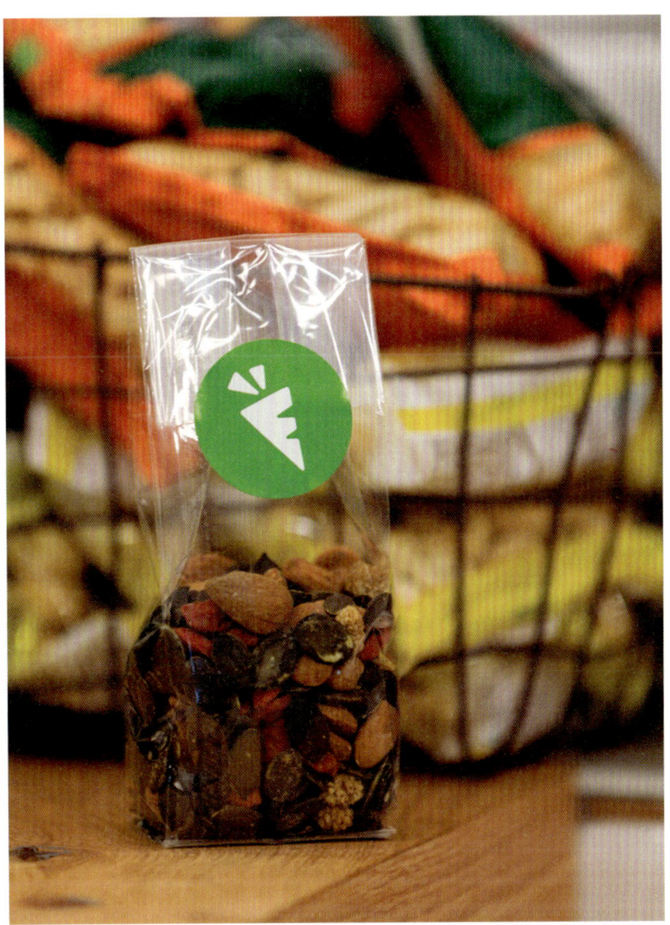

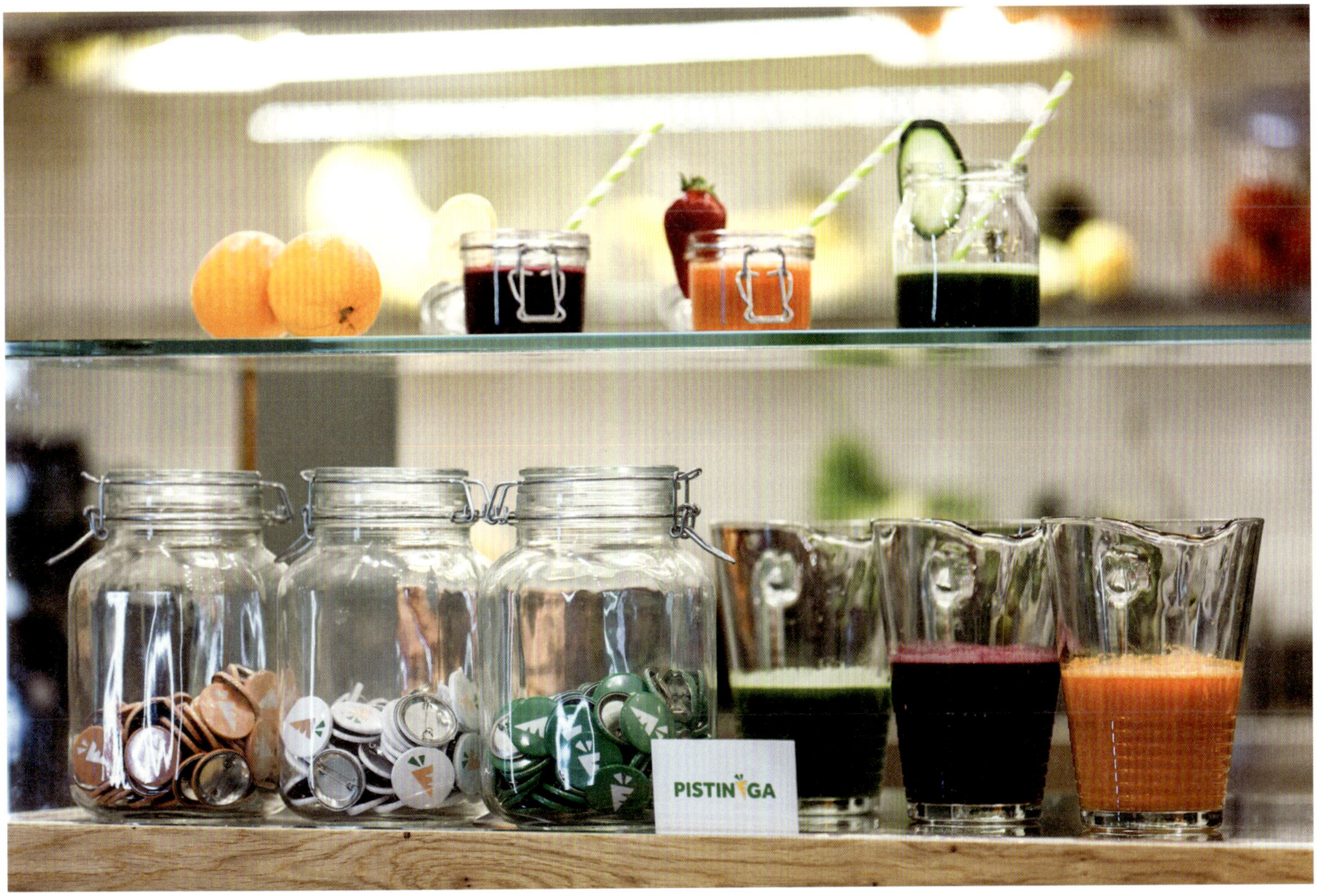

Jinnam Agricultural Corporation

Located in Munkyung-Si, South Korea, Jinnam Agricultural Corporation is a company producing fermented food, such as soybean paste and chili paste. Established in 1915 by Bong Seon Lee, Jinnam has been sincerely making their products with fresh ingredients harvested from their village. Inspired by the scenery of Munkyung, the designer drew an imaginary village where people are working at farms to make high quality products. The village was drawn based on two Korean letters, "Jin" and "Nam." The package and promotional items are printed in offset printing. Embossing is applied on promotional brochures to show the name of brand. Gold foil appears on labels and boxes, which make the design really shine.

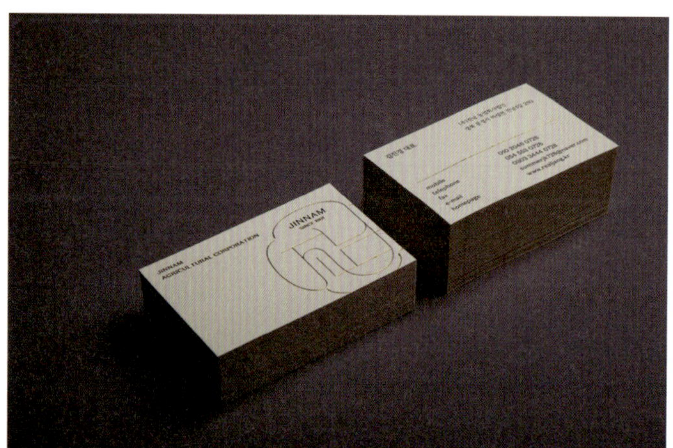

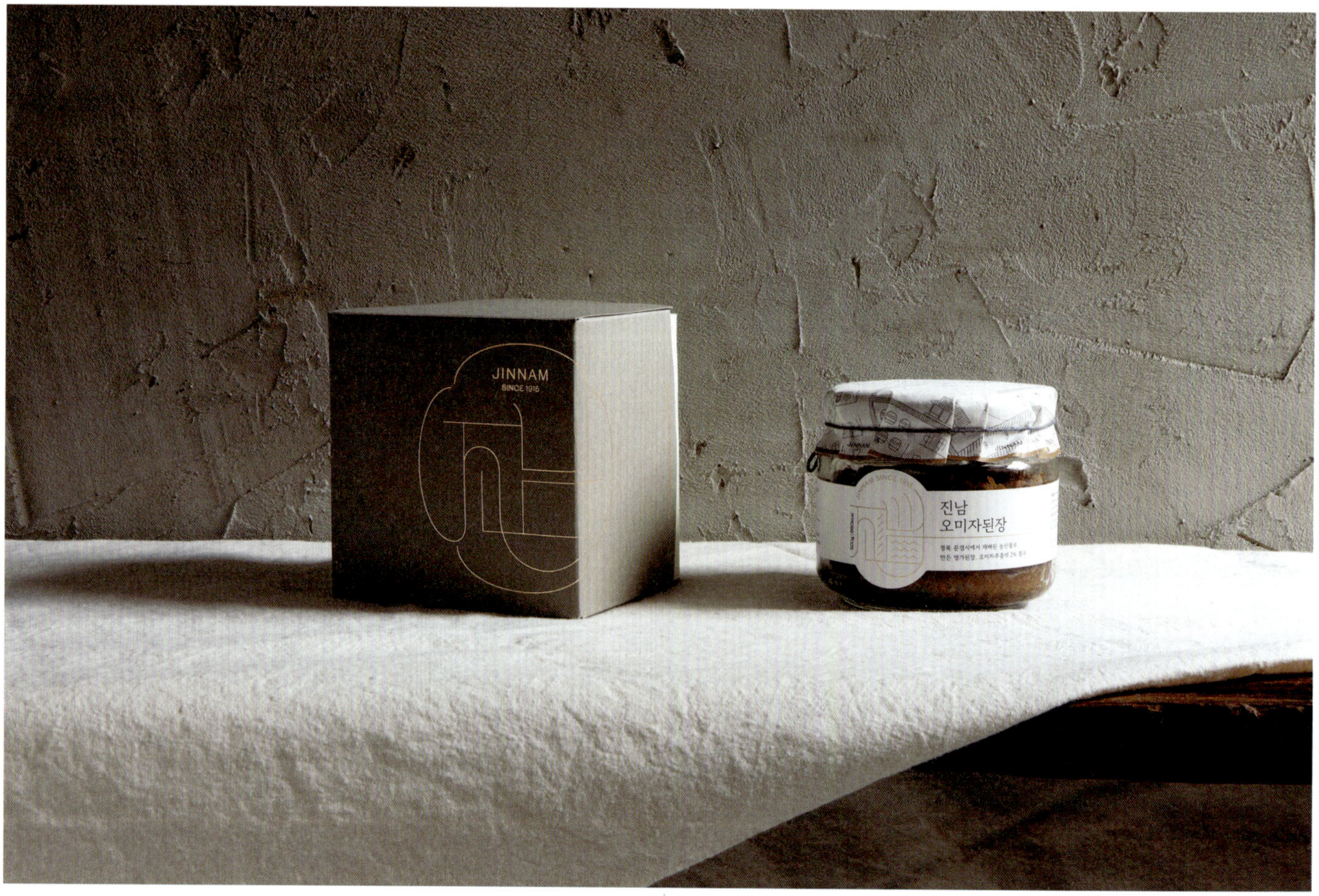

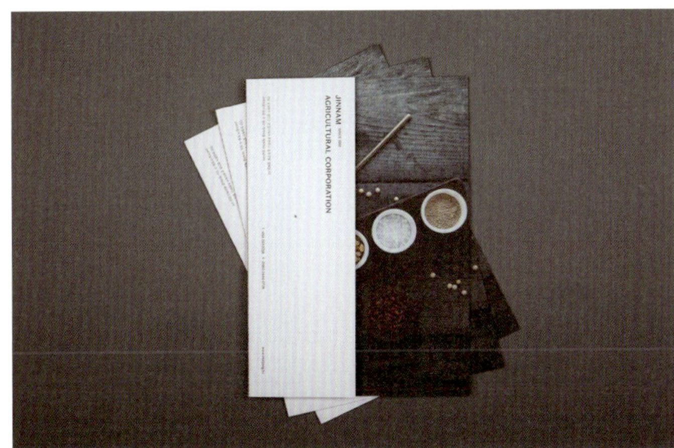
JINNAM
AGRICULTURAL CORPORATION

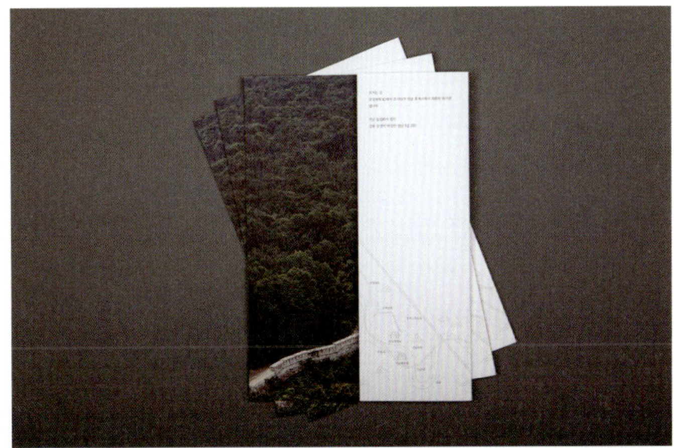

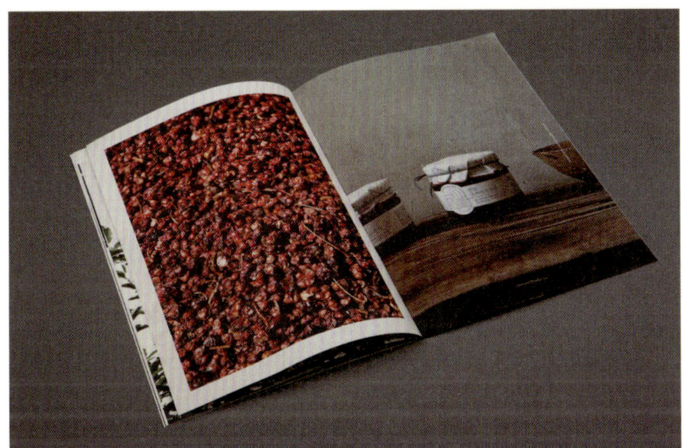

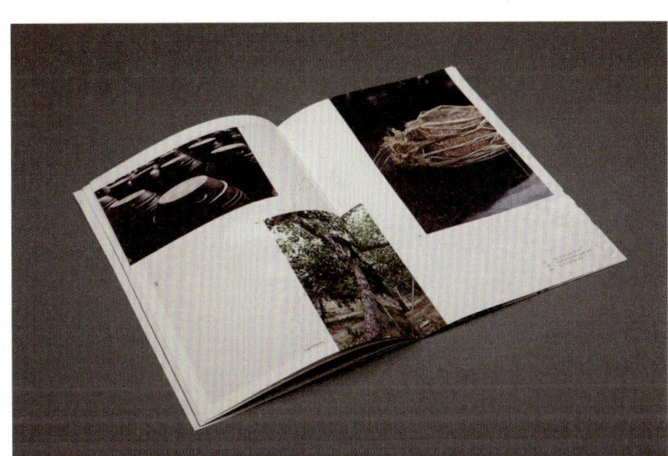

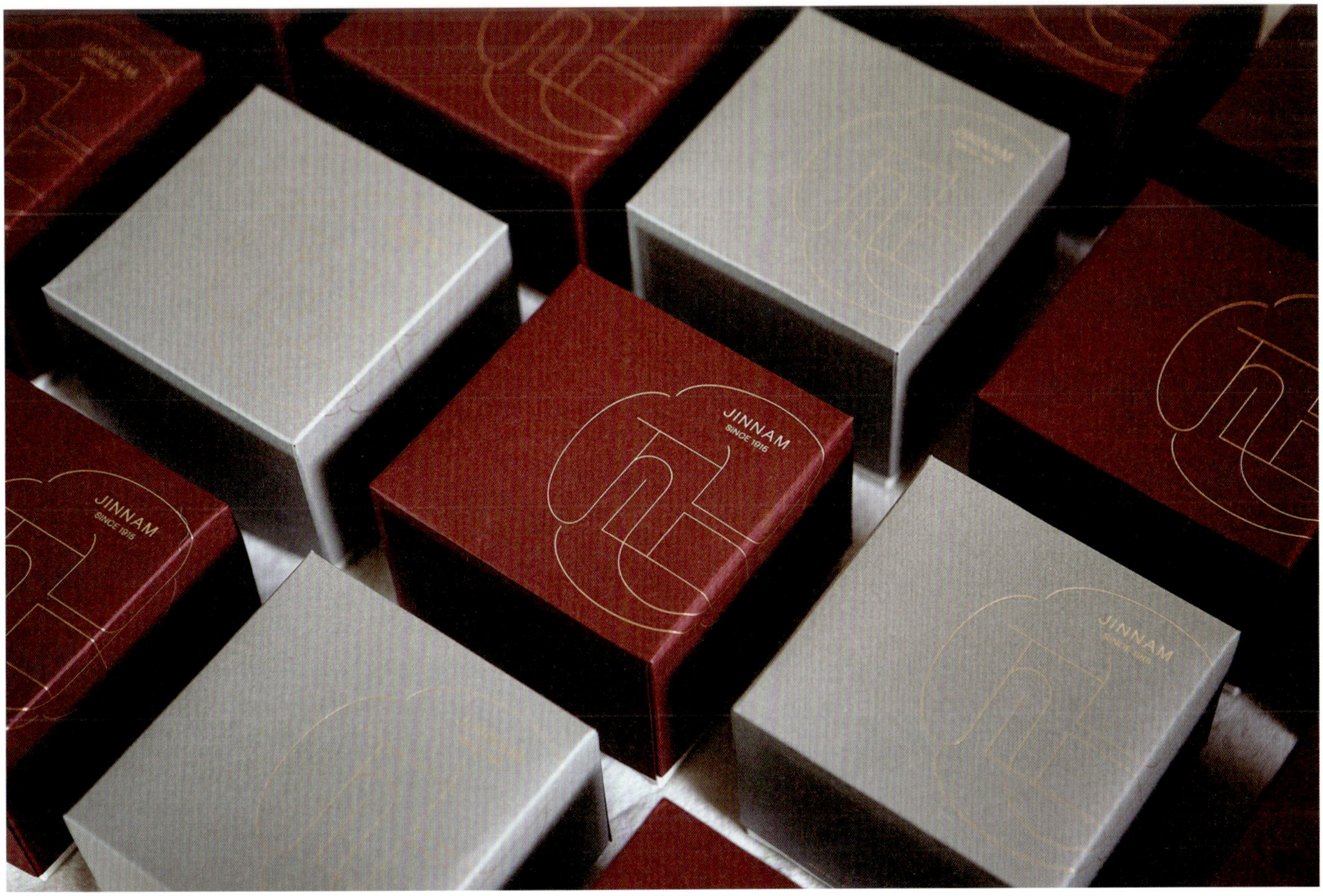

Taipei Metro / Year of the Monkey Commemorative Tickets

- PVC plastic, specialty papers
- Pantone spot color, gold foil

To celebrate the 20th anniversary of the Taipei Metro system, this One-Day Pass Ticket design features 20 unique city images with 20 Taiwan macaque monkeys looking for celestial peaches. In Taiwanese culture peaches represents longevity, and 2016 is the Year of the Monkey according to the Chinese zodiac. 20 Taipei city spots, depicted in a semi-abstract style with minimal forms and vivid colors, reflect the lively and bustling atmosphere of Chinese New Year.

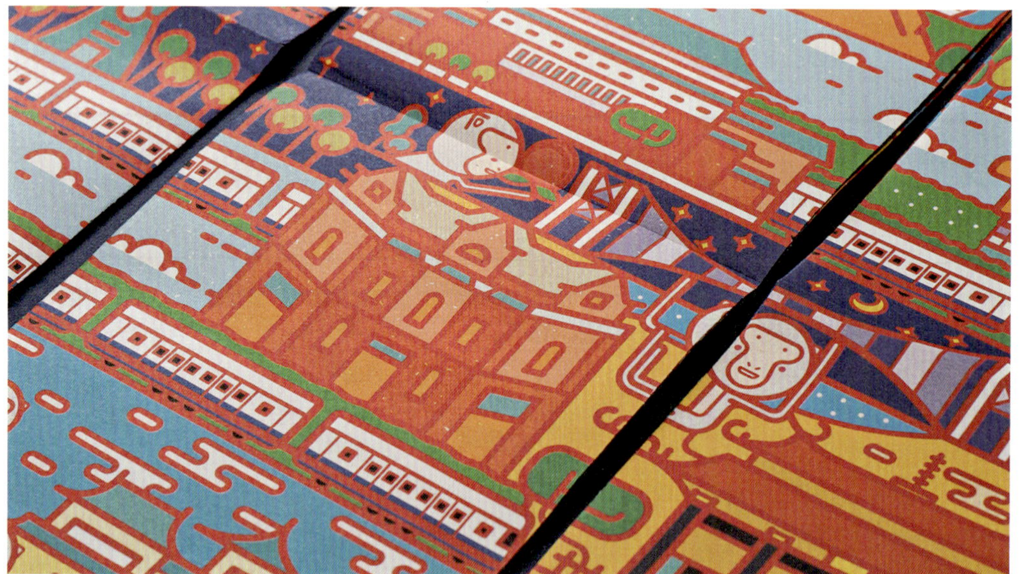

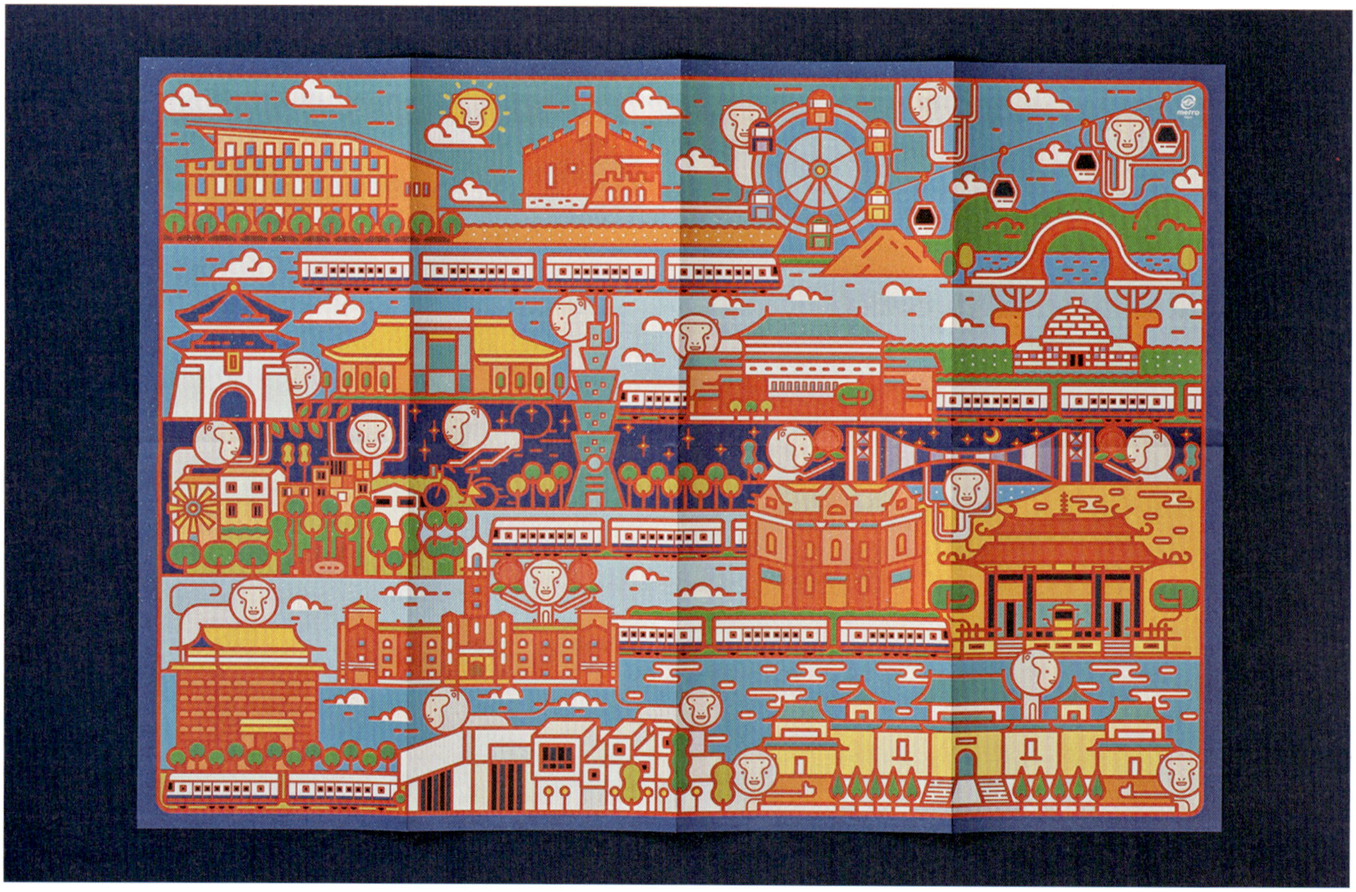

D: Kuocheng Liao & Midnight Design

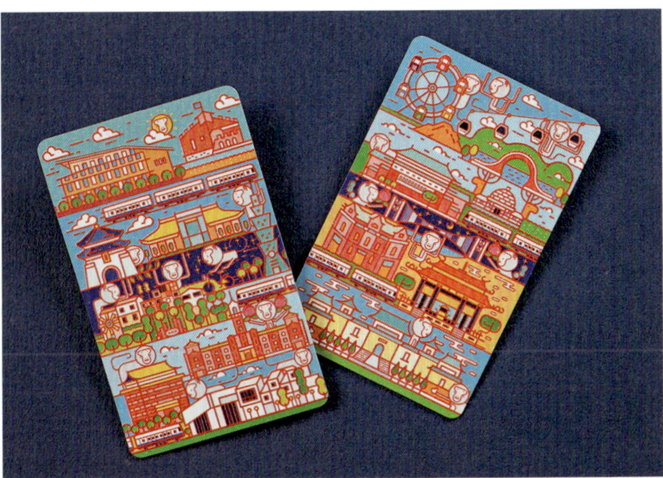

Card #01—Taipei Public Library Beitou Branch, Fort San Domingo, Chiang Kai-shek Memorial Hall, Sun Yat-sen Memorial Hall, Daan Forest Park & Treasure Hill International Art Village, Taipei 101, The Grand Hotel Taipei, Presidential Office Building, Taipei Fine Arts Museum

Card #02—Taipei Children's Amusement Park, Taipei Maokong Gondola & Dahu Park, Taipei Zoo & Taipei Botanical Garden, National Museum of History, Bitandiao Bridge, Ximen Red House, Mengjia Longshan Temple, and National Palace Museum.

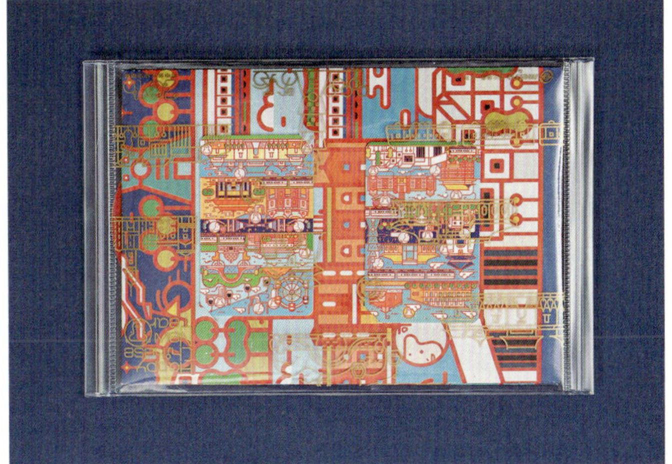

The package design references the tradition of Chinese New Year, during which eating candies is said to bring good luck and fortune. The front side of the packaging tells the story of macaque monkeys looking for celestial peaches, with the images printed in metallic gold, considered the luckiest color for the New Year, echoing the festive tone and adding fine details.

The contents include various sizes of posters, New Year couplets, and red envelopes. The multi-layered package design not only looks festive, but its vivid color palette also evokes an energetic and bright mood for imagining the great happiness of embracing the Chinese New Year.

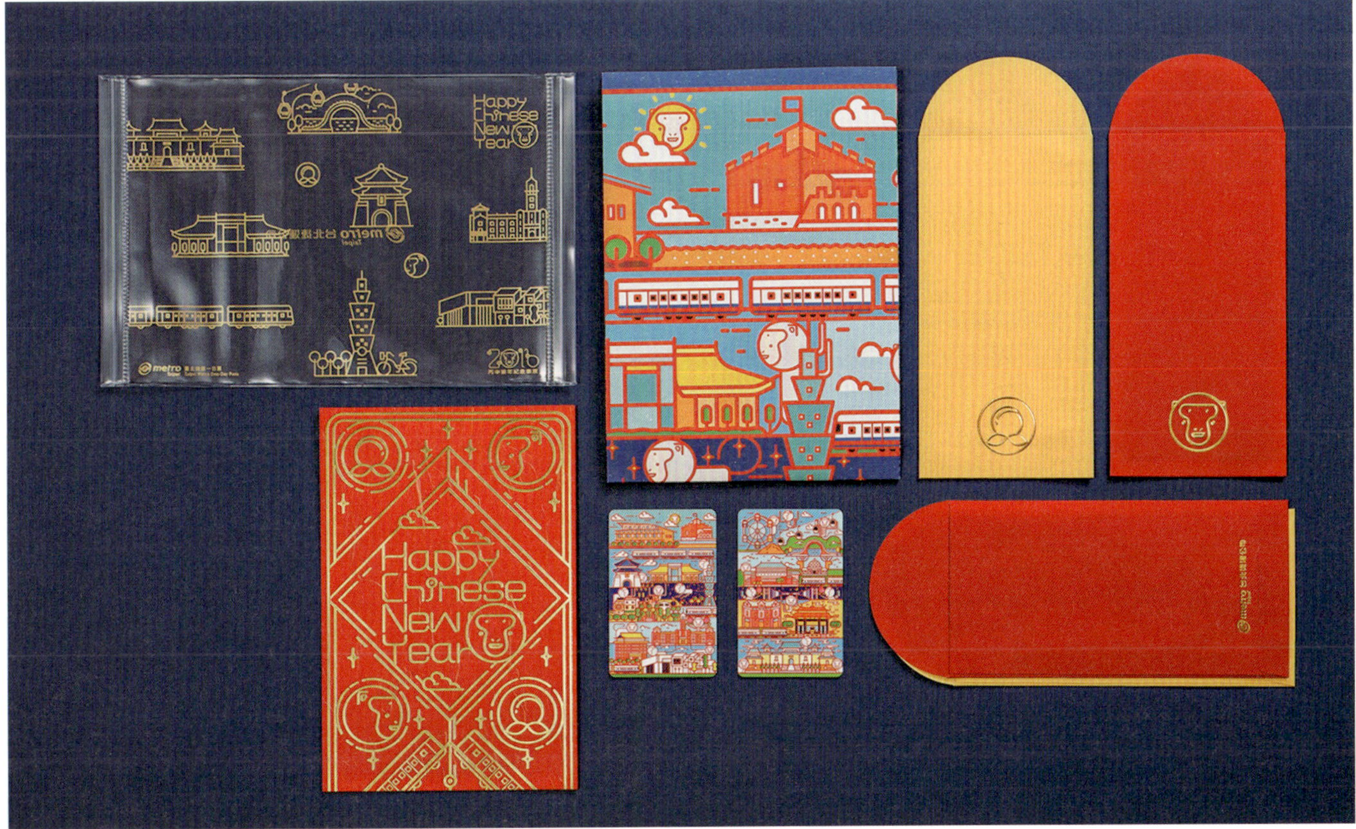

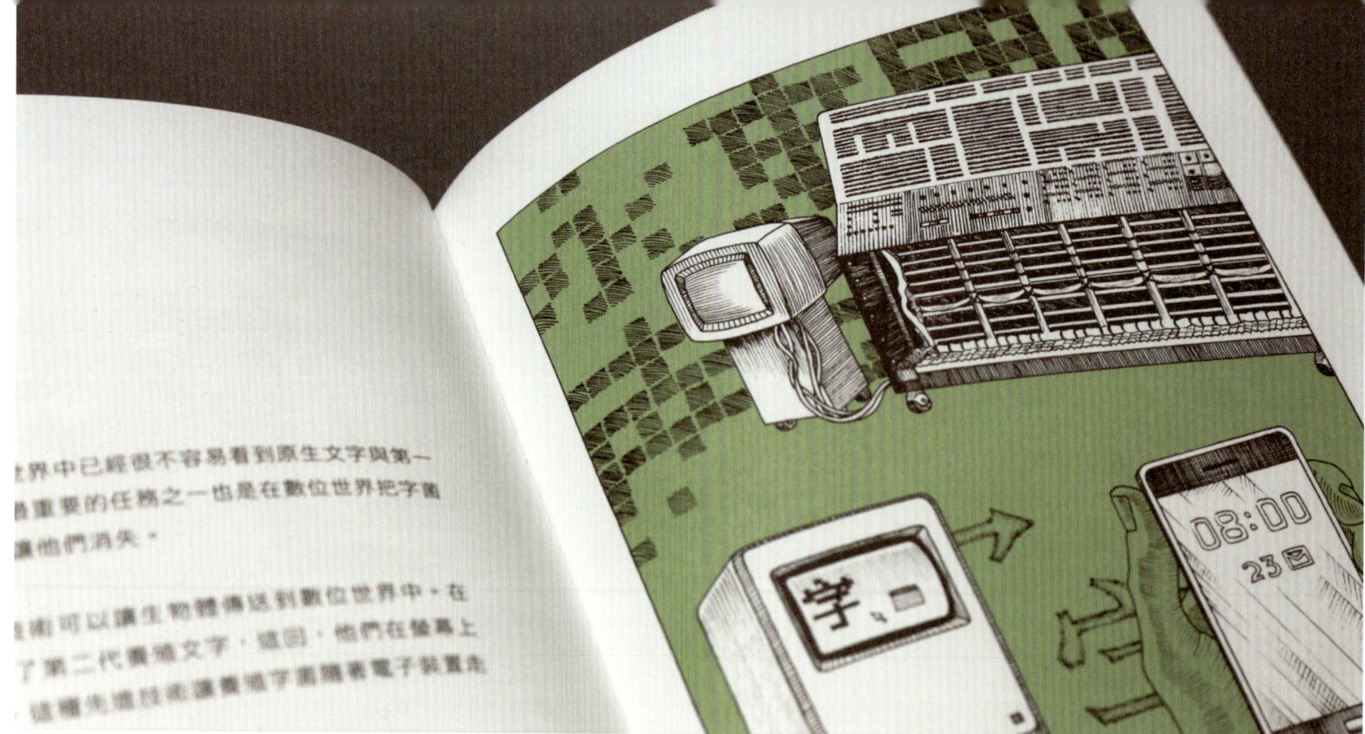

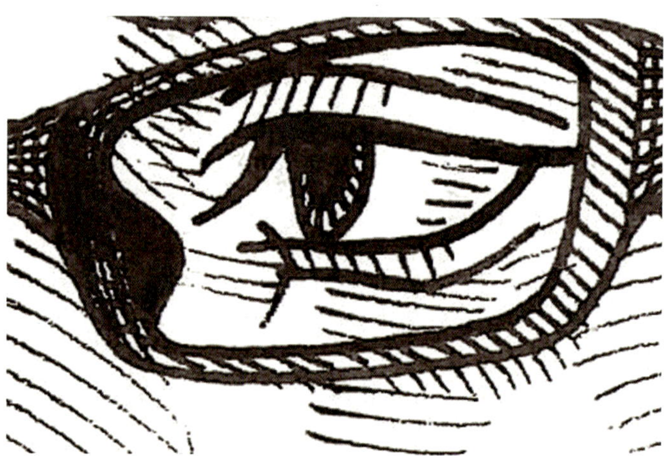

Scaned by platform type scanner

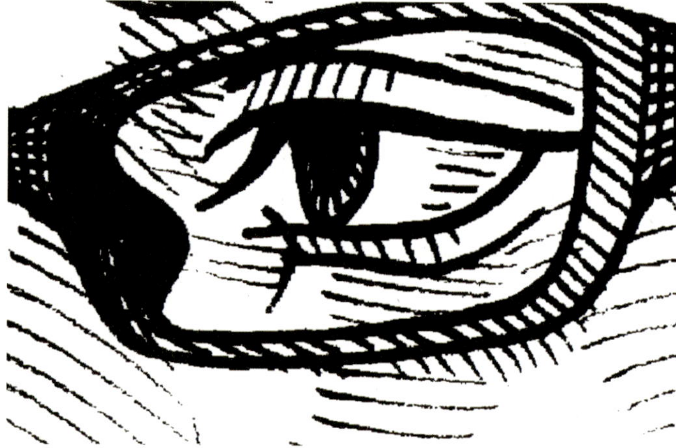

Scaned by roller type scanner

Story of Chinese Fonts

Cover: 158g white kraft paper; Inside page: 147g wood-free paper

Pantone 773 U, black ink

Story of Chinese Fonts is a complimentary book for the customer who has made a donation to Justfont's* new font. In order to present the key visual in the best printing result, the staff used a high-class roller scanning machine to scan the illustrations and convert them to digital files, then rearranged them. Smooth and non-reflective wood-free papers were used as inner sheets, whereas the cover was made from white kraft paper. The spot color is green. Before it is pulled into the ink fountain, it has to be changed a little. Based on the color of paper, a clean and saturated printing will result.

*Justfont: a Taiwan-based organization dedicates to Chinese web font.

D: Jesé graphic and printing design Co. Ltd

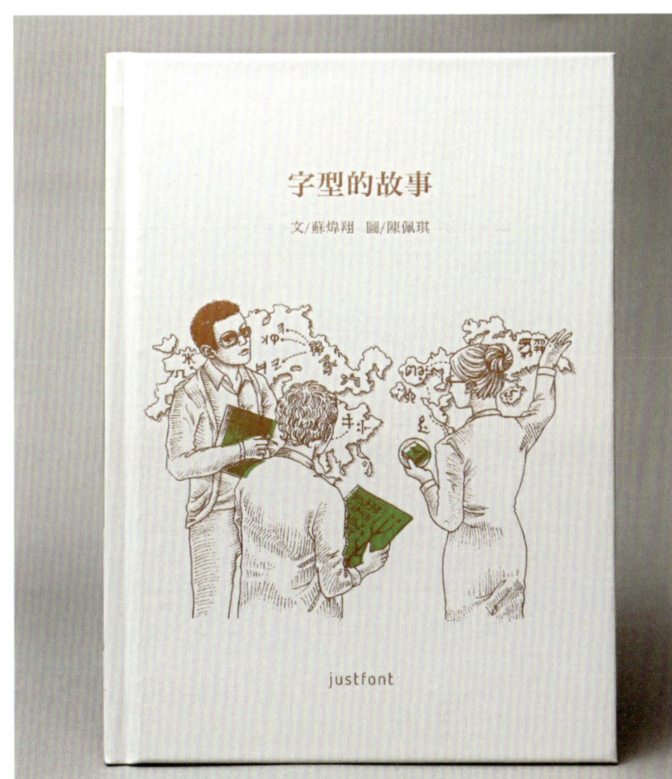
字型的故事
文/蘇煒翔 圖/陳佩琪
justfont

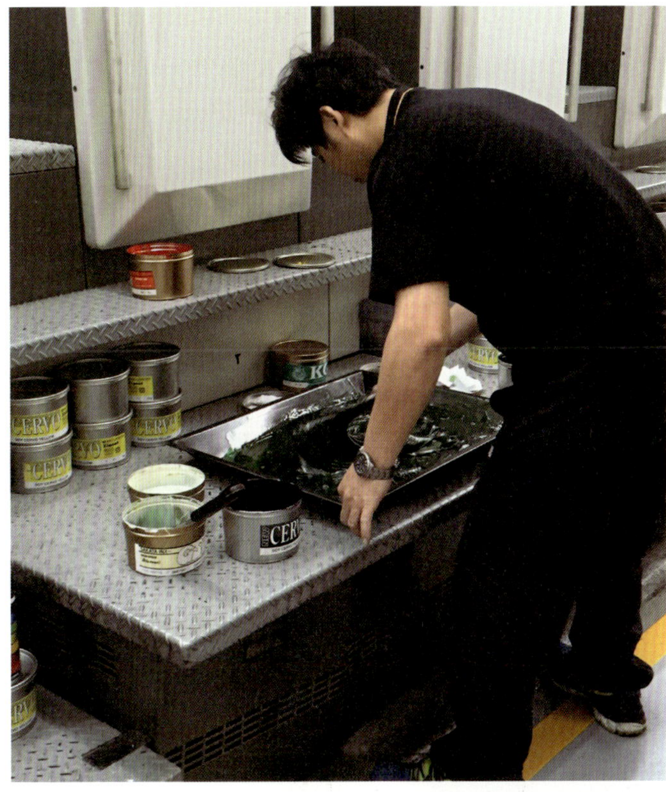

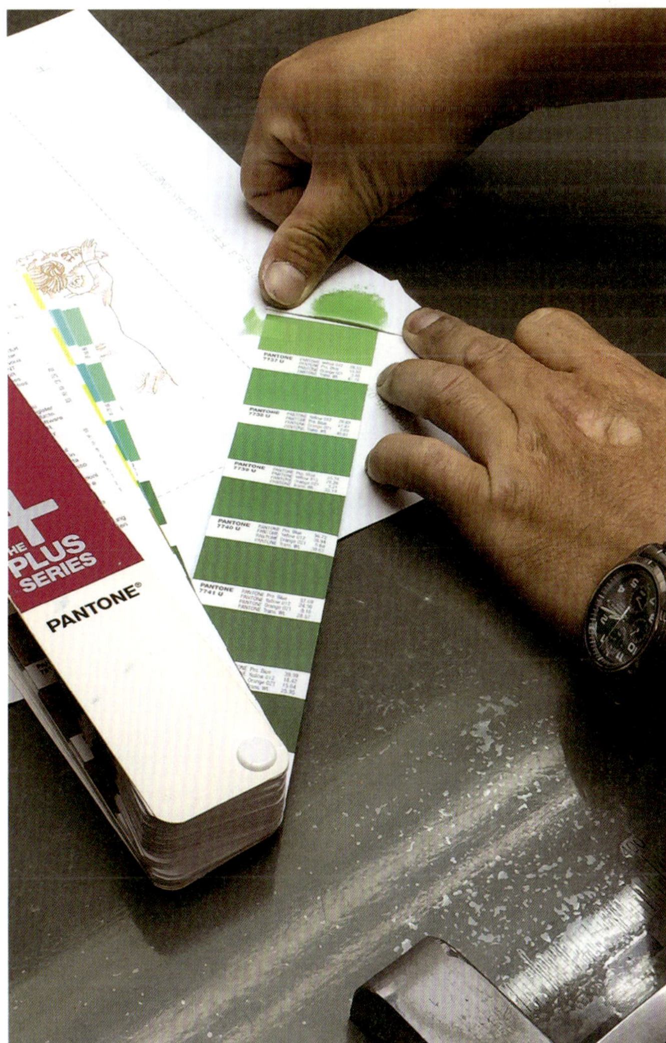
THE PLUS SERIES
PANTONE

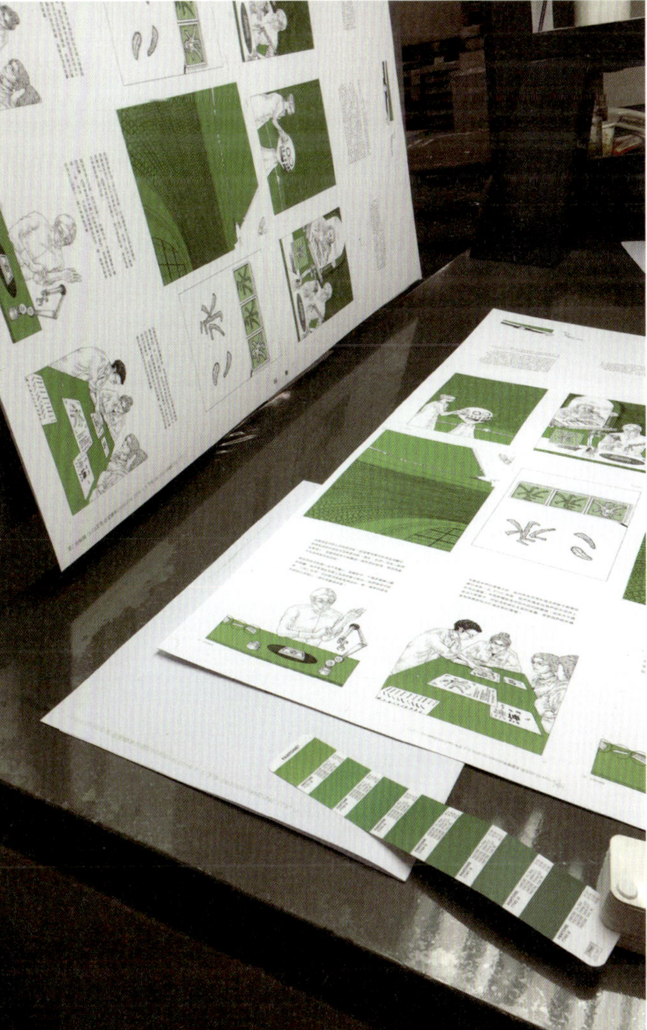

P.S. - Secrets of the Barguzin Skeleton

Cyclus Offset paper, Eksa cardboard

Pantone 2736, BLACK, UV

This book is about the discovery of a skeleton that may belong to the Hungarian poet Sándor Petőfi. It provides an overview of the related events and documents. The design was inspired by spy stories in which secret information can be made visible only under UV light. Similarly, the reader can go on a hunt for secrets in this book. It consists of three layers: the actual story, articles from the time of the discovery, and the UV layer, which contains handwritten comments and annotations by the author.

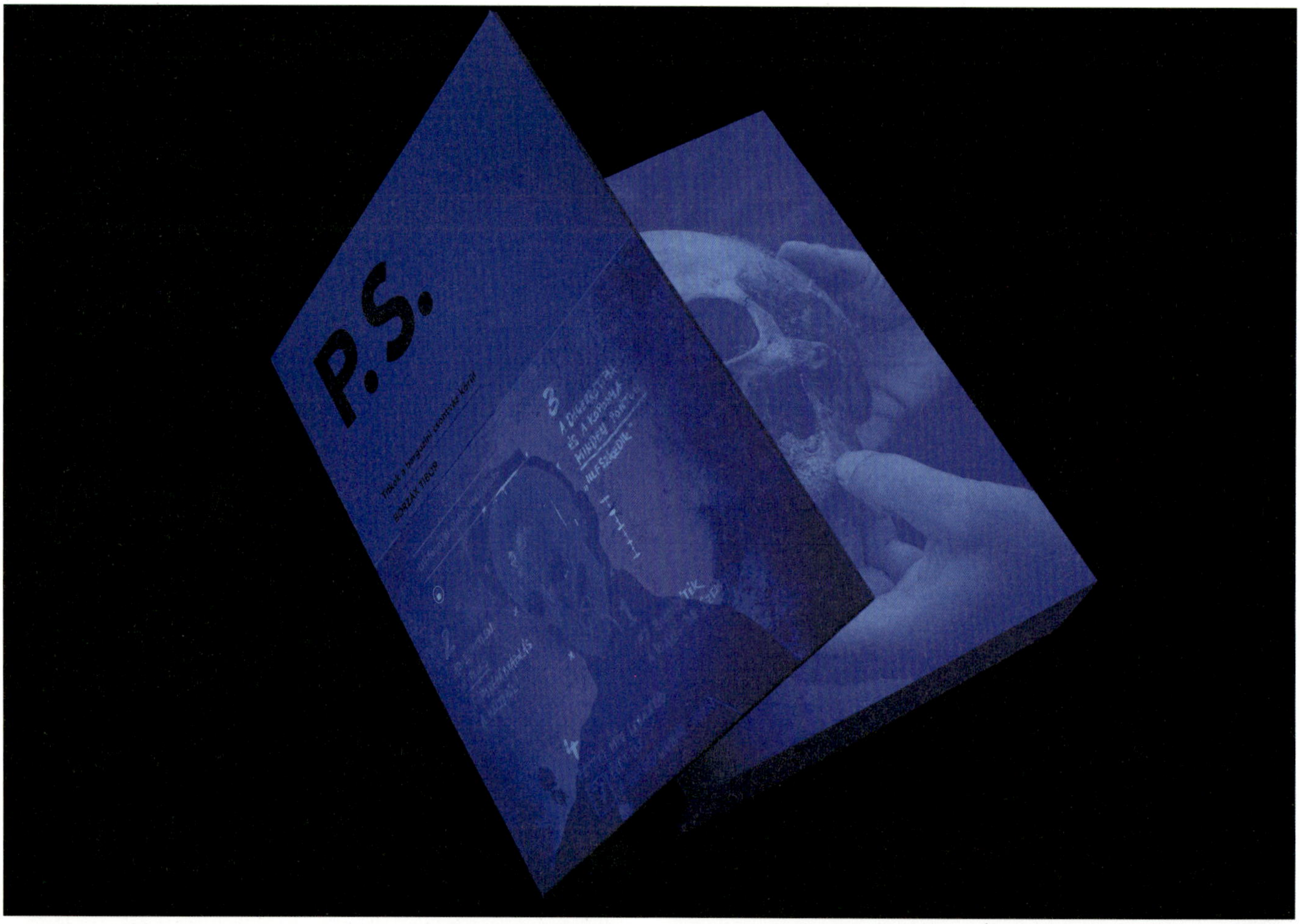

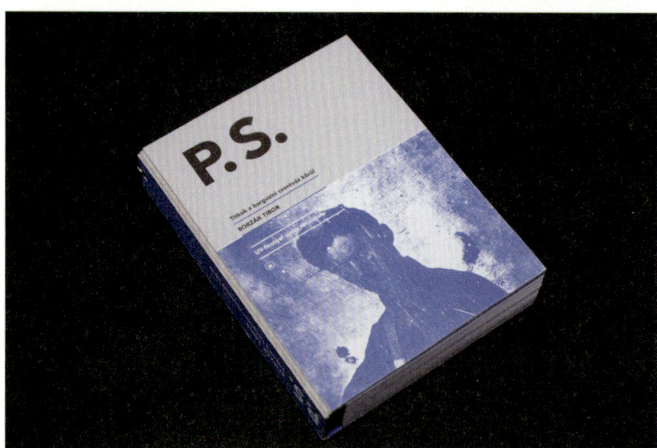

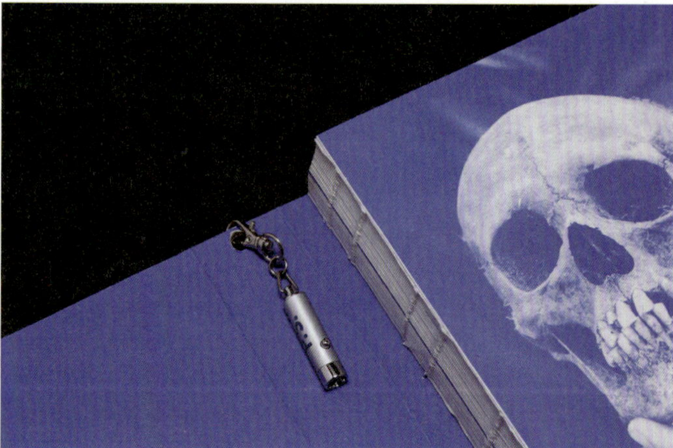

D: Marton Borzak

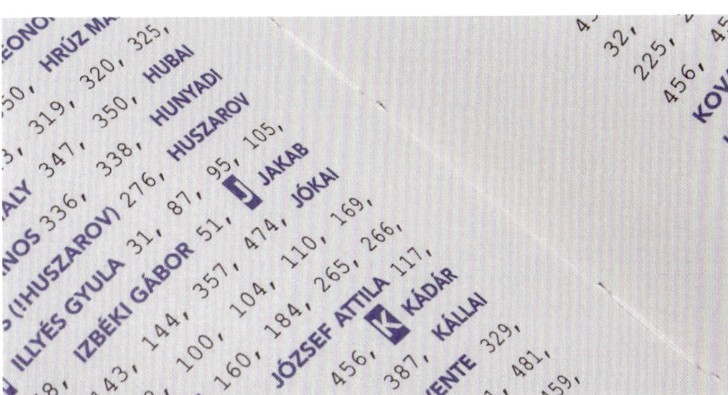
HUBAI
HUNYADI
HUSZAROV
JAKAB
JÓKAI
ILLYÉS GYULA
IZBÉKI GÁBOR
JÓZSEF ATTILA
KÁDÁR
KÁLLAI

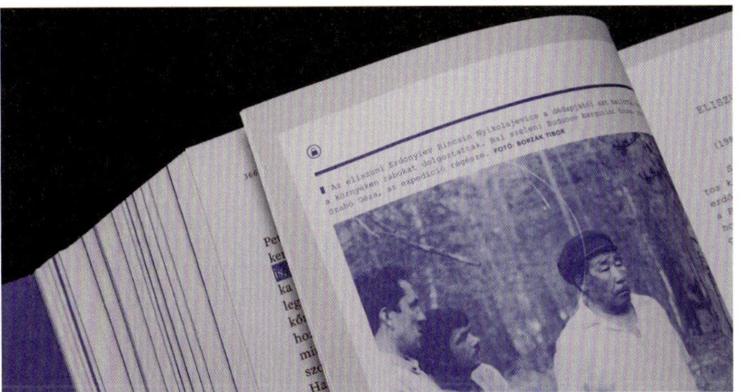

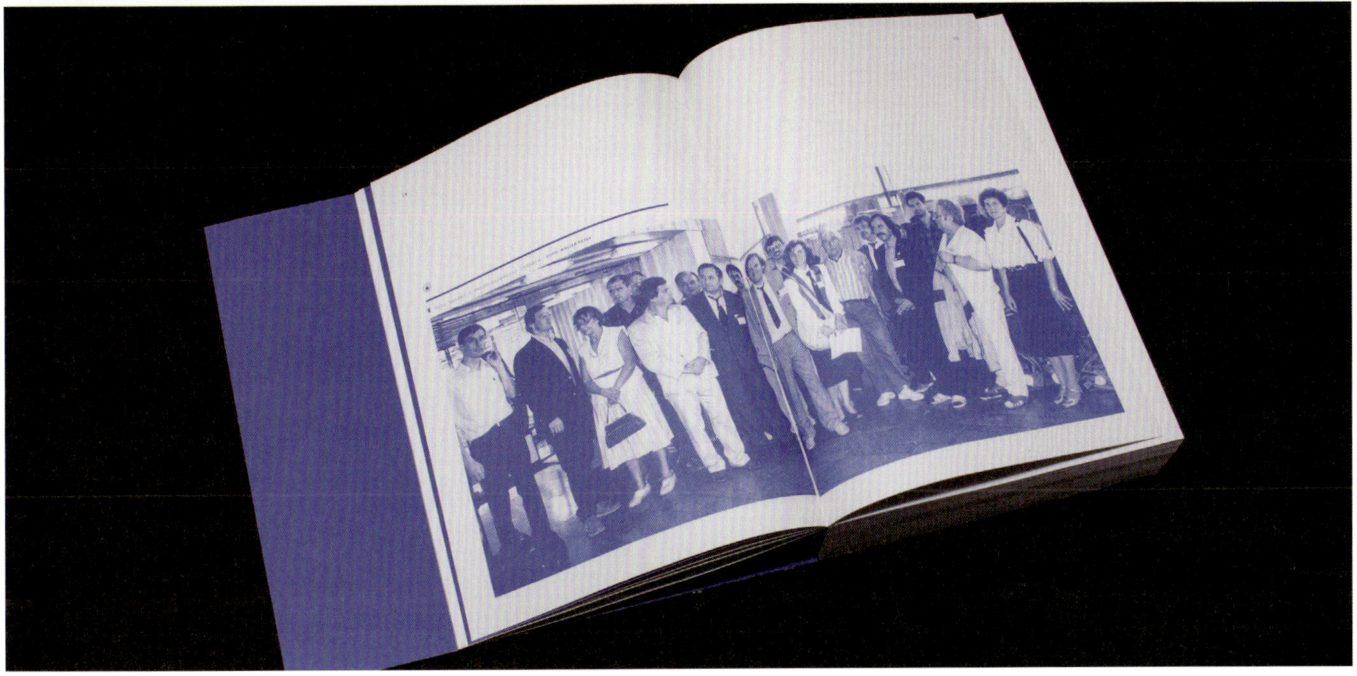

Unicer General Catalogue 2017

Cover: 350g semi matt coated paper
Interior: 170g semi matt coated paper

Unicer presents a wide range of ceramic tiles of many different shapes, textures, and materials. The design of their catalogue reflects the tiles: with bold colors and a variety of geometric figures filled with various patterns, representing all the possible combinations you can create. Using UV varnish on the bright colors created volume on the figures and added textures to the various shapes.

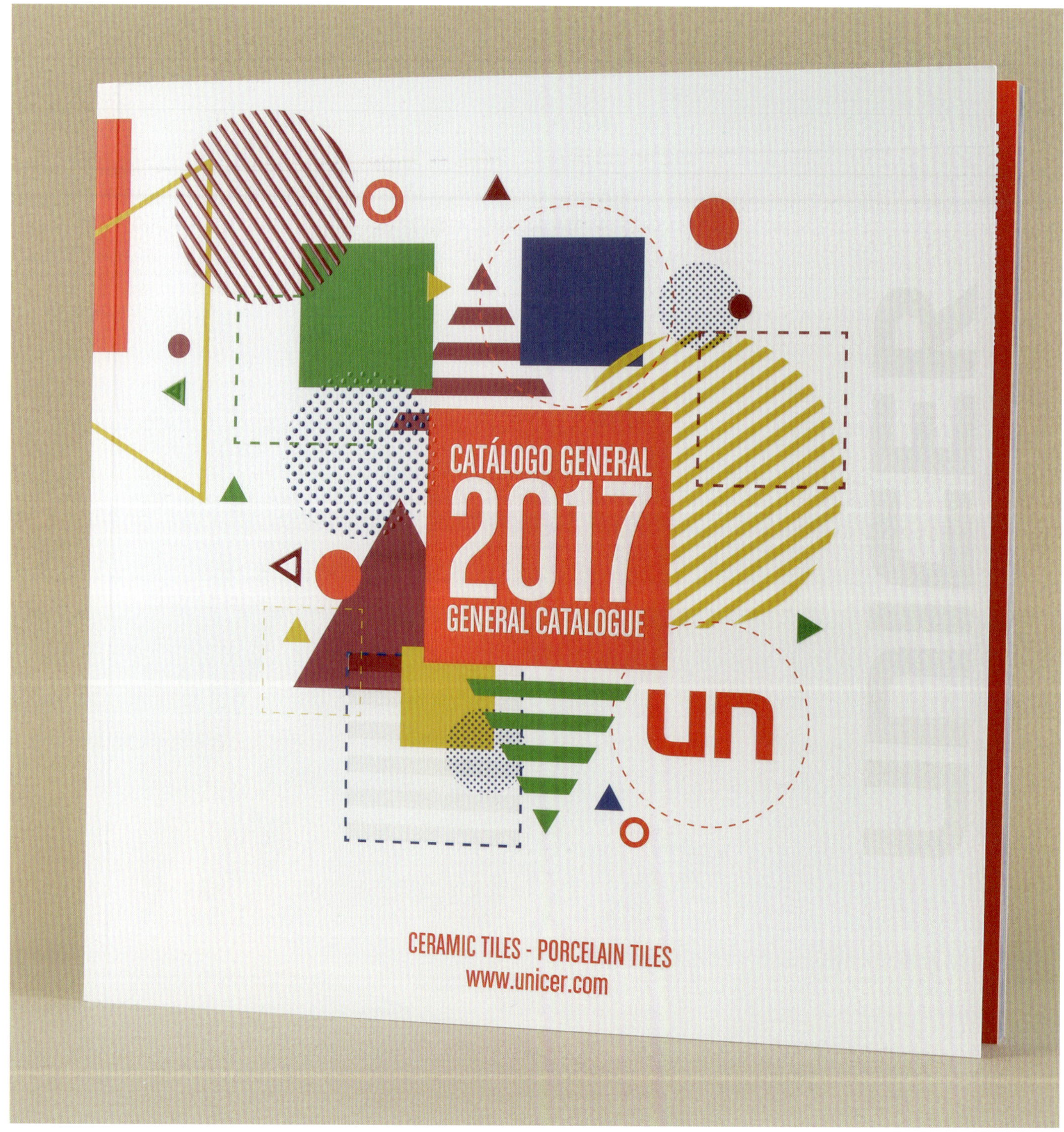

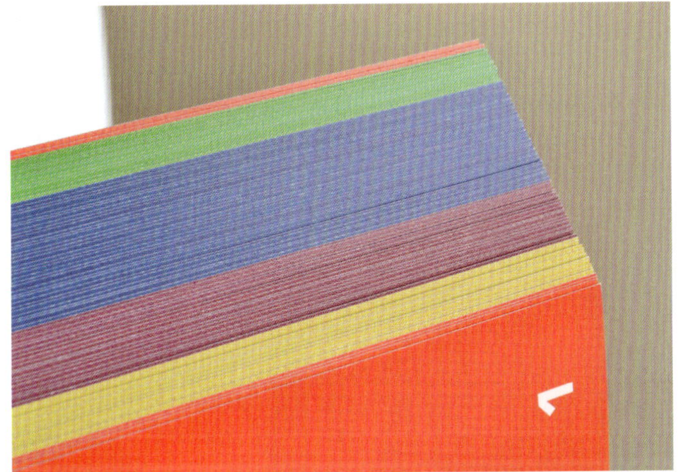

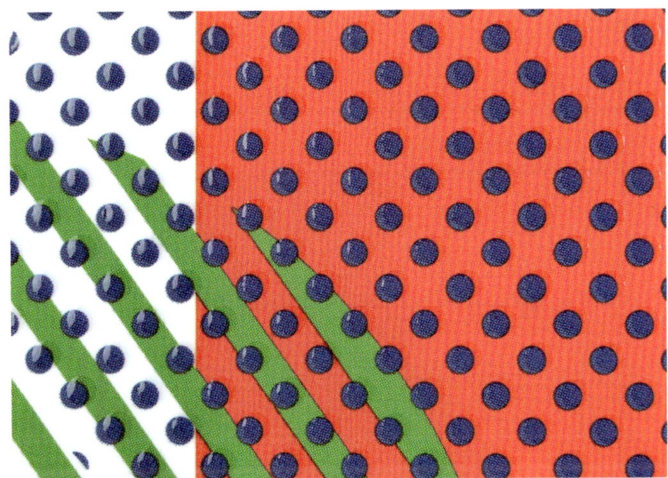

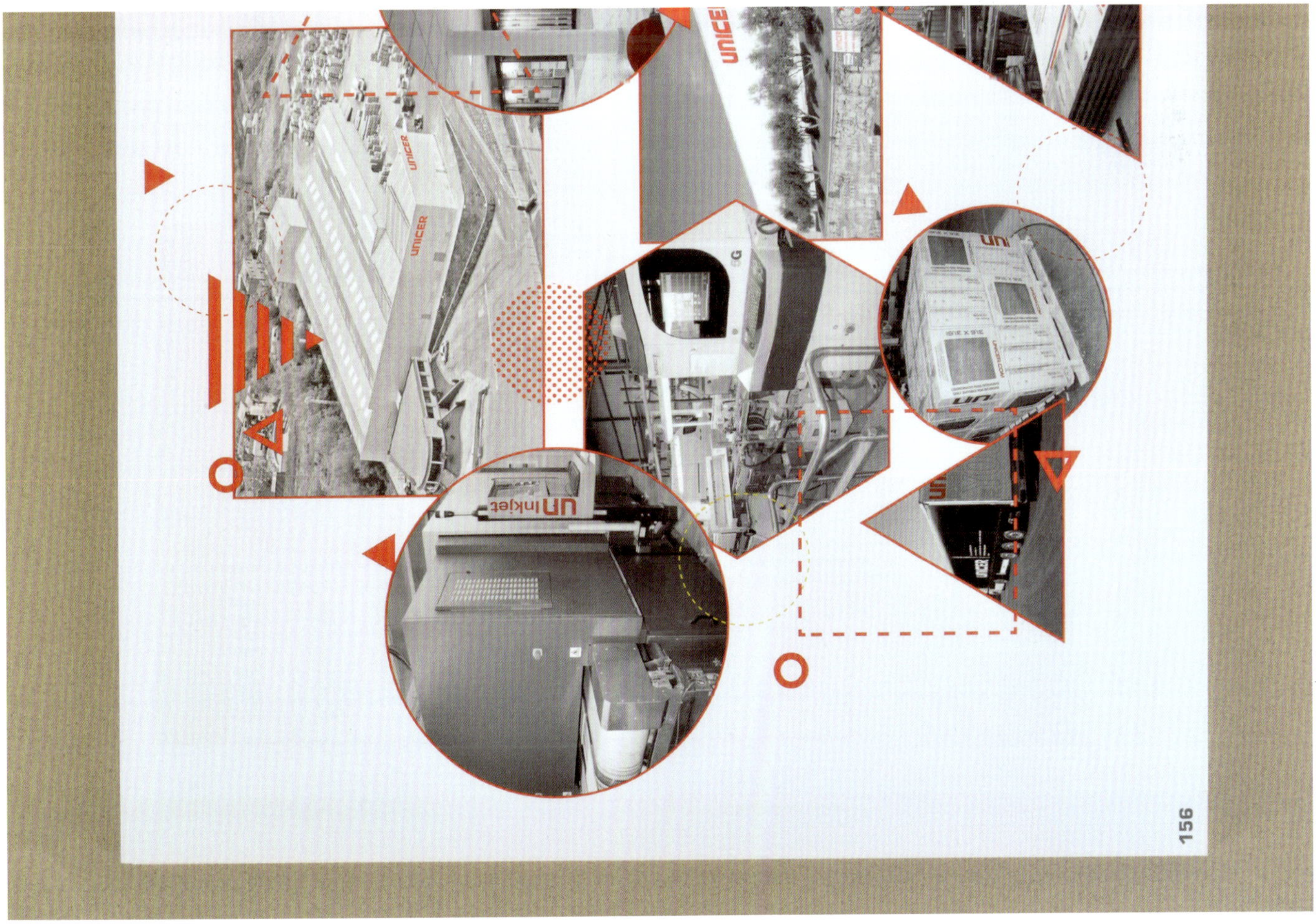

Design Development of Key Visual

- paper
- four fluorescent inks:
  TOKA FLASH VIVA DX 300 (Ceres Red)
  TOKA FLASH VIVA DX 610 (Saturn Yellow)
  TOKA FLASH VIVA DX 630 (Persephone Green)
  TOKA FLASH VIVA DX 850 (Apollo Cyan)
  Megami Super Black

Design Development of Key Visual is a design book introducing many outstanding designs using key visuals. The sub-title is "Promotional ideas to get lines of sight," so the designer depicted two lines of sight abstractly. Simultaneously, the main visual expresses development of design with spreading shapes. The designer wanted this book to stand out with colors, therefore, four fluorescent inks and black ink are used. Polypropylene processing was employed after offset printing to protect the colors.

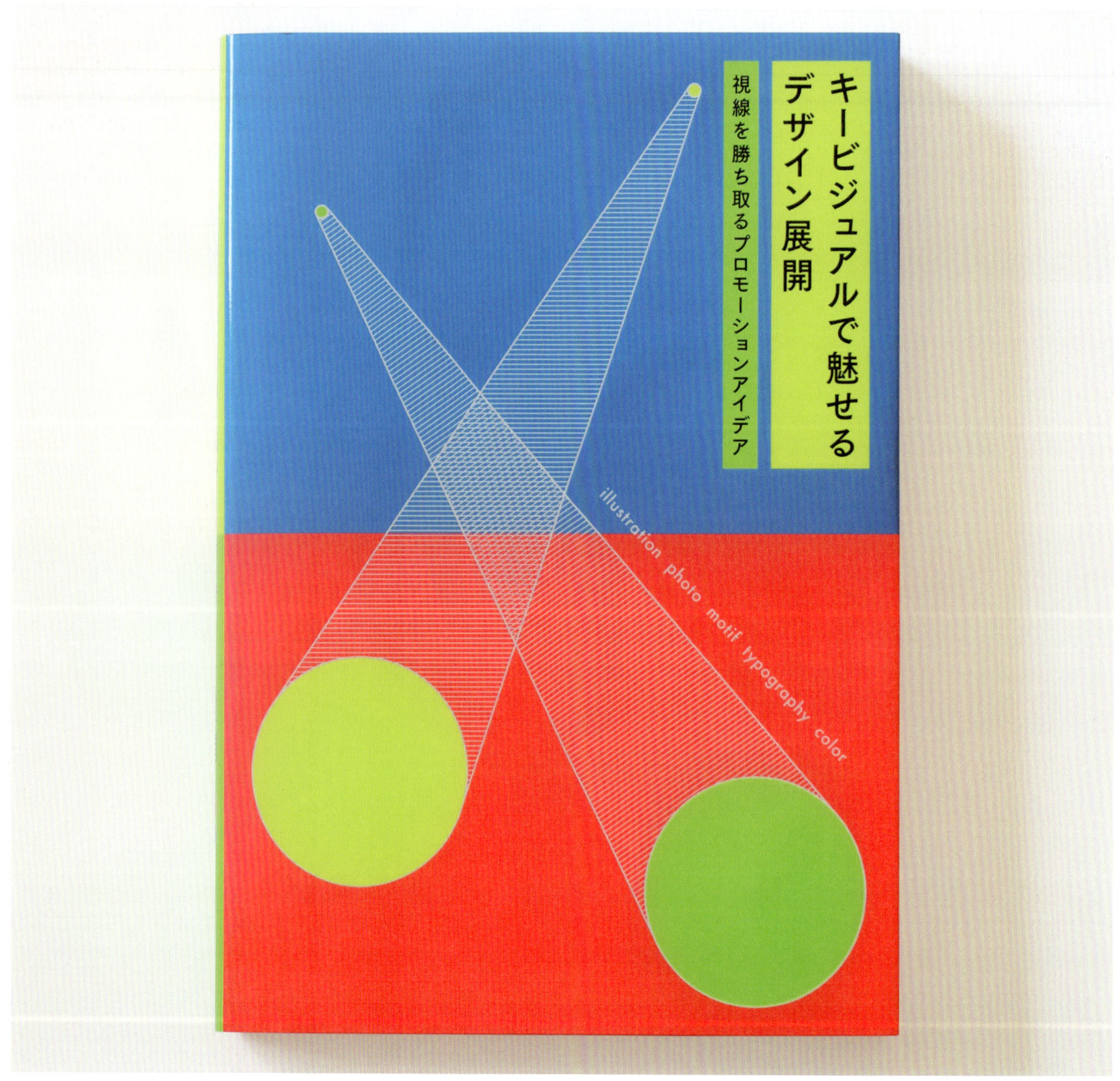

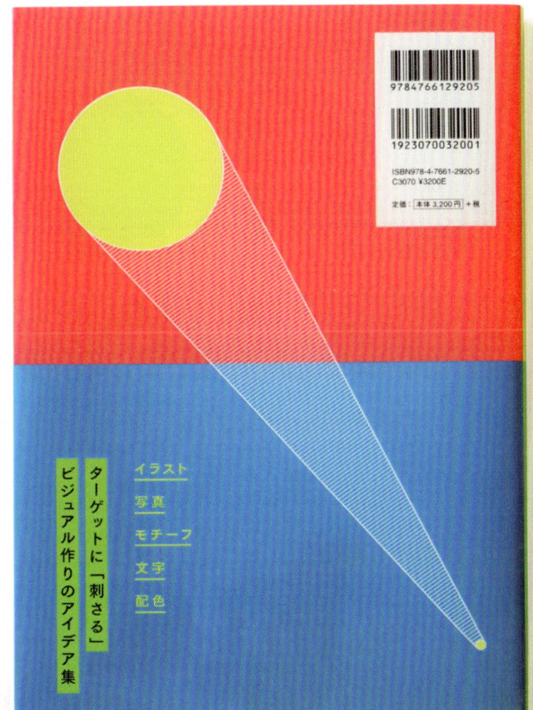

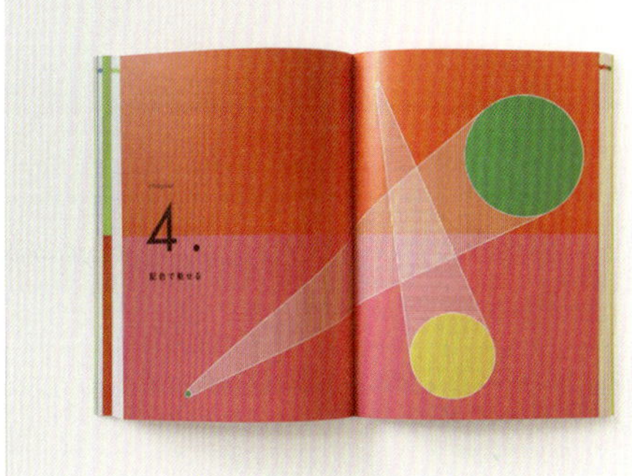

INTRODUCTION

ターゲットに「刺さる」
ビジュアル作りのアイデア集

日々世に送り出される新しいサービスや商品などの様々なプロモーション。ロゴ制作やブランディング同様に、デザイン制作者はビジュアルコンセプトの提案からはじまり、グラフィックの制作や運用を行なっています。いかにクライアントや商品などの価値を引き出し、コンセプトを消費者に的確に伝えるか。コンセプトを視覚化し、そのキーとなるビジュアルを様々な広告物にデザイン展開していく具体的な事例を多数収録するのが本書です。

写真・モチーフ・配色・文字・イラストにカテゴリー分けし、ターゲットに向けて、様々なキービジュアルを用いたデザイン作品を掲載しました。ポスターや冊子などの印刷物、ロゴ、ディスプレイ、Web、動画、ノベルティなど、様々な展開事例をご紹介します。広告制作やブランディングに活用できる1冊として、みなさまのデザイン制作の一助となりましたら幸いです。

本書制作にあたり、ご多忙な中、多大なご協力を賜りました方々に、心より御礼申し上げます。

CONTENTS

略号表記について
制作者クレジットにおいて、以下の略号を用いております。

CL クライアント
DF デザイン制作会社
AD アートディレクター
D デザイナー
IL イラストレーター
PH フォトグラファー
AG 広告代理店
P プロデューサー
DIR ディレクター
CD クリエイティブディレクター
CW コピーライター
W ライター
PL プランナー
CP クリエイティブプロデューサー
AE アカウントエグゼクティブ
ST スタイリスト
HM ヘアメイク
M モデル

それぞれの制作会社への、本書に関するお問い合わせはご遠慮ください。

Ready-Made Painting

This book is an album of paintings collected from the "Ready-Made Painting" art exhibition sponsored by Ying Art Center. Offset printing is the chosen printing method.

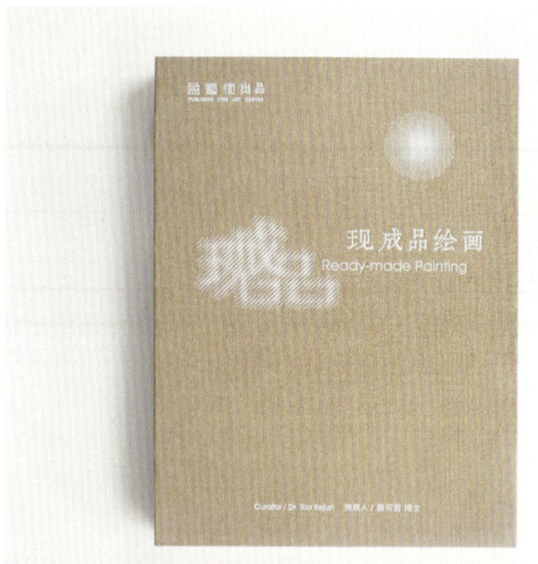

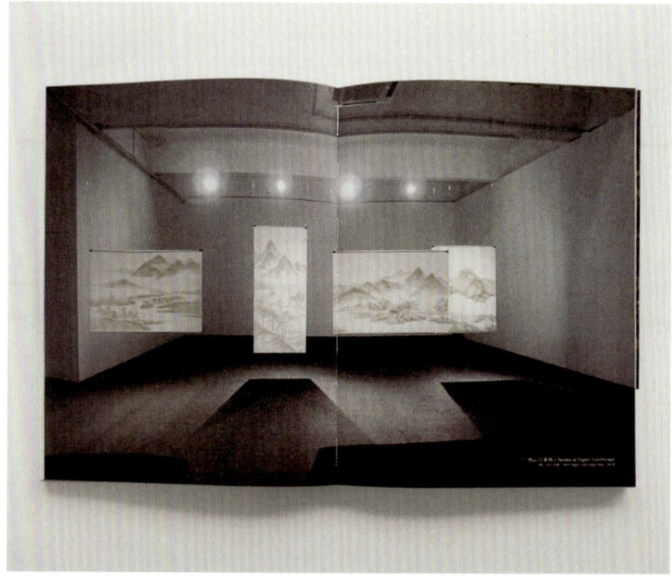

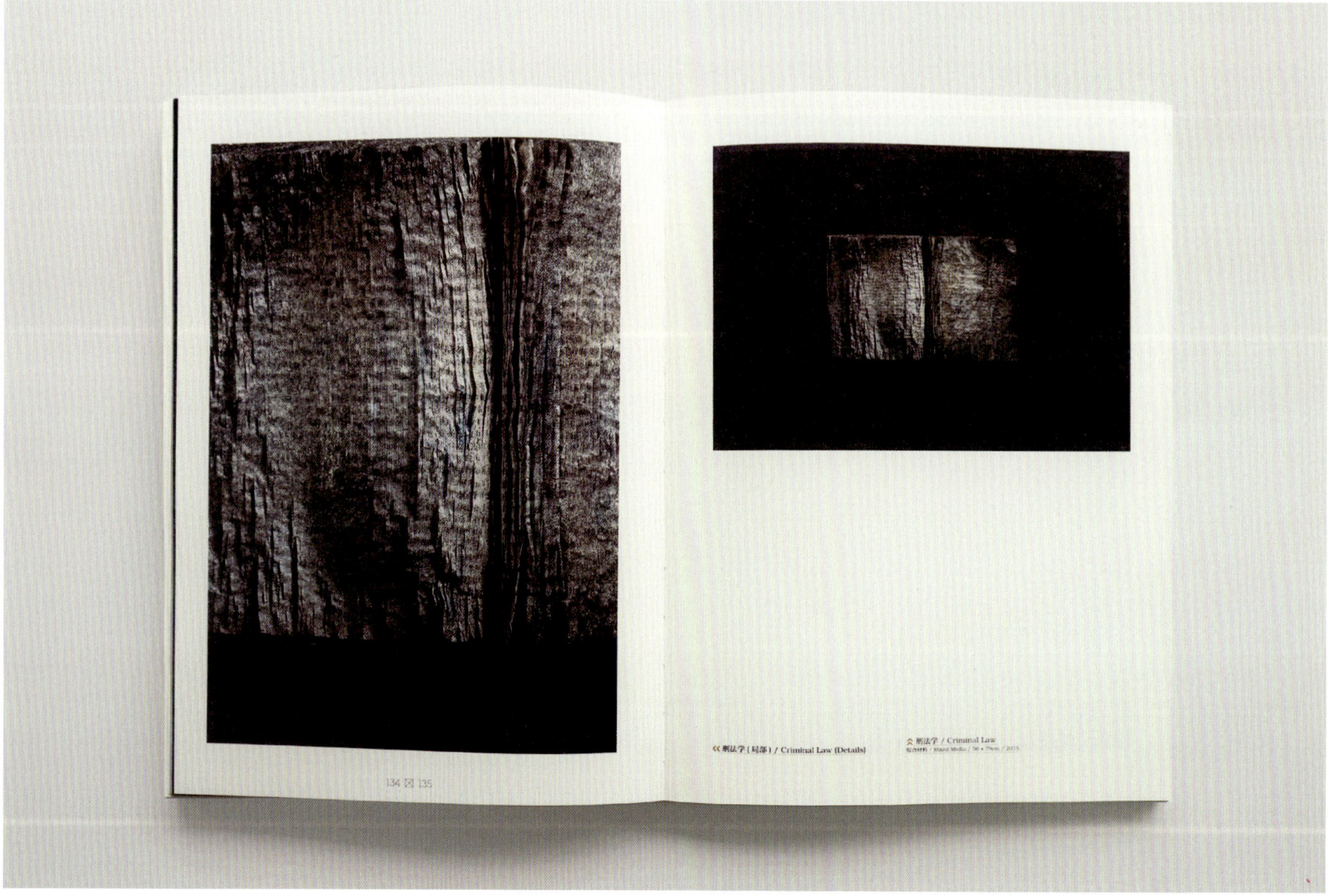

Porcolipsis

180g uncoated paper

Pantone 2985 U, Pantone 194 U

Porcolipsis is an infographic poster about the Catalan pork industry and its excesses. Designed in the illustrative style of traditional stationary from local butcher and meat shops, it is naïve and positive - creepy and gory. Traditional offset printing was the chosen method for this poster, because the client needed a quick and affordable way to get a large amount of copies distributed.

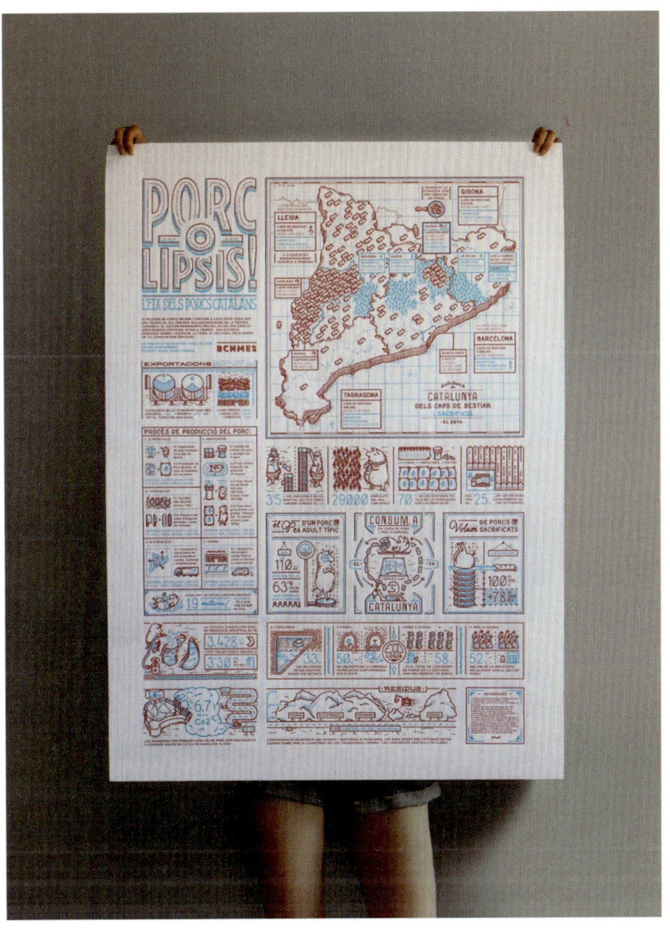

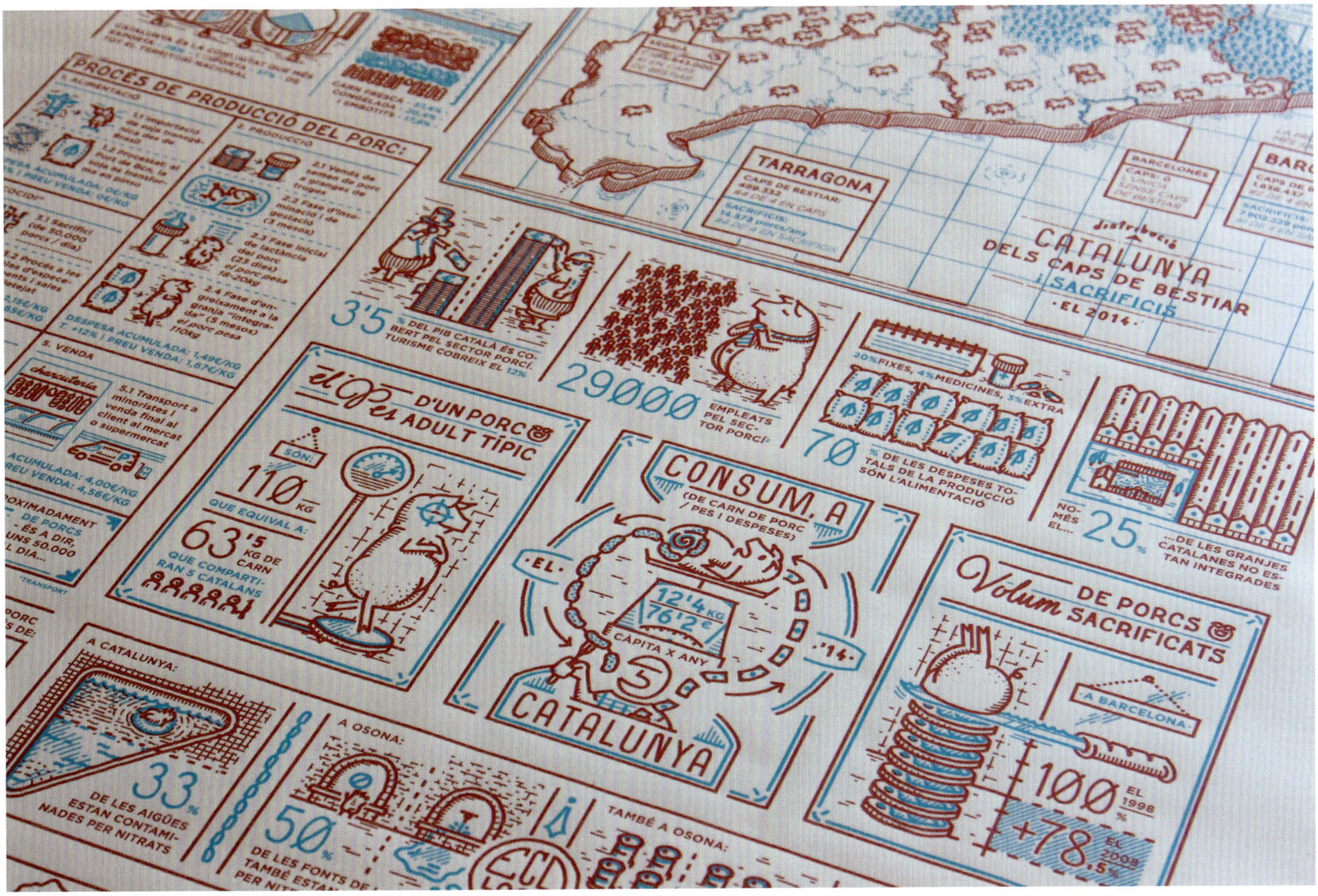

D: Angel Sanz Correa

Arts On The Black River

offset uncoated paper

Pantone Spot Color Print (7429 U, Pantone Yellow, 151 U, 1925 U, 2758 U, Pantone Warm Red, 1235 U)

"Arts On The Black River" is an independent cultural event that takes place at the lovely surroundings of the Nera River valley near Narni, Itlay. The festival aims to create a connection between nature, art, and all kinds of culinary delights. Combined with local foods and wine, people can enjoy a variety of art performances such as music, dance, and theater. Big headlines combined with illustrations in a monochromatic deep blue color scheme suggest characteristic elements of the event such as music, river, nature, dance, food, and other delights. The color palette refers to the atmosphere of a sunset. To better translate this mood visually, the designer used Pantone Spot Colors. Colors play a main role in this project, and using Pantone allowed the designers to add strength to the printed materials.

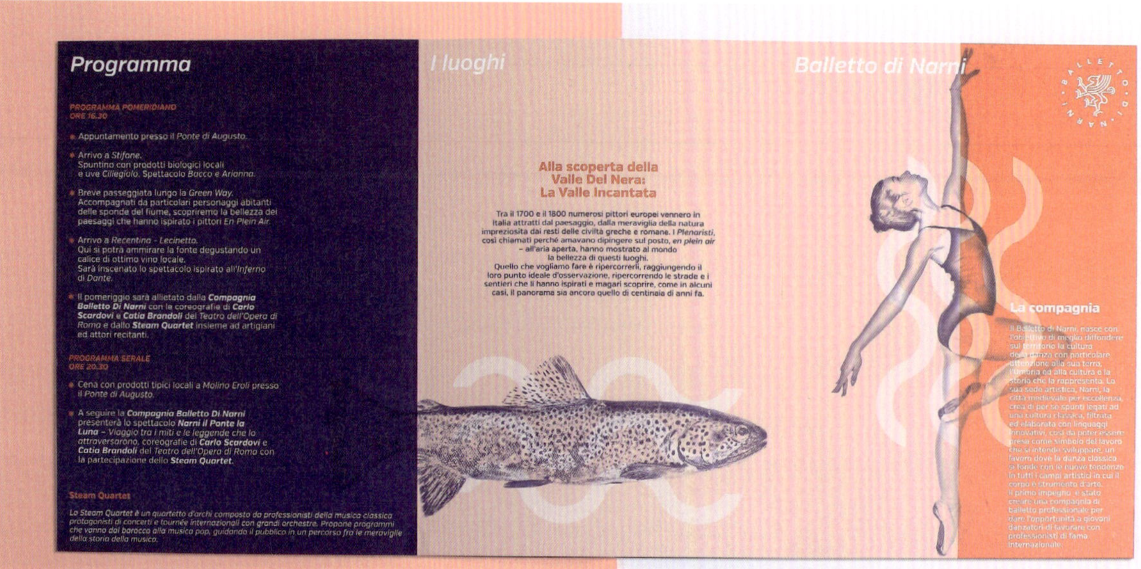

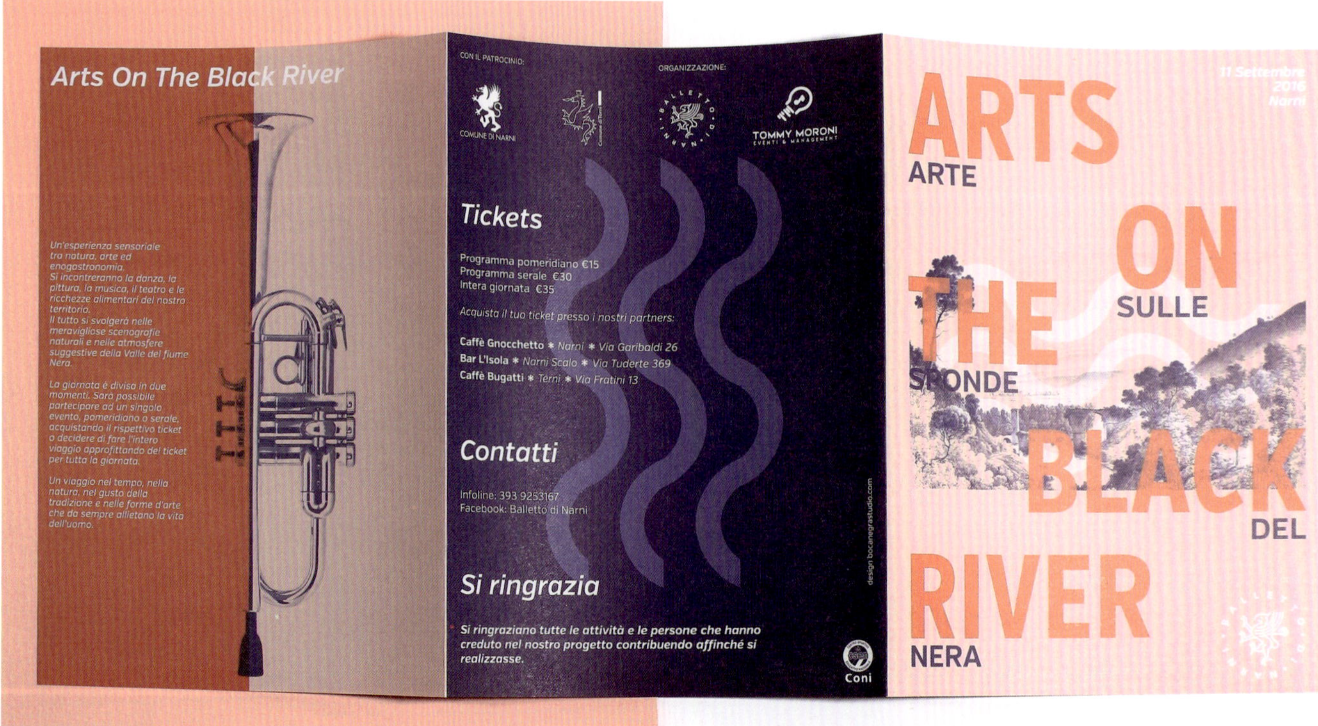

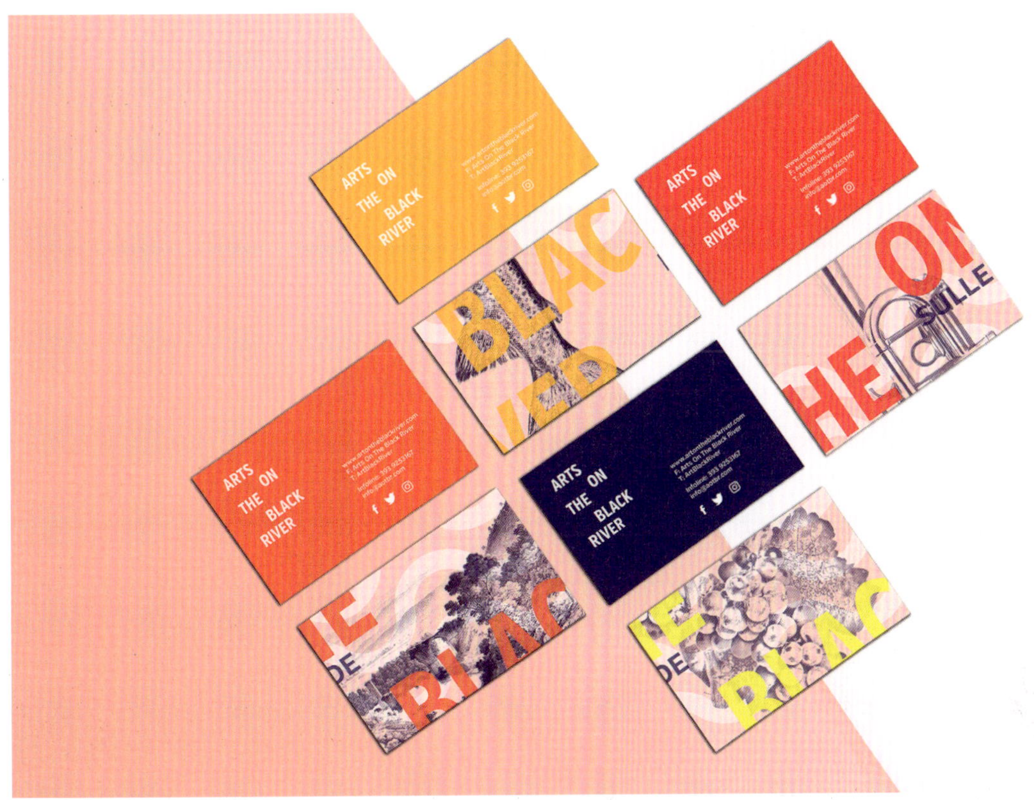

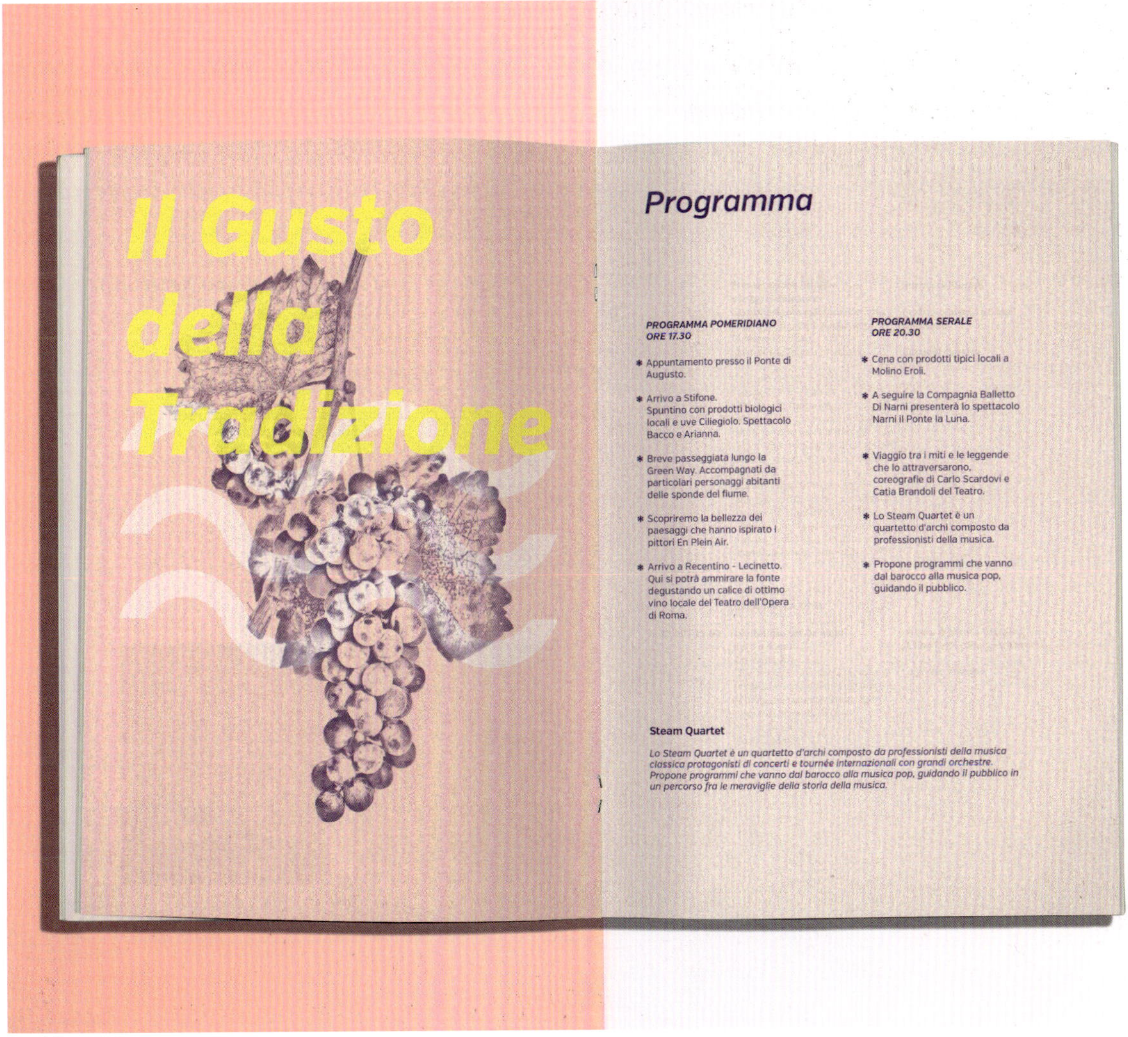

Il Gusto della Tradizione

Programma

PROGRAMMA POMERIDIANO
ORE 17.30

* Appuntamento presso il Ponte di Augusto.
* Arrivo a Stifone. Spuntino con prodotti biologici locali e uve Ciliegiolo. Spettacolo Bacco e Arianna.
* Breve passeggiata lungo la Green Way. Accompagnati da particolari personaggi abitanti delle sponde del fiume.
* Scopriremo la bellezza dei paesaggi che hanno ispirato i pittori En Plein Air.
* Arrivo a Recentino - Lecinetto. Qui si potrà ammirare la fonte degustando un calice di ottimo vino locale del Teatro dell'Opera di Roma.

PROGRAMMA SERALE
ORE 20.30

* Cena con prodotti tipici locali a Molino Eroli.
* A seguire la Compagnia Balletto Di Narni presenterà lo spettacolo Narni il Ponte la Luna.
* Viaggio tra i miti e le leggende che lo attraversarono, coreografie di Carlo Scardovi e Catia Brandoli del Teatro.
* Lo Steam Quartet è un quartetto d'archi composto da professionisti della musica.
* Propone programmi che vanno dal barocco alla musica pop, guidando il pubblico.

Steam Quartet

Lo Steam Quartet è un quartetto d'archi composto da professionisti della musica classica protagonisti di concerti e tournée internazionali con grandi orchestre. Propone programmi che vanno dal barocco alla musica pop, guidando il pubblico in un percorso fra le meraviglie della storia della musica.

One Fine Dinner Journal

90g Munken Print Cream paper

One Fine Dinner Journal is a monthly magazine published by CFC Publishers. Each issue picks a specific region and introduces food, culture, and travel information about that area. Also one discovers postcards, along with journals containing recipes related to each region. So far three issues have appeared: *Athens*, *Madrid*, and *Dijon*.

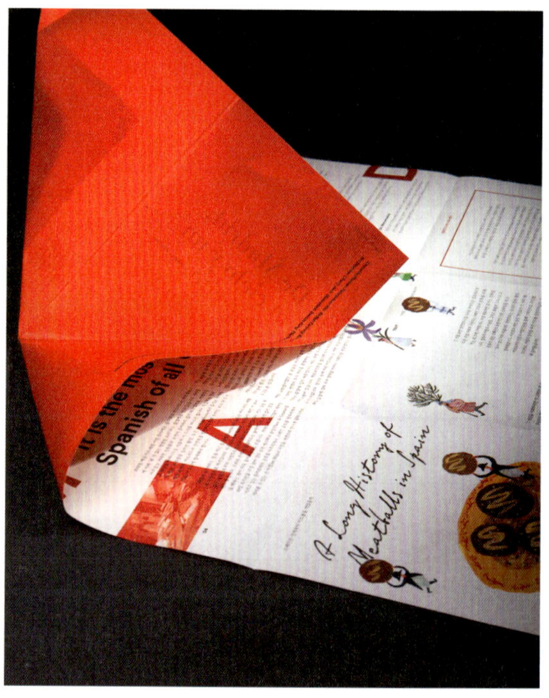

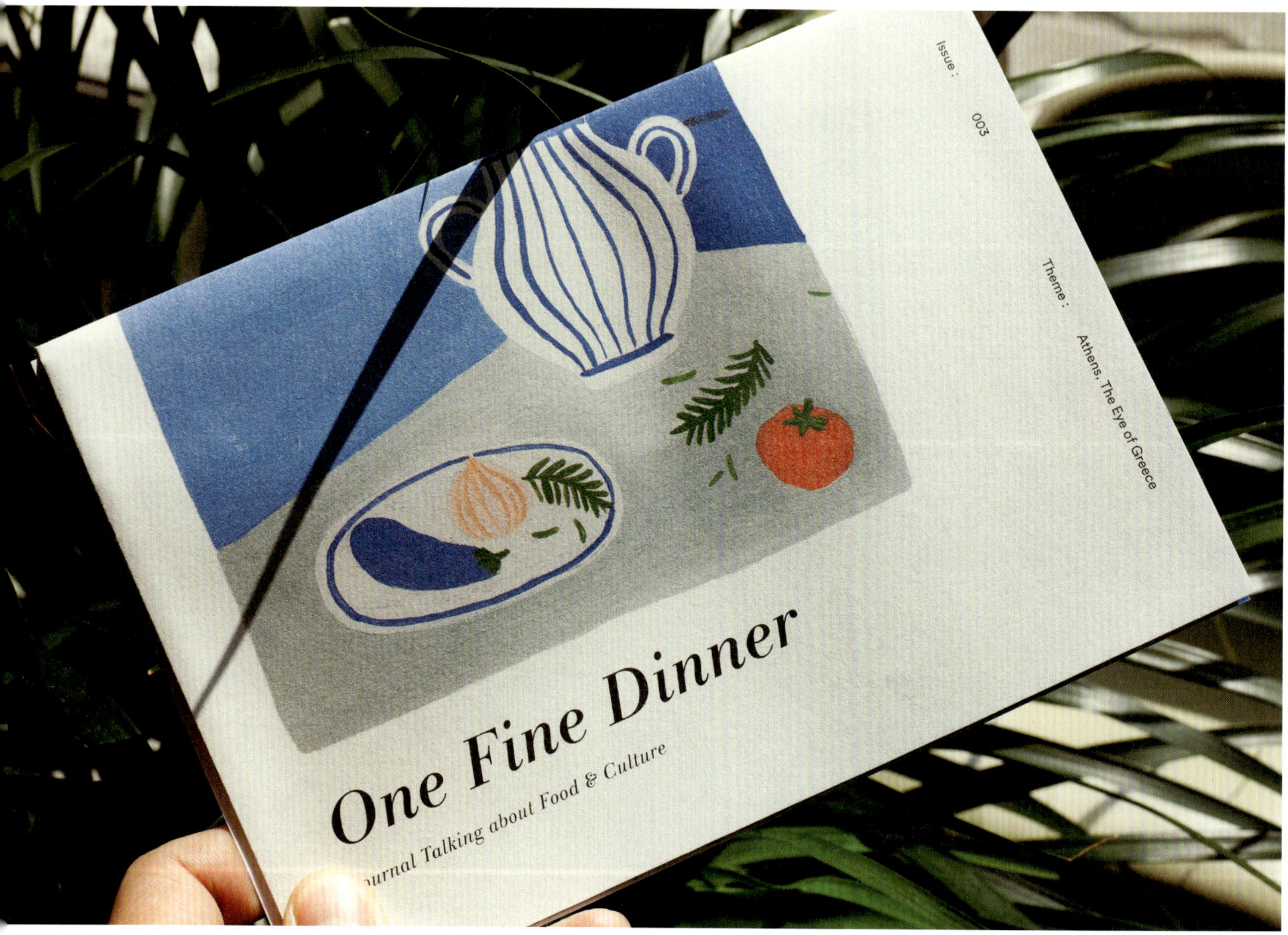

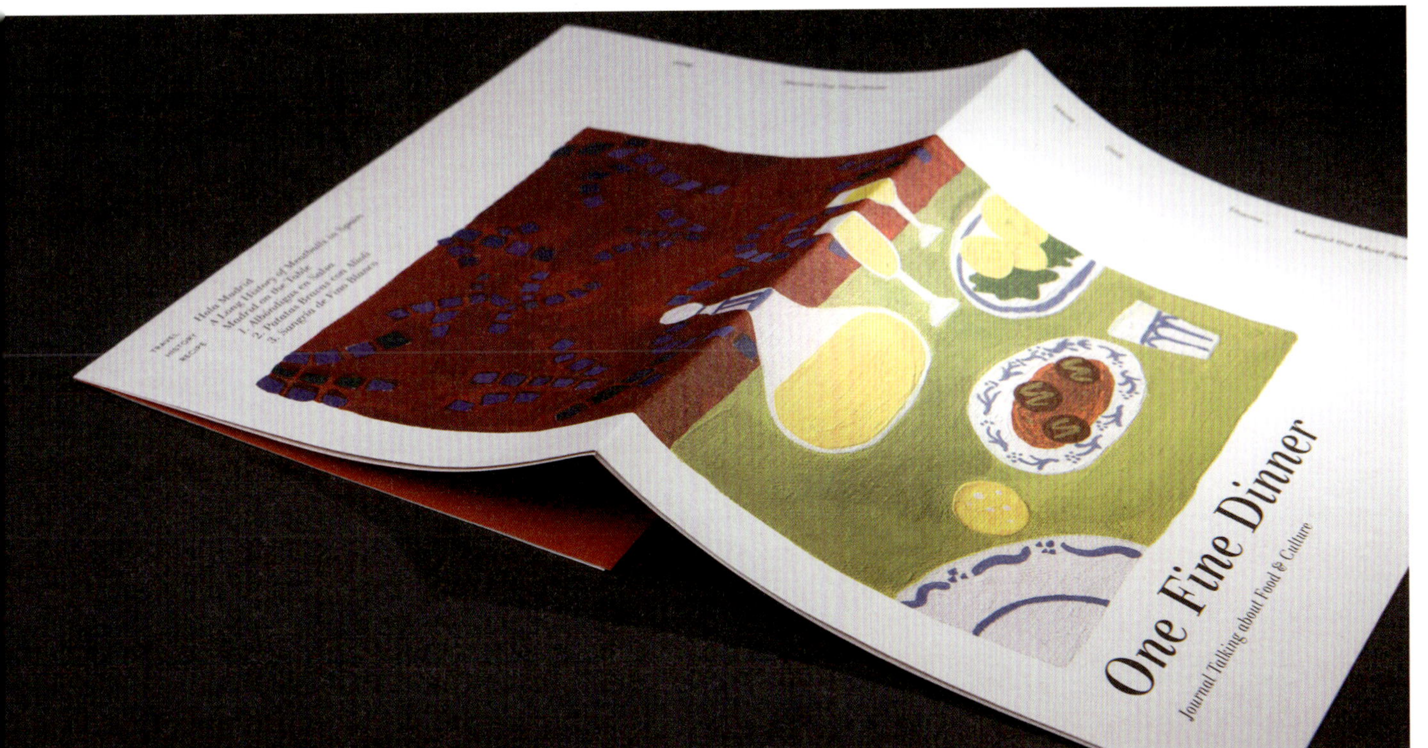
One Fine Dinner
Journal Talking about Food & Culture

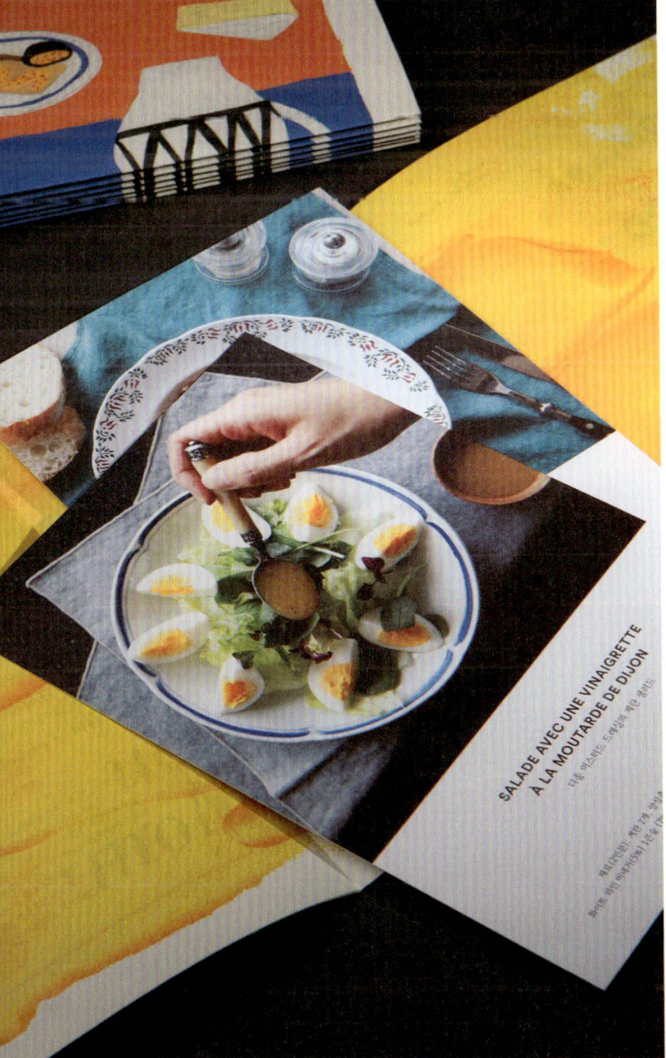
SALADE AVEC UNE VINAIGRETTE
À LA MOUTARDE DE DIJON

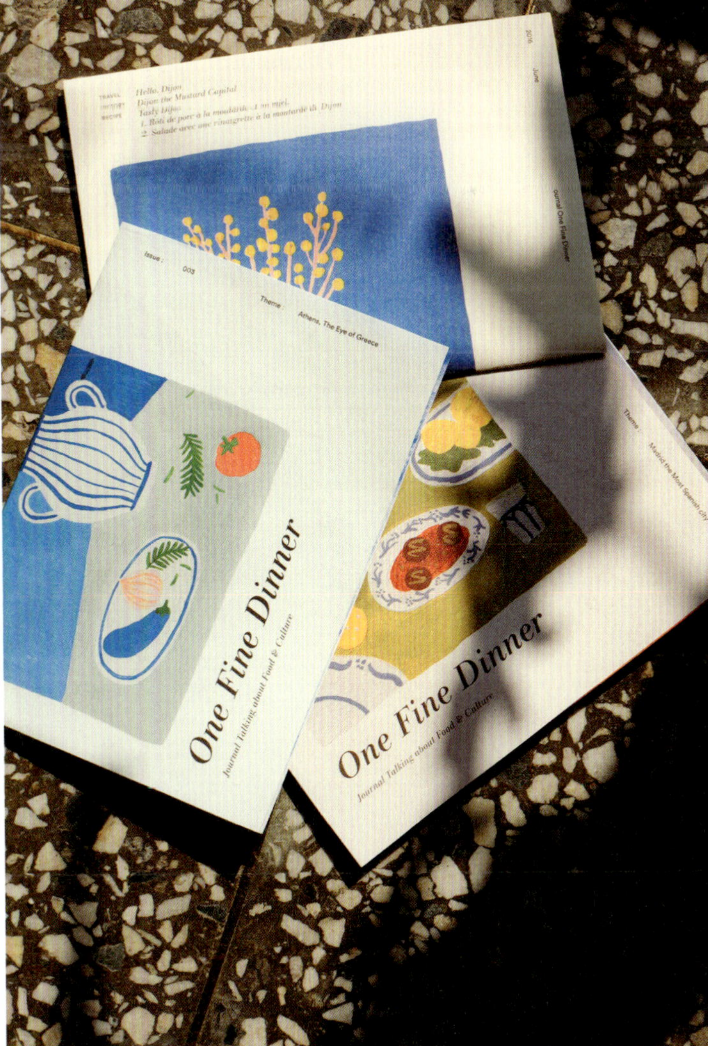
Theme / Athens, The Eye of Greece
One Fine Dinner
Journal Talking about Food & Culture
One Fine Dinner
Journal Talking about Food & Culture

ART WORKER

ART WORKER is a thematic student newspaper. At the heart of the concept lies the phenomenon of illustration. Authors introduce readers to the history of illustration, masters from this field of art, modern trends, and best works of this area. The newspaper offers a facile, close to student-life style that is at the same time a bit sidy.

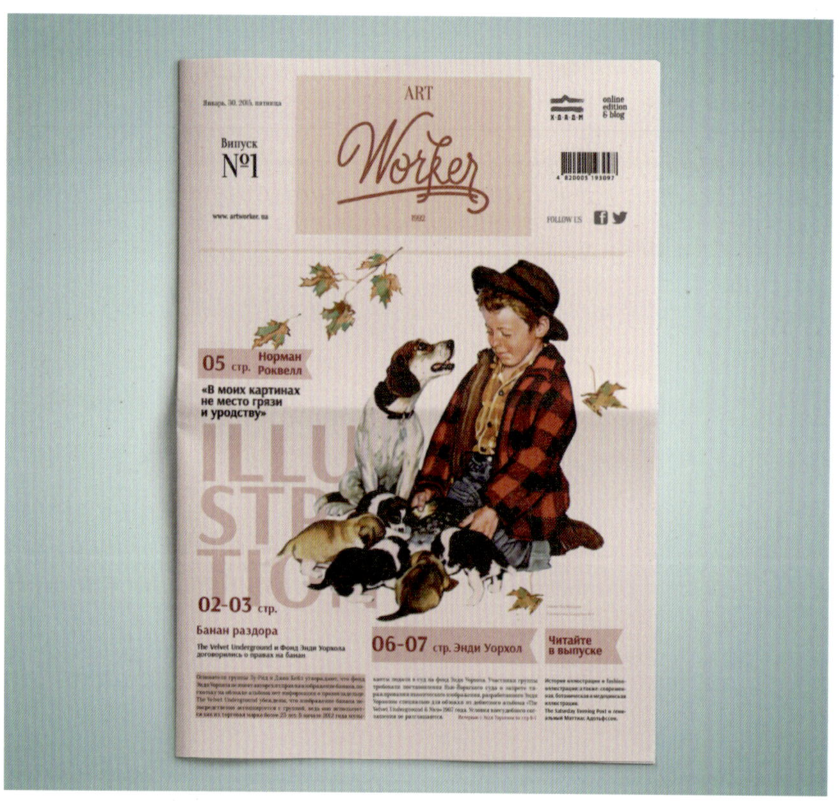

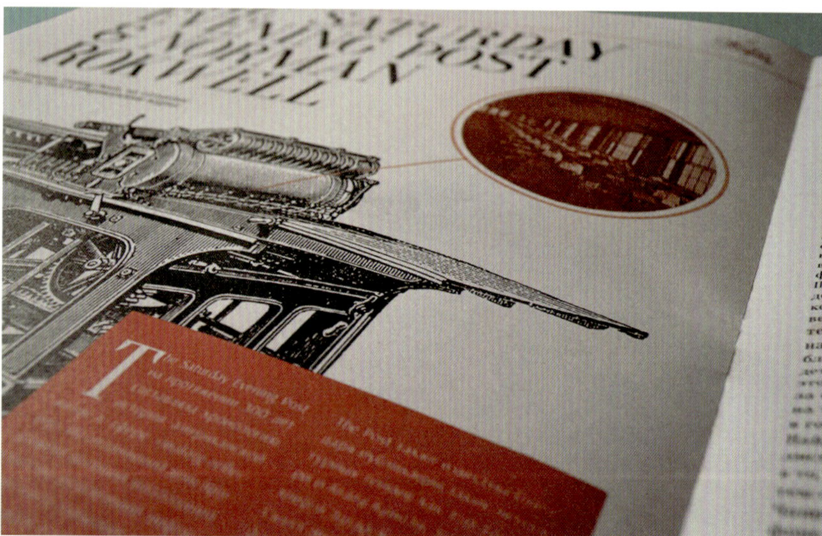

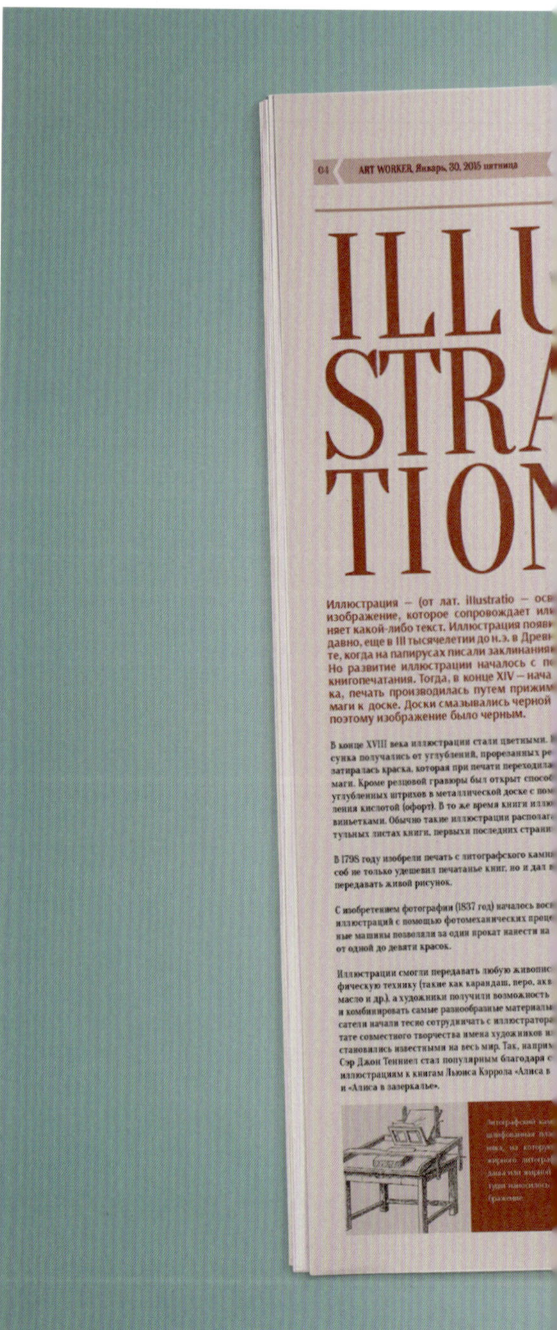

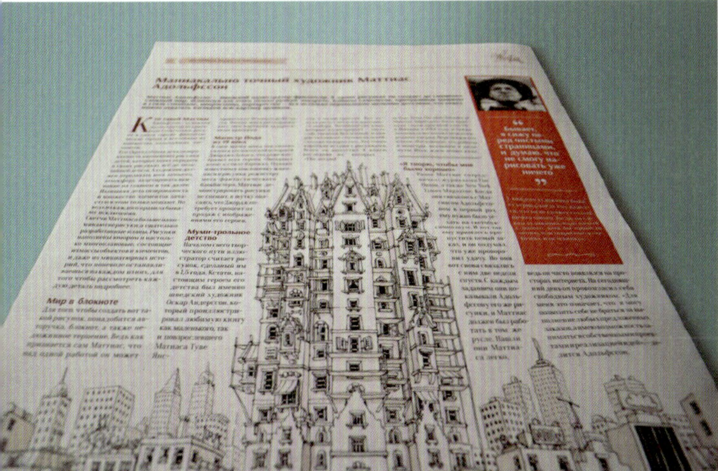

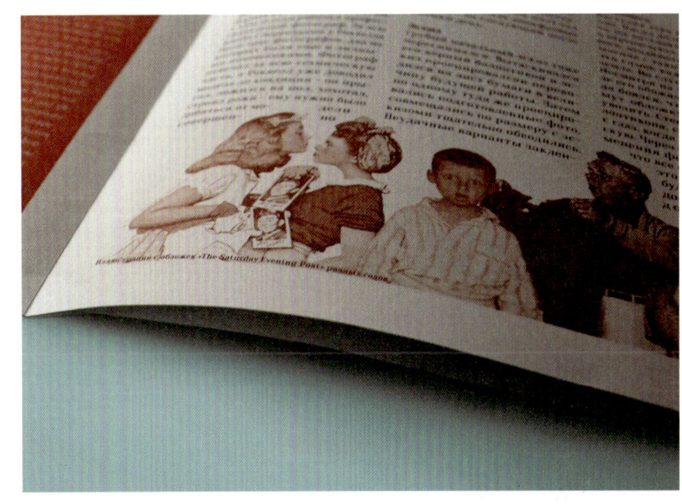

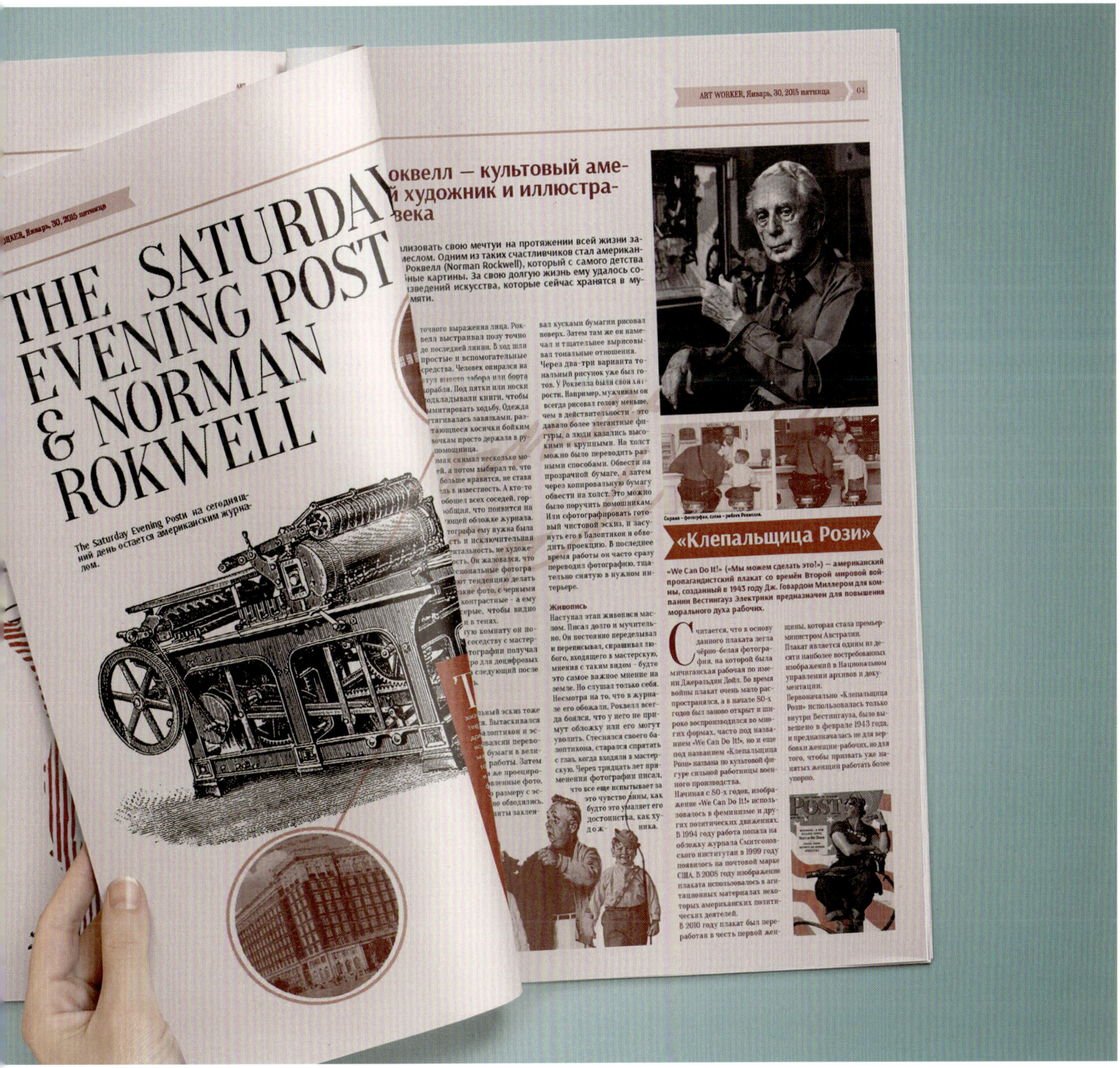

ART WORKER, Январь, 30, 2015 пятница
THE SATURDAY EVENING POST & NORMAN ROKWELL
The Saturday Evening Post на сегодняшний день остается американским журналом.
«Клепальщица Рози»
«We Can Do It!» («Мы можем сделать это!») — американский пропагандистский плакат со времён Второй мировой войны, созданный в 1943 году Дж. Говардом Миллером для компании Вестингауз Электрик предназначен для повышения морального духа рабочих.

Ethan Lee Photography #2

Yi-Hsien Lee is a famous photographer based in London. His works lend the design a sense of tranquility, so he used a darker tone to address that. Some areas of the work were printed in an offset printing manner, and a laser hot-stamping technique was applied in some parts.

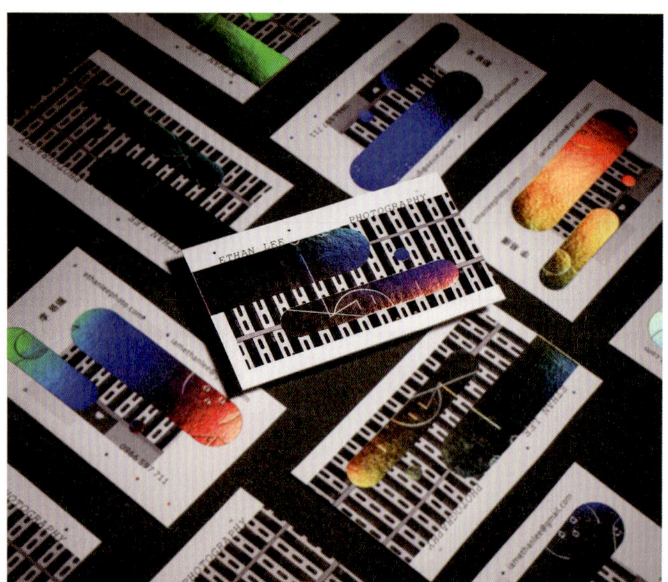

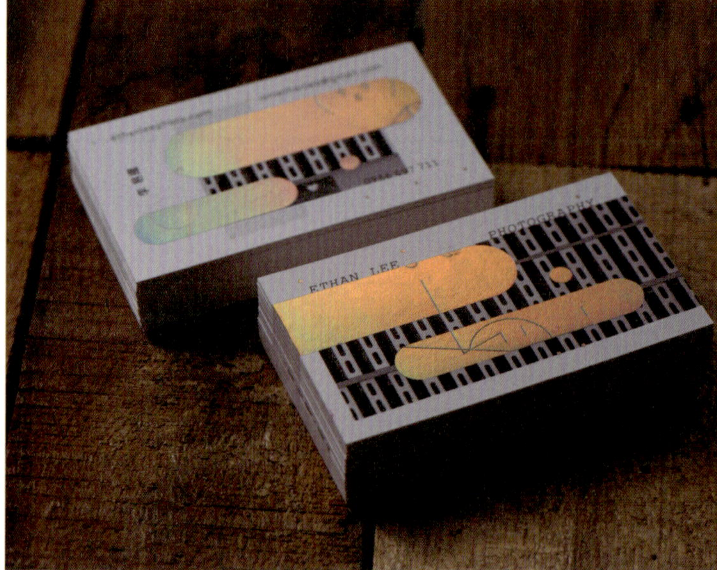

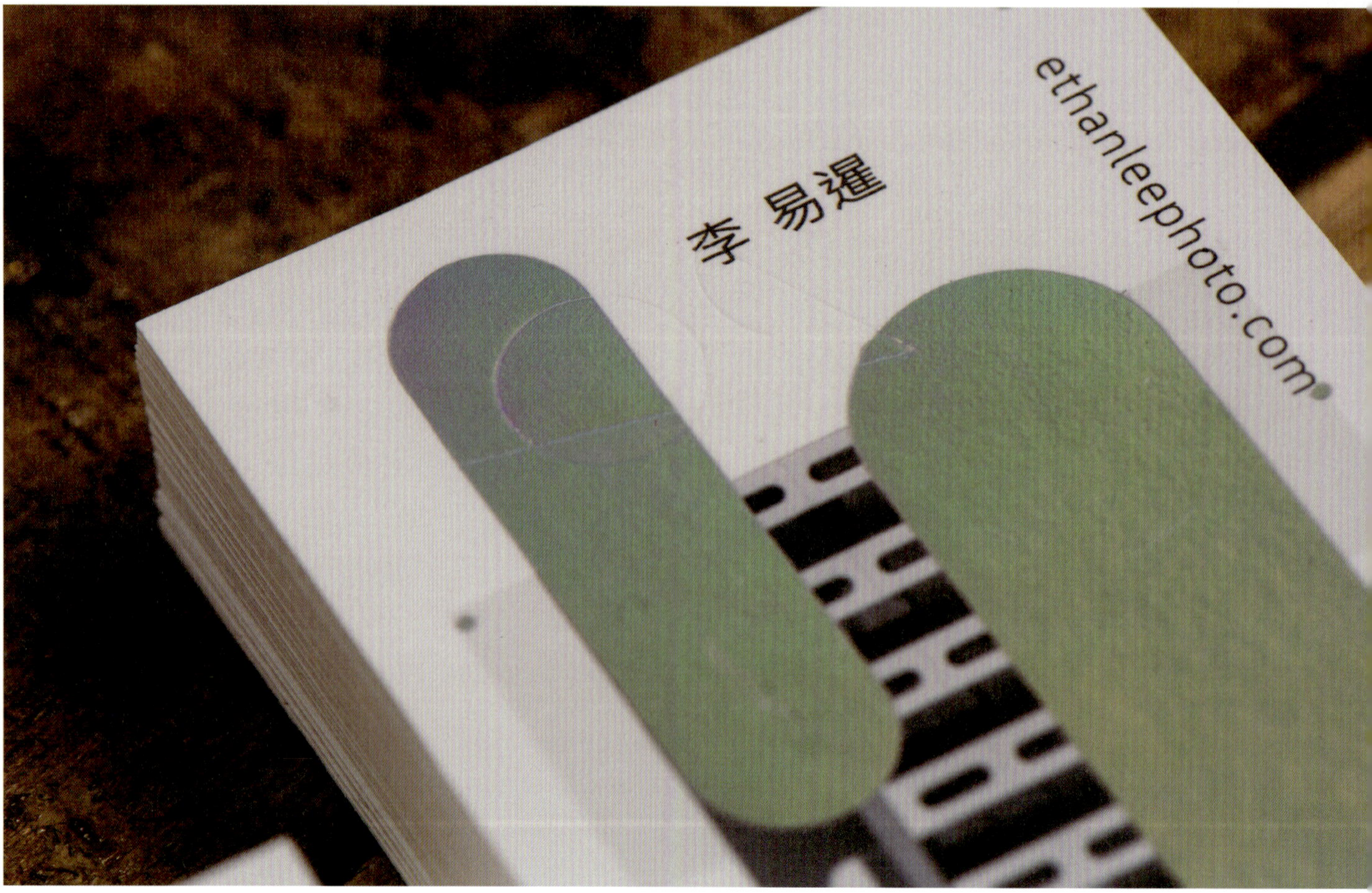

D: Sion Hsu

Chinese New Year of Rooster Gift Box

specialty paper

4 color printing paste

The designers hope to get the younger generation to pay attention to ancient Chinese culture and foods. So they used the theme of "the chicken eats millet." The designers created the package vision by redesigning the Chinese traditional patterns in a modern design language, while trying to be concise. They choose offset printing and printed on specialty paper in order to make the design more suitable for mass production.

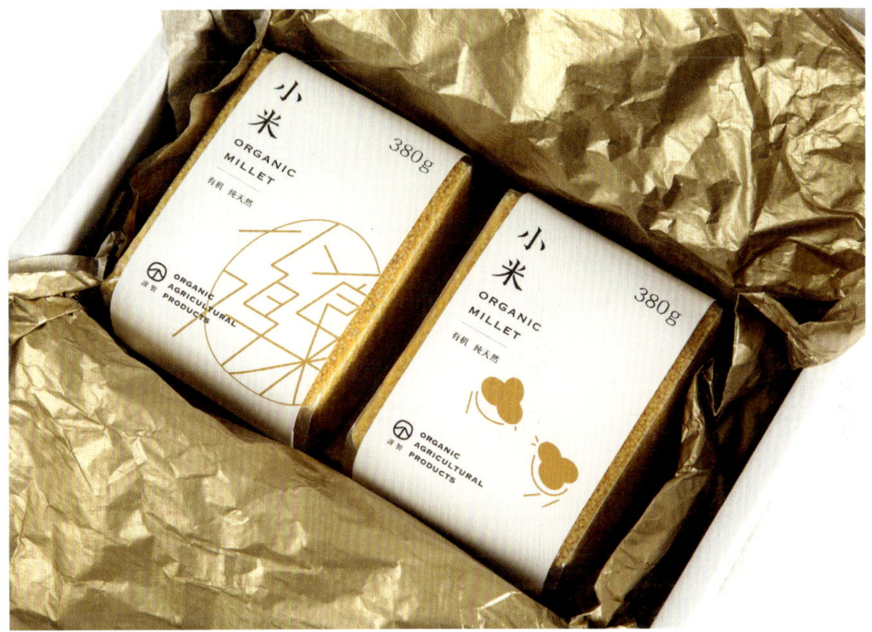

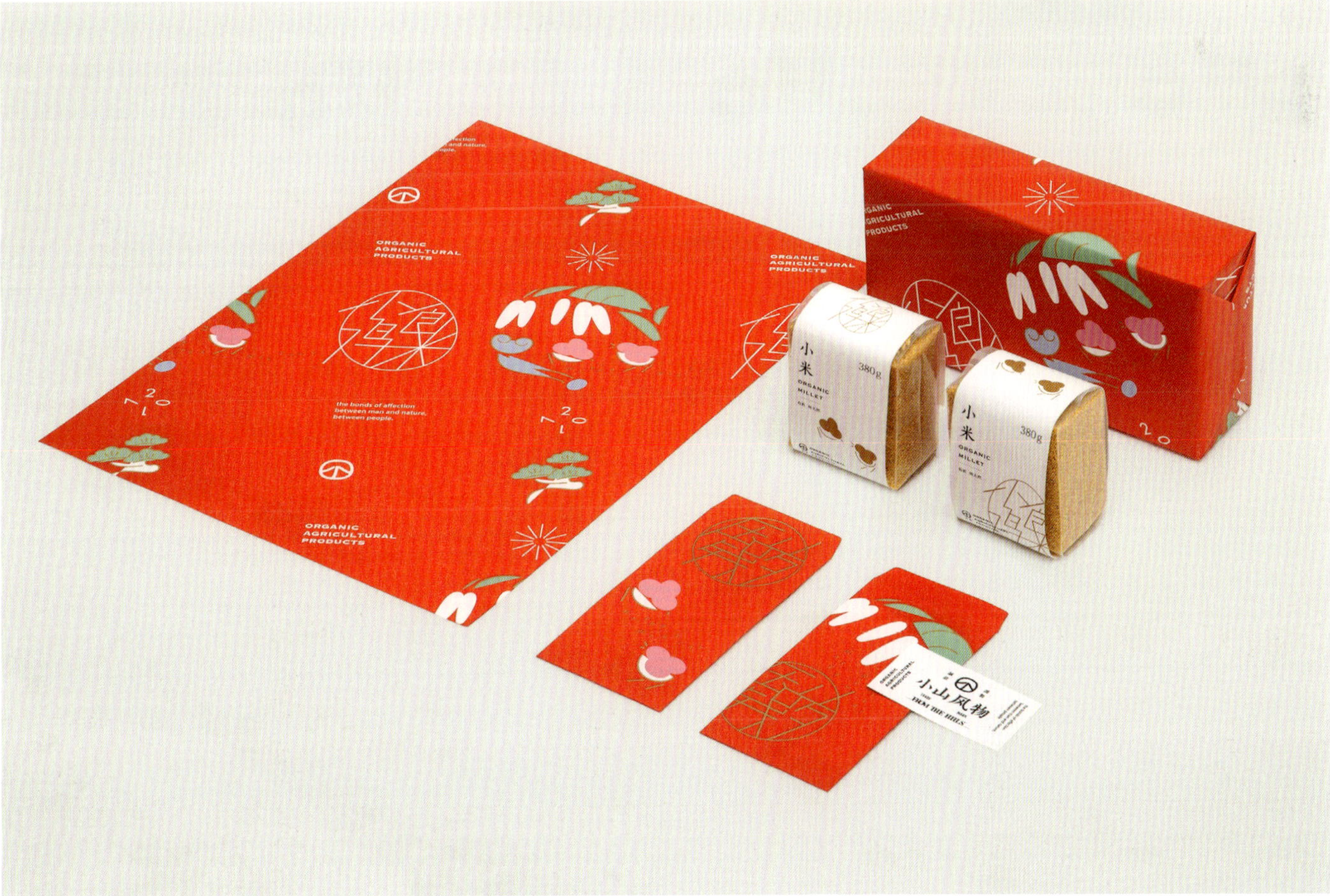

Leonie Rudelt Osteopathie

paper, cardboard

Leonie Rudelt offers osteopathy for children. The concept behind this branding was inspired by toy blocks for children. The designer chose geometric shapes used for the logo as well as a graphic element. The business cards show different sections of the graphic elements and can be combined and therefore used as toys for the children waiting for their appointments.

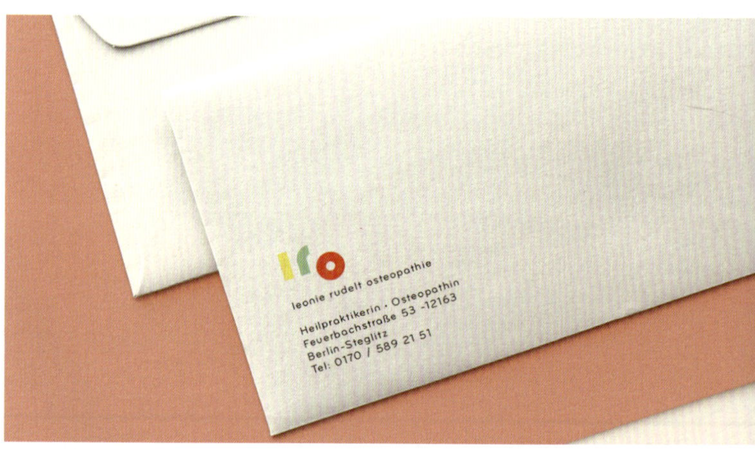

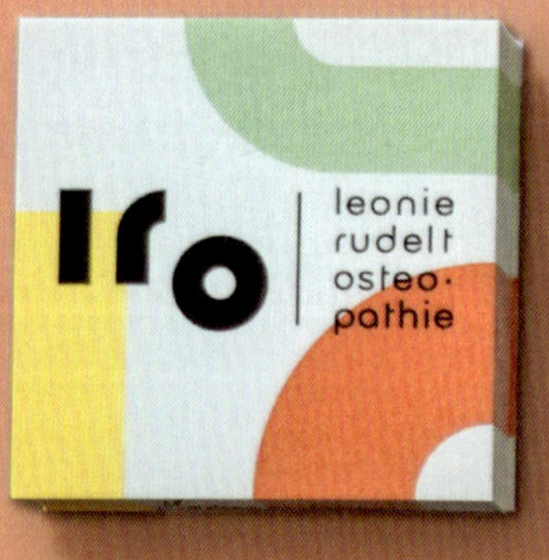

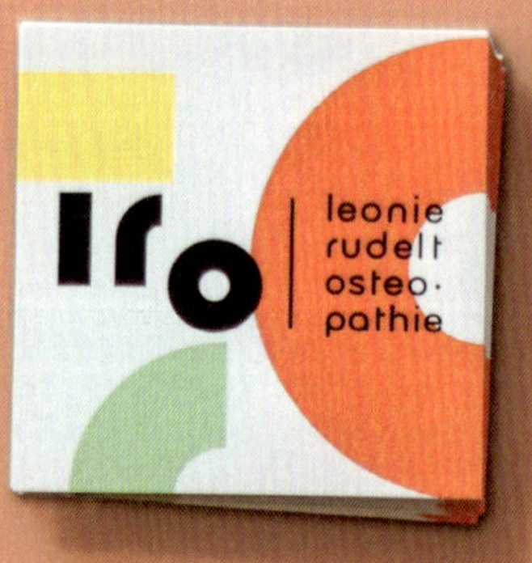

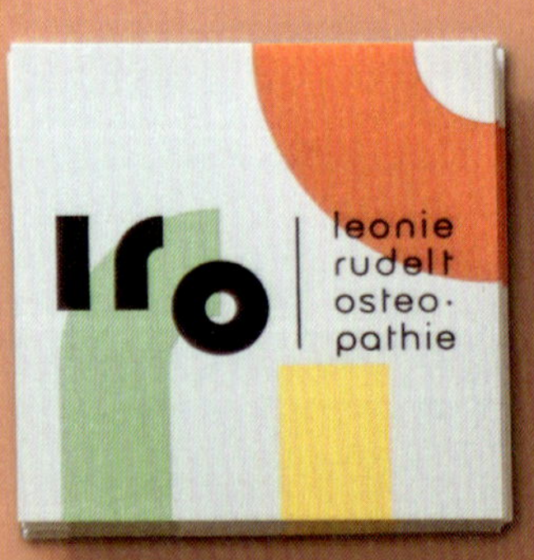

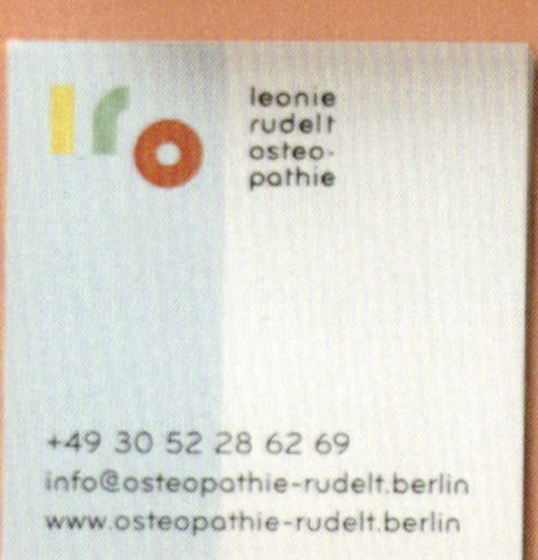

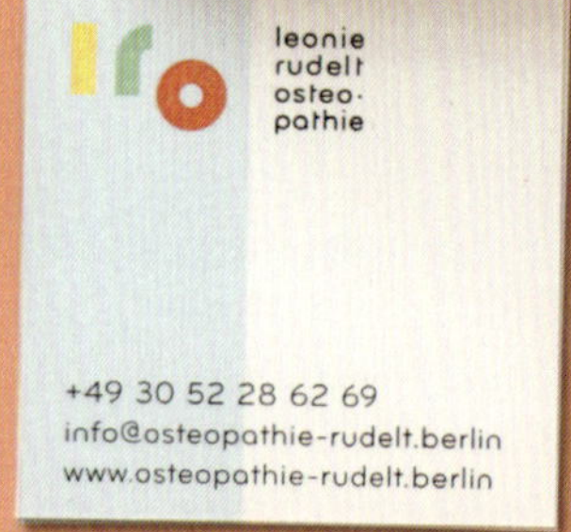

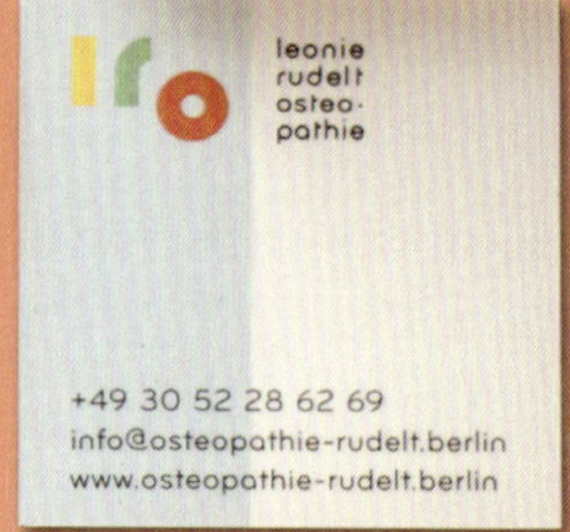

D: Alessia Sistori

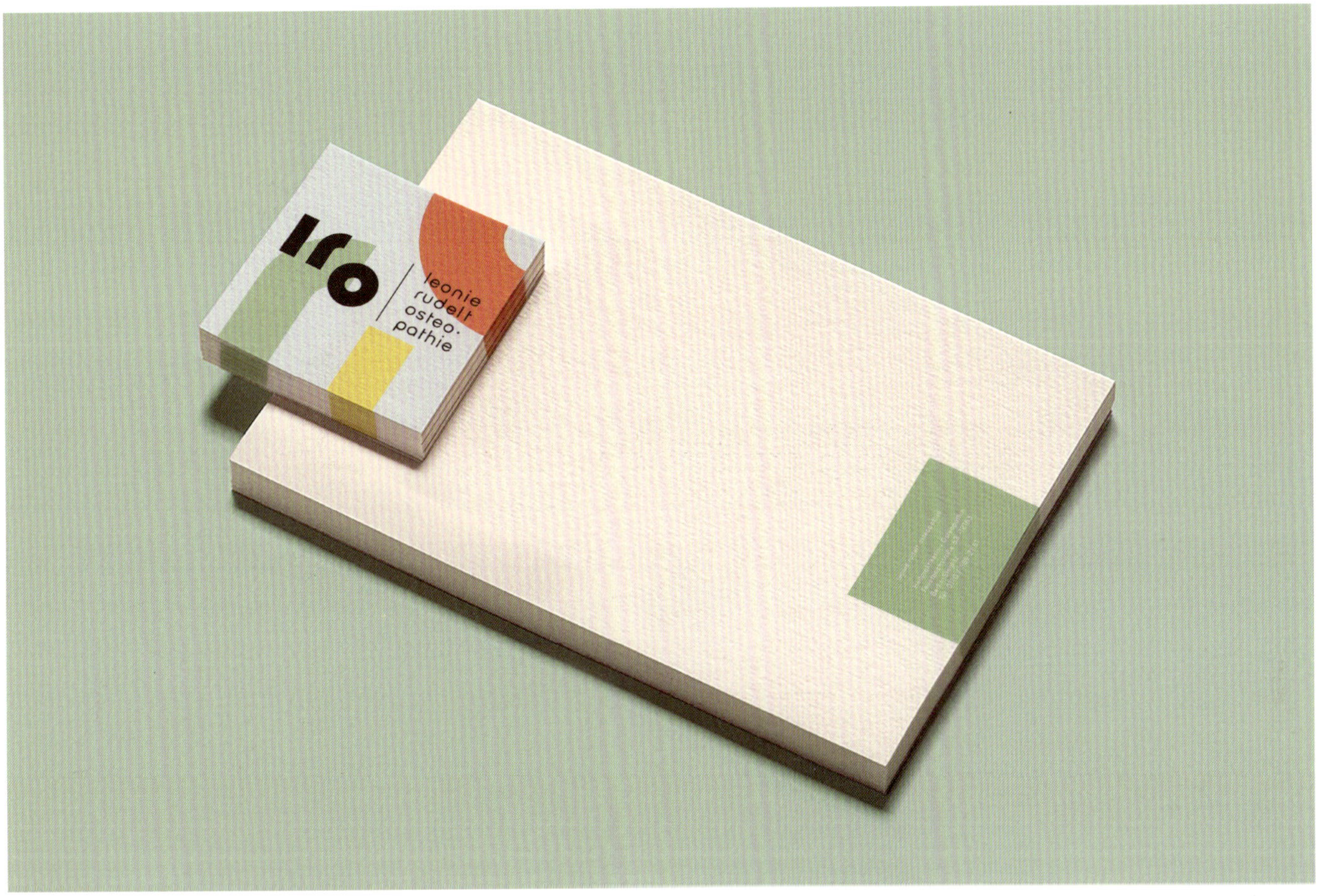
lro
leonie
rudelt
osteo.
pathie

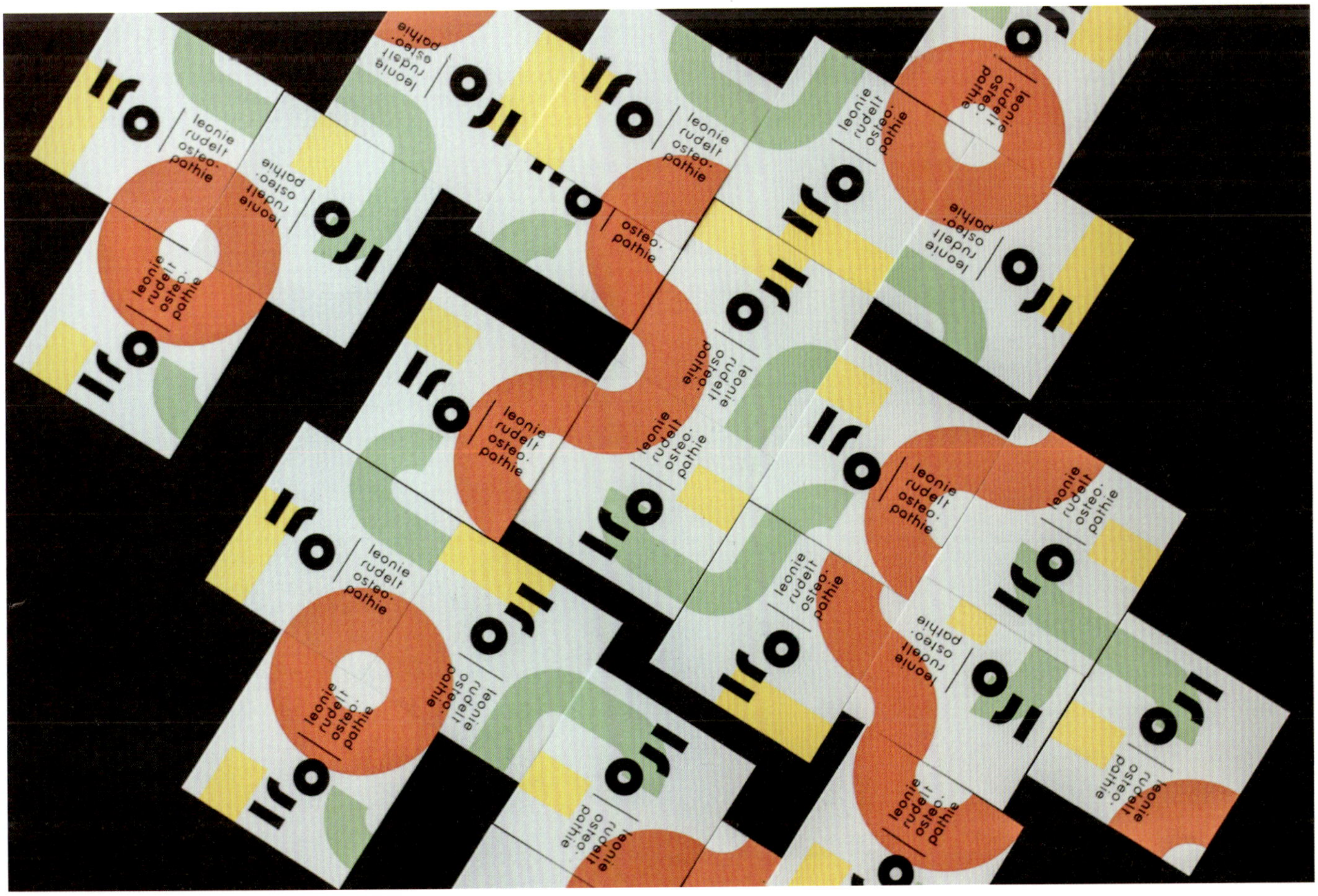
lro
leonie
rudelt
osteo.
pathie

ZOUKHROF

200g matt (DL envelop/brochure), 250g matt (business card)

CMYK 4 colors

ZOUKHROF is an Arabic word which means ornament and pattern. ZOUKHROF is also a form of decoration used in the Arab world since ancient times. They used the word "ZOUKHROF" to be their agency's name because of its artistic and creative impact, which represents the mission and vision of their agency. ZOUKHROF is a multinational marketing and advertising agency located in Syria. The designer used the Square shape which is the most used shape in Arabic ornaments and designed a word mark inspired from the Kufi Square font. And the flexibility part for the agency appears in the letters dots and there movement to the axes.

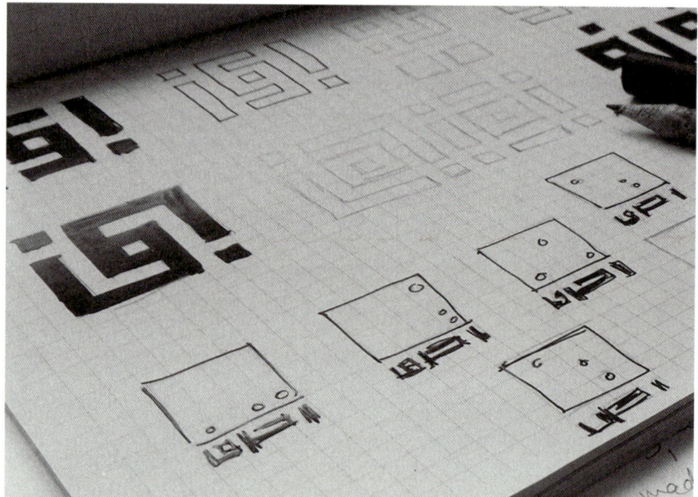

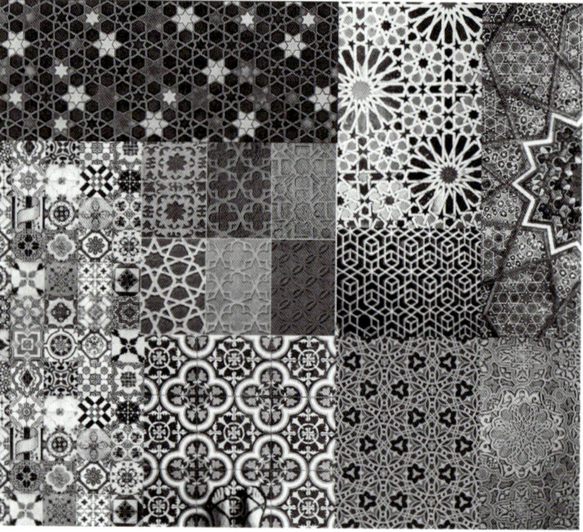

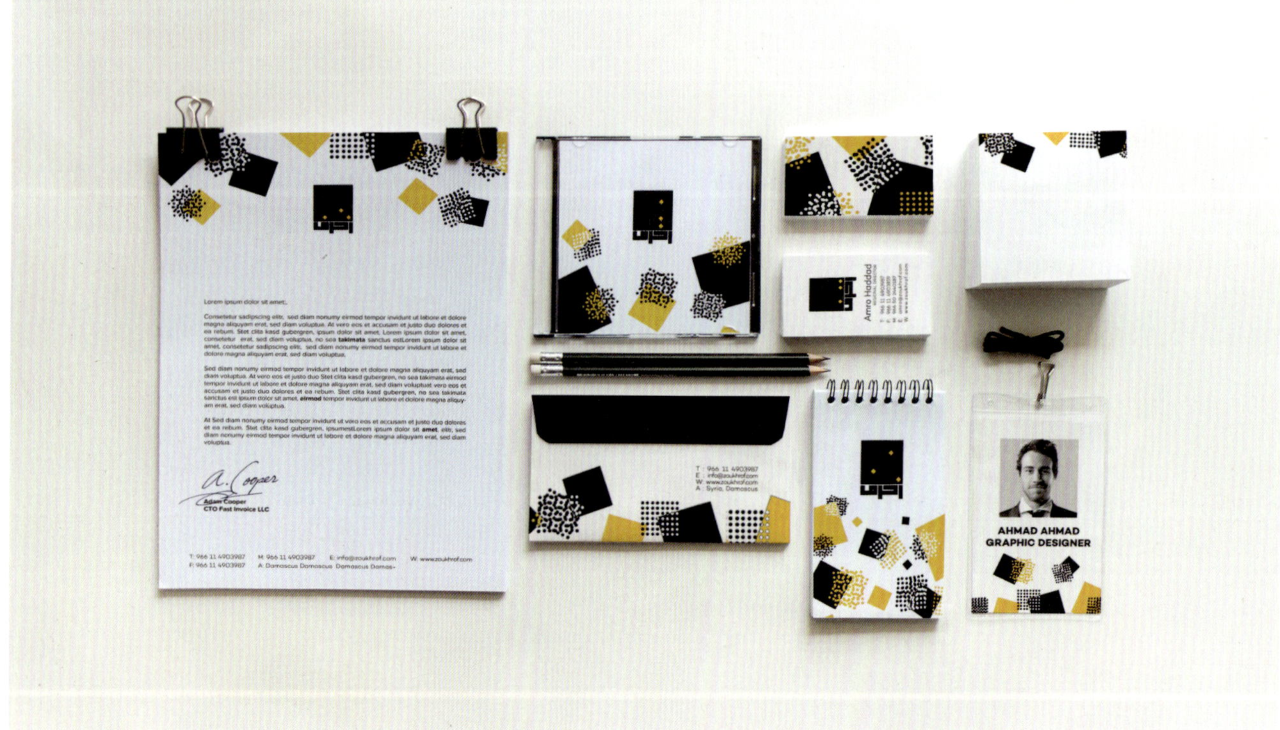

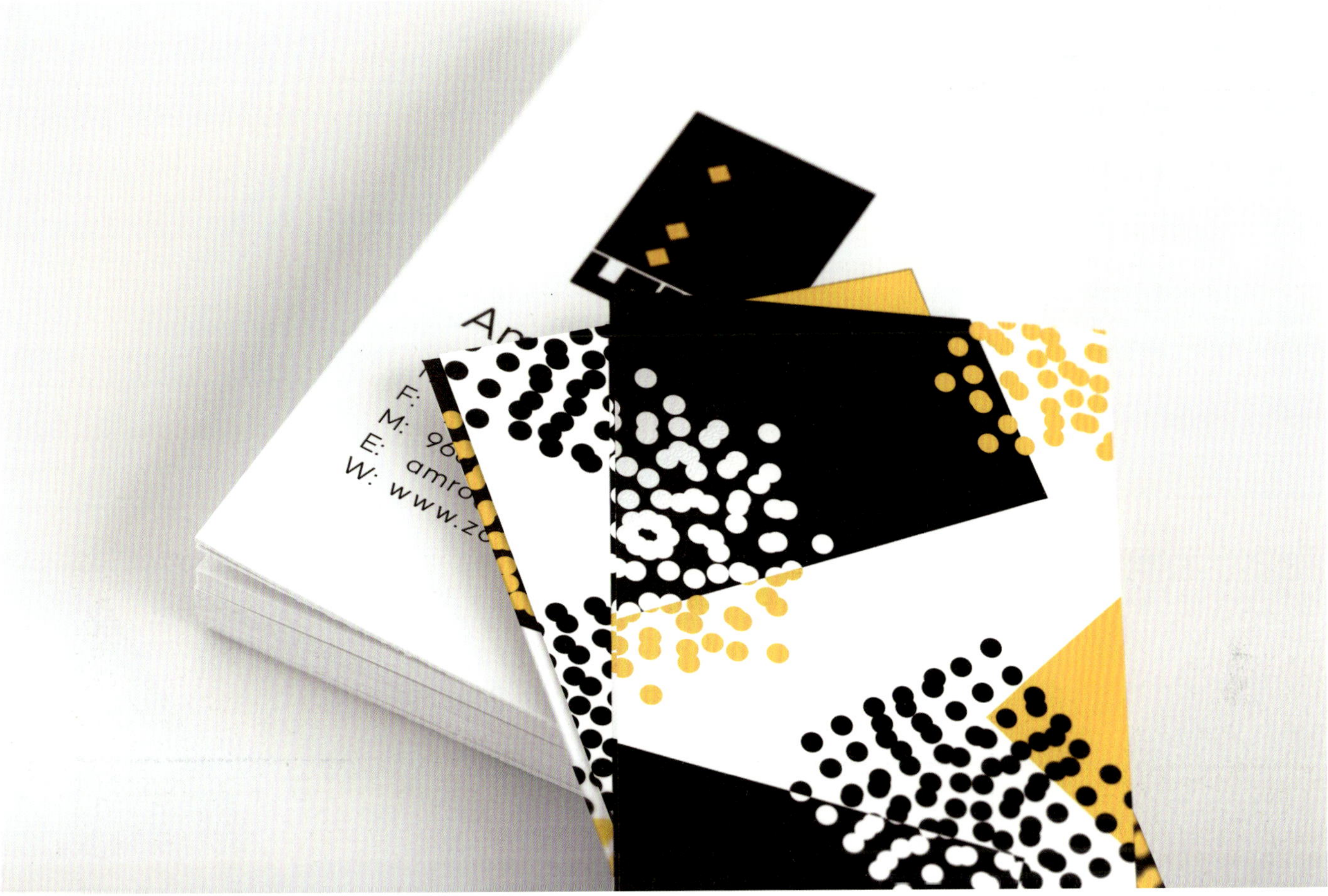

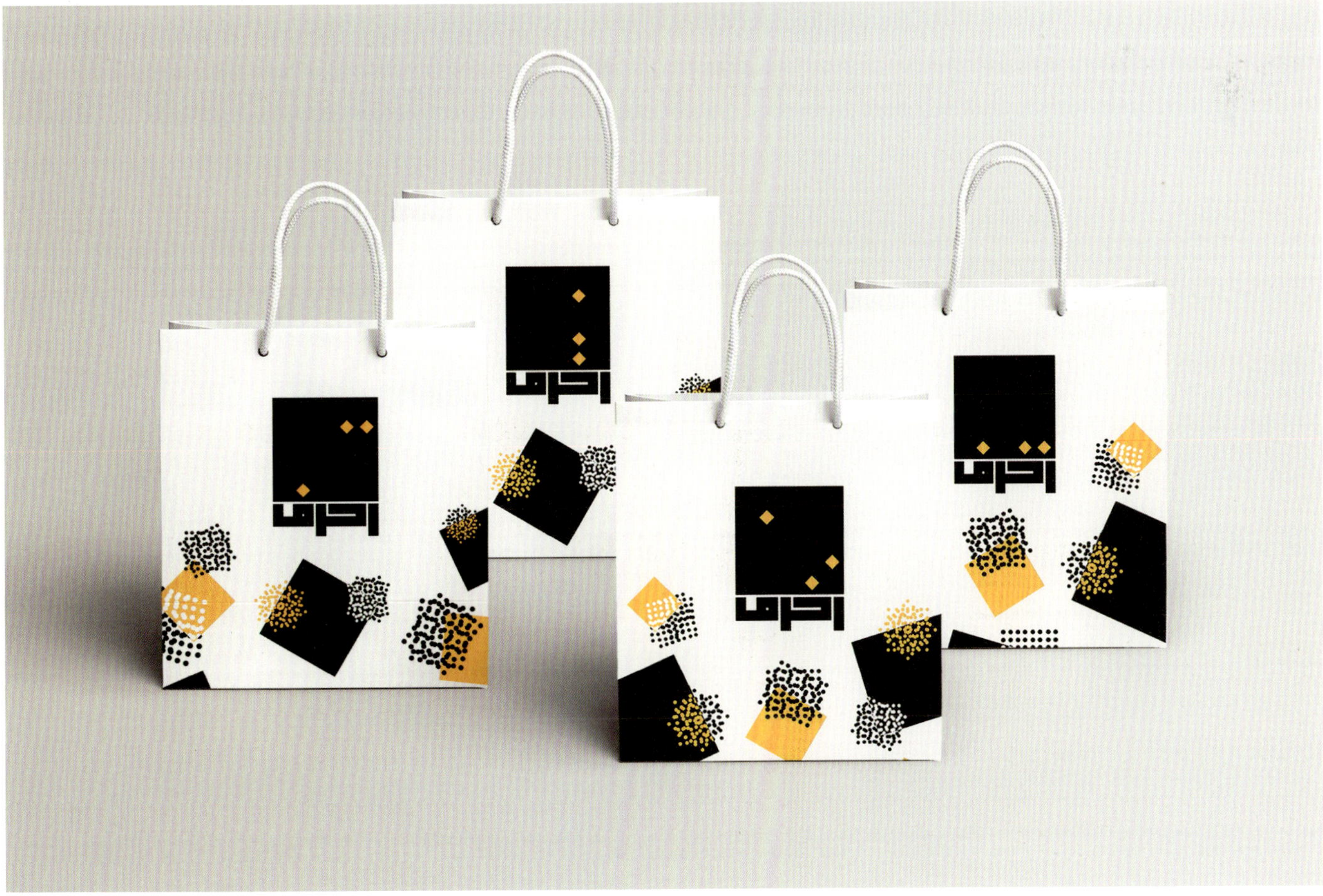

Sewoon Plaza and Makers Graphic Design

120g Snow White

CMYK, Gold spot color, Pantone 802 C

"Sewoon Plaza" is an electronic product shopping mall in Seoul that boasts a long tradition. And "Makers" are young people who make a variety of ideas using electronic devices. "Sewoon Plaza and Makers" is an event that will showcase to the public the results of collaborations between young "Makers" and people working at Sewoon Plaza. The designer made electronic objects, electronic devices, and electronic boards as graphic object. And he printed a gold spot color on blue to reveal the characteristics of the machine. The main graphics were used as posters, websites, and printed materials.

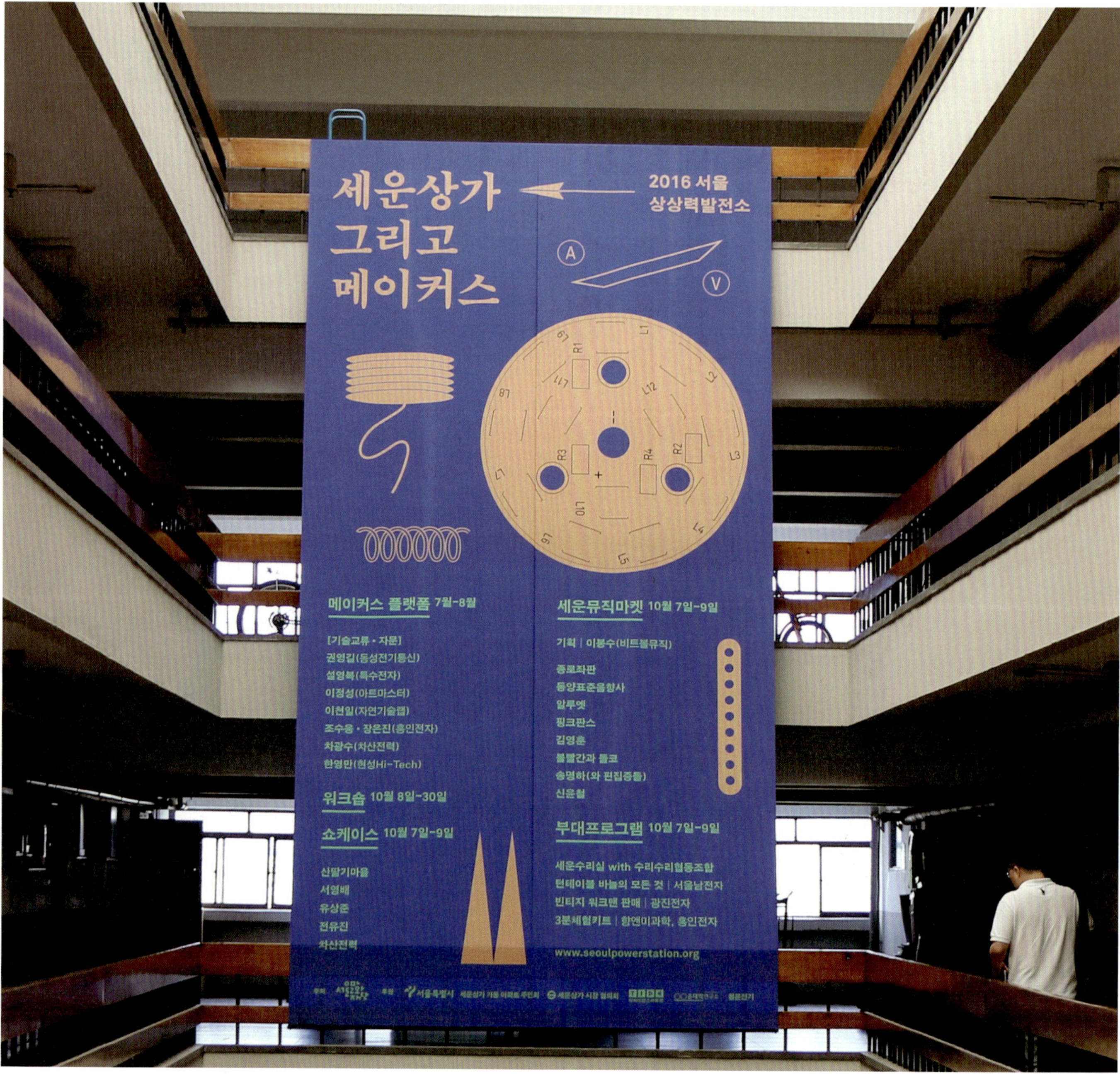

 D: Kisung Jang

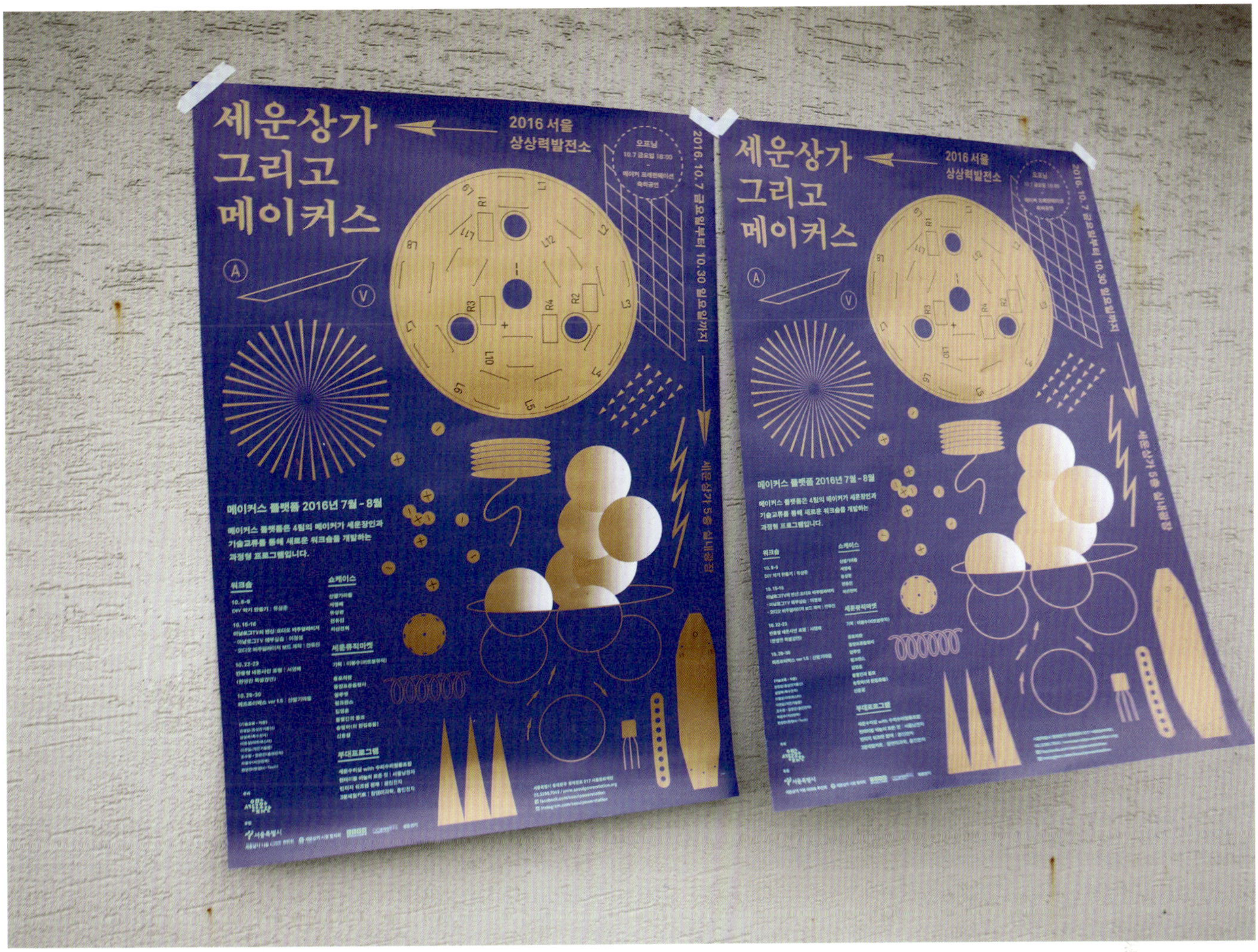

세운상가
그리고
메이커스
2016 서울
상상력발전소
2016. 10. 7 금요일부터 10. 30 일요일까지
메이커스 플랫폼 2016년 7월 - 8월
세운상가 5층 실내광장

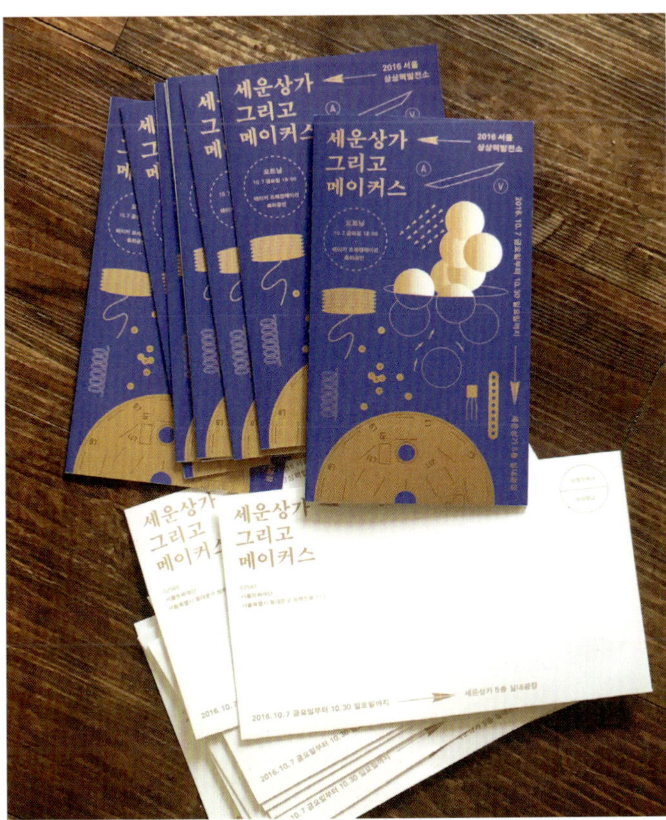
세운상가
그리고
메이커스
2016 서울
상상력발전소

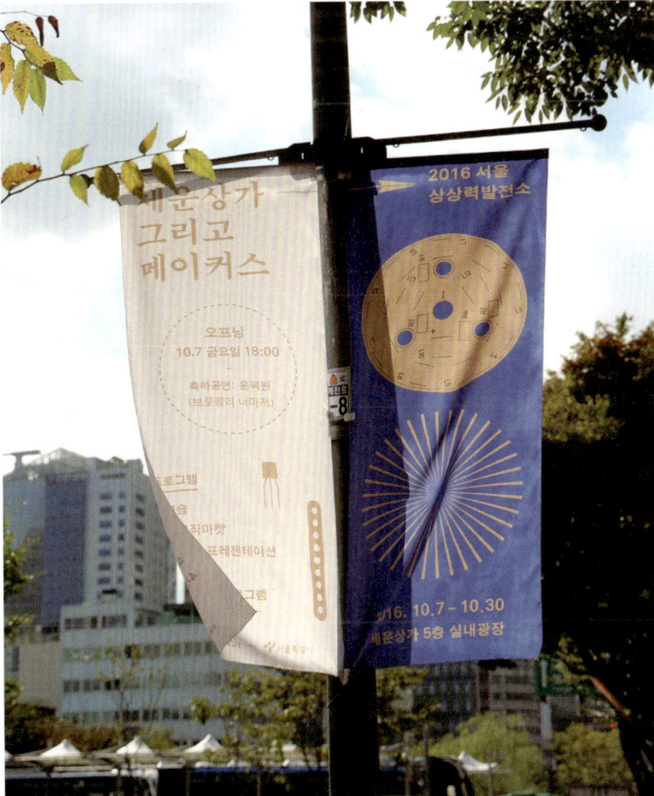
세운상가
그리고
메이커스
오프닝
10.7 금요일 18:00
축하공연: 윤덕원
(브로콜리 너마저)
2016 서울
상상력발전소
2016. 10.7 - 10.30
세운상가 5층 실내광장

LUSO DESIGN SHOW

This initiative is a short selection of the best of designs created by designers, brands, and factories based in some Portuguese-speaking countries. The selections aim to showcase a variety of different businesses where design and creativity are key factors adding value to a product or brand. A multi-directional approach to each exhibit, presenting both the result of design process as well as the process itself, provides a glimpse of what lies behind design.

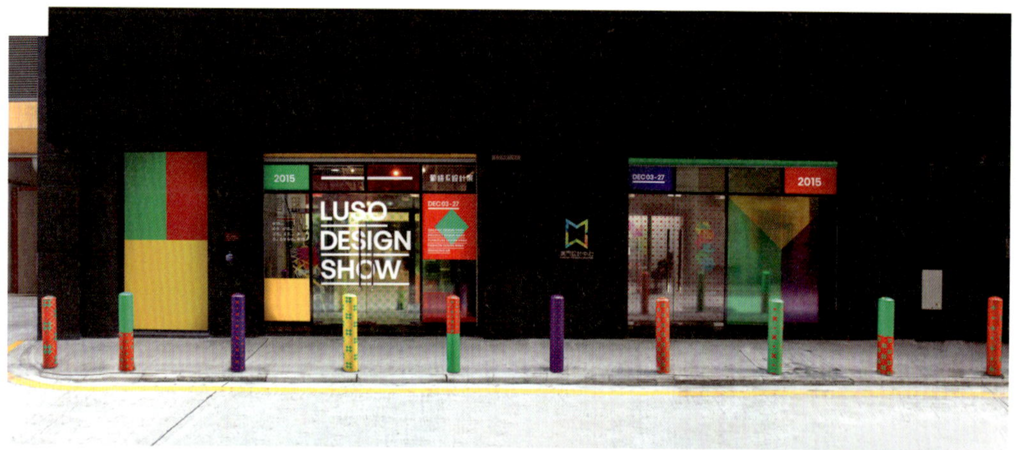

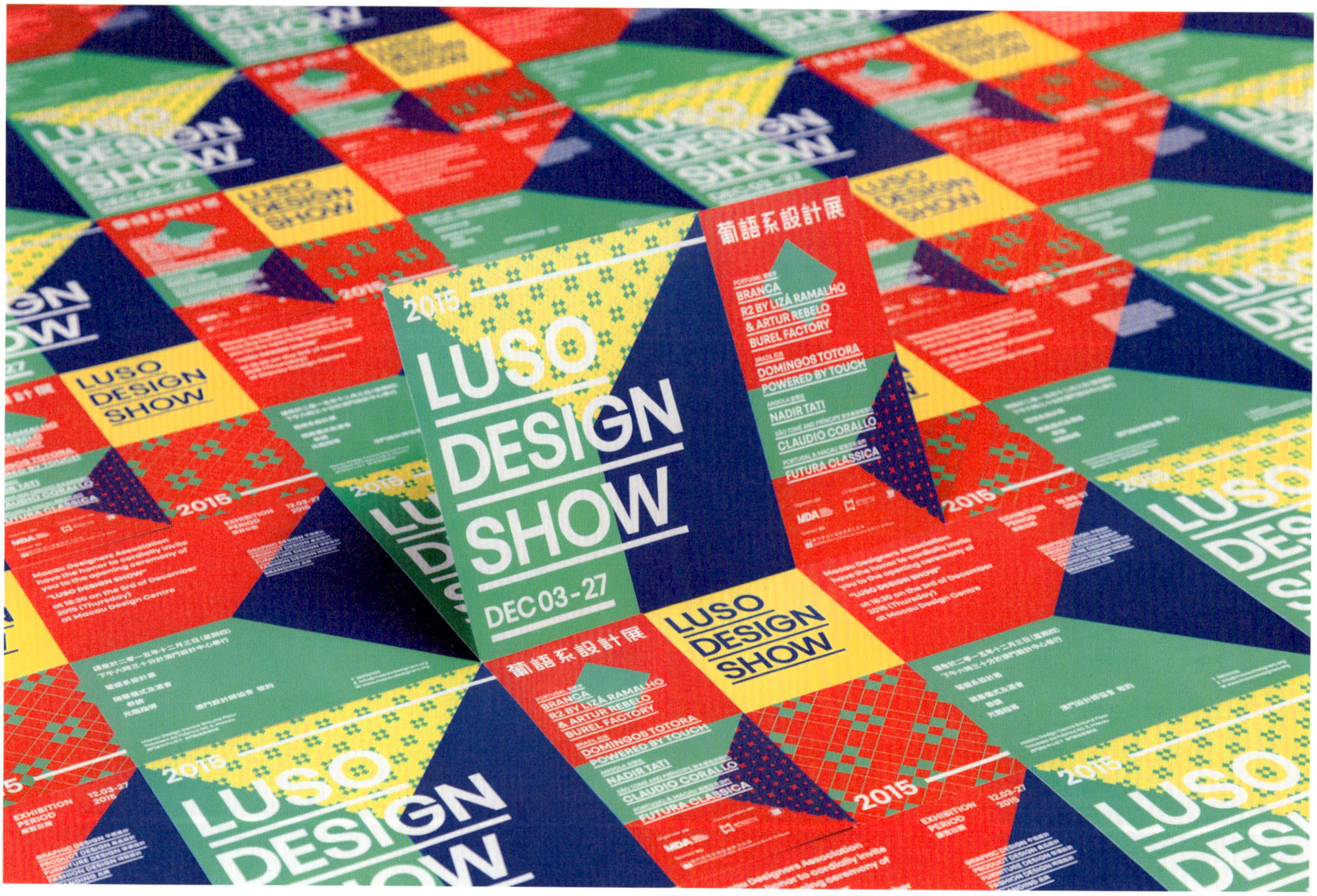

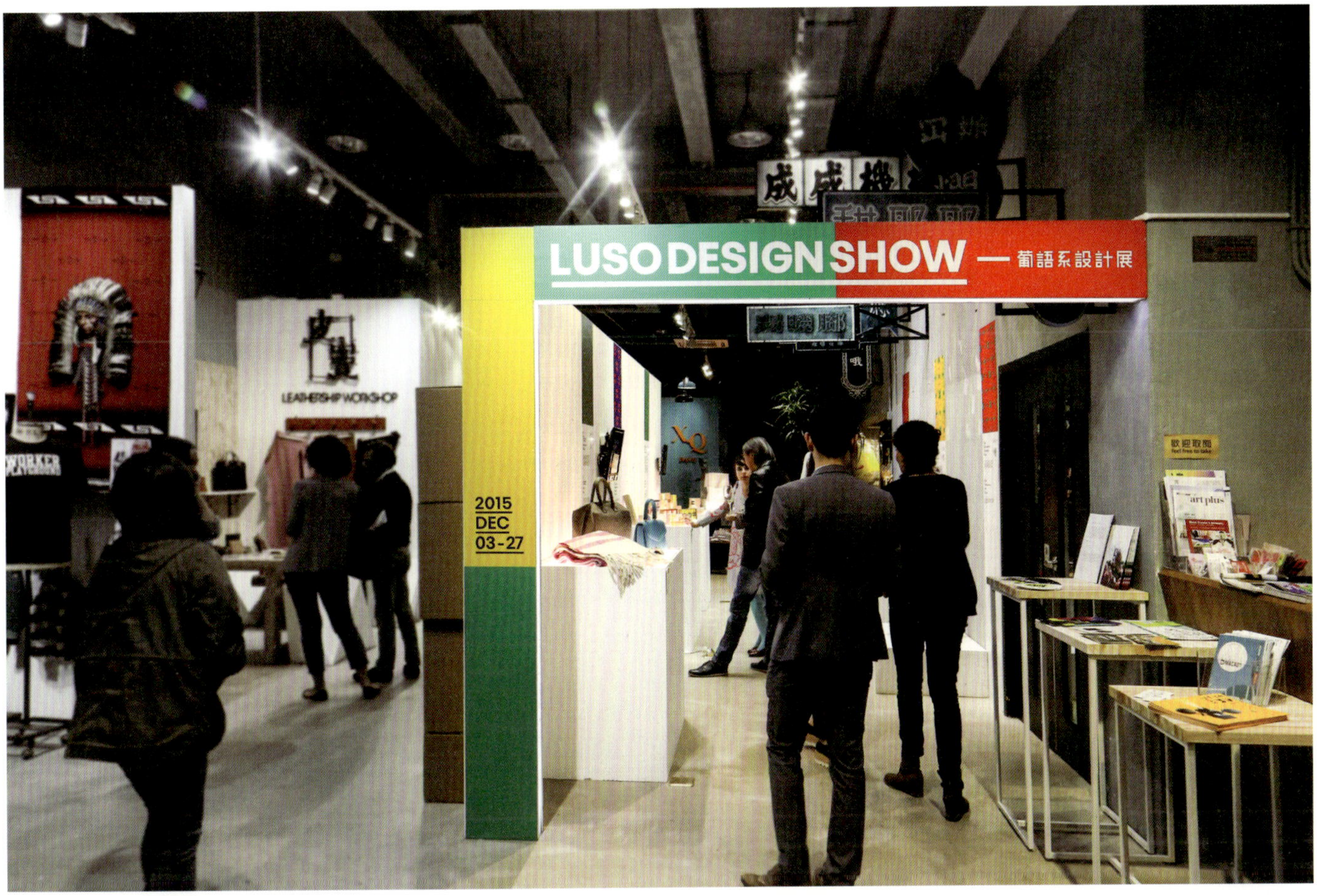

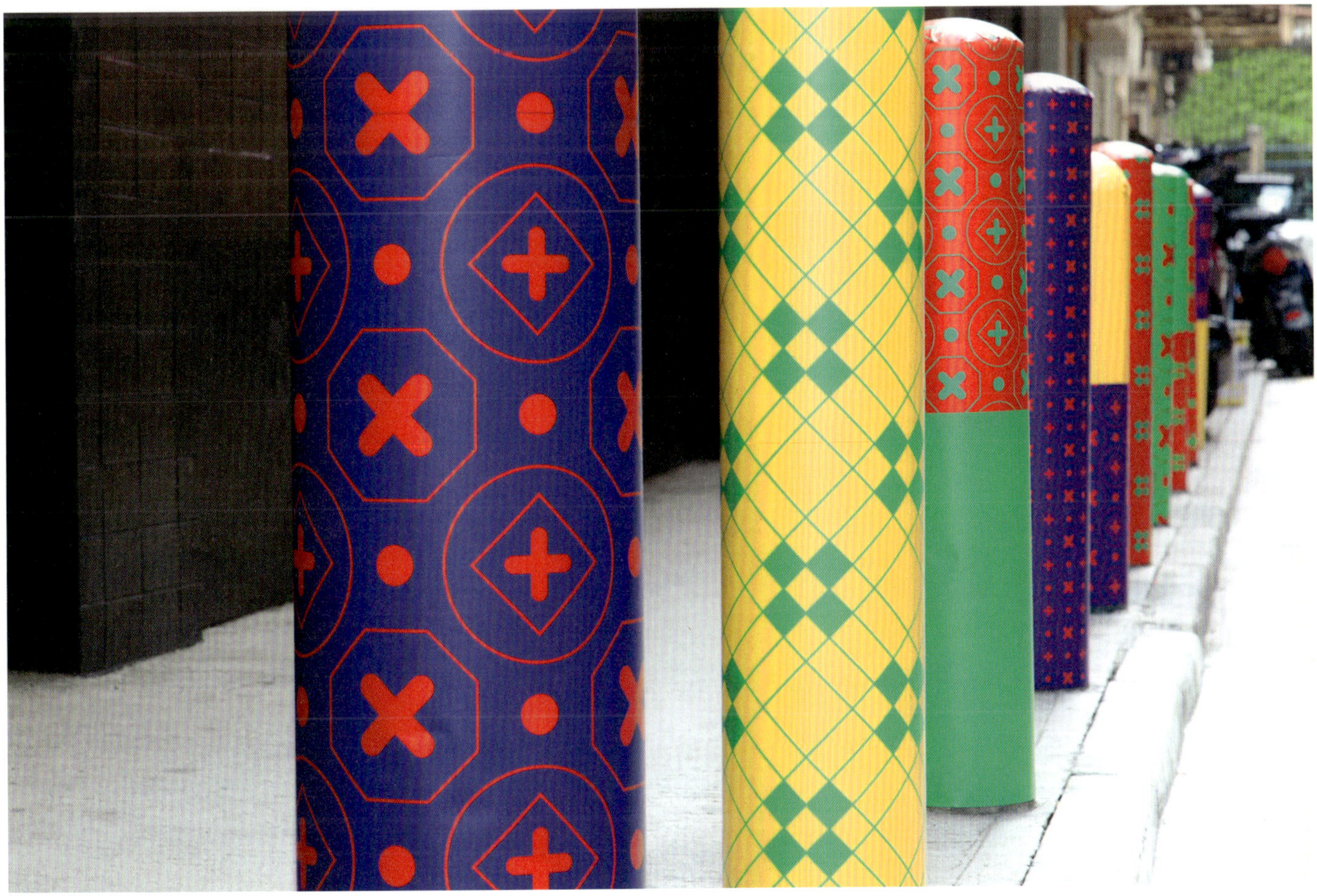

Commemorating the 150th Anniversary of the Birth Dr. Sun Yat-sen

light weight coated paper

Pantone Neutral Black C

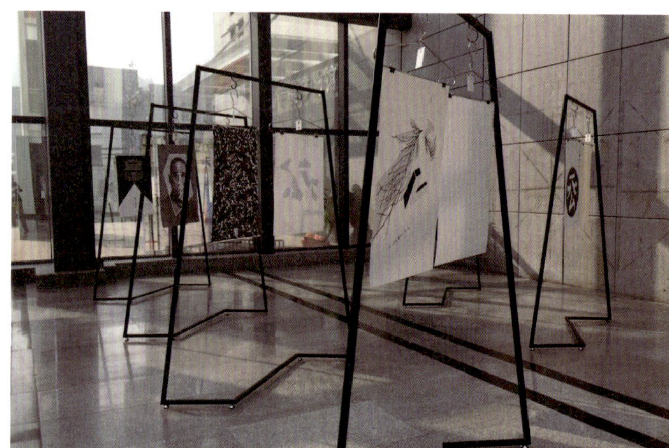

This memorial poster is designed from the perspective of Taiwan. In Taiwan, the image of Dr. Sun Yat-Sen is applied to the design of NT$100 note, which is used most widely. As time goes by, modern people usually connect Dr. Sun Yat-Sen with the notes. Therefore, the image of the note is used as the topic of the poster, constructed with geometric shapes in salute to his democratic revolutions. The poster not only serves his memory but also tries to raise viewer's awareness about the influence of historical figures on what is happening now. The offset printing method was used to achieve an optimal effect.

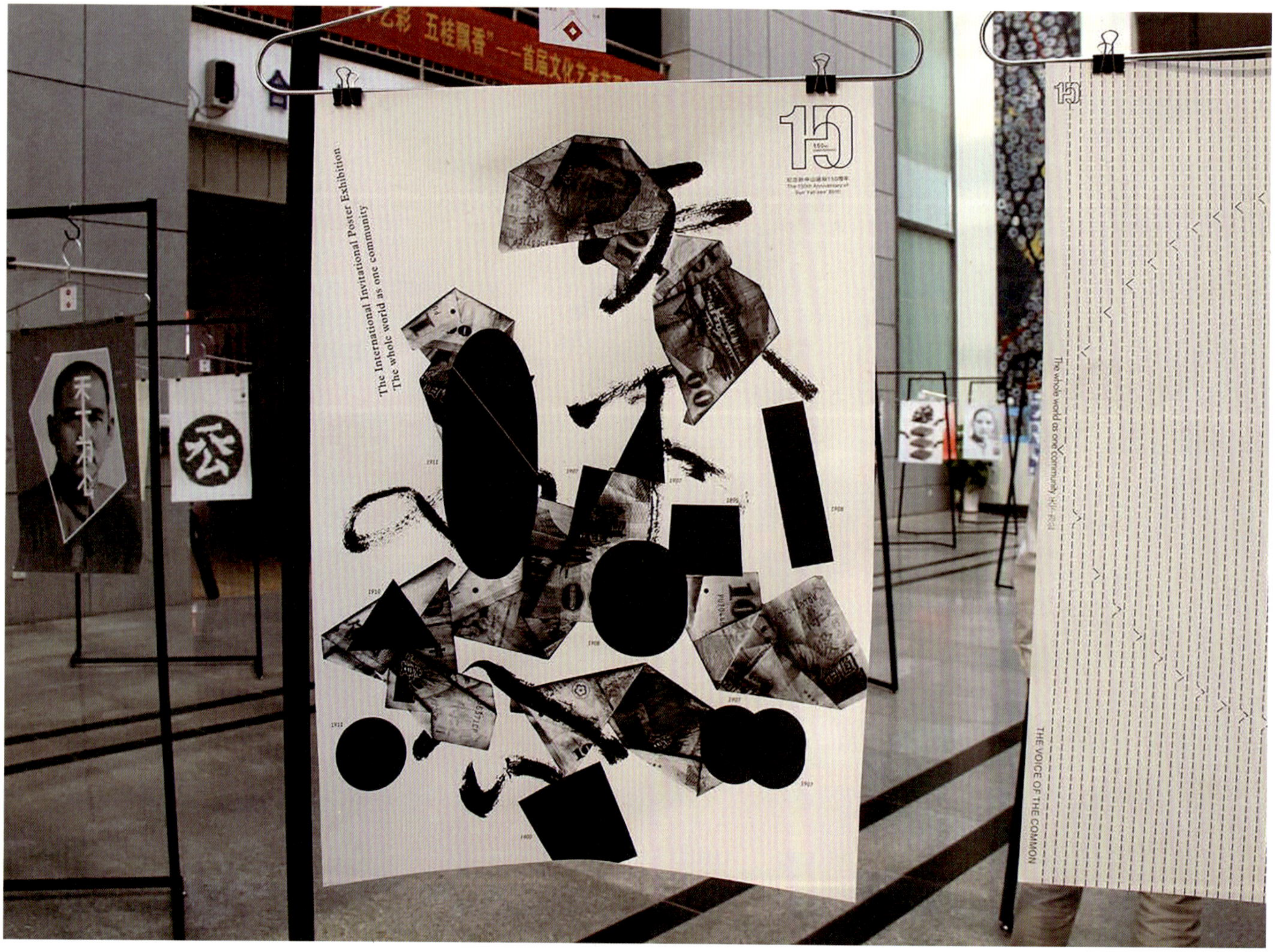

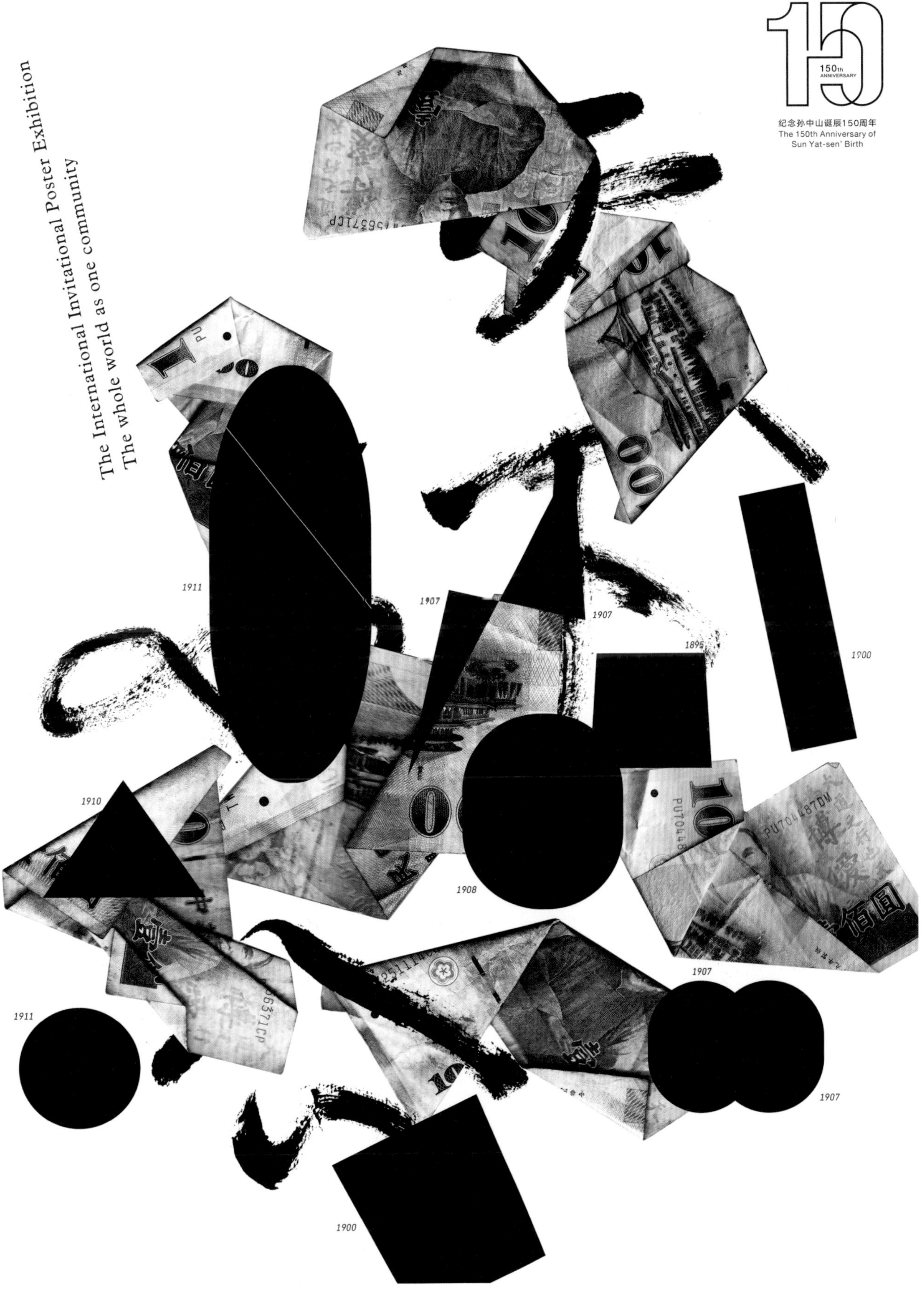

150th ANNIVERSARY
紀念孙中山诞辰150周年
The 150th Anniversary of
Sun Yat-sen' Birth
The International Invitational Poster Exhibition
The whole world as one community
1911
1907
1907
1895
1900
1910
1908
1907
1911
1907
1900

De Martino

The restyling of this logo considered the impressive wealth of centuries of family history, a history that has been condensed into a pictogram joined by the family's name, a solution that recalls the medieval heraldic tradition. The use of symbols, mostly of the four alchemical elements—fire, land, air, water—and Sant'Antuono, the patron of those who work with fire and a votive image cared for by the family, offers a complex design: compact and modern. The work is printing in an offset printing manner.

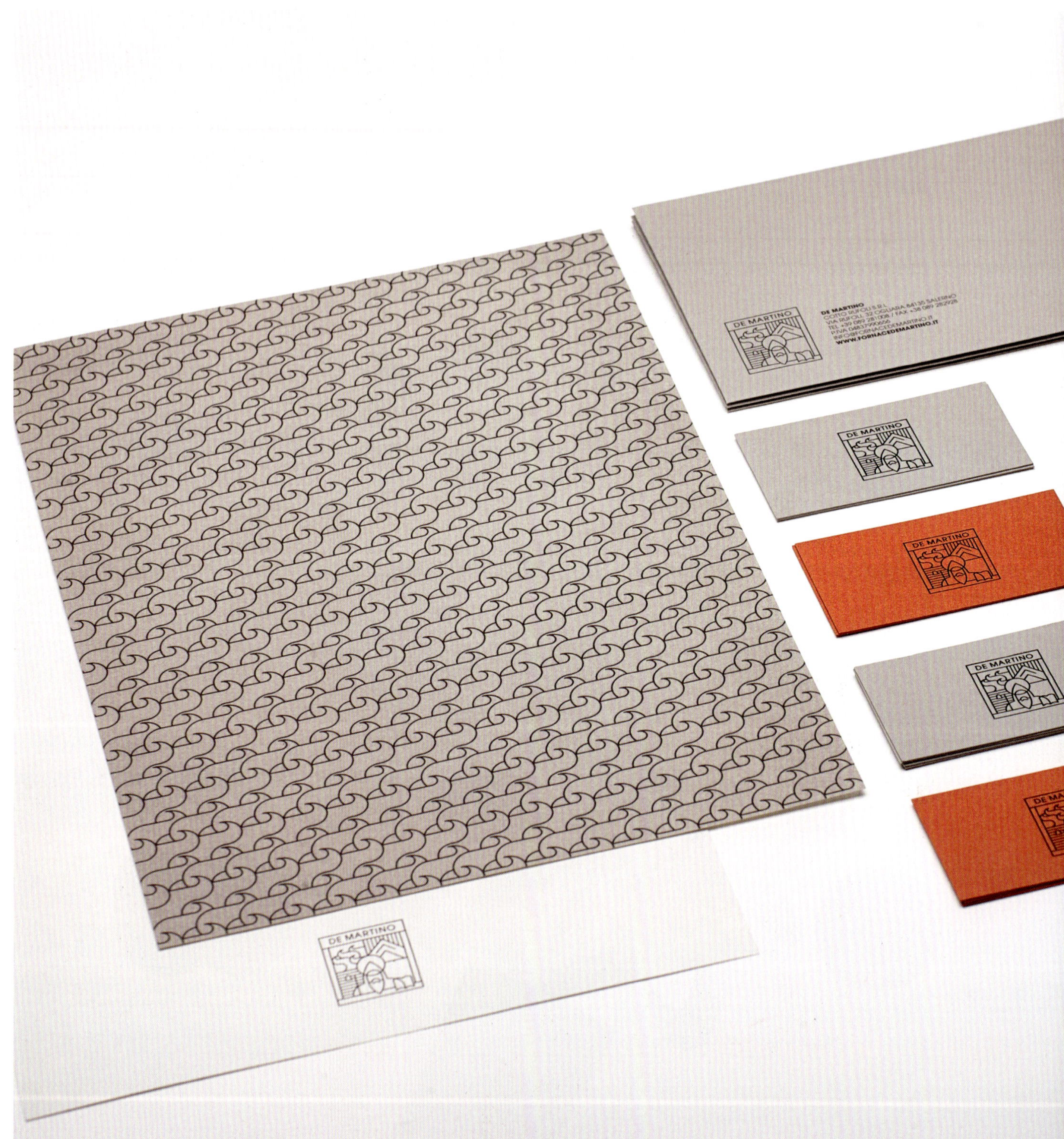

***D*:** Mario Cavallaro, Stefano Marra, Annamaria Varallo, Simonetta Pagliuca, Carla Del Regno

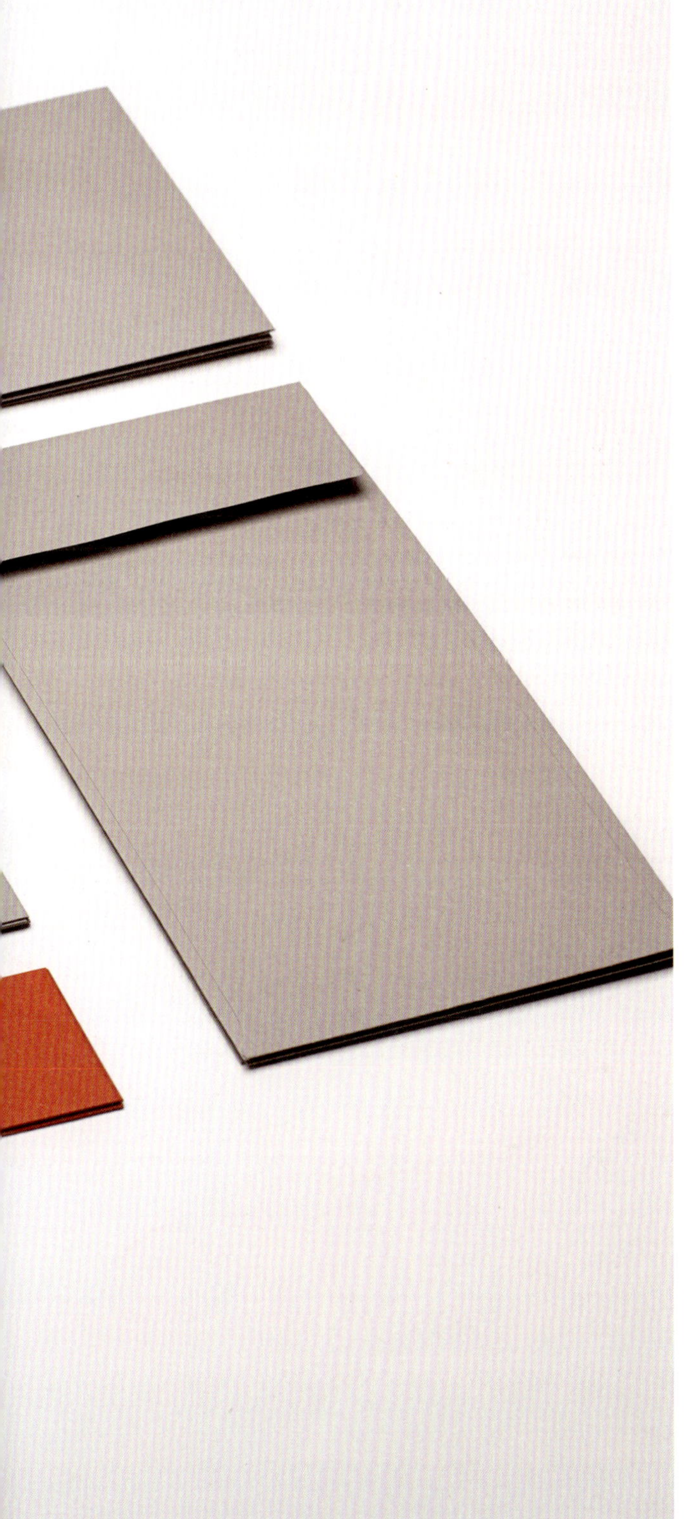

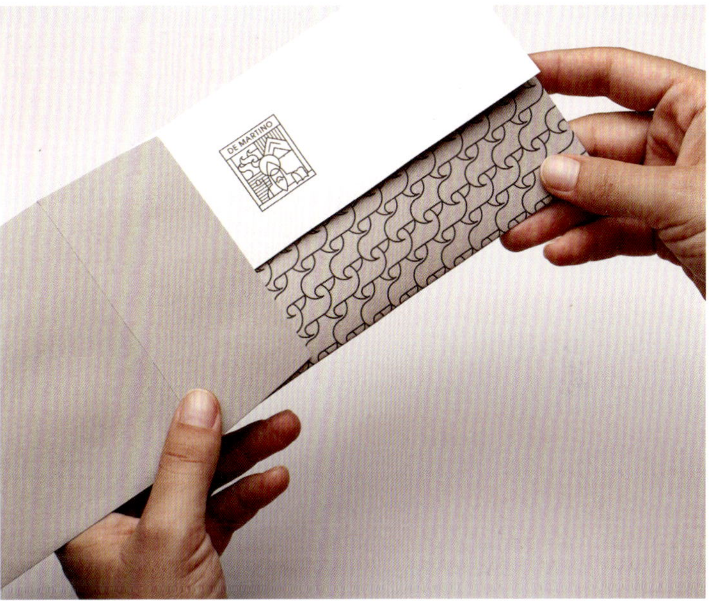
DE MARTINO

DE MARTINO
DE MARTINO
COTTO RUFOLI S.R.L
VIA RUFOLI, 32 OGLIARA 84135 SALERNO
TEL +39 089 281008 / FAX +38 089 282928
P.IVA 04837990656
INFO@FORNACEDEMARTINO.IT
WWW.FORNACEDEMARTINO.IT

ONE THING

The album aims to express the idea of "Try your best to do things that you most want to do." The technique of machine embroidery was used to convey the idea. The CMYK offset printing method was used to print the album.

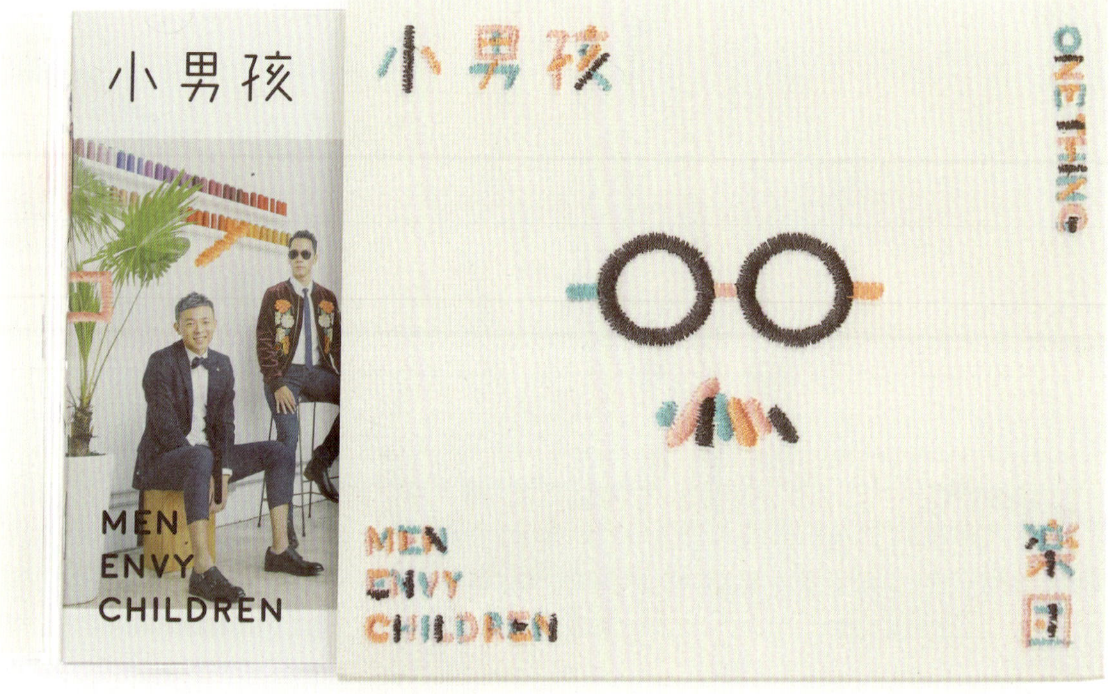

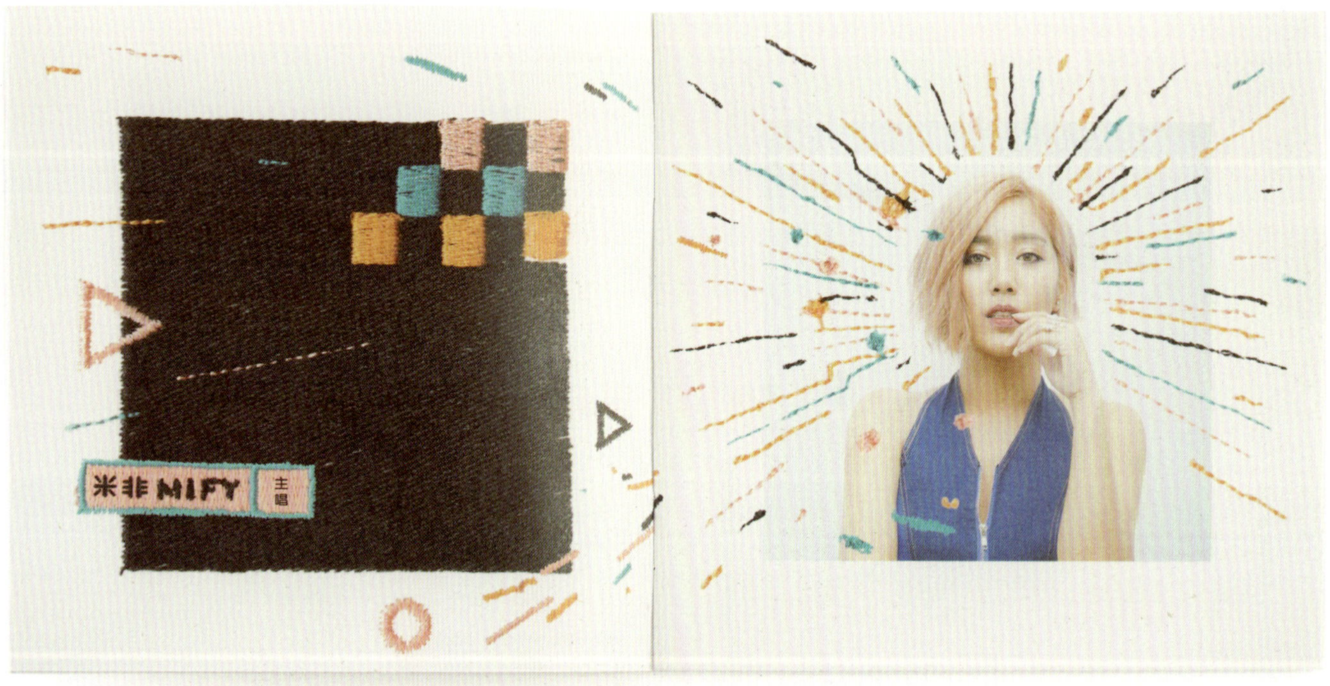

 D: Joy Fang, FKWU

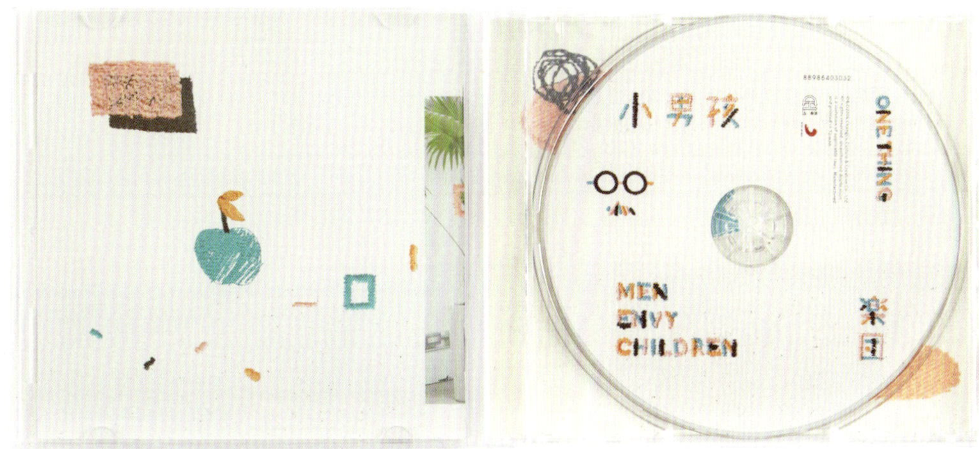
小男孩
ONE THING
MEN
ENVY
CHILDREN
楽団

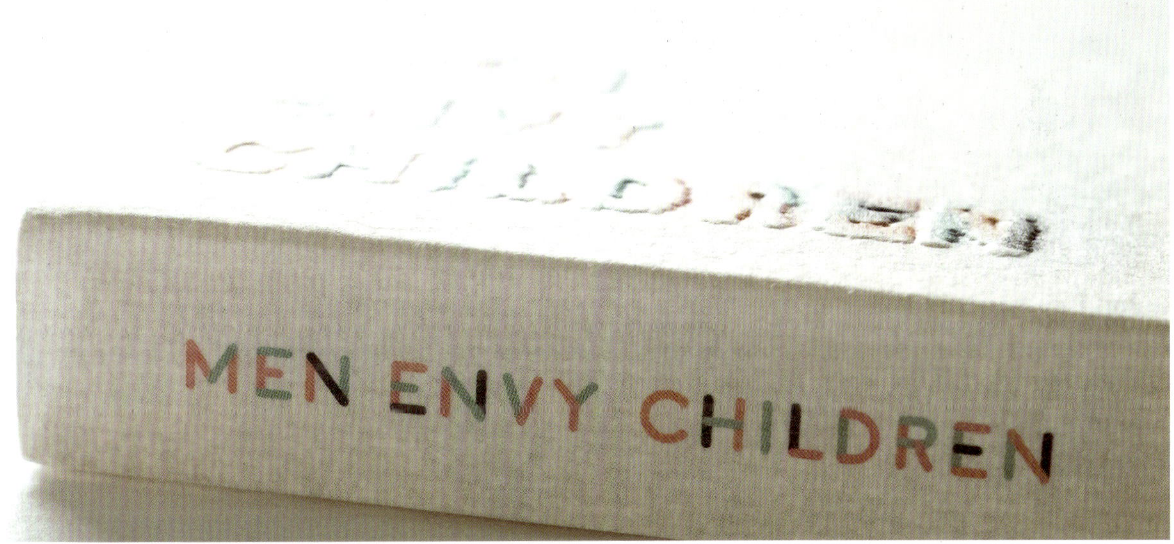
MEN ENVY CHILDREN

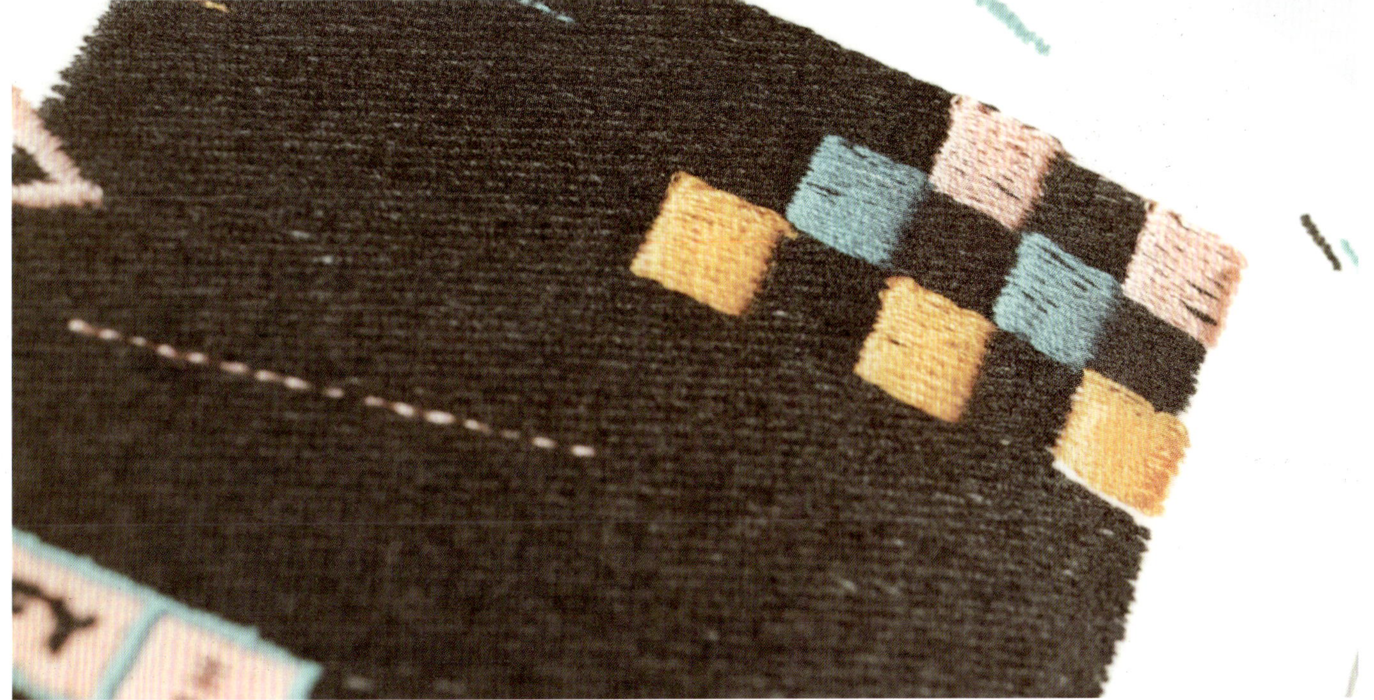

Morning Bound for Midnight—Diamond Zhang

Zhang thinks that no matter how long midnight might be, morning will come eventually. The cover of the album finds Zhang contemplating around midnight, with white flowers signifying morning and black flowers signifying night. The main visual theme is black and white. The PVC cover is printed in UV offset printing. And the song book is printed on black paper with white UV ink as well as white paper with CMYK offset printing.

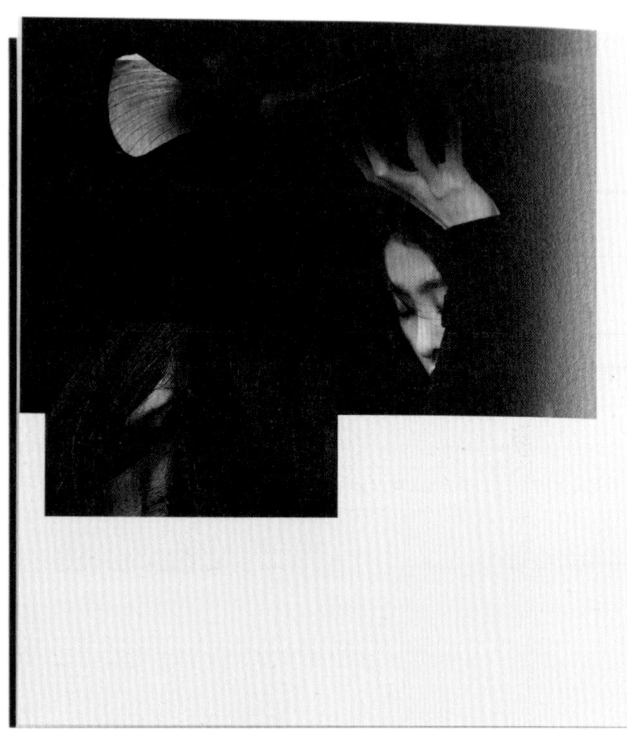

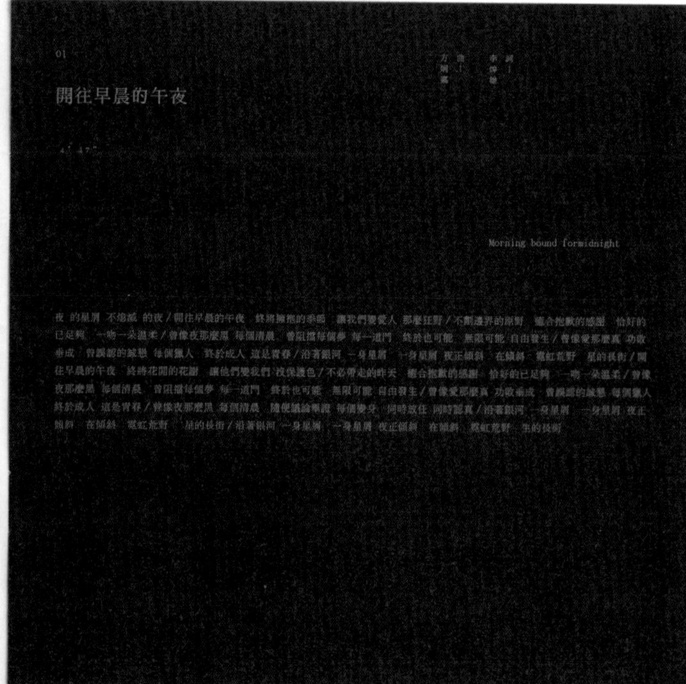

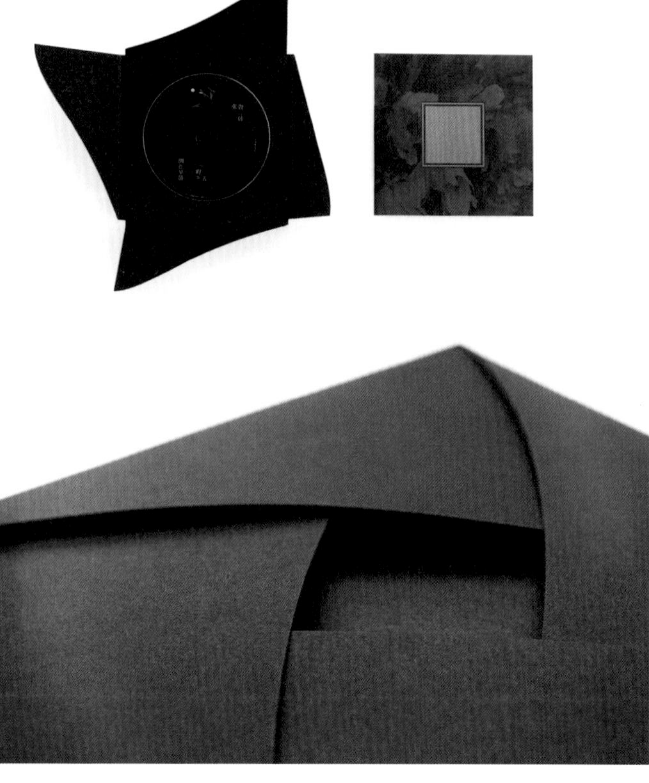

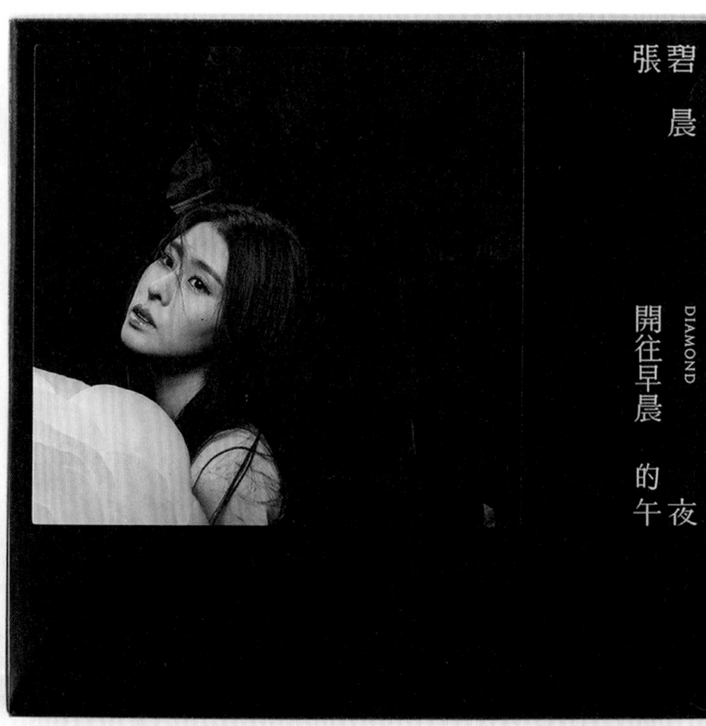

***D*:** Joy Fang

The Cave in the Forest

This is a 3-color lithography work created by the designer. The illustration was from the light event in the forest in Roztoky in the Czech Republic. She used both ink and chalk, made the two pictures on a stone, and printed it at the same time in order to use the same colors.

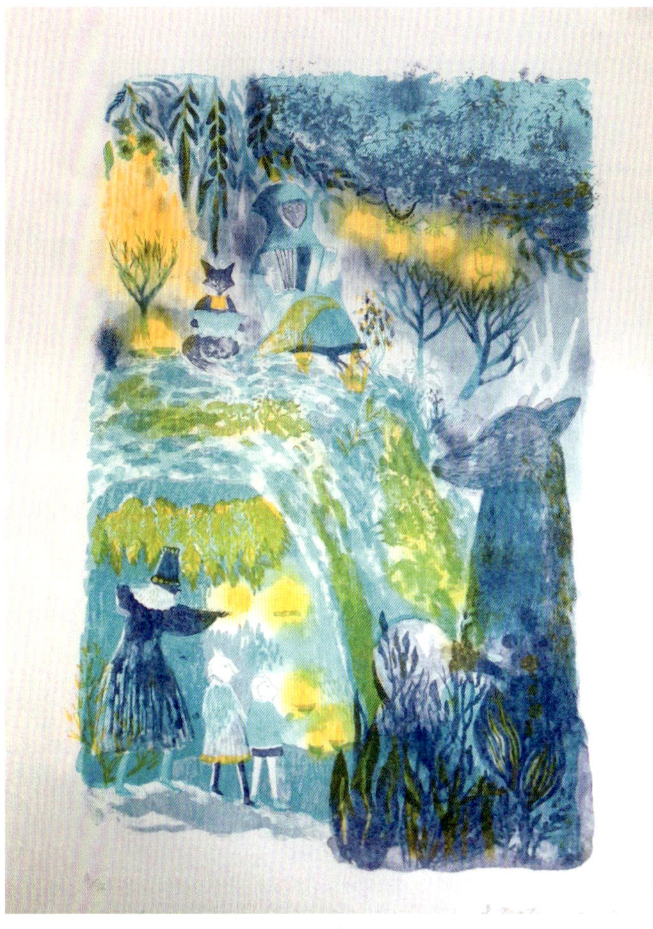

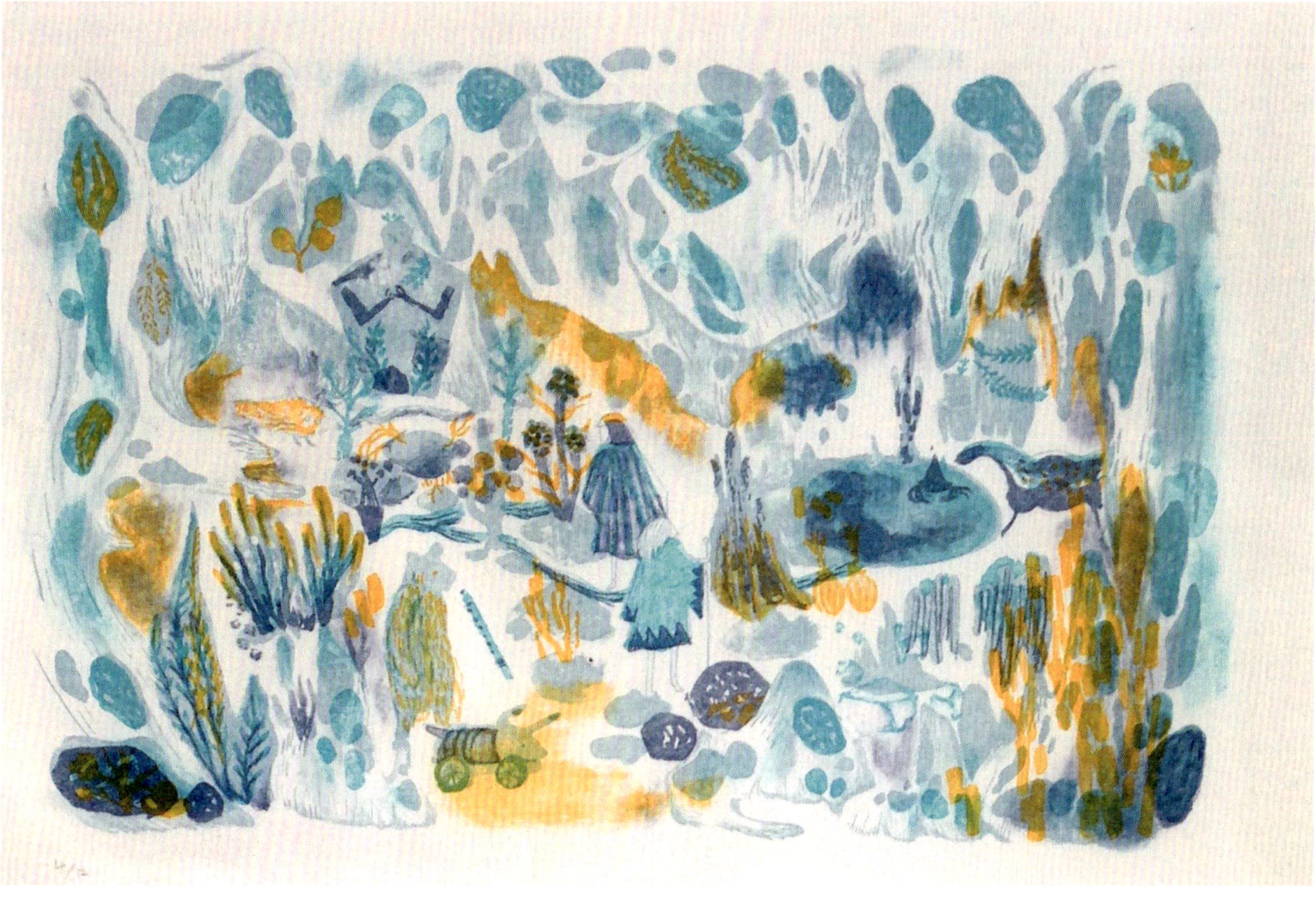

D: Saki Matsumoto

UMPRUM Animation Studio Newsletter

This is a newsletter from UMPRUM animation studio in Prague, Czech Republic. The illustration collects from students the characters of the animation. She chose to create in two colors, with an old offset printing machine.

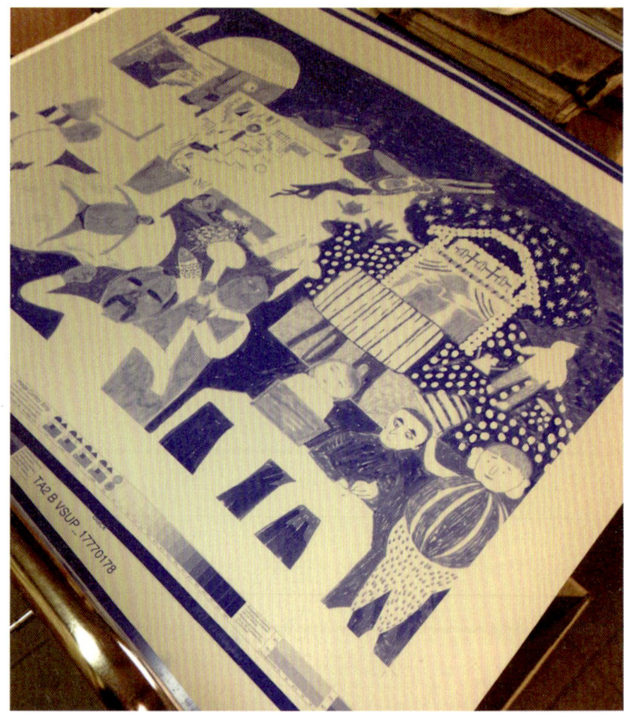

Printer: Jaroslav Jand'ourek

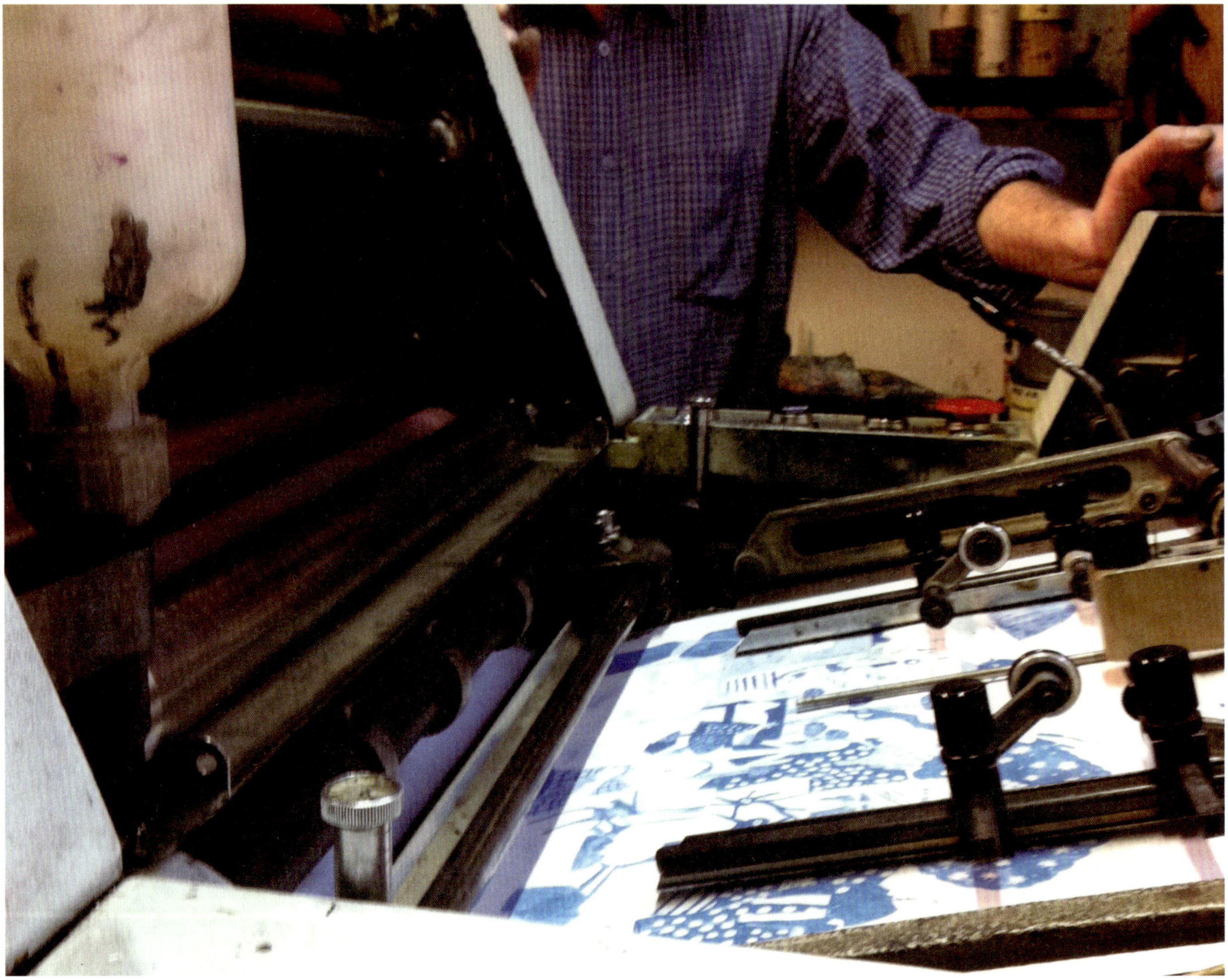

D: Saki Matsumoto

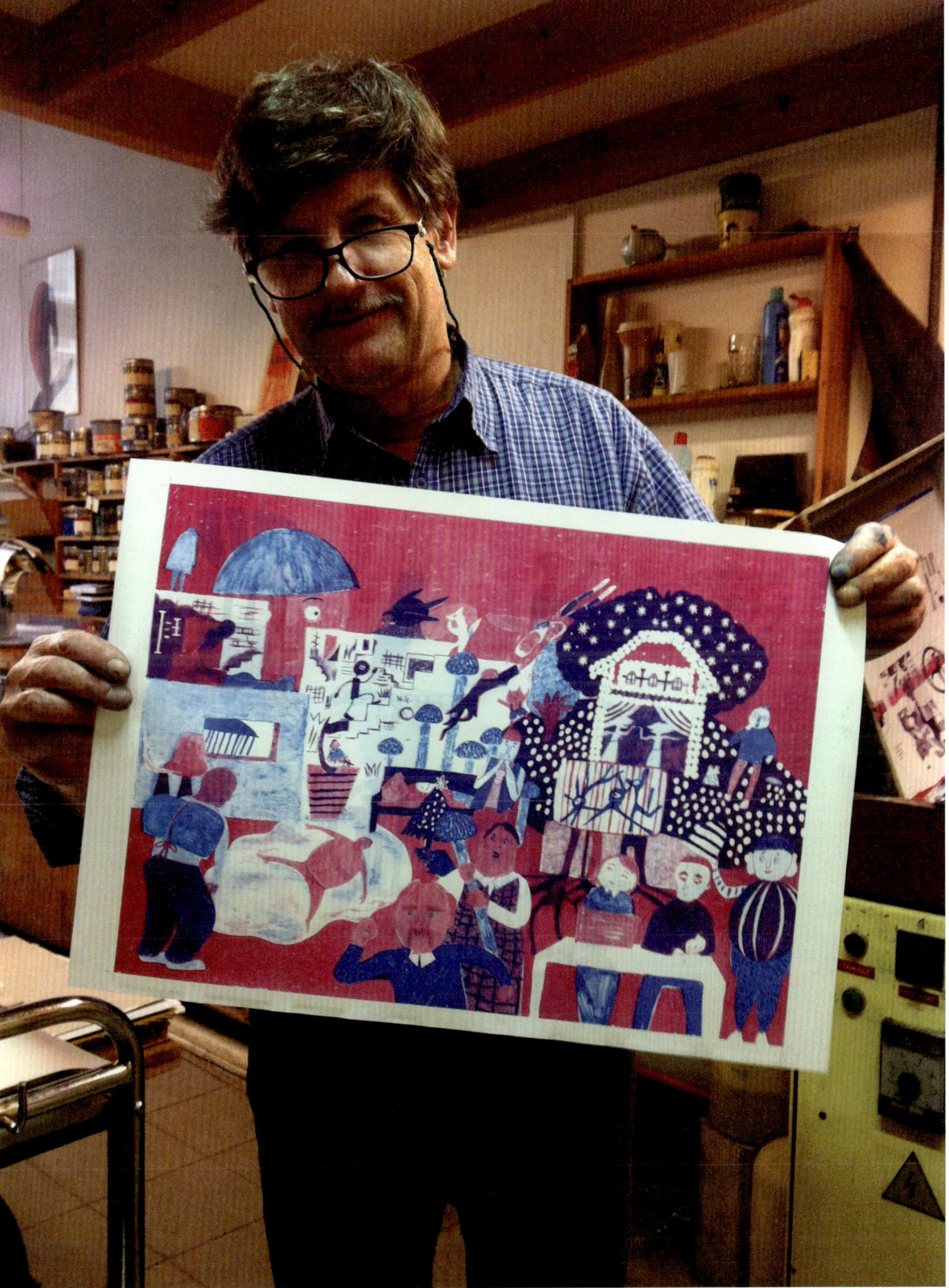

Raven 2

Nature creates the most wonderful patterns and structures, and the designer often inspires them in her works and combines them with traditional ornaments. She used a simple, traditional Finnish ornament as a contrast to thick feathers. The technique is 4-color offset printing.

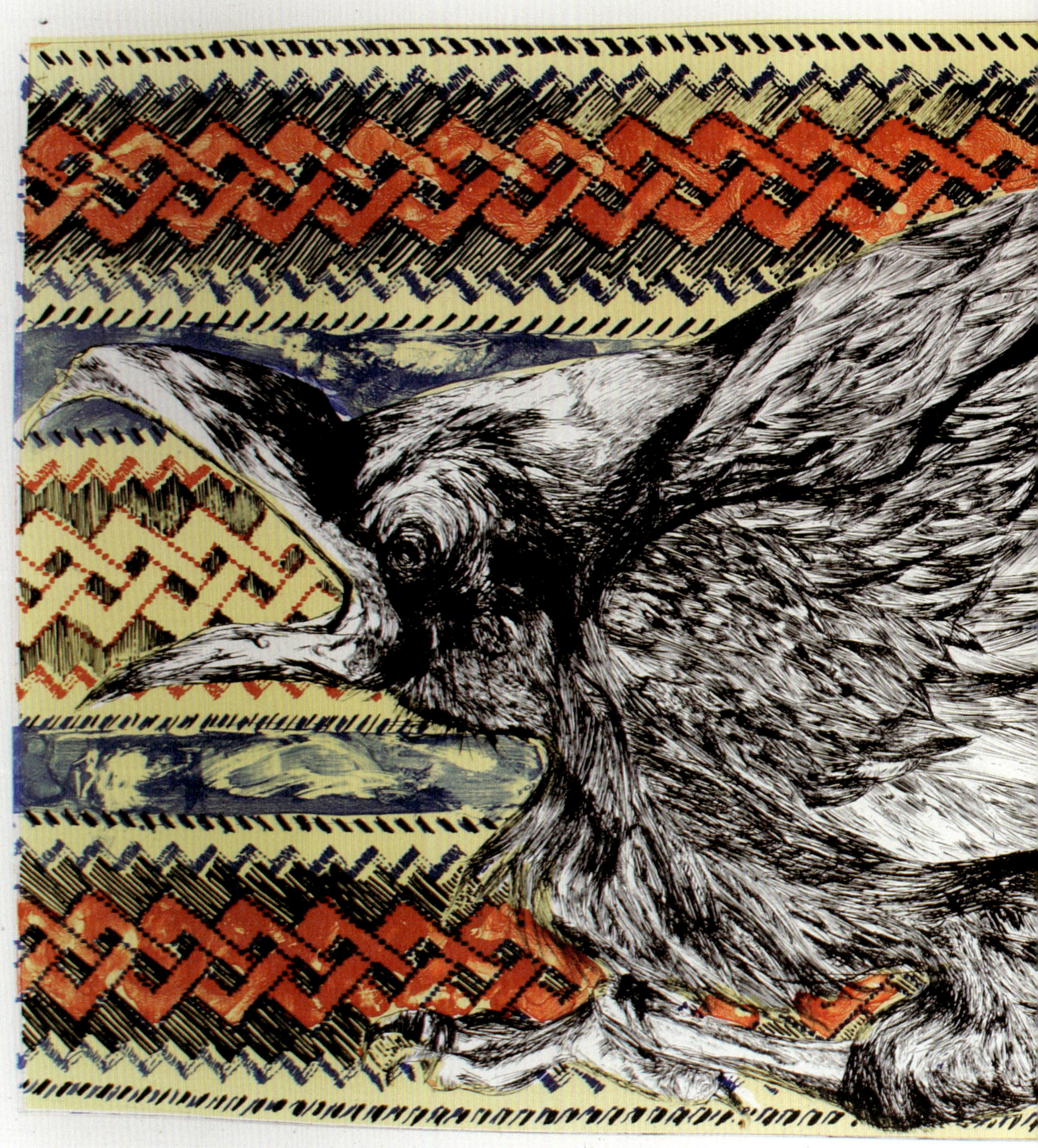

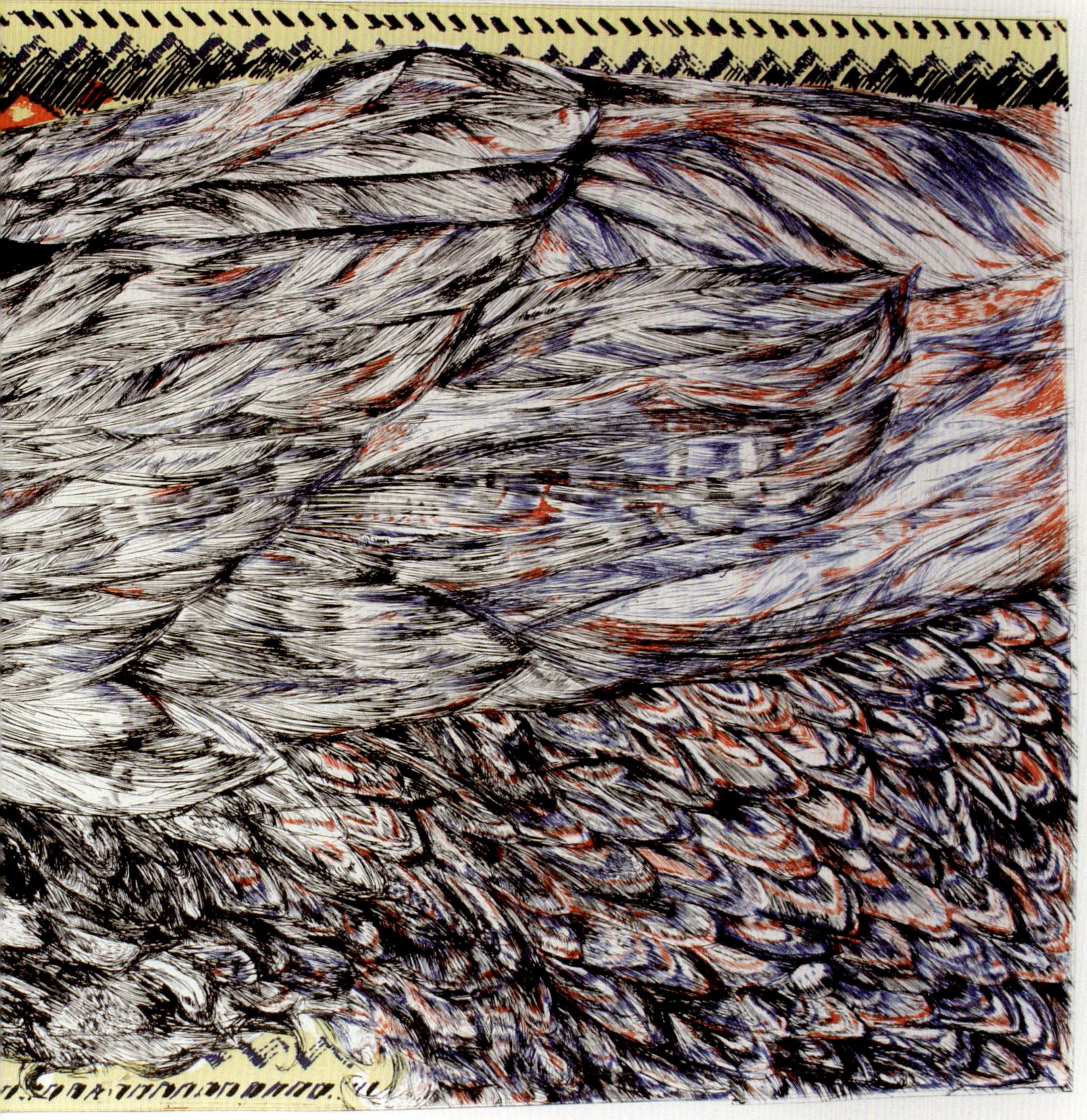

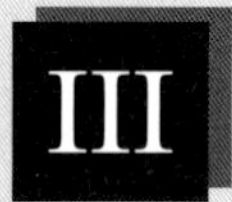

Intaglio Printing

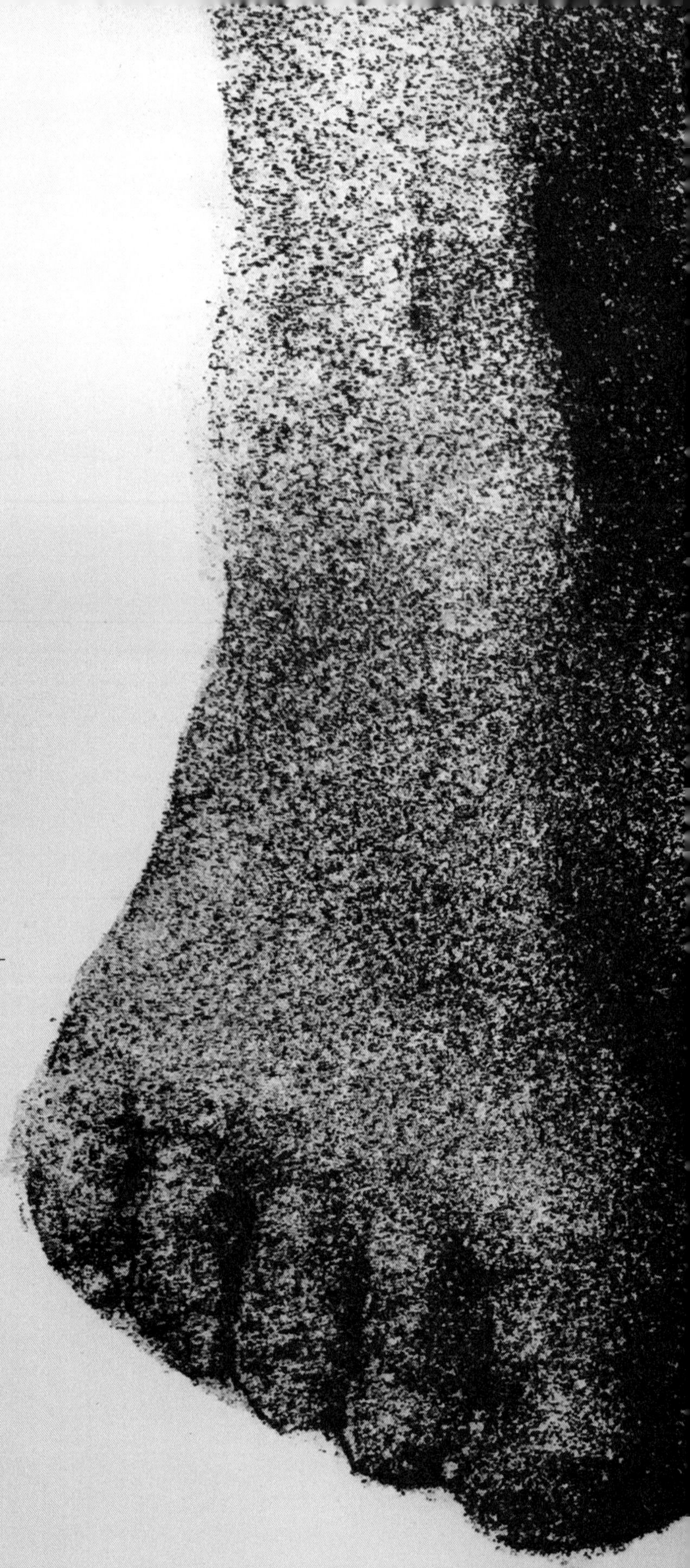

Intaglio Printing

1 Introduction

Intaglio printing is a direct printing method. The graphic part is sunken below the zero line. During the printing process, the sunken graphic part is filled with ink. The depth of the image is determined by the depth of the sunken part.

2 Application

① packaging ② bank notes, stamps and securities ③ decorative materials ④ magazines, catalogs, and so forth.

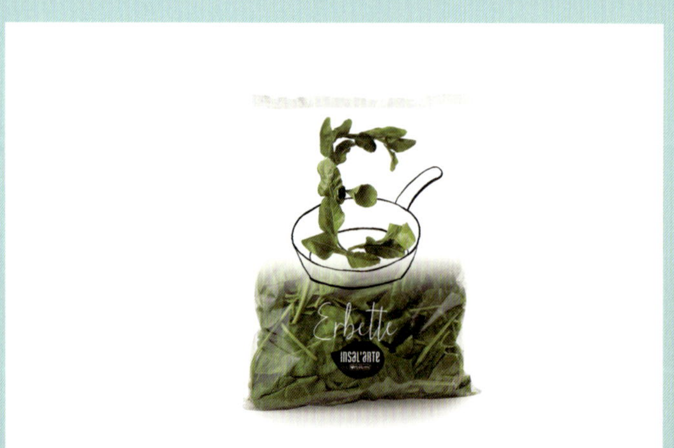

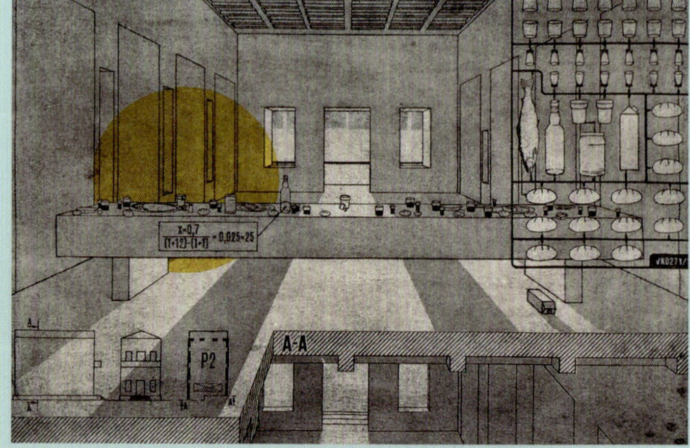

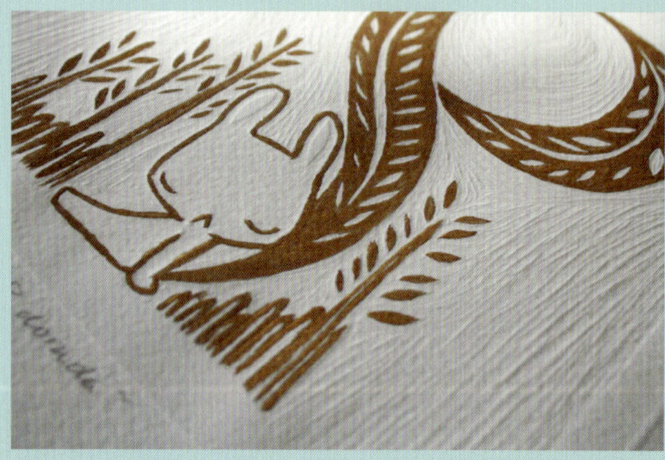

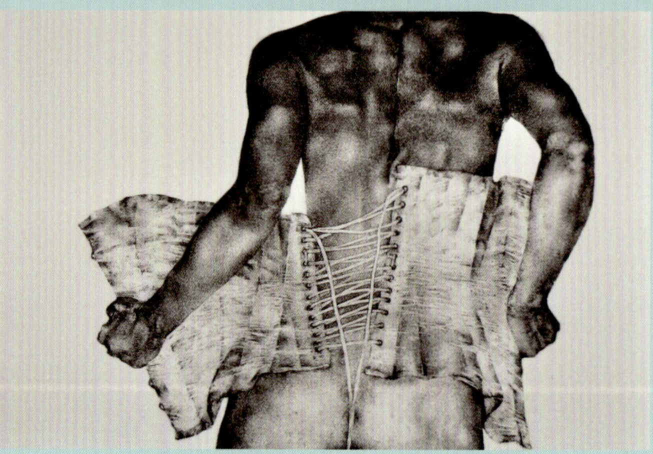

3 Features

- Sunken printed surface
- Reverse reading of the graphics
- Direct printing method
- Extra 45° network of figures and graphics

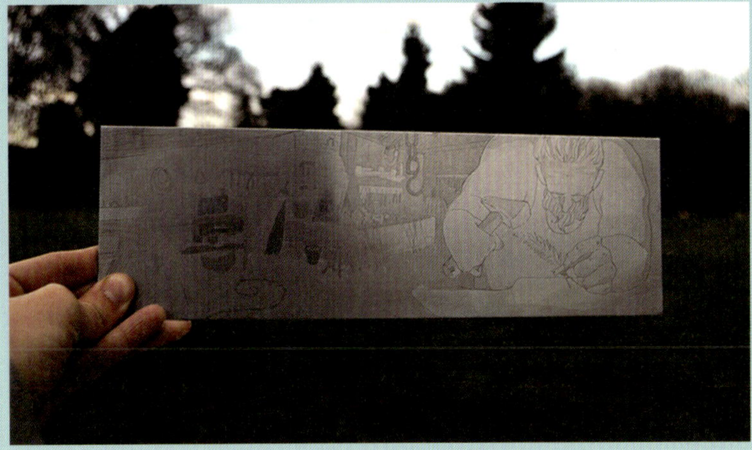

The surface of the metal plate is uneven.

4 Merits and Demerits

- A versatile printing option works well on a variety of projects .
- Thick printed ink layer, bright colors, high saturation.
- Durable printing plates.
- Fast printing speed.

- Complex pre-press plate making process and high cost.
- High content of harmful gas in the workshop which does great damage to workers' health.

A printed work of intaglio printing.

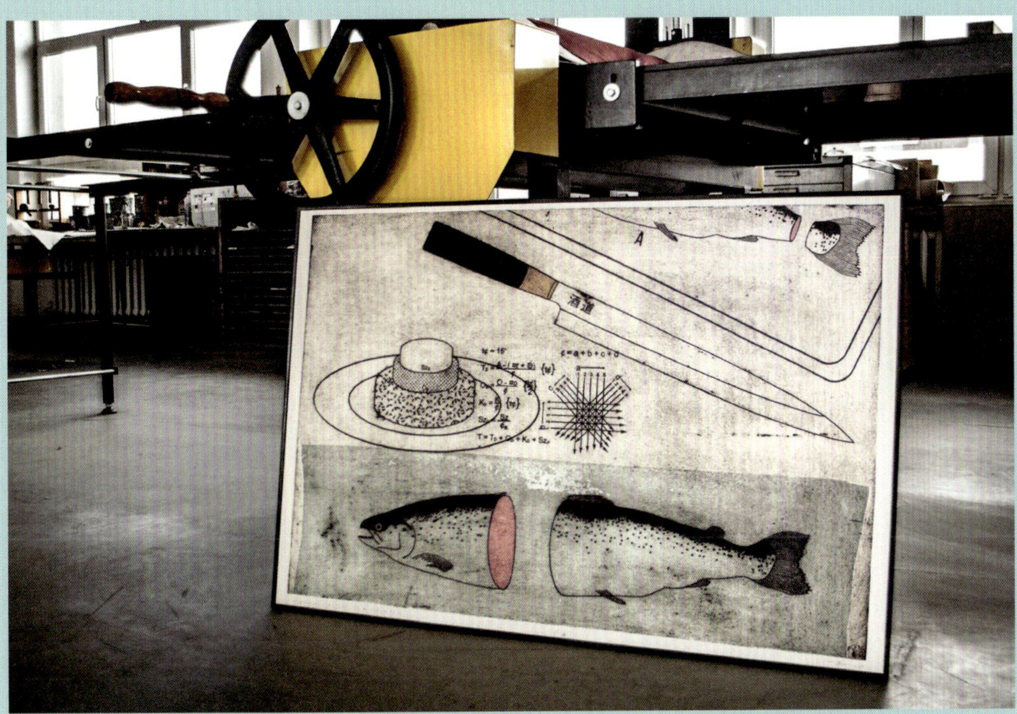

5 Mechanism

A Function View

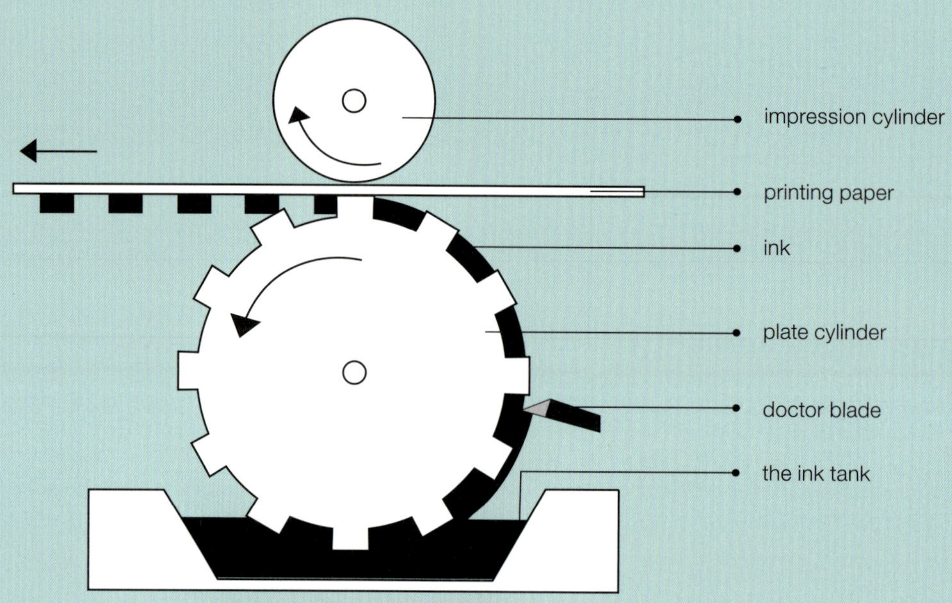

B Top View

C Side View

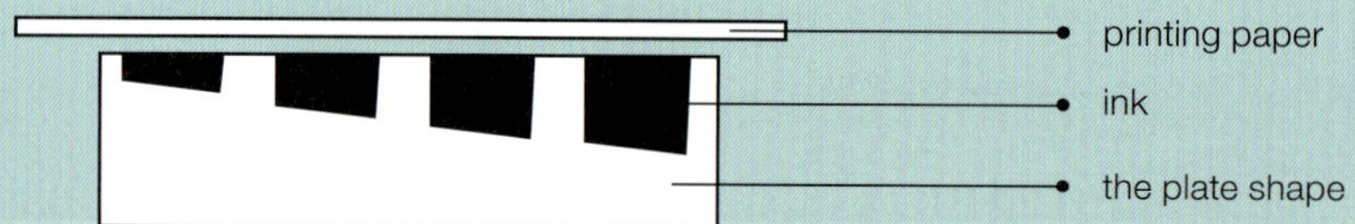

D Printing Method

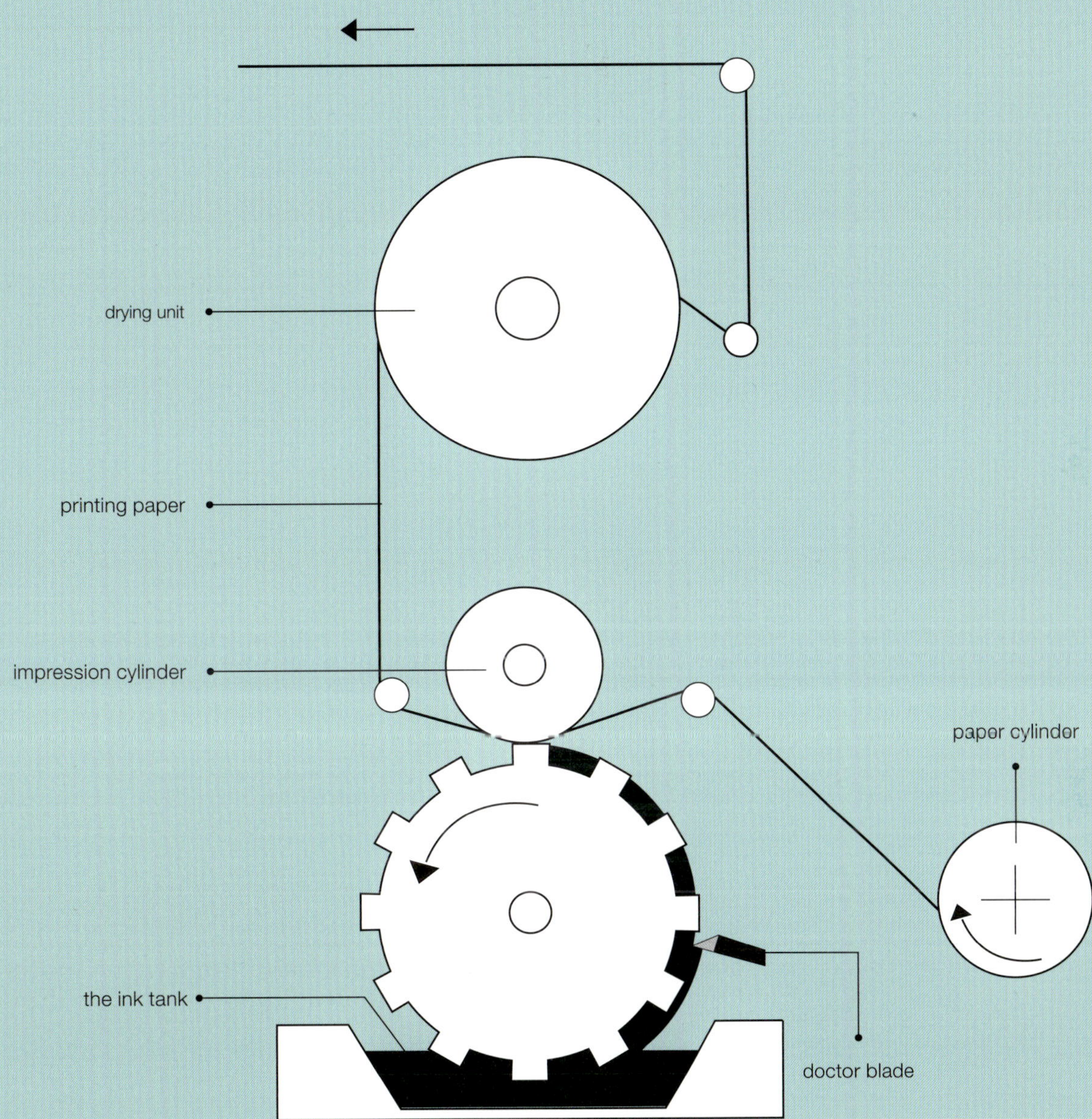

Principle

To print an intaglio plate, ink is applied to the surface by wiping or dabbing the plate to push the ink into the recessed lines, or grooves. The plate is then rubbed with tarlatan cloth to remove most of the excess ink. A damp piece of paper is placed on top of the plate, so that when going through the press the damp paper will be able to be squeezed into the plate's ink-filled grooves. The color reproduction of intaglio printing is very strong, thus the printed image has a three-dimensional thickness.

E Structure

Generally, an intaglio printing press consists of a sheet-conveying device, a printing unit, an inking unit, and a delivery unit. A variety of objects can be printed in an intaglio printing method. The printing speed should be adjusted properly during printing. A registration system in the press ensures an accurate color register.

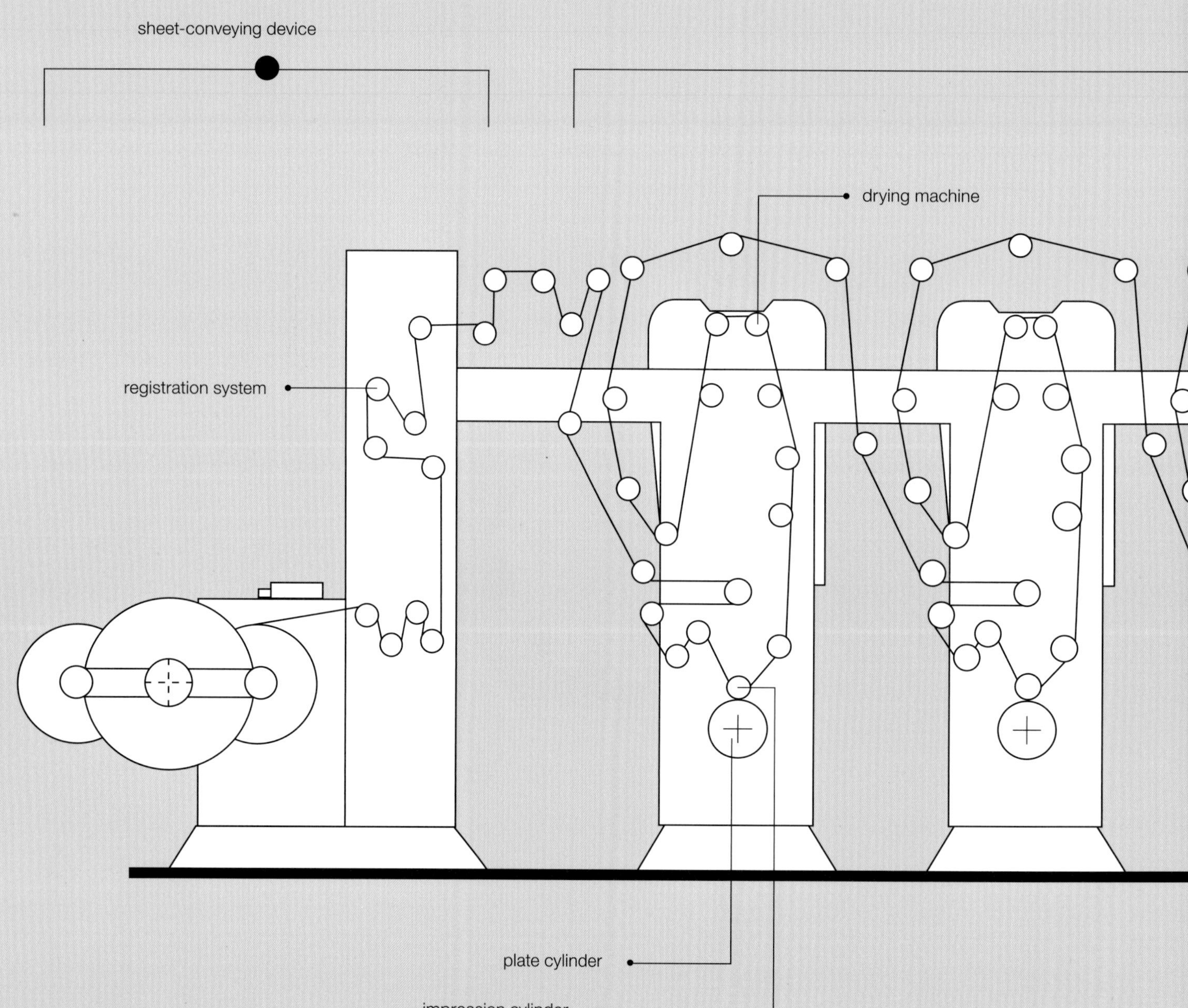

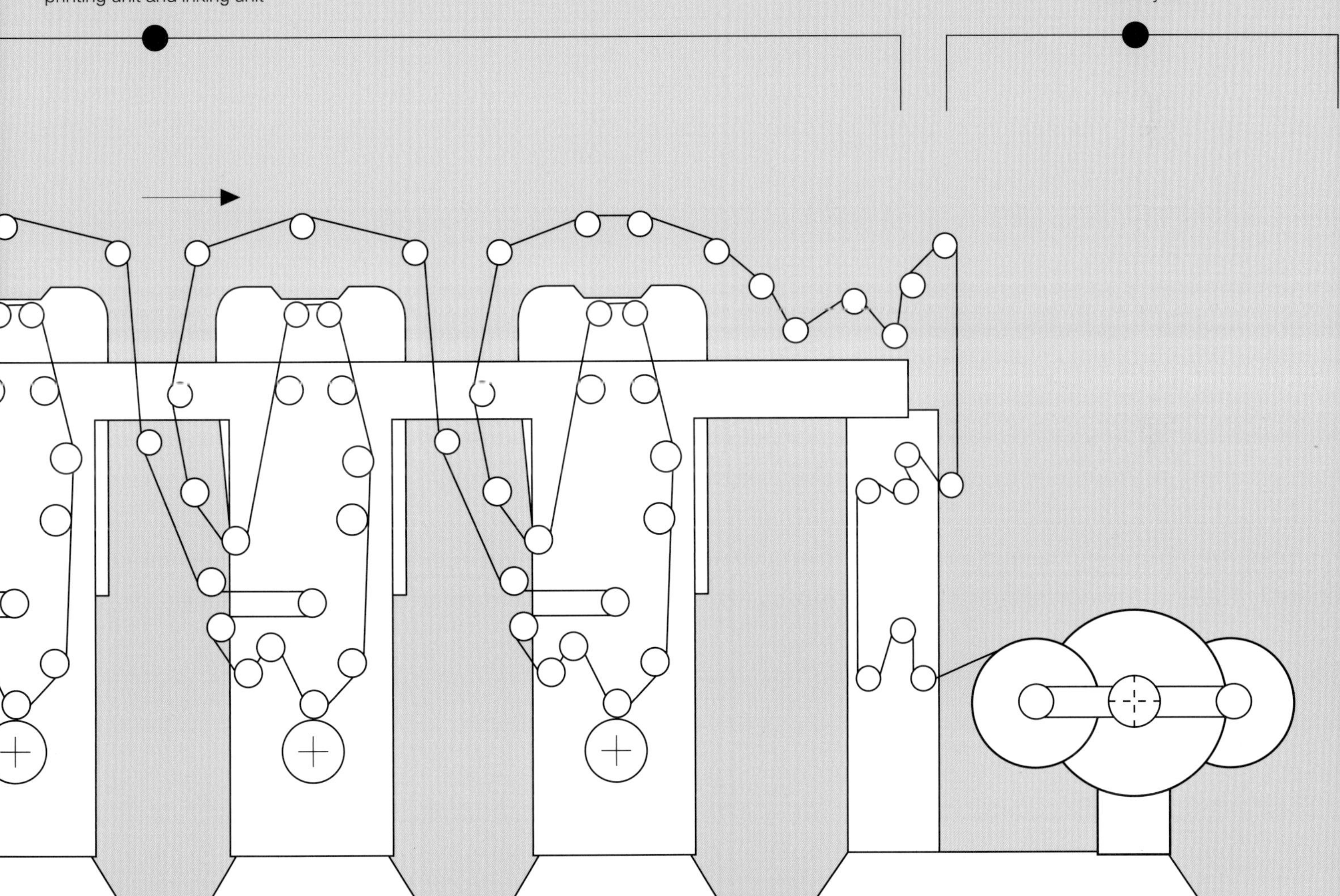
printing unit and inking unit
delivery unit

6 Plate Making

There are two ways of making intaglio printing plates: engraved gravure and corrosion gravure.

a. Engraved gravure

According to the knife-control method, engraved gravure can be divided into hand-carved gravure, mechanical engraving gravure, and electronic engraving gravure.

(1) Hand-carved gravure

Hand-carved gravure is hand carved by a technician with a knife in the plate cylinder surface in accordance with the original manuscripts. The plate materials available are copper or steel plate. It requires heavy manual labor, high plate-making costs, and long cycles. But hand-carved gravure has clear lines and a strong print level that is difficult to forge. It is used mostly for the production of securities and high-quality works of art gravure printing.

(2) Mechanical engraving gravure

Mechanical engraving is the use of mechanical control of the knife on the surface of the cylinder to conduct engraving production. It reduces the heavy manual labor with high plate-making speed, shorter cycle and lower cost. It is used mainly in the production of printed securities gravure.

(3) Electronic engraving gravure

It is engraved by the electronic control device on the surface of the plate cylinder. In the use of an electronic engraving machine, in accordance with the principle of optoelectronics, the carving knife is controlled to carve out a hole on the surface. Its area and depth change at the same time.

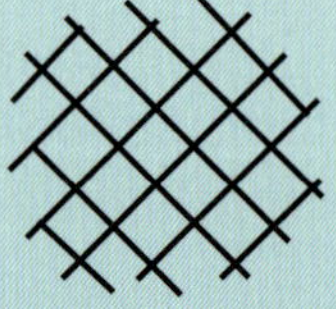

a.square mesh

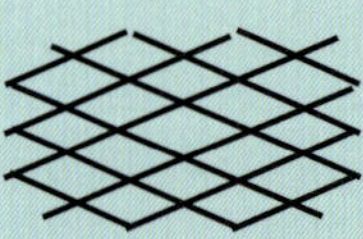

b.flaser mesh

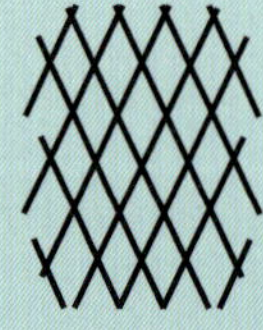

c.extended mesh

The shapes of mesh

b. Corrosion gravure

Process

Because the corrosion method is controlled manually, the stability of plate making, the density of plates and the clarity of texts is of poor quality. Usually it is used for plastic soft package printing.

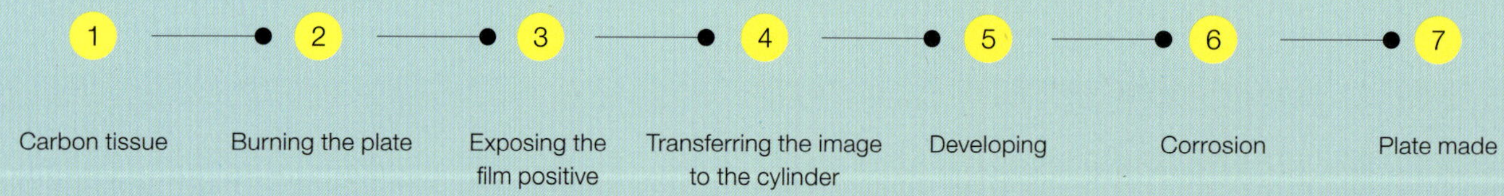

7 Printing Process

Studio: Terrible Producciones

Designer: Juan Santiago Sierra Salas

Terrible Producciones is based in Bogotá, Colombia, it was founded in order to respond a demand and to concentrate the knowledge of printmaking. They focused on small printmaking series for upcoming artists, experimental projects, and sometimes they work as a teaching space for students. They want to regain the value of handmade design projects and create a cultural focal point for printmaking in the city.

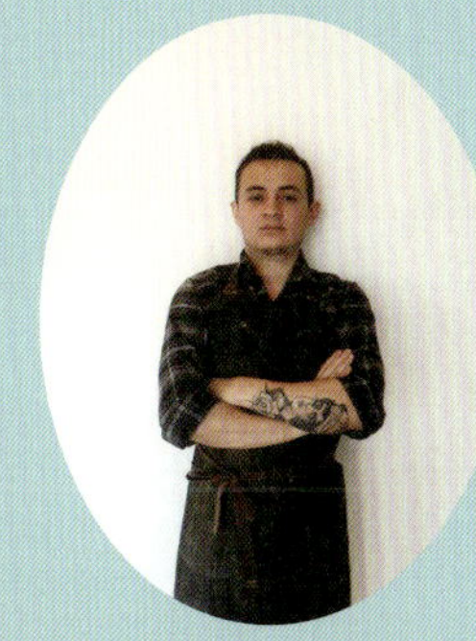

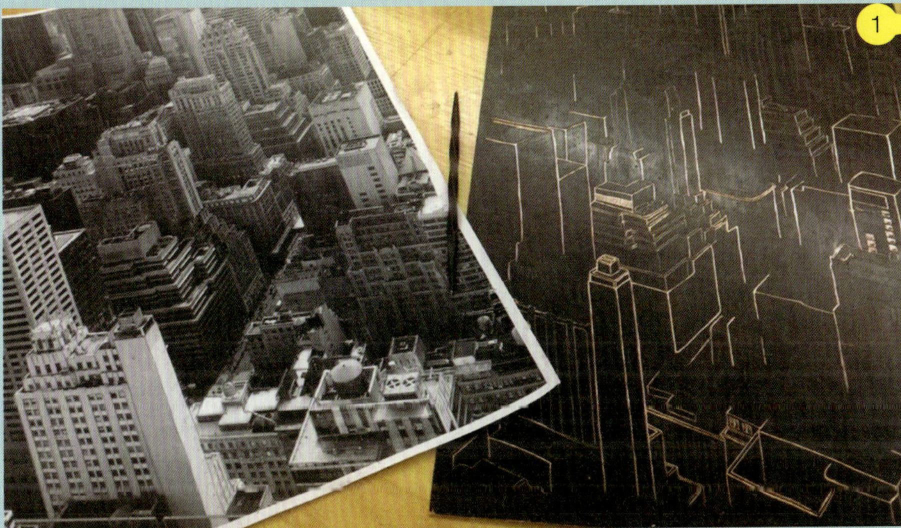

1 Designers choose to use manual engraving for plate making, first of all, to draw the pattern on the copperplate.

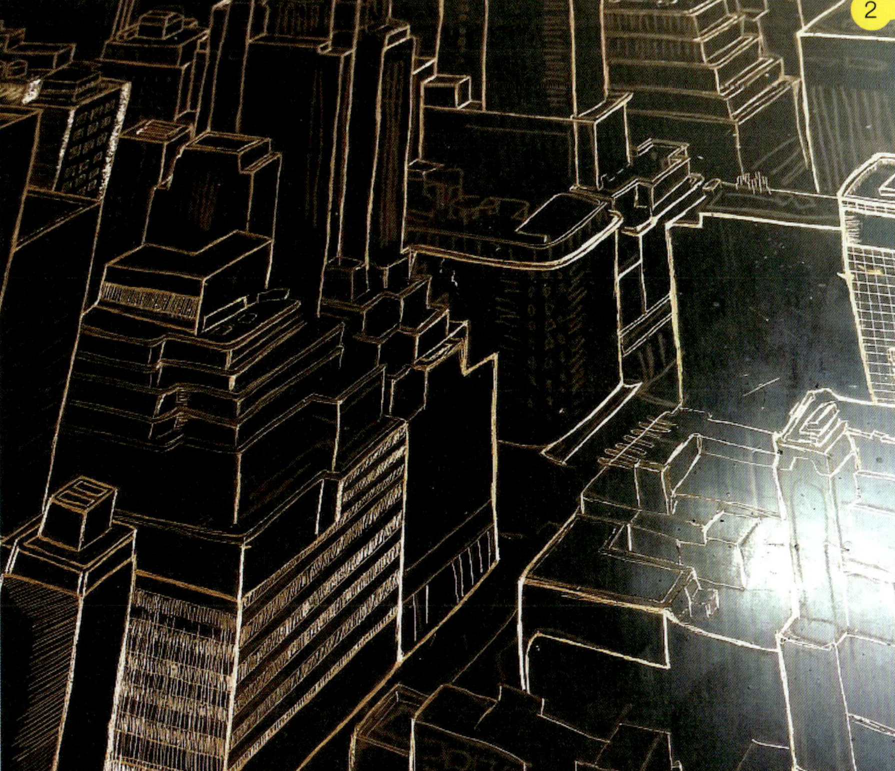

2 Then with an etching tool the ground is removed on the parts to be recorded with ink on the paper. It does not need to be hard marks. Any scratch on the hard ground that will make the metal visible will suffice.

Photo by Juan Santiago Sierra Salas

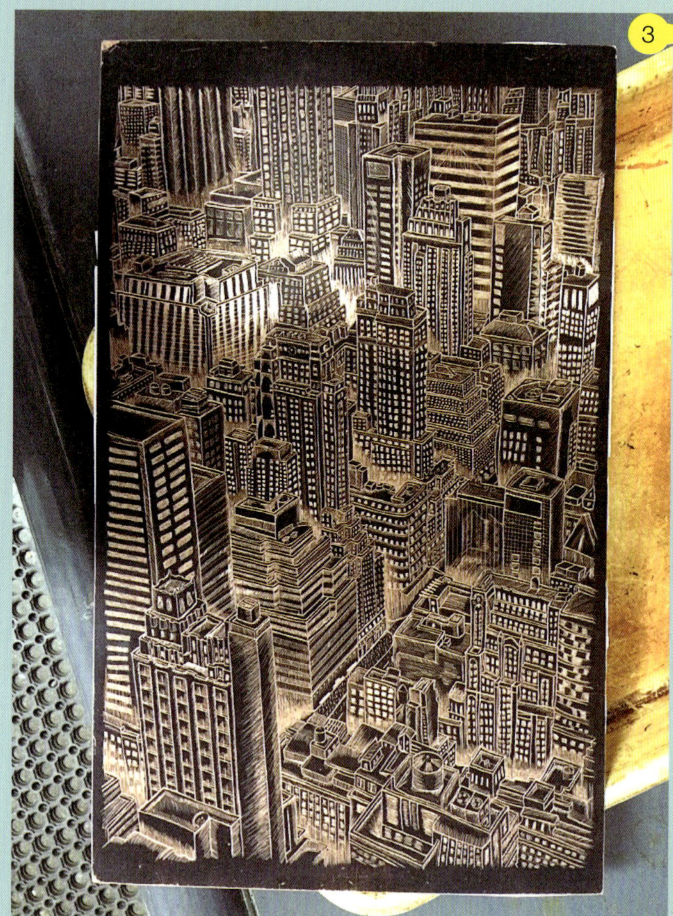

3 Then the plate needs to be covered on the back in order to protect it from the acid that can make the metal plate thinner. Depending on the acid water proportions the time needed varies, but remember that deeper ink lines should be longer times. One is able to see the plate's sparkly lines when finished.

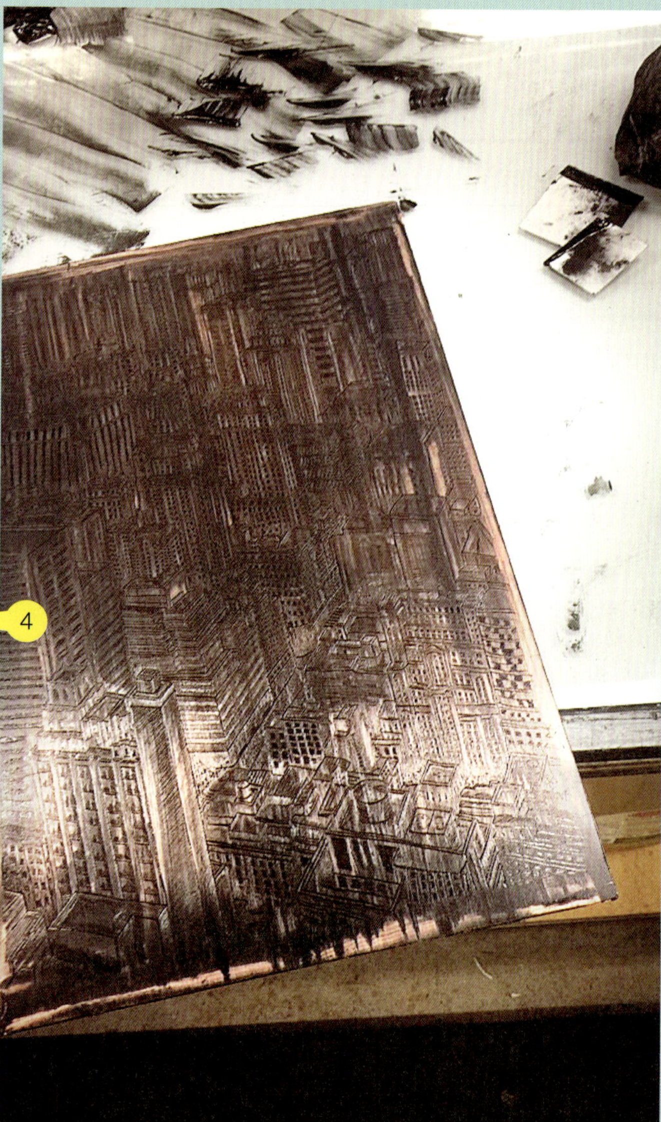

4 After washing the acid with water and removing hard ground, the ink needs to be applied with force in an even layer using a spatula or cardboard.

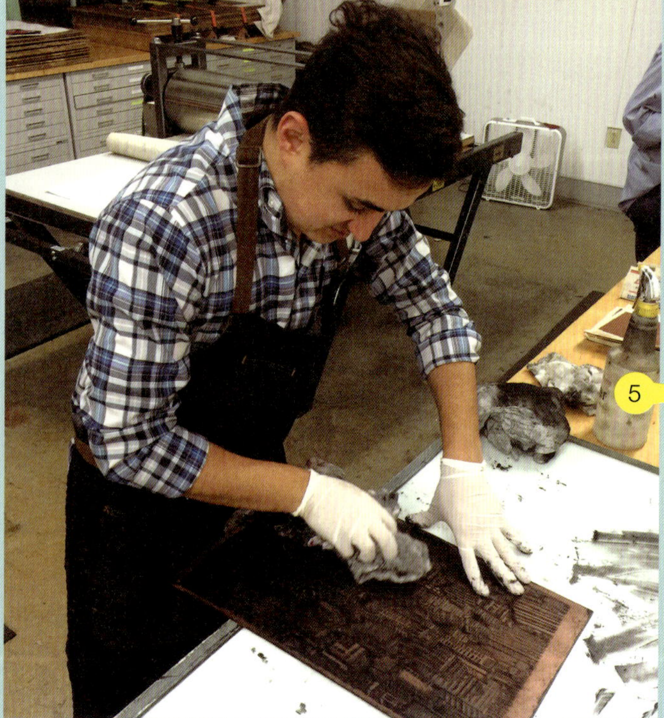

5 Using a medium gauze, you will be able to clean the extra ink on the plate from the areas that will be highlighted, and for small details you can use tissue papers or even a cotton bud.

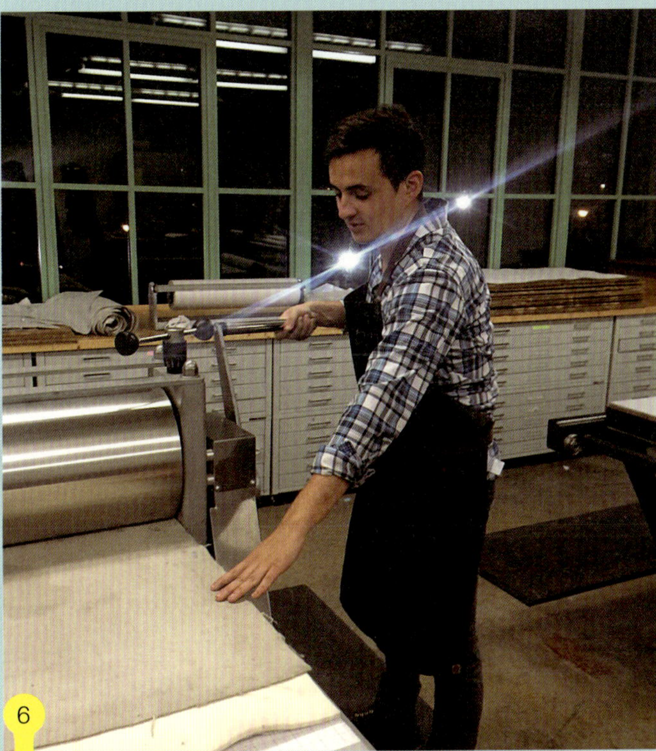

6

Therefore the plate is placed in the intaglio press using protective layers of fabric and placing the paper, which, for better results must be cotton based and previously wetted.

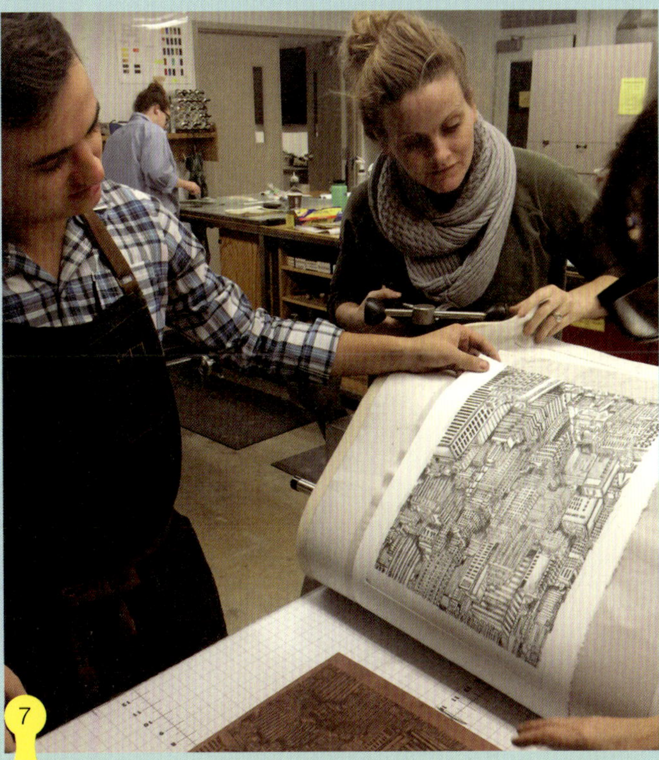

7

Finally the etching print is done and ready.

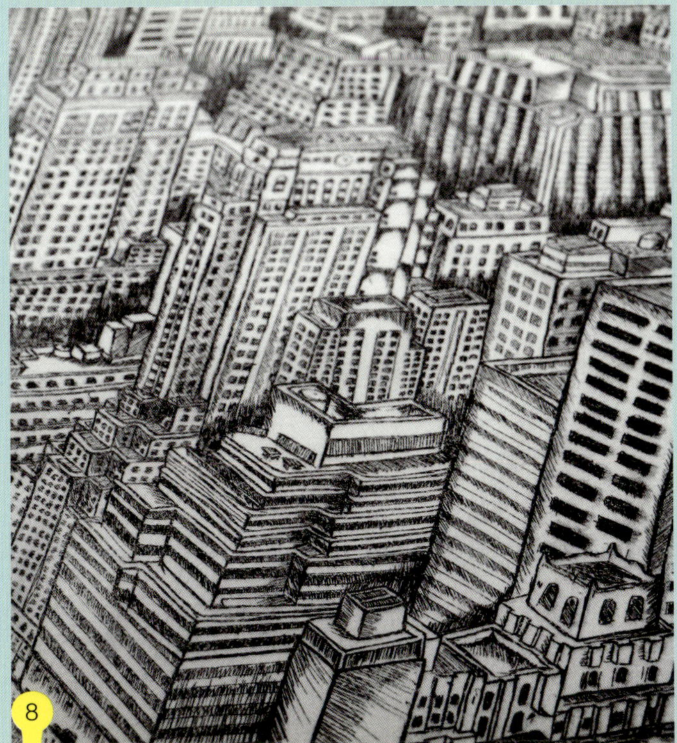

8

Details can be appreciated in the highlighting areas where less ink has been applied.

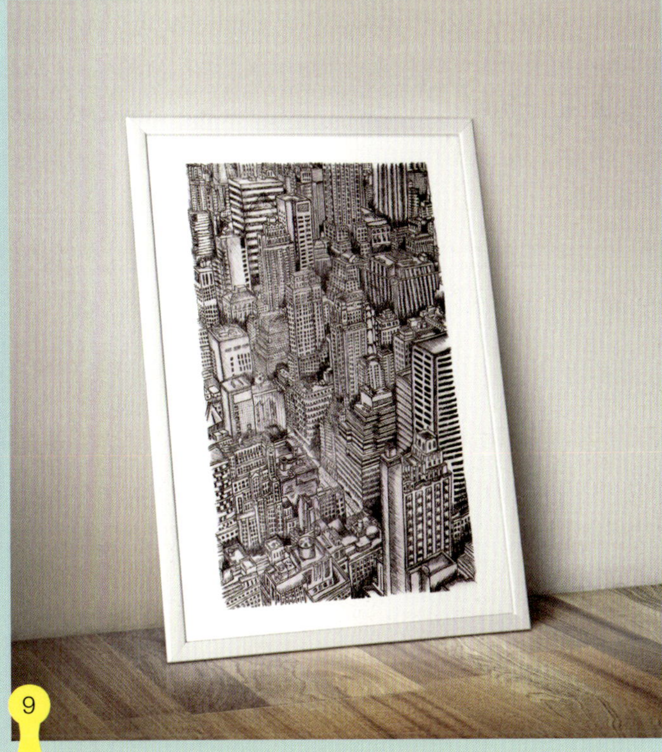

9

The final printing product.

8 Printed Works

: Substrates

: Printing Inks

D : Design

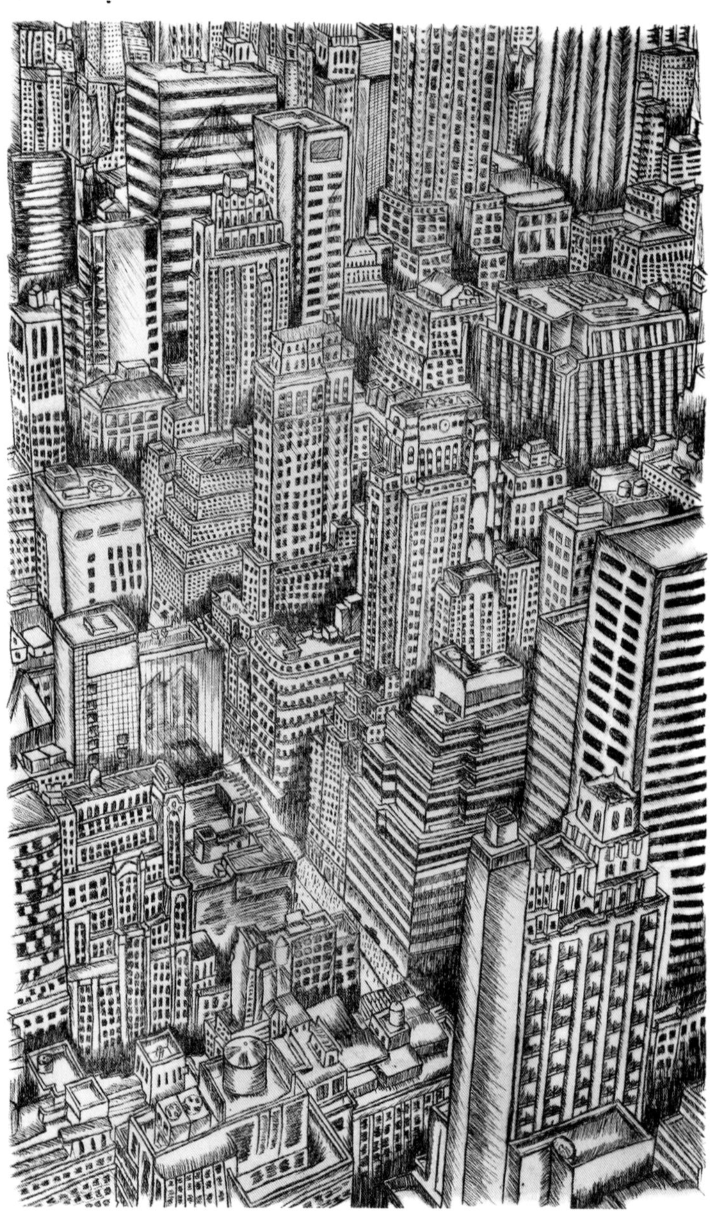

Etching NYC From the Top of the Rock

Somerset 100% Cotton

Charbonnel Black Luxe, Cardinal Red, Cobalt Blue, Deep Yellow

This design is based on a photograph the designer took from the Rockefeller Center in NY, in which he tries to reflect the amount of detail that each building contains, how each one of them combines to form unique patterns, and even to think about the stories that could be happening inside. Etching was the technique he used because is the one that allowed him to manage the thin lines and the minimal windows in better ways than any other technique. Also it let the designer graduate the depth of the engraving lines by measuring the ground and the acid-burning time.

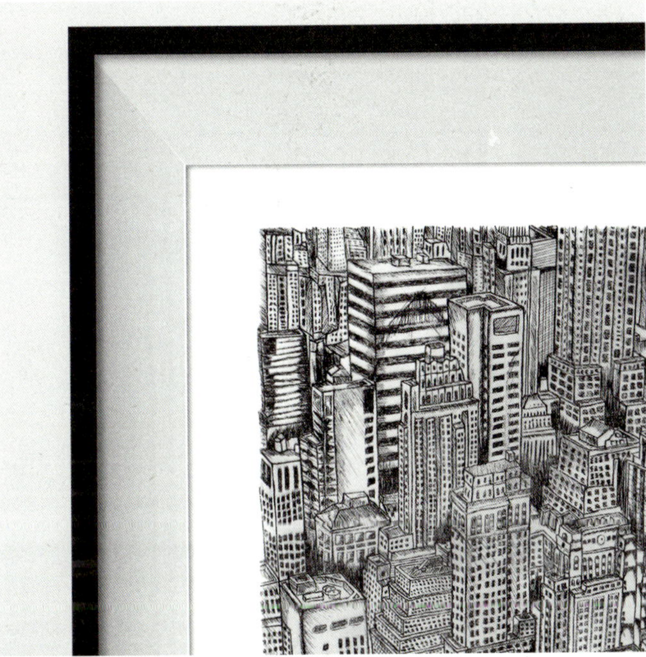

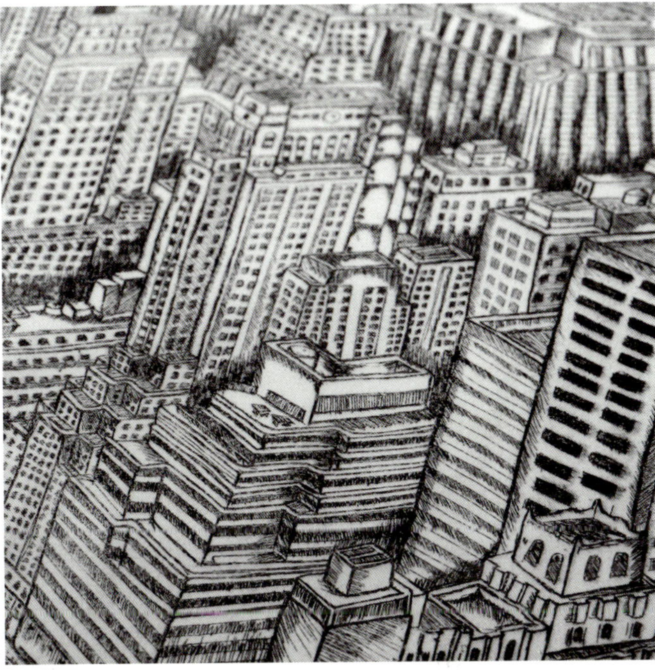

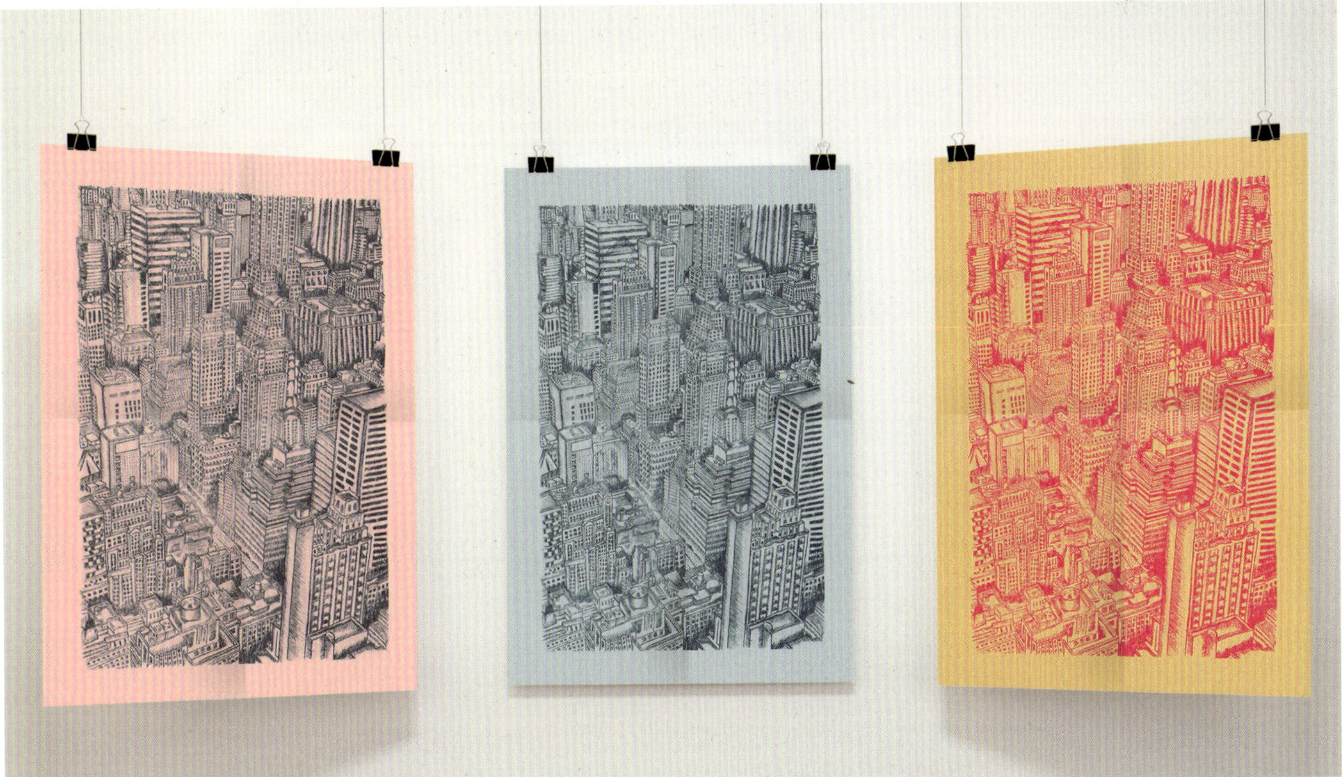

D: Juan Santiago Sierra Salas

The Body of Matter

- Fabriano Rosaspina Bianco paper
- Offset ink Novavit F918 Supreme Bio (black)

The basic source of the designer's inspiration is her own subjective experience of the world and the observation of everyday events and daily life. She often depicts women who are turned around, from behind, wearing tights, taking off their nightdresses, or putting them on. The women are shown in transient moments. The works are done using variants of aquatint. The design is made on a plate with a diamond spar, which provides the speckled look of the final product. Ready prints often resemble aquatint, and by using this method an artist can achieve a great number of tones without different exposure times and acid concentrations.

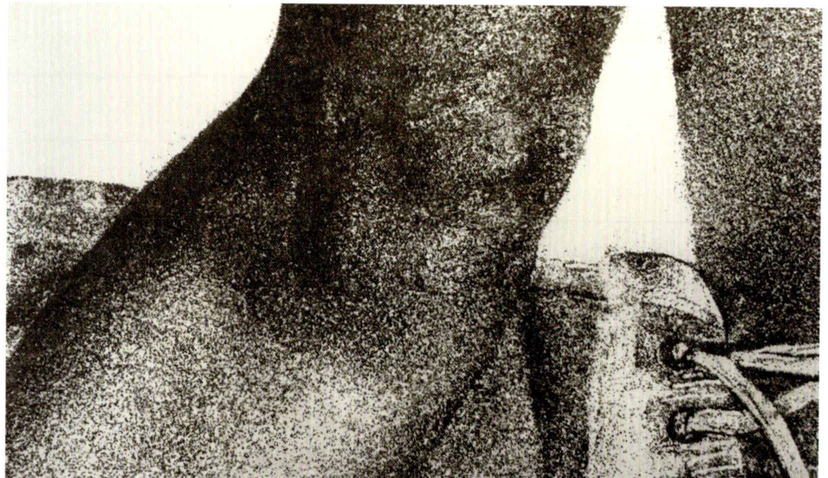

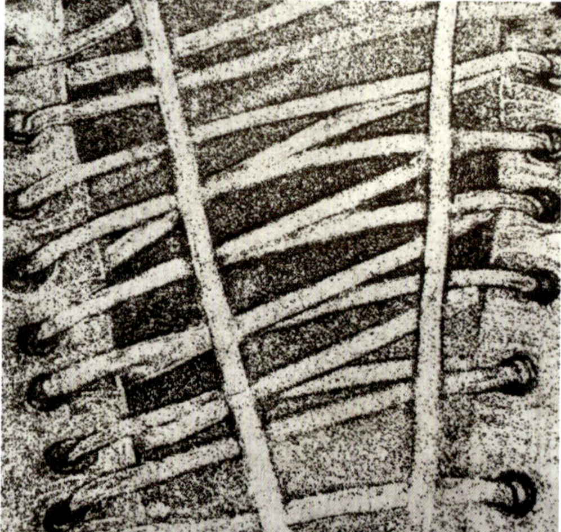

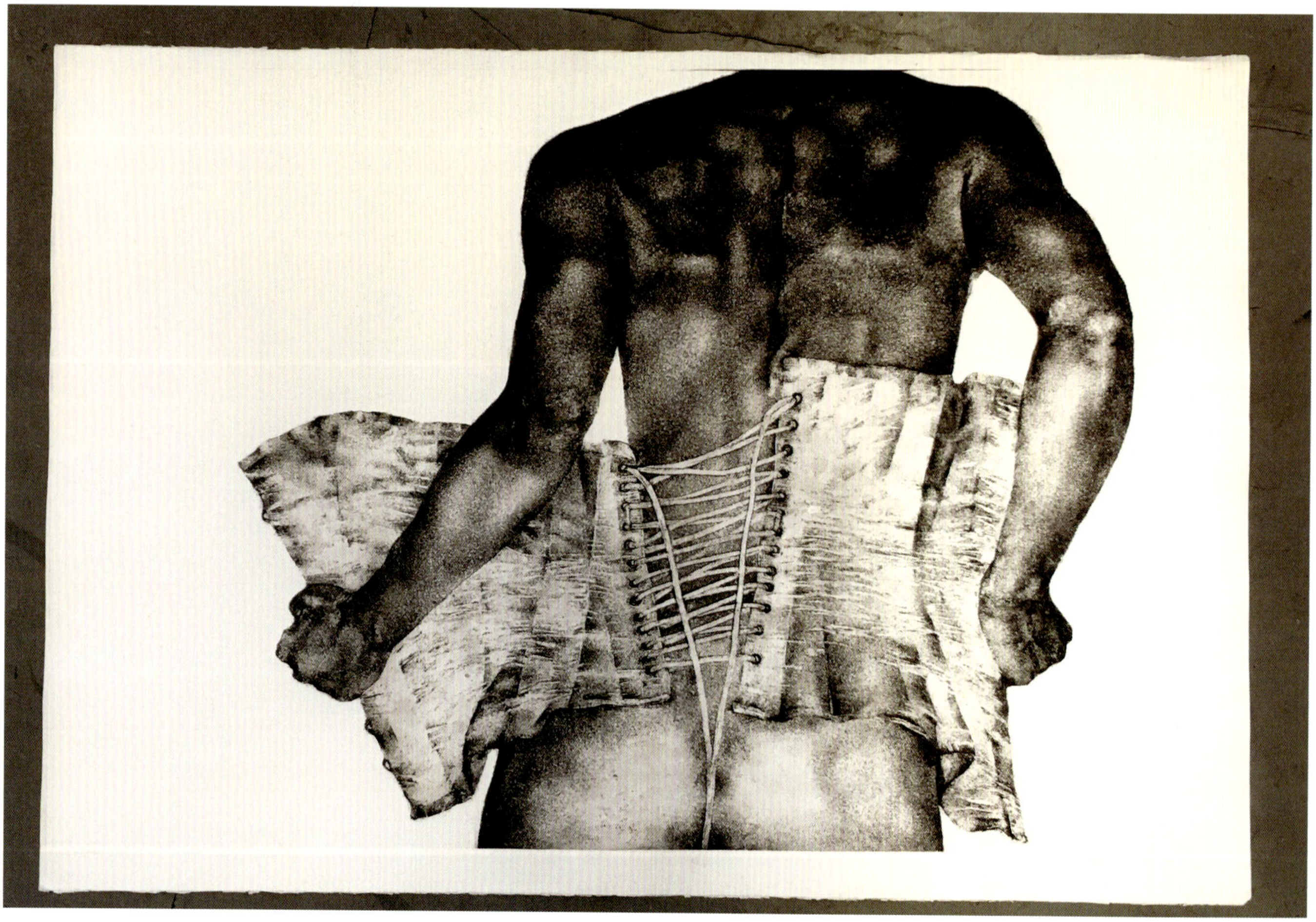

D: Agnieszka Lech-Bińczycka

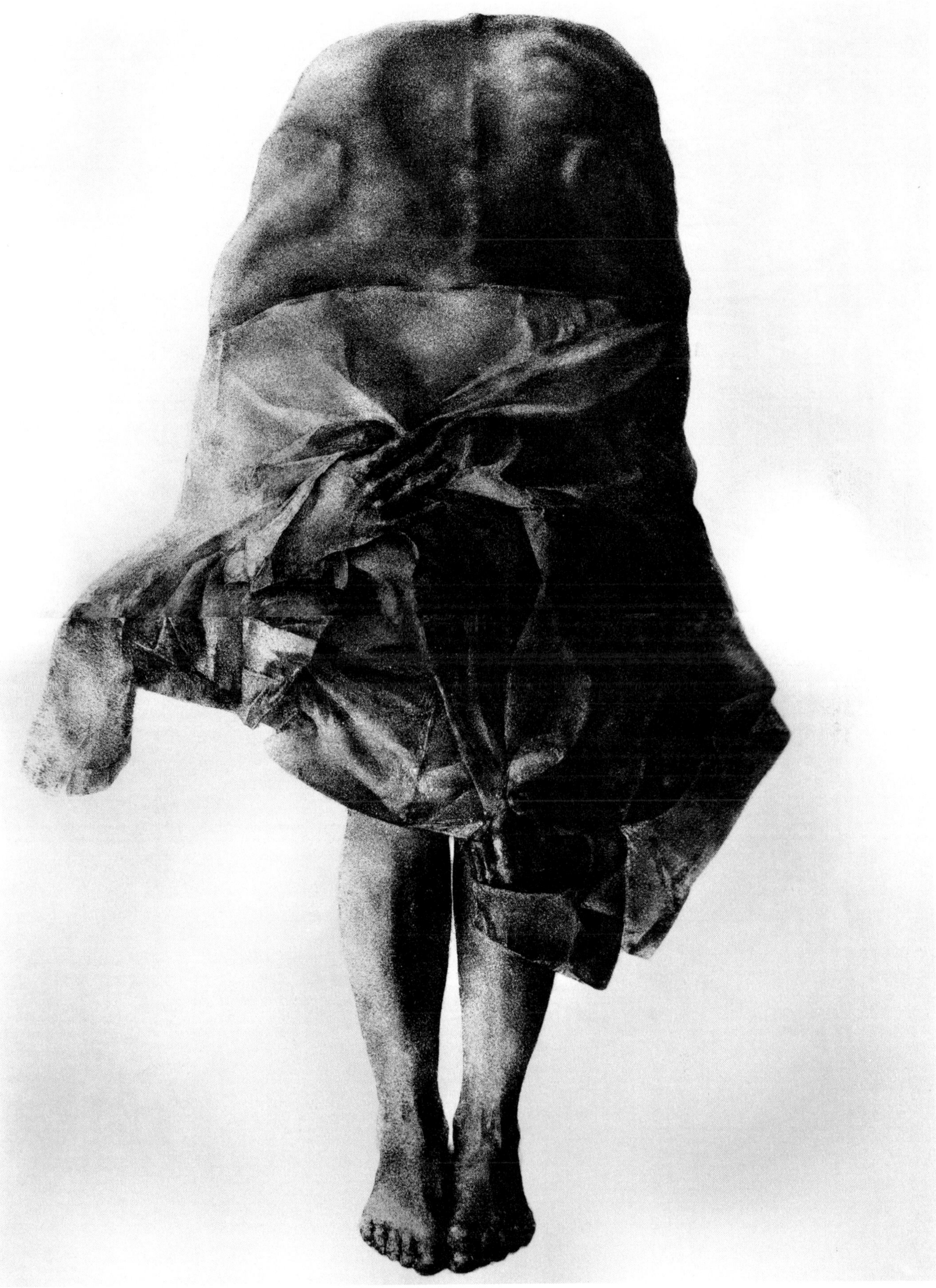

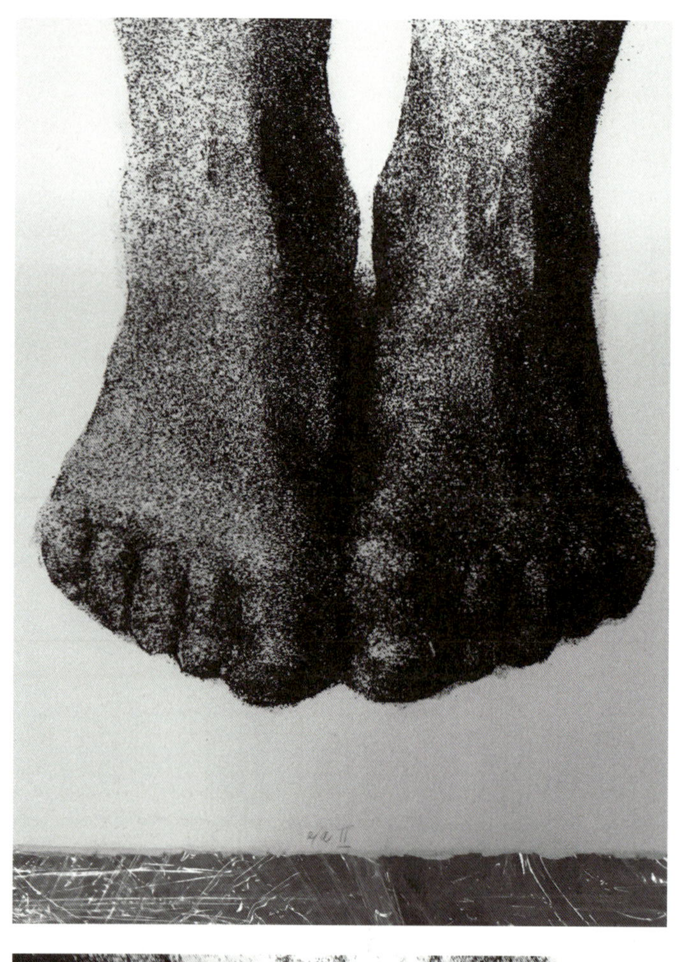

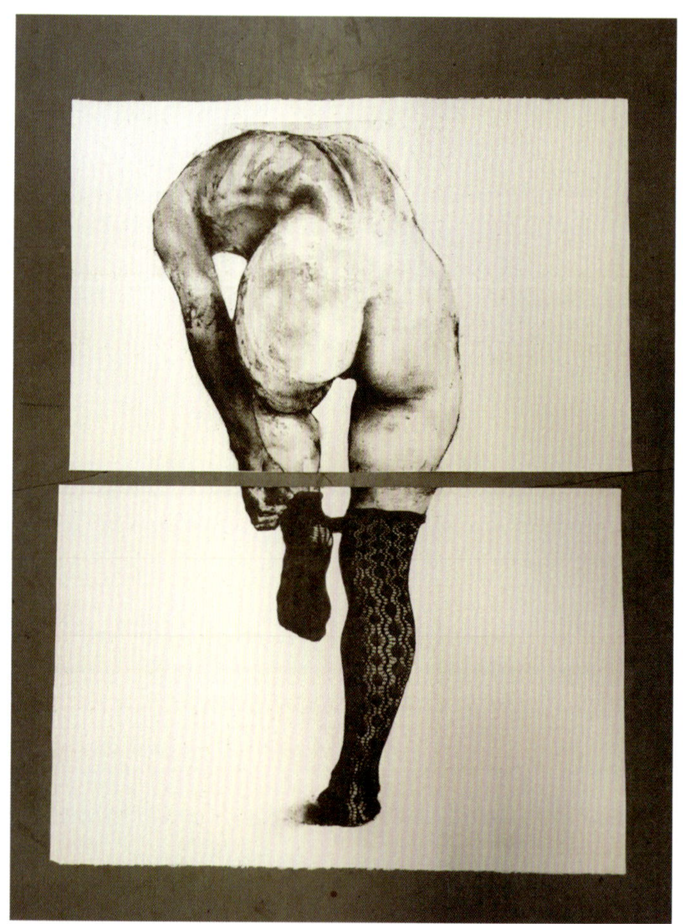

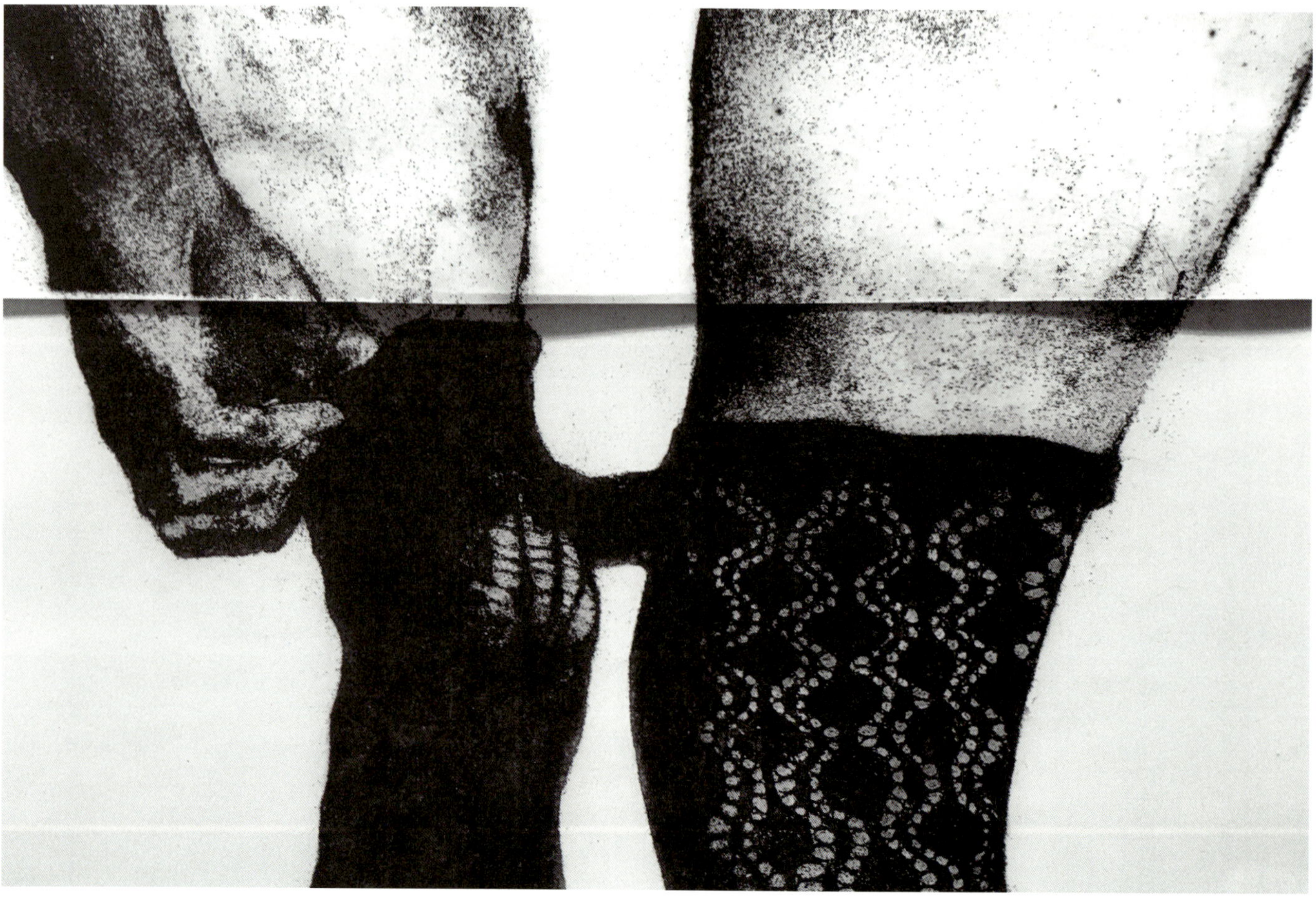

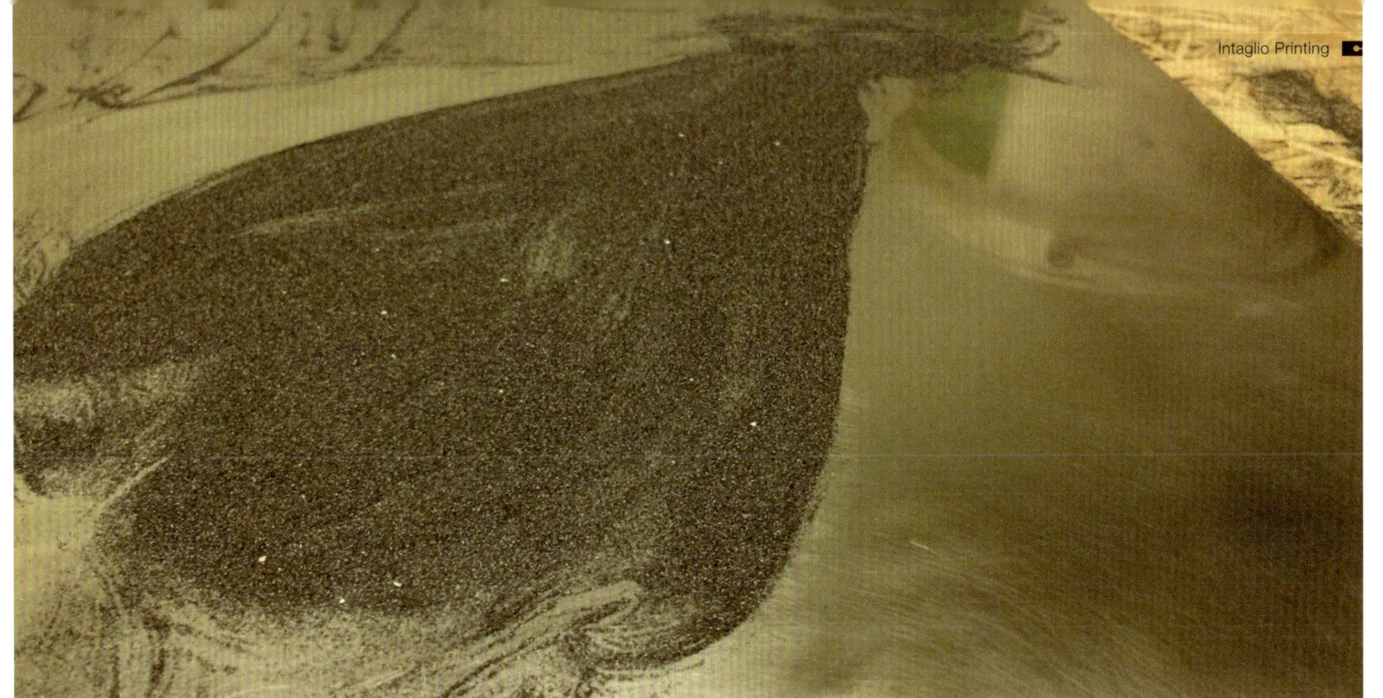

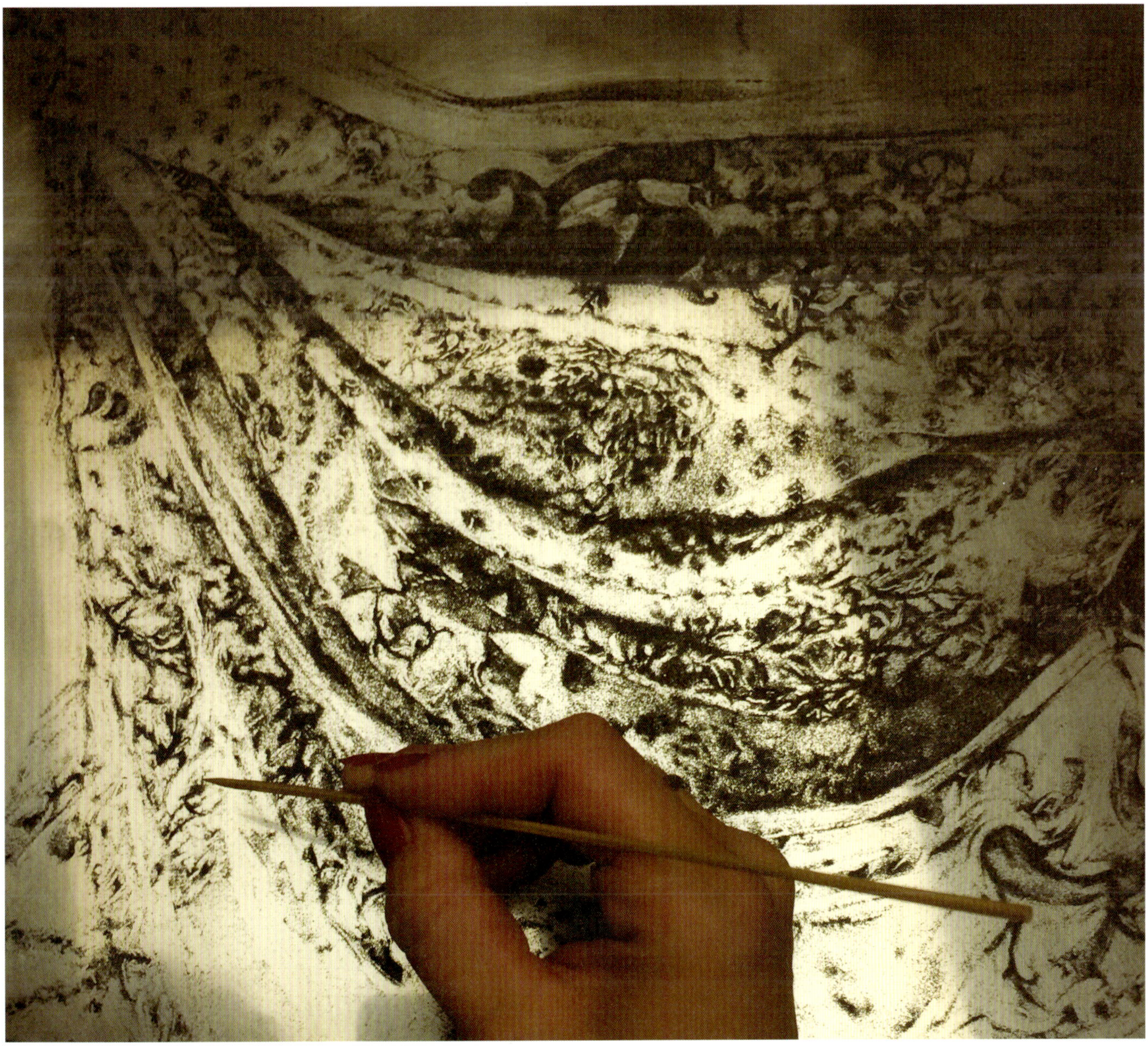

He Who Doesn't Drink

350g Handmade paper Hahnemühle and crepe color

offset printing ink, acrylic spray paint

The print "He who doesn't drink" bounds the *Norma 2.0 series*. The composition includes a variety of elements linking to other works within the series, although shown in a brand new context, as a part of the new composition. The configuration evokes *The Last Supper* by Lenoardo da Vince. It shows the interior of the cenacle: empty, however, of people. Yellow color refers to the symbols of Judas, being at the same time an emphasis of his place at the table. The title of the painting is connected with a Polish saying: "The one who doesn't drink is the one who narks." It refers to the era of Communism times, when person who hasn't been drinking has very often been the informer.

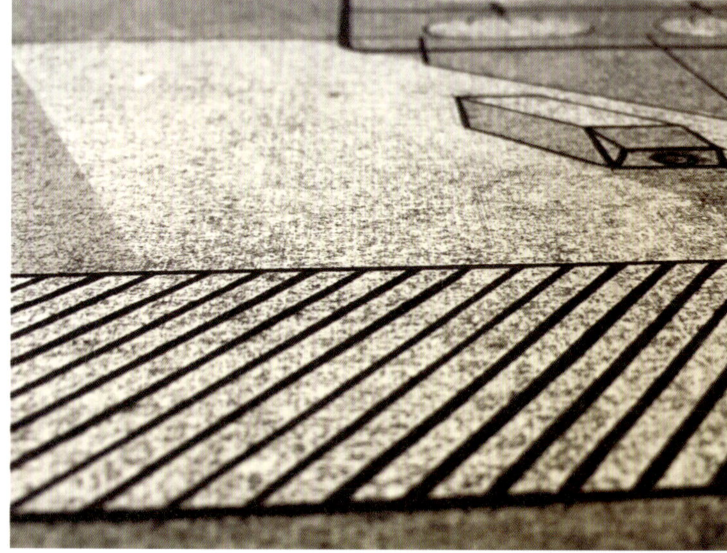

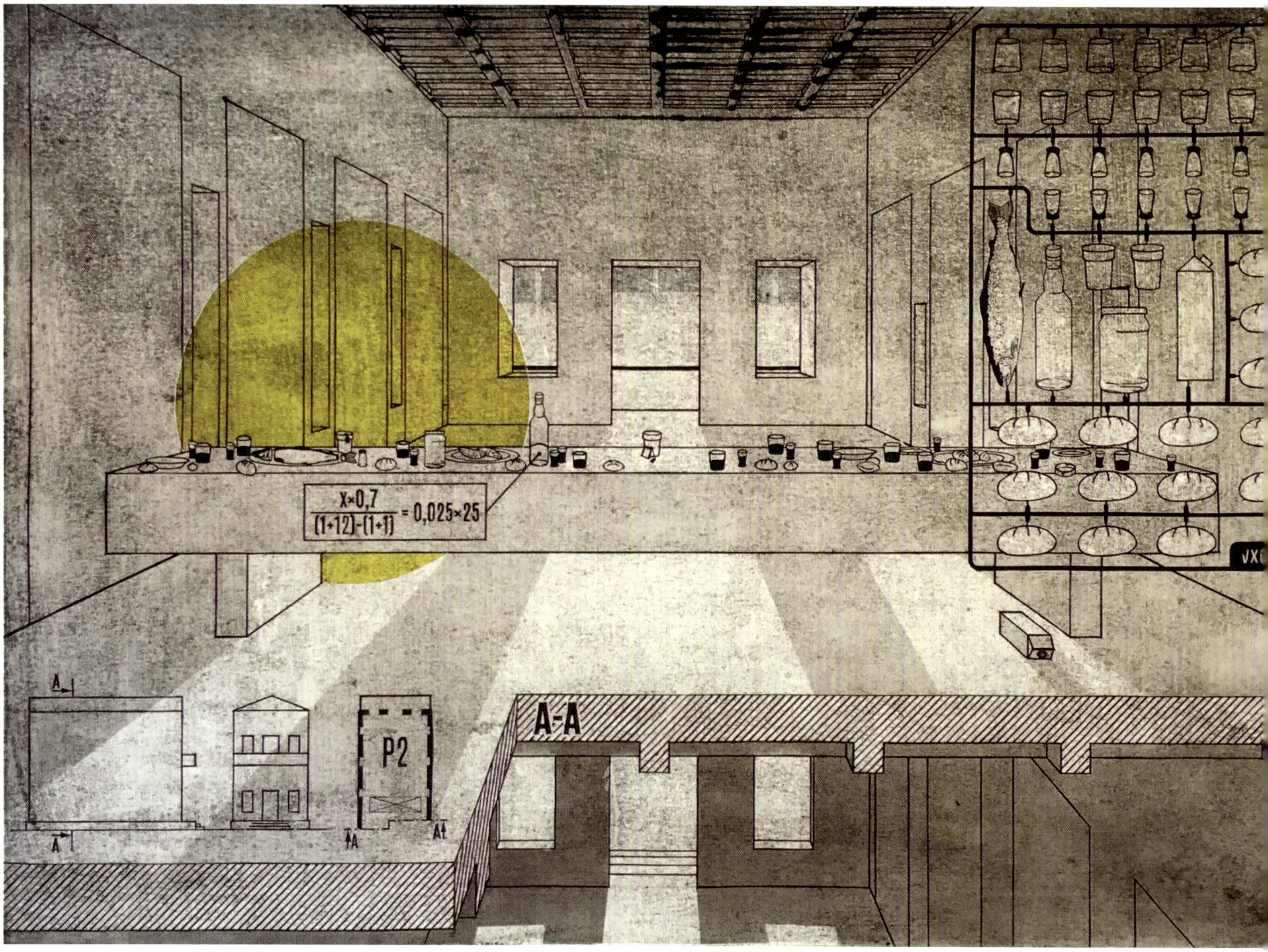

D: Jacek Machowski

Untitled - Not to Irritate Anyone

350g Handmade paper Hahnemühle and crepe color

offset printing ink, acrylic spray paint

A work that is a part of the *Norma 2.0 series*, this print is executed as form of a triptych. Each of the parts shares similar composition, analogical to the character's performance of a scene and without highlighting the main person—Jesus. It suggests an image of suffering in a cool, schematic, and suppressed way, having gotten rid of emotions. The lack of the title offers the opportunity for the audience to interpret the work freely and to search out its polyvalent layers of meaning.

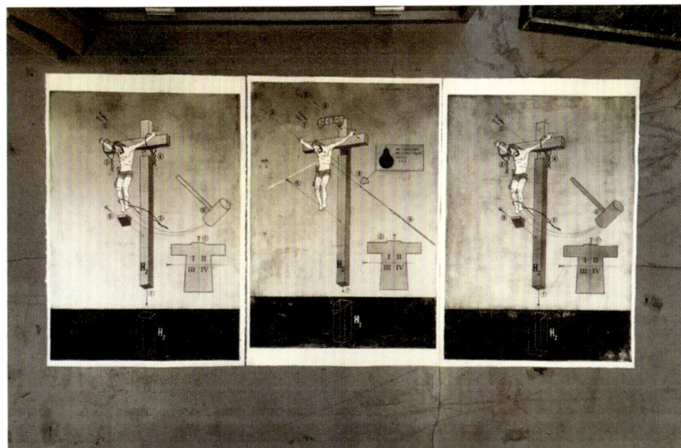

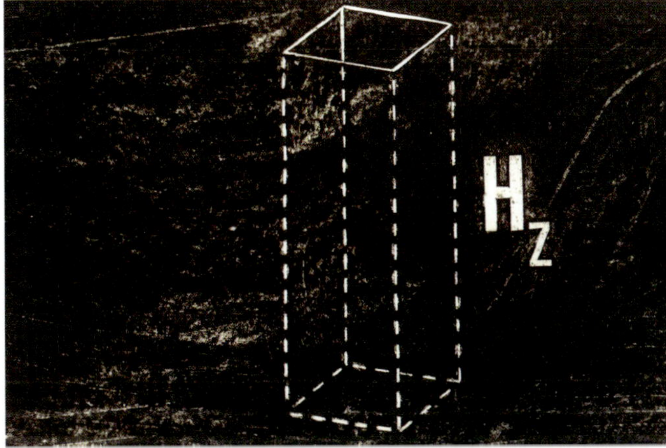

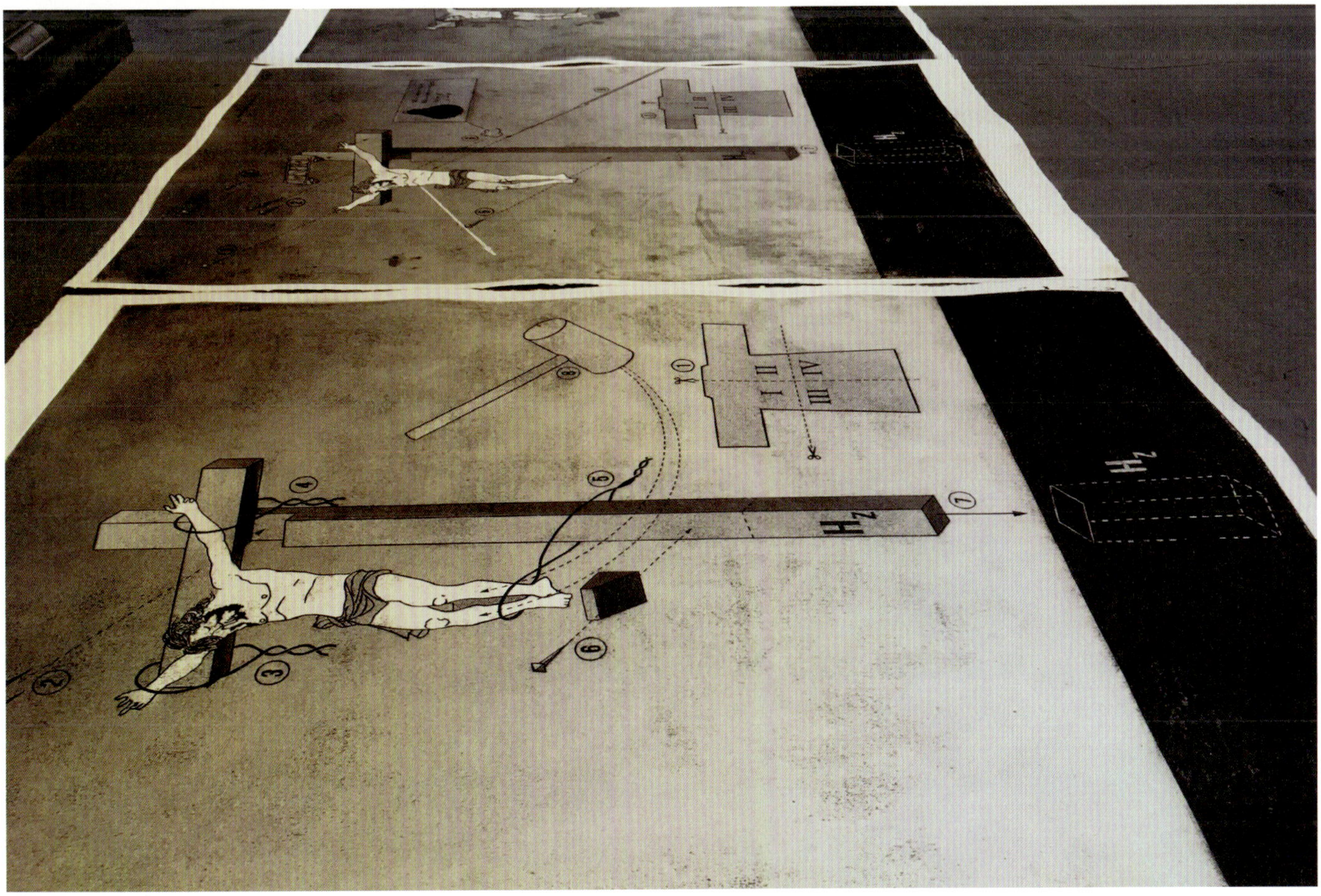

D: Jacek Machowski

Improvisation for Grażynka

- 350g Handmade paper Hahnemühle and crepe color
- offset printing ink

This print is a part of the *Norma 2.0 series*. The title "Improvisation for Grażynka" borrows from the *Józef Gielniak* series. The work alludes to the Jacek's lecturer of history of art, Dr. Grażynka Ryba (the Polish word *ryba* means "fish" in English).

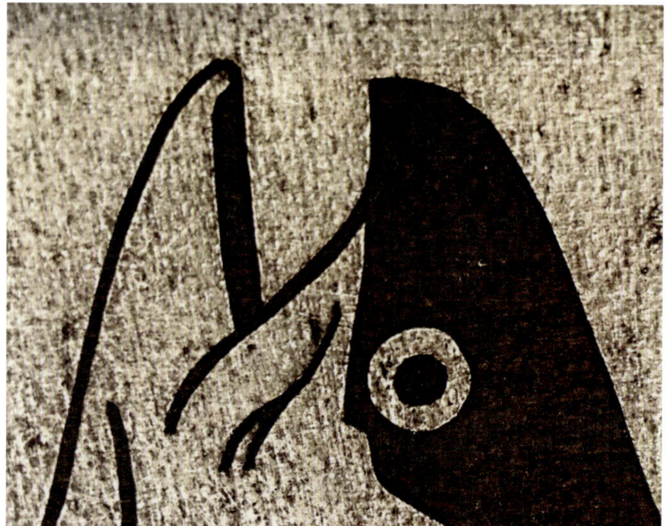

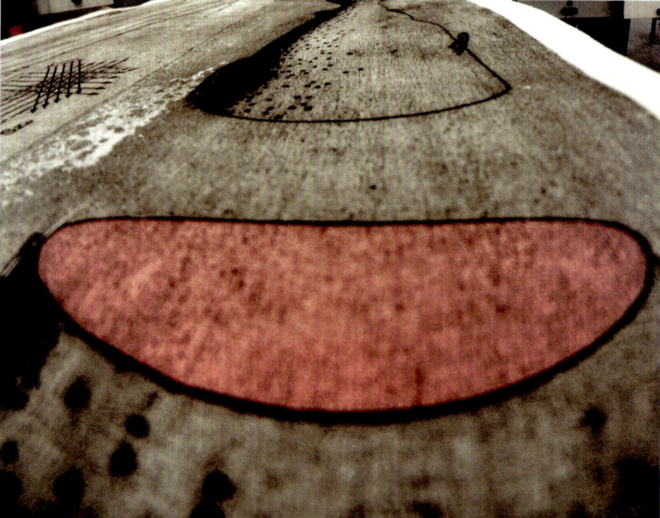

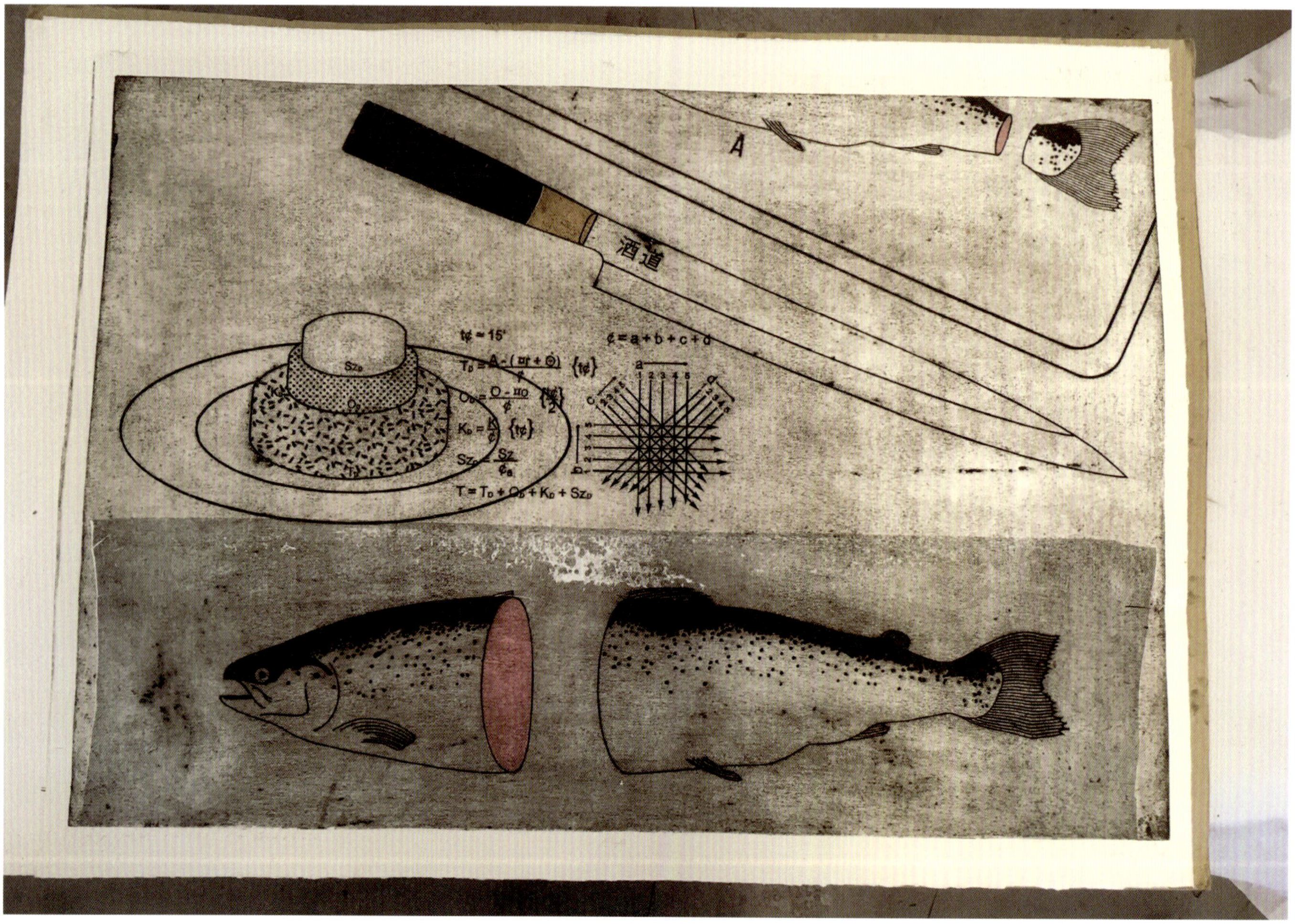

The Effect of Gravity on Pickling Jar

350g Handmade paper Hahnemühle and crepe color

offset printing ink, acrylic spray paint

This print is a part of the *Norma 2.0 series*. It shows literally what has been put down in the title: the relation of the gravity and the atmospheric pressure within the pickling process.

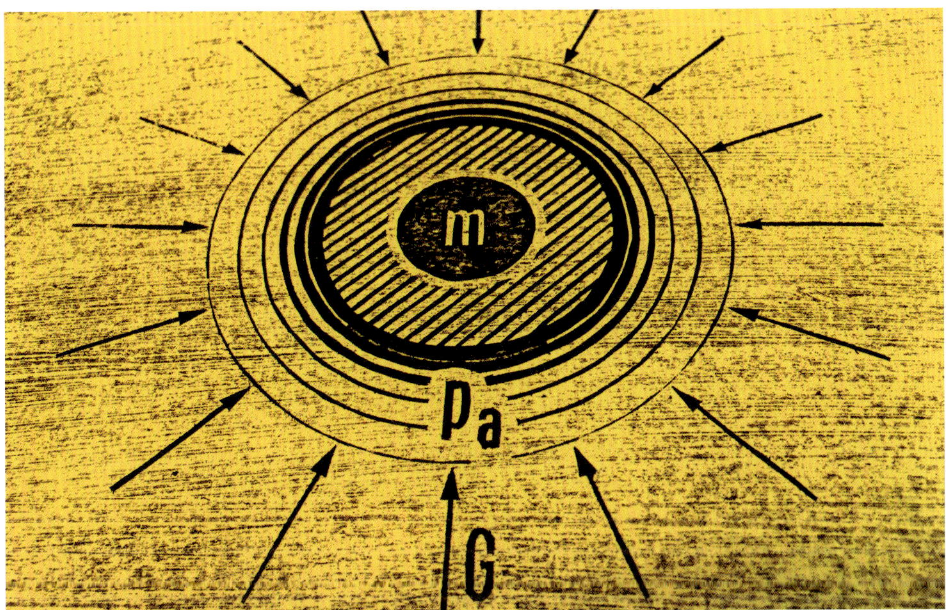

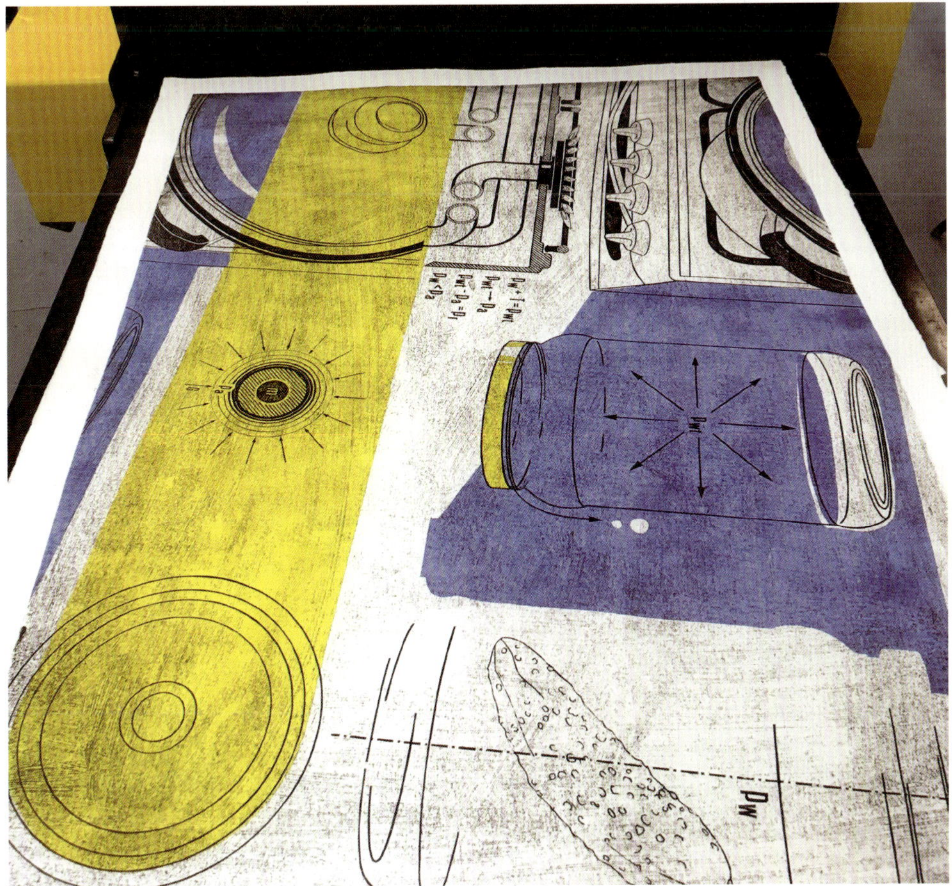

***D*:** Jacek Machowski

A Feather Forge

"A Feather Forge" is an intaglio print inspired by the painting *An Iron Forge* by Joseph Wright of Derby. It illustrates the contrast of the blacksmith's labor by showing that he is able to use his strength and tools to transform cold iron into beautiful and delicate pieces. The feather is a symbol of the enlightenment brought by the Smith's work and represents the finesse he was able to achieve. The technique chosen to create this piece was etching and aquatint, because metal is the main work material of the blacksmith.

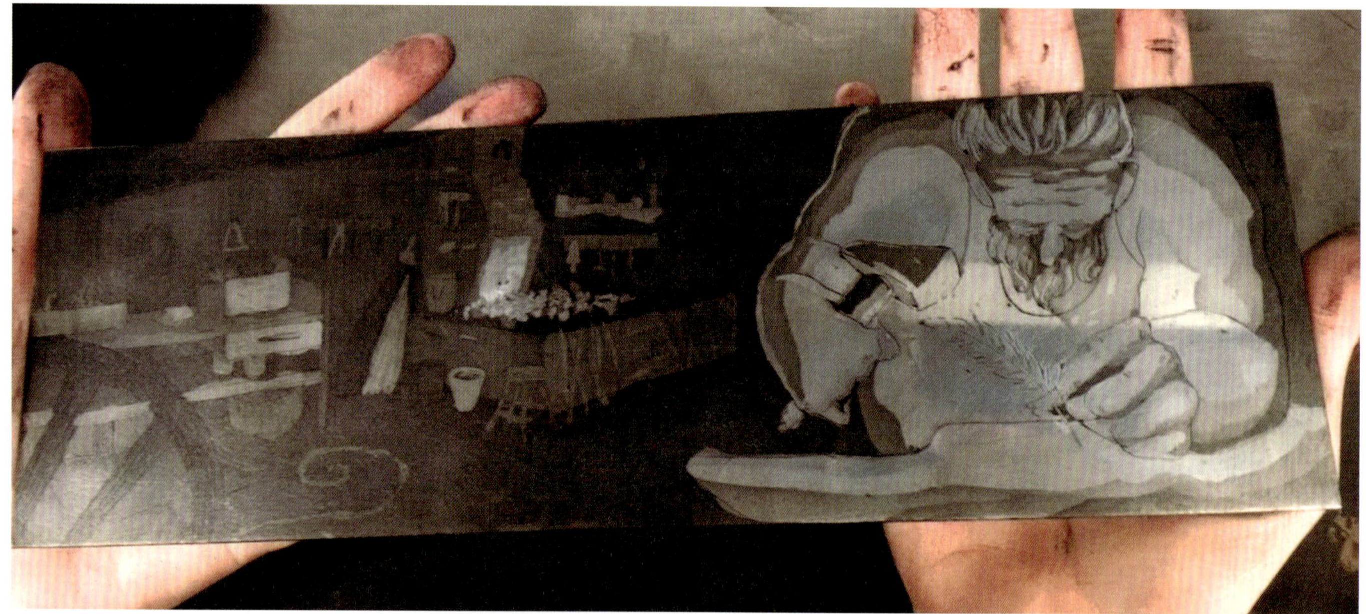

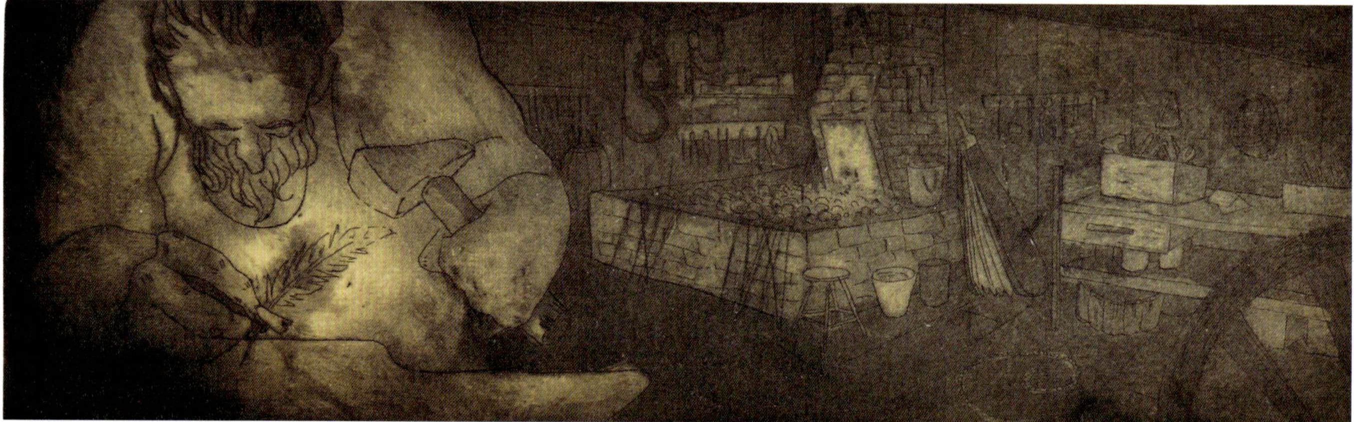

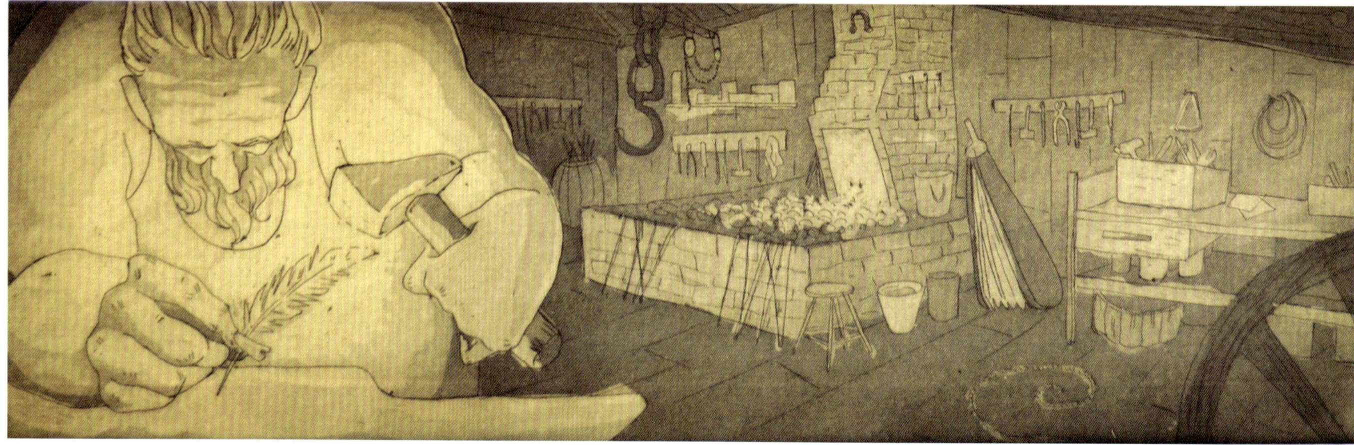

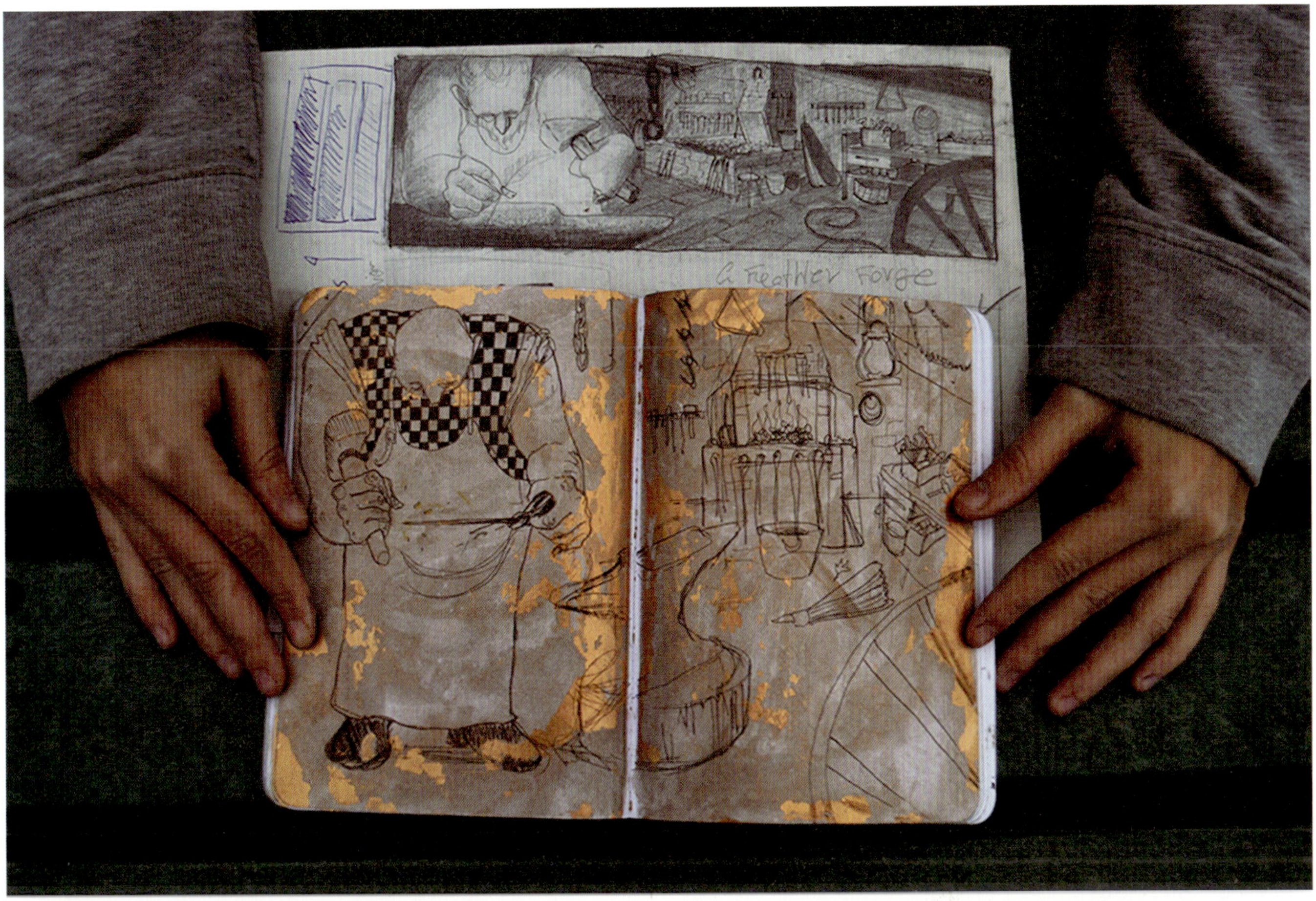

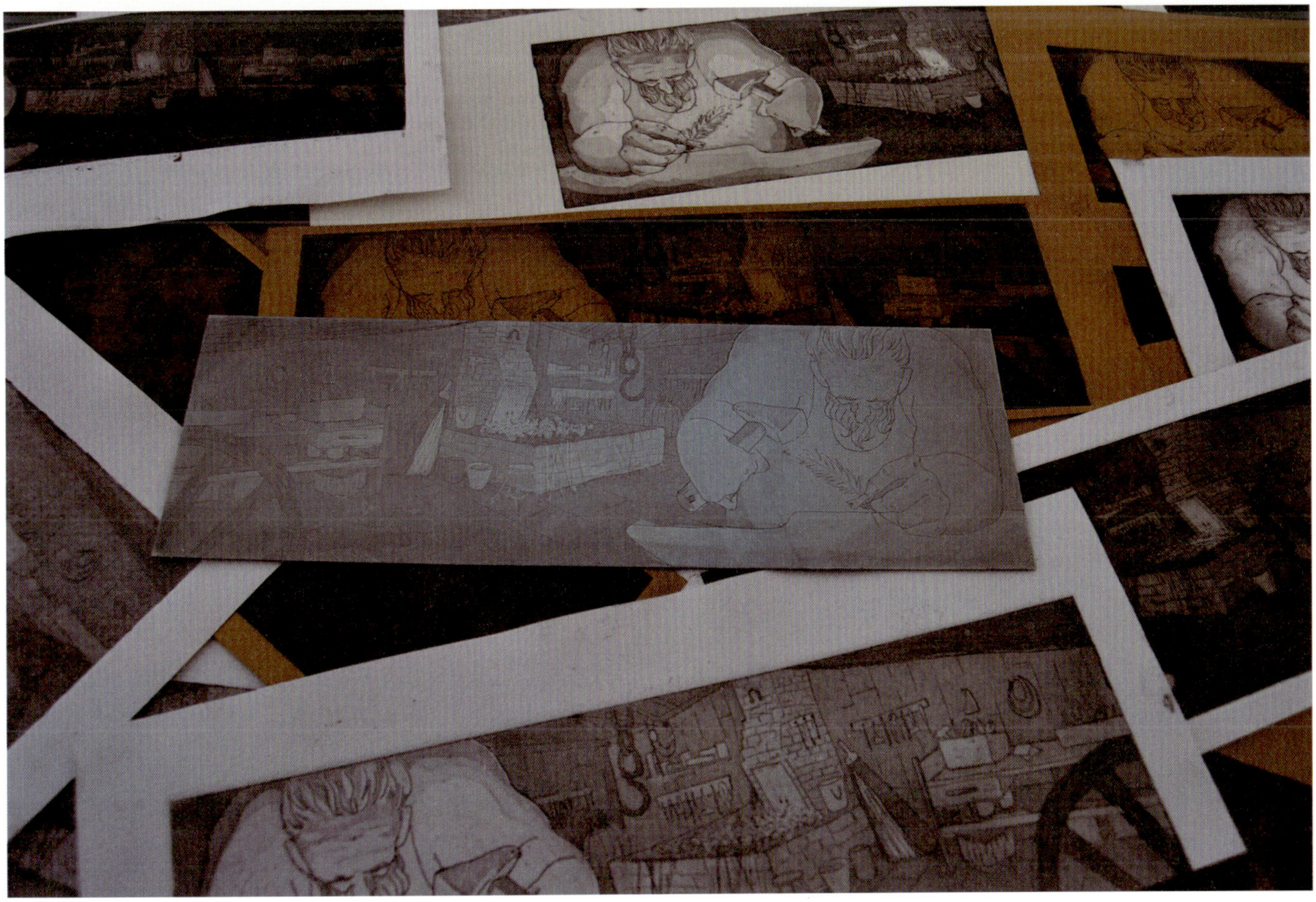

Doctor, My Foot Hurts

Fabriano Rosaspina cotton paper

Charbonnel black intaglio ink

"Doctor, My Foot Hurts" is a single illustration depicting a box-headed person in a doctor's waiting room. The girl misses her right foot, which waits by her side, and a little flower has grown from the wound. This situation stands as a metaphor of loss, and need for help, while the flower may represent a glimpse of hope. The designer chose to add aquatint shadows to lend her illustration a darker atmosphere.

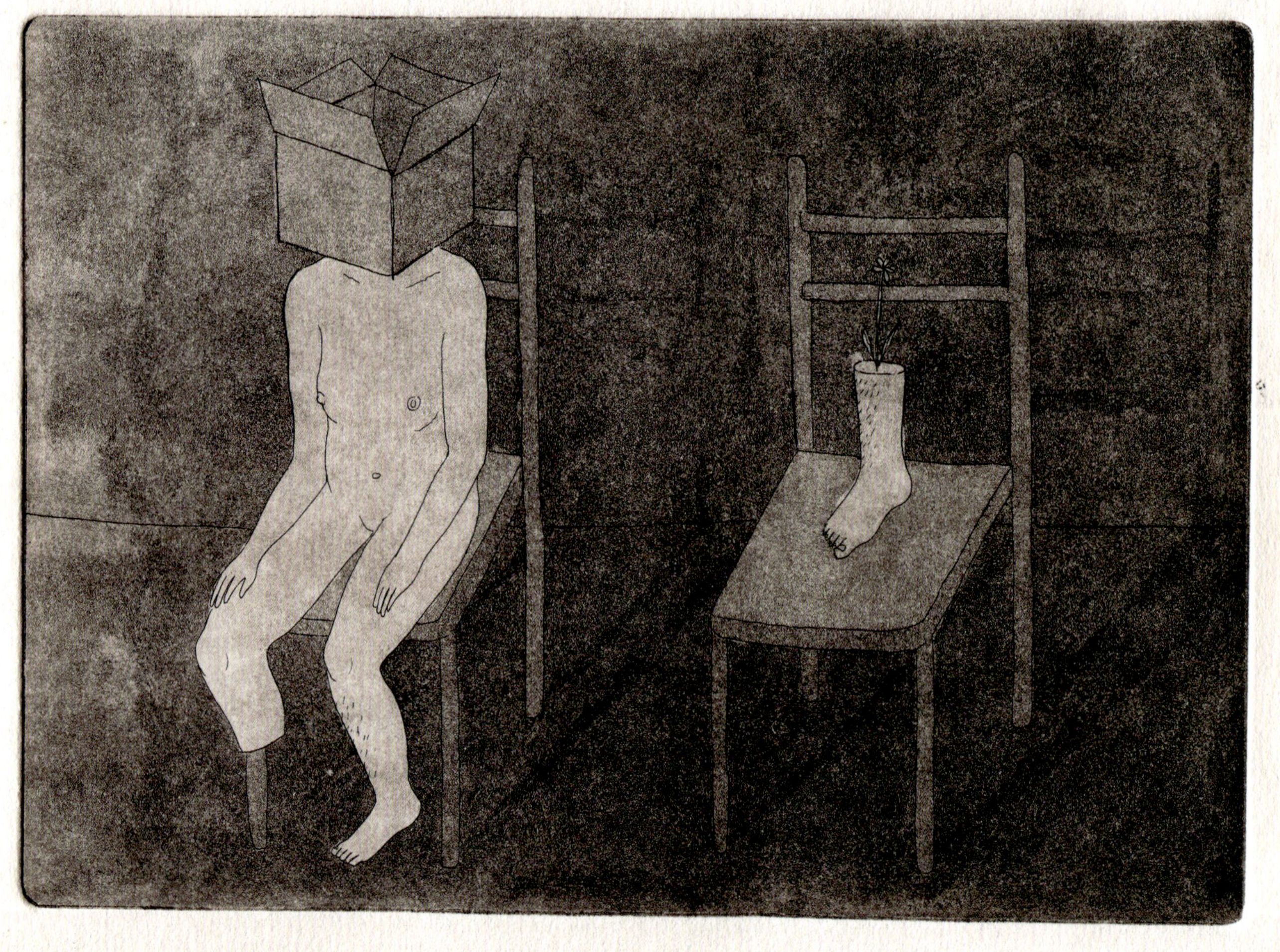

Dead Flowers

Fabriano Rosaspina cotton paper

Charbonnel black intaglio ink

"Dead flowers" is a single illustration that may look like a simple still life but it isn't. The designer tried to represent the memory of this person who every morning changes water to these by now dead and dry flowers. It is like her or his attempt to keep a certain feeling or memory alive, which may seem useless to some but actually keeps her going on.

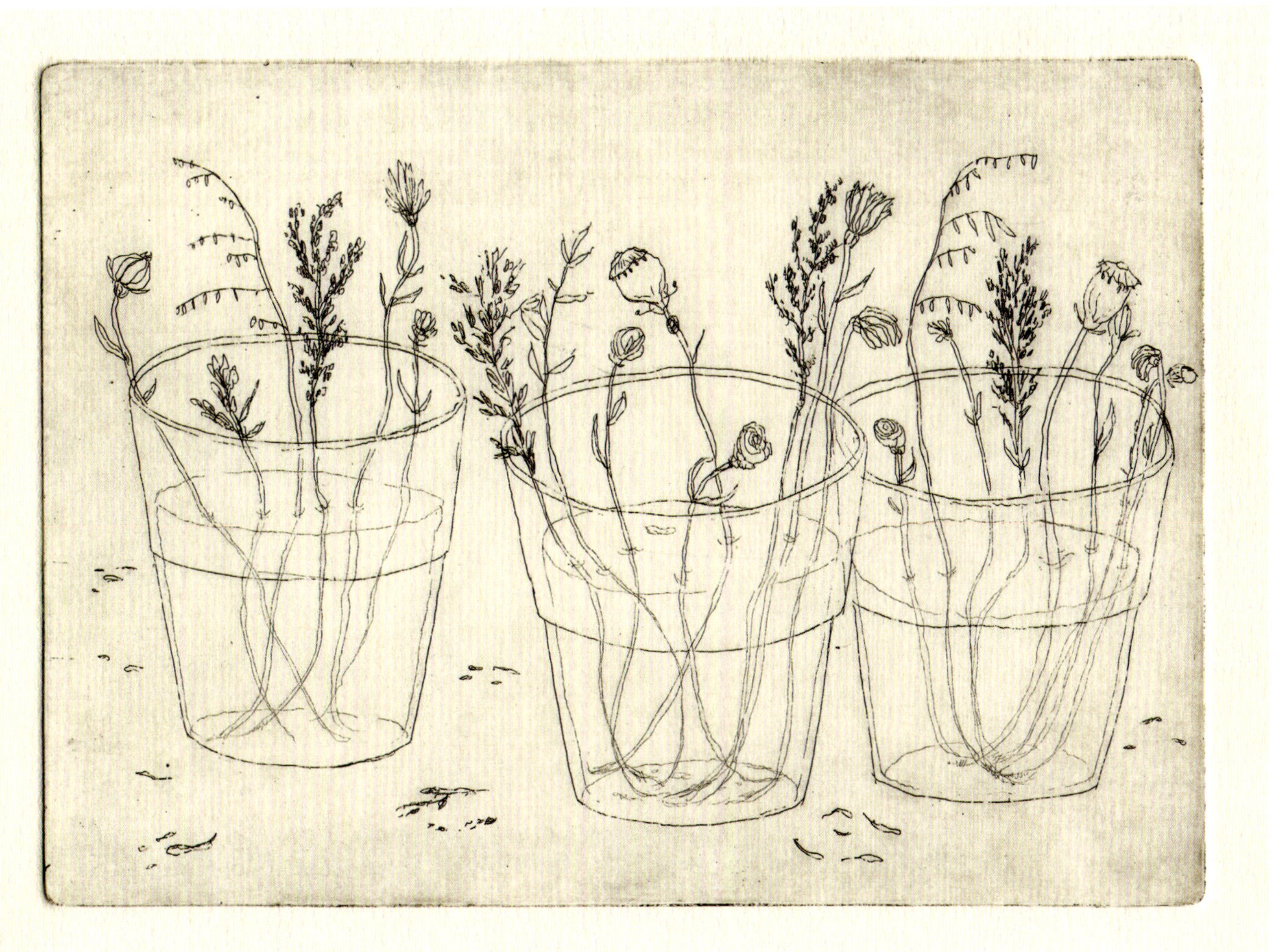

A Series of Thematic Graphic Works

paper

etching paint

These works are created through an etching technique. It is a style favored by the designer because it helps him to deliver the initial vision of a picture born in his imagination.

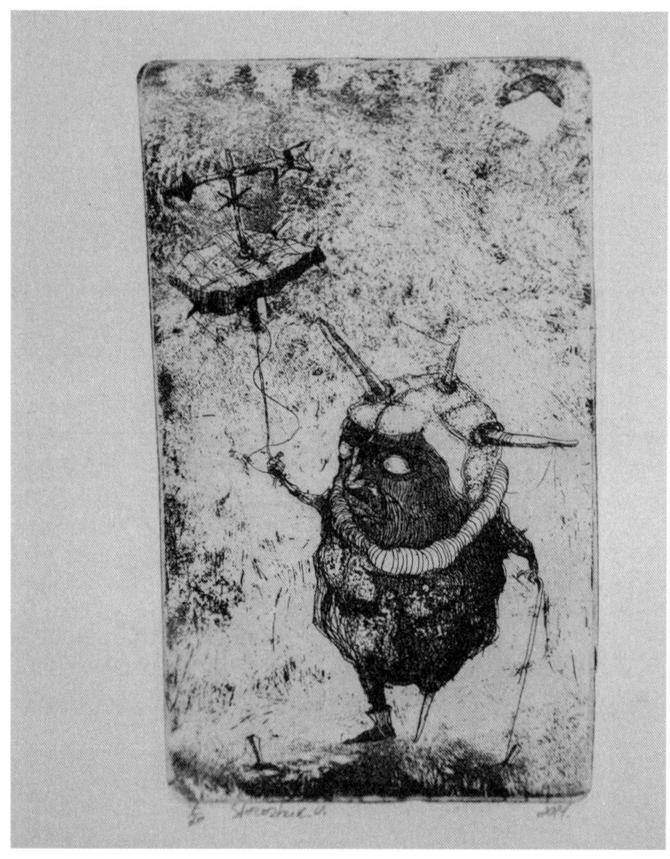

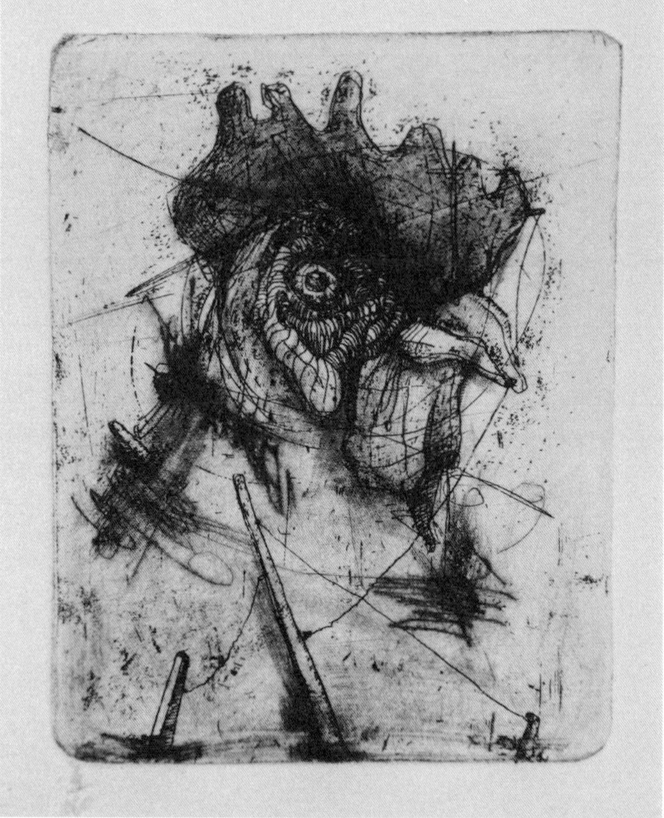

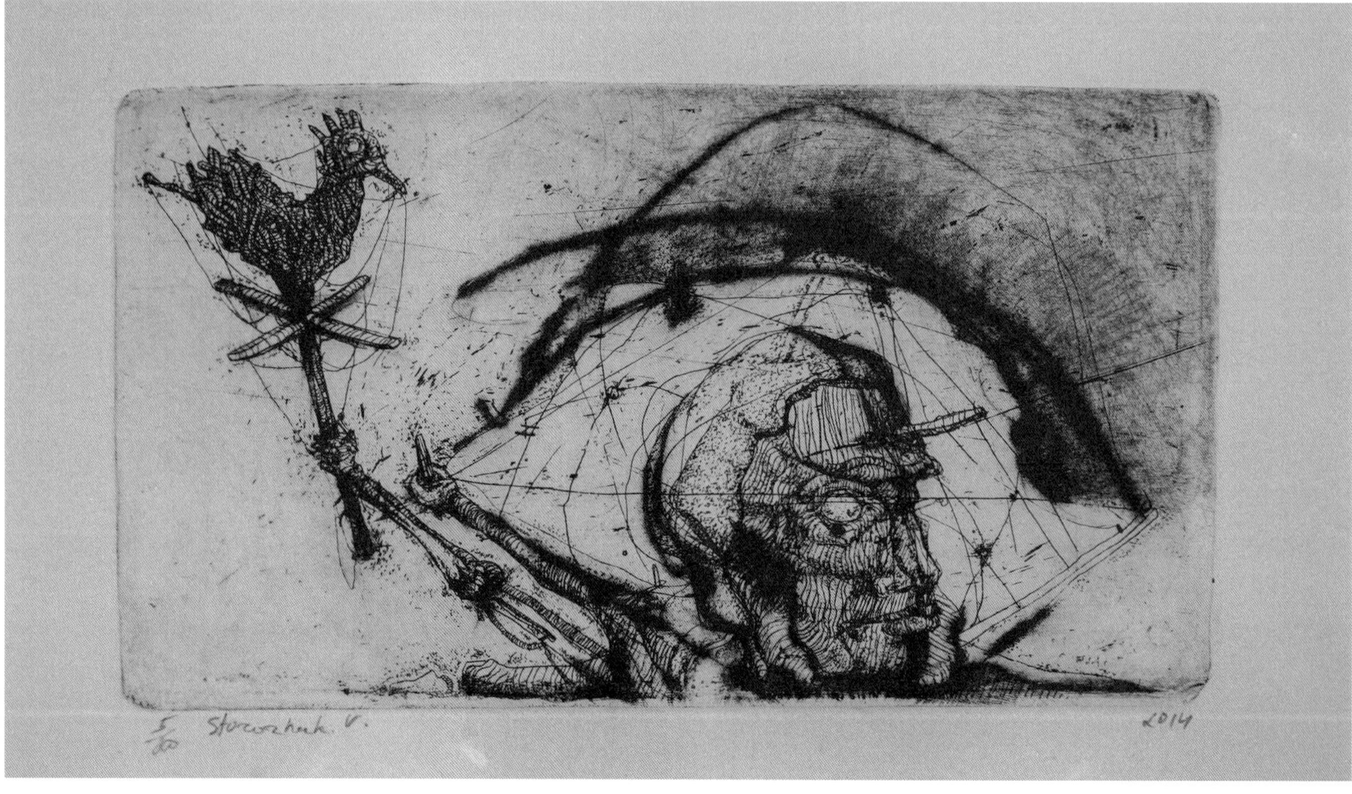

The Letter "P"

Fabriano paper

golden acrylic paint, offset blue ink

The letter "P" is an illustration project combining illustration and typography, drawing inspiration from the capital letters of the Middle Ages and the forms and textures of nature. The project has been developed using a handmade engraving technique, using a carved wooden base to generate relief by pressing on a heavy surface. The piece has also been painted in detail manually with gold paint and offset ink.

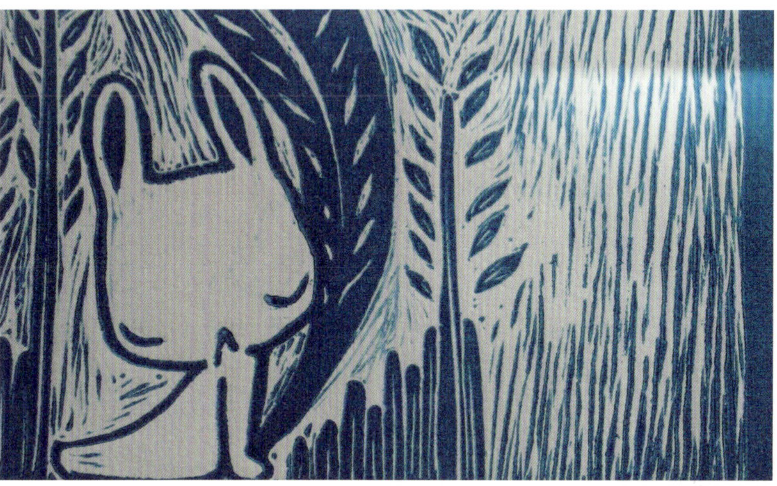

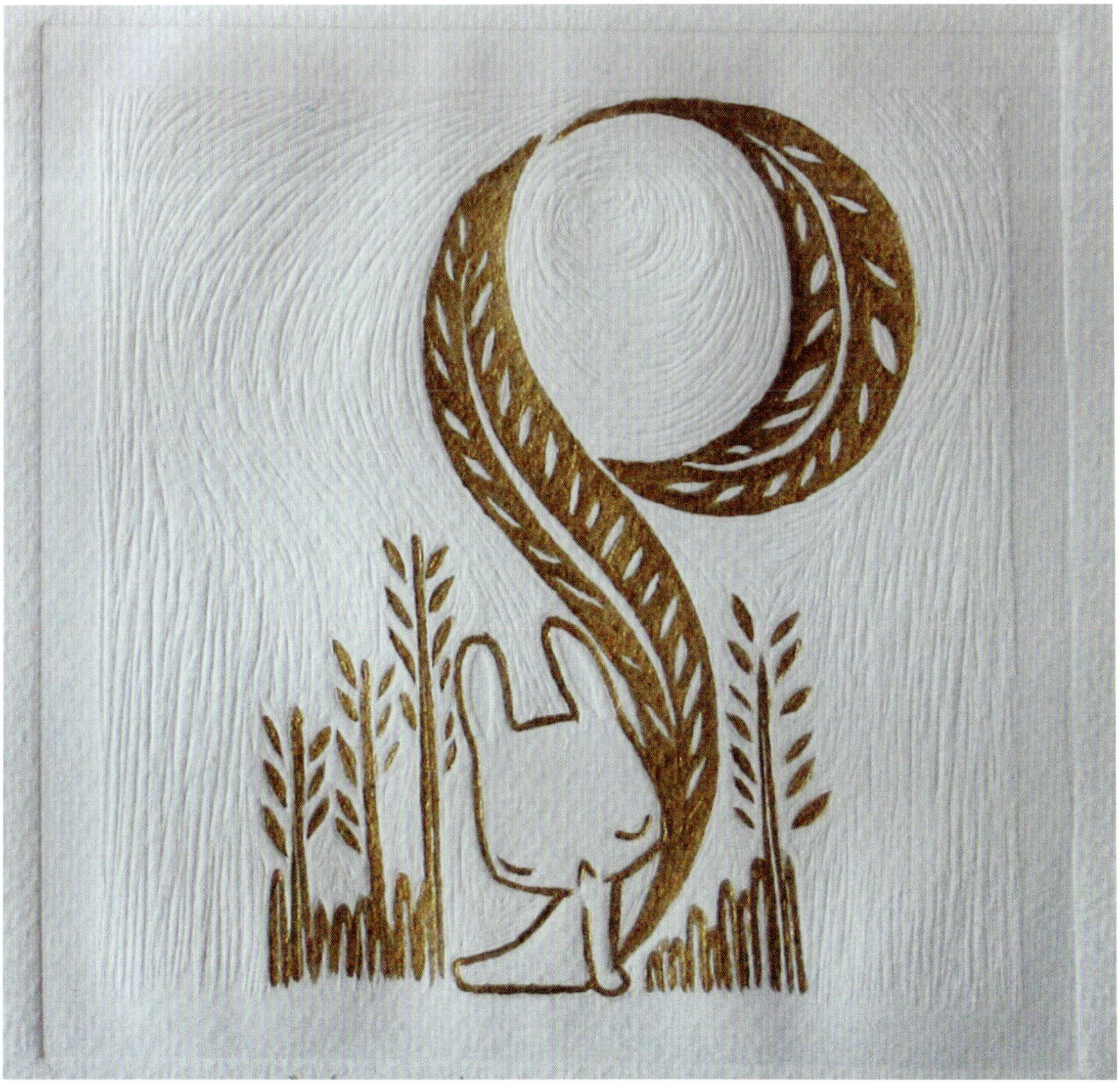

D: Carlos Franco Leyva

Domingo's

25 micro BOPP laminated to 25 micron BOPP

2 spot/6 Pantone colors

This family-owned manufacturer of traditional Hispanic salty snacks wished to sell pork rind products to natural food store consumers. The designers analyzed the company history and product qualities while researching the target market, and decided the key positioning features would be the old-fashioned cooking process and the Gaytan family story. In honor of the founder they chose "Domingo's" as the brand name. To evoke the time period of the 1920s, baseball-style hand-lettering and distinctive period fonts were used. A re-discovered photograph of the original store focused the design on the heritage of the company. Rotogravure reproduction was used to project a high-level of quality to the consumer.

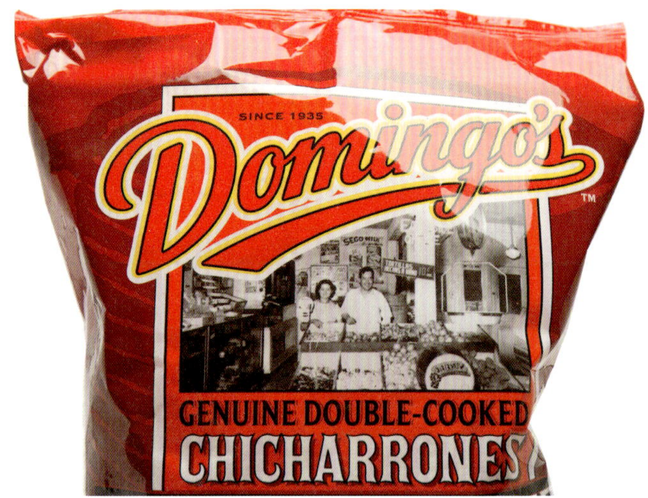

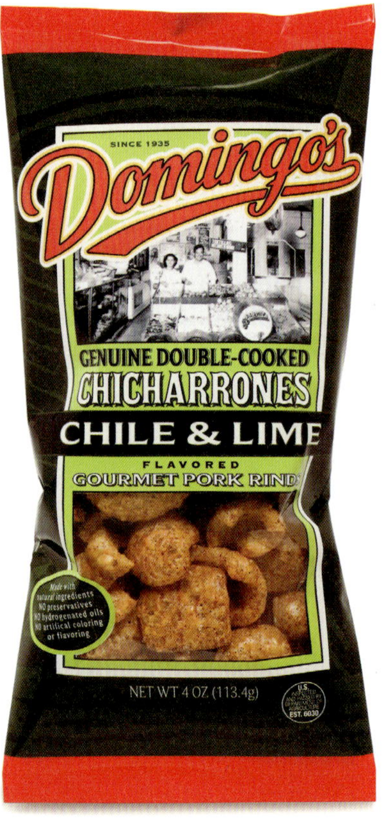

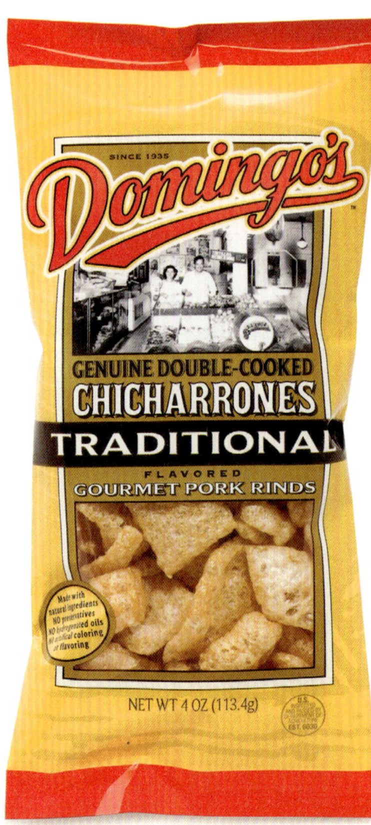

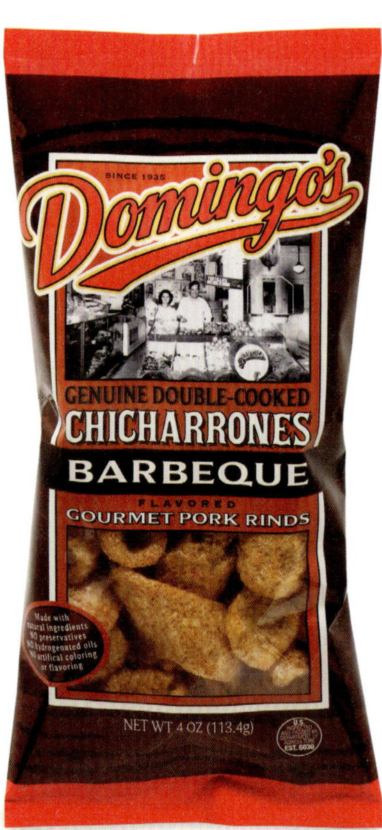

D: Mark Oliver

INSAL'ARTE

Every package of fresh salad in a polypropylene bag shows the initial letter of the product inside. For the realization of every letter there has been created a sculpture made with salad leaves, and then photographed, using the salad contained in the package. The result not only shows the fresh product contained in the package but also creates immediate recognizability when shelf stocked and the possibility to establish customer interaction: having the entire alphabet at one's disposal. After many attempts, the studio chose rotogravure printing machines, which produce a soft fading effect and shiny colors as in the pictures.

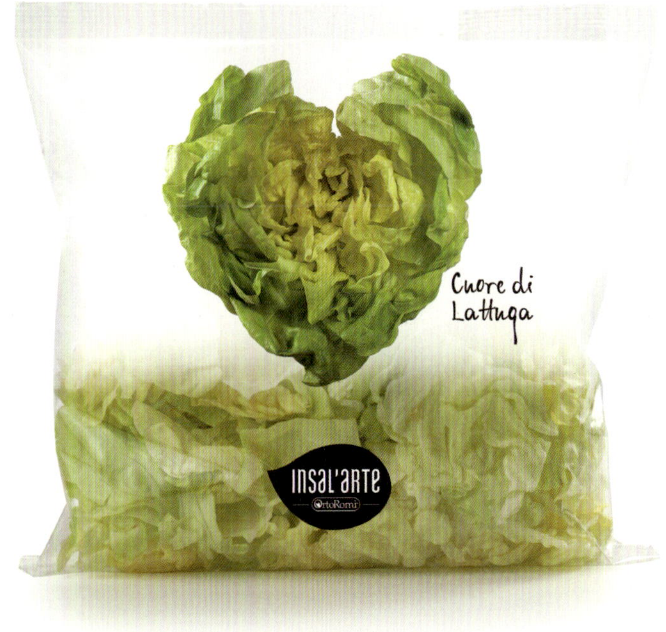

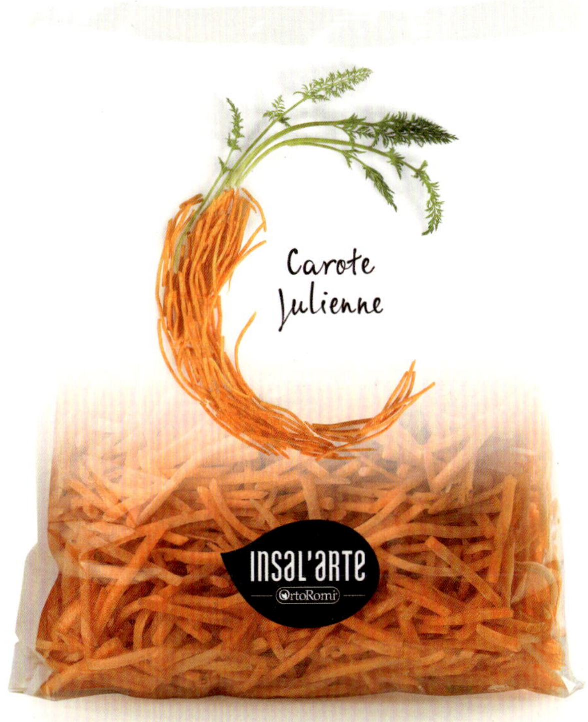

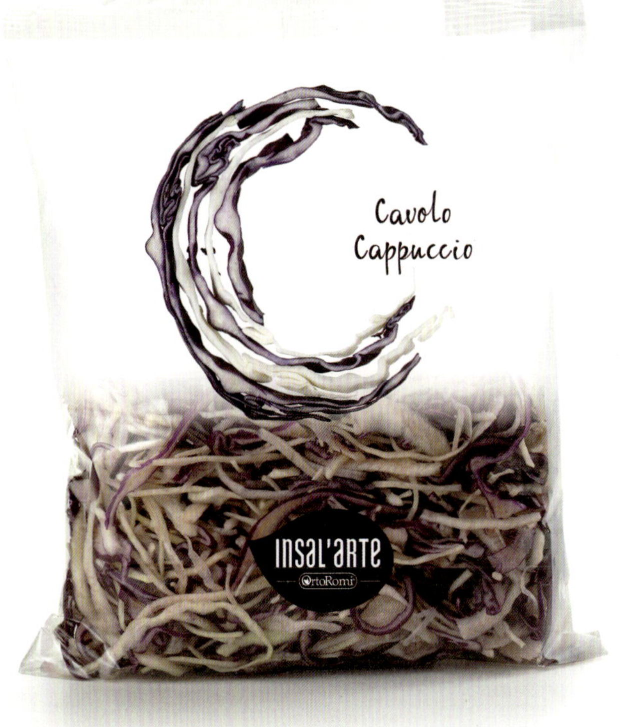

***D*:** Mirco Luzzi

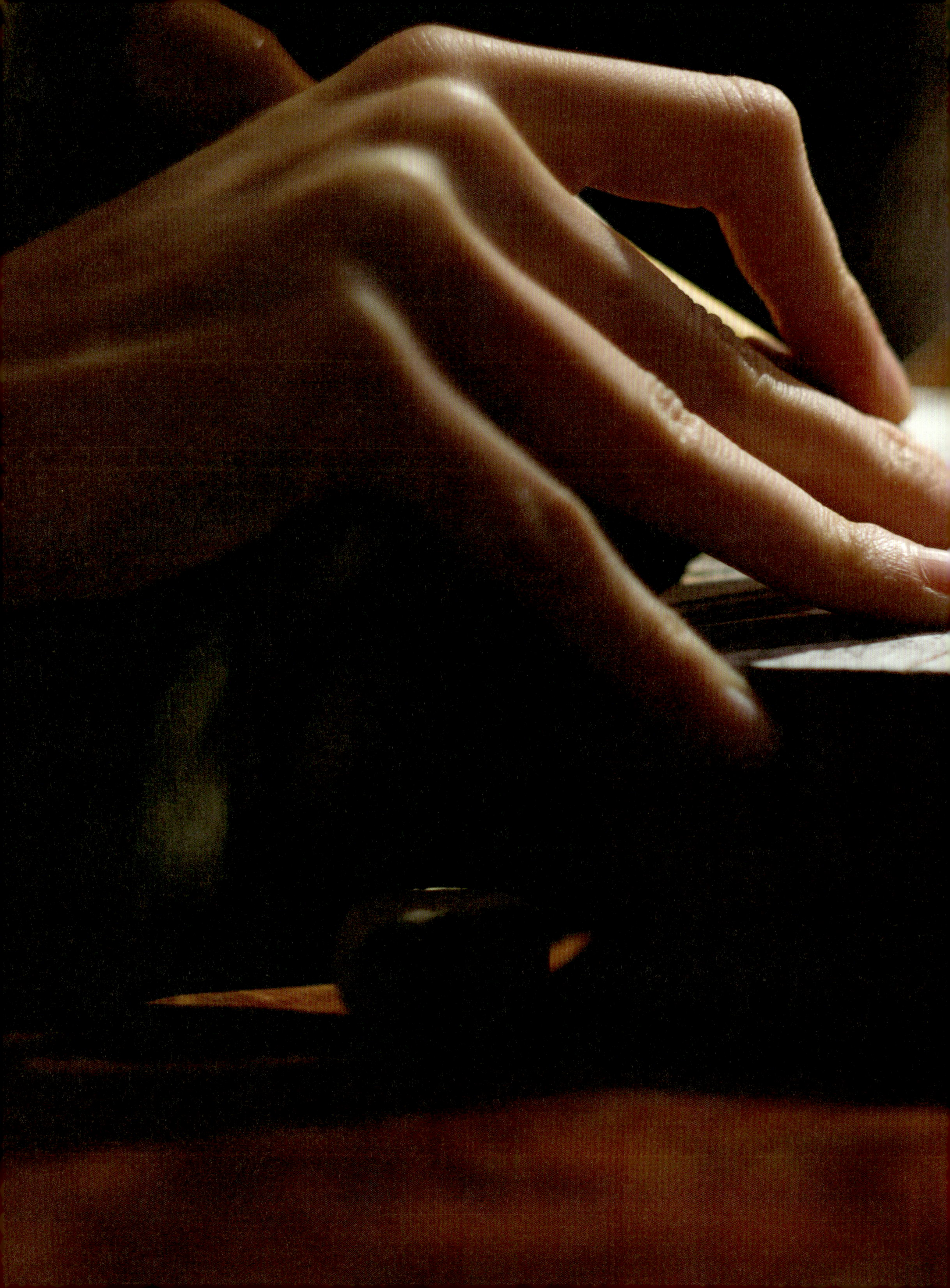

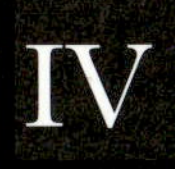

Relief Printing

Relief Printing

1 Introduction

Relief printing is a process where protruding surface faces of the printing plate or block are inked. It is one of the oldest forms of printing, and improvements have been made during its course of development. Woodblock printing was invented in the beginning of the Tang Dynasty (618 - 906). Texts or images were engraved on wood. The surface of the wood block was then inked and covered with a sheet of paper. The text or images were printed by gently brushing the paper over the engraved characters. It is one of the oldest forms of printing. Nowadays, flexography is the most commonly used relief-printing method.

2 Application

① book covers ② greeting cards ③ envelopes ④ business cards ⑤ wedding invitation
⑥ woodblock printing and the newspapers in the early Republic of China

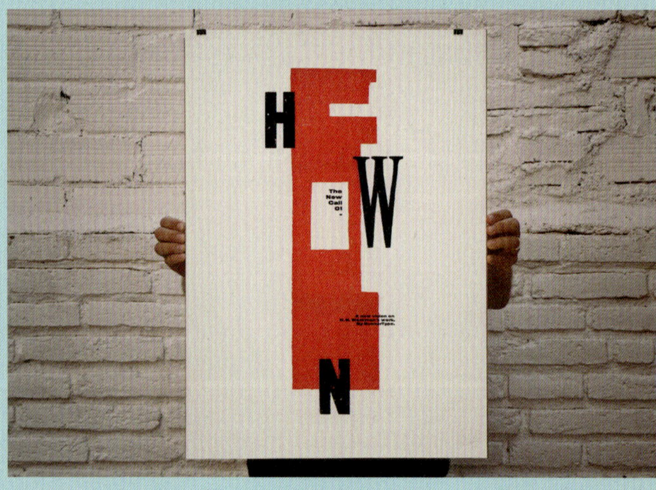

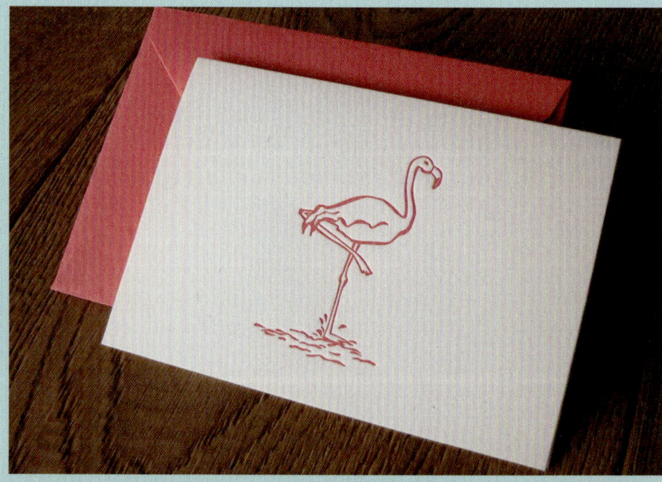

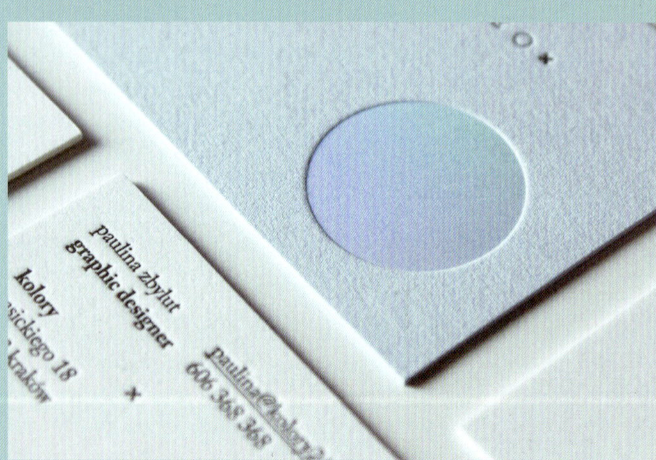

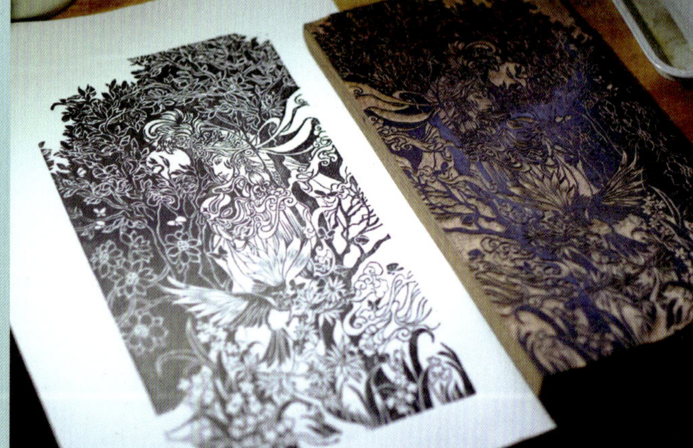

3 Features

- Raised printing face
- Reversed images or text
- Direct printing method

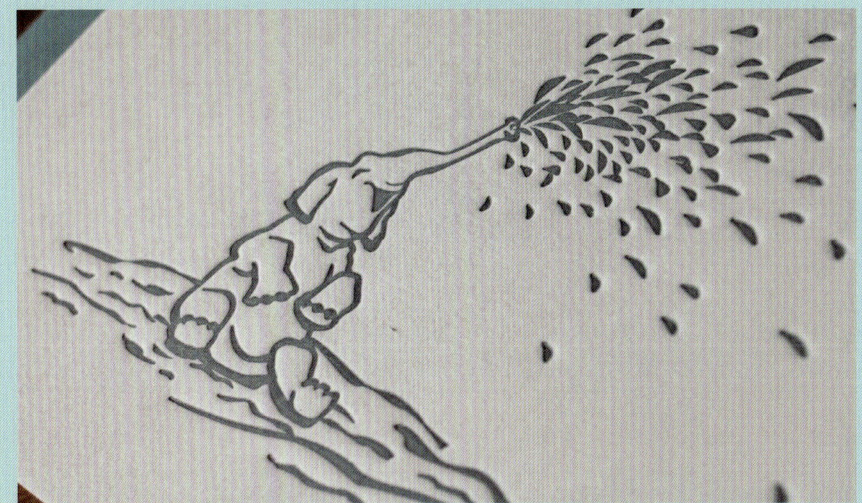

The pressure applied on the substrate produces a characteristic rim on the edges of the printed lines.

4 Merits and Demerits

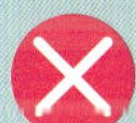

- Suitable for mass printing
- Characteristic rims on the edges of the printed lines
- Thick ink expression
- Performs well when printing objects with a rough surface

- High cost of plate making and printing
- Complex plate-making process

A poster printed by a Heidelberg letterpress machine.

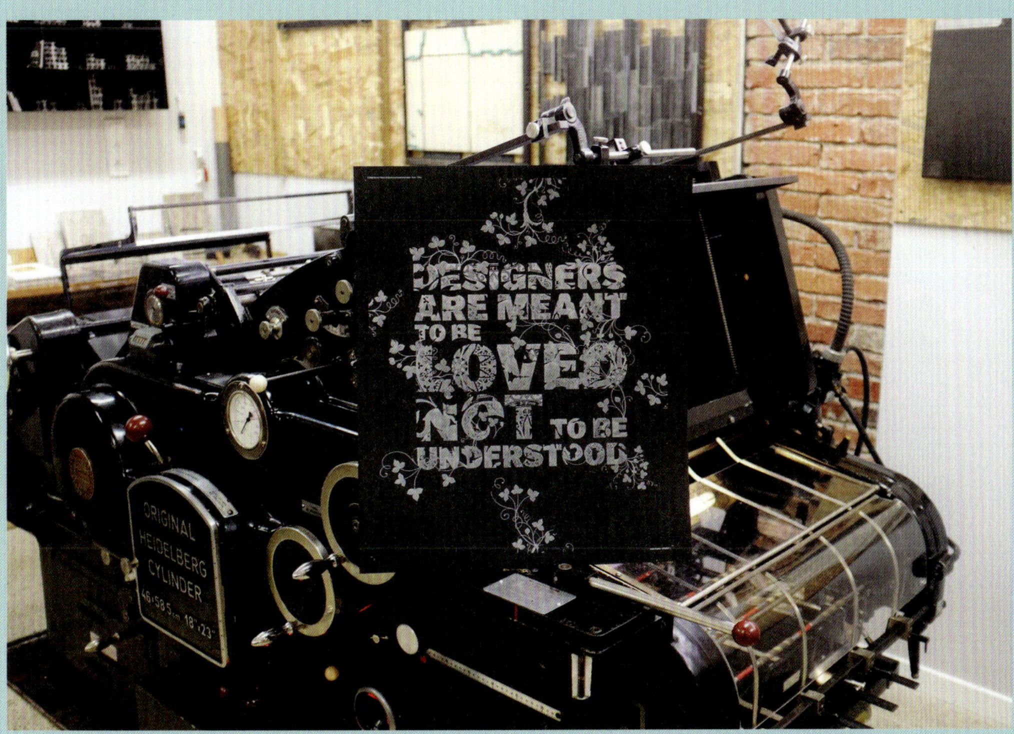

5 Mechanism

A Function View

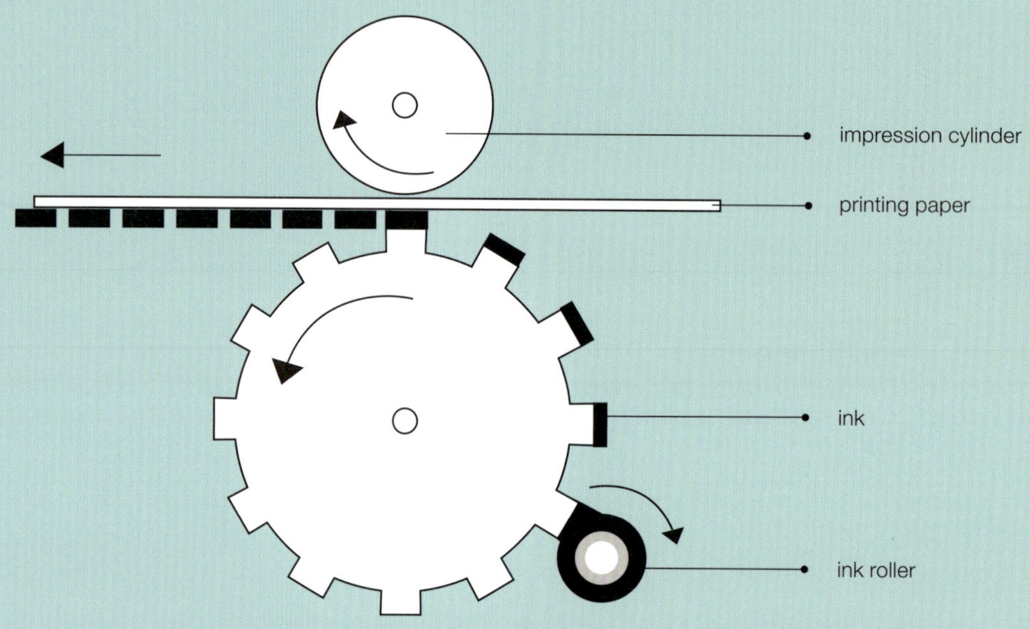

B Top View

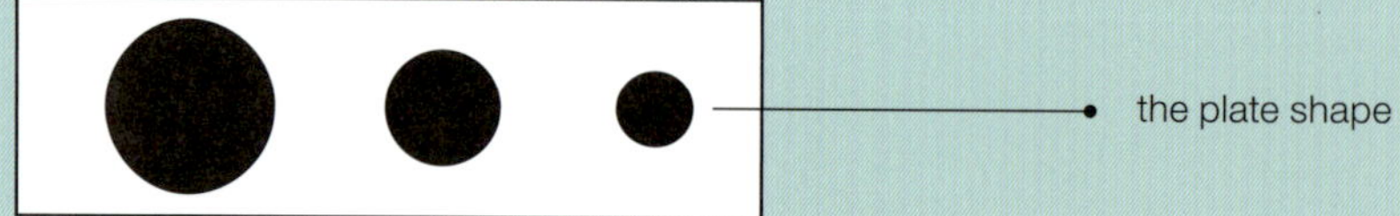

C Side View

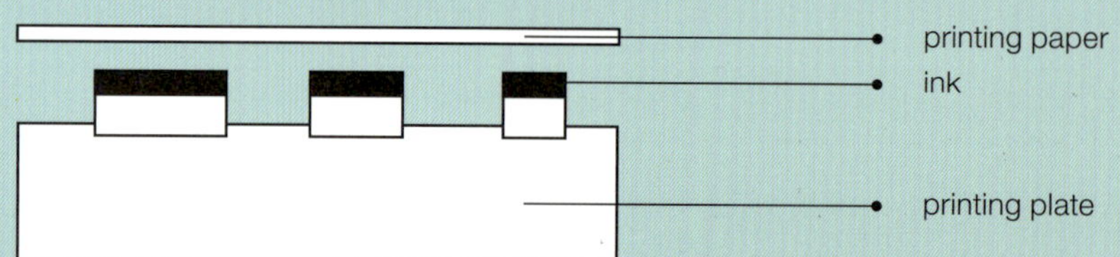

D Printing Method

1. rotary letterpress machine

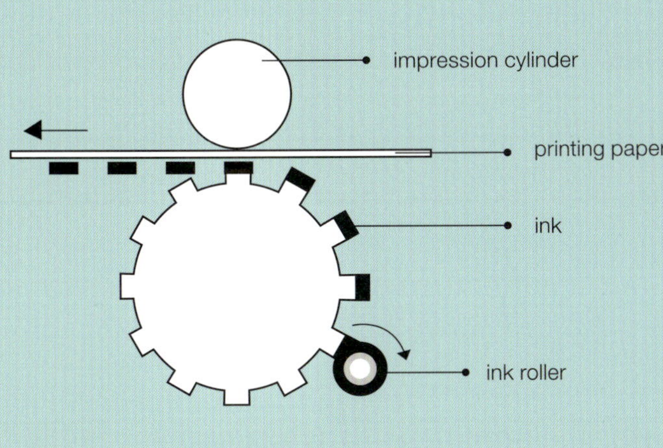

2. platen press

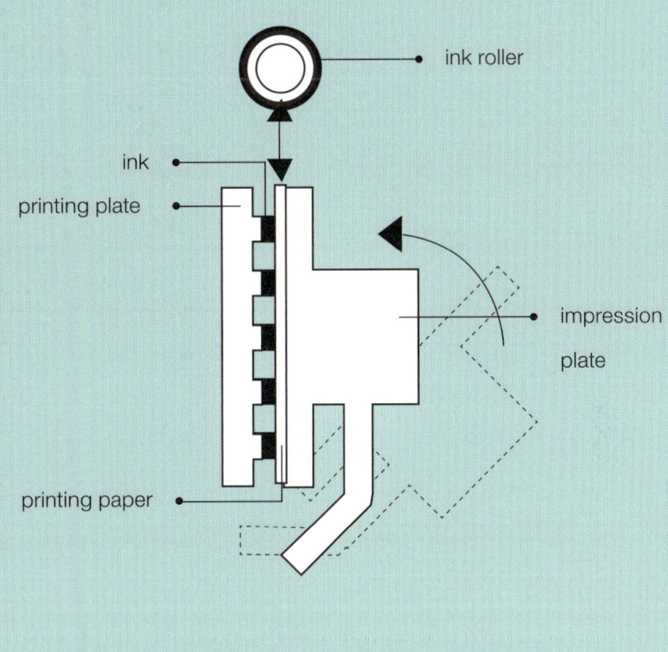

3. flat-bed cylinder press

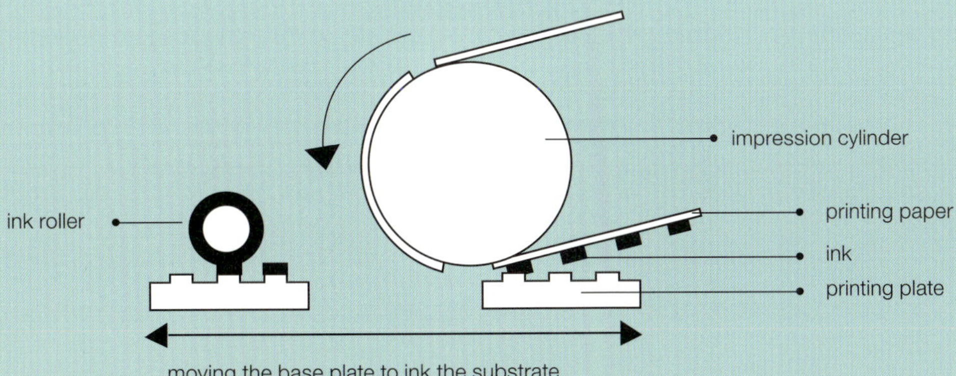

Principle

The inked area on the printing plates is higher than on the non-inked area, it causes an uneven surface on paper through printing pressure, and it can create a marginal zone: a printing area larger than it should be due to a side leakage of ink. Relief printing produces good printed outputs. The ink reproduction rate is 70% to 80%.

E Structure

A relief printing press consists of a sheet feeder, a printing unit, and a delivery unit. The picture below is an illustration of a central cylinder type press, in which the substrate is fixed tightly on the central impression cylinder. Thus the accuracy of the color register is quite high.

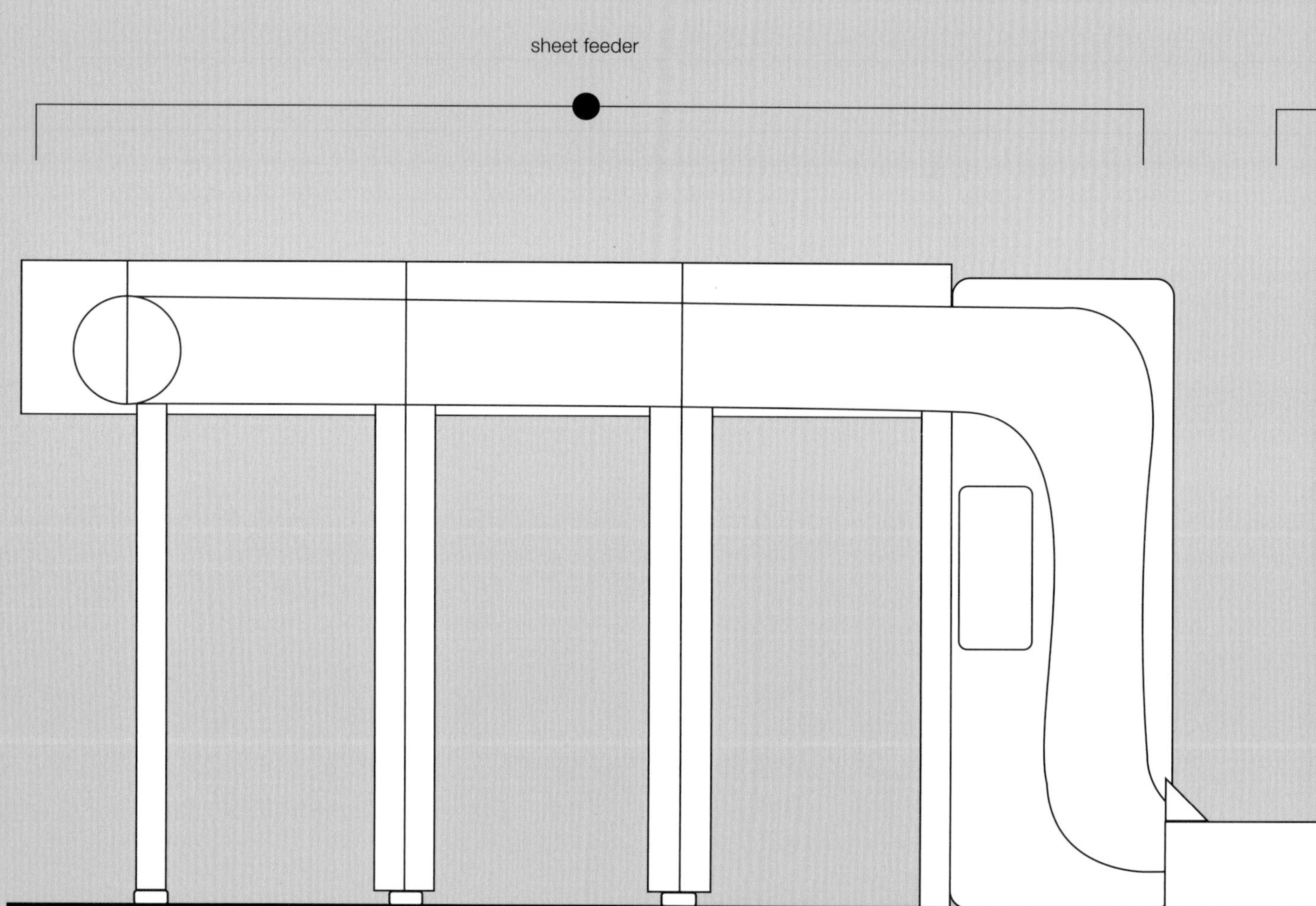

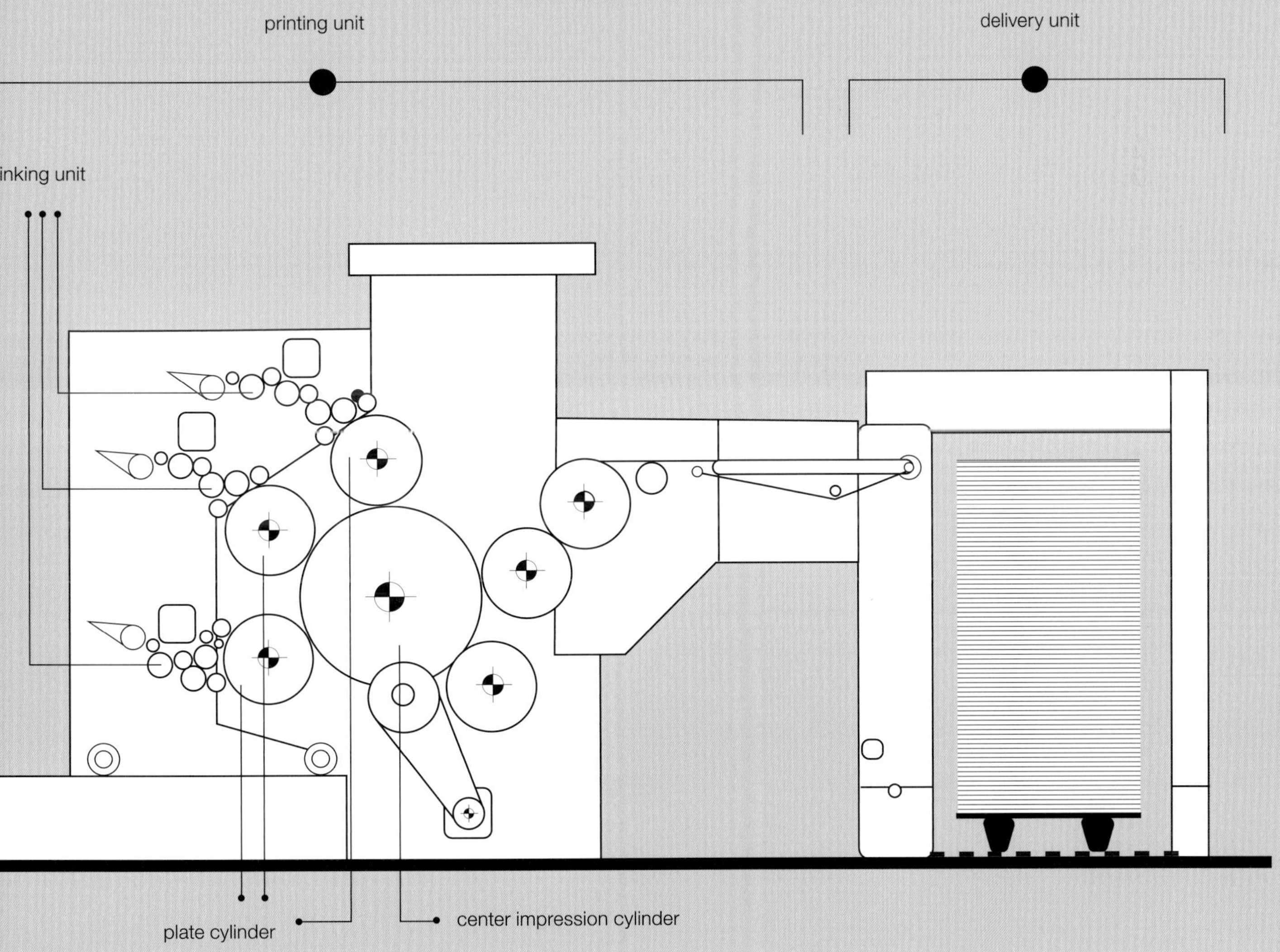
printing unit
delivery unit
inking unit
plate cylinder
center impression cylinder

6 Plate Making

There are two kinds of plates in relief printing: (a) metal plates made from copper, zinc and lead, and so on. (b) photopolymer plates, rubber plates, and flexographic plates.

a.The process - take zinc and copper plates for example

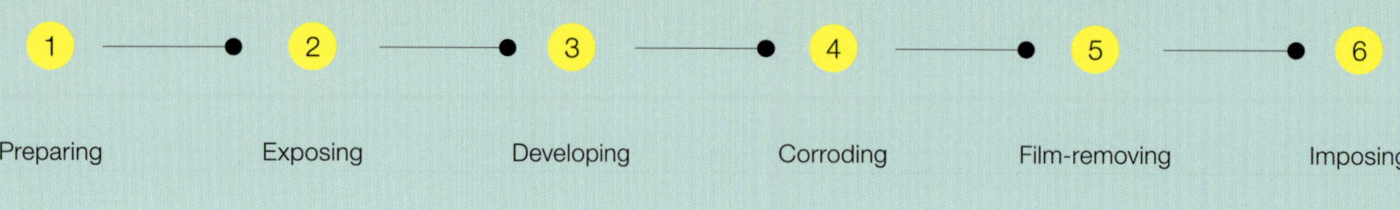

1 Preparing

Choose a zinc or copper plate with a desired thickness and cut it into a proper size. Remove the greasy dirt and the oxidation film on the surface. Polish the surface with wood charcoal to increase its absorbability to emulsion. Put the ready metal plate in a coating machine and apply an even coat with emulsion on the plate. Then dry the plate in a warm environment with a temperature of 70°C.

2 Exposing

Lay the film positive on the coated copper or zinc plates firmly, for exposure. The parts exposed to light will react to form a water-insoluble and corrosion-resistant high-molecular polymer.

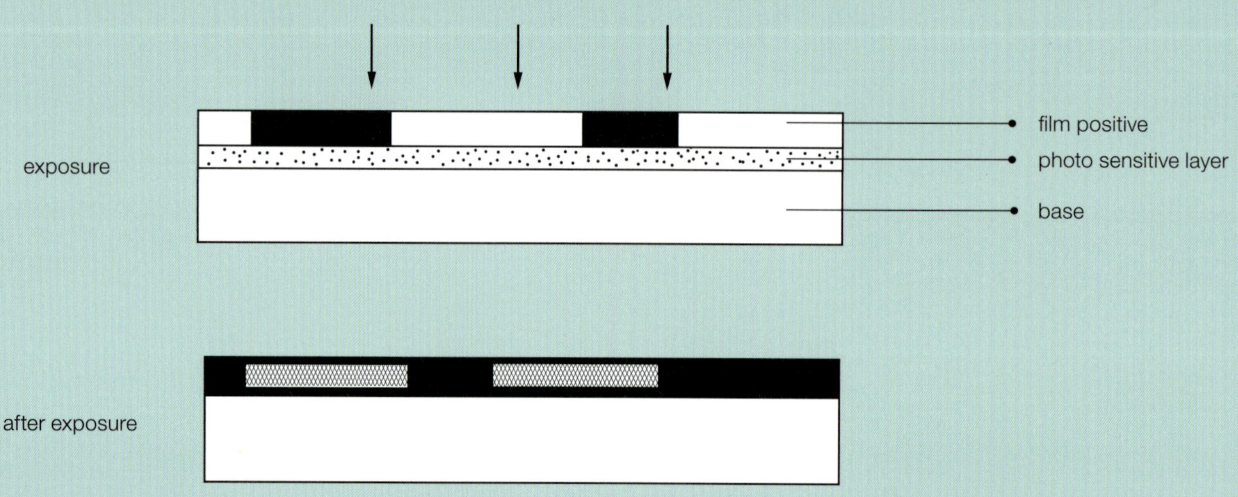

3 Developing

Once the exposure is done, rinse the plate in water to develop the image. The parts are not exposed will be washed away and the exposed parts become hard and remained on the surface. Place the plate in a bath of the methyl violet 5BN to develop the image more clearly. Then bake the plate to increase the corrosion resistance of the coating.

4 Corroding

Use chemical methods to etch the non-image area of the plate. The image area will become a raised surface. Either powder etching or powderless etching could be used.

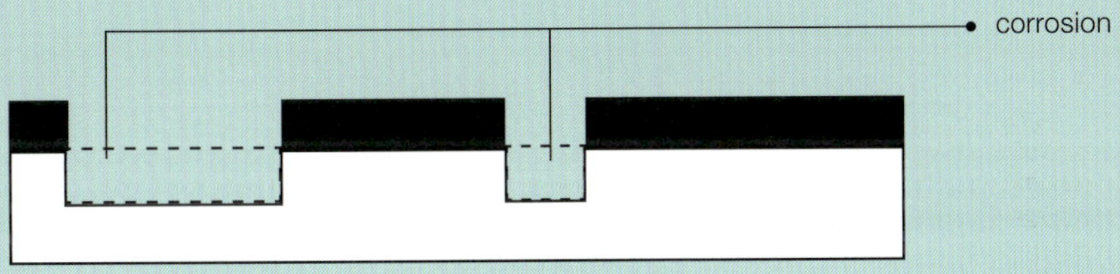

5 Film-removing

Remove the resistant layer.

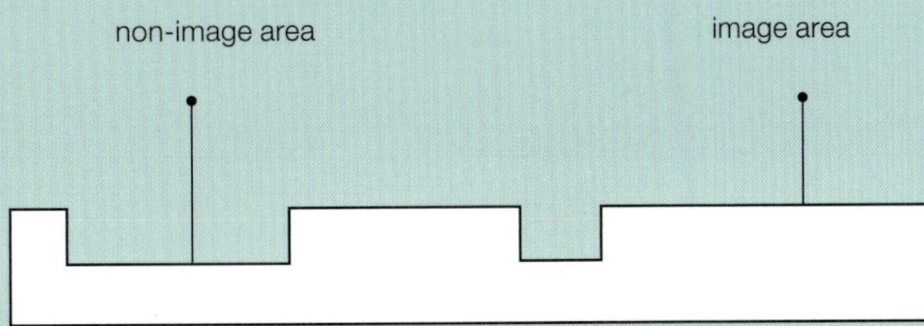

6 Imposing

Several plates could be assembled to convert into one plate to save materials and cost.

b.The process - take photopolymer plates as an example

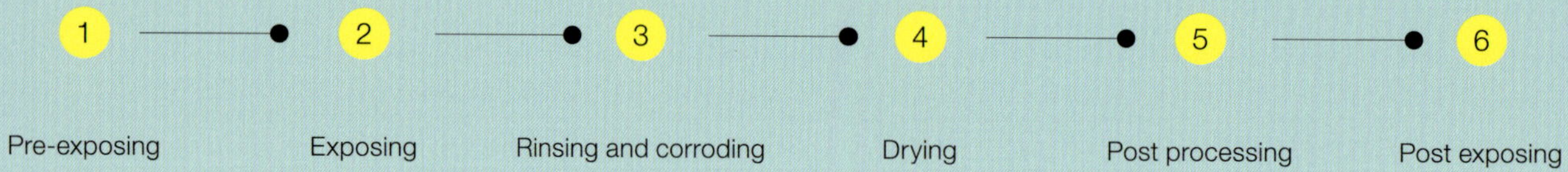

1 Pre-exposing

Expose the reverse side of the plate without any film to increase its thickness. The longer the exposure time is, the thicker the plate is. A thick plate is more durable.

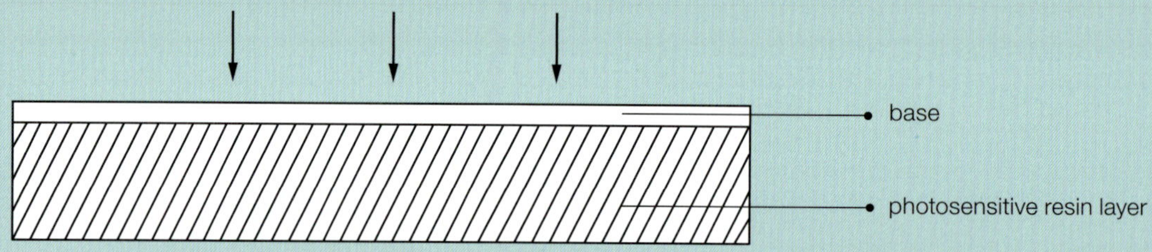

2 Exposing

Lay the negative film on the photopolymer plate for exposure. The exposure time is important because it determines the clarity of the image and the height of the raised parts. The longer the exposure time, the lower the raised part.

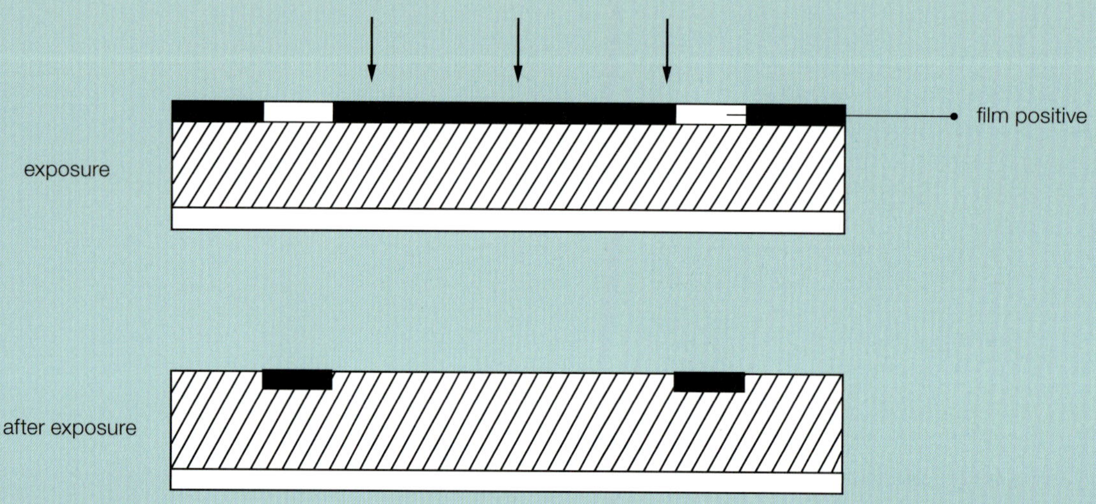

3 Rinsing and corroding

The parts that are not exposed dissolve and can be washed away, whereas the exposed parts become hard and remain a raised surface in the shape of the design.

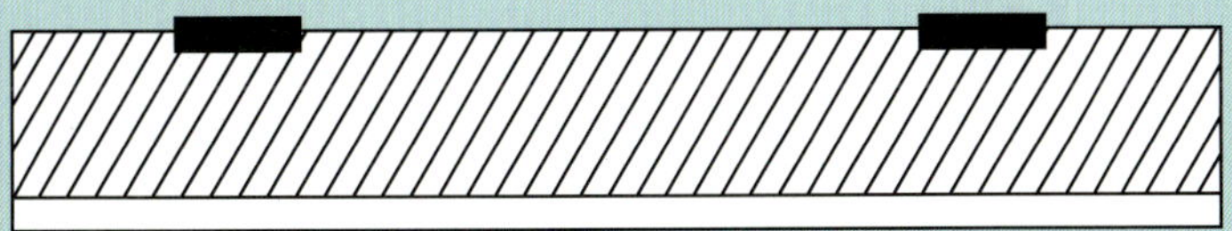

4 Drying

Dry the plate. The drying temperature should be around 60°C, and the time should be 30 minutes. If the temperature is too high, the plates may be out of shape.

5 Post processing

When the plate is dry, wash away the residue on the surface. Use a clean cloth and solvent to scrub the plate and then dry it for 5 minutes.

6 Post exposing

Exposing the plate for a certain amount of time to solidify the plate.

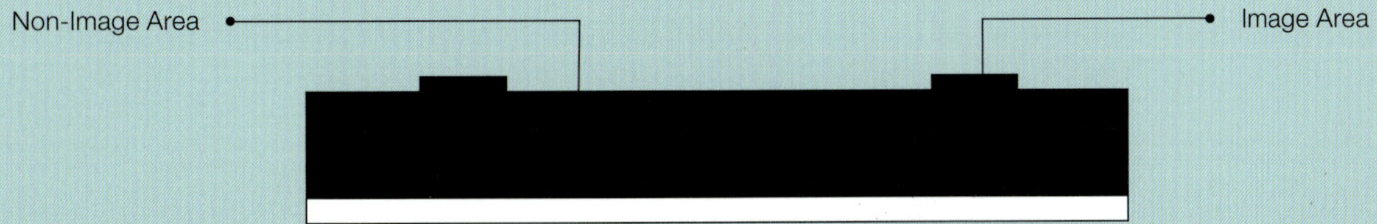

7 Printing Process

Studio: Reykjavík Letterpress

Designer: Hildur Sigurdardottir & Olof Birna Gardarsdotti

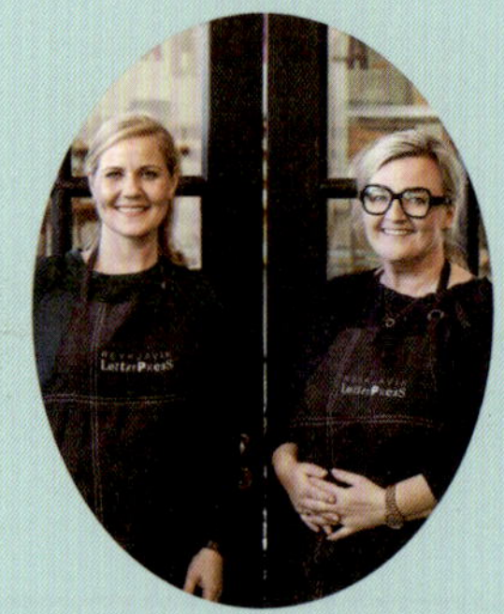

Reykjavík Letterpress is a design studio established in 2010 by two graphic designers—Hildur Sigurdardottir and Olof Birna Gardarsdotti. As well as offering their service of graphic design, the studio specializes in the letterpress technique which is one of the oldest forms of printing. The studio designs and prints all kinds of wonderful goods such as business cards, hangtags, notebooks, greeting cards, invitations to weddings, coasters, napkin and so on. They ranked No.2 on the top 10 list of "World's Finest Letterpress Studios."

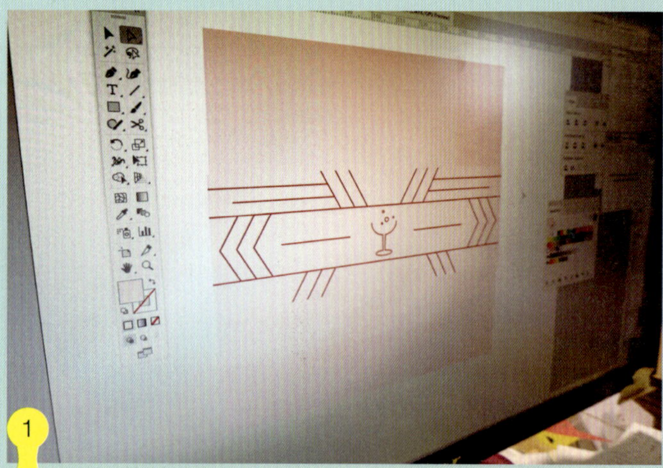

1 The designer worked on the computer to create the artwork.

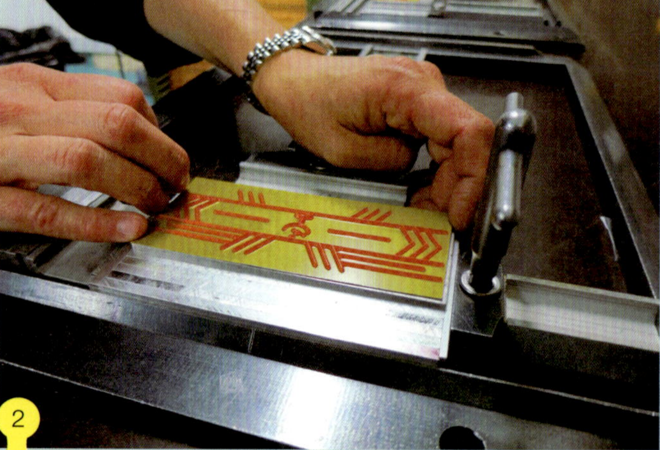

2 Putting the ready-made photo-polymer print plate in place.

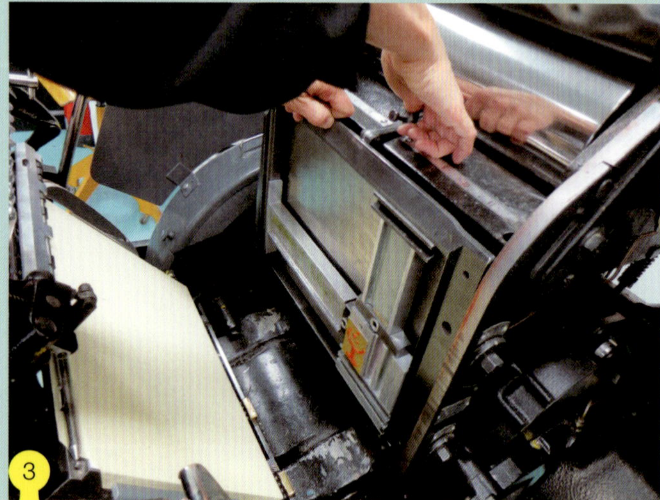

3 Fastening the print-plate securely in the frame and placed it in the machine.

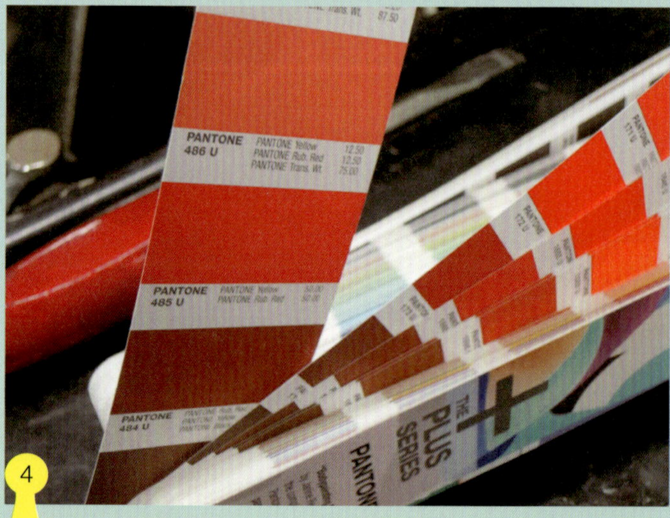

4 The Pantone system.

Photo by Reykjavík Letterpress

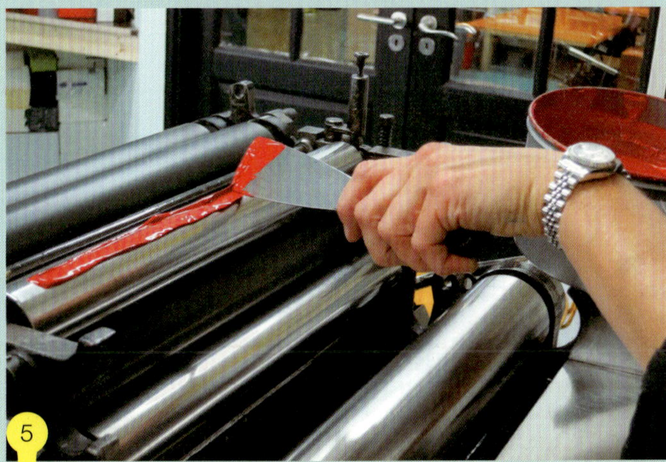

5 Using the Pantone color system to ink the machine.

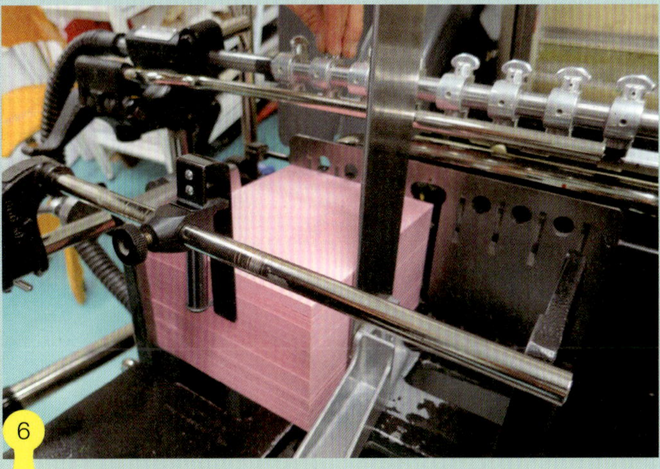

6 Adjusting paper on the paper tray.

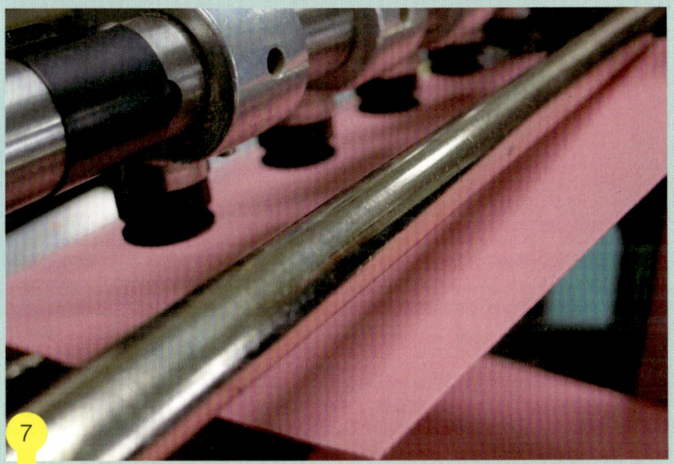

7 Suckers that suck up one sheet at a time to print.

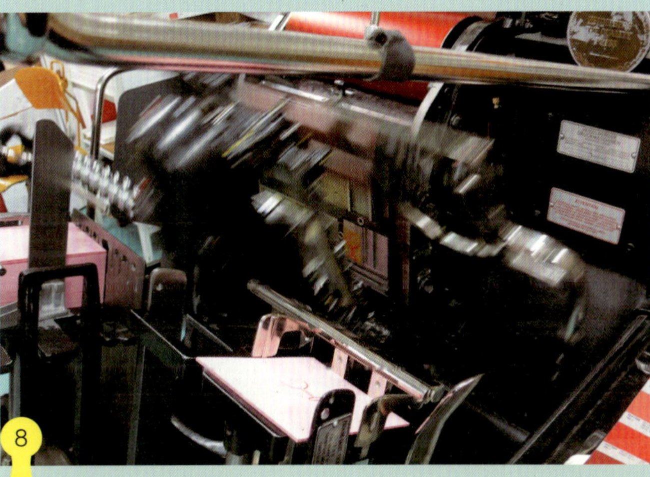

8 Start printing.

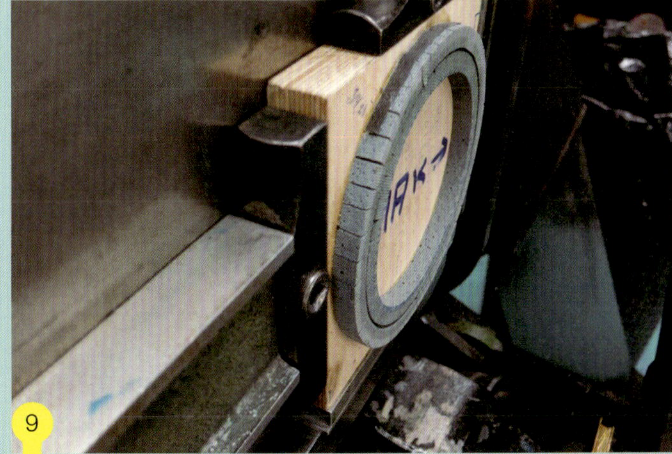

9 Putting die cutter in place.

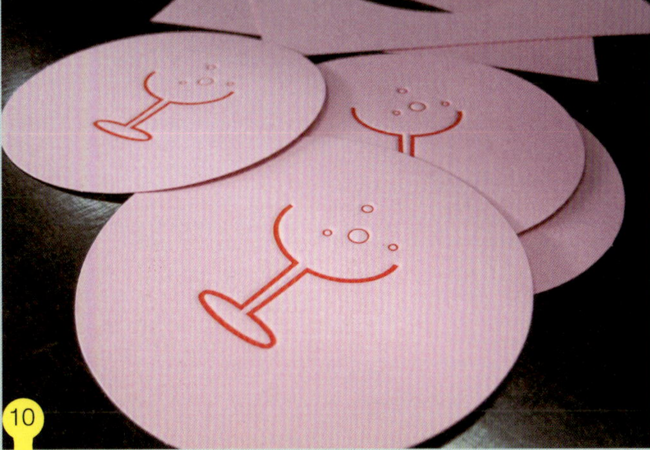

10 Coasters die-cut.

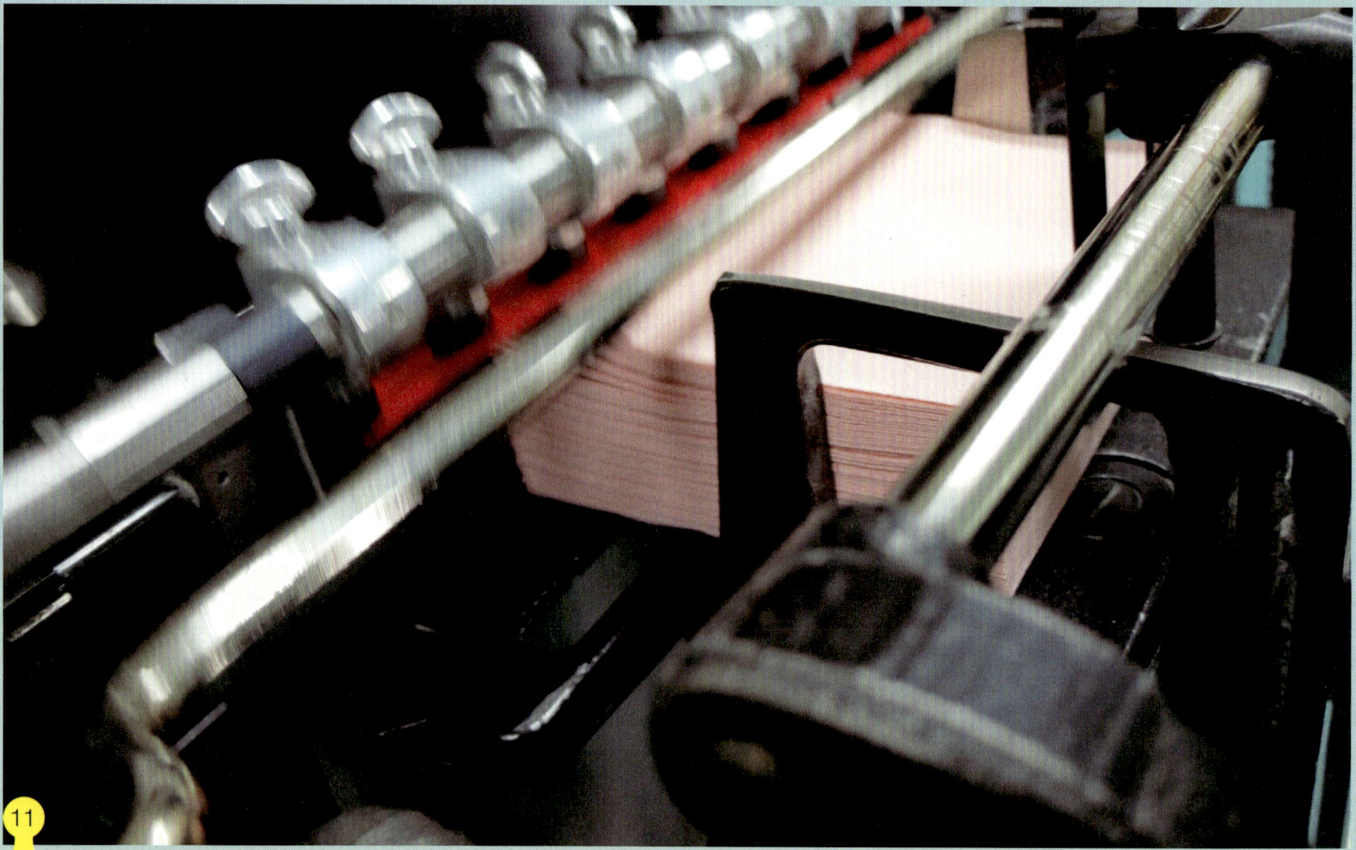

11

Printing napkins.

Final napkin and coaster.

12

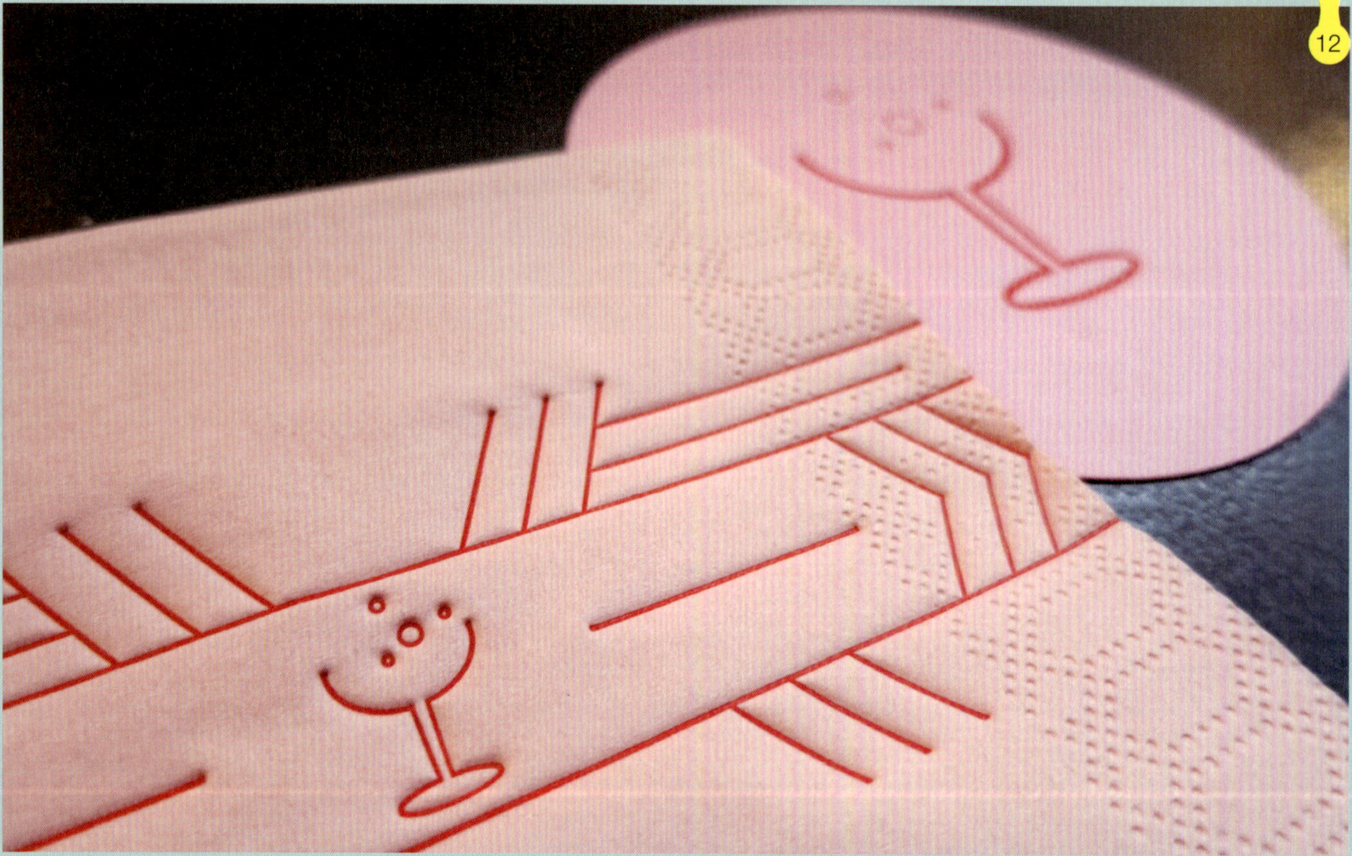

: Substrates

: Printing Inks

D : Design

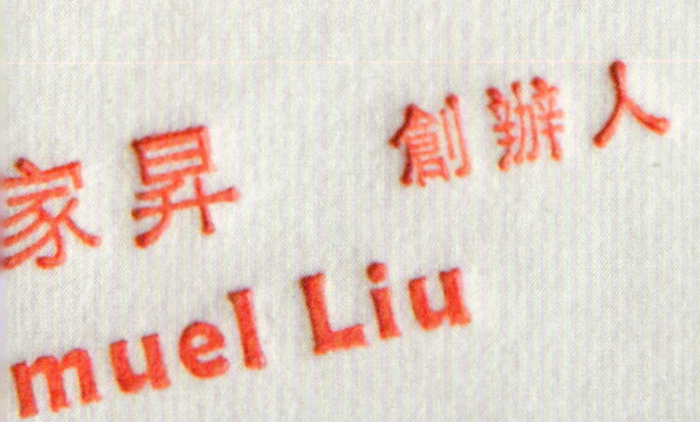

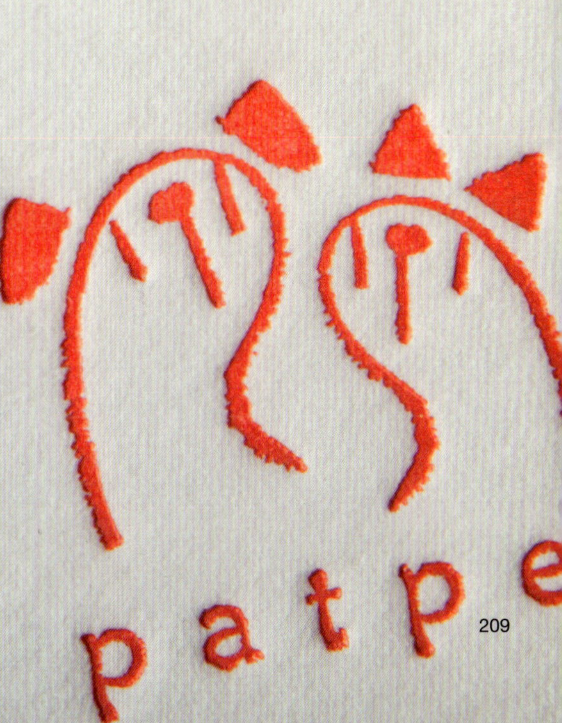

Fade to Blue

Chung Yufeng, a pipa (琵琶) player, and David Chen, a U.S. born blues guitarist, combined the unlikely sounds of Chinese pipa and blues guitar in a collaborative music project called "Fade to Blue (藍・掉)." The CD is a live recording consist of only 2 instruments, a Chinese pipa and an acoustic blues guitar with no other backing instrument. It is a dialogue between 2 musicians and 2 instruments, between the east and the west, a man and a woman from different cultural and musical backgrounds. In order to capture the purity of their collaboration, only 2 color (red and blue inks) were used on the entire album. The red symbolizes the pipa/the female musician/the East and Chinese text. While blue ink represents the West/the blues guitar/ the male and also all the English text he wrote. Letterpress printing is also used to reinforce raw and organic culture of their performance.

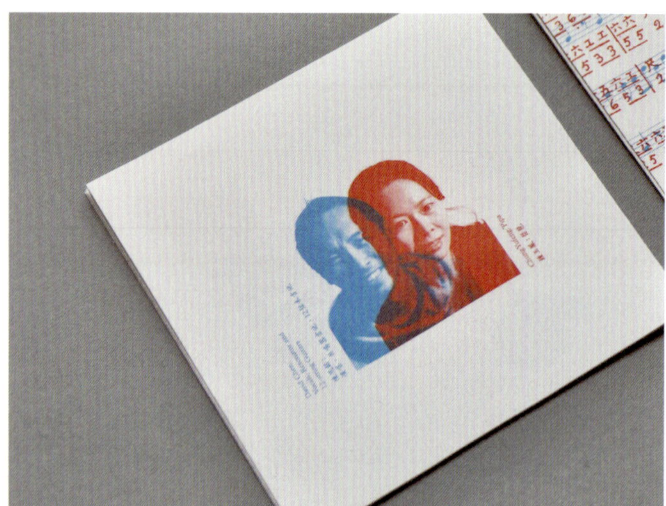

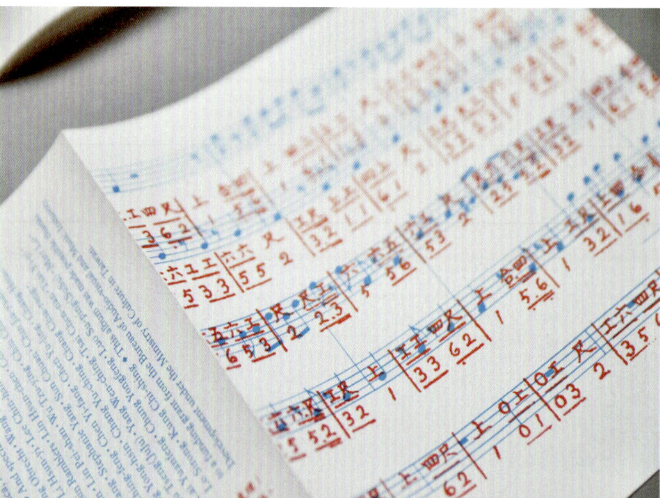

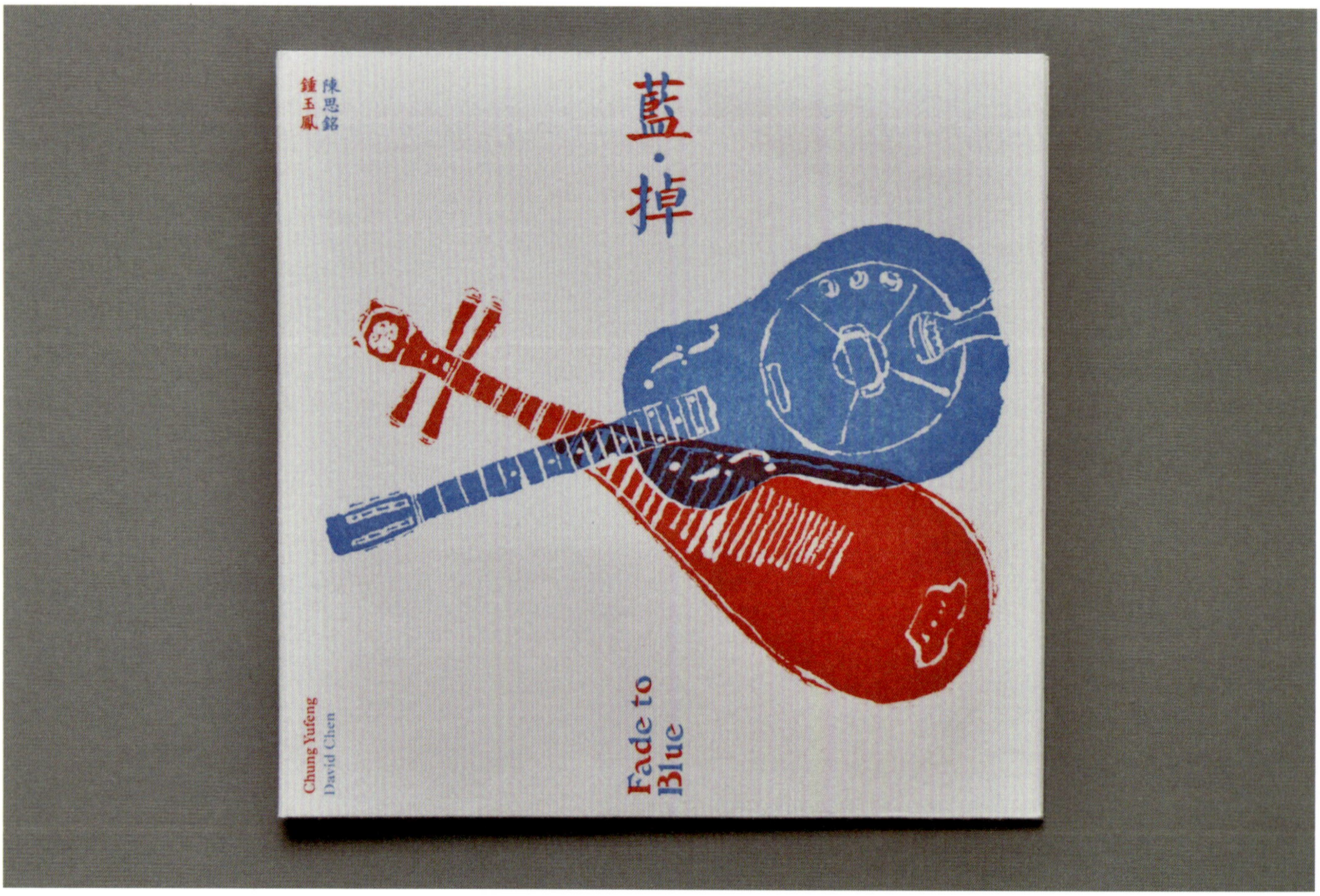

D: Andrew Wong, Karen Tsai, Fong Ming Yang

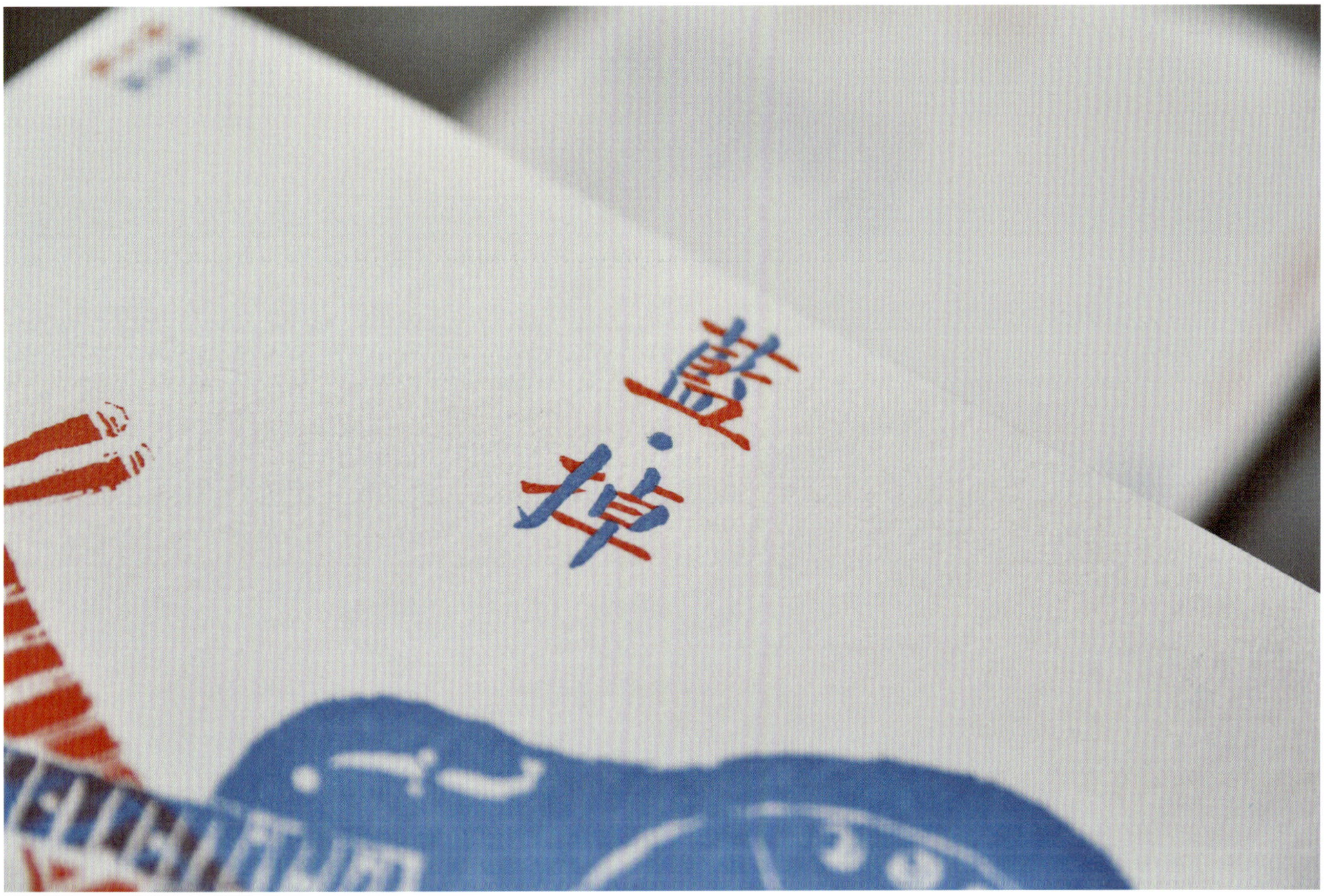

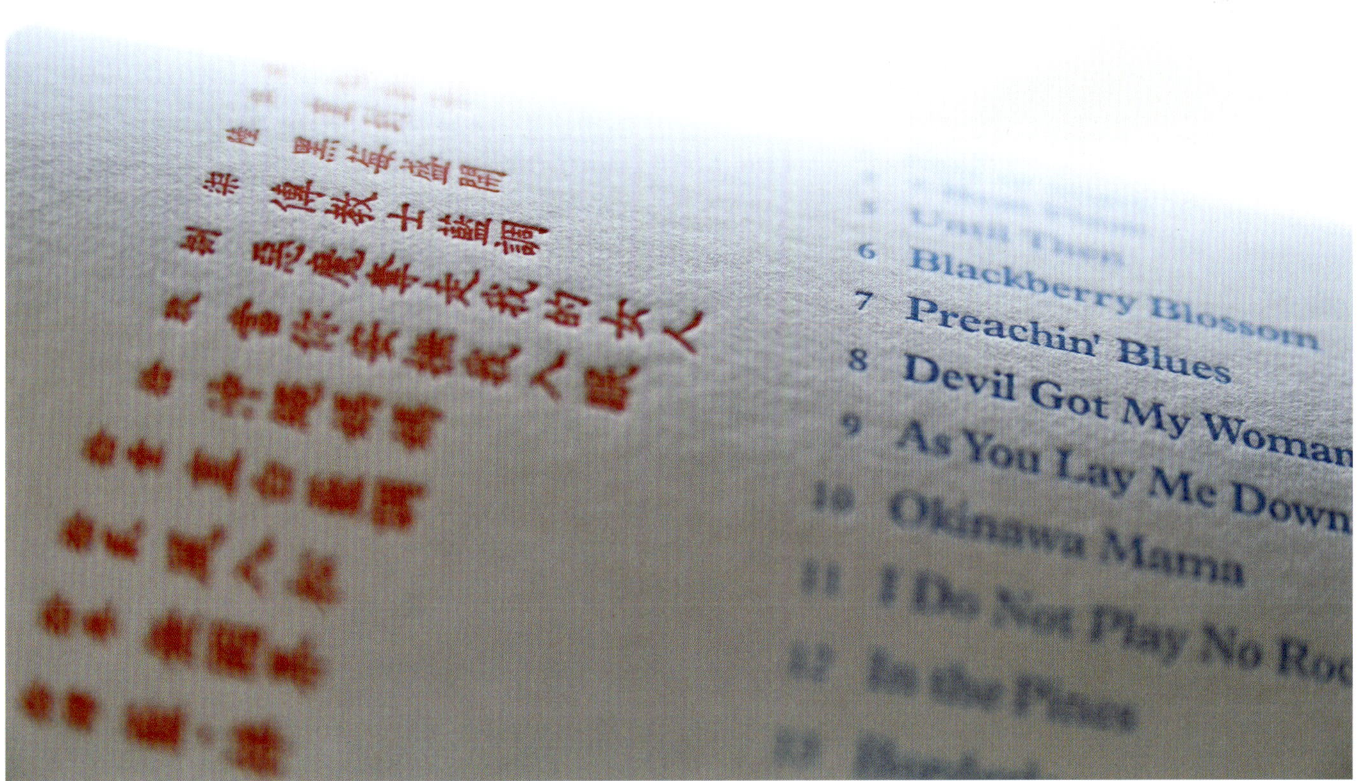
傳教士藍調
惡魔奪走我的女人
Until Then
6 Blackberry Blossom
7 Preachin' Blues
8 Devil Got My Woman
9 As You Lay Me Down
10 Okinawa Mama
11 I Do Not Play No Roc
12 In the Pines

Antalis Promo Cards

850g Cordenons - Wild

rubber base inks

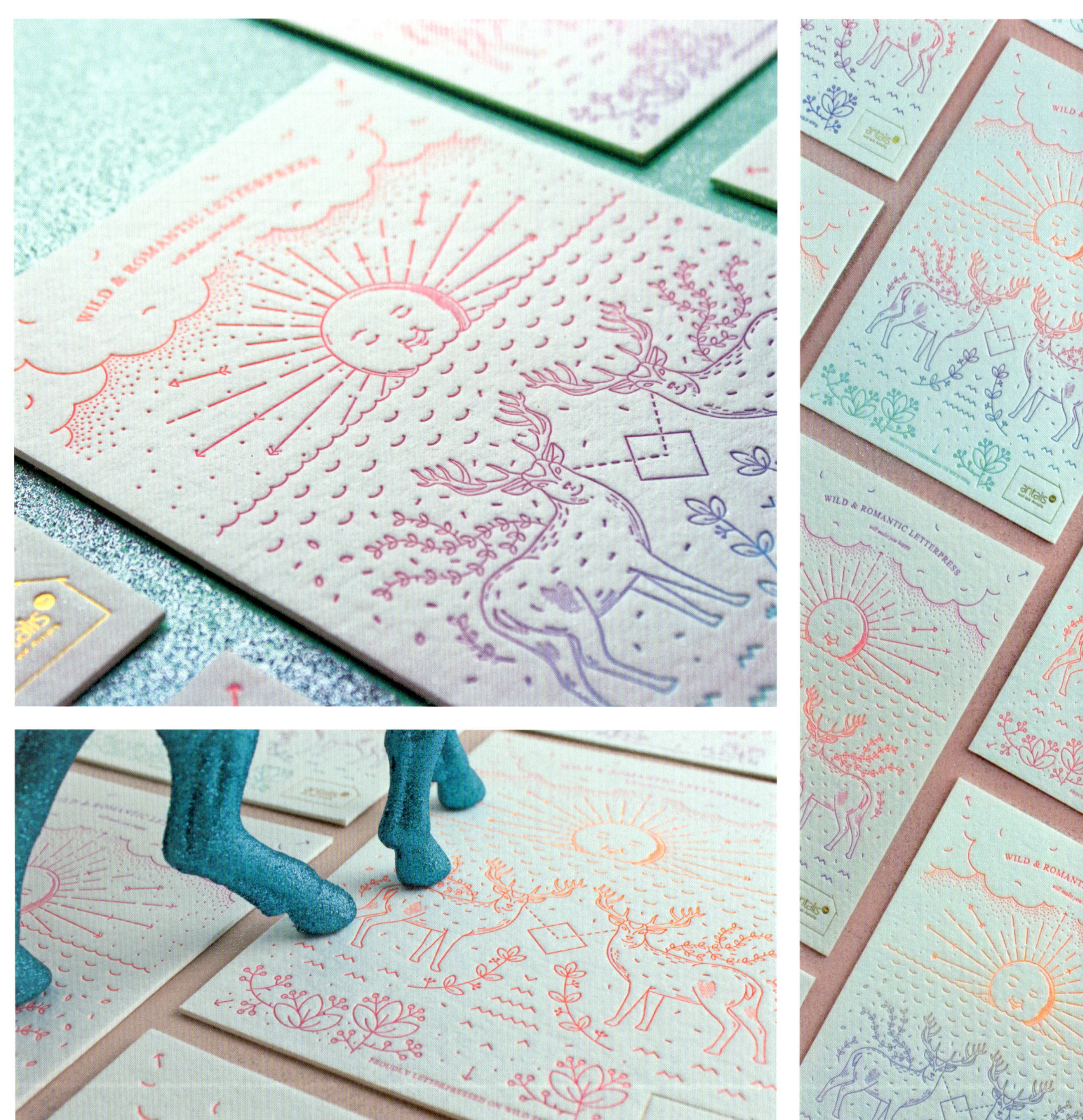

D: Paulina Zbylut/Kolory

The designers were asked to create a card to promote a paper from the Antalis catalogue – Cordenons, Wild 850g. They were well aware of the pros and cons of this paper, because they had enjoyed the pleasure of using it many times before in various designs. To show this paper in the best possible light, the designers have chosen letterpress rainbow roll printing.

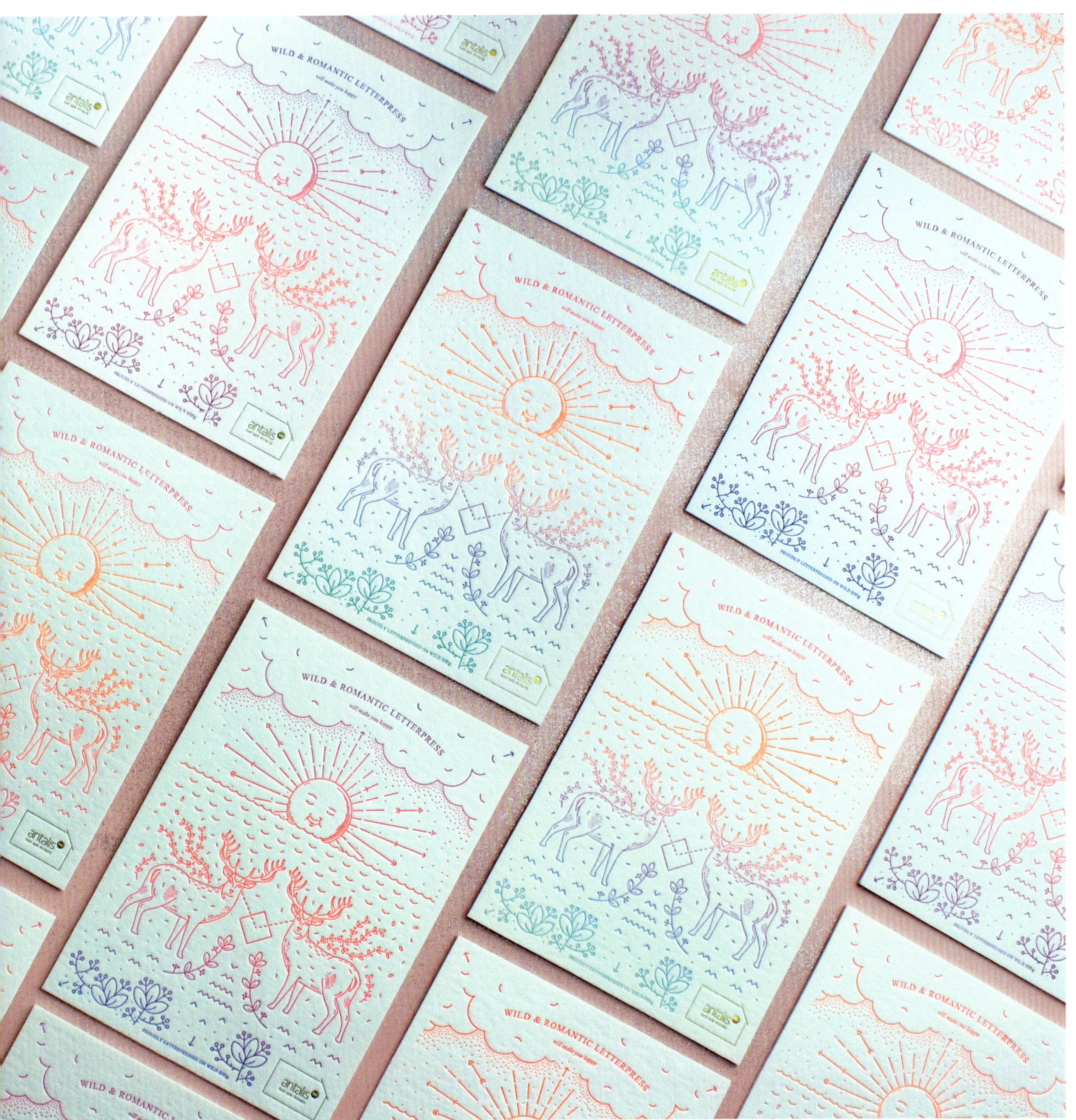

Wedding Invitation "Garden Party"

450g cotton paper

letterpress ink, oil based

The designer's friend wanted a special wedding invitation. The kind you keep on a shelf long after you have kissed the bride and eaten the cake. When the designer was told the theme was "Garden Party" she knew letterpress was the right technique. It let her explore a lush variety of patterns and textures. Some of them were more intricate like leaves, tree bark, checkered shirts, or striped summer dresses. Others were subtle, like the crease a gentleman's pant would make as he leads his lady on the dance floor.

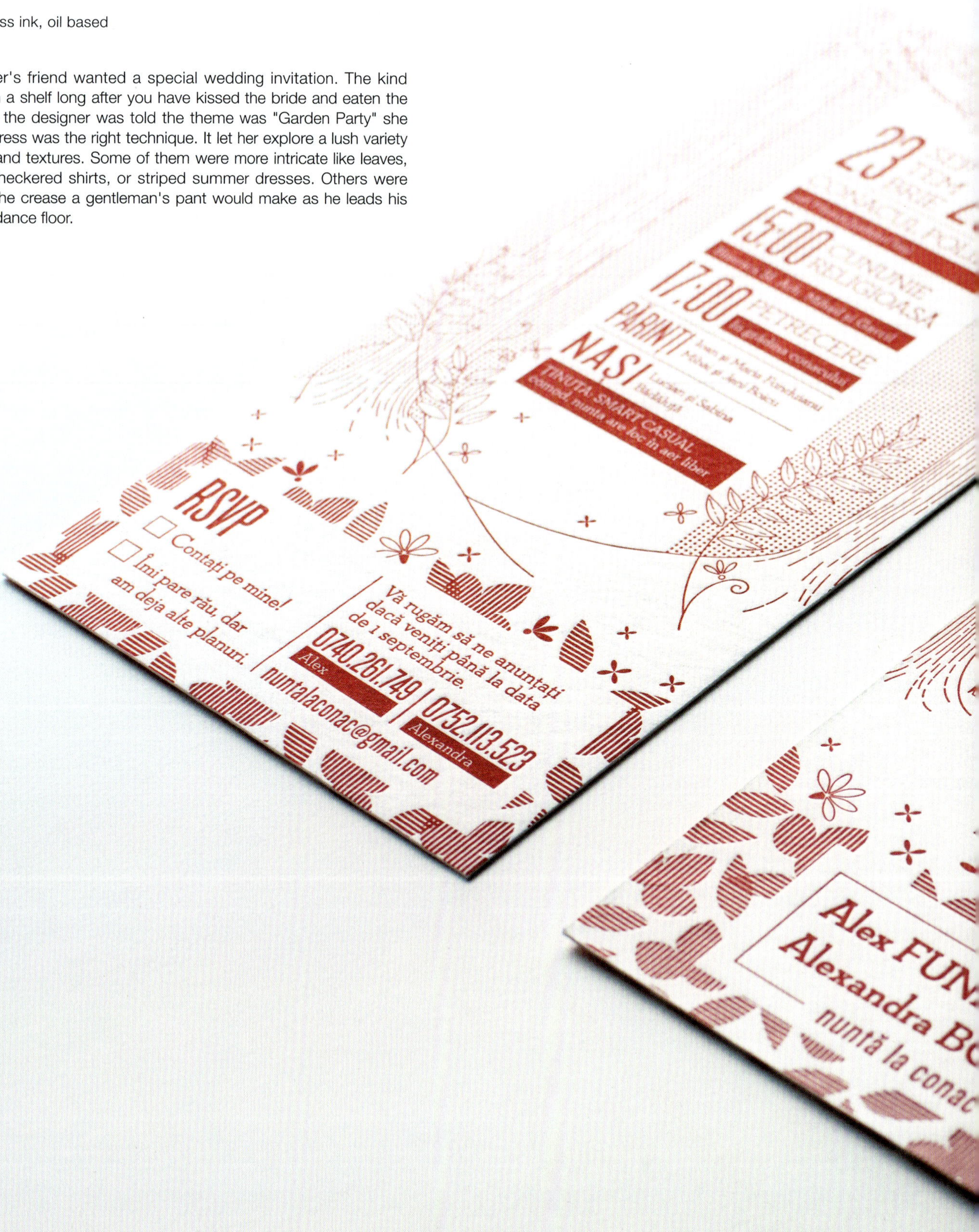

D: Alexandra Mîrzac

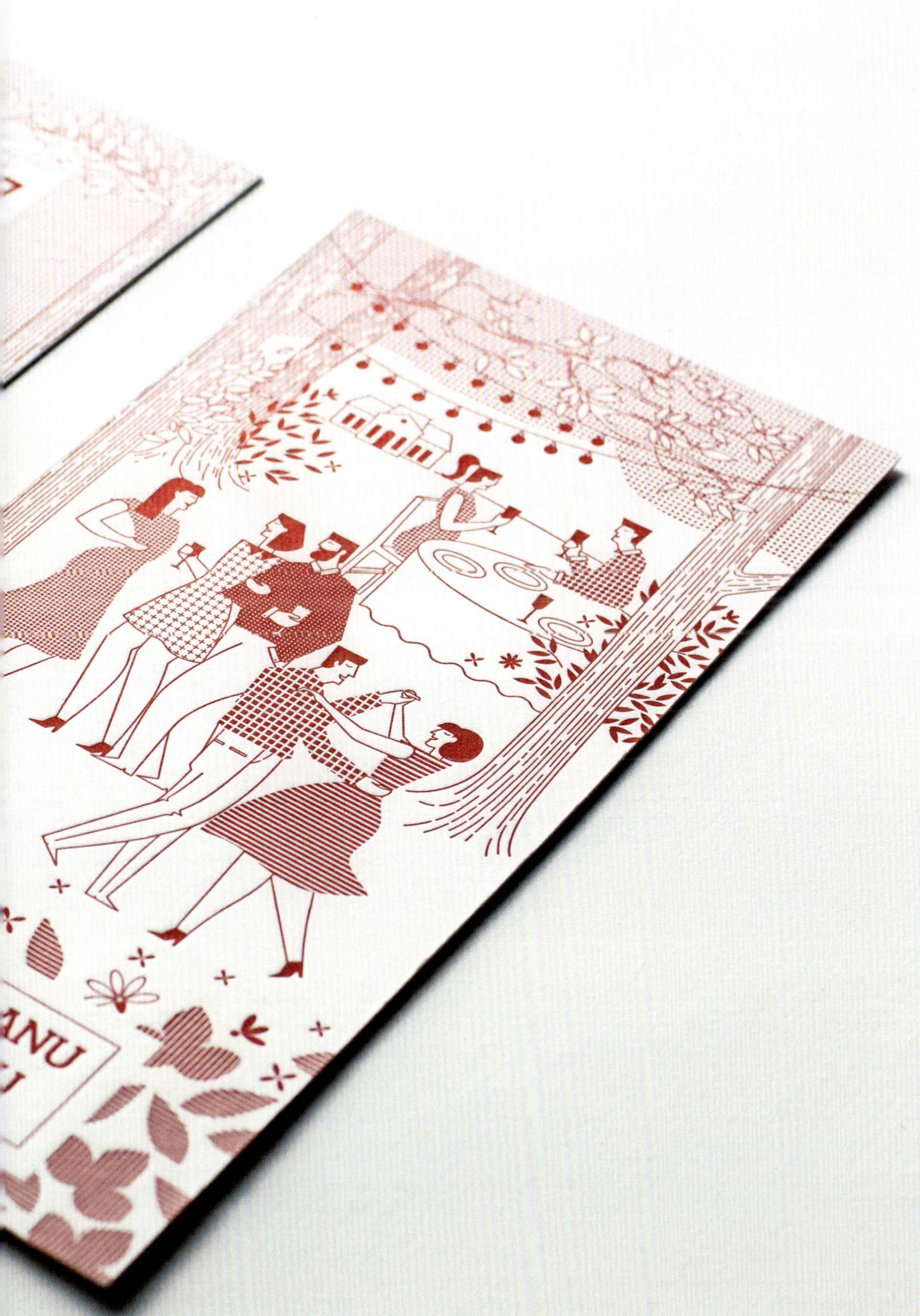

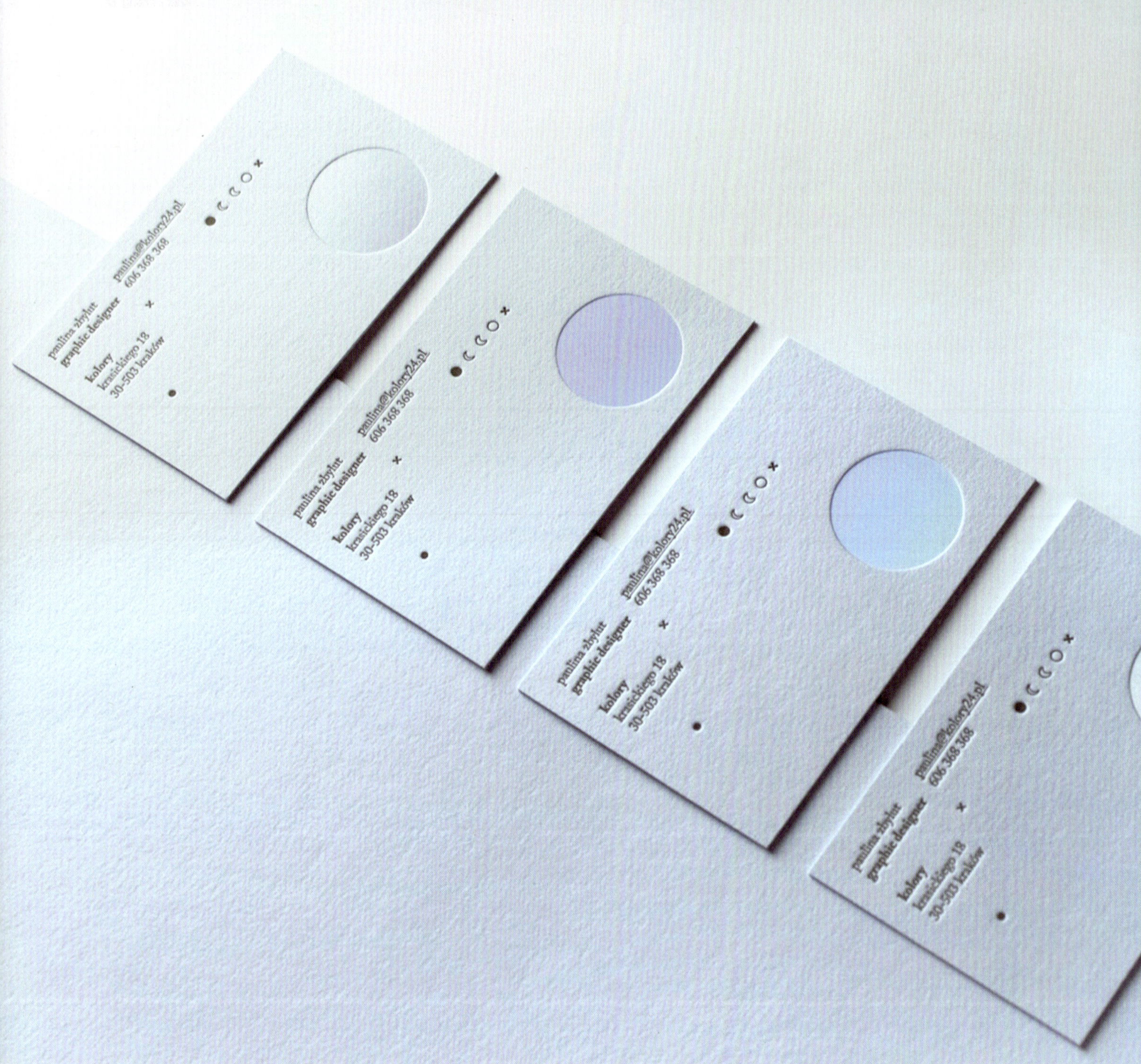

Holographic & Letterpress Business Cards

600g Gmund Cotton Paper

holographic foil for hot-stamping, black rubber base ink for letterpress

The designer wanted to create business cards that would combine printing technologies and materials that are not such obvious choices. They chose letterpress and hot-stamped relatively large surfaces, which is not especially recommended for the cotton paper they choose. They had a great time doing the printing, and the final result was a highly positive surprise.

 D: Paulina Zbylut/Kolory

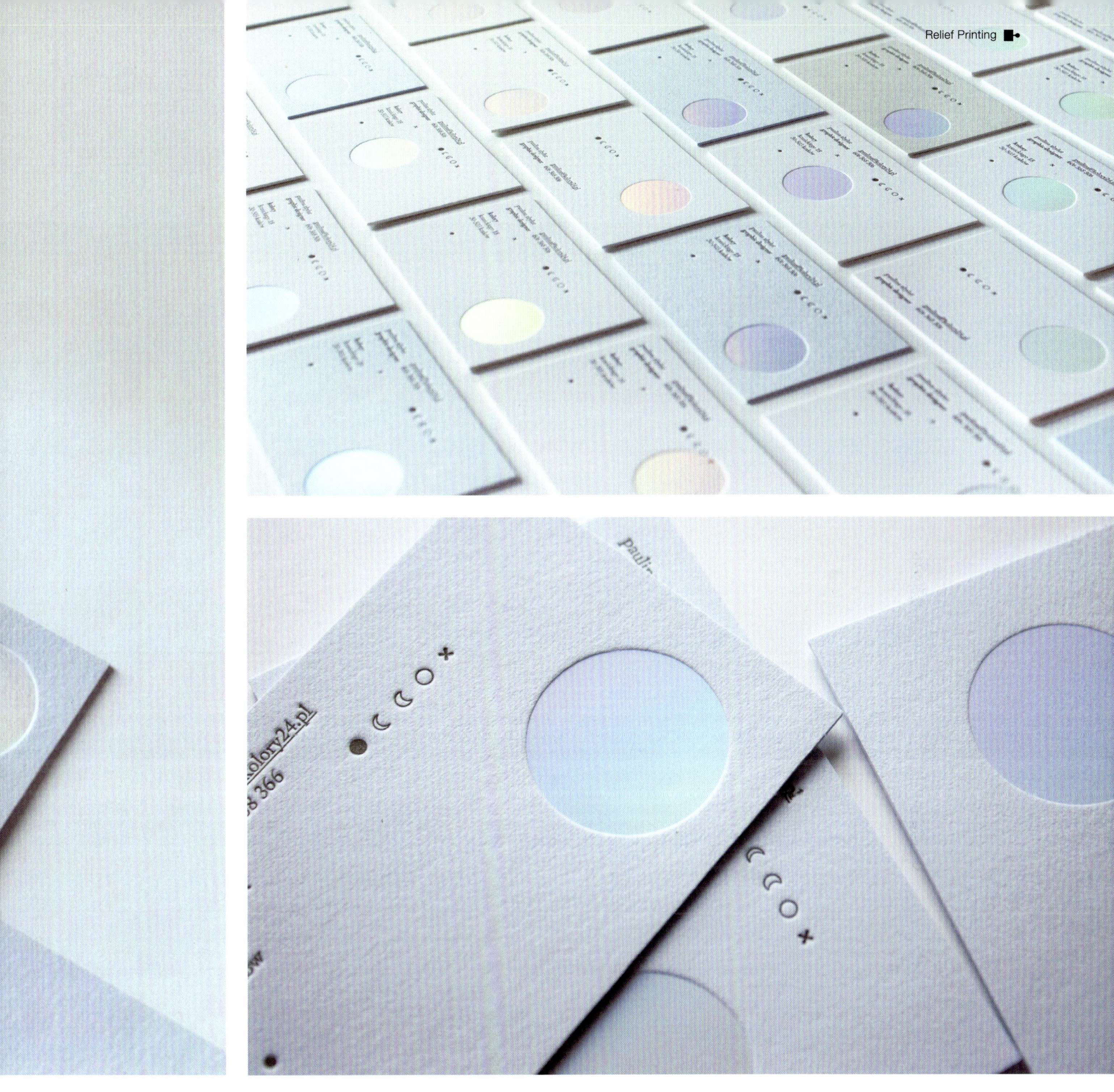

Christmas Card

- 520g Luna Paper
- Pantone eco-friendly soyabean ink

The illustration printed on "Christmas Card" is drawn by illustrator Li Qiguai, clean and simple lines are suitable for letterpress printing.

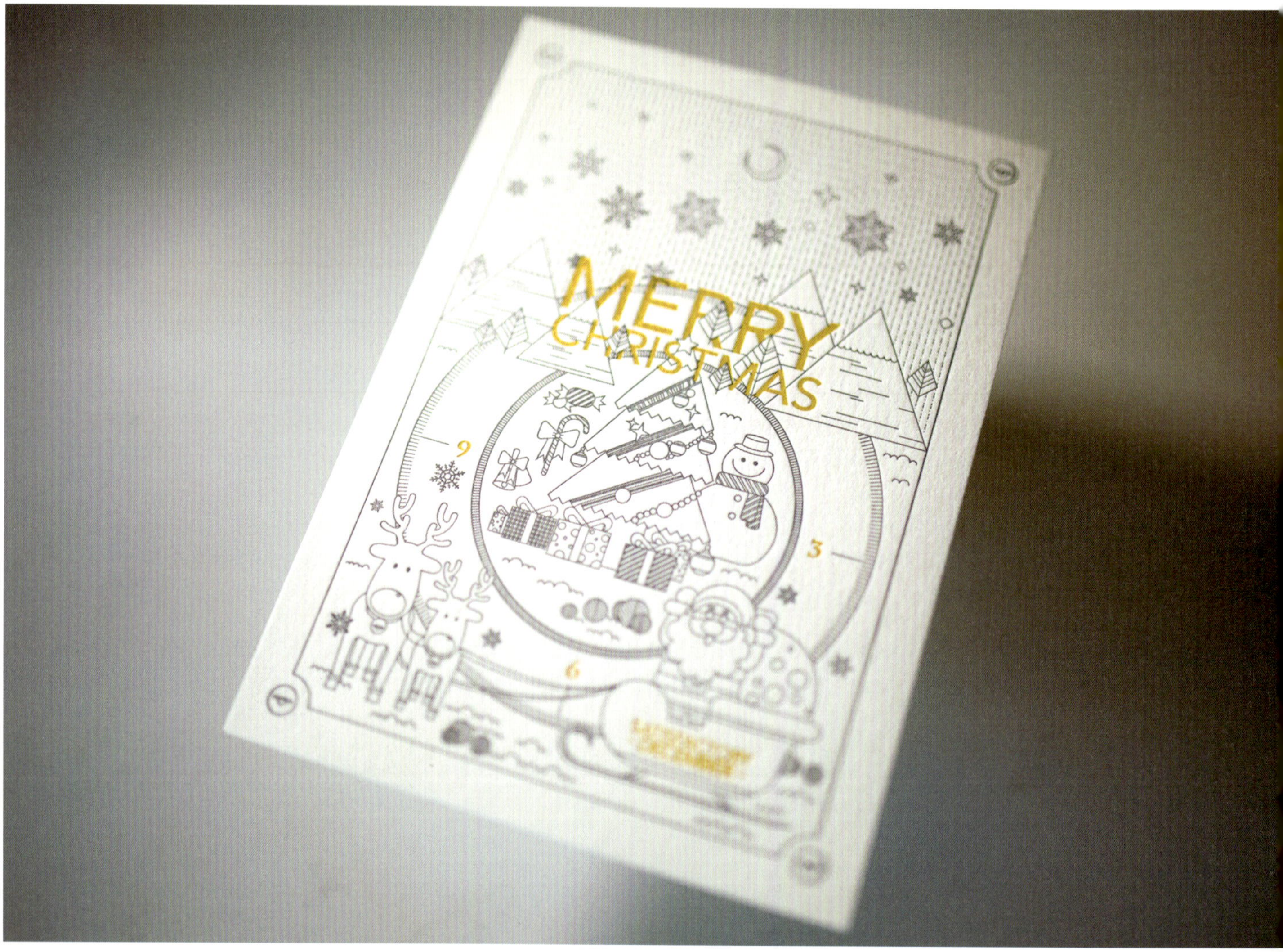

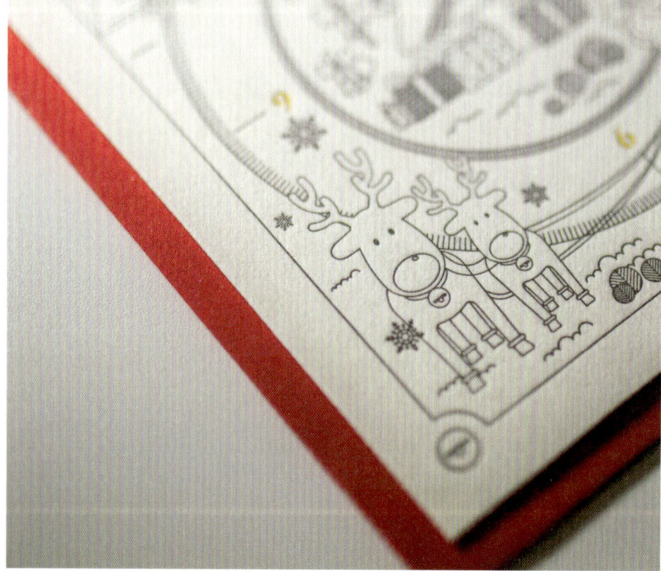

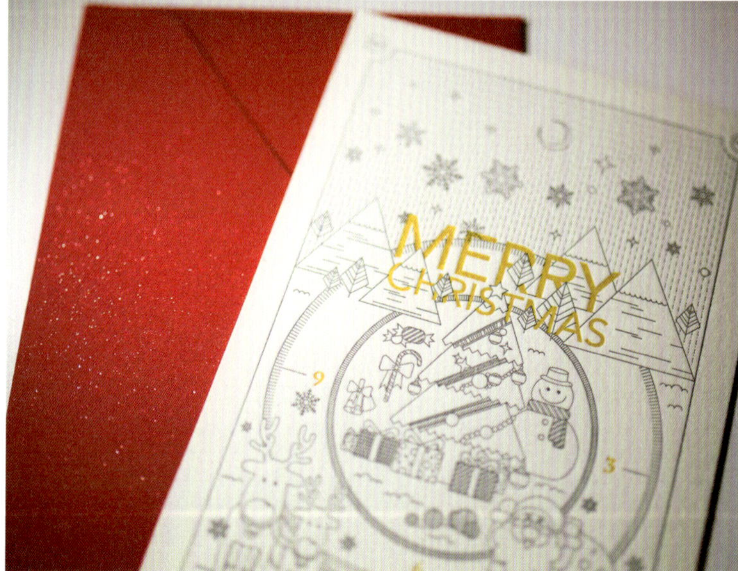

Patpet

300g Cordenons - Wild

Pantone 185 U

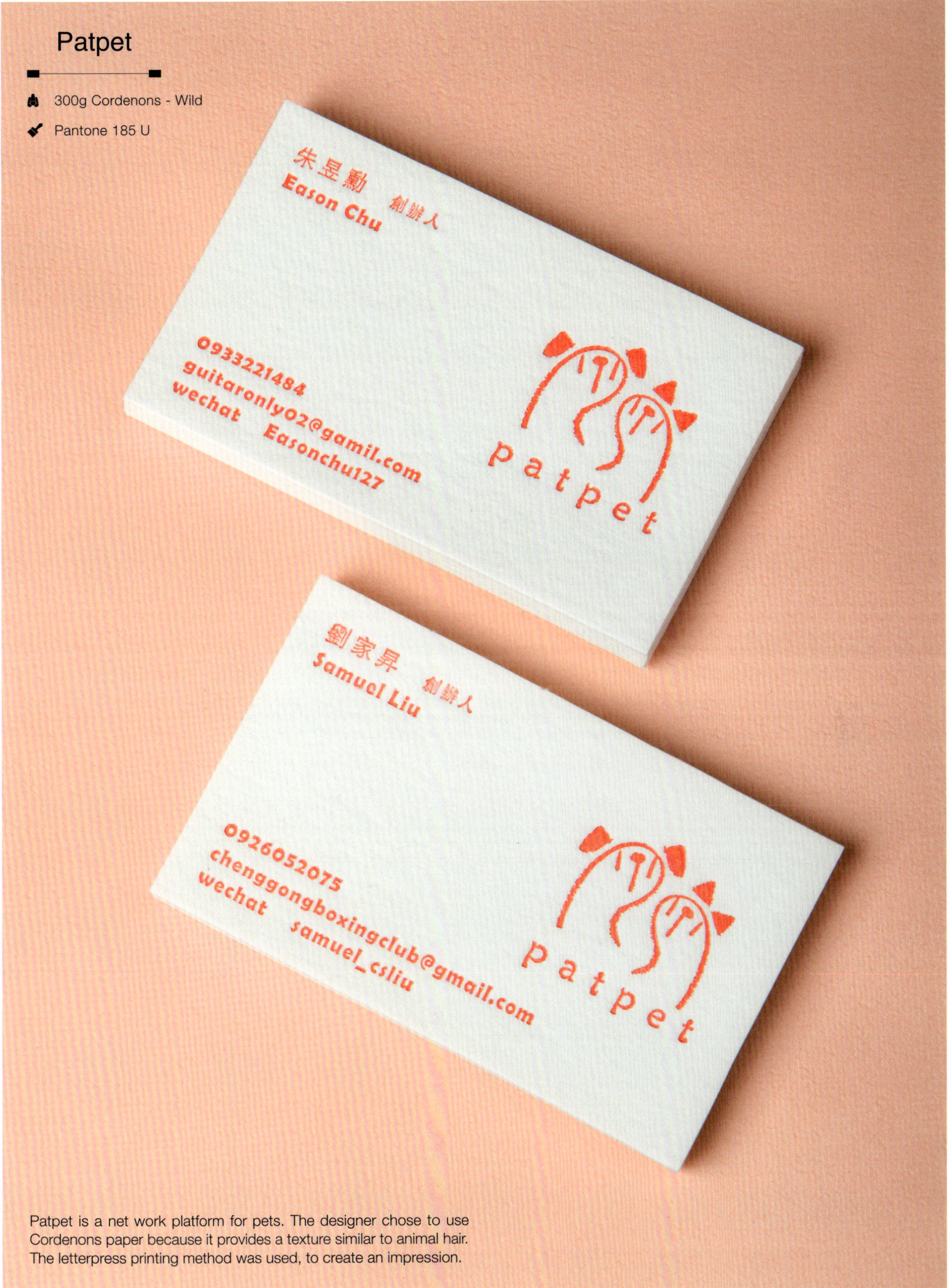

Patpet is a net work platform for pets. The designer chose to use Cordenons paper because it provides a texture similar to animal hair. The letterpress printing method was used, to create an impression.

D: Chun-Ta Chu

Photo by Chuan-Shun Huang

Greeting Cards and Hangtags

300g Munken Rough Pure Paper

eco-friendly ink

The designers make their own line of products, which includes greeting cards, hang tags, napkins, notebooks and such. These products are a part of that, and the thought was to have colorful cards for kids of all age (0 - 100 years) and for people to decorate their gifts with. Letterpress printing is their way of printing. They think everything looks good letterpressed!

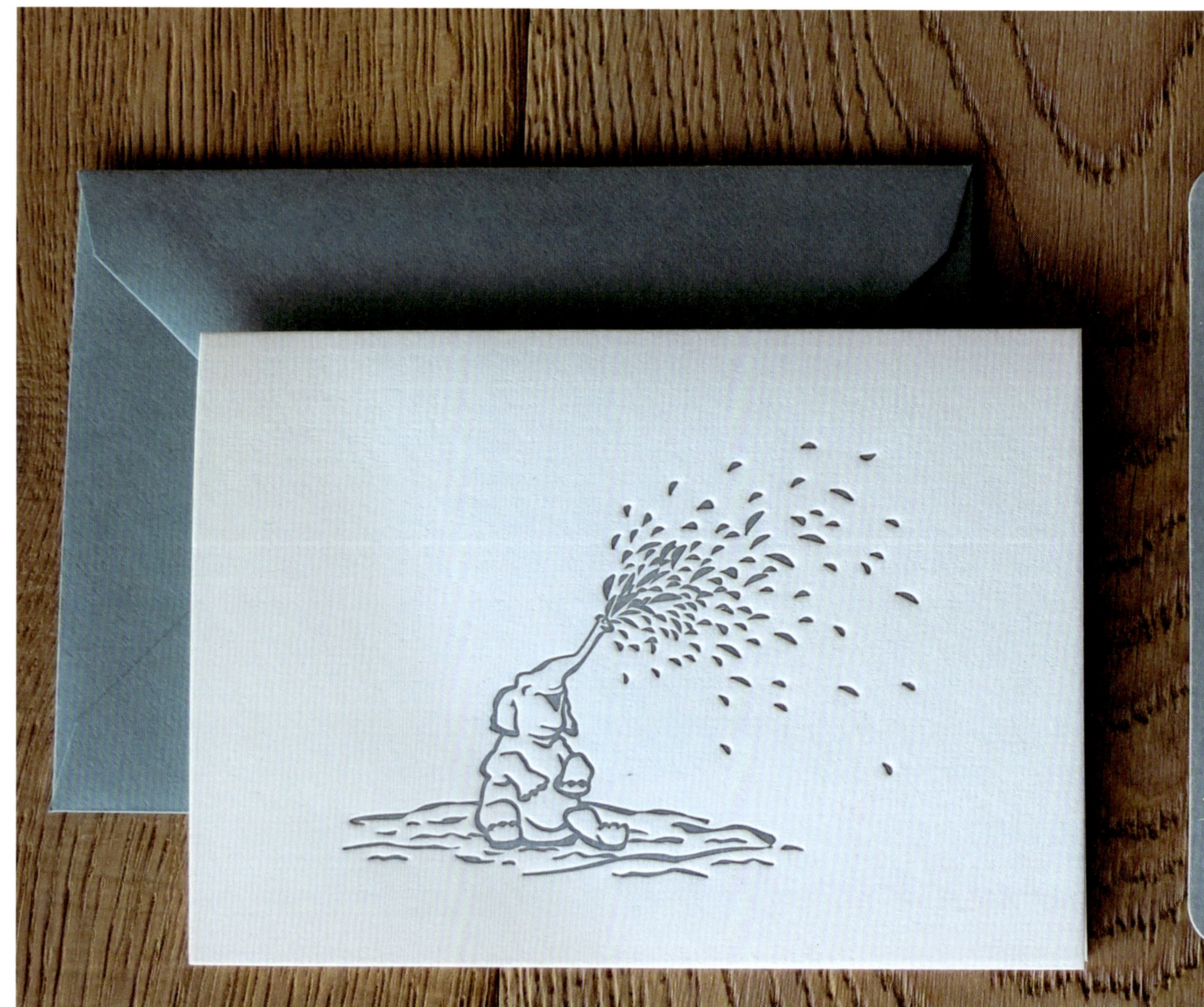

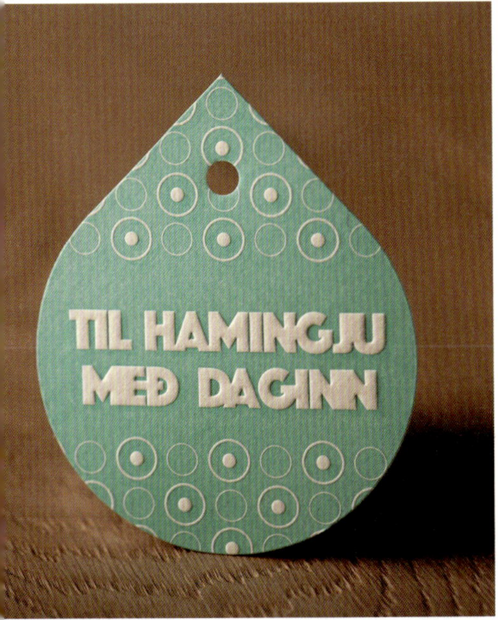
TIL HAMINGJU
MEÐ DAGINN

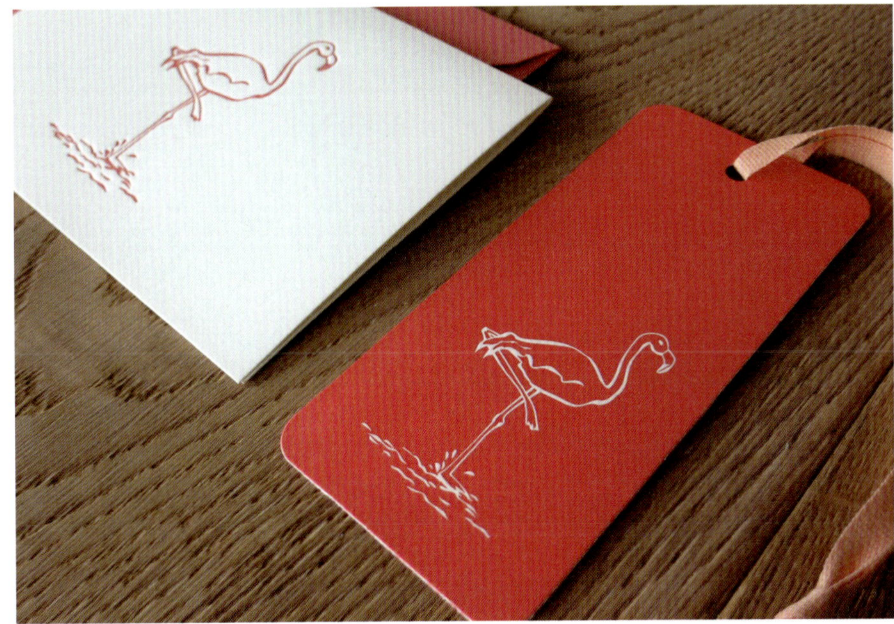

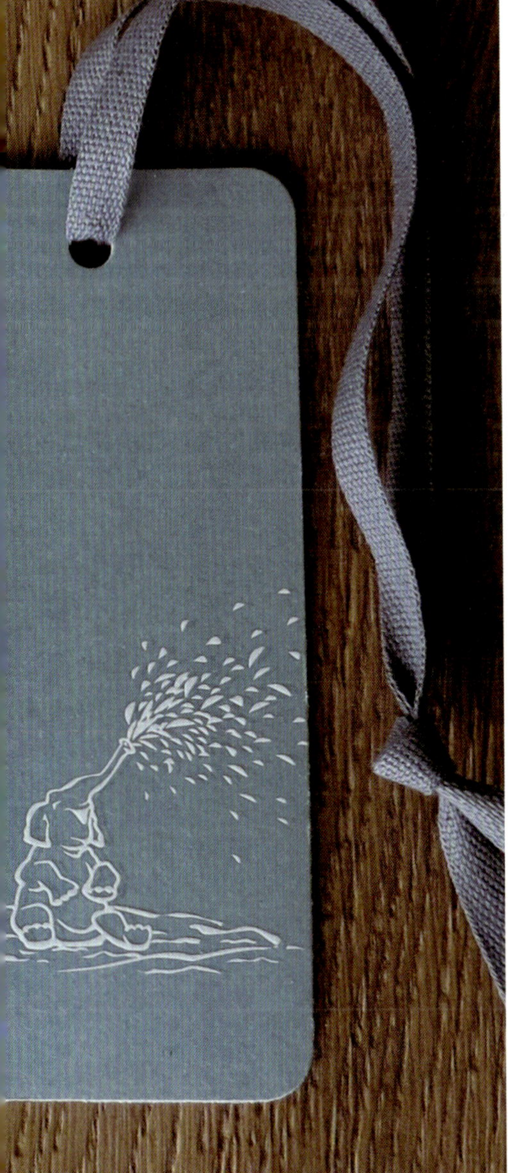

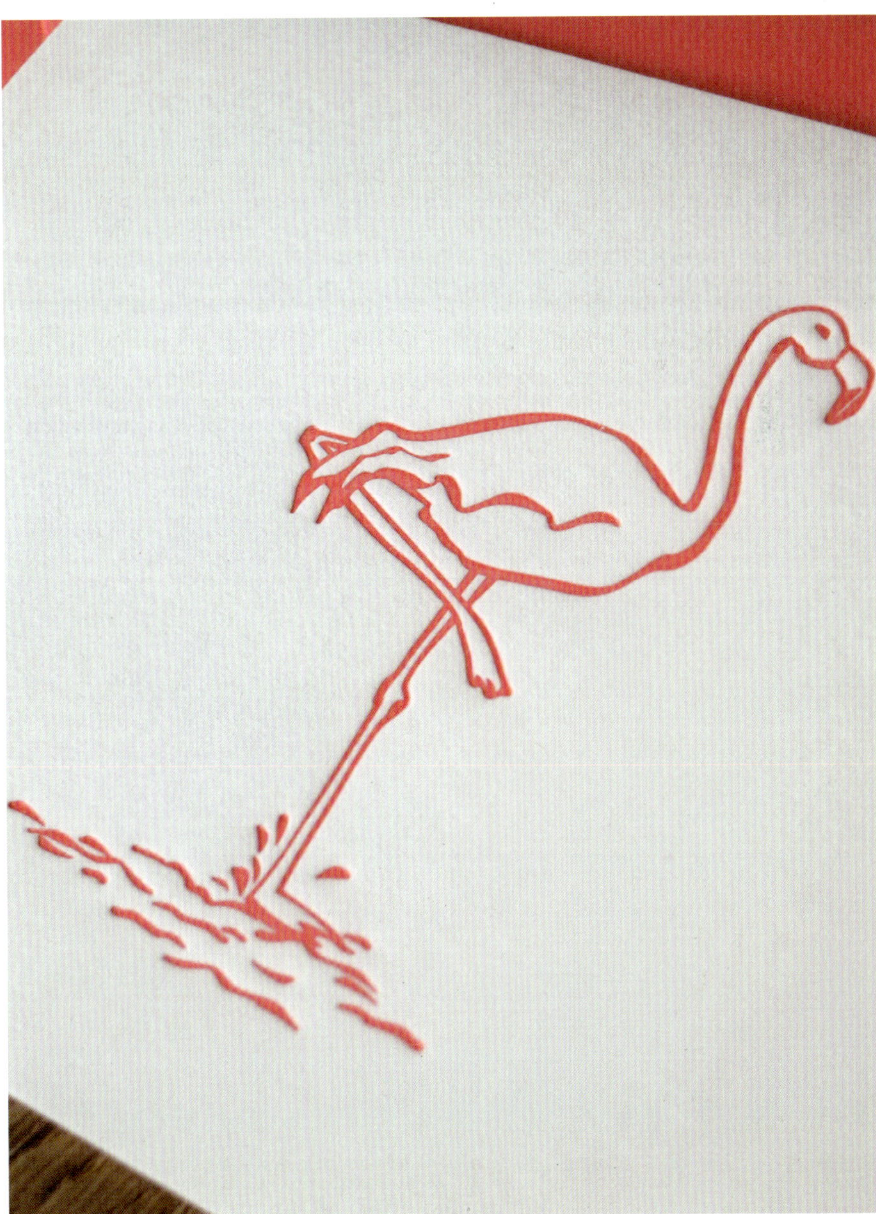

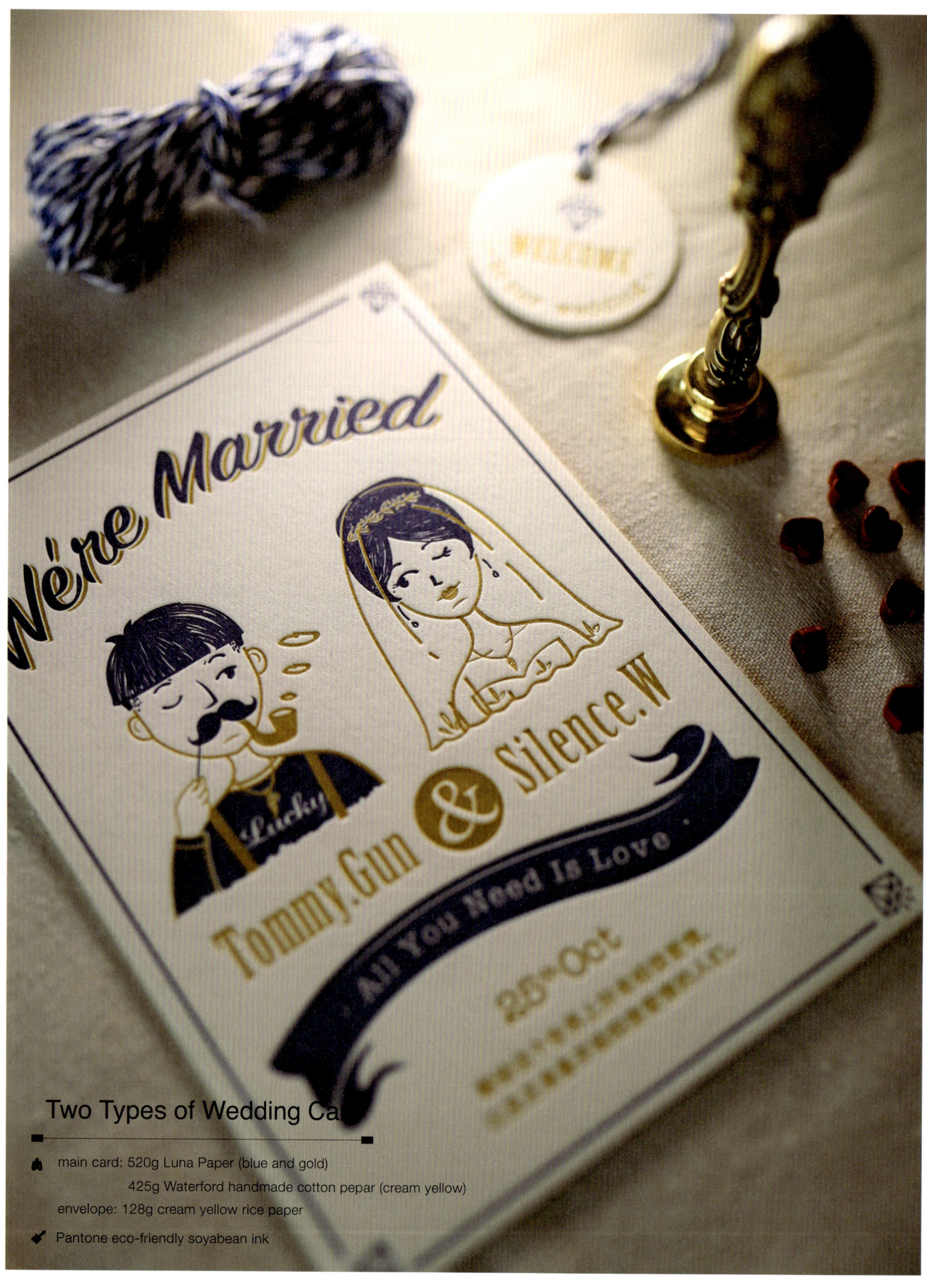

Two Types of Wedding Ca

- main card: 520g Luna Paper (blue and gold)
  425g Waterford handmade cotton pepar (cream yellow)
  envelope: 128g cream yellow rice paper
- Pantone eco-friendly soyabean ink

The image and text on the wedding invitation is printed in a letterpress manner. People will be filled with happiness and joy when they receive their exquisite wedding invitation.

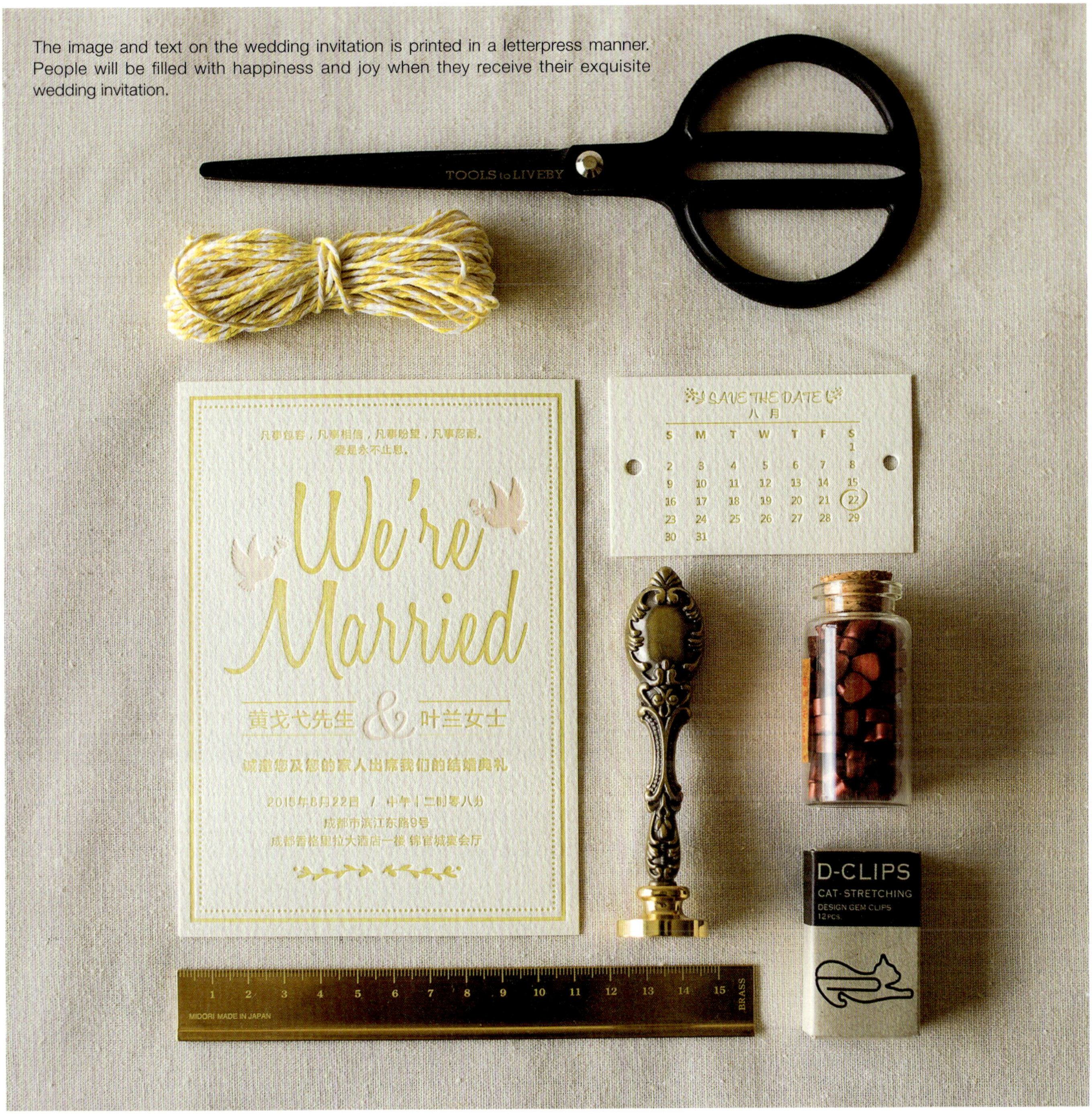

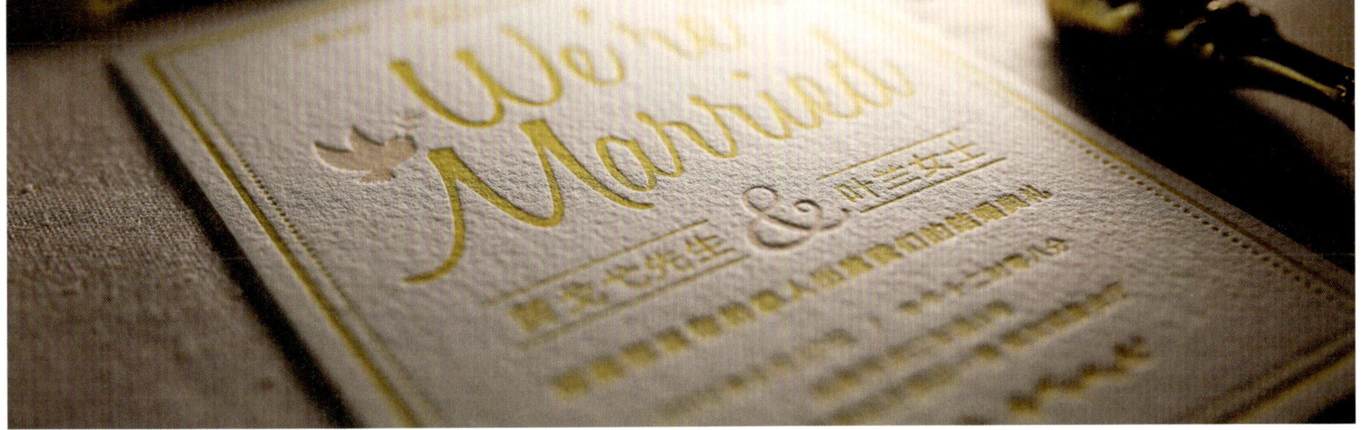

Ryan's Scribble

300g Somerset cotton paper

Pantone eco-friendly soyabean ink, Prismacolors

Sister Regina hopes to print some of the graffiti produced by his 18-month-old-brother Ryan as a printed matter, so DK PRESS was commissioned to make letterpress printing. First, they used illustrator to redraw the lines of the graffiti, then make it into printing plates. Second, they printed the lines using Somerset cotton paper, with a better grain sense. It is worth nothing that the small Ryan in the graffiti process continues to draw when ink is exhausted. That produces some dents that the studio reproduces in embossing. After the letterpress printing was completed, the studio according, to the "Bauhaus" and "the odyssey," used the Prismacolors color palette to paint in manual way. Every painting is art.

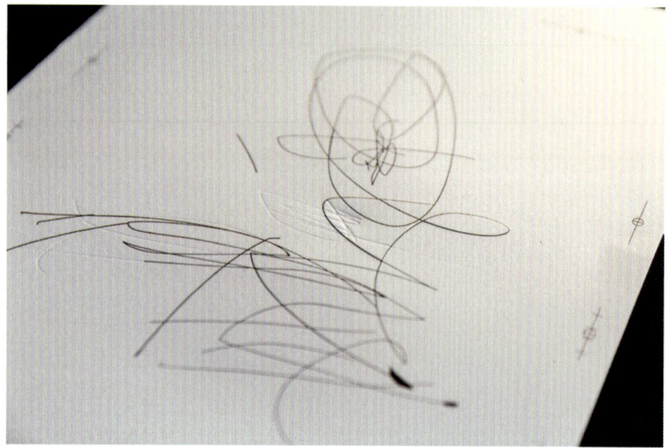

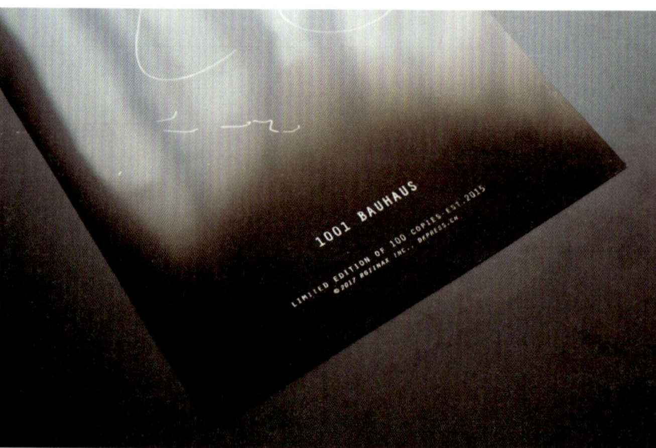

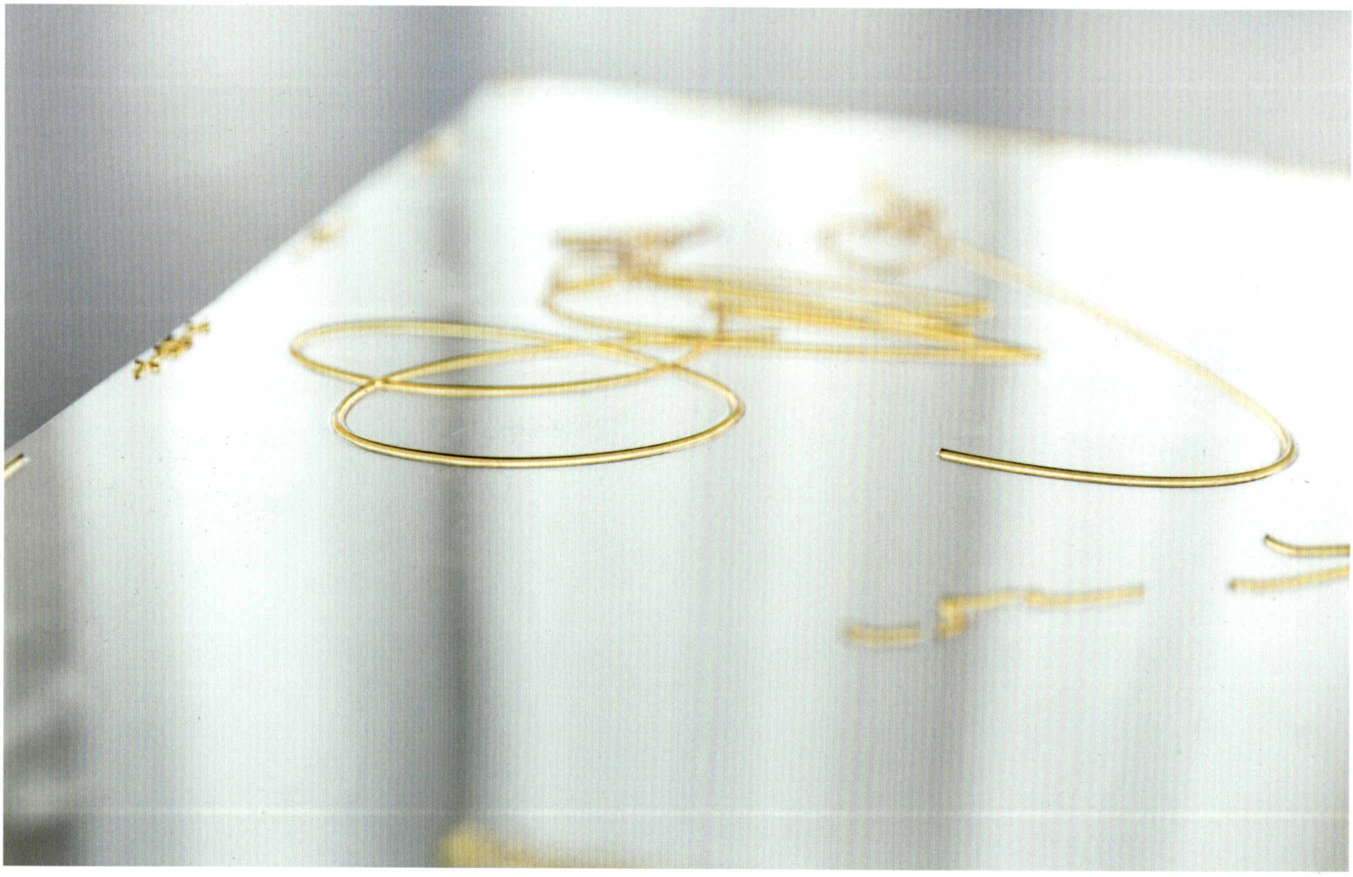

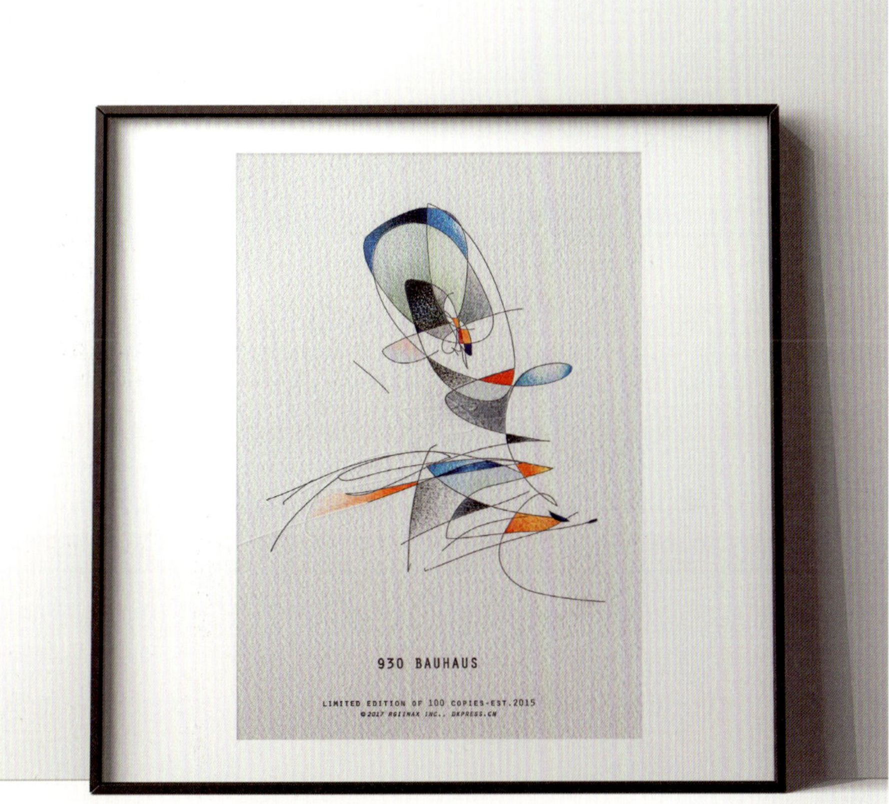
930 BAUHAUS
LIMITED EDITION OF 100 COPIES·EST.2015

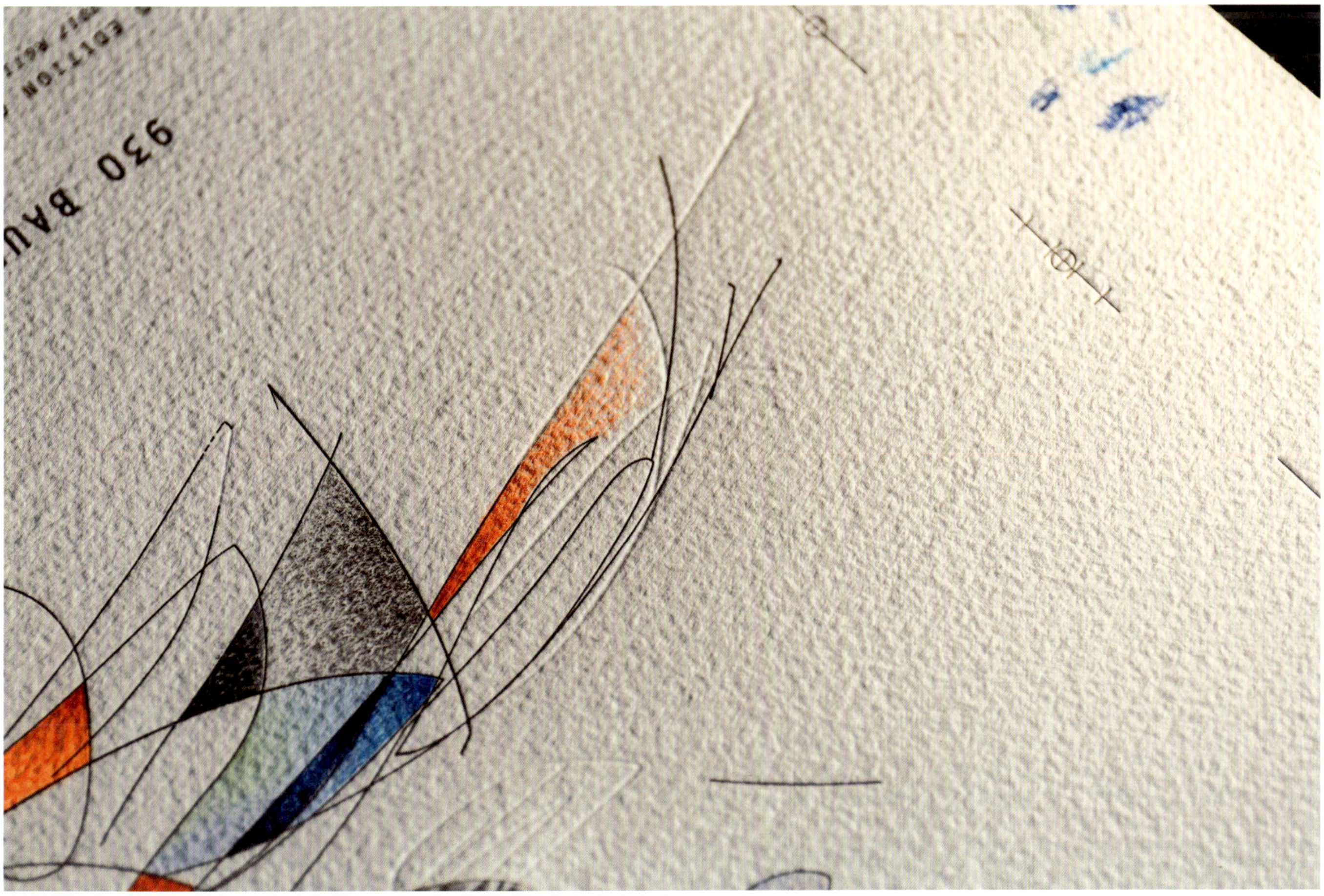

Collectors' daily - YANG CHEN HUA Solo Exhibition

- 350g Kagula paper
- hot foil, black spot color ink

As an artist and collector, Yang Chen Hua collects rare stones, dead wood, antiques, decorations, vessels, and plants. The invitation card for his solo exhibition was printed on light paper via letterpress: suggesting a feeling of age and delicacy.

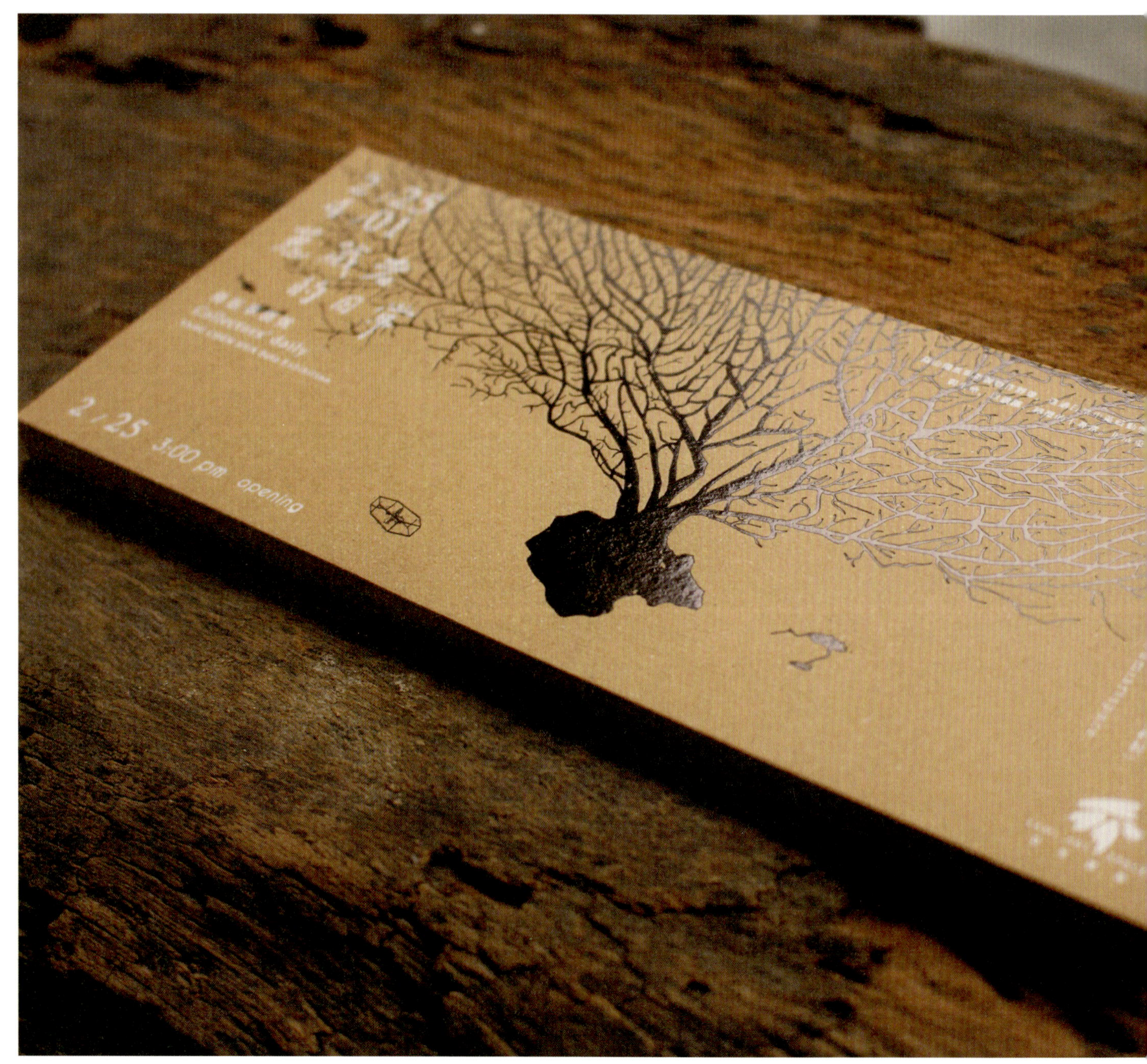

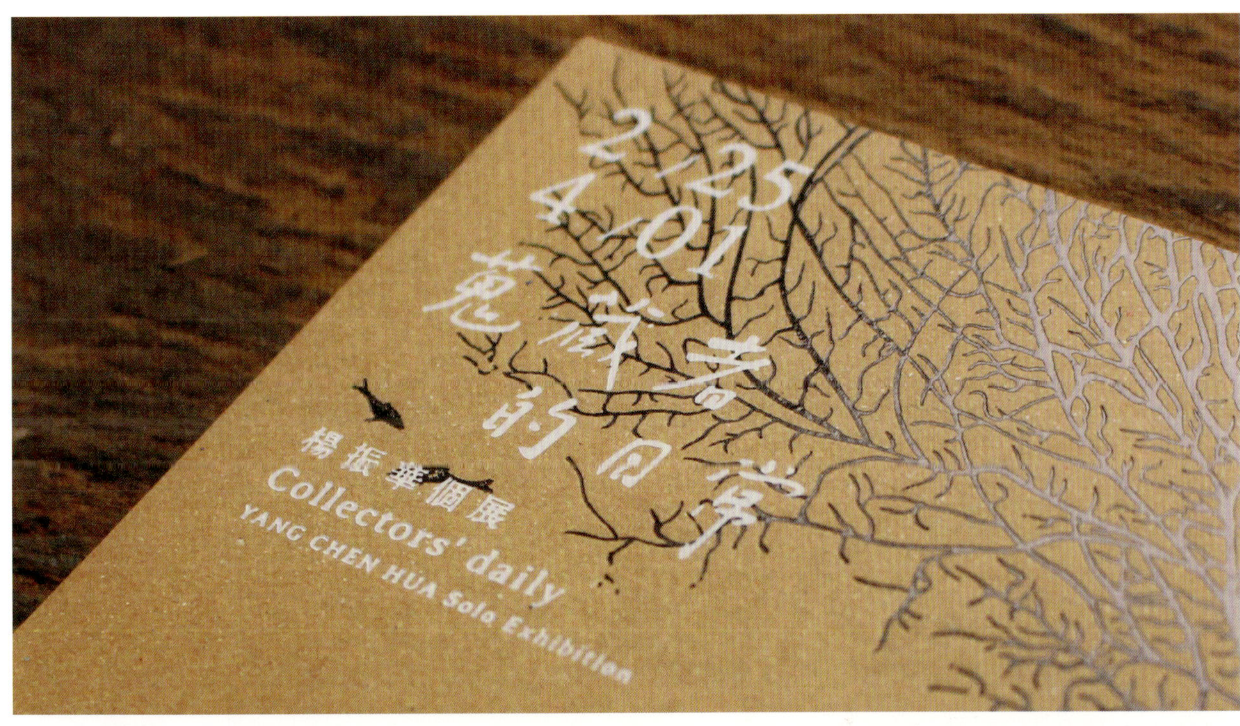
2/25
4/01
楊振華個展
Collectors' daily
YANG CHEN HUA Solo Exhibition

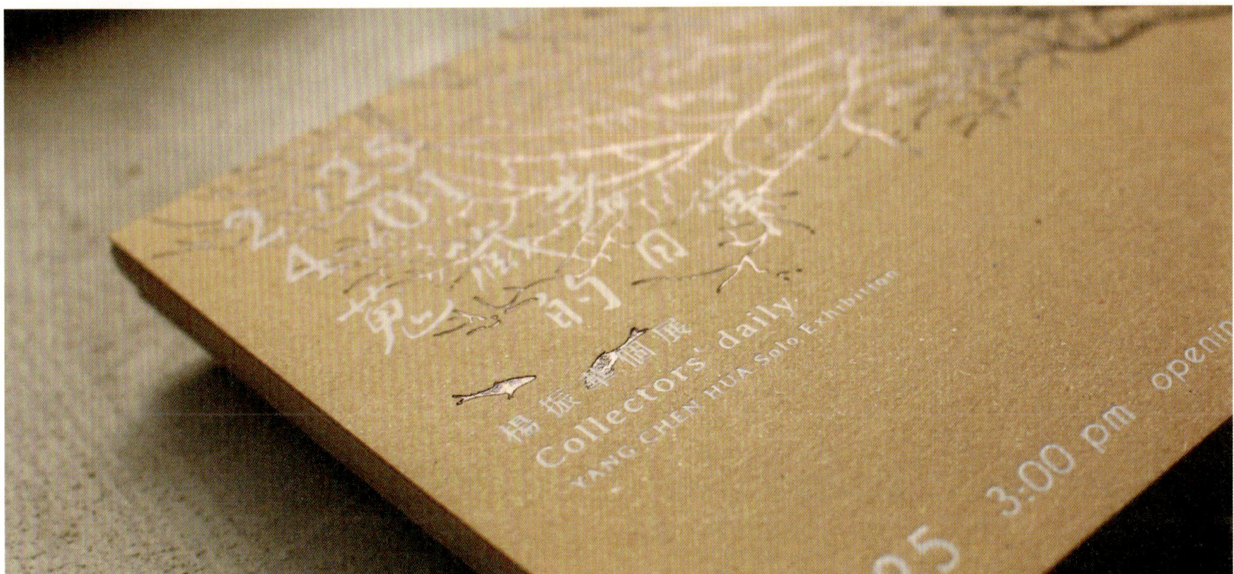
Collectors' daily
YANG CHEN HUA Solo Exhibition
3:00 pm

COOPERY 1956

The designer found a tiny picture of her great-grandmother in the family photo album. On the back of the photo was written the year: 1956. This photo fascinated her with its number of patterns and ornaments, although it was only a few centimeters wide. She decided to create a great linocut, multiplying and adding to the multiplicity of patterns.

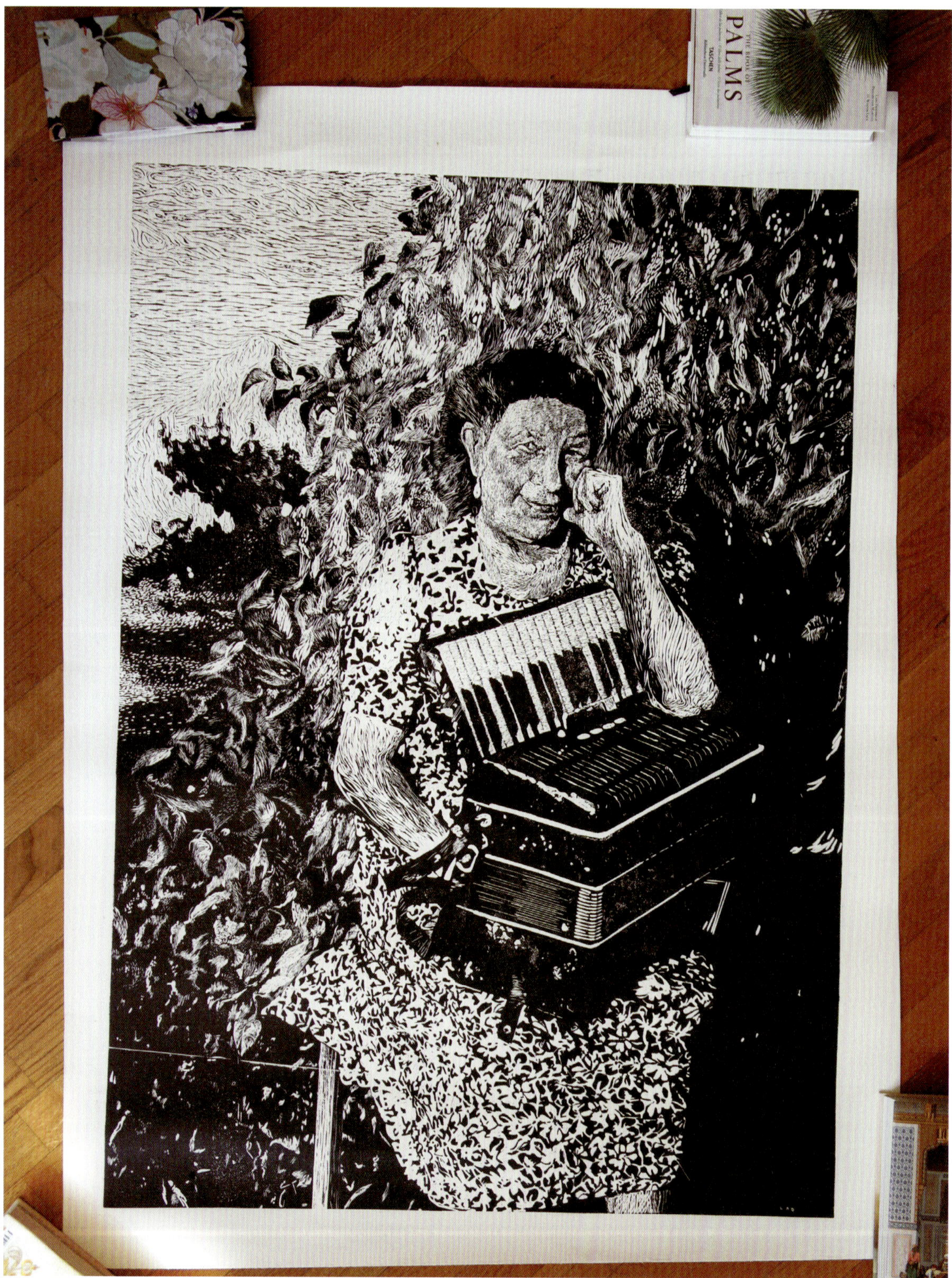

D: Klaudia Lademann

Corner

Fabriano Rosaspina cotton paper

Schmincke water-based ink

"Corner" is a 2-color linocut illustration printed during a 2 day live performance at the CRACK! Festival in Rome – 2017. Each day she changed the line's block color, producing two different limited editions existed. She tried to represent the weight of a part of the self, the big head looking away from the maimed body holding it. For the designer, the corner of a room has always been an evocative way to represent space as empty and disturbing as the weird human figure itself.

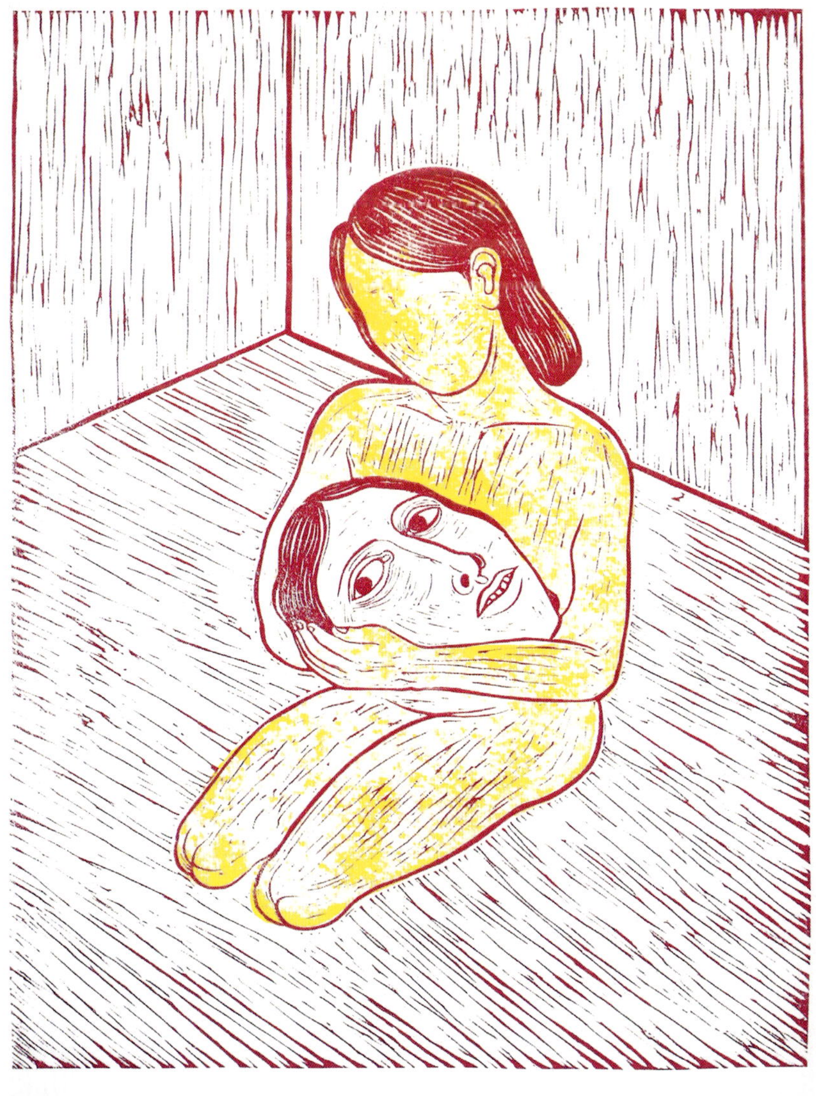

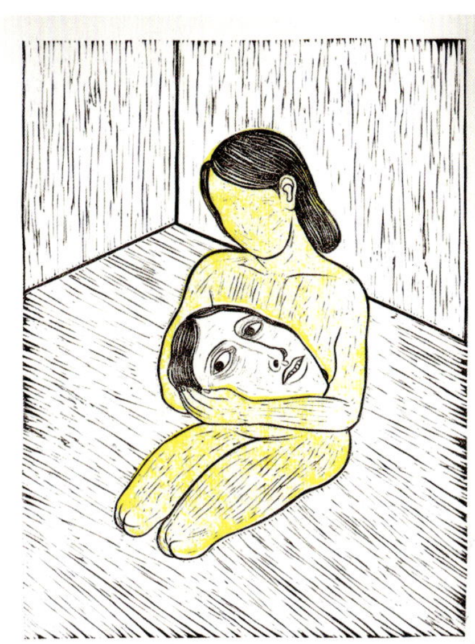

Touch

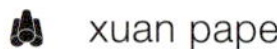

xuan paper

printing oil

Woodcut is a relief printing technique used in printmaking. The artist carves an image into the surface of a block of wood, typically with gouges, leaving the printing parts level with the surface while removing the non-printing parts. Areas that the artist cuts away carry no ink, while characters or images at the surface level carry the ink to produce the print. The designer used rosewood from South America for this project.

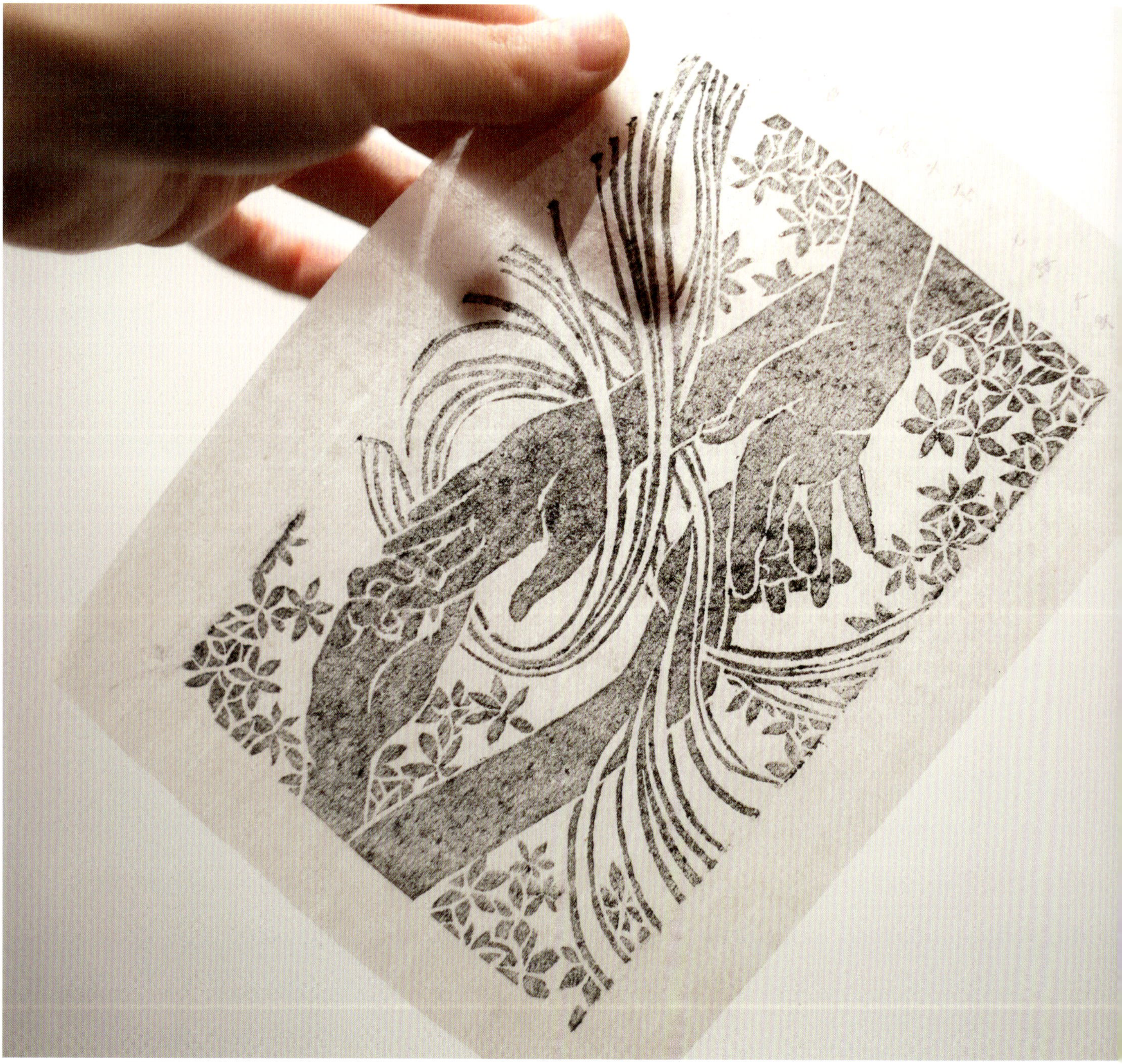

D: Danian Zhong

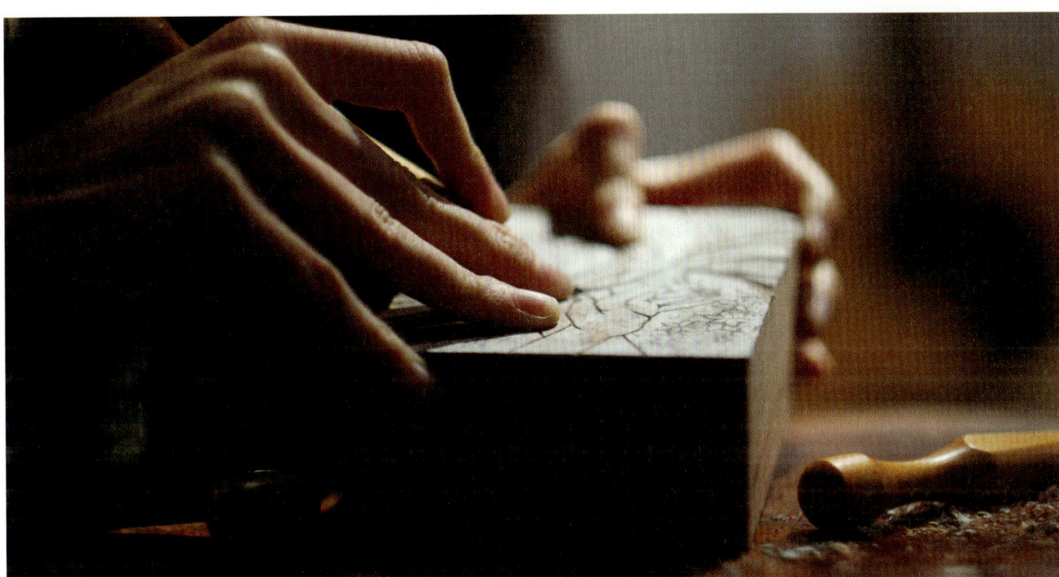

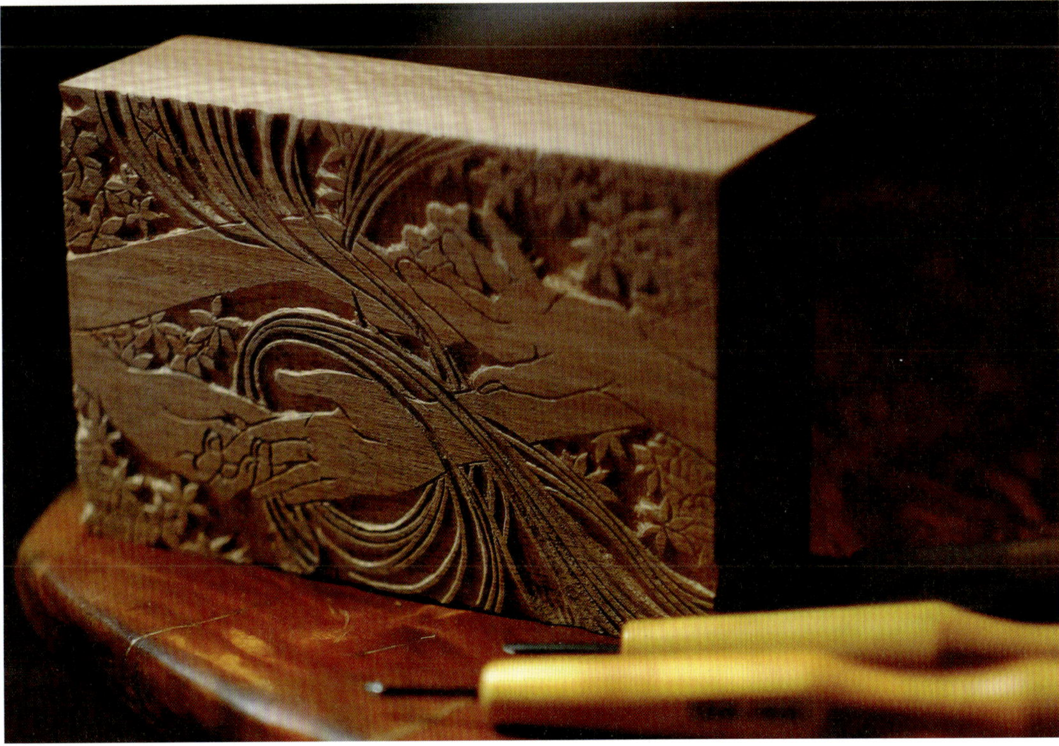

Through

tissue paper

printing oil

Woodcut is a relief printing technique used in printmaking. The designer used black walnut to do this project. She thinks walnut is ideal for sculpture and furniture making due to its high density.

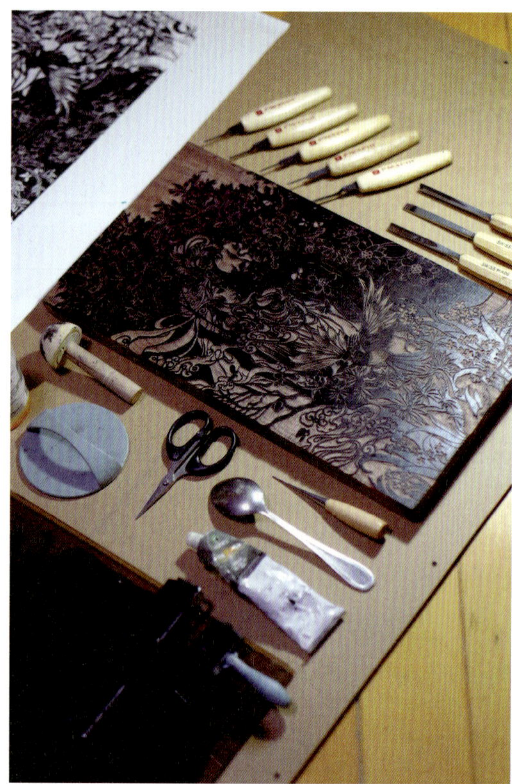

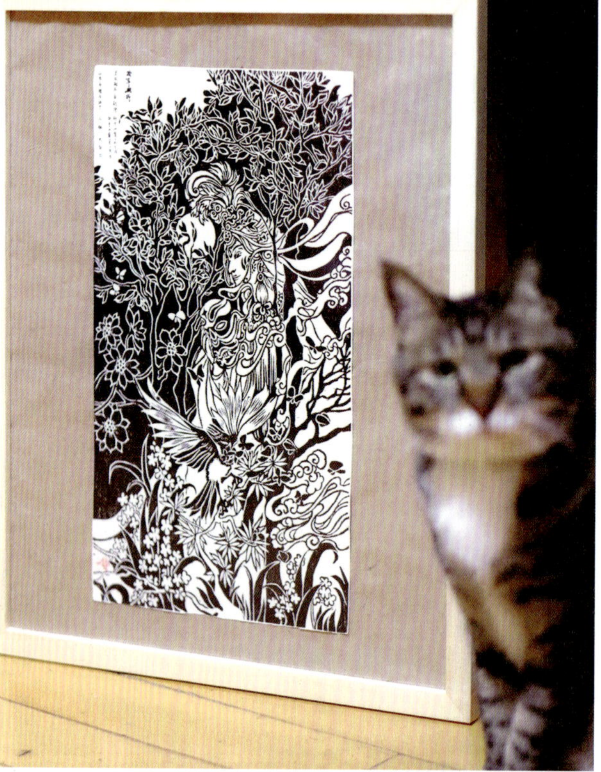

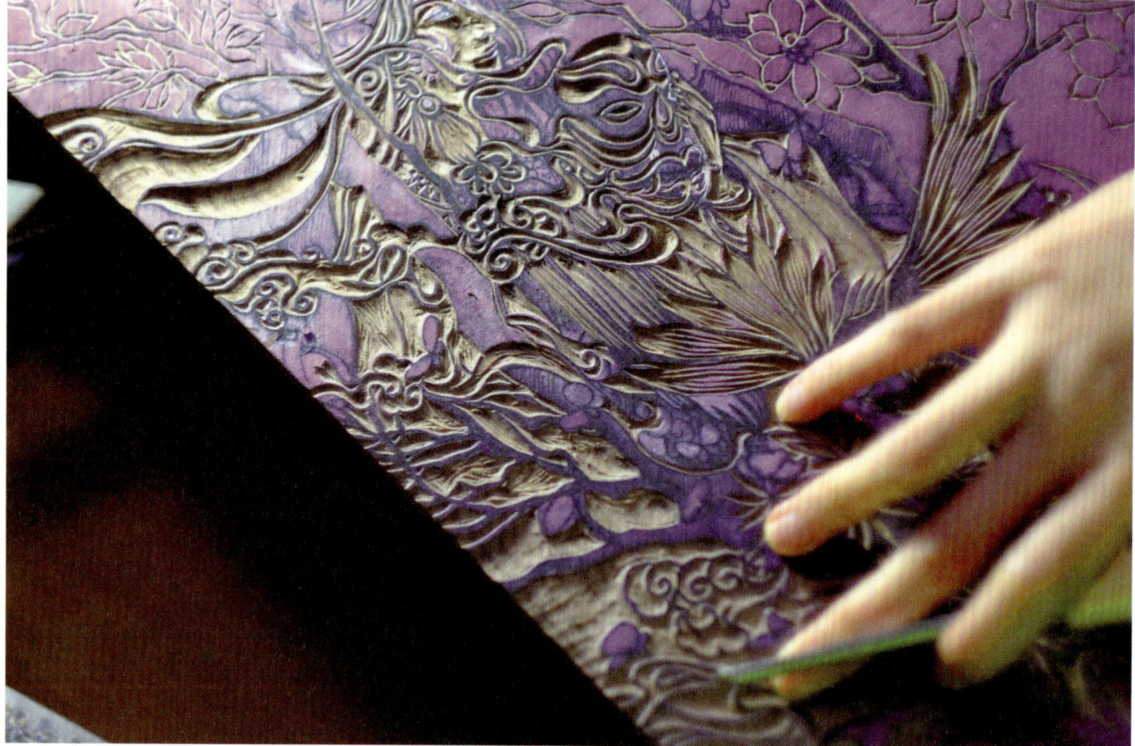

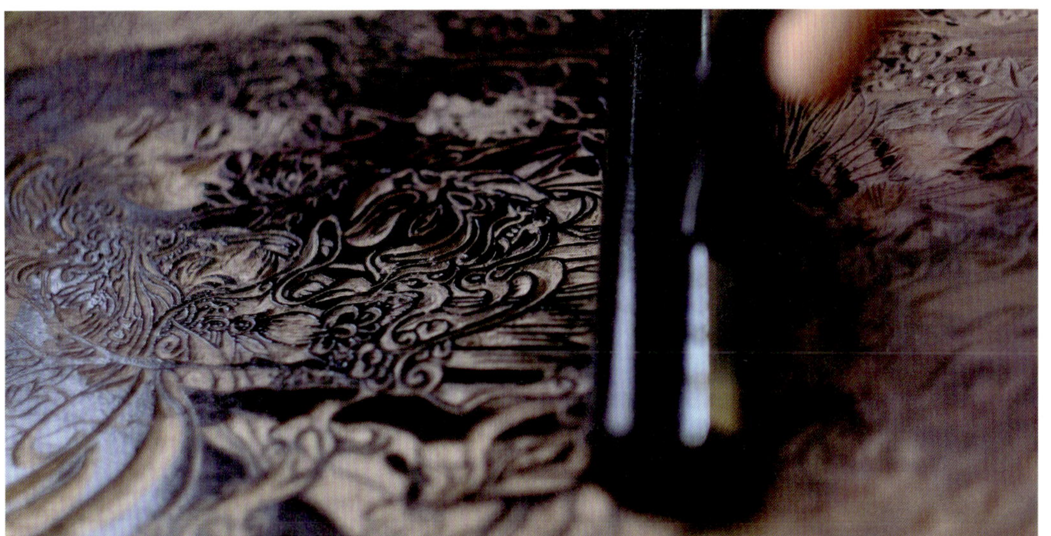

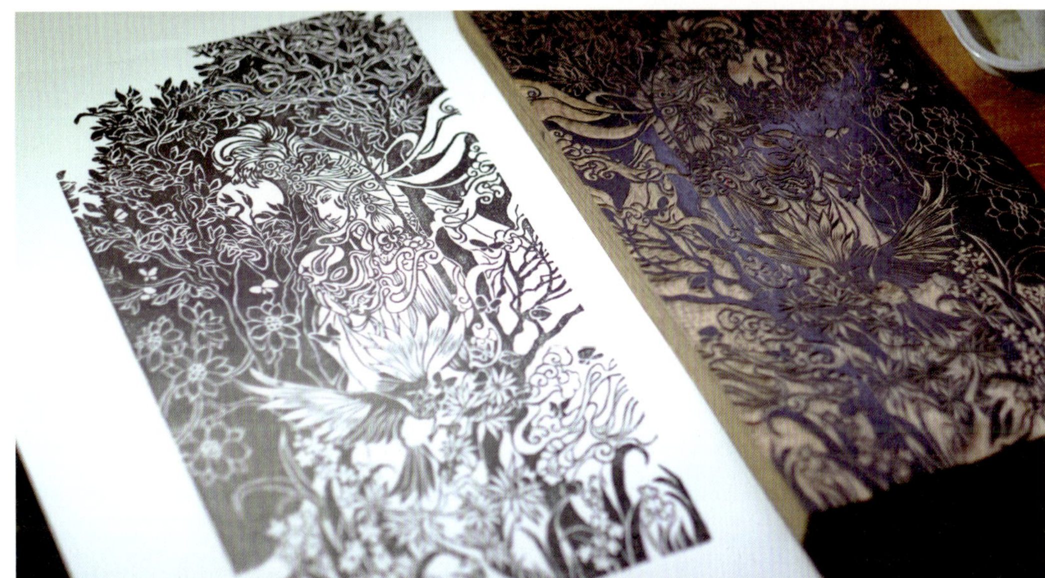

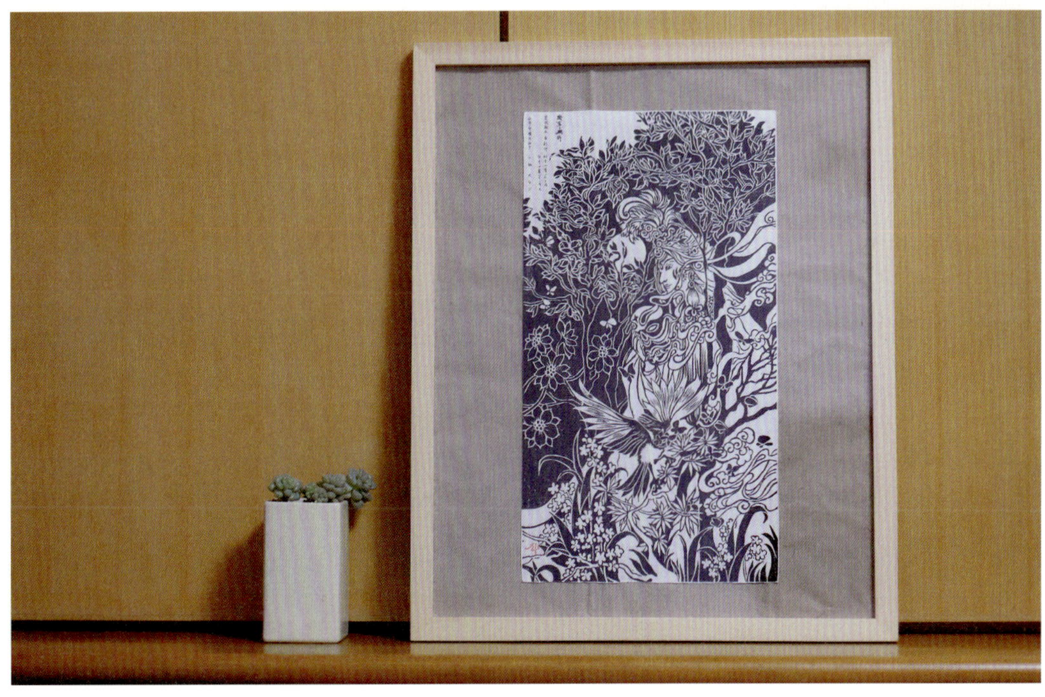

The New Call

175g Colorplan Natural, G.F. Smith's

offset ink

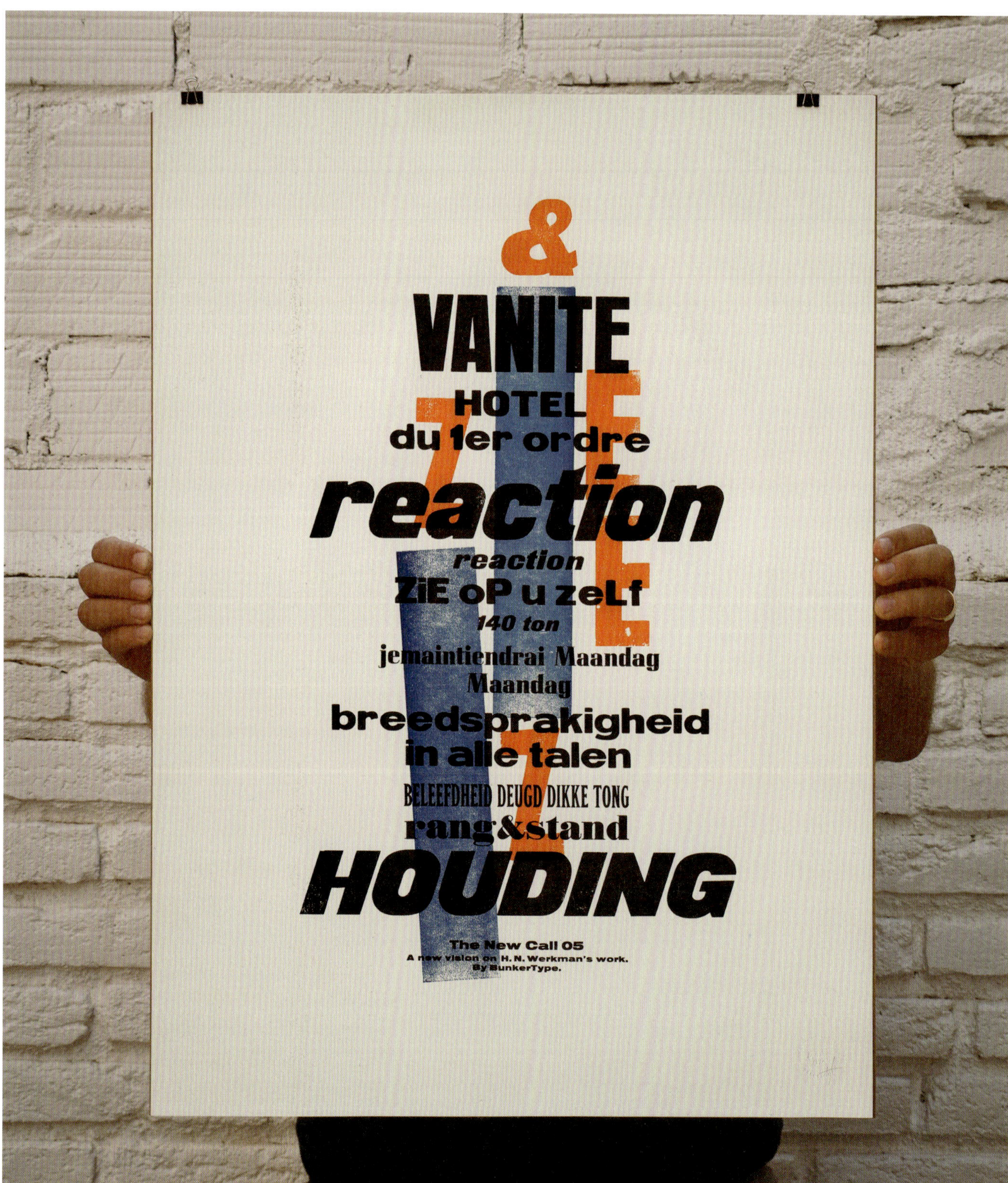

 D: J. Morentin

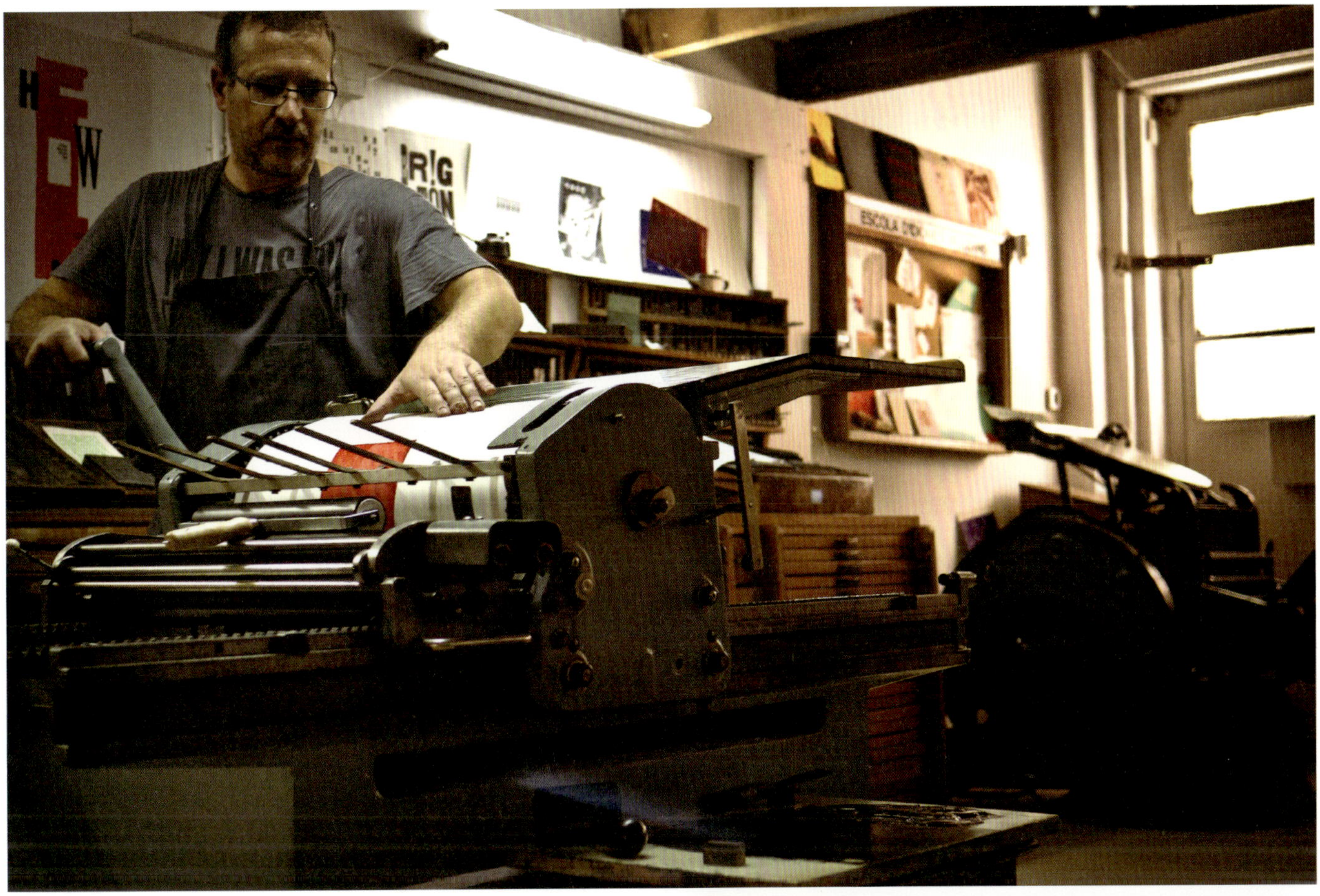

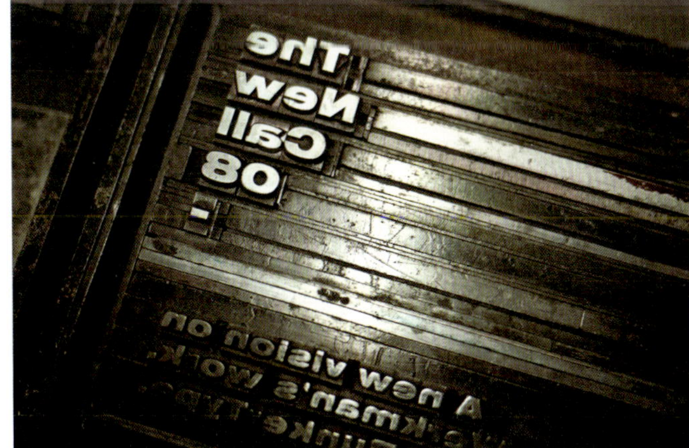

The New Call is a project of reinterpretation of the work of HN Werkman, specifically of one of its most paradigmatic pieces: the magazine *The Next Call*, one of the boldest publications of European avant-garde art during the interwar period. About 40 copies of each of the 10 reinterpretations of the collection were printed.

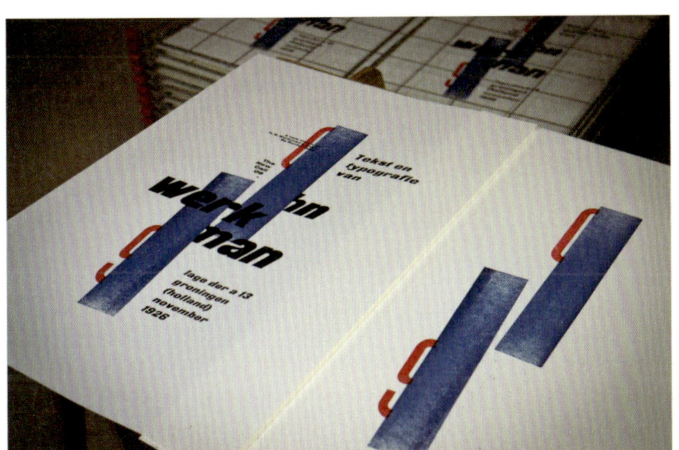

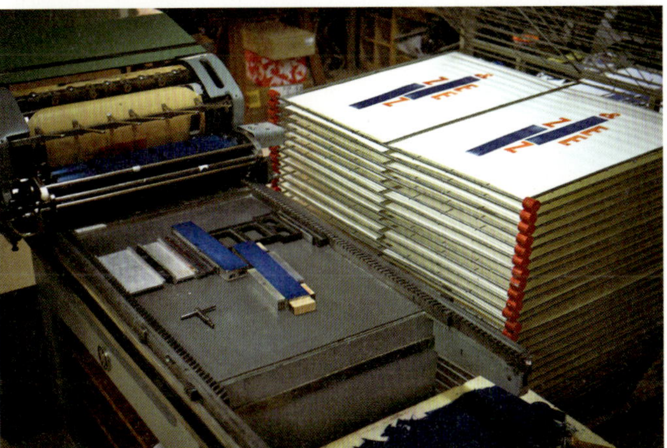

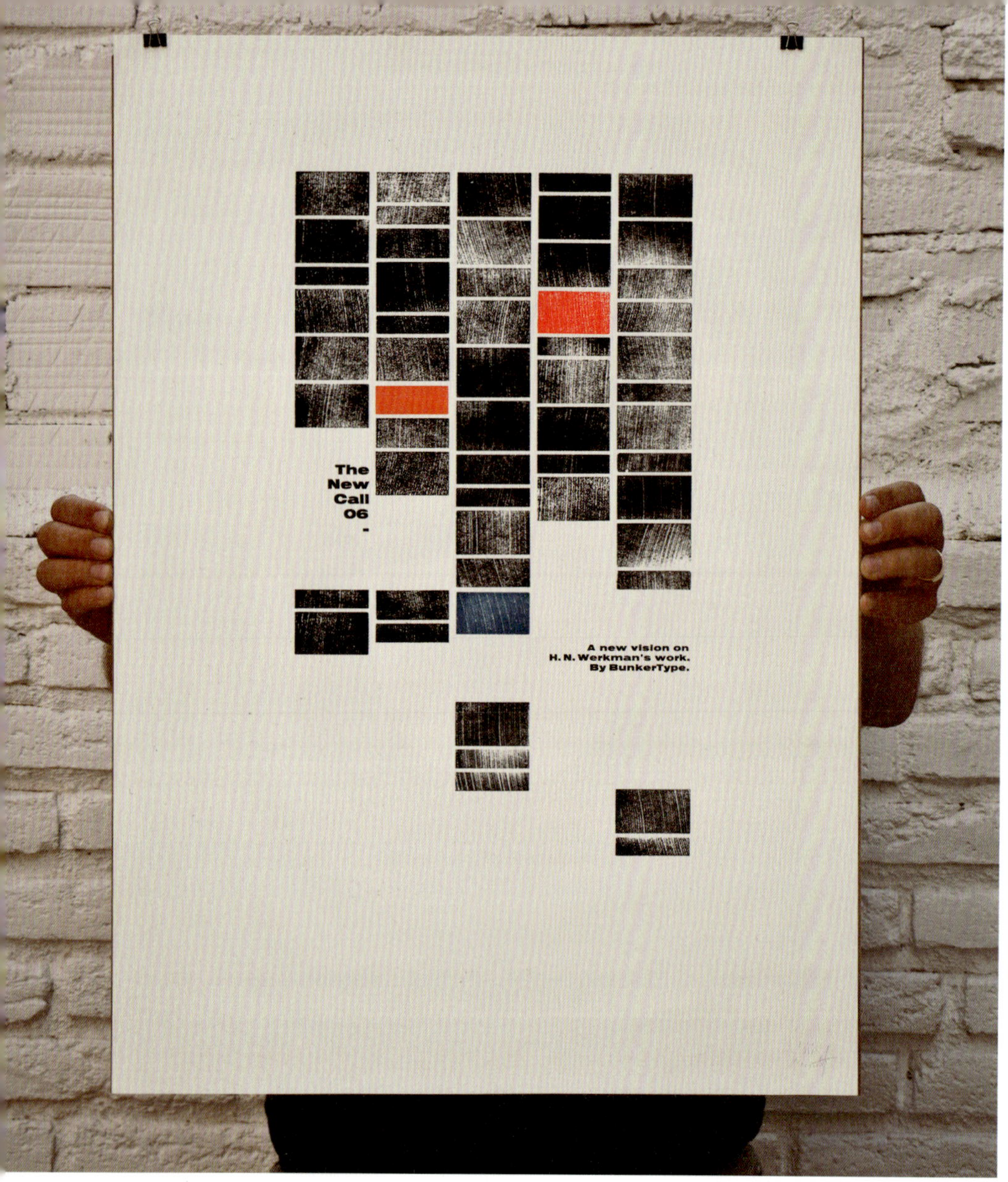

The New Call 06 -

A new vision on H. N. Werkman's work. By BunkerType.

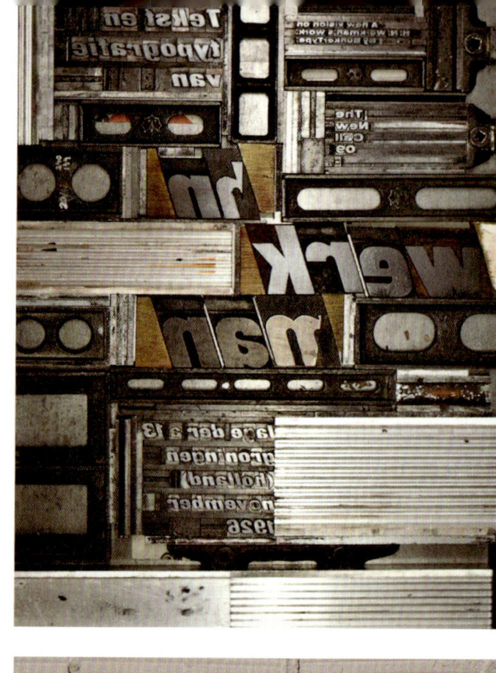

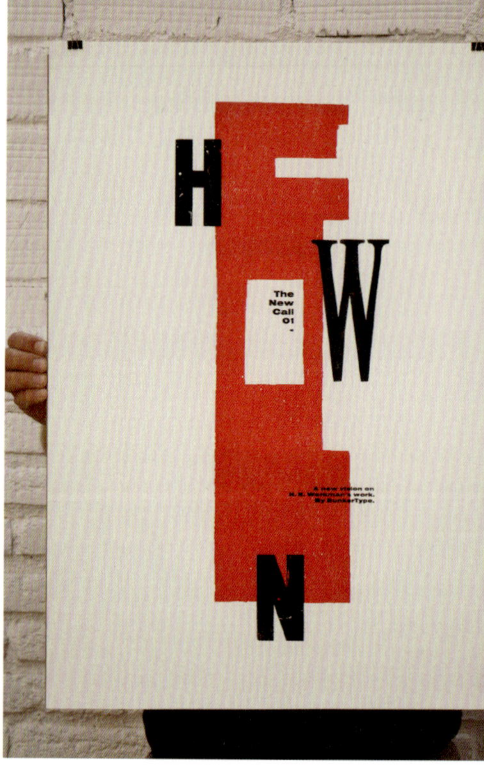

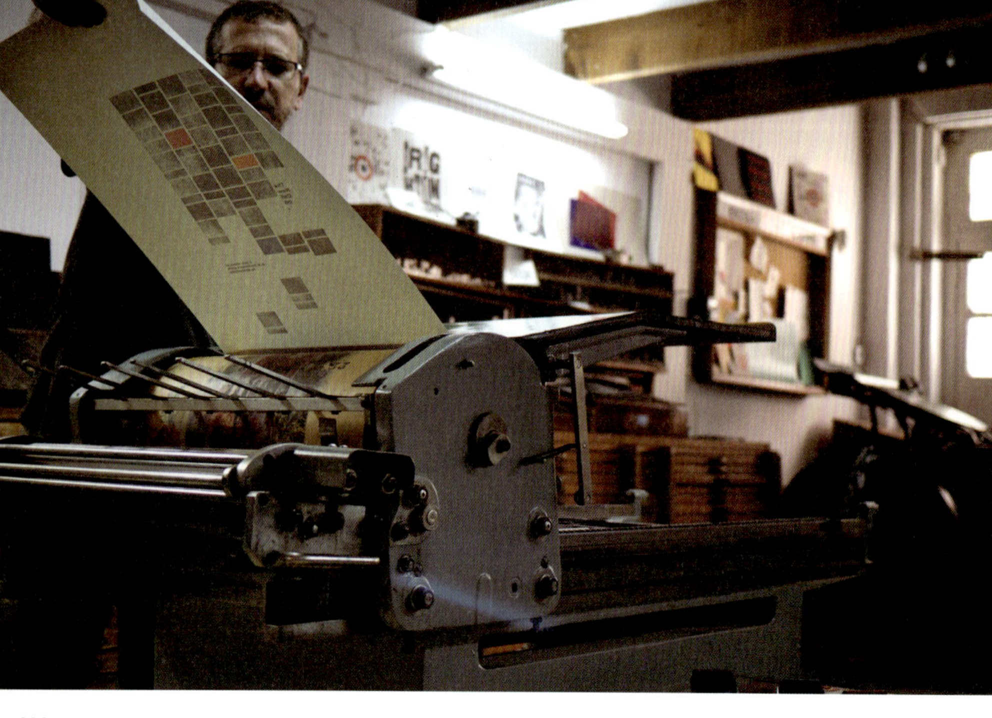

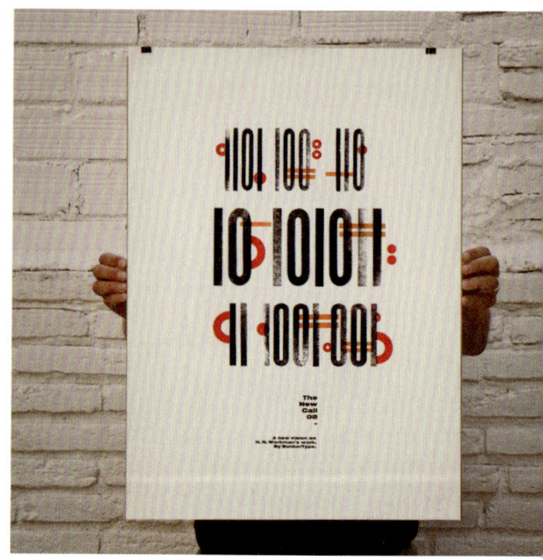

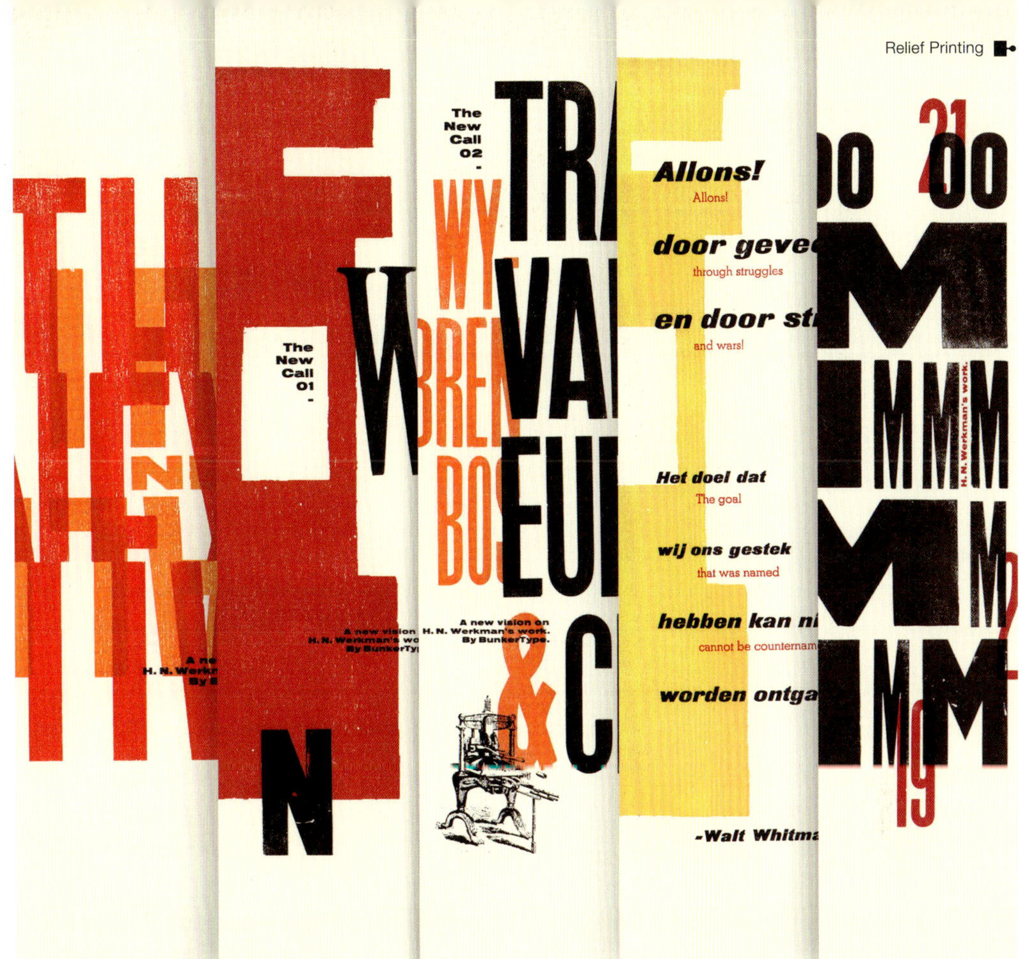
The
New
Call
01
The
New
Call
02
A new vision on
H. N. Werkman's work.
By BunkerType.
Allons!
Allons!
through struggles
and wars!
Het doel dat
The goal
wij ons gestek
that was named
H. N. Werkman's work.

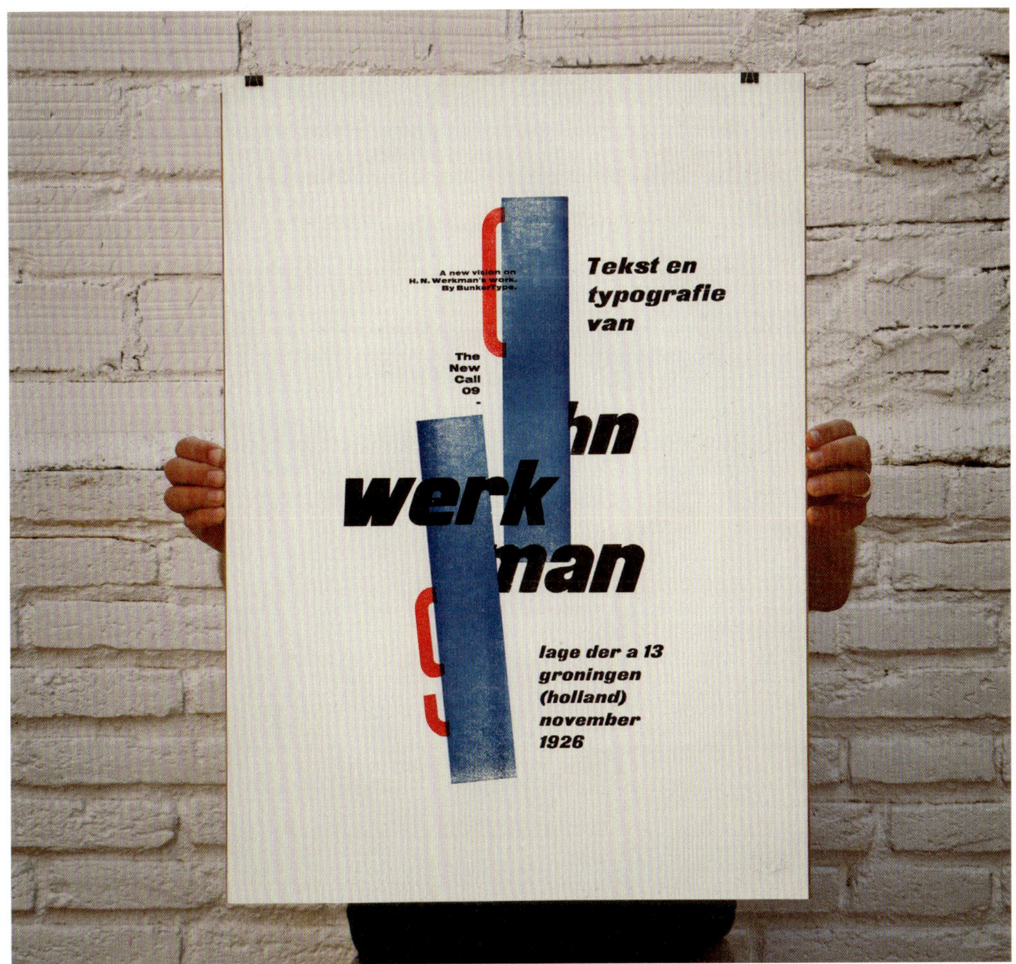
A new vision on
H. N. Werkman's work.
By BunkerType.
Tekst en
typografie
van
The
New
Call
09
werk
lage der a 13
groningen
(holland)
november
1926

Spain… is different

Materica Gesso Fedrigoni's paper

offset ink

Spain is different is an artistic project of protest based and constructed exclusively from the elements that German designer Gerd Arntz created for the *Isotype* (International System of Typographic Picture Education) project in the 1930s. In the project, Gerd Arntz created a visual universe of about 4,000 pictograms on any subject thinkable. The work *Spain is different* participates, not only in the language of Arntz, but also in its critical spirit, portraying a society resigned and submissive to the inequalities and abuses of the elites and their leaders. The work is printed in a letterpress manner with metal and wood movable types.

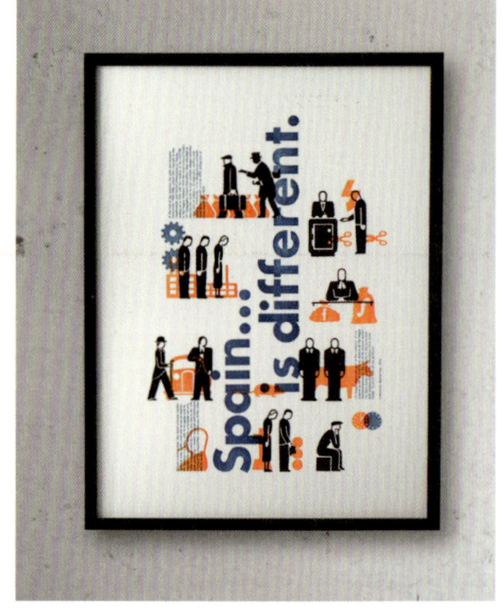

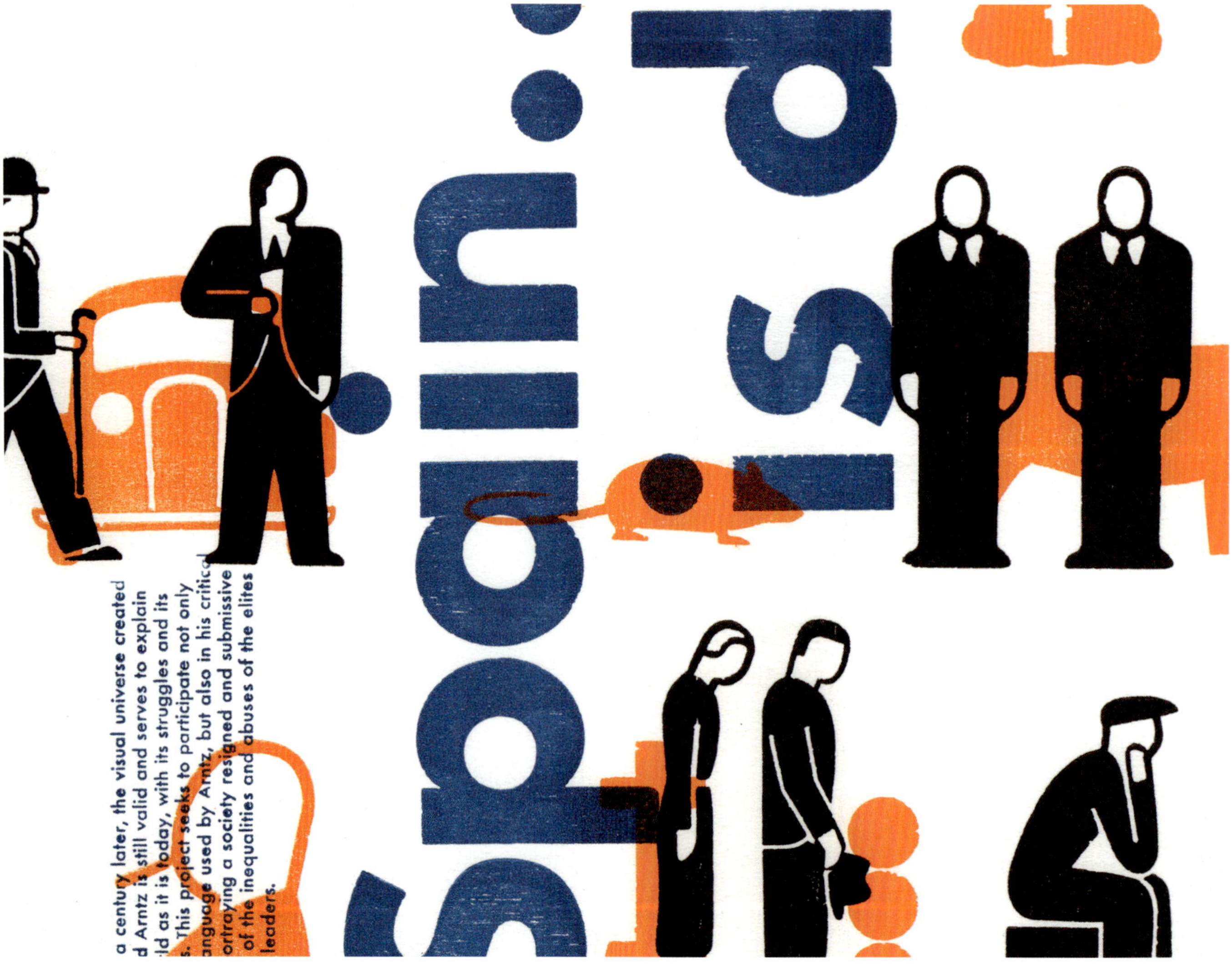

D: J. Morentin

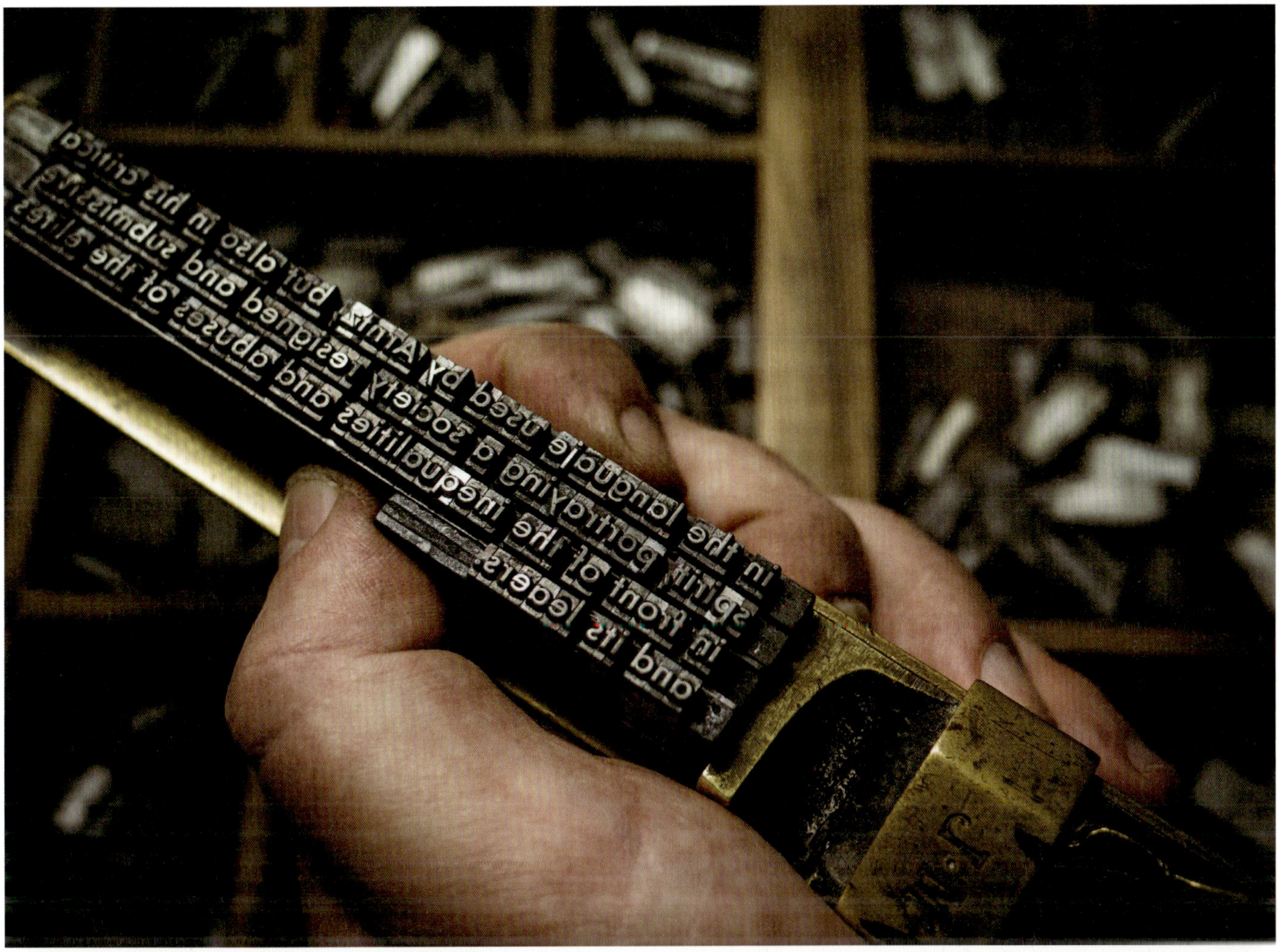

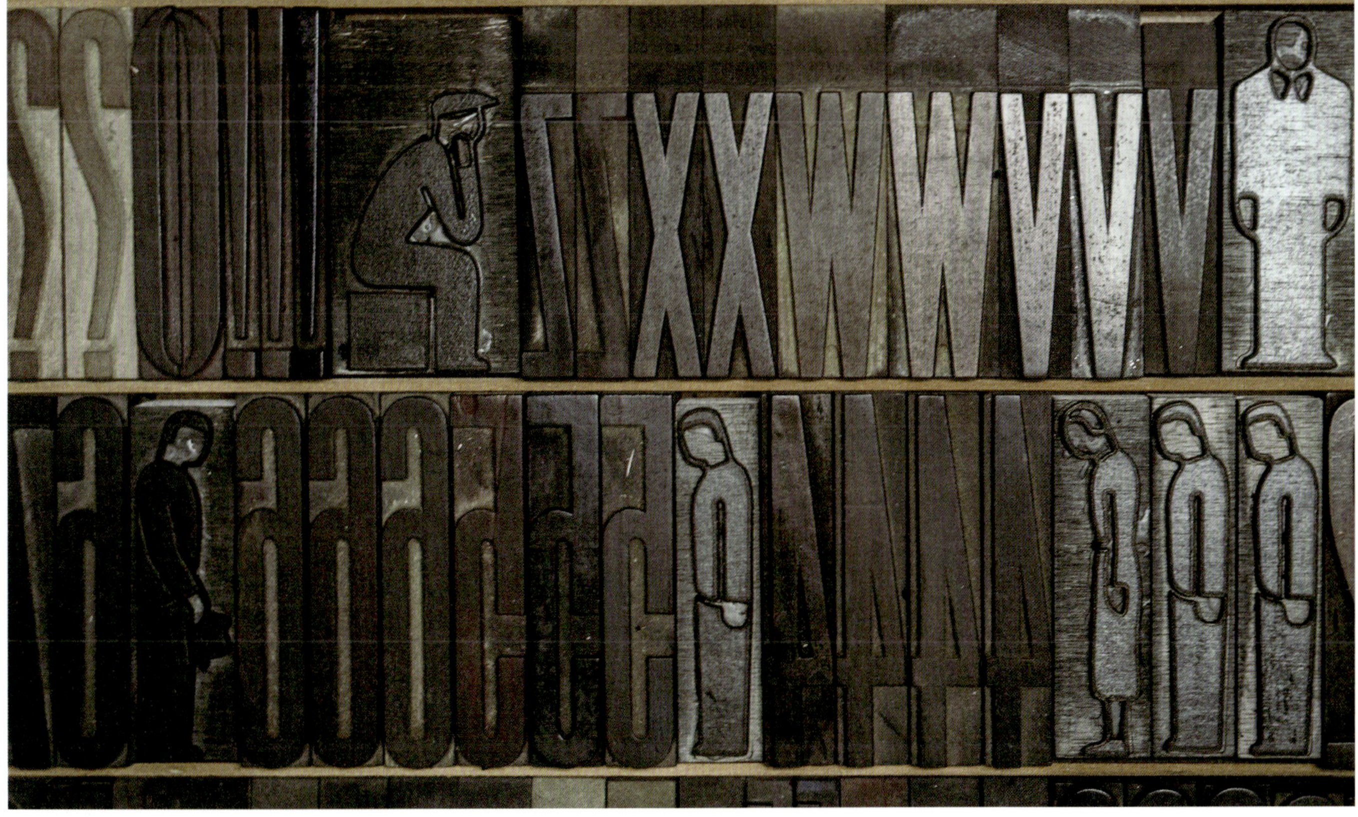

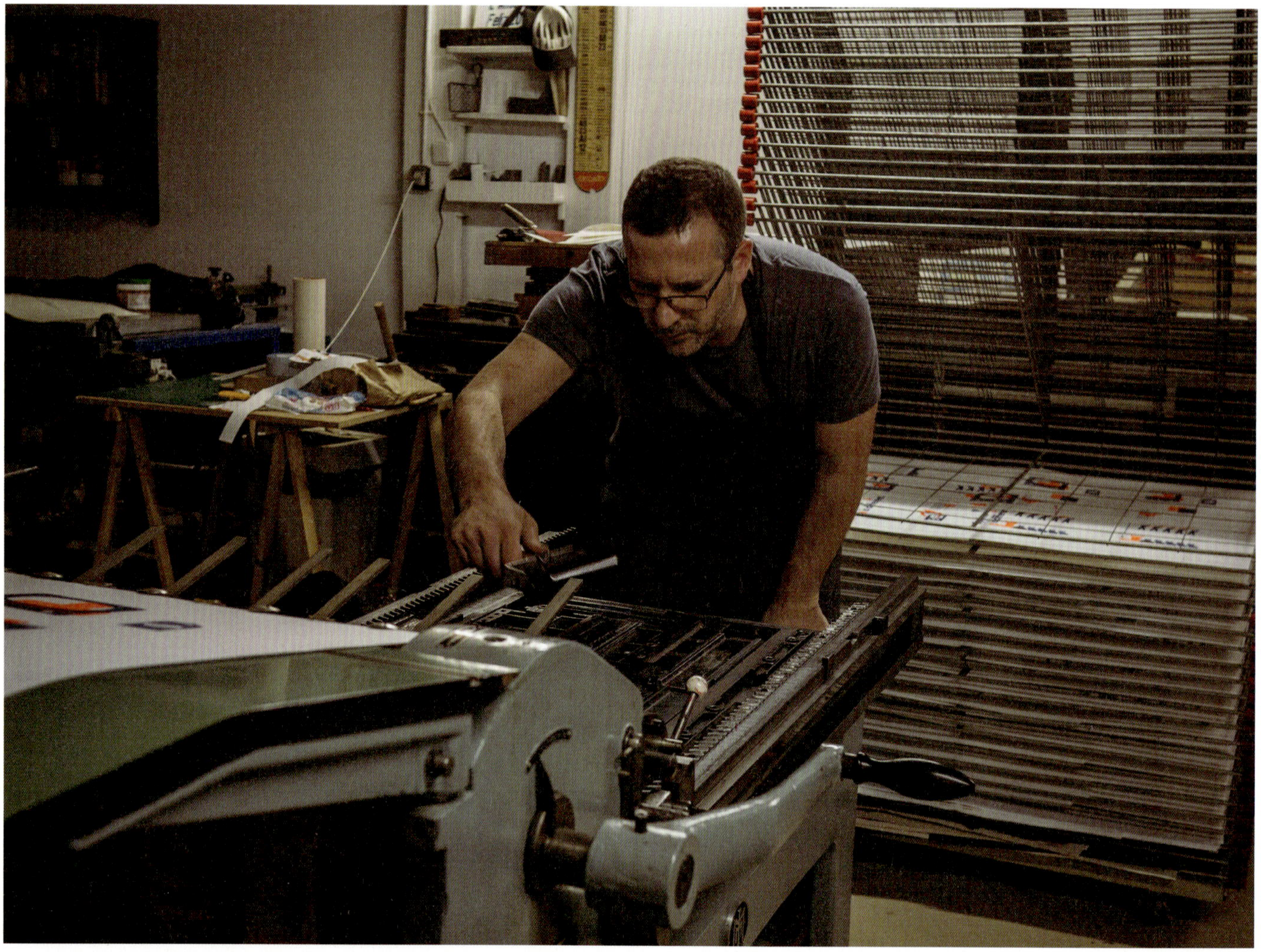

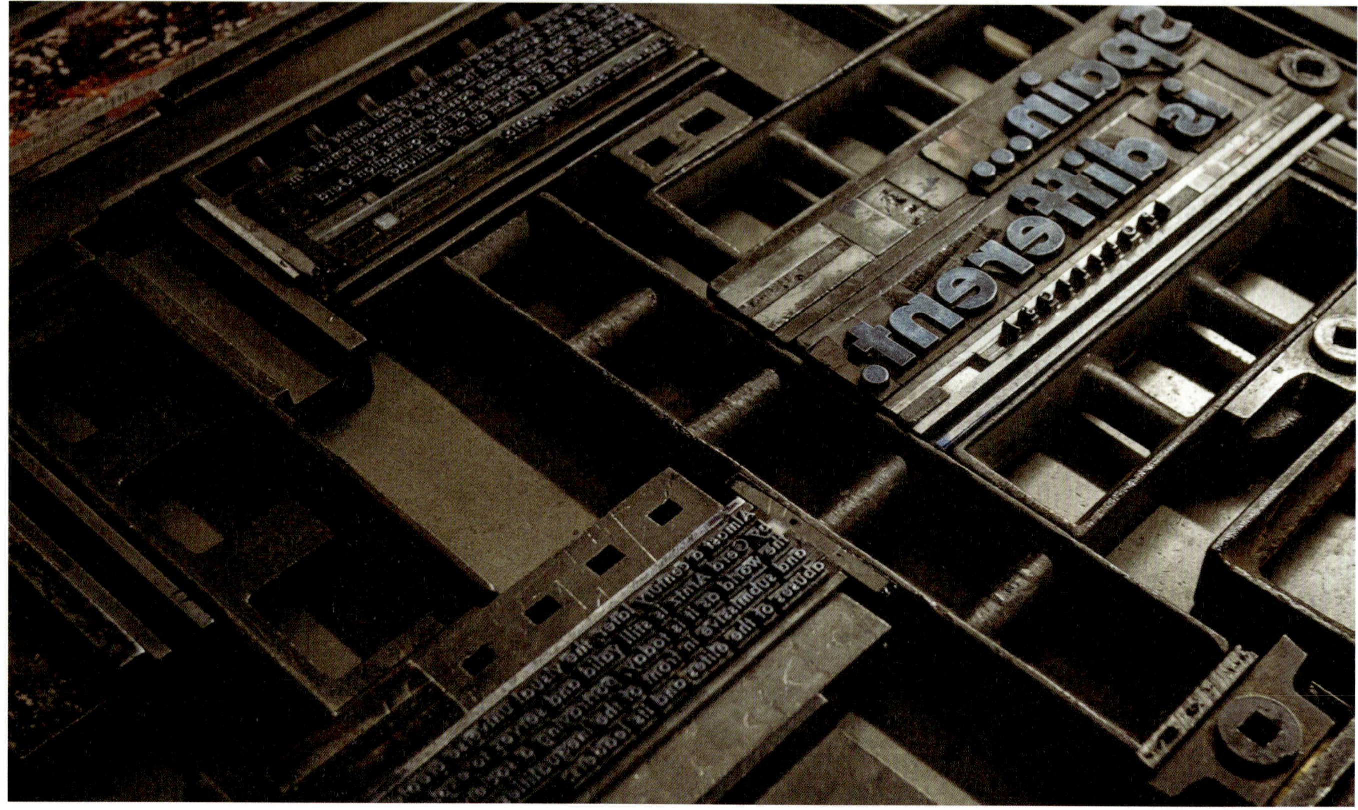
Spain...
is different!

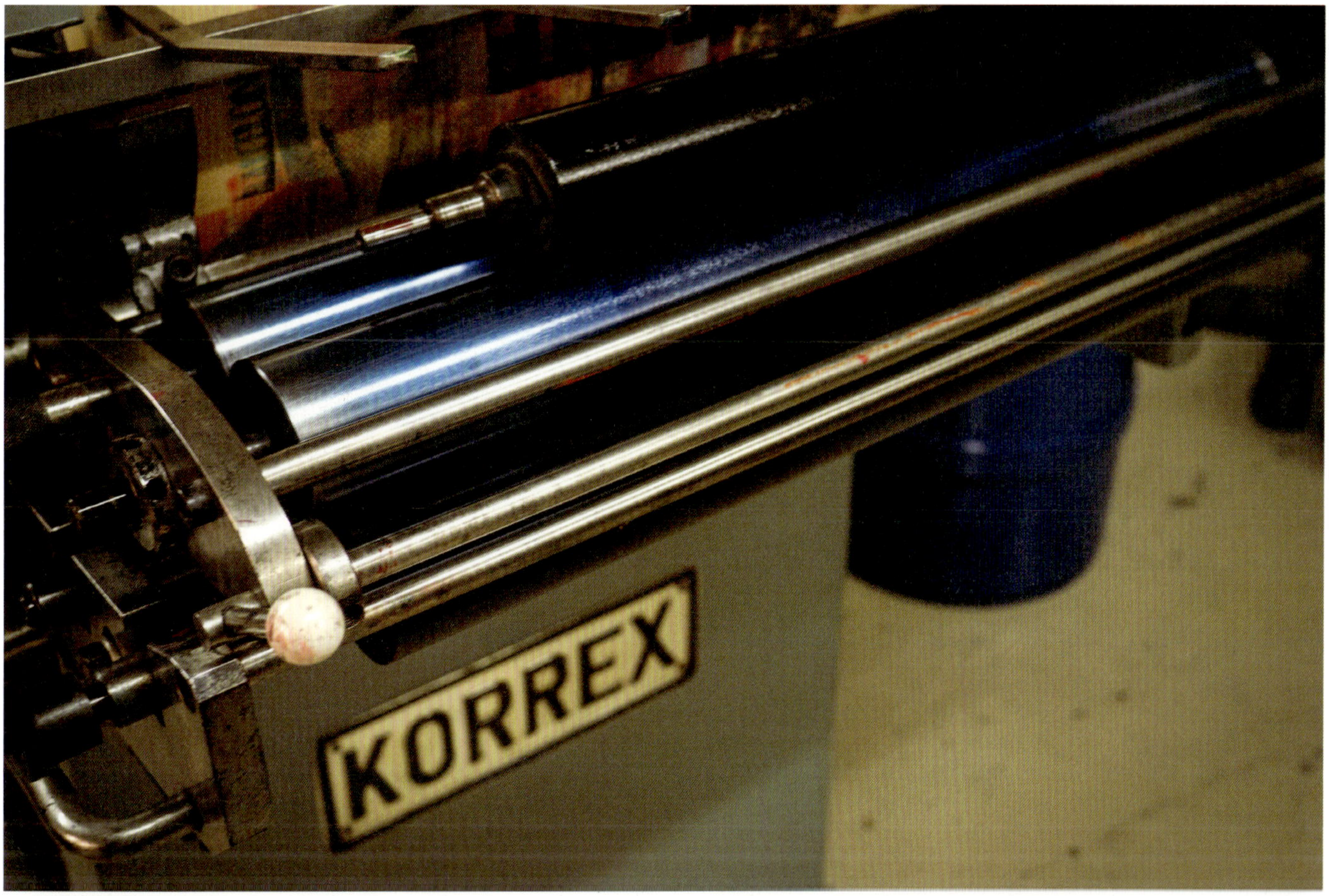
KORREX

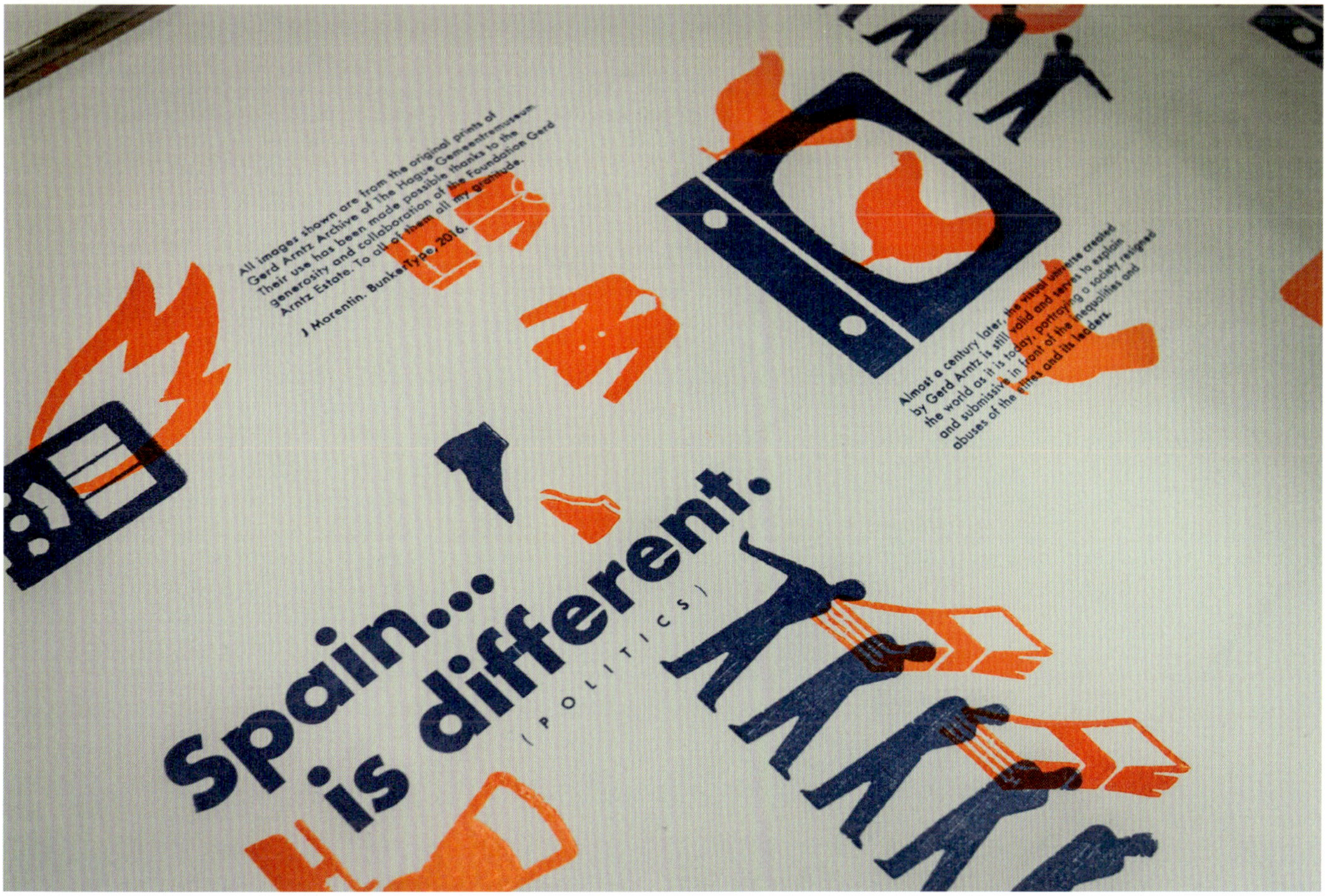
All images shown are from the original prints of
Gerd Arntz Archive of The Hague Gemeentemuseum.
Their use has been made possible thanks to the
generosity and collaboration of the Foundation Gerd
Arntz Estate. To all of them all my gratitude.
J Morentin. BunkerType, 2016.
Almost a century later, the visual universe created
by Gerd Arntz is still valid and serves to explain
the world as it is today, portraying a society resigned
and submissive in front of the inequalities and
abuses of the elites and its leaders.
Spain...
is different.
(POLITICS)

The Letterpress Posters

350g white paper, 350g black paper

The concept behind these letterpress printed posters is to create a typographic illustration based on an inspirational sentence about design or creativity. This was made possible only as the designer collaborates with Studio Pression, the printer. When Mr Cup created the visual design for these posters, he was not sure how much details could be printed and how it would look like at the end. The result was above his expectation, the relief is impressive and the feeling of looking at your creating printed in letterpress is unique! Each design is limited to 100 prints, all hand signed.

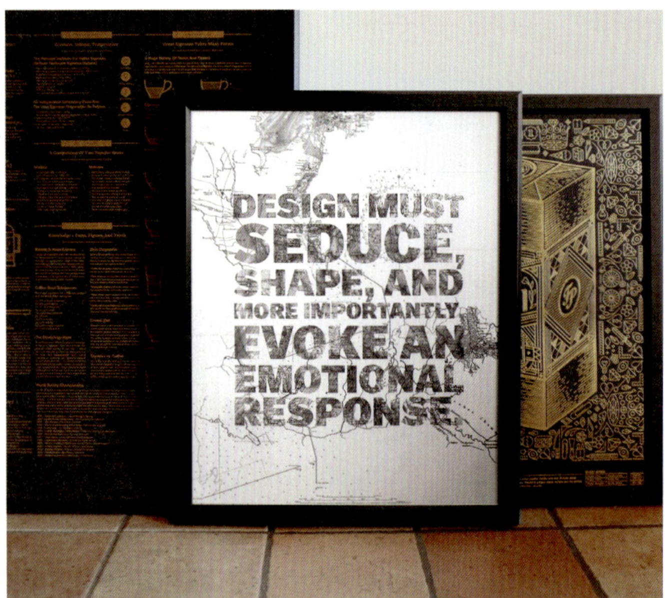

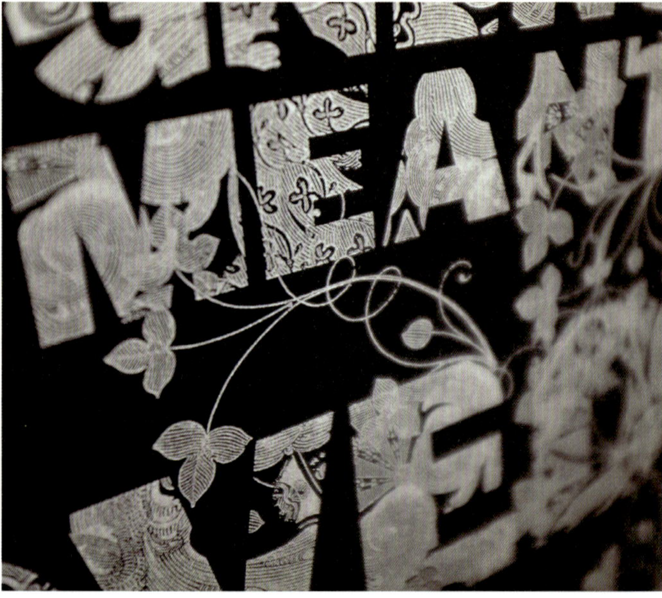

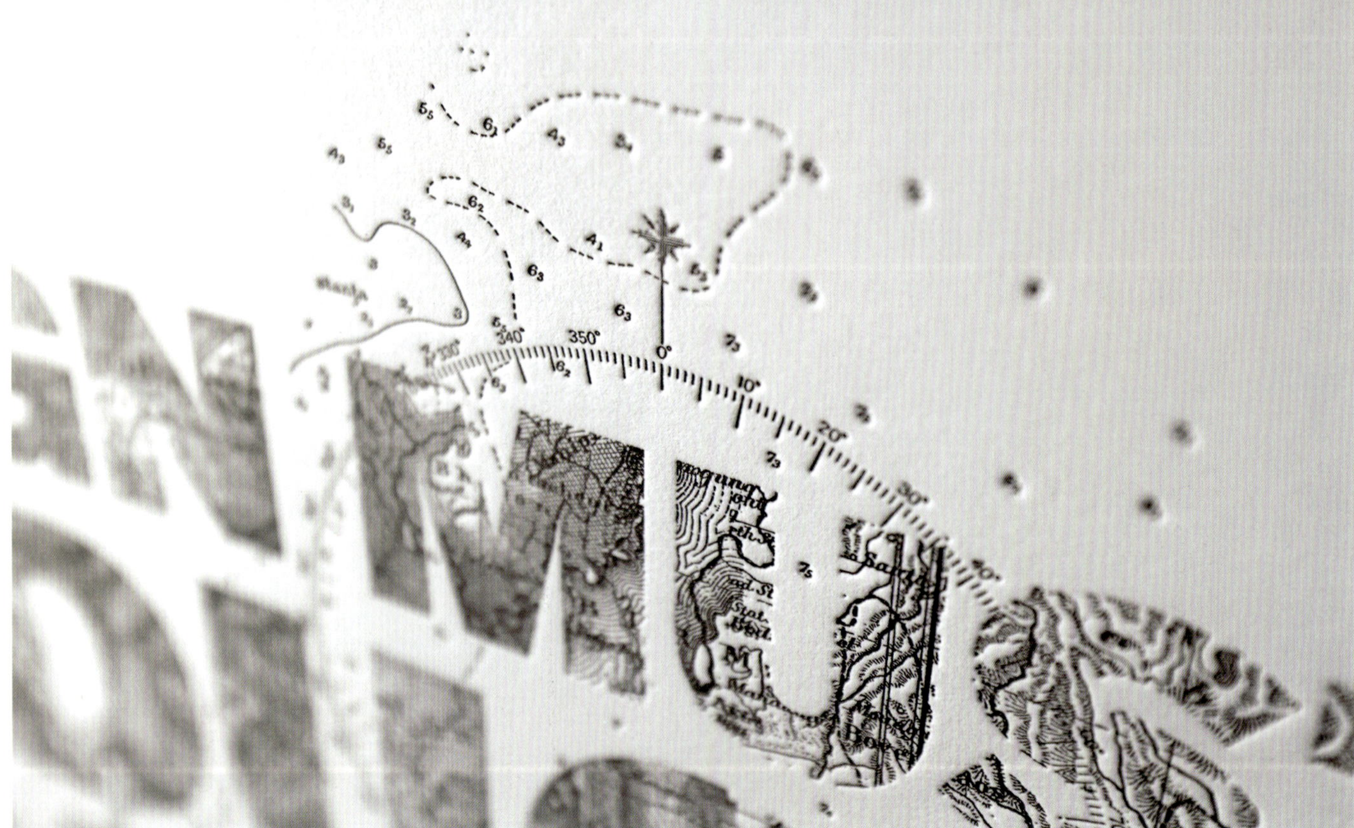

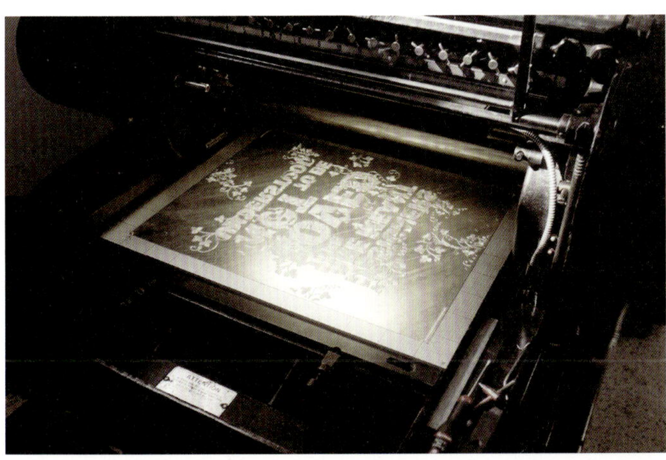

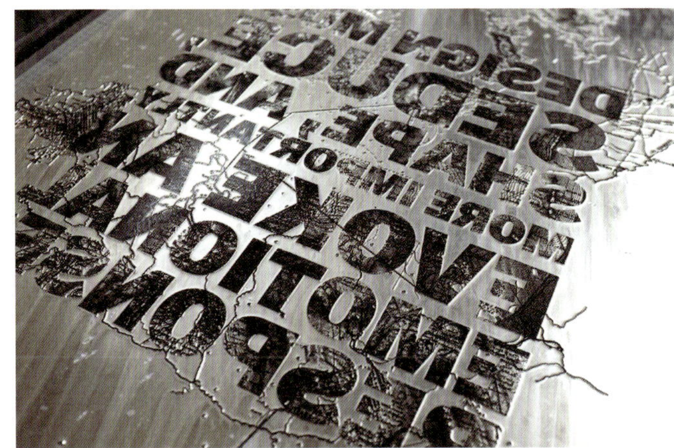

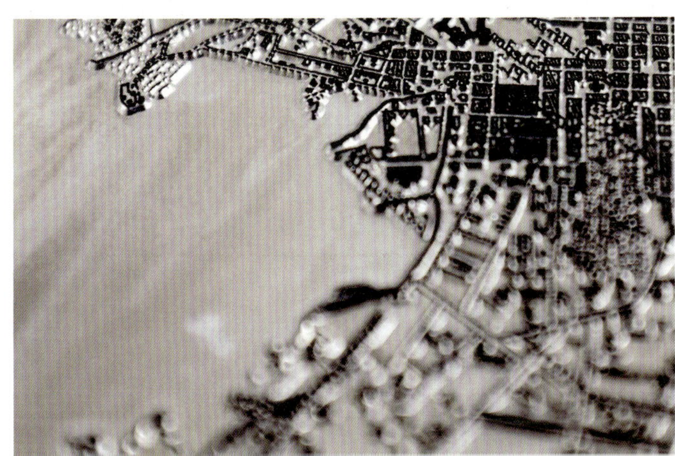

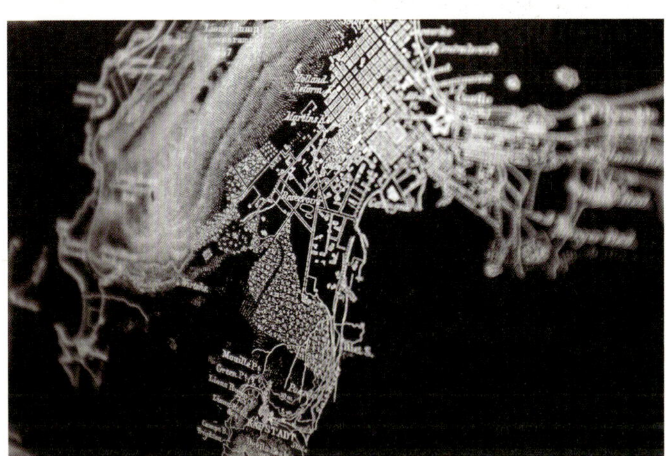

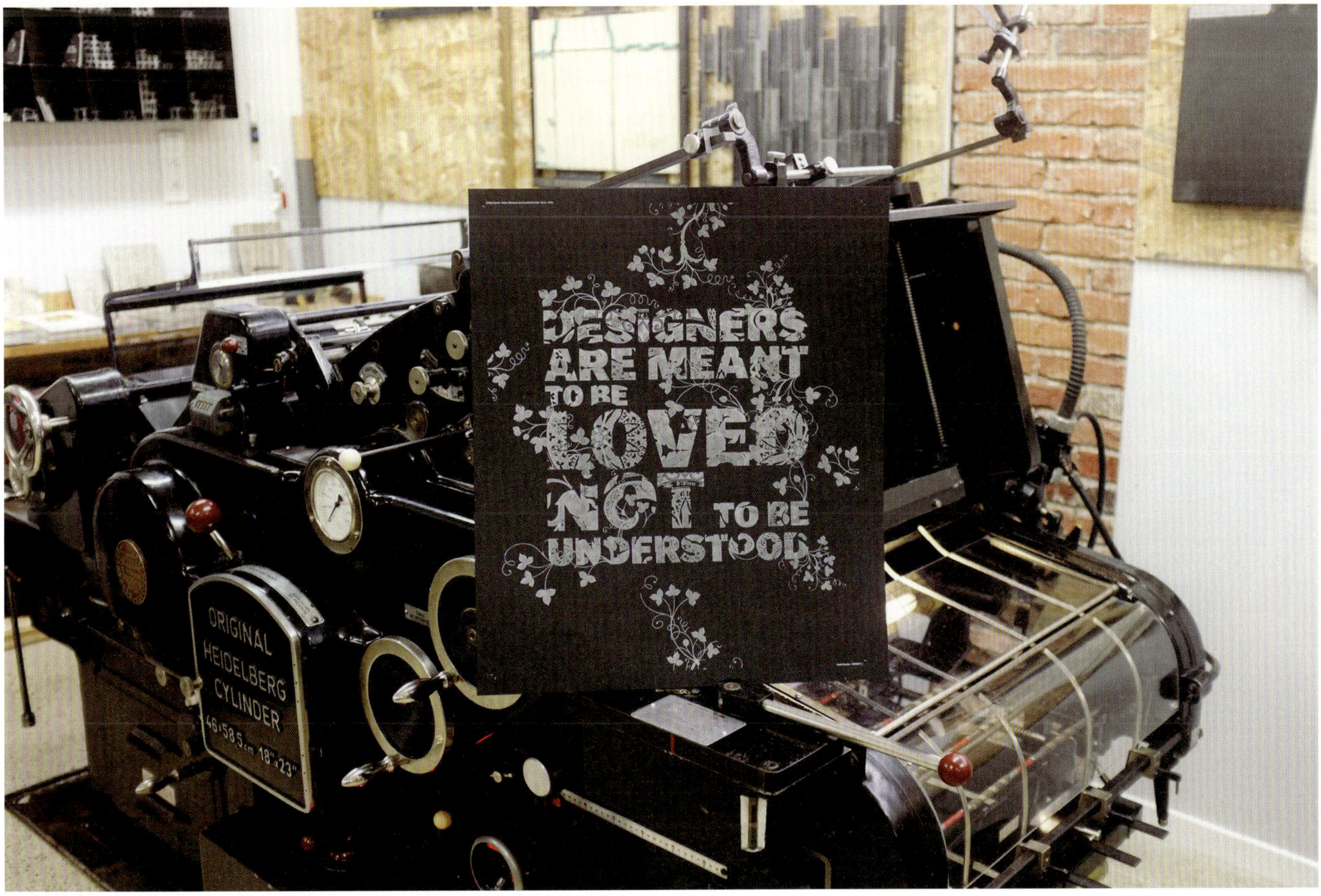

2016 Letterpress Calender

700g French paper

The calendar is composed of 14 cards printed on 700g French paper. Two editions were done, a special edition which comes with a copperplate-printed black cover, with a second blind printed design, and with copperplate foil edging! The normal edition has a 2-color cover printed on white paper. Each page was printed in one color, according to the season!

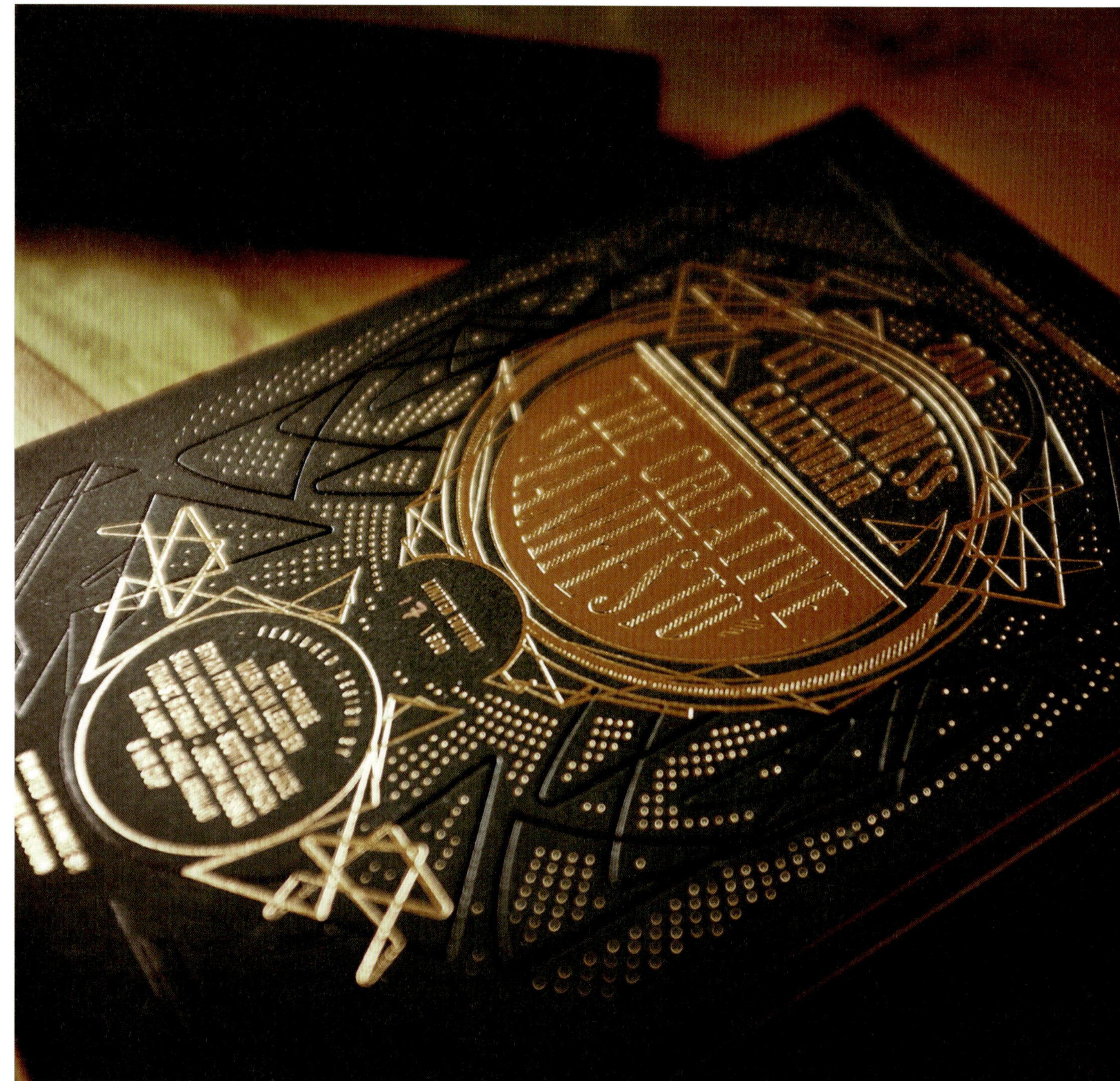

***D*:** Mr Cup

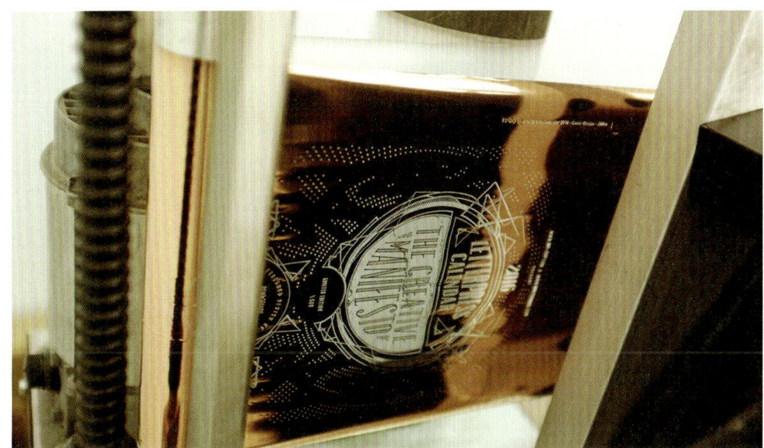

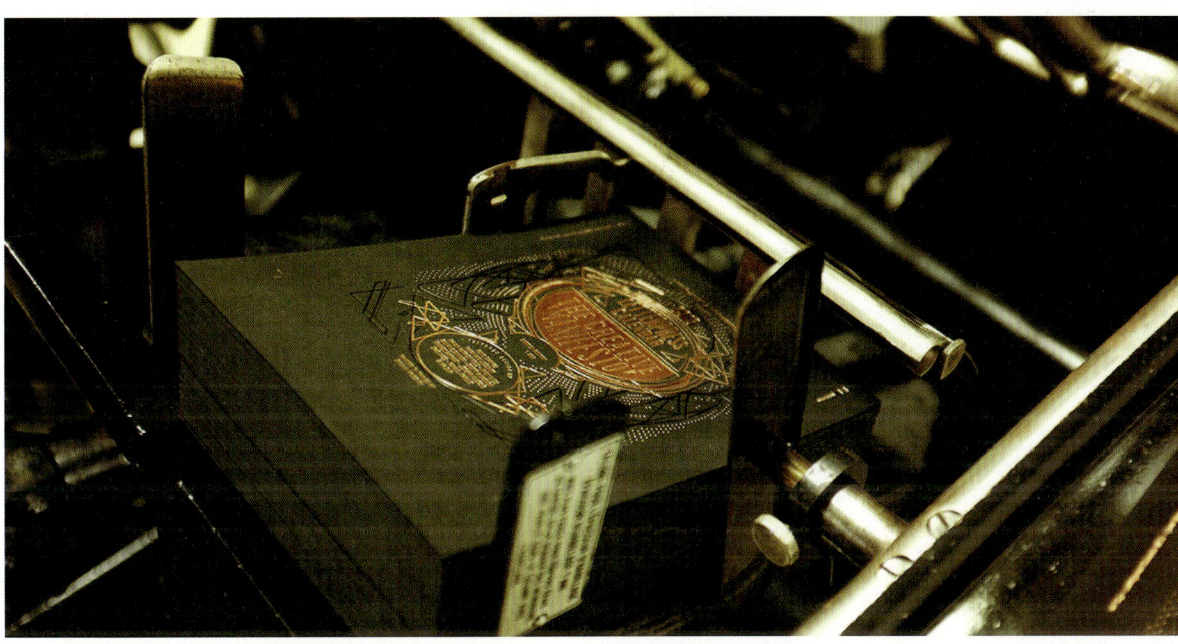

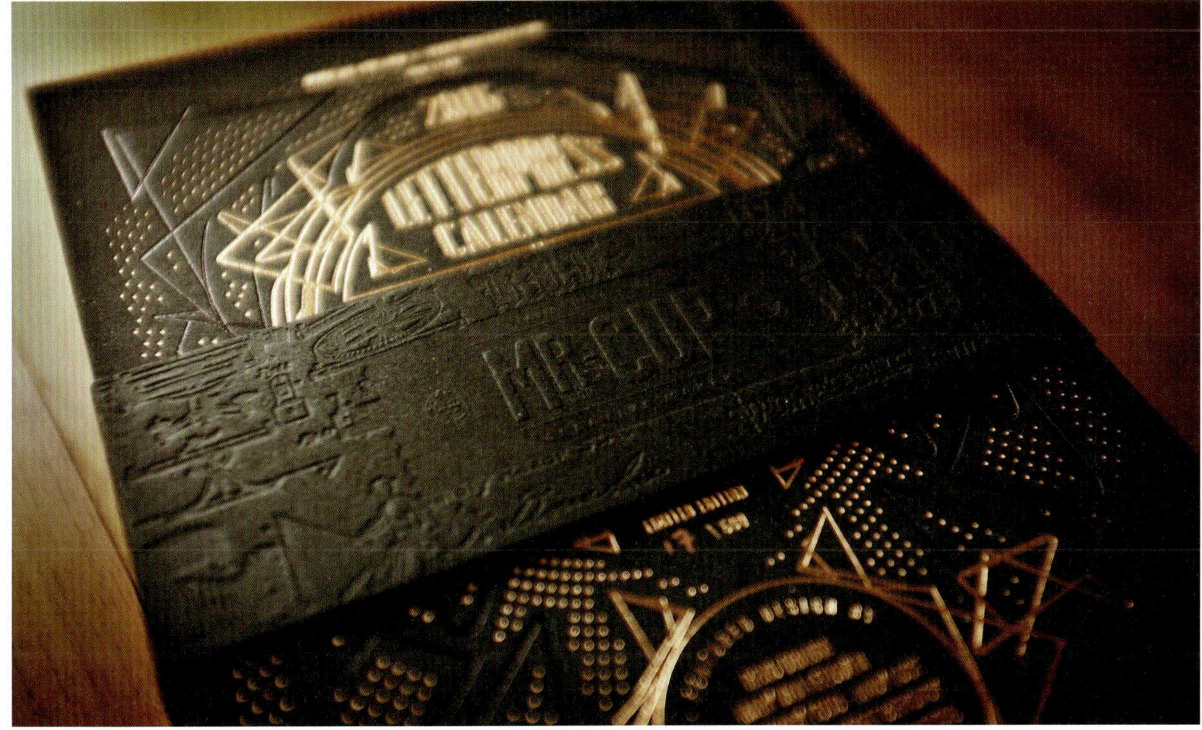
LETTERPRESS
CALENDAR
LIMITED EDITION

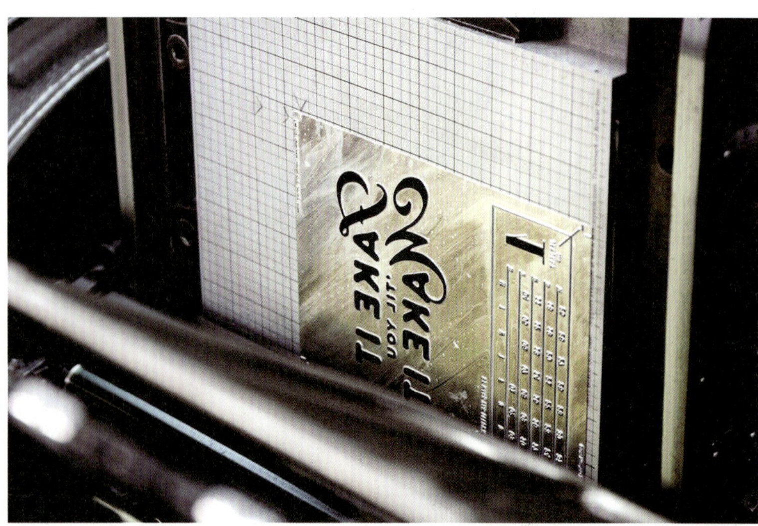

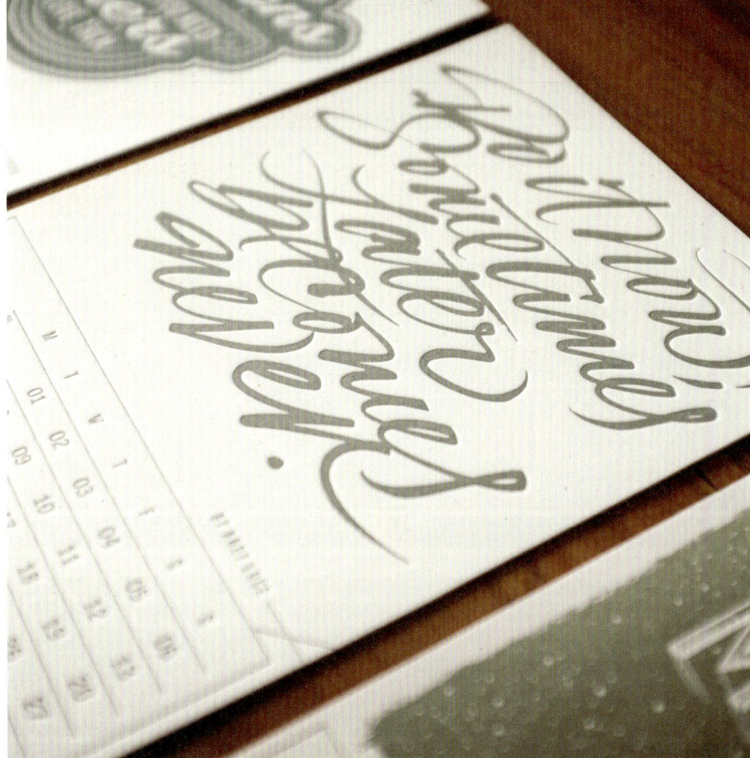

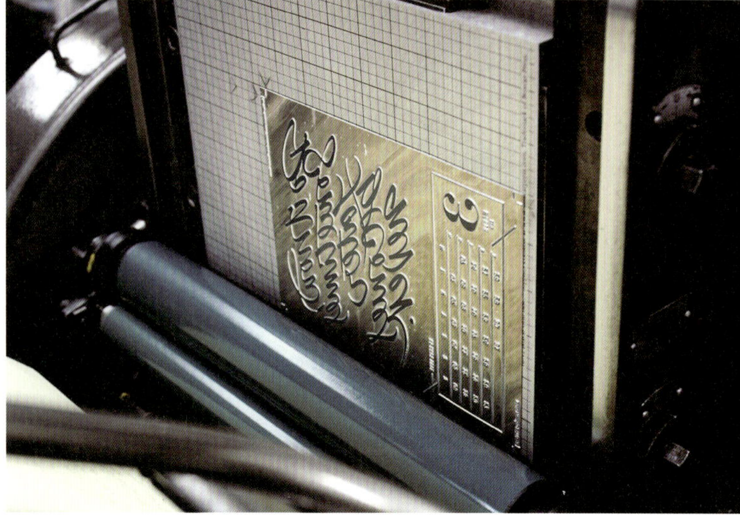

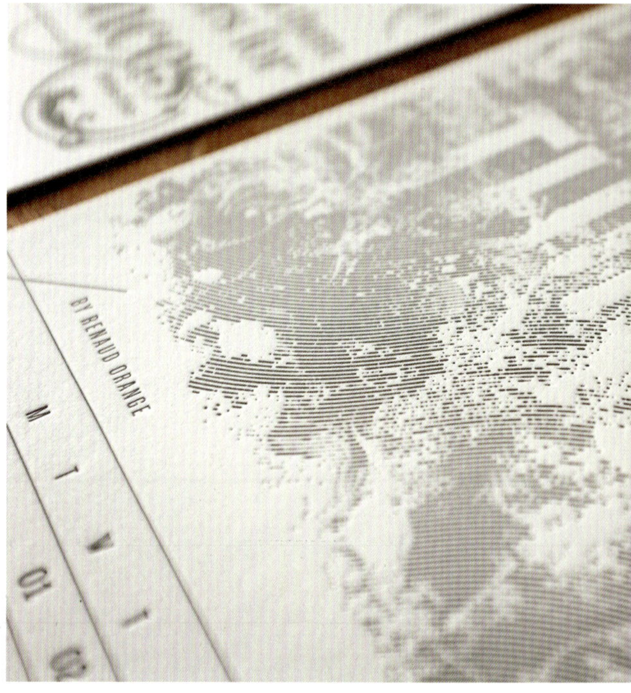
BY RENAUD ORANGE

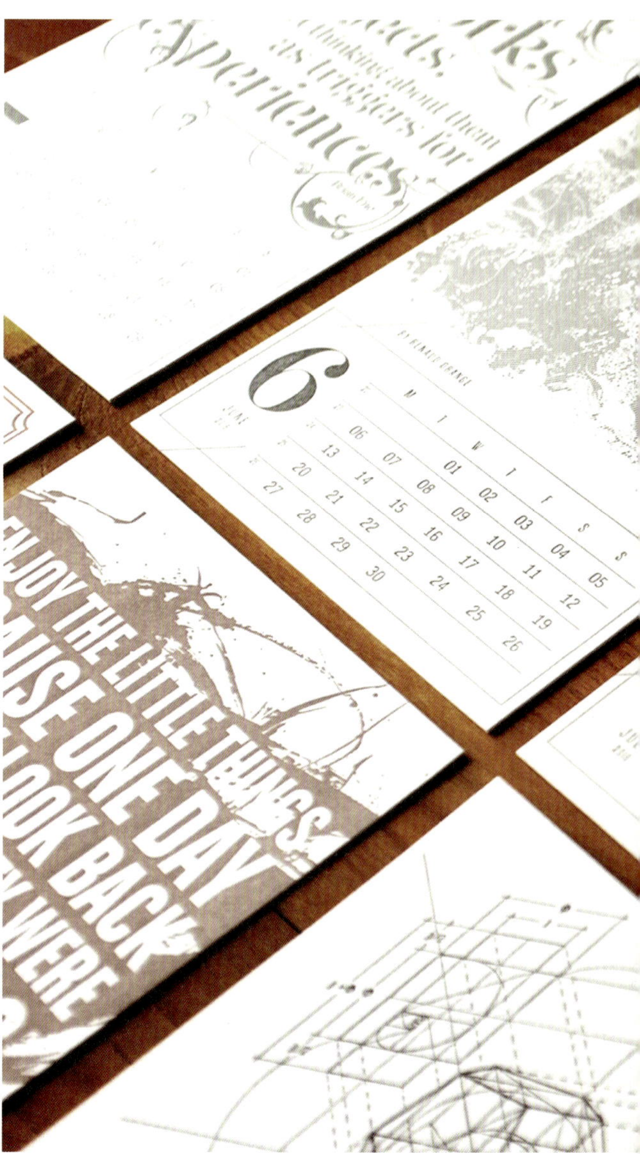
ENJOY THE LITTLE THINGS

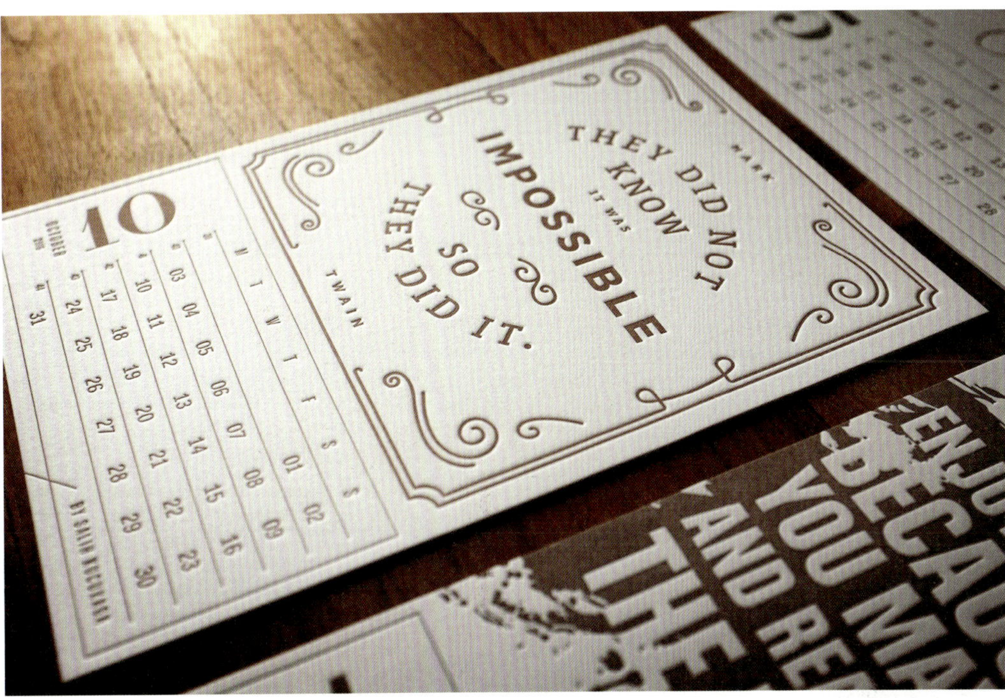
THEY DID NOT
KNOW
IT WAS
IMPOSSIBLE
SO
THEY DID IT.
MARK
TWAIN
10
OCTOBER

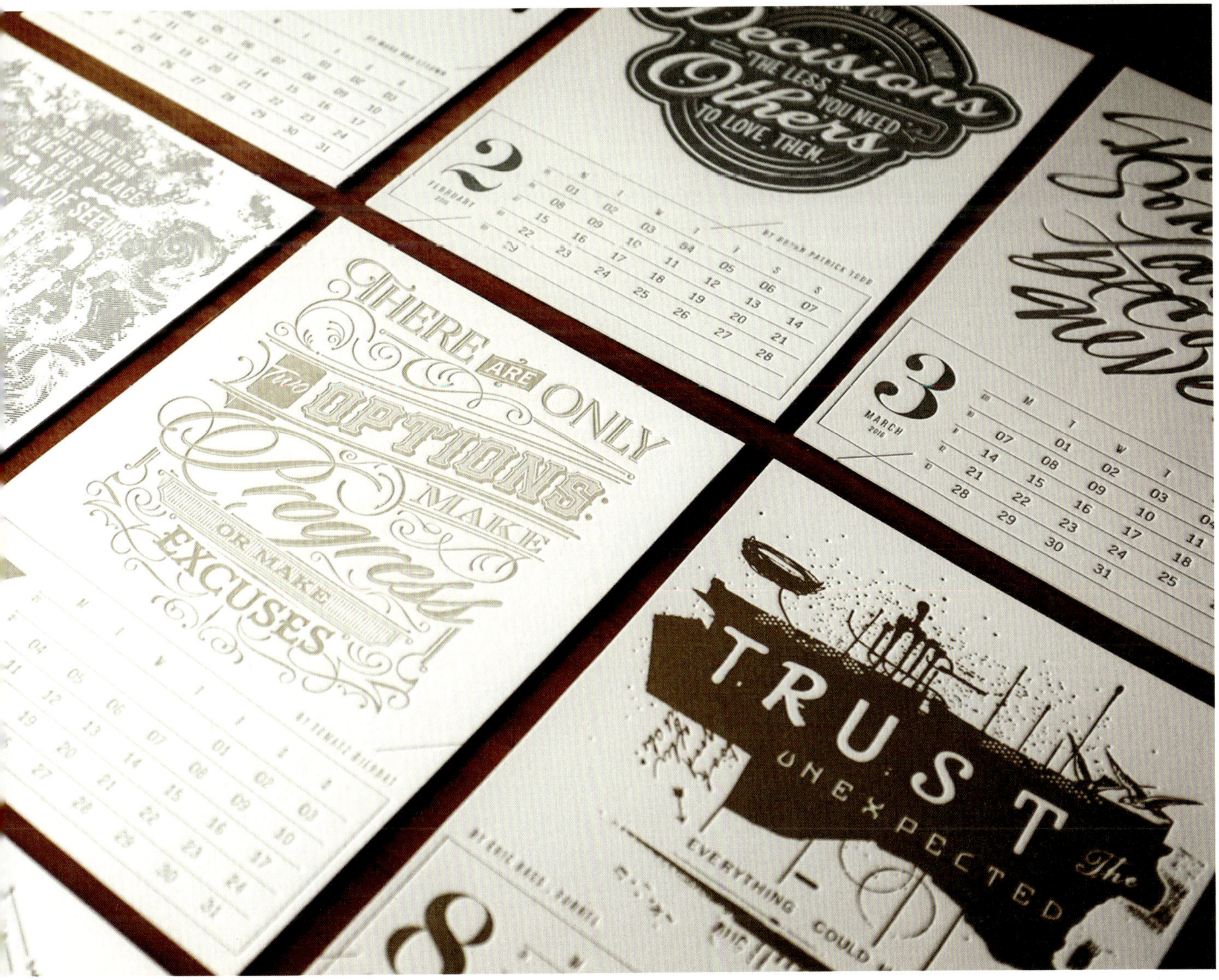

2017 Letterpress Calender

700g Colorplan paper

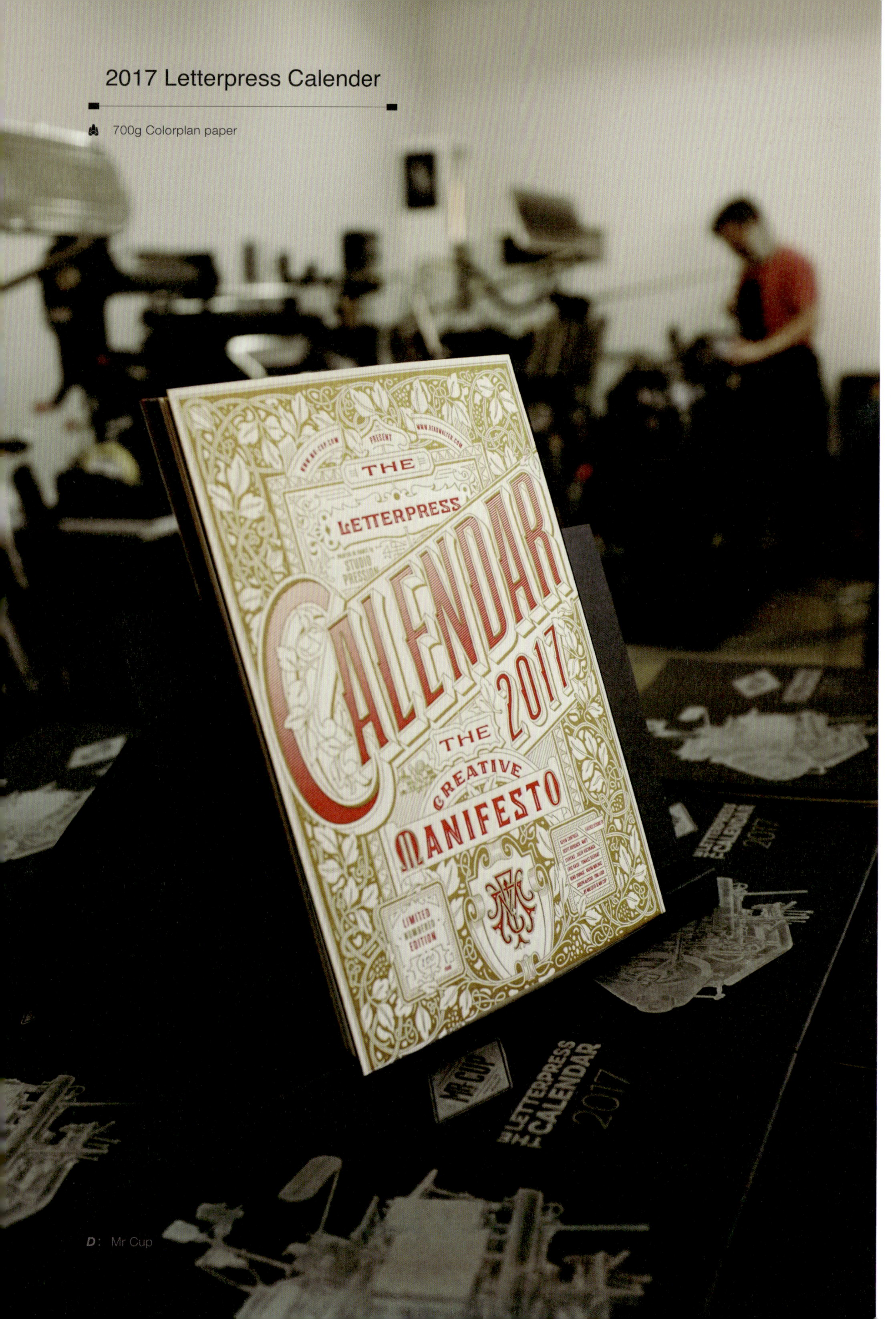

D: Mr Cup

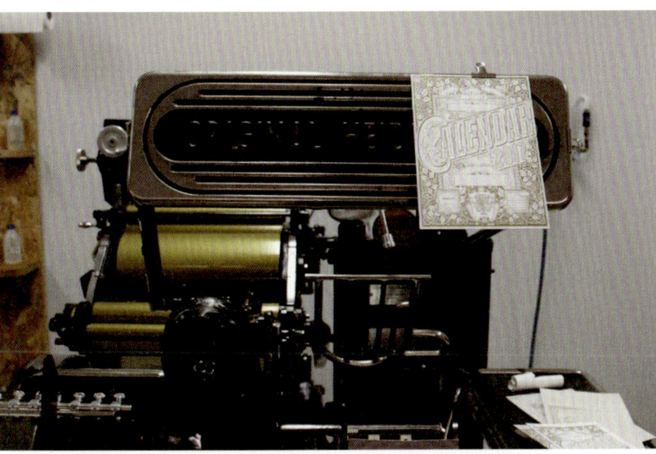

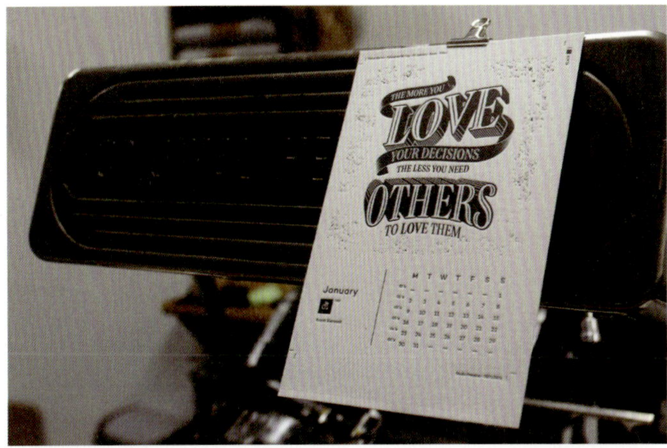

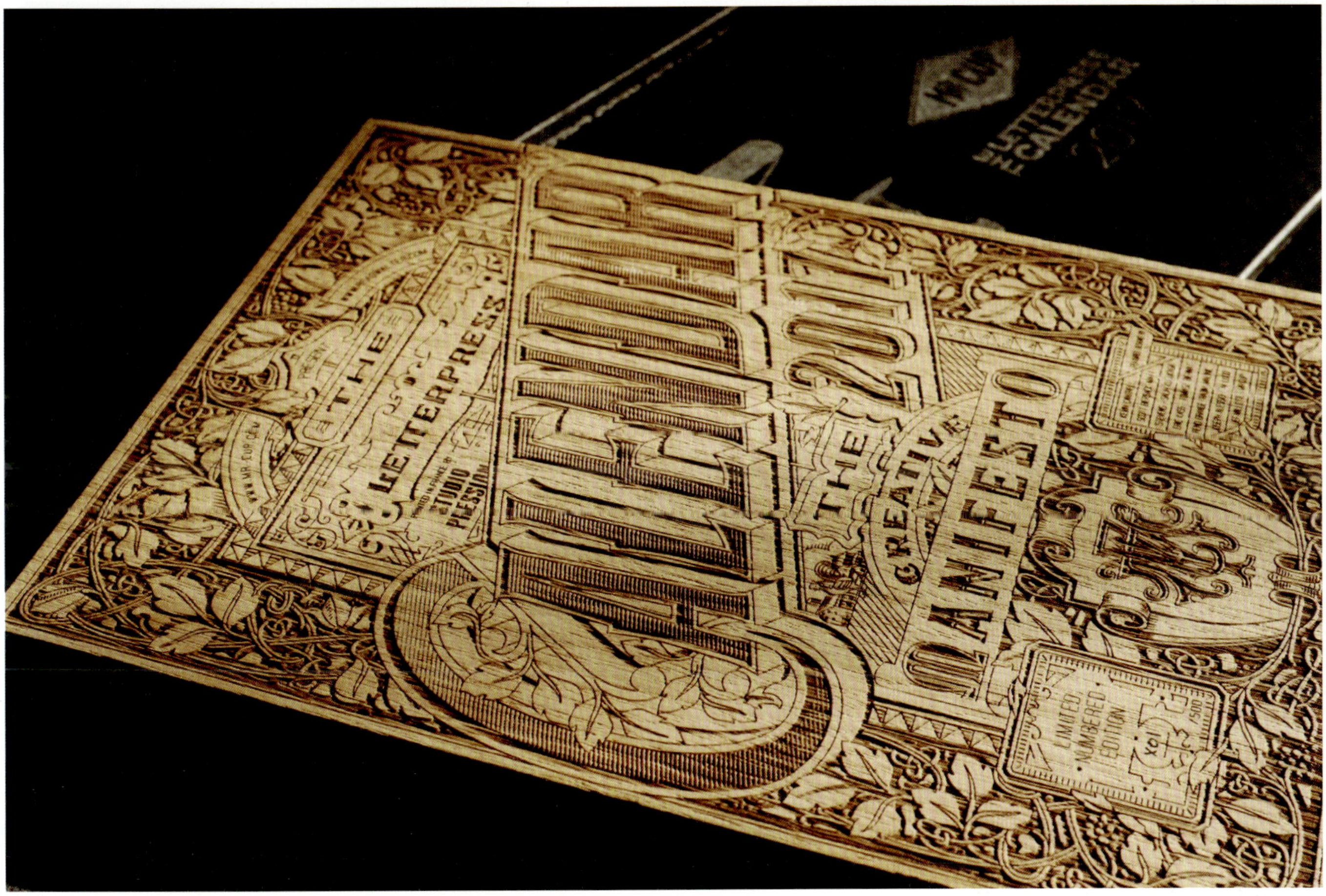

The front cover of the Deluxe edition is laser engraved on wood and limited to 200 first copies. The normal edition cover is printed on white paper with two colors. It is a numbered, limited edition. The calendar is composed of 13 cards printed on 700g Colorplan papers: six light-color papers with black printing/six dark-color papers with light printing. It comes in a black silver printed cover, which unfolds to be used as a stand for the calendar!

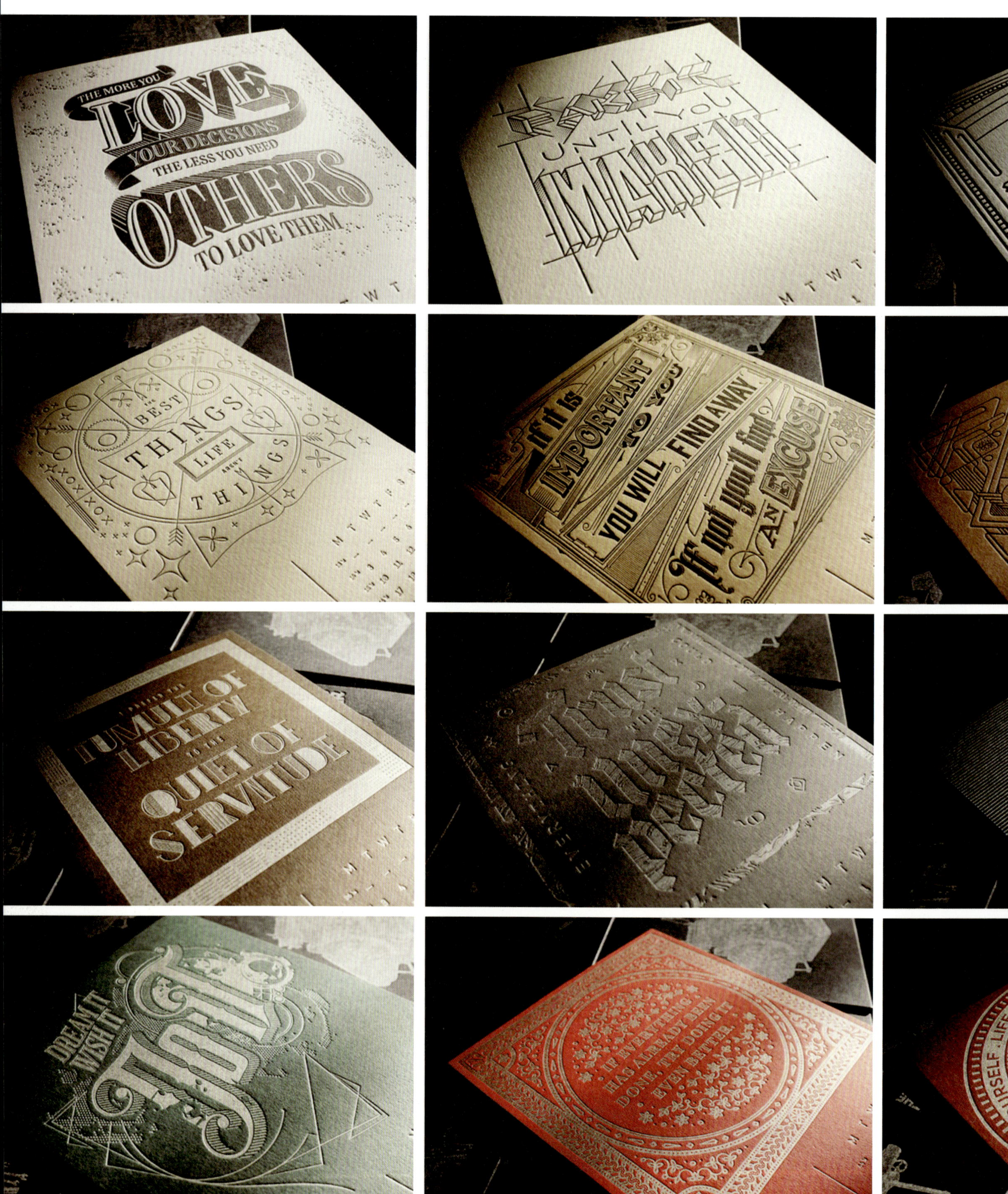
THE MORE YOU
LOVE
YOUR DECISIONS
THE LESS YOU NEED
OTHERS
TO LOVE THEM
UNTIL YOU
MAKE IT
BEST
THINGS
LIFE
THINGS
If it is
IMPORTANT
TO YOU
YOU WILL FIND A WAY
If not you'll find
AN EXCUSE
TUMULT OF
LIBERTY
QUIET OF
SERVITUDE
DREAM IT
WISH IT
IF EVERYTHING
HAS ALREADY BEEN
DONE, TRY DOING IT
EVEN BETTER.

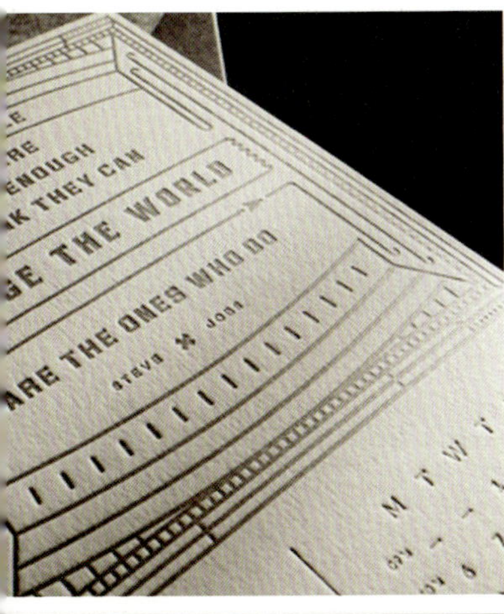
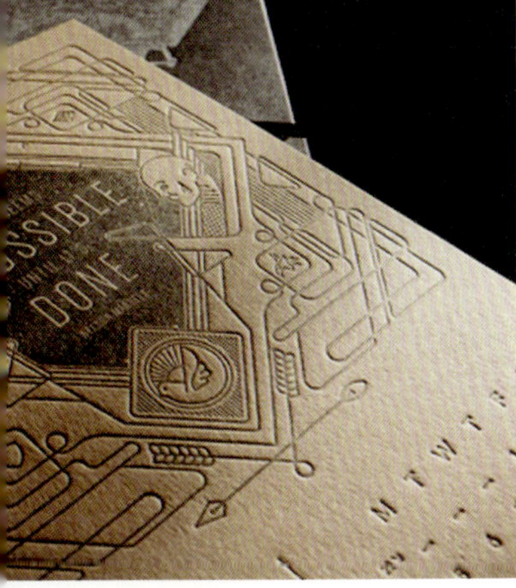
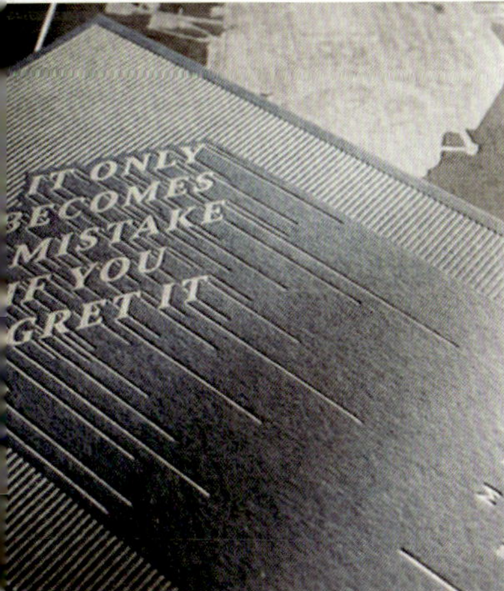
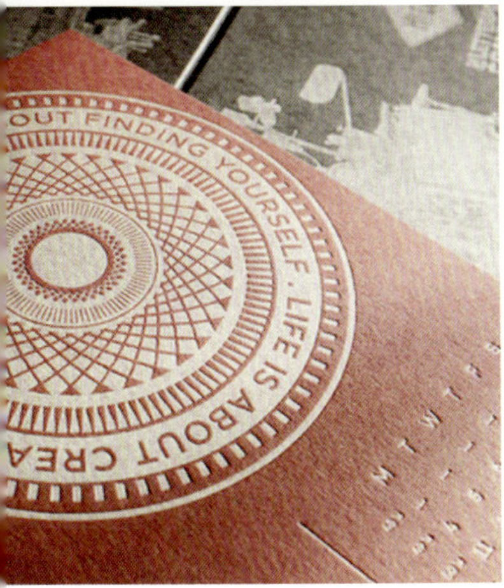
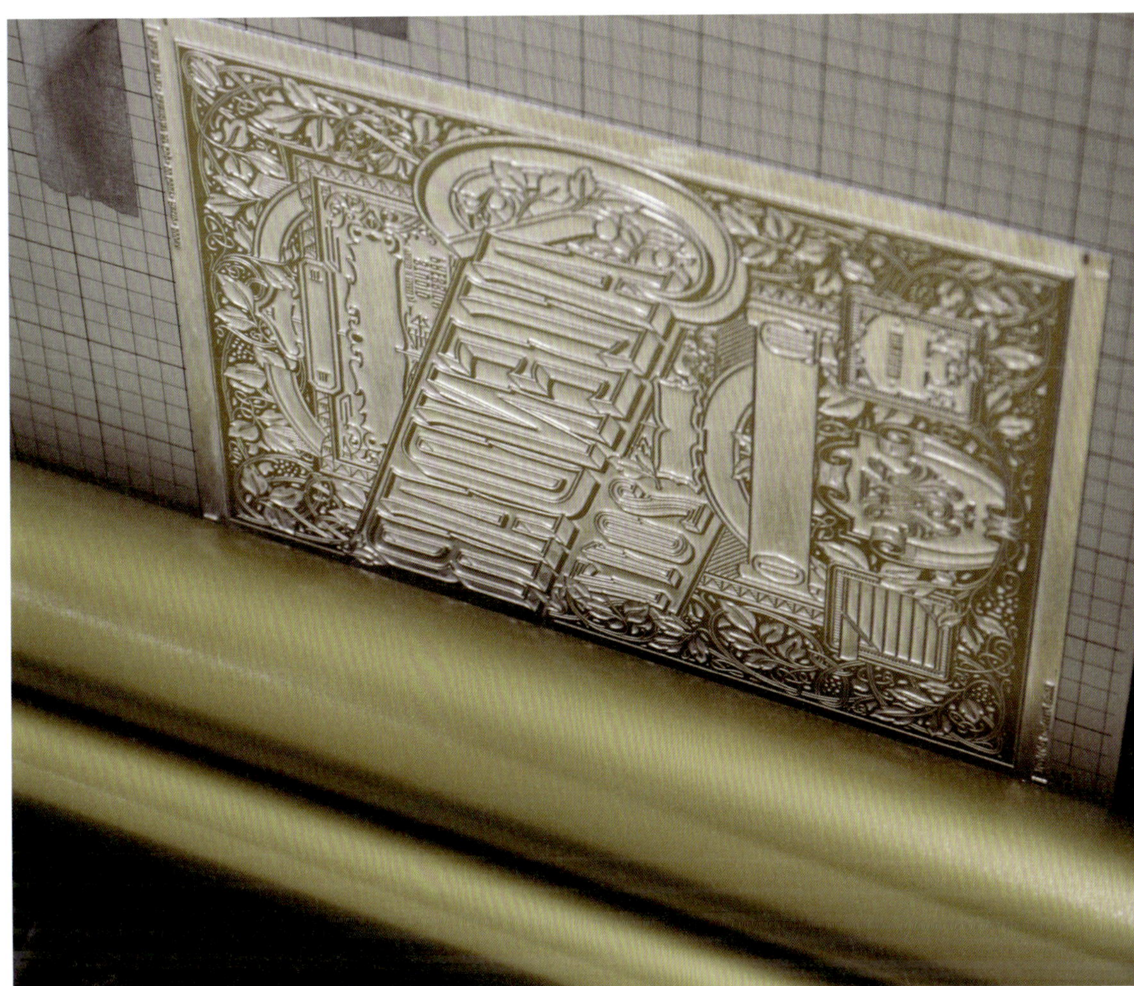
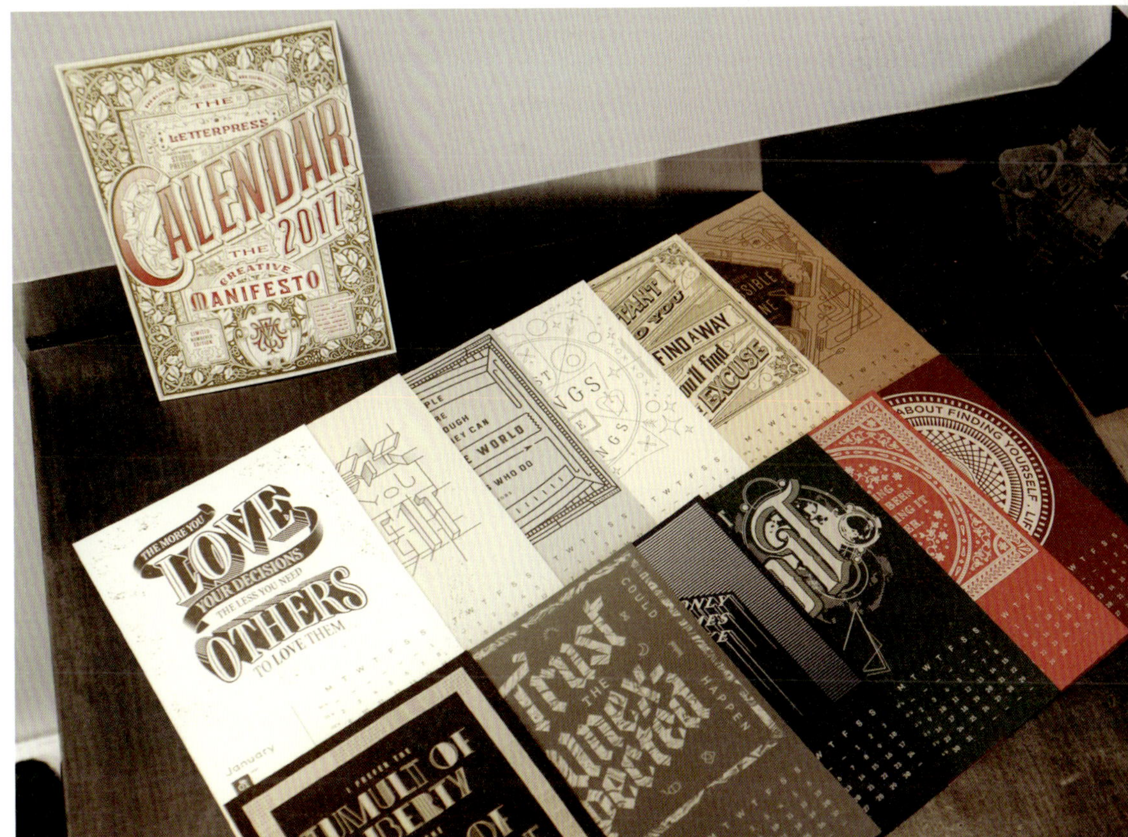

Ceramide Care

Primax with Matte UV Coating

Ceramide Care™, a ground-breaking new formulation for natural hair-care products needed to stand out on the shelf and appeal to 18~33-year-old millennials shopping in the natural channel. A progressive flexographic process was utilized which combined custom inks and label material to achieve the desired effect for shelf impact.

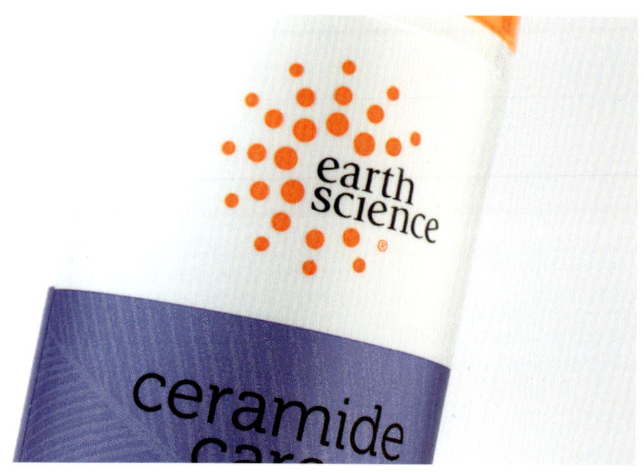

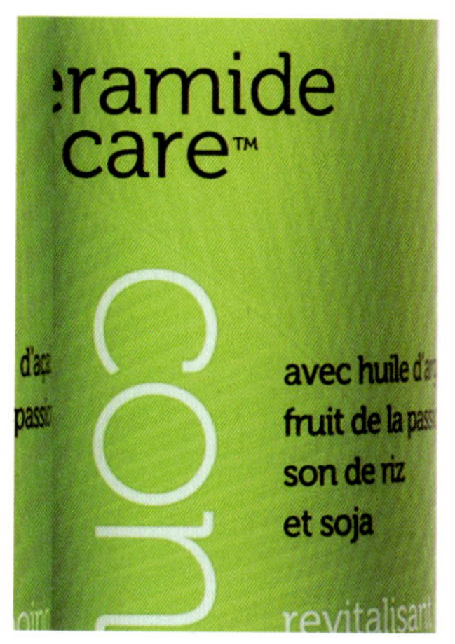

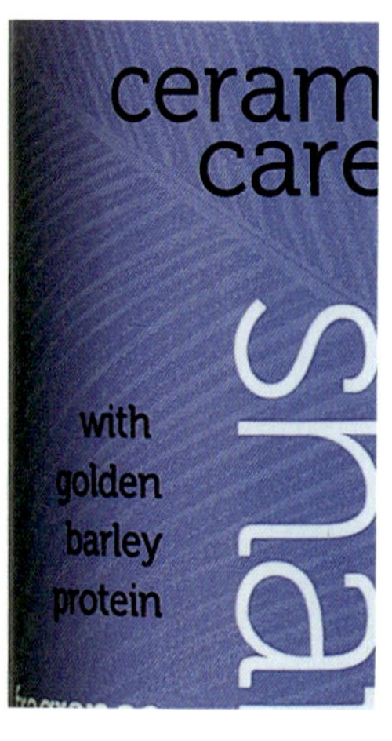

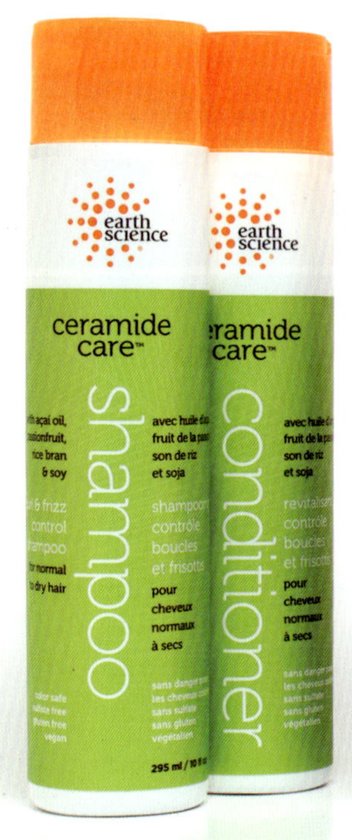

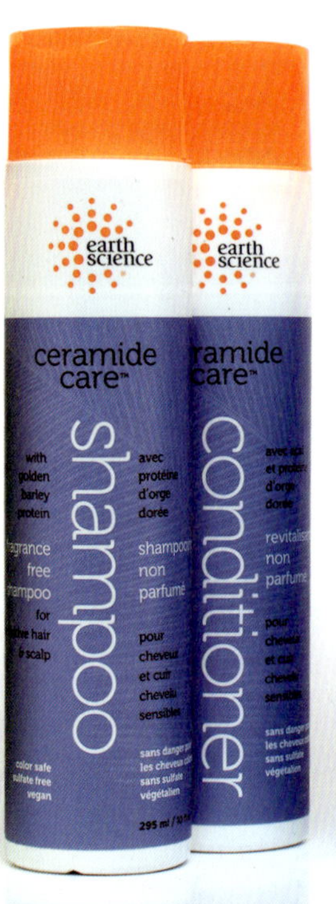

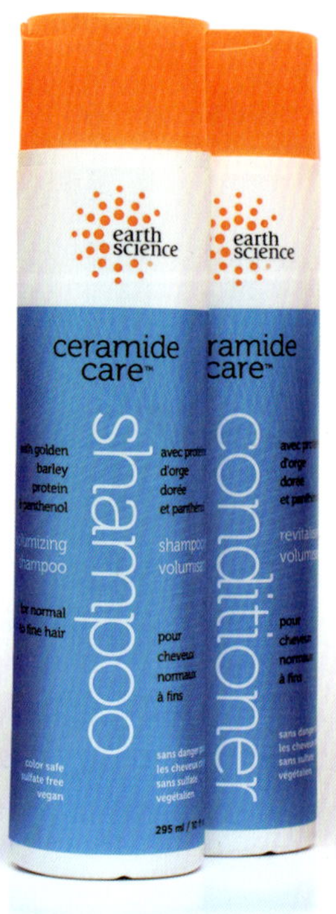

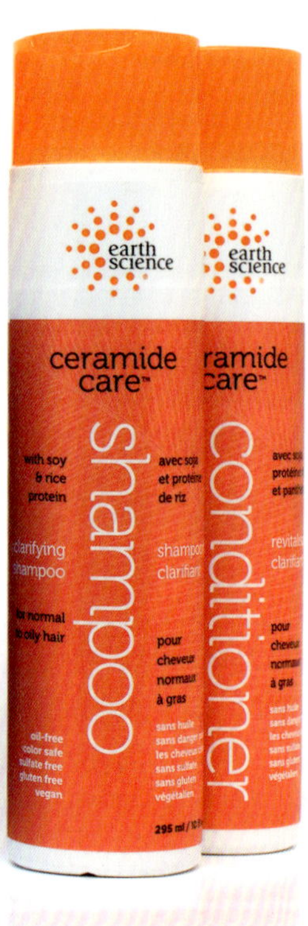

 D: Mark Oliver

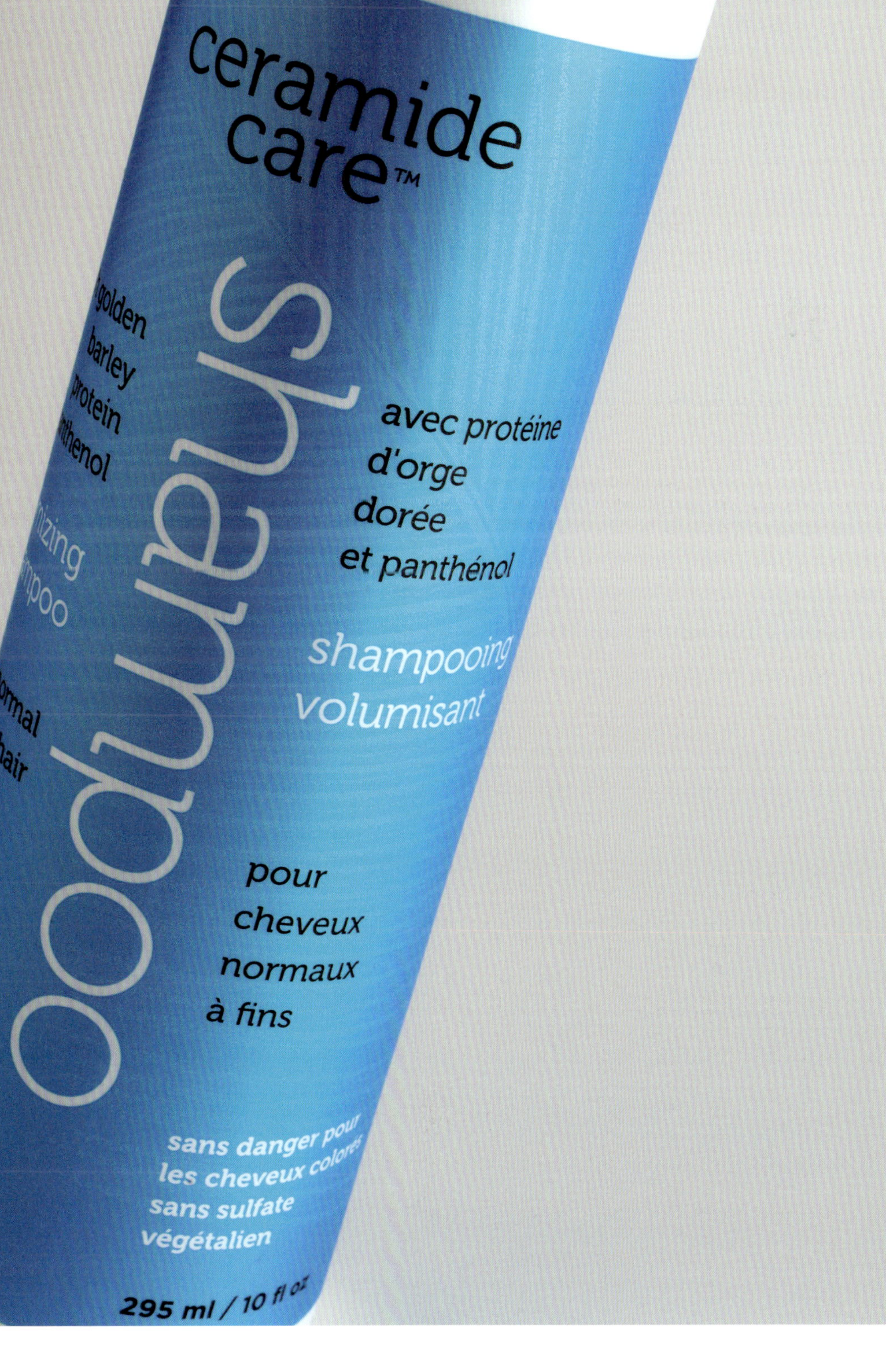
earth science
ceramide care™
golden
barley
protein
shampoo
avec protéine
d'orge
dorée
et panthénol
shampooing
volumisant
pour
cheveux
normaux
à fins
sans danger pour
les cheveux colorés
sans sulfate
végétalien
295 ml / 10 fl oz

INDEX

ACKNOWLEDGEMENTS

We would like to thank all the designers and contributors who have been involved in the production of this book; their contributions have been indispensable to its creation. We would also like to express our gratitude to all the producers for their invaluable opinions and assistance throughout this project. And to the many others whose names are not credited but have made helpful suggestions, we thank you for your continuous support.

FUTURE PARTNERSHIPS

If you wish to participate in SendPoints' future projects and publications, please send your website or portfolio to editor01@sendpoints.cn.